Microsoft® Office Word 2010 Inside Out

Katherine Murray

Published with the authorization of Microsoft Corporation by:
O'Reilly Media, Inc.
1005 Gravenstein Highway North
Sebastopol, California 95472

Printed and bound in the United States of America.

1 2 3 4 5 6 7 8 9   QGT   5 4 3 2 1 0

Microsoft Press titles may be purchased for educational, business or sales promotional use. Online editions are also available for most titles (http://my.safaribooksonline.com). For more information, contact our corporate/institutional sales department: (800) 998-9938 or corporate@oreilly.com. Visit our website at microsoftpress.oreilly.com. Send comments to mspinput@microsoft.com.

Acquisitions and Development Editors: Juliana Aldous and Kenyon Brown
Production Editor: Kristen Borg
Production Services: Octal Publishing, Inc.
Technical Reviewer: Todd Meister
Indexing: Denise Getz
Cover: Karen Montgomery
Compositor: Octal Publishing, Inc.
Illustrator: Robert Romano

978-0-735-62729-1

Contents at a Glance

Part 1: Word 2010: Make an Immediate Impact

Chapter 1
Spotlight on Microsoft Word 2010 3

Chapter 2
Managing Your Documents with
Backstage View 33

Chapter 3
Right Now Document Design with
Word 2010 69

Chapter 4
Templates and Themes for a
Professional Look 101

Chapter 5
Customizing Page Setup and
Controlling Pagination 139

Chapter 6
Setting Up Your Layout with Page
Backgrounds and Columns 173

Part 2: Creating Global Content: From Research to Review

Chapter 7
Creating and Reusing Content 201

Chapter 8
Navigating Your Document . . . .

Chapter 9
Translating Text and Working
with Languages 267

Chapter 10
Editing, Proofing, and Using
Reference Tools 289

Chapter 11
Formatting Your Document 331

Chapter 12
Applying and Customizing Quick Styles 379

Chapter 13
Working with Outlines 413

Chapter 14
Printing Documents Professionally 435

Part 3: Make Your Point, Clearly and Visually

Chapter 15
Clarifying Your Concepts in
Professional Tables 463

Chapter 16
Create Compelling SmartArt
Diagrams and Charts 493

Chapter 17
Adding and Editing Pictures
and Screenshots 523

Chapter 18
Adding the Extras: Equations, Text
Boxes, and Objects 561

Chapter 19
Command Attention with Borders
and Shading 587

Part 4: Word 2010 As a Team Effort, Anywhere, Always

Chapter 20
Securing Your Word Documents 613

Chapter 21
Sharing Your Documents 641

Chapter 22
Collaborating and Co-Authoring
in Real Time 667

Part 5: Word 2010 Interactive

Chapter 23
**Preparing Tables of Contents
and Indexes**............................705

Chapter 24
Special Features for Long Documents......731

Chapter 25
**Blogging and Using the
Word Web App.**........................747

Chapter 26
**Creating Mailings Large
and Small**..............................761

Chapter 27
**Customizing Documents with
Content Controls**......................789

Chapter 28
Working with Macros in Word 2010........811

Table of Contents

Acknowledgments. xxiii
Conventions and Features Used in This Book. xxv
Introduction xxvii

Part 1: Word 2010: Make an Immediate Impact

Chapter 1 **Spotlight on Microsoft Word 2010**. **3**

Imagining Word 2010. 3
What's New in Word 2010? 4
    Enhancing Your User Experience 5
    Better Authoring Features. 7
    Use Word 2010 Anywhere. 11
Finding Your Way Around the Word 2010 Window 13
    Get What You Need, Intuitively 13
    Exploring the Ribbon 14
    Keep Your Favorite Tools in Reach with the Quick Access Toolbar. 16
    Using Dialog Launchers. 17
    Working with Galleries. 19
    Making Quick Formatting Changes with the Mini Toolbar. 20
    Getting a New View of Your Document 21
    Finding What You Need Quickly with the Navigation Pane 24
    Displaying Rulers and Gridlines 26
    Viewing More Than One Page at a Time 28
    Working with Multiple Documents 28
Understanding and Tailoring the Status Bar 30
What's Next?. 31

What do you think of this book? We want to hear from you!

Microsoft is interested in hearing your feedback so we can continually improve our books and learning resources for you. To participate in a brief online survey, please visit:

microsoft.com/learning/booksurvey

Chapter 2   Managing Your Documents with Backstage View **33**

Introducing Backstage View 34
    The Tabs Area... 35
    The Groups Area 36
    The Preview and Properties Area........................ 37
Working with Document Properties in the Info Tab 38
    Converting Documents from Earlier Versions of Word 46
    Protecting the Document 47
    Checking Document Compatibility 50
    Recovering Draft Versions of Your Files 52
    Recovering Unsaved Files 54
Accessing Recent Files.. 55
Starting a New File... 57
Previewing and Printing Documents 57
Saving and Sending Your Documents 58
Getting Help in Word 2010 60
Setting Word Options.. 62
    Choosing General Program Preferences................... 64
    Customizing the Word 2010 Ribbon 64
    Setting Up the Microsoft Word Trust Center............... 66
What's Next?... 68

Chapter 3   Right Now Document Design with Word 2010. .... **69**

Starting Out with Word 2010 Designs 69
    Beginning with a Template 69
    Coordinating Your Document Design...................... 72
    Saving Your Favorite Templates 74
    Opening Recent Documents............................ 75
    Inputting Data....................................... 77
Performing Basic Editing Tasks 78
    Selecting Text.. 79
    Copying, Cutting, and Pasting 80
    Using the Office Clipboard 83
    Undoing, Redoing, and Repeating....................... 85
Creating Theme-Enabled Documents 87
    Experimenting with Themes 87
Saving Documents... 91
    Performing Simple Saves............................... 91
    Saving Files with the Save As Dialog Box 92
Designing Instant Documents... 95
    An Annual Report 96
    Business Letterhead 97
    A Newsletter 99
What's Next?... 100

Chapter 4   **Templates and Themes for a Professional Look** **101**

Where Does Your Document Get Its Design?. 102
Templates 101: Behind the Scenes 102
Understanding How Templates Work 105
Getting the Scoop on the Normal Template 106
Using Templates from the New Documents Dialog Box 109
Creating Custom Templates. 112
Thinking Through Your Template Design. 113
Attaching Templates to Documents 117
Working with Global Templates 119
Modifying Existing Templates 122
Changing the Template File 122
Changing a Template While Working in a Document 123
Using the Organizer to Rename, Delete, and Copy Styles 123
Protecting Templates 125
Applying Themes in Word 2010 126
What's in a Theme?. 128
Themes, Quick Styles, and Galleries. 129
Changing a Theme. 130
Changing Theme Colors 131
Choosing a New Font Selection 131
Selecting Theme Effects. 133
Creating a Custom Theme 134
Creating Your Own Color Scheme 135
Customizing Theme Font Sets 136
Saving Your Custom Theme 137
What's Next?. 137

Chapter 5   **Customizing Page Setup and Controlling Pagination** **139**

Basic Page Setup Options. 139
Planning Your Document 142
Simple Margins and Orientations 145
Changing Margin Settings. 145
Choosing Orientation. 147
Selecting Paper Size and Source 148
Choosing a Paper Size 148
Selecting the Paper Source 149
Multiple Page Settings. 150
Working in Sections. 151
Creating a Section. 153
Inserting Text Wrapping Breaks 155
Controlling Page Breaks. 156
Creating a Page or Section Border. 158
Removing Page and Section Breaks 158
Adding Page Numbers 159

Adding Headers and Footers 160
   Creating Headers and Footers 161
   Editing Headers and Footers 163
   Deleting Headers and Footers 167
Saving Page Setup Defaults to the Current Template 168
Adding and Controlling Line Numbers 170
   Deleting Line Numbers 171
What's Next? 172

Chapter 6   **Setting Up Your Layout with Page Backgrounds and Columns 173**
The Nature of Complex Documents 173
Layout and Design Fundamentals 175
   Considering Content Delivery 178
Designing Backgrounds and Watermarks 178
   Adding and Customizing a Page Background 179
   Adding Watermarks to Printed Documents 183
   Editing a Watermark 184
Adding Columns 187
   Planning Your Columns 187
   Creating a Multicolumn Document 188
   Creating Columns for Part of a Document 191
   Creating Unequal Column Widths 192
   Changing Column Width on the Ruler 193
   Flowing Text into a Column Layout 194
   Beginning a New Column Layout 195
   Inserting Column Breaks 196
   Removing Column Breaks 197
What's Next? 197

Part 2: Creating Global Content: From Research to Review

Chapter 7   **Creating and Reusing Content 201**
Creating Content Today 201
   What Does It Mean to Reuse Content? 202
   Ways You Can Reuse Content in Word 2010 203
Entering Text 203
   Ink for Everyone 204
   Importing Documents 204
   Placing Objects 207
   Inserting Building Blocks 208
Creating a Cover Page 208
Formatting Text as You Go 210
   Specifying Fonts and Sizes 213
   Applying Text Attributes 215
   High-End Typography in Word 2010 216
   Text Effects to Really Wow 'Em 218
   Additional Text Formats 220

Changing Case. 220
Using the Highlight Tool 221
Changing Text Color. 222
Clearing Formatting Attributes. 223
Positioning Your Text 223
Inserting Symbols and Special Characters. 224
Inserting Symbols 224
Inserting Special Characters 227
Inserting Date and Time Elements 228
Creating and Using Building Blocks 230
Inserting Existing Building Blocks 232
Creating Building Blocks 234
Modifying Building Block Properties. 238
Deleting Building Blocks 239
Creating Catalogs of Content 240
What's Next?. 243

Chapter 8   **Navigating Your Document** **245**
A Quick Look at Navigation in Word 2010 245
Finding Content with the Navigation Pane. 246
Browsing by Headings 248
Browse by Page. 249
Browse by Search Results. 251
Navigating with Browse Object 252
Finding Text and Elements Within the Current Document. 253
Finding Instances of Formatting. 256
Finding Special Characters Using Codes. 257
Moving Through the Document with Go To 259
Creating Bookmarks for Document Navigation. 260
Changing the View 261
Displaying and Arranging Windows 262
Splitting the Document Window 262
Viewing Pages Side by Side. 263
Switching Among Multiple Windows 264
Navigating Using Shortcut and Function Keys. 264
What's Next?. 266

Chapter 9   **Translating Text and Working with Languages** **267**
Translating Content in Word 2010 268
Setting Up Languages. 269
Adding a Language 269
Setting a Proofing Language 270
Adding Keyboards for Languages 271
Changing Languages As You Type. 273
Using the Mini Translator 274
Translating Selected Text 277
Translating Entire Documents 278

Changing and Adding Translation Services 279
    Choosing a Different Service 280
    Adding a New Translation Service 281
Using Bidirectional Text 282
Working with the Document Grid 283
    Specifying Document Grid Settings 284
    Displaying the Drawing Grid 285
Working with Other Translation Tools 285
What's Next? 287

Chapter 10   **Editing, Proofing, and Using Reference Tools** **289**
Editing Tools in Word 2010 289
Spell It Right! 290
    Looking at Error Notifications 291
Proofing Your Document 295
    Controlling Proofing Display and Exceptions 296
    Configuring Spelling and Grammar Options 298
    Managing Custom Dictionaries 301
Judging Your Document's Readability Level 306
AutoCorrecting Your Document 307
    Controlling AutoCorrect Changes 308
Adding References in Word 2010 312
    Referencing in Style 315
Adding and Managing Sources 315
    Incorporating Other Source Lists 317
Inserting a Citation 317
    Editing Citation and Sources 318
Generating a Bibliography 319
Adding Footnotes and Endnotes 320
    Inserting Footnotes and Endnotes 321
    Customizing Footnotes and Endnotes 321
    Moving and Copying Footnotes and Endnotes 323
    Deleting Footnotes and Endnotes 323
Inserting Cross-References 325
    Adding a Cross-Reference 326
    Modifying, Moving, and Updating Cross-References 327
What's Next? 329

Chapter 11   **Formatting Your Document** **331**
Paragraph Basics in Word 2010 332
Managing AutoFormat Effectively 334
    Adjusting AutoFormat Choices 336
    Changing Options for AutoFormat As You Type 336
Formatting Paragraphs by Aligning and Indenting Text 338
    Using the Ruler to Align Paragraphs 339
    Aligning Paragraphs by Using the Paragraph Dialog Box 341

Addressing Spacing Issues 343
    Specifying Line Spacing 345
    Adjusting Spacing Above and Below Paragraphs 346
Controlling Alignment by Using Tabs. 347
    Using the Ruler to Set Tabs 349
    Creating Tabs by Using the Tabs Dialog Box 351
    Clearing Manual Tabs. 352
Controlling Line and Page Breaks. 353
Taking Control of Hyphenation. 354
    Hyphenate an Entire Document Automatically 355
    Hyphenating All or Part of a Document Manually 356
Creating Drop Caps in Existing Paragraphs. 357
Creating Effective Lists 358
    When Bullets Work 359
    When Numbers Matter 360
Creating a Quick List 361
    Creating Lists While You Type. 362
    Ending a List the Way You Want. 363
Enhancing Bulleted Lists. 364
    Choosing a New Bullet from the Bullet Library 364
    Using a Custom Bullet 364
    Changing the Bullet Font. 365
    Changing a Bullet Symbol 366
    Using a Picture Bullet 367
Improving Numbered Lists. 367
    Choosing a Numbering Scheme. 368
    Modifying the Numbering Style 368
    Continuing Numbering 370
    Restarting Numbering 371
    Converting a Bulleted List to a Numbered List (or Vice Versa). 371
Changing List Indents 372
Creating and Using Multilevel Lists. 373
    Applying a Multilevel List 373
    Creating a New List Style. 375
What's Next?. 378

Chapter 12   **Applying and Customizing Quick Styles. 379**
Style Design with Users in Mind 379
    Style Fundamentals. 381
Exploring the Quick Style Gallery and Quick Style Sets 384
    Applying and Modifying Styles Using the Quick Style Gallery. 385
    Switching and Modifying Quick Style Sets. 386
    Custom Quick Style Sets 387
Working with the Styles Pane 390
    Mastering the Styles Pane 391
Creating and Modifying Styles 395
    Modifying Existing Styles. 397
    Additional Style Options 398

Style Management Tools 400
   Inspecting Styles 401
   Reveal Formatting Task Pane 401
   Managing Styles 404
   Keyboard Shortcuts for Styles 409
What's Next? 411

Chapter 13   Working with Outlines 413
Getting Started Outlining in Word 2010 413
The Basics of a Good Outline. 414
Eleven Reasons to Outline Your Next Complex Project 415
Viewing a Document in Outline View 417
   Exploring Outlining Tools 419
Creating a New Outline 421
Choosing Outline Display 422
   Displaying Different Levels of Text. 423
   Showing the First Line of Text. 424
   Removing and Showing Formatting 425
Working with Headings in Outline View 426
   Adding a Heading. 426
   Applying Outline Levels. 426
   Promoting and Demoting Headings 426
Displaying Outline and Print Layout View at the Same Time. 428
Changing Your Outline 429
   Expanding and Collapsing the Outline 429
   Moving Outline Topics. 429
Printing Your Outline. 431
The Navigation Pane vs. Using Outline View 433
What's Next? 434

Chapter 14   Printing Documents Professionally 435
Printing in a Greener World. 435
The (Almost) One-Click Print Process in Word 2010 436
   Previewing Your Document. 438
   Zooming In on the Details. 439
   Making Changes While Previewing 441
Printing Quickly and Efficiently 443
   Printing Selected Text. 444
   Printing Hidden Text. 445
Canceling a Print Job. 446
Setting Print Options. 447
   Printing More than One Copy of a Single Document. 447
   Printing Ranges 448
   Printing Odd and Even Pages 449
   Printing Document Elements 450
   Printing Several Pages per Sheet 452
   Scaling Printed Documents 453

Specialized Printing 454
    Printing Envelopes 456
    Creating Labels 458
What's Next?. 460

Part 3: Make Your Point, Clearly and Visually

Chapter 15   **Clarifying Your Concepts in Professional Tables** **463**
Creating Tables Today. 463
Choose Your Method: Creating Tables in Word 464
    Adding a Quick Table. 465
    Using the Row and Column Grid to Create a Table. 467
    Inserting a Table and Specifying AutoFit Options. 467
    Drawing a Table. 468
    Converting Text to a Table 469
    Inserting an Excel Spreadsheet. 470
Creating Nested Tables. 471
Editing Tables 472
    Displaying Table Formatting Marks. 472
    Selecting Table Cells. 474
    Copying and Pasting Table Data 474
    Inserting Columns and Rows. 476
    Inserting Cells 476
    Deleting Columns, Rows, and Cells 477
    Moving Rows and Columns. 477
    Merging Cells. 477
    Splitting Cells 478
Enhancing Your Tables with Formatting 480
    Changing Table Format by Using Table Styles. 480
    Creating Custom Table Styles 482
    More Formatting Fun. 484
Positioning Tables in Your Document. 485
    Flowing Text Around Tables 485
    Sorting Table Data 486
Resizing Tables 487
    Understanding AutoFit. 487
    Resizing an Entire Table 488
    Setting Preset and Percent Table Sizes 488
    Changing Column Width and Row Height. 489
    Distributing Data Evenly in Rows and Columns. 489
    Changing Text Direction 489
Working with Functions in Tables. 490
What's Next?. 491

Chapter 16   Create Compelling SmartArt Diagrams and Charts **493**

Adding SmartArt Diagrams 493
    Creating the SmartArt Diagram 494
    Adding and Formatting Diagram Text 496
    Making Formatting Changes in the Diagram 497
Creative Charting 499
Introducing Word 2010 Chart Types 499
Creating a Basic Chart 501
    Changing the Chart Type 503
    Creating a Chart Template 503
    Understanding the Chart Tools 505
Entering Chart Data 506
    Working with the Datasheet 507
    Changing the Data Arrangement 508
Editing and Enhancing Chart Information 509
    Choosing a New Chart Layout 510
    Applying a Chart Style 511
    Adding a Chart Title 512
    Working with Axes 513
    Add Gridlines and Trendlines 515
    Displaying and Positioning a Legend 516
    Working with Data Labels 517
Formatting Charts 518
    Changing the Format of Your Chart Elements 519
    Formatting Shapes 520
What's Next? 522

Chapter 17   Adding and Editing Pictures and Screenshots **523**

Adding Art to Your Word Documents 523
    Inserting Pictures 524
    Adding Clip Art 526
    Adding Shapes and Lines 530
Editing Pictures 532
    Applying Artistic Effects 532
    Editing and Adjusting Images 534
    Cropping Pictures 535
    Resizing Pictures 537
    Rotating Pictures 538
Removing Picture Backgrounds 539
Enhancing Pictures 541
    Applying Picture Styles to Your Images 541
    Adding Captions to Pictures 543
Modifying Shapes and Lines 544
    Applying Shape Styles 545
    Adding and Formatting Shape Text 546
    Modifying Lines and Fills 546
    Formatting Shadows and 3-D Effects 549
    Applying and Customizing 3-D Effects 551

Adding Screenshots and Clippings 553
Arranging Art on the Page 553
    Aligning Objects 553
    Grouping and Ungrouping Objects 555
    Controlling Object Layering 556
    Choosing Art Position 556
    Controlling Text Wrapping 557
What's Next? 559

Chapter 18   **Adding the Extras: Equations, Text Boxes, and Objects 561**
Inserting Mathematical Equations 561
Using Math AutoCorrect 568
Adding and Linking Text Boxes 570
    Adding Text Boxes 572
    Inserting Text into Text Boxes 574
    Formatting Text Boxes 574
Linking Text Boxes to Flow Text 578
    Moving Between Linked Text Boxes 580
    Copying or Moving Linked Text Boxes 580
    Breaking Text Box Links 582
    Deleting Linked Text Boxes Without Losing Text 582
Adding Objects to Your Word Document 583
    Insert an Object 584
    Create a New Object 584
    Adding an Existing Object 585
What's Next? 585

Chapter 19   **Command Attention with Borders and Shading 587**
Adding a Simple Border 587
Creating Enhanced Borders 588
    Dressing Up Your Border 590
    Selecting Line Styles for Borders 592
    Choosing Color 593
    When You Need to Match Colors Exactly 594
    Controlling Border Width 596
Creating Partial Borders 596
Adding a Border to a Page 597
    Creating a Page Border 598
    Adding an Artistic Border 599
Adding Borders to Sections and Paragraphs 600
    Bordering Sections 600
Adjusting Border Spacing 601
Inserting Horizontal Lines 603
Adding Borders to Pictures 604
Adding Table Borders 605
Applying Shading Behind Content 606
    Applying Shades to Tables and Paragraphs 607
    Shading Considerations 608
What's Next? 609

Part 4: Word 2010 As a Team Effort, Anywhere, Always

Chapter 20   **Securing Your Word Documents** **613**

Protection Features in Word 2010 614
Working with Protected View 615
  Choosing What's Displayed in Protected View 616
  Changing File Validation 617
Marking a File As Final 618
Encrypting Documents 620
  Removing Protection 621
Applying Editing Restrictions 622
Removing Personal Information and Hidden Data 625
  Removing Personal Information 625
Preparing PDF and XPS Files 626
  Understanding PDF and XPS 627
  Saving Your Document As PDF and XPS 627
Signing Your Documents with Digital Signatures and Stamps 628
  Getting a Digital ID 628
  Creating a Digital ID 629
  Attaching a Digital Signature to a File 630
  Adding a Stamp 631
  Viewing Signatures 631
  Removing a Signature 632
Working with the Trust Center 633
  Viewing and Removing Trusted Sources 635
Setting Permission Levels 636
  Customizing Permissions 637
  Applying Permissions to Documents 638
Checking Document Accessibility 638
Ensuring Document Compatibility 639
What's Next? 640

Chapter 21   **Sharing Your Documents** **641**

Sharing Documents in Word 641
Word 2010 New Sharing Options 644
A Closer Look at SharePoint Workspace 2010 646
  Creating a New Workspace 646
  Checking Out and Checking In a Document 649
  Create and Save a New Document 650
Setting Up and Using Windows Live SkyDrive 651
  Sharing a File 652
  Save Your Document to a Shared Space 653
Working with Network Locations 654
  Creating a Network Location 654
  Linking to FTP Sites 654

Accessing Resources Stored in Network Locations...........................655
Saving Documents to a Network Location................................655
Using Workgroup Templates...656
Sharing Word Documents via E-Mail 658
Setting E-Mail Priority 659
Flagging a Message for Follow-Up 660
Requesting Receipts...660
Delaying Delivery 661
Include Voting Buttons..662
Using Word to Send Faxes 663
Creating and Sending a Fax...663
Choosing a Fax Service..664
What's Next?...666

Chapter 22   **Collaborating and Co-Authoring in Real Time 667**
Benefits of an Organized Revision Process 667
Familiarizing Yourself with Markup Tools 668
Setting Reviewer Name..671
Configuring Colors Associated with Reviewers 672
Viewing Comments and Revisions 673
Adding and Managing Comments Effectively 675
Inserting Comments...675
Inserting Voice and Handwritten Comments......................676
Tracking Changes...677
Tracking Changes While You Edit.....................................678
Customizing the Appearance of Changed Lines 680
Configuring Balloon and Reviewing Pane Options 680
Balloon and Reviewing Pane Styles 681
Showing and Hiding Balloons..681
Adjusting Balloon Size and Location for Online Viewing.......682
Printing Comments and Tracked Changes 684
Reviewing Comments and Tracked Changes 685
Navigating Your Comments 686
Responding to Comments...687
Deleting Comments 688
Accepting and Rejecting Proposed Edits 689
Comparing or Combining Documents.......................................693
Comparing Two Versions of a Document 694
Combining Revisions from Multiple Authors.....................696
Co-Authoring Documents in Word 2010....................................697
Editing Simultaneously and Saving Changes.....................698
Contacting Your Co-Author 700
Troubleshooting Co-Authoring 701
What's Next?...702

Part 5: Word 2010 Interactive

Chapter 23   **Preparing Tables of Contents and Indexes** **705**

Creating Effective Reference Tables 706
Creating a Table of Contents 707
     Using a TOC Style 707
     Creating a Customized TOC 708
     Adding TOC Entries Manually 710
     Compiling the Manual TOC 711
     Choosing a TOC Format 711
     Editing and Updating a TOC 712
Preparing a TOC for the Web 714
Customizing a TOC 714
     Matching Entry Styles to TOC Levels 715
     Changing TOC Styles 715
Adding Indexes 716
     What Makes a Good Index? 717
     Indexing with Word 718
Creating Index Entries 718
     Marking Index Entries 719
     Creating Subentries 720
     Selecting Repeated Entries 721
     Formatting Entries 722
     Adding Cross-References 722
     Specifying Page Ranges 722
Generating the Index 723
     Choosing the Index Format 724
     Choosing Index Alignment 725
     Changing the Way Entries Are Displayed 725
     Changing Index Columns 726
Updating an Index 727
AutoMarking Entries with a Concordance File 728
What's Next? 730

Chapter 24   **Special Features for Long Documents** **731**

What Goes into a Long Document? 732
Building a Table of Figures 732
     Adding Captions 732
     Generating a Table of Figures 734
Adding a Table of Authorities 734
     Adding Citations Manually 735
     Generating the Table of Authorities 736
When Master Documents Make Sense 736
     Master Document Mayhem and Workarounds 737
     Getting Started with a Master Document 738
     Creating a Master Document 740

Creating Subdocuments 741
Importing Data for Subdocuments 741
Working with the Master and Subdocuments 742
What's Next? 745

Chapter 25   **Blogging and Using the Word Web App** **747**
Everybody Blogs 747
Starting a New Blog Post 750
Entering Text 752
Inserting a Web Link 752
Adding a Category to Your Post 753
Adding a Picture to Your Post 755
Configuring Your Blog Account 755
Using the Word Web App 757
Save Your Document to Windows Live SkyDrive 757
Open Your Document in the Word Web App 757
Working with the Word Web App 758
What's Next? 759

Chapter 26   **Creating Mailings Large and Small** **761**
Mail Merge Overview 762
Know Your Merge Terms 763
Starting the Mail Merge Project 763
Selecting the Document Type 764
Starting Out with the Main Document 765
Using the Current Document 765
Starting from a Template 766
Starting from an Existing Document 767
Choosing Your Recipients 768
Creating a New List 768
Using an Existing Recipient List 770
Choosing Outlook Contacts 771
Choosing and Sorting Recipient Information 771
Filtering Your Recipient List 773
Adding Merge Fields 774
Inserting an Address Block 775
Choosing a Greeting Line 776
Inserting Merge Fields 777
Matching Fields with Your Database 778
Adding Word Fields 780
Previewing the Merge 781
Finding a Specific Entry 782
Checking for Errors 782
Merging the Documents 783
Merge to a New Document 783
Choosing Merge Print Options 783
Merge to E-Mail 784
Creating a Directory 784

Printing Envelopes and Labels. 785
    Creating Labels 787
What's Next?. 788

Chapter 27   Customizing Documents with Content Controls. 789
Understanding the Word 2010 Content Controls 789
Creating the Document 790
    Displaying the Developer Tab. 790
Adding and Formatting Static Text 792
Adding Content Controls 794
    Control Types in Word 2010 795
    Adding a Control. 798
Changing Content Control Properties 799
    Adding Titles and Tags. 800
    Styling Your Control 801
    Locking Controls 803
    Adding Content to Lists 803
    Mapping Controls to XML. 804
Using Content Controls. 805
Protecting Documents 805
Adding Legacy Controls 808
Adding ActiveX Controls. 808
    ActiveX Controls and the Trust Center 809
    Adding an ActiveX Control 809
    Changing Control Properties 810
    Programming a Control. 810
What's Next?. 810

Chapter 28   Working with Macros in Word 2010. 811
A Bit About VBA and Macros. 812
Saving Macro-Enabled Documents and Templates. 813
Recording a Macro 814
    Setup and Planning. 814
Running Macros. 818
    Adding a Macro to the Quick Access Toolbar 818
    Assigning a Keyboard Shortcut to a Macro 822
    Running a Macro Automatically. 824
Editing Macros 826
    The Visual Basic Editor 829
Additional Macro Options 830
    Renaming a Macro, Module, or Project 830
    Deleting and Exporting Macros and Modules. 832
    Importing Macros and Modules. 833
Protecting Your Macros 835

Digitally Signing Macros. 835
    Creating a Self-Signed Digital Signature. 836
    Third-Party Digital Signature 836
    Digitally Signing a VBA Project. 837
What's Next?. 839

Index **841**

Acknowledgments

Microsoft Word 2010 Inside Out represents a kind of milestone for me. After a year of writing about various Microsoft Office 2010 programs and features (in a variety of formats), *Microsoft Word 2010 Inside Out* is the culmination of all we've learned and developed throughout the beta and launch of Word 2010. I think this version of Microsoft Word is the best yet. Echoing the maturation of the software, this book has also found a voice and purpose in sync with the times, offering readers many practical examples, plenty of how-to information, and a flexibility designed to help content creators prepare what they need for a variety of formats and distribution channels.

Growth and development never happens in a vacuum but requires a supportive environment—complete with wind, sunlight, and rain—to produce the best results. A huge thank you goes out to the following people for contributing to the tending and nurturing of this project:

- Juliana Aldous, who was responsible for acquiring this project when we started many months ago (and who has since moved into a new role at Microsoft Learning), a big thanks for catching the vision and being enthusiastic about the new ideas and approach I wanted to take in these pages;

- Claudette Moore, my agent at Moore Literary Agency, for her always-helpful suggestions, insights, and encouragement when there's a lot to do and not much time in which to do it! Thanks, Claudette; as always, you make these projects possible—and even fun.

- Kenyon Brown, senior editor, for overseeing this book, (our most recent in a whole series of Office 2010 projects) with his characteristic professional style and holistic management skills. Keeping everyone moving, in sync, and on schedule is no simple task, but Ken seems to do it naturally.

- Todd Meister, technical editor, for his careful and insightful review of all content in this book. Tech editing isn't easy when a book project spans the process of beta development and software release, and Todd not only makes the task look simple, but offers corrections and great suggestions in a supportive and collaborative way.

- Bob Russell at Octal Publishing, for a great copy edit, complete with fun and thoughtful comments and suggestions that helped make this a better book;

- Kristen Borg, Production Editor, for her careful and kind project management as the book moved through editing, review, and production;

- Sumita Mukherji, for her friendly and helpful scheduling and coordination of the project early-on; and

- Dianne Russell, also at Octal Publishing, for the beautiful, clean, and effective layout and design you now hold in your hands.

Conventions and Features Used in This Book

This book uses special text and design conventions to make it easer for you to find the information you need.

Text Conventions

Convention	Feature
Abbreviated menu commands	For your convenience, this book uses abbreviated menu commands. For example, "Choose Tools, Forms, Design A Form" means that you should click the Tools menu, point to Forms, and select the Design A Form command.
Boldface type	Boldface type is used to indicate text that you enter or type.
Initial Capital Letters	The first letters of the names of menus, dialog boxes, dialog box elements, and commands are capitalized. Example: The Save As dialog box.
Italicized type	Italicized type is used to indicate new terms.
Plus sign (+) in text	Keyboard shortcuts are indicated by a plus sign (+) separating two key names. For example, Shift+F9 means that you press the Shift and F9 keys at the same time.

Design Conventions

Note
Notes offer additional information related to the task being discussed.

Cross-references point you to other locations in the book that offer additional information on the topic being discussed.

CAUTION

Cautions identify potential problems that you should look out for when you're completing a task, or problems that you must address before you can complete a task.

INSIDE OUT — This Statement Illustrates an Example of an "Inside Out" Problem Statement

These are the book's signature tips. In these tips, you'll get the straight scoop on what's going on with the software—inside information on why a feature works the way it does. You'll also find handy workarounds to different software problems.

TROUBLESHOOTING

This statement illustrates an example of a "Troubleshooting" problem statement.

Look for these sidebars to find solutions to common problems you might encounter. Troubleshooting sidebars appear next to related information in the chapters. You can also use the Troubleshooting Topics index at the back of the book to look up problems by topic.

Sidebar

The sidebars sprinkled throughout these chapters provide ancillary information on the topic being discussed. Go to sidebars to learn more about the technology or a feature.

Introduction

Maybe you've noticed: creating simple documents today is *so* 2009. In this new decade, the emphasis has shifted from designing, creating, editing, and printing real hold-in-your-hands documents to creating content that can be used in a variety of smart, efficient ways. You might create content about a new product, for example, and instead of simply printing a fact sheet that you hand to all your sales reps, you save one version as a PDF, send another in an e-mail message, post some of the content to a blog, include some of the description in a catalog, and forward the Word file to peers around the globe.

What's more, you'll rarely create these content pieces alone. The use of teams is growing throughout industries of all types, and with good reason. When you work collaboratively, each person on a team can contribute his or her expertise, without tying up anybody's time around the clock. Shared review enables many people with many perspectives to provide feedback so the content is the best that it can be. Team work, when it works well, can make a huge difference in the type and quality of materials you create. When team work *doesn't* work well, of course, it's another story. Luckily, Word 2010 includes some great new features that help you to reduce or dissolve collaboration challenges.

Another big change in the way we work has brought about changes in Word 2010. Today, thanks to the advent of the mobile phone and the wanderlust spirit of today's information enthusiast, we know it's possible—and we increasingly want—to work anywhere, anytime. You know those moments that seem wasted on the train out of the city? Now you can use them to finish reviewing a document you need to share with your team in the morning. You can access your Word files—and edit, format, review, and share in real time—from any point you have Web or smartphone access.

With these major changes in the way we work and where we work underway, Word 2010 is positioned to be a state-of-the-art word processing program that really is there for you. With the tools you need to produce any kind of content you want and the flexibility to enable you to create, edit, and share that content from almost any point on the globe, Word 2010 pops the lid on anything that was holding you and your creativity back before.

Get Busy with Word 2010

With all that being said, the book you now hold in your hands is a major revamp from previous versions of *Microsoft Word Inside Out*. As Word users, our need for content creation has been kicked up a few notches, and this book responds accordingly. In the pages that follow, you'll find that the emphasis on creating all kinds of content, with anyone, from anywhere, flows through the examples, features, and projects. We hope you'll find examples that speak to the way you use Word every day to accomplish the goals of your business, department, company, or school.

The various parts and chapters in this book help you to explore the whole Word 2010 landscape from a variety of entrance points. The parts focus generally on the types of overall tasks you are likely to want to complete, and individual chapters within each part zoom in on a specific tool or technique (or range of techniques) related to that task. Along the way, you'll find notes, Inside Out tips, and troubleshooting ideas, as well as some "green" ideas and sidebars offering additional information that can help boost your understand or application of Word 2010 concepts.

Some Assumptions About You

The *Inside Out* series is designed for readers who have some experience with Word and are pretty comfortable finding their way around the program. You don't have to be a power user or Word developer by any means; you aren't necessarily a technology enthusiast (like your author) although you do like the idea of using programs in a way that is efficient and effective so you can accomplish what you want to accomplish without a lot of fuss and bother.

For this reason, *Microsoft Word 2010 Inside Out* touches only briefly on some of the basic topics that you'll find covered in more detail elsewhere. Although we want the coverage in a book this size to be as complete as possible (we want you to get what you paid for), we also focus in on techniques and topics that are likely to appeal to readers who have already mastered many of the basics in Word.

If you find that you'd like to brush up on Word 2010 basics in addition to taking on the topics you'll find covered fully in this book, you may want to check out any or all of the following books:

- *Microsoft Word 2010 Plain & Simple,* by yours truly (Microsoft Press, 2010)

- *Microsoft Word 2010 Step by Step,* by Joyce Cox and Joan Preppernau (Microsoft Press, 2010)

Tip
Remember that although nothing replaces the book experience when you need to refer to a technique or look something up in a reference work, there are other learning opportunities available to you online. Visit Microsoft Learning for online learning courses related to Word 2010 and the other Office 2010 programs.

About This Book

Microsoft Word 2010 Inside Out helps you learn to master Word 2010 in the way you're most likely to use the program, following a linear process that looks something like this:

- Create a new document

- Apply a template and make layout choices

- Choose your theme for color and style

- Add content

- Translate phrases and documents

- Edit your content and use reference tools

- Apply and customize Quick Styles

- Add tables, diagrams, art, and more

- Co-author and share your documents with your team, near and far

- Work almost anywhere with the Office Word Web App

- Use Word 2010 for special projects, like blogging, mailings, long documents, and more

- Tackle the high-end Word features, including macros and forms

Each chapter provides the detail you need to know in order to accomplish those various tasks successfully, and you'll find tips and cautions along the way to steer you away from trouble spots and help you optimize the time you spend creating content.

How This Book Is Organized

Microsoft Word 2010 Inside Out gives you a comprehensive look at the various features you will use whether you create long or short projects for print or online uses. The chapters are organized according to the types of tasks you are likely to be performing. Here's the general roadmap for the book:

Part I, "Word 2010: Make an Immediate Impact," starts with the obvious: the way the world has changed in relation to technology and the way we work, and how that is reflected in the new features you'll find in Word 2010. After a tour of the new features, you explore Backstage view and find out about the best ways to create a new document, apply and tweak a template, set up a page, adjust a layout, and apply themes.

Part II, "Creating Global Content: From Research to Review," focuses on the ways you pull together different elements to create your Word document, translate it for a global audience, and edit, proof, and use reference tools as you polish up your words. In this part, you also learn the ins and outs of Quick Styles and find out how to create them on your own. You use the new Navigation Pane to find just what you want when you want it, reorganize content with Outline view, and spend a little time with the streamlined print process.

Part III, "Make Your Point Visually," shines a light on one of the big improvements in Word 2010. As it becomes easier to grab and insert photos in our documents and content pieces, the overall look of the files we create is improving. Today you can create a professional marketing piece in under an hour that used to take weeks (no kidding) at a commercial print shop. Not only are the cost and quality under your control, but the images you choose to portray and the styles and artistic effects that you select enable your content to rival that produced by expensive firms or elaborate marketing departments. Also in this part, you learn how to add screenshots to your content and reflow text around the art elements on your pages.

Part IV, "Word 2010 as a Team Effort—Anywhere, Always," helps you tackle the challenge of creating content in a global workplace that likely needs that content to be produced in different ways for different audiences. The reality of localizing content is that programs need to include translation tools that are easy to use and extend—and Word 2010 has just those sorts of translation tools. With the new language features in Word 2010, you can choose from a variety of languages and set up multiple levels of control for translations, whether you want to translate entire documents, sections, or words and phrases on the fly.

Part V, "Word 2010 Interactive," moves things to a new level as you consider the different ways you can share the content you create. Whether you are generating an enormous master document that combines subdocuments contributed by a number of team members; blogging for a global audience; or designing and completing mass mailings to your customer base, donor list, or parent population; you'll find what you need to complete your projects in this part of the book. This part also includes more specialized high-end Word 2010 techniques related to designing and distributing documents that use content controls and automating tasks using macros.

Getting Started

So as you can see, there's a lot to cover no matter how you plan to produce and offer your Word 2010 content to the world. The great news is that Word 2010 is in sync with the times and can grow right along with you as you stretch your own capabilities to master the features you need. The next chapter gets you started on that path by introducing you to the new and improved features in Word 2010.

PART 1

Word 2010: Make an Immediate Impact

CHAPTER 1

Spotlight on Microsoft Word 2010. 3

CHAPTER 2

Managing Your Documents with
Backstage View 33

CHAPTER 3

Right Now Document Design
with Word 2010. 69

CHAPTER 4

Templates and Themes for a
Professional Look. 101

CHAPTER 5

Customizing Page Setup and
Controlling Pagination 139

CHAPTER 6

Setting Up Your Layout with Page
Backgrounds and Columns 173

Spotlight on Microsoft Word 2010

Imagining Word 2010 3

What's New in Word 2010? 4

Finding Your Way Around the Word 2010 Window 13

Understanding and Tailoring the Status Bar 30

What's Next? 31

For most of us, the phrase *word processing* doesn't bring to mind exciting images of movement, color, sound, and images. It doesn't promise a lot of fun and connection like the phrase *social networking* does. It doesn't hint at an unlimited world of information or draw you closer to what fascinates you like the phrase *web browsing* does.

But that's all changing with Microsoft Word 2010.

The newest version of Word offers new and improved features that make it easy for you to make your documents look better than ever. You can control the format, enhance your text, and apply artistic filters to images to make your documents really shine. You can easily translate content on the fly, access your documents from almost anywhere, blog and share content with social media sites, and share your content with colleagues in a number of different formats with just a few clicks of the mouse. And you can access your content in a variety of ways—from the server, your desktop PC, your smartphone, or any device with Web access.

This chapter encourages you to envision the types of projects you'd like to create with Word 2010 and spotlights the new and improved features that will help get you there. Along the way, you'll learn about the Word 2010 window, explore the Ribbon, and find out more about Word options, the Trust Center, and tweaking program features to your liking.

Imagining Word 2010

So how will you use Word 2010? Maybe one of the following scenarios fits what you have in mind or reflects tasks you might want to try in the future:

- Create a four-color annual report with photos of your staff, services, and office.

- Design a new product brochure with high-quality typography.

- Download the latest version of a document from shared server space so that you can review, edit, and upload the content later.

- Draft a letter to your top-level donors.

- Post an entry to your blog.

- Edit a book chapter simultaneously with others on your team.

- Review and edit your document while you're on the road.

The content you create today is likely to be much different from the ho-hum documents you drafted, printed, and photocopied a dozen years ago. Thanks to the advent of Web and mobile technologies, change is happening at an ever-increasing rate, and it's touching the way we create, edit, and share our information—printed and otherwise. Yesterday you were working on documents, one at a time, using revision marks and then waiting for your documents to come back from review. To move a file from one computer to another, you either e-mailed it or saved it to a disk or USB drive.

As today's Word user, you are probably not tied to a single computer as you create, edit, review, and share the content you create. You might use one computer at home and another at work; perhaps you check e-mail on your smartphone and log in to the office server from remote places that offer Web access. No longer are you working on one document at a time and then sending it to another member of your team for review—now your group might be viewing, editing, discussing, and commenting on the document in real time. And nobody is stuck at a stand-alone or networked PC any longer; now editing on your smartphone is a real option, as is logging in to your files using the Word Web App.

The idea is to give you a consistent user experience with Word 2010 no matter which device you might be using. Whether you open and work with files on the Web, review content on your smartphone, or edit documents on your PC, you'll be able to access and leverage the content you create in an almost unlimited number of ways.

What's New in Word 2010?

Word 2010 is an exciting new release because not only have software developers been listening to the requests and feedback of users like you all over the globe, but they have also taken into account the way the work world is changing. With Word 2010, you can take advantage of features that enable you to share files in real time, work seamlessly with your corporate server, edit content simultaneously, and dramatically improve the pictures and the look of your text.

The changes in Word 2010 offer new and improved features in three key areas:

- **Creating a better user experience.**   The Ribbon—which was introduced with Word 2007—can now be fully customized, which means that you can create your own tabs and tab groups. And now Backstage view brings together all the tools you need to set program preferences, work with files, and protect and share your content. Other user experience enhancements include the Navigation pane, which enhances the power of your search capabilities, and Paste with Live Preview, which enables you to preview various paste options before you add content to your document.

- **Improvements in authoring.**   Co-authoring, also known as simultaneous editing, is the big story in authoring features for Word 2010, but you'll also find great new image features and text effects that help your content really stand out. What's more, now you can use high-end typographic features through the OpenType fonts that support them, including ligatures, kerning, stylistic sets, and more.

- **Word power in new contexts.**   The idea of taking Word beyond the desktop becomes reality in Word 2010. Now you can move from desktop to Web to smart-phone to server—and back again—using any of the various access choices for Word 2010. You can also run Word 2010 on 64-bit systems to take advantage of the full processing power your computer possesses.

The sections that follow give you a quick introduction to each of these features in more detail.

Enhancing Your User Experience

Word 2010 is all about flexibility—putting more power in your hands and giving you the tools to tailor the program to work the way you do. These are some of the top enhancements that will make your user experience a more pleasant one in Word 2010:

- **Customizable Ribbon.**   You can easily add your own tabs and tab groups to the Ribbon in Word 2010. Suppose that you regularly create reports introducing the new products your company introduces. You can add tab groups that give you easy access to the tools you use for preparing, formatting, and reviewing the documents you are charged with producing (see Figure 1-1).

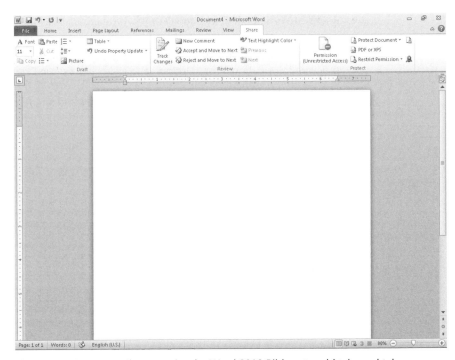

Figure 1-1 You can easily customize the Word 2010 Ribbon to add tabs and tab groups (as demonstrated on the Share tab in this image) that fit the way you use the program.

> For specific steps on tailoring the Ribbon to include the tools and tabs you want, see Chapter 2, "Managing Your Documents with Backstage View..

- **Navigation pane.** The Navigation pane combines the best of the Find tool with Outline view and thumbnail displays, giving you three different ways to navigate the content in your document. You can search by heading, by thumbnail, or by text phrase. Additionally, you can use Word's Find and Replace tools from the Navigation pane and browse through the objects in your document as well.

- **Paste with Live Preview.** Word users copy, cut, and paste information all the time. In fact, Word users undo paste operations more than any other—at least in part because in previous versions of the program, you didn't always get the results you expected when you pasted information. Whether you are copying and pasting text, pictures, objects, headings, lines, charts, diagrams, or shapes, you need to make choices about the way in which you want the information pasted into your document. The new Paste with Live Preview makes it possible for you to preview the way the information will look before you click to paste it in your document. This builds more flexibility into a very common task, saving you time and trouble by enabling you to paste the information the way you want it—the first time.

- **Backstage view.**   In Backstage view you have access to all the tools you'll use to create, save, open, share, protect, and print the files you create. Backstage view simplifies many of the most common file management tasks and gives you access to program information, Word Options, and Help choices (see Figure 1-2).

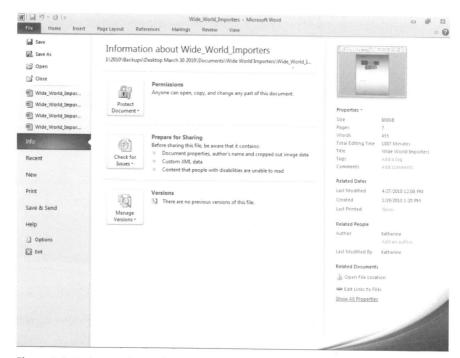

Figure 1-2 Backstage view pulls together all the tools you need to work with files and program preferences.

Better Authoring Features

Many different features in Word 2010 are designed to improve your authoring experience so that you can create content that accomplishes the goal you're reaching for. Some of the top authoring features include:

- **Co-authoring in real time.**   Word 2010 lets more than one person work in a file at the same time. You can communicate with other authors as you work and easily see where changes are being made in the document (see Figure 1-3). What's more, the co-authoring feature helps you resolve any editing conflicts that might arise (for example, perhaps you and a co-author have edited the same paragraph in different ways and Word can help you resolve the issue).

Chapter 22, "Collaborating and Co-Authoring in Real Time," shows you the ins and outs of co-authoring and walks you through the process of resolving authoring conflicts in your files.

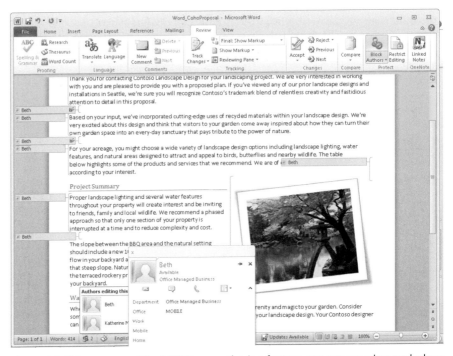

Figure 1-3 When you use Word 2010's co-authoring feature, you can see when and where others are making changes in a shared file.

- **Better translation tools help you talk to the world.**   With Word 2010, you can choose the language you want to use for a number of translation and on-screen features. You can customize help text and program prompts, or translate text, sections, or entire documents on the fly using the Mini Translator (see Figure 1-4), the Research task pane, or whole-document translation services.

You learn how to set up the language you want to use and choose your translation preferences in Chapter 9, "Translating Text and Working with Languages."

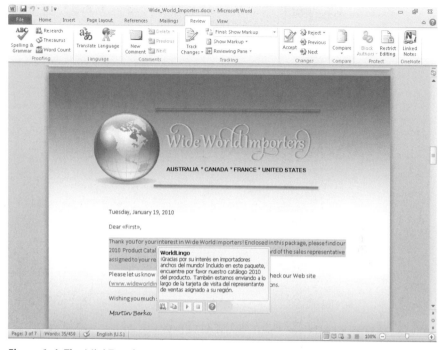

Figure 1-4 The Mini Translator pops up over your Word window and enables you to copy, look up, or listen to the translation.

- **Check what you mean—as well as what you say.**   The new contextual spelling checker helps you check your document for errors in usage as well as spelling. Did you say "there" when you meant to say "their"? Or did you use "loose" instead of "lose"? The new contextual spelling checker points out these and other errors so that you can make sure your document is as grammatically accurate as possible.

- **Improve pictures with artistic effects and enhanced editing.**   Word 2010 now includes specialized filters that you can apply to the images you place in your documents. Instead of including a regular photo of a new product, for example (although you might want to include that elsewhere in your document), you can stylize the image by applying one of any number of cool effects, such as glass, pencil sketch, plastic wrap, and more (see Figure 1-5). You can also control the balance, saturation, contrast, and more in your photos by using the expanded editing capabilities—you can even remove the picture background, which you'll learn more about in Chapter 17, "Adding and Editing Pictures and Screenshots."

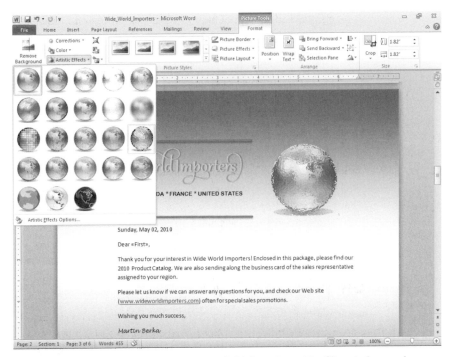

Figure 1-5 With Artistic Effects, you can apply high-end graphics filters to images in your documents.

> **Tip**
> Word 2010 also includes enhancements to SmartArt. Find out about SmartArt's new features in Chapter 16, "Create Compelling SmartArt Diagrams and Charts."

- **Show others your screen.** If you create training materials or want to share a picture of what you see on-screen, you'll enjoy the new Insert Screenshot feature in Word 2010. As part of the Illustrations group, you can either grab a portion of the screen or insert an entire screen image in your current document. You'll find out more about adding screenshots in Chapter 17.

- **Enhance text with text effects and support for OpenType features.** New text features in Word 2010 enable you to apply new effects to the content and headings in your document, such as glows, reflections, 3-D effects, and much more. You can also take advantage of high-end typography features available with some OpenType fonts, including ligatures, stylistic sets, and number styles to extend the look you want to create.

Chapter 7, "Creating and Reusing Content," introduces you to the ways that you can use text effects to spruce up the look of your text and increase your font choices with OpenType support.

> ## Tip
>
> **Expanded inking capabilities.** Word 2010 now includes improved support for ink users via an expanded pen palette, enhanced touch sensitivity, and the ability to incorporate and convert inked content to digitized text and equations. Turn to Chapter 7 for more information on using ink capabilities in Word 2010.

Use Word 2010 Anywhere

When was the last time you sat at your desk all day long and worked on one continuous document? We thought so. Word 2010 takes into account the needs of today's user, who is often on the go, juggling multiple projects, and working seamlessly with others down the hall or around the world. New features that help you take Word 2010 beyond your desktop PC include:

- **The Word Web App.**   Now you can access your Word 2010 files and review, edit, update, format, and share them normally from any point where you have Web access. Using your SharePoint Workspace or Windows Live SkyDrive account, you can access your saved files and work with them in a Web version of the Word 2010 interface you're accustomed to (see Figure 1-6). This means you don't need to carry a flash drive or e-mail documents to yourself in order to access them in different places.

- **Seamless saving to the server.**   Working with others means that you might be regularly saving the files you create in a shared server space or posting your documents to Windows Live SkyDrive so that others can access them. You can save your files to your shared space as easily as you save a document on your hard drive in the office. Another detail, simplified.

Figure 1-6 The Word Web App makes it easy for you to work on your files from any point you have Web access.

- **Using Word Mobile 2010.**   In addition to having the flexibility to work on your Word files from the Web or saving to your server, you can also access and work with your files from your smartphone. Using a streamlined Microsoft Office 2010 interface designed for the small screen, you can view, edit, format, update, and share your documents easily from your phone.

> **Note**
> Office Mobile 2010 is not part of the Office 2010 suites and must be purchased separately.

Finding Your Way Around the Word 2010 Window

It turns out that we're still dealing with the aftermath of the Office 2007 user interface redesign. People had greatly divergent views on the overall approach that the designers of Office 2007 were reaching for—and many people just plain didn't like the Ribbon. Early reactions were generally positive—people were intrigued by the idea that Office designers went "back to the drawing board" when they began brainstorming about the new look and feel of the user interface. Experienced users were wary—why fix what's not broken?—and power users wondered whether the simplified design would make it impossible to use the shortcuts, macros, and more they had come to rely on to expedite their document tasks.

Word 2010 (along with all the other Office 2010 applications) carries forward the purpose and intent of the new user interface, this time offering increased flexibility—now you can customize the Ribbon to suit your needs. Shortcut keys still work, macros are easier to create than ever, and we realize—as the software continues to move forward—that we haven't lost any of the familiar tools that we were worried about misplacing in the new design.

Get What You Need, Intuitively

But, you know, everybody's different. One of the lessons I think Word 2007 taught was that not everybody was in agreement that "new = better." The intention to create an interface that was easier to use and ultimately uncluttered the workspace was a good one. And the design philosophy behind the Ribbon—bringing you just the tools you need when you need them, organized around specific tasks you want to complete—was also sound. But learning a dramatically new interface and getting comfortable finding your favorite tools and options when you need to get things done can be a bit of a headache—one many Word users suffered through on the way to a more intuitive word processing experience.

When you open Word 2010 for the first time, the screen that meets your eye is open and inviting. Figure 1-7 shows the Word 2010 window. The Ribbon appears at the top of the screen, with tabs that group the tools you need for the various tasks you'll undertake in Word.

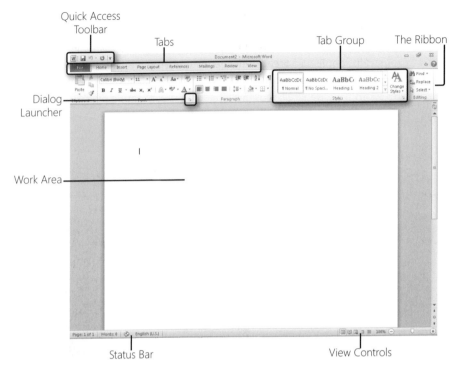

Figure 1-7 The Word 2010 window.

Exploring the Ribbon

The Ribbon across the top of the window organizes the tools in tabs, which reflect the different tasks you are likely to want to accomplish with the program. For example, when you create the document, the Home tab provides the commands you are likely to use as you start out. When you want to add pictures, shapes, diagrams, and more, you find the tools you need on the Insert tab. When you're ready to share your document with others, the Review tab offers a variety of tools for preparing the file for review and working with the review copies when you receive them.

The Ribbon, as it appears by default, includes all the following elements:

- **Tabs (Home, Insert, Page Layout, References, Mailings, Review, and View).** Tabs stretch across the screen just below the window's title bar. You can also customize the Ribbon by adding tabs and tab groups that provide tools you use most often.

- **Groups.** These are collections of tools available on the Ribbon when a specific tab is selected. For example, on the Insert tab, the groups displayed include Pages, Tables, Illustrations, Links, Header & Footer, Text, and Symbols.

- **Contextual tabs.**   Contextual tabs help keep the window uncluttered by displaying task-related tools only when an object is selected in the document. When you select a picture, for example, the contextual Picture Tools tab appears along the top of the Ribbon. The commands displayed when the tab is selected all relate to the object you've selected (see Figure 1-8).

Figure 1-8 Contextual tabs display tools related to the specific object you select in the document.

Note

The Ribbon is fully displayed by default when you begin working with Word. If you want to minimize the Ribbon to increase room on the screen, press Ctrl+F1 or click the Minimize The Ribbon button, located to the left of the Help tool just above and at the right end of the Ribbon. The Ribbon reduces to the tabs only. To redisplay the Ribbon, press Ctrl+F1 again or click Expand The Ribbon. A quick way to reduce and alternately display the tabs is to double-click one of the tabs. The first double-click hides the Ribbon; the second redisplays it.

You can tailor the Word 2010 interface to fit your own style. Now you can add tab groups, create new groups, reorder tools, and rename groups already displayed. You'll find everything you need to make these changes in Word Options. See Chapter 2 to find out the specifics.

Keep Your Favorite Tools in Reach with the Quick Access Toolbar

In the upper-left corner of the screen you'll find the Quick Access Toolbar, which offers, within clicking distance, favorite file-management tools you are likely to use often. When you first launch Word 2010, the Save, Undo Typing, and Repeat Typing tools appear in the Quick Access Toolbar. You can click the Customize The Quick Access Toolbar arrow to display a list of additional tools and options that you can use to tailor the tools offered there (see Figure 1-9).

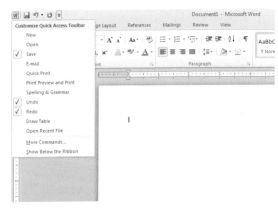

Figure 1-9 You can tailor the Quick Access Toolbar to include the tools you use often and want to make available while you work.

You can customize the Quick Access Toolbar a couple of different ways. First, you can simply click the tool you want from the Customize Quick Access Toolbar list. If the tool doesn't appear in the list, you can click More Commands, navigate to the tool you want to add, and click it. You can also add a tool to the Quick Access Toolbar by right-clicking the tool in the Ribbon, and then click Add To Quick Access Toolbar (see Figure 1-10).

> ### Tip
> The changes you make to the Quick Access Toolbar in one document carry through for other documents as well. To return the Quick Access Toolbar to the default display, click the Customize Quick Access Toolbar and choose More Commands. In the Customizations area, click the Reset arrow and choose Reset Only Quick Access Toolbar, and then click OK.

Figure 1-10 Add favorite tools to the Quick Access Toolbar easily.

> **Note**
>
> If you add a number of tools to the Quick Access Toolbar, you might want to give it more room by displaying the toolbar in its own row below the Ribbon. To do so, Right-click anywhere on the Ribbon and choose Show Quick Access Toolbar Below The Ribbon. To return the display of the toolbar to its original state, right-click the Quick Access Toolbar and choose Show Quick Access Toolbar Above The Ribbon.

Using Dialog Launchers

The Ribbon is great for providing you with groups of tools that are related to the task you're trying to accomplish, but sometimes it's helpful to see all the options you have available so you can make the best choice. In those situations, having a traditional-style dialog box comes in handy. Dialog boxes are available for some groups on the Ribbon. Those groups that do have a dialog box display a small, boxed arrow symbol, called a *dialog launcher*, in the lower-right corner of the group. For example, the Font group on the Home tab has a dialog launcher in the lower-right corner. When you click the launcher, the dialog box appears (Figure 1-11).

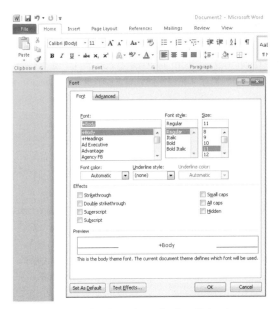

Figure 1-11 Dialog launchers display dialog boxes.

Options for displaying dialog boxes are also available at the bottom of any gallery that offers additional options. For example, when you click Columns in the Page Setup group on the Page Layout tab, a gallery of column settings appears. Click the More Columns option (see Figure 1-12) at the bottom of the gallery to launch the Columns dialog box.

Figure 1-12 Click the More Columns command at the bottom of the gallery to display additional options.

Working with Galleries

Word 2010 includes all sorts of galleries—themes, styles, picture styles, and more—that graphically display the range of choices from which you can click the design, color, layout, and style you want. You will see galleries displayed in different ways, depending on your screen resolution and the size of the Word window. The Ribbon was designed to adjust to the size of the screen, so in some cases you might see galleries appear as selections on the Ribbon, while other galleries appear as drop-down items.

Basically you'll see galleries presented in one of three ways in Word. Some galleries are shown as part of a group on the Ribbon (similar to the Picture Styles gallery shown in Figure 1-13); you can click the More button in the lower-right corner of the gallery to display the full collection of choices. Other galleries (such as those available for Themes, Margins, and Position commands) display as drop-down galleries from which you can make your selection.

Figure 1-13 Some galleries display choices in the Ribbon.

Other galleries open as a palette of choices, like the Corrections gallery shown in Figure 1-14. Using galleries, you can easily see at a glance which color combination, format, color scheme, transition, or chart type you want. The choices you see in the galleries are connected with the theme you've selected (if any) for your document. This helps you be sure that when you're choosing a chart type, for example, it reflects the colors, fonts, and effects used in other parts of your document.

To choose an option in a gallery, simply click your choice, and the setting is applied to the current document or selected object.

Figure 1-14 Some galleries open as palettes from which you can easily click your choice.

> **Tip**
> You can easily preview how the new selection will look by hovering your mouse over the option you're thinking about selecting. The effect of the choice will show in the selected object or text in your document. In this way, you can try out different choices before you commit to one by clicking it.

Making Quick Formatting Changes with the Mini Toolbar

If you're like other Word users, many of the choices you make while you're working on a document have to do with formatting. Word 2010 includes the Mini Toolbar to bring the most common formatting options to you so you don't have to leave your creative zone to choose the options you want to apply. Whenever you select text, the Mini Toolbar appears above the selection (see Figure 1-15). If you want to use the Mini Toolbar, move the mouse toward it and select the option you want; otherwise, move the mouse pointer away from the toolbar and it will fade away.

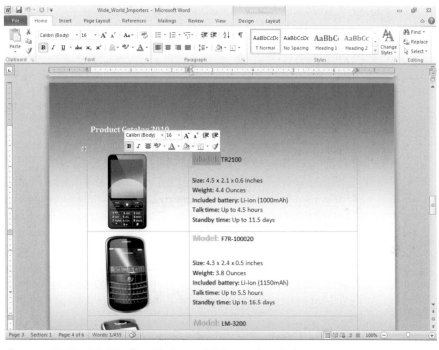

Figure 1-15 The Mini Toolbar displays quick formatting choices whenever you select text.

> **Note**
>
> If you find the Mini Toolbar distracting or don't think you'll use it, you can simply turn the feature off. On the File tab, choose Options; in the General tab of the Word Options dialog box, clear the Show Mini Toolbar On Selection check box, and then click OK. Now the Mini Toolbar is disabled and will not appear the next time you select text. (It will appear, however, when you right-click selected text.) To reactivate the Mini Toolbar, display the Word Options dialog box again and reselect the check box.

Getting a New View of Your Document

While you're working on your document, you can easily change to a different view by clicking one of the view tools in the bottom-right corner of the Word window or by choosing a view in the Document Views group on the View tab. You can also use the new Zoom slider (in the lower-right corner of the Word window) to enlarge or reduce the display of the document. Word offers you many different ways to view your work, depending on the type of document you're creating and the task at hand:

- **Print Layout** This view, which is used by default when you create a new document, seems to be the view most people use as they create and edit their documents. It shows how the document will look when printed. In this view, you can see headers and footers as well as footnotes and endnotes. The edges of the page and the space between pages are also visible as you type and edit.

> ### Tip
> You can alternately suppress and display the top and bottom margins of your document in Page Layout view by double-clicking the space between the pages. By default, Page Layout view shows a gap between pages. If you position the pointer over the page break, the pointer changes to two arrows and a tooltip prompts you to double-click the space to remove it. Double-clicking at that point removes the space between the pages and enables you to view text before and after the break in a continuous paragraph. To return the page display to the default setting, position the pointer over the page break line and double-click.

- **Full Screen Reading** This view gives you the maximum amount of space on the screen, giving you more room to review and comment on the content. Note, however, that Full Screen Reading view does not display the document as it will look in print—that's the job of Page Layout view. By default, when you first begin using Full Screen Reading view, the functionality is limited to only reviewing and commenting. If you want to be able to type and edit in Full Screen Reading view, click View Options in the upper-right corner of Full Screen Reading view and choose Allow Typing.

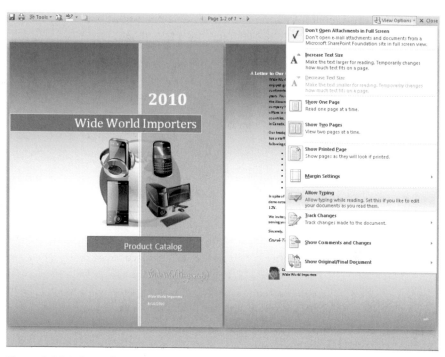

Figure 1-16 Using Full Screen Reading view, you can view, comment on, and edit your document with a maximum amount of room on the screen.

- **Web Layout**   This view displays the page as though it were a Web page. The first thing you will notice when you select the Web Layout view tool is that the page margins are not used, and depending on the content of your document, the format of your document might seem skewed (see Figure 1-17).

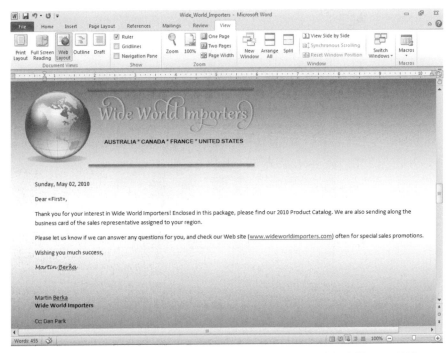

Figure 1-17 Web Layout view shows you what your document will look like as a Web page.

- **Outline** With this view, you can see the document in outline form, with headings and subordinate text indented so that you can easily identify and work with sections in a long document.

- **Draft** This view is a fast, no-frills mode that many people prefer to use when they need to write or edit something quickly. Note that some elements—such as headers and footers—are not visible while you're working in Draft view.

Finding What You Need Quickly with the Navigation Pane

An exciting new feature in Word 2010 combines the Document Map and Thumbnail features with a powerful search tool to help you to find content you need quickly using whatever method works best for you. On the View tab, select the Navigation Pane checkbox in the Show group; the Navigation pane appears on the left side of your Word 2010 window (see Figure 1-18).

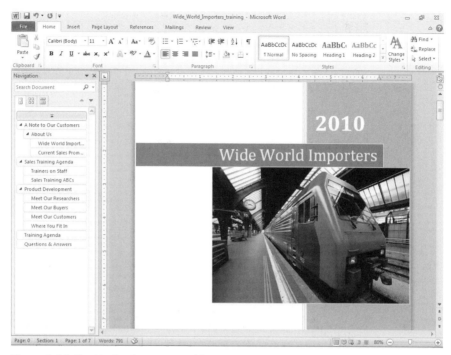

Figure 1-18 The Navigation pane enables you to view, move through, and search your document by heading, page view, or text search.

The Navigation pane offers three different tabs that move you through the information in your document by one of these methods:

- **Browse the headings in your document.**   When you click this tab (shown in Figure 1-18), Word 2010 displays a list of headings in your document. Clicking on any of these heading will bring you directly to the point in the file where the heading appears.

- **Browse the pages in your document.**   This tab displays thumbnail images of the pages in your document. Again, you can move to a specific page by clicking on an image in this view.

- **Browse the results from your current search.**   This tab shows the results of a search performed using a word or text phrase you enter in the Search Document box. The results are listed and highlighted, as shown in Figure 1-19. Move to the result in the file by clicking the result you want to see.

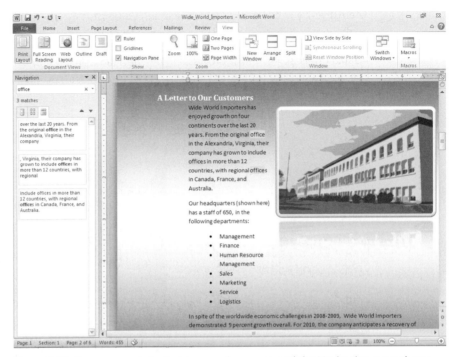

Figure 1-19 You can search for text in your document, and the Navigation pane shows you every place the word or phrase appears.

> **Tip**
> You can also search for specific objects in your document using the Browse Object features. For more about searching and navigating your document, see Chapter 8, "Navigating Your Document."

Displaying Rulers and Gridlines

When you are working on a document in which the alignment and sizing of elements is important, you will want to turn on rulers and gridlines to ensure that items line up on the page and meet the measurements you need. The controls for both items are found in the Show/Hide group on the View tab.

You can display and hide rulers quickly using a tool located at the top of the vertical scroll-bar. The rulers are displayed by default, so to hide the them, click the View Ruler button. To redisplay the rulers, click the tool a second time.

Alternatively, you can display vertical and horizontal rulers by selecting the Ruler check box on the View tab. To hide the rulers, clear the Ruler check box.

Adding gridlines is a similar process. On the View tab, select the Gridlines check box. Gridlines appear on your document to which you can easily align pictures, quotes, or other elements on your page (see Figure 1-20).

Figure 1-20 Gridlines help you to align pictures, charts, and other elements in your document.

> **Note**
>
> If you don't like rulers cluttering up your work area and you want to remove the vertical ruler in Print Layout view, you can turn it off using Word Options. On the File tab, choose Options, and then choose Advanced and scroll down to the Display options. Clear the check box for Show Vertical Ruler In Page Layout View. Click OK to save your changes. When you return to Print Layout view, the vertical ruler will be gone.

Viewing More Than One Page at a Time

The Zoom group on the View tab includes five different tools with which you can change the size and number of pages you view on the screen at any one time. Page Width view is selected by default, but you can easily change the view to match your own comfort level.

To change the size of the text, click the Zoom tool to open the Zoom dialog box. You can choose one of the preset sizes or specify your own by clicking in the Percent box and typing a new value (see Figure 1-21). You can also change the number of pages displayed by choosing the Many Pages option and then dragging to select the number of pages you want to display on the screen. The Preview window shows you how your document will look, and the sample text area shows how readable (or not!) your text will be. When you've made changes you are happy with, click OK to save them.

Figure 1-21 Use the Zoom dialog box to change the way your document is displayed.

In addition to changing the page display in the Zoom dialog box, you can also easily switch among multipage views by clicking the One Page, Two Pages, or Page Width tools in the Zoom group on the View tab. Each of these tools behaves the way you would expect—One Page shows you the whole page at the cursor position; Two Pages displays the page on which the cursor is active and the next full page in the document; and Page Width magnifies or reduces the size of the document so that it fits the width of the Word window.

Working with Multiple Documents

When you are working on a big project, chances are that you will have more than one document open at the same time. If you're copying and pasting your research notes into a new journal article you're writing, or if you're incorporating the latest fundraising figures into the annual report, you'll need an easy way of moving among open documents while you work. The View tab includes the Window group which gives you the means to do just that.

When you want to easily move among open Word documents, use the Switch Windows tool. When you click Switch Windows, a list appears that shows you the various open windows (see Figure 1-22); just click the one you want to see.

Figure 1-22 Click Switch Windows and choose the document you want to view to move among open files.

Use the New Windows tool when you want to open a new copy of the current document in a new window. You might use this tool when you need to edit or compare different portions of a large document instead of endlessly scrolling back and forth. When you're ready to close the copy, click the close button in the upper-right corner of the screen.

The Arrange All, Split, and View Side By Side commands all enable you to choose how you want to view the open documents. If you have more than two documents open at once, clicking View Side By Side displays the Compare Side By Side dialog box, as shown in the following image. Here, you can choose the other open document you want to compare with the current one. Select your choice and click OK to display the document.

> **Note**
> Depending on the number of open document windows and your screen resolution, when you use the Arrange All command, the Ribbon might disappear. This happens due to the auto scale feature of the Ribbon. To return to the full view of the Ribbon, simply resize the height of the document window.

When you use the View Side By Side command, Word sets the default to Synchronous Scrolling, which means that as you scroll through one document, the other document scrolls automatically as well. This is helpful for comparing documents in which you're looking for paragraphs, sections, or even phrases that might be slightly different.

Understanding and Tailoring the Status Bar

The status bar, which is located in the lower-left corner of the Word 2010 window, provides useful information about your current document. By default, the status bar shows you:

- The location of the cursor position

- The number of pages in the document

- The number of words

- Whether any proofing errors exist

- The selected language you are using if you have installed more than one language keyboard preference

> **Note**
> You might also see in the status bar an indicator that lets you know whether any macros are currently being recorded in your document.

Page: 2 of 7 | Words: 451 | English (U.S.)

The status bar includes four key elements:

- The Page area shows the number of the current page and the length of your document. You can also click this area to display the Go To tab in the Find and Replace dialog box.

- Word displays a continually updating word count on the status bar as well. If you select text, Word shows you how many words of the total word count are selected (for example, 50/451). Click this area to display the Word Count dialog box, in which you can view additional statistics on number of characters, paragraphs, and more.

- To detect errors, an ongoing spelling and grammar checker continuously reviews your document content. Click this icon to go to the error and see options for correcting it.

- If you have installed more than one language and keyboard preference for your version of Word 2010, the language you have selected as the default appears in the status bar to the right of the proofing indicator. Click this option to display the Language dialog box and choose the language used for the spelling and grammar checker.

In addition to the controls that show in the status bar by default, you can add or remove options by right-clicking anywhere on the bar. The Customize Status Bar list appears, presenting statistics about your document and showing you which features are currently enabled (see Figure 1-23). Additionally, the Customize Status Bar list provides the status of various elements that show you the status of the file; for example, in Figure 1-23, you can see that there is no macro currently being recorded and that Permissions and Track Changes are both turned off for the current file.

Figure 1-23 The Customize Status Bar list displays the status of various features in your document and enables you to add or remove additional options.

What's Next?

This chapter introduced you to some of the leading new features in Word 2010, so now you can begin to experiment with the program, whether you want to make good documents look great, share your content easily with colleagues, or access your files from the Web. The next chapter introduces you to Backstage view, where you can manage your files and program information in one convenient place in Word 2010.

Managing Your Documents with Backstage View

Introducing Backstage View. 34

Working with Document Properties in the Info Tab. . . . 38

Accessing Recent Files. 55

Starting a New File. 57

Previewing and Printing Documents. 57

Saving and Sending Your Documents. 58

Getting Help in Word 2010 60

Setting Word Options 62

What's Next? 68

Working with your documents in Word 2010 isn't all about creating content. Once you design your page, enter your text, format it the way you want it, add your illustrations, and do your proofreading pass, you need to think about what you want to *do* with the file. Will you print it? Share it? Close it and go to lunch?

This chapter is all about what you do with the files you create in Word 2010. While you're creating your document, you will be making decisions about who can access it and when, what kind of editing you want them to do, what kinds of tags and comments you add to the file, and much more. In order to manage that type of information, perform file management tasks, and set program preferences in Word, you will use the new Backstage view. This view pulls together in one convenient place all the commands you need to set program preferences, work with your Word files, get help, and save, share, and print your files.

Backstage view was designed with the idea of giving you an easy way to access all the tools you need as you manage your documents. Because today we have so many different ways to use and share the content we create, having one central location for file-management tasks is more important than ever. We need to be able to use a consistent process to find, save, create, open, and share our files—and that process should be similar, no matter which Office 2010 program we are using.

The Ribbon was designed to bring you just the tools you need while you're working on various tasks in your document. The idea was to reduce both the clutter on the screen and make the commands in the program easier to find and use. Backstage view was designed with a similar goal in mind, except that the focus of the commands is different. Now instead of using commands to create, format, and work with the content in your document, Backstage view gives you the tool you need to work with the document itself.

Introducing Backstage View

You'll find Backstage view on the File tab, which is located at the far left end of the Ribbon. This takes you to a window that looks similar to the Word 2010 document window—same color scheme and fonts—but provides a multicolumn interface, with tabs stretching down the left side of the window (see Figure 2-1).

Figure 2-1 Backstage view shares a color and font scheme with the Word 2010 window, but the interface lets you know you've entered a new realm.

At the top of the tabs column, you find four selections called *fast commands* in Office 2010. These are the common operations you perform regularly in Word—Save, Save As, Open, and Close. When you click Save, Save As, or Open, the familiar dialog boxes open from which you can navigate to the folder you need and save or open a file, depending on your selection. When you click Close, Word 2010 prompts you to save the file if needed and then closes the current document. Pretty straightforward.

Below the fast commands, by default a set of four recent documents is displayed. From this list, you can conveniently reopen files you've used most recently without needing to navigate to the folder in which they are stored. You can change the number of files displayed in this portion of the Backstage tab column by clicking the Recent tab and changing the Quickly Access This Number of Recent Documents entry at the bottom of the Recent files list.

The Tabs Area

The Backstage tabs column offers a set of six tabs, organized according to the different ways you will want to work with your files. Here's a quick definition of what you'll do with each tab:

- **Info**   Use the options on the Info tab to display document properties; set user permissions for your document; inspect the document before sharing it and run accessibility and compatibility tests; and recover or delete draft versions of documents you've worked on previously.

- **Recent**   When you click Recent a listing of documents you've already worked on appears in the center column of the view. You can scroll through the list, click a file to open it, or "pin" a file to the list (this causes it to remain at the top of the list and not scroll out of view) so that you can access is easily later. Further, at the bottom of the Recent file list, you can click the Recover Unsaved Documents link to open a dialog box that gives you access to versions of files you have closed without saving. You can also set the number of recent documents you want to be displayed on the tab area beneath the Close tool.

- **New**   The New tab displays your options for creating a new document in Word. You can choose to start with a blank file, a blog post, an existing or sample template, or create a new file based on an existing one. Additionally, you can browse through literally dozens of Office Online templates. After you find the document you want to create, click it and a thumbnail image of the template appears in the preview pane on the left. Click Create to create the document.

- **Print**   The Print tab is where you can preview and set print options for your file. The preview shows you in real time the changes you make in the print selections. For example, if you change the orientation of the page from portrait to landscape, Print Preview shows the change. You can set the options you want for the print job and then click Print to complete the operation.

> ### Tip
> Print is one of the great—and greatly simplified—features now available in Backstage view. The whole print process has been simplified so that you can preview, set options, and print your document all in a single screen. To find out more about printing your documents in Word, see Chapter 14, "Printing Documents Professionally."

Chapter 2

- **Save & Send** The Save & Send tab lists the various options you have for sharing your document. Depending on whether you are part of a team or use either Share-Point Workspace or Windows Live SkyDrive for your files, you might have the following options or others in the Save & Send area: Send Using E-mail, Save To Web, Save To SharePoint, Publish As Blog Post. When you choose any of these options, additional selections—for example, the location of the SharePoint site to which you want to save the file—become available in the pane on the right. In the File Types area on the tab, you can select the type of the file you're saving or create a PDF/XPS document.

- **Help** The Help tab in Word 2010 provides you with information about your software registration and your product ID and version. It also provides access to tutorials, searchable help, and links to program updates.

The final choice in the tabs column isn't a tab *per se*—it's the Options command. Clicking Options in Backstage view displays the Word Options dialog box, where you can control a wide range of settings related to various aspects of the program.

The sections that follow offer more detail about the different tasks you'll accomplish in Backstage view. Because the Info tab provides access to file information you won't find anywhere else in Word 2010, many of the techniques described in this chapter concern this tab and the actions you carry out in it. You will also find information about each of the tabs and their basic functions and get pointers to specific chapters where techniques are described in greater detail. Along the way, you'll discover a few tips and techniques for tailoring the program to handle your documents the way you want them to be handled.

The Groups Area

The middle column of Backstage view displays groups of tools related to the tab you've selected. Although each of the tabs displays a very different set of tools—some of which require additional choices—the idea is always the same: the groups area allows you to take action on a specific task or file. In the groups area, you choose the command you want to use or the file you want to work with. The groups area for the Print tab is displayed in Figure 2-2. As you can see, you choose the print options for the current file in the groups area of Backstage view.

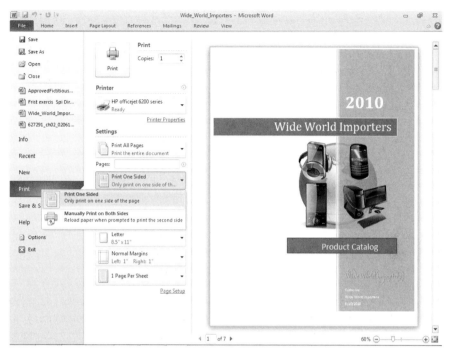

Figure 2-2 The groups area on the Print tab enables you to choose the settings for Print options for the current file.

The Preview and Properties Area

The column on the right side of Backstage view also varies depending on the tab you've selected. On the Info tab, this column displays the document properties for your file. On the Print tab, you can preview and page through your document. On the Help tab, this area displays information about your version of Word 2010 and gives you access to your product ID (see Figure 2-3).

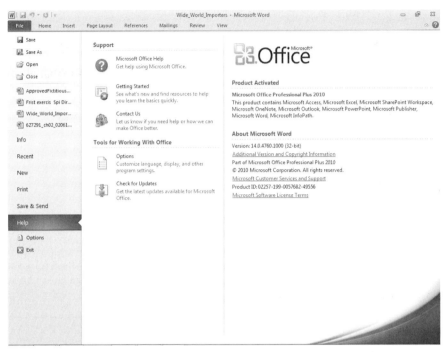

Figure 2-3 The right column in Backstage view gives you additional information about the current document and the choices you make in the groups area of the view.

Working with Document Properties in the Info Tab

Have you noticed that in earlier versions of Word, there's no easy way to display your document's properties without taking up a large portion of the document window? You might want to know, for example, when the file was last modified, who has been working on the document, or whether the file has been printed recently. You can find out all this—and more—by viewing the properties on the Info tab.

By default, Word 2010 provides the following document properties:

- **Size**   Displays the file size of the current document

- **Pages**   Shows the number of pages

- **Words**   Gives you a total word count of the entire document

- **Total Editing Time**   Lists the number of minutes the file has been open since it was created

- **Title**   Displays the title you've given the document

- **Tags**   Enables you to add tags to identify the document content and topic

- **Comments**   Lets you add a note that stays with the file so that others viewing or editing the file can see it

You can also find out when the document was last modified, when it was created, and when it was last printed. This information is for viewing only; there's nothing you can do to change the date information displayed (except, of course, modify or print the document).

Adding and Using Document Tags and Comments

Tagging provides an important and easy way to identify the content in such a way that you can find it easily again later. Suppose, for example, that you are creating copy for a new catalog your department is producing. If you create a document with blurbs for the catalog copy, you could add the tag *catalog*—or, if you want to be more specific, two tags, such as *catalog, smartphone*—so that others compiling the content later can search and find your document for inclusion in the larger catalog file.

> **Tip**
>
> If you work as part of a team that is working together to produce content for a specific project, meet and discuss the tags you are going to use before you start using them. Because tagging provides you with a system for locating and grouping files, you want to be sure you're all using the same tags; otherwise, the benefit of tagging is lost because the files won't be found together in a search.

Likewise, you can add comments to your document to make an overall comment that is not visible to people who are viewing your document. You can add a note to your editor about a section you are working on, but when others view the file in Final view, the comment won't be visible.

> **Tip**
>
> If you are working with others who use earlier versions of Word (Windows or Mac versions), be sure to let them know you have added comments to the file. Recently I sent an article to a publisher who was using Word for the Mac and a comment I inserted in the file was published as a footnote! When using comments across multiple program versions, be sure to be clear and let everyone know comments are included in the file—just in case.

Chapter 2

The process for adding tags and comments to your document is a simple one.

1. Click the File tab to display Backstage view.

2. The Info tab is displayed by default. Click Add A Tag in the Tags area in the right column.

3. Type one or more tags, separating the tags with commas—for example, *catalog, smartphone, fall* (see Figure 2-4).

4. Save and close your document.

Figure 2-4 Enter tags for your document by clicking the Add A Tag area and typing the tags you want to use.

You can use the tag and comment information you use in your Word 2010 document when you are viewing your files at the operating system level. For example, suppose that you are looking for a specific Word document in which you discuss different smartphone models. The tags you entered in your Word 2010 document will help you locate the catalog file. (Note, however, that a file you've just created might not show up because the operating system needs to have a chance to include the file in a file index before it is displayed in search results.) Here's how to do it:

1. Click the Windows 7 Start button.

2. Type **smartphone** in the search box.

3. Click the file you want from the list that appears (see Figure 2-5).

Figure 2-5 You can easily locate a specific file using the tags you entered in Word 2010.

The tags and comments you add on the Info tab of Backstage view stay with the file and are visible when you choose a file in a folder in Windows 7 as well. In Figure 2-6, you see that when you click the file, the tags appear in the details at the bottom of the folder window. You can also display all the file's properties by right-clicking the file, choosing Properties, and then clicking the Details tab.

Right-click
file

Tags

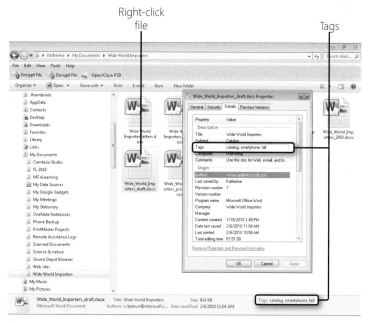

Figure 2-6 The tag information you entered is visible when you select the file in Windows 7.

Chapter 2

> **Tip**
>
> If you use the document with SharePoint, properties you specify might also appear as fields in document libraries.

INSIDE OUT The Tag Information I Specify Doesn't Seem to Be Showing Up When I Select the File in the Operating System

The tag information you add to the document through Word 2010 does remain with the file; however, the search indexer might need time to index the newly saved document. Additionally, Windows 7 might not locate the file until you save *and* close (not simply save) the document. Save and close the file before you search for it using your operating system, and the file should appear as part of the results list displayed after you search for the tag.

For more information on inserting and working with the document property controls in your document, see Chapter 7, "Creating and Reusing Your Content."

Adding and Contacting Co-Authors

You can also add, modify, and make contact with your co-authors for the current file from the Info tab. To add a co-author to your document, follow these steps:

1. Click in the Related People area.

2. Place your cursor in the Add An Author box and type the name of the co-author you want to add.

   As you begin typing, Word searches for contacts in your local or global Outlook contacts lists that match the text you enter.

3. Click the co-author you want to add from the list that appears or finish typing the name in the box, and press Enter.

   The names are added to the Author list, as you see in Figure 2-7.

Figure 2-7 On the Info tab, you can create a list of co-authors who work on the current document.

> **Note**
>
> Adding authors to the Author list does not give them the permissions they need to share the document; nor does it make the document available to them in any kind of shared folder, such as a folder available on SharePoint Workspace or Windows Live Sky-Drive. In order to take advantage of the full co-authoring features in Word 2010, you need to give your co-authors the necessary permissions to work in the file and save the file to a location they can access. You learn more about the entire co-authoring process in Chapter 22, "Collaborating and Co-Authoring in Real Time."

Why add co-authors to the Author list? For one thing, compiling a list of people working on the current document gives you access to the people you might need to contact related to various aspects of the project. Then if you want to contact one of your co-authors, you can simply click the name of the person on the Info tab and choose the way in which you want to communicate.

If you are working with Office Communicator or Microsoft Exchange, a presence indicator lets you know who among your co-authors is currently online and available for contact and who is not. In Figure 2-7, for example, Beth's presence icon shows green, which means she is available for online contact. Rosemary's presence icon, on the other hand, shows yellow, which means she is currently away and unavailable for contact. When you click the name of a co-author, the contact card appears, giving you four different ways to contact the person, as shown in the following illustration:

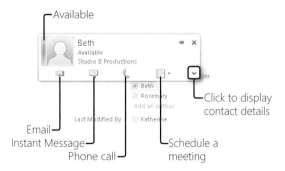

> **Tip**
>
> You'll learn more about the various ways of contacting your co-authors in Chapter 22.

Finding and Linking to Additional Files

Another valuable option on the Info tab of Backstage view is found in the Related Docu-ments area. Because few of the documents we create today actually stand alone, know-ing where and how to access similar content is important (and can save you a lot of time searching through folders and drives on the server).

Both selections in the Related Files area—Open File Location and Edit Links To Files—are live selections, meaning that you can click them to move directly to the task you want to perform. When you click Open File Location, Word 2010 will ask you to confirm that the location you are accessing is a safe one; click Yes to continue, and Word 2010 opens the fol-der where the current file is stored. Now you can look for additional files, open collateral documents, or do the research you need to do. Perhaps, for example, you want to see what tags have been assigned to other files in your document folder. When you're finished in the folder, click the Close box to return to the Word 2010 Backstage view.

The Edit Links To Files selection enables you to check, modify, and update links to any objects you've embedded in your document. If you do not have other objects in your docu-ment, this option will not appear. Clicking this selection displays the Links dialog box, as shown in Figure 2-8.

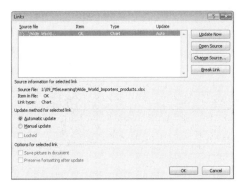

Figure 2-8   Use the Edit Links To Files selection on the Info tab to review, change, and update links to objects embedded in your document.

To learn more about embedding objects and working with links in Word 2010, see Chapter 18, "Adding the Extras: Equations, Text Boxes, and Objects."

Customizing Document Properties Display

The document properties shown by default on the Info tab of Backstage view are the ones most commonly used by the majority of Word users, but your needs or interests might dictate storing more specialized information about the file. You can change the document properties collected and displayed on the Info tab by clicking the Properties arrow (see Figure 2-9).

Figure 2-9 You can change the way document properties are displayed to suit your needs.

When you click Show Document Panel, the Document Properties panel appears at the top of your document. This panel is where you can view and modify document properties easily (see Figure 2-10). The Document Properties panel shows you any properties that currently store document information as well as the current folder location of the file. The Keywords field reflects the tags you add so that the file can be located easily in a search. You can review and change the information as needed and then close the panel by clicking the close box in the upper-right corner.

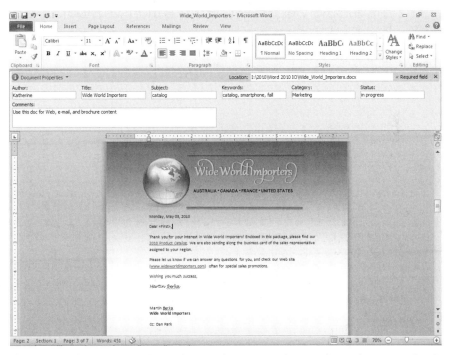

Figure 2-10 The Document Properties panel appears at the top of your document, showing all properties currently entered for the file.

Chapter 2

When you choose Advanced Properties, the Properties dialog box appears, giving you the option of entering and working with document properties by entering information in the General, Summary, Statistics, Contents, and Custom tabs.

To learn more about customizing your document to use document properties in content controls, see Chapter 27, "Customizing Documents with Content Controls."

Tip

By clicking Show All Properties at the bottom of the Properties panel on the Info tab you can add additional properties fields so that you can view and modify those settings as well. The additional properties include Status, Template, Categories, Subject, Hyperlink Base, and Company. You might use Status, for example, to update the progress on the document or use Categories to indicate which department has ownership of the project.

Converting Documents from Earlier Versions of Word

When you are working with documents created or saved in previous versions of Word, the document is automatically opened in *Compatibility Mode*. Word 2010 shows you that Compatibility Mode is in effect by displaying [Compatibility Mode] in the title bar of the document. When you display the Info tab for a file created in a previous version of Word, you will see the Compatibility Mode group, which contains the Convert command. Using this command, you can convert the file to Word 2010 format so that all the features in the latest version of the program are available to you as you work on the file.

Tip

Will you worry about maintaining compatibility with others who aren't using Word 2010 if you convert the file? Microsoft has made a converter available free of charge for users who aren't interested in upgrading their version of Microsoft Office but still need to trade files with Office 2010 and Office 2007 users. This way you get the best of both worlds—you can share files with other users and still get the best the program has to offer. You'll find the Microsoft Compatibility Pack available on the Microsoft Downloads site.

To convert the file to Word 2010 format, simply click Convert (see Figure 2-11). A message box appears, alerting you that the file will be converted into the new format. Click OK to complete the operation.

Figure 2-11 To convert the file from an earlier version of Word, click Convert on the Info tab of Backstage view.

Chapter 2

CAUTION

The document will be converted to the new file format, given the new file extension (.docx for macro free documents or .dotm for macro enabled documents), and a copy of the original will not be preserved. Though you can save a converted document back to the Word 97-2003 file format, if you have any conversion concerns, you should make a backup copy of your document prior to using the Convert tool or use Save As to save your document in the new file format instead. For more information about saving documents, see the section titled "Saving and Sending Your Documents," on page 58.

Tip

Why Convert? Many of the new features available with both Word 2007 and Word 2010—for example, quick styles, SmartArt, photo effects, and more—are not available in older file formats. To take full advantage of the latest features designed to enhance the look and function of your document, convert the file to Word 2010 format.

Protecting the Document

If you share files regularly—both within and outside your organization—you know how important it is to safeguard the information you create. You might want to prepare a file in such a way that others can't change it; ensure that others can only make certain changes—such as fill out a form, respond to questions, or edit only a specific section.

Word 2010 makes it easy for you to set varying levels of protection for your document, and the Permissions group on the Info tab shows you which features are in effect for your current file. Here's how to protect your document in Backstage view:

1. Click the File tab to display Backstage view.

2. In the Permissions group, click Protect Document.

3. Click the option that best reflects the type of protection you want to add to the file:

   - **Mark As Final**   This option makes your document as read-only so others can't change it.

   - **Encrypt With Password**   Word prompts you (twice) to assign a password so only those with the password can open the file.

     Note that although password protecting a document in this way is suitable protection for some documents, for highly sensitive information you also need other means of protection as well.

   - **Restrict Editing**   With this option, you can choose the level of editing you want various users to be able to perform.

   - **Restrict Permission By People**   This enables you to set the limits of editing by role so people with specific functions are given the permissions you specify.

   - **Add A Digital Signature**   You can add a digital signature to the document to help ensure the authenticity of the file.

Figure 2-12 shows how as you make choices to protect your document. Your selections are displayed in the Permissions group so you can always keep track of the protection features in use in the current document. When you return to the document window via the File tab, you see that the message bar shows the new level of protection and provides a button you can click for more information (see Figure 2-13).

Figure 2-12 Use the Protect Document tool in the Permissions group to add protection features to your document.

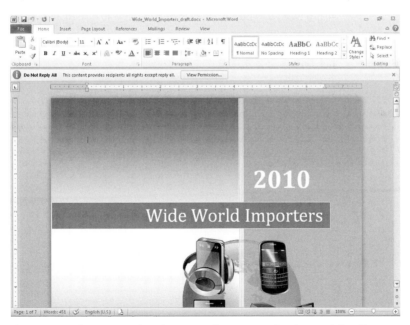

Figure 2-13 The message bar shows you that a protection feature is in effect.

Checking Document Compatibility

In the Prepare For Sharing group on the Info tab, you'll find the Check For Issues tool (see Figure 2-14). This tool contains three checkers you can use to ensure that your document is ready for sharing with others outside your organization. The following list describes each:

- **Inspect Document**   Word will let you know whether the file contains any sensitive personal or business information, hidden comments, or XML data you might not want to share.

- **Check Accessibility**   This ensures that users with varying levels of ability will be able to read your file.

- **Check Compatibility**   This checks your document to locate any features that will not be available to people who are using previous versions of Word.

Both the Inspect Document and Check Accessibility features are covered in Chapter 21, "Sharing Your Documents," so this section focuses on showing you how to check the compatibility of the documents you create and use in Word 2010.

The Word 2010 Compatibility Checker helps you identify which elements in your document are not fully supported in previous versions of Word. If there's any possibility that your document will be viewed by people who use earlier versions of Word, use the Compatibility Checker to ensure that you know how your document will look to all recipients.

Figure 2-14 You can check file compatibility on the Info tab of Backstage view.

> **Note**
>
> Word 2007 and Word 2010 use the same file format (.docx), so saving to a previous version of Word means saving to the Word 97-2003 format or earlier.

The Compatibility Checker evaluates your document and displays a report that lets you know how things in your file will change (see Figure 2-15). For example, the following list provides some of the more common changes made when you save a Word 2010 document to a previous version format:

- Building block information becomes static text

- OpenType font features are removed

- Citations and bibliographical entries cannot be updated

- Charts become single elements

- Text effects are removed

- Content Controls become static text

- Embedded objects can no longer be edited

- Equations are converted to images

- SmartArt graphics are converted to single objects that cannot be edited

- Text box positioning might change

- Tracked moves are shown as deletions and insertions

Figure 2-15 The Microsoft Word Compatibility Checker lets you know how features will change when you save a Word 2010 document to an earlier format.

If you are not sure what a summary item means, you can click the Help link below the number of occurrences in the Summary area to view additional information.

After you review changes, click OK and then either save the document in Word 97-2003 format knowing what changes will take place or make changes in your document and run the Compatibility Checker again.

Recovering Draft Versions of Your Files

Most computer users have experienced losing data at one time or another—whether because of a badly timed power outage, a glitch in the program, a sudden lockup, or forgetful moment. To help reduce the risk of losing data, Word includes the AutoRecover and Background Saves features, which are both activated by default. These two features work together to help save your information without interrupting your workflow too much. Here's what they do:

- **AutoRecover**   Creates temporary files of open documents. These files are used if your system crashes or if there's a power failure. These files are considered temporary because they are deleted when you either close the open documents or exit Word.

- **Background Saves**   Allows you to continue working in Word while you save a document. A flashing disk icon appears on the status bar when a background save is taking place. You can toggle background saves off and on using the Allow Background Saves option found in Word Options in the Advanced section under the Save options.

Note

If you attempt to save a long document while Word is still performing a background save, you might get a Same Name error because Word uses the same file name to complete both save operations. If this occurs, simply wait a moment until the background save is complete and then save the document normally. You can tell when a document is being saved by looking for the Save message and Save Progress bar on the status bar at the bottom of the Word window.

Changing the AutoRecover Save Interval

By default, the AutoRecover feature in Word stores unsaved changes made to an active file every 10 minutes. You can turn off the AutoRecover feature or change the frequency of AutoRecover saves by changing the Save settings in the Word Options dialog box. Click the File tab to display Backstage view then click Options. Click the Save section and change the setting in Save AutoRecover Information Every __ Minutes option.

Keep in mind that the AutoRecover feature isn't a replacement for saving your files. AutoRecover only temporarily saves changes made to active documents. It is specifically a tool designed to help you recover a file after a system crash. You need to continue to save and back up your documents regularly.

> **Note**
>
> By default, Word does not automatically create backup files. To turn on the automatic backup feature, select the Always Create Backup Copy check box in the Save section on the Advanced tab in Word Options. The backup copy will have the words, Backup Of, added at the beginning of the file name and will have a .wbk file extension. Note the backup copy is a version of the document that you saved prior to the most recent save.

If you experience a system crash while working in Word, the application displays a Document Recovery task pane along the left side of the Word window after you restart your system and reopen Word. The Recovery task pane shows up to three versions (Recovered, AutoSaved, and Original) of each Word file that was open at the time of the crash. The most current version (usually the recovered version) is shown at the top of the group of related files. You can select which files you want to save from among the recovered versions of documents that appear in the Document Recovery task pane.

To open a recovered document, click the entry in the Document Recovery task pane or click the arrow next to the item then click Open. In addition, you can save or delete a recovered file or view repairs made to a recovered file by clicking the item's arrow and then selecting the desired command.

> **Recover the Most Recent Versions of Files**
>
> When you see versions of the same file listed in the Document Recovery task pane's Available Files list box, keep in mind that an AutoRecover file is usually in better shape than an original file. Be sure to check the Last Saved time listed with each recovered document to verify that you're recovering the most recent version. If later during the same session you determine that you would rather use a different version, click the Recovered button on the status bar to reopen the Document Recovery task pane.

After you've made your recovery decisions, click Close in the lower-right corner of the Document Recovery task pane to close the pane. If you determine that you want to use a different recovered document after you've closed the Document Recover task pane, click the Recovered button on the status bar to reopen the task pane.

Chapter 2

When you close a recovery file without saving it, the recovery file is deleted—you can't recover a deleted recovery file. Furthermore, when you close Word after recovering documents, you will not be able to re-access the various saved versions whether you deleted them or not. If you are not sure which file to save, consider saving all of the recovered files with different names so you can compare and review the files without losing any of them. After you are sure which file you want to keep, you can delete the files you don't need in the same manner you delete any other Word file.

Recovering Unsaved Files

Although Word's ability to recover files after a lockup can help you avoid losing important content you've created, what is there to help you if you forget to save a file and the power goes out? Now Word 2010 provides a way to recover documents that you didn't have a chance to save. Gathered from those background saves you barely notice, the Recover Unsaved Documents feature gives you access to those versions of the file you didn't think to keep. You can then open, save, and work with the content as you like.

You'll find this feature on the Info tab of Backstage view. To access the content in unsaved versions of your file, follow these steps:

1. Click the Manage Versions button and choose Recover Draft Versions from the list that appears (see Figure 2-16).

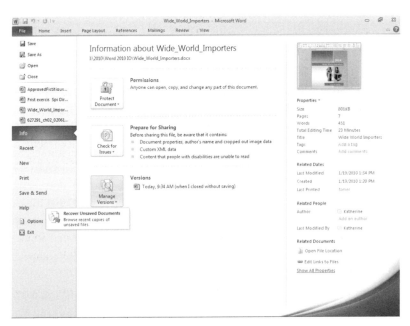

Figure 2-16 Access unsaved drafts of your document by choosing Manage Versions on the Info tab of Backstage view.

2. In the Open dialog box, Word displays the folder containing the unsaved drafts. Select the file you want and click Open.

3. The message bar alerts you that the file is a draft version and prompts you to click Save As if you want to save the file and use the content (see Figure 2-17).

Click Save As to display the Save As dialog box then choose the folder and file name for the saved file.

4. Click Save to complete the process.

Figure 2-17 When you open a draft version of the file, Word 2010 prompts you to save the file.

Accessing Recent Files

Use the Recent tab in Backstage view to choose your most recent documents—and identify your favorite most recent documents—from a nice, long list (see Figure 2-18). The scrollable list provides access to a maximum of 22 of your most recent documents; you can click the pushpin to "pin" the document to the list so that it does not scroll off as you continue to open and work with files.

The number of files that appear beneath the fast commands area in the Backstage tabs column is determined by the value set in Quickly Access This Number of Recent Documents, located at the bottom of the Recent files list. If you want to increase the number of documents displayed there, increase the value in the box. The documents displayed in that area of the Recent tab will show pinned documents first, followed by the most recent documents in your Recent files list.

> **Tip**
> You can change the number of files displayed in the Recent Documents list by clicking Options, choosing the Advanced tab, and then in the Display area, entering a new value in the Show This Number of Recent Documents field.

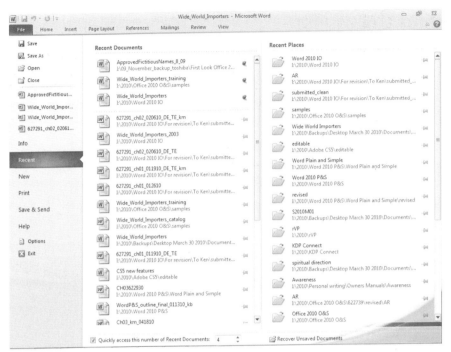

Figure 2-18 The Recent tab in Backstage view gives you one-click access to a long list of recent files.

You can also click the Recover Unsaved Documents link at the bottom of the list to display the Open dialog box and access the content of any files you closed without saving. This link gives you another way to access the Recover Draft Versions functionality available through the Manage Versions selection on the Info tab.

> ### Tip
> If you find that you regularly return to the document you were using most recently, you can streamline the task of opening that recent file by adding Open Recent File to the Quick Access Toolbar in the top-left corner of the Word window. Click the Customize Quick Access Toolbar arrow at the right end of the toolbar and choose Open Recent File from the list. Now you can simply click the tool to open the document you worked with most recently.

Starting a New File

The New tab in Backstage view provides everything you need to start a new document, blog post, or template in Word 2010 (see Figure 2-19). The three-column format enables you to find the type of file or template you want to create and preview the document template in the panel on the right. When you've selected the item you want to create, click the Create button.

You learn more about creating and working with new documents in Chapter 3, "Right Now Document Design with Word 2010."

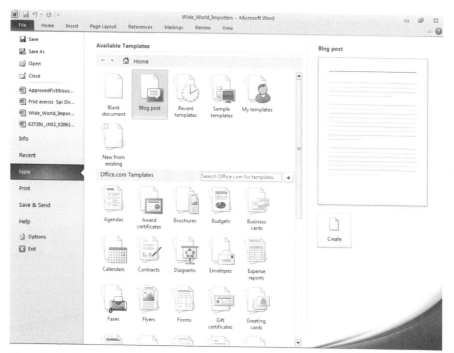

Figure 2-19 The New tab contains everything you need to easily find the type of new file you want to create and get started.

Previewing and Printing Documents

Printing and previewing have become easier than ever before, thanks to the redesign and reorganization of the Print and Preview tools in Office 2010. Now Print is available to you through Backstage view, and you can easily set print options, preview your document, and browse through the file all within a single window (see Figure 2-20). And when you're ready to print the file, just click the Print button. Nice.

Chapter 2

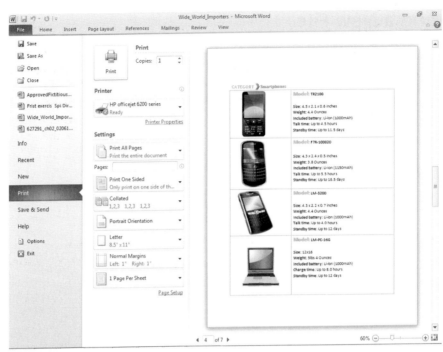

Figure 2-20 With the Print tab, you can set print options, preview, and print your file within one easy-to-use window.

For the ins and outs of setting print options, preparing to print different types of documents, and optimizing your printing, see Chapter 14.

Saving and Sending Your Documents

Sharing is a big story in Word 2010. Because the nature of the way we work on documents has been changing over recent years, Word now includes features that enable you to save and send your files to others easily while still ensuring they are as secure as possible.

On the Save & Send tab in Backstage view, you can specify where and how you want to share the files you create. As you see in Figure 2-21, you can opt to share your document by e-mail, save it to the Web, post it to your SharePoint server space, or publish it as a blog post.

> **Tip**
>
> Wondering where you'll save your file on the Web? Windows Live SkyDrive is a free file-sharing utility available at *www.skydrive.live.com* and is often used by home and small business users. Microsoft SharePoint is a server technology that is typically used by larger businesses at the enterprise level. Microsoft Office Professional Plus includes SharePoint Workspace 2010, so users who have access to Microsoft SharePoint can take their files offline and share them easily with others in a collaborative workspace.

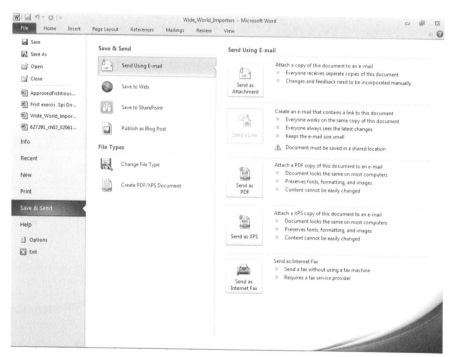

Figure 2-21 You will use the Save & Send tab to choose how you want to share the documents you create in Word 2010.

The Save & Send tab provides you with various options for sharing your files; you can also set up the necessary accounts (for example, when you click Save To Web, you are given the option to sign in to your Windows Live account or sign up for one if you don't already have one). After you sign in to Windows Live, you can save your file to Windows Live SkyDrive by clicking the Save To Web tool and prepare to share the files from that online point.

If you currently work with SharePoint, clicking Save to SharePoint will display a list of your current SharePoint locations; simply click the folder where you want to store the file.

You learn more about saving and sharing documents and working with co-authoring in Chapter 21.

You'll also find what you need to save your document as a PDF or XPS file, send the file as an Internet fax, and change the file type for the current document so that you can save the file in other formats. Table 2-1 lists the other file formats in which you can save your Word 2010 file.

Table 2-1 **Alternate File Formats in Word 2010**

Format	Description	Format	Description
*.doc	Word 97-2003	*.odt	OpenDocument Text
*.dotx	Template	*.txt	Plain Text
*.rtf	Rich Text Format	*.mht, *.mhtml	Single File Web Page
*.dotm	Word Macro-Enabled Template	*.dot	Word 97-2003 Template
*.pdf	PDF format	*.xps	XPS Document
*.xml	Word XML Document	*.XML	Word 2003 XML Document
*.wps	Works 4.x Document	*.wps	Works 6 – 9 Document

Getting Help in Word 2010

You can easily get help from any point in Word 2010 by clicking the small Help button on the right side of the Ribbon, as shown in the following image:

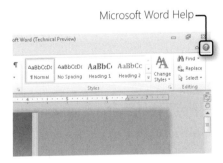

Microsoft Word Help

This displays the Word Help dialog box shown in Figure 2-22. You can search for a specific word or phrase related to the information you'd like to see, click a link to display an article or dive deeper into a specific category, or display the table of contents so that you can browse all Help topics.

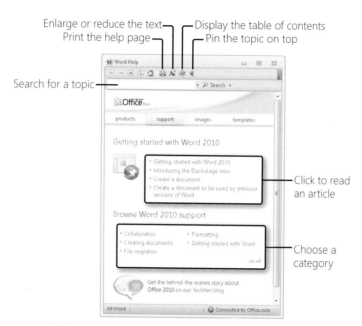

Enlarge or reduce the text
Print the help page
Display the table of contents
Pin the topic on top
Search for a topic
Click to read an article
Choose a category

Figure 2-22 You can find specific information related to the tasks you want to accomplish with Word.

On the Info tab, you can click the Help tab to display a variety of different links that can assist you in learning more about Word and getting software support (see Figure 2-23). At the top of the Support column in the center of the Backstage view, you see the Microsoft Office Help selection. Clicking this link displays the Word Help dialog box shown in Figure 2-20. The Getting Started selection takes you online to a page that provides a number of articles covering the basics in Word.

If you have specific questions that you haven't been able to answer using Microsoft Office Help or the Getting Started articles, you can click Contact Us to enter your question in Microsoft support. You can find answers to common problems here and access product centers with more information about specific techniques in the different Office 2010 programs.

In the Tools For Working With Office group, you can change your preferences for the way Word operates by clicking the Options link on the Help tab. Clicking this item displays the Word Options dialog box (something you can also do using the Options selection at the bottom of the Backstage tabs column). Finally, choosing Check For Updates takes you to the Microsoft Update page, which enables you to search for the latest updates for your version of Office 2010 and downloads any new changes (with your permission, of course) to your computer.

Chapter 2

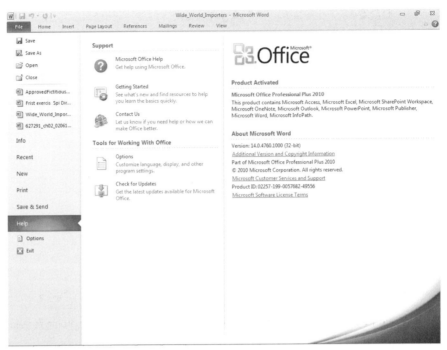

Figure 2-23 The Help tab gives you several options for finding information about Word, and the right column lists your software version and registration number.

Setting Word Options

Your last stop in the tabs column of Backstage view (before the Exit command, anyway) is Options. You use Word Options to set your preferences for the way Word 2010 behaves as you work with the various aspects of the program (see Figure 2-24). The Word Options dialog box includes 10 tabs, each organized to help you set preferences for a different set of program features. Table 2-2 introduces you to the different types of settings you can change in Word Options.

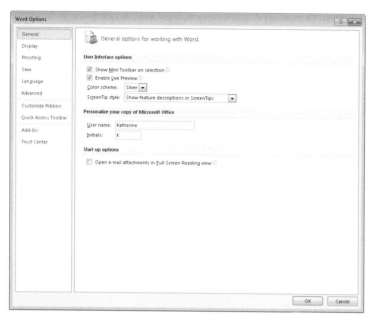

Figure 2-24 Use Word Options to set up the program to work according to your preferences.

Table 2-2 Setting Word Options

Use This Category	To Do This
General	Set options related to Word 2010 startup options, your own user account, and general items about the user interface
Display	Control page display, formatting marks, print options
Proofing	Choose options for correcting and formatting text and setting spelling and grammar options, dictionaries, languages, and exceptions
Save	Indicate file locations, choose whether to save fonts in the file or not), and choose save options for saving to the server
Language	Choose an editing language, display and help language, and ScreenTips language
Advanced	Set more specialized options for editing, AutoComplete, image size and quality, display considerations, charts, sound options, units of measurement, and layout options
Customize Ribbon	Add new tabs and tab groups to tailor the Ribbon to include the tools you want to display
Quick Access Toolbar	Set the tools—and the arrangement of tools—in the Quick Access Toolbar
Add-Ins	Manage program add-ins, custom templates, and more
Trust Center	Set levels of privacy and protection for the Word 2010 documents you create and share

Choosing General Program Preferences

The options available on the General tab of the Word Options dialog box enable you to select your choices about some of the big-picture items in Word 2010, such as the following:

- Whether you want the Mini Translator tool to appear when selected

- Whether you want Live Preview to be used when you hover the mouse over selections in a gallery

- Which color scheme you want to apply to Word 2010 (Blue, Silver, or Black)

- Whether you want ScreenTips to provide feature descriptions (or be displayed at all)

- Whether the program includes your name and initials in the file

- Whether you want e-mail attachments to be opened in Word's Full Screen Reading view

Simply select your options and click OK to save your changes. The preferences you choose will be applied to all documents you create or edit in Word.

> **Tip**
>
> You will see Word Options mentioned throughout this book at points related to specific content. For example, you learn about setting your preferences for editing and proofing in Chapter 10, "Editing, Proofing, and Using Reference Tools."

Customizing the Word 2010 Ribbon

Although user reactions to the Ribbon were mixed after the launch of Word 2007, the Ribbon does a great job of organizing tools and groups as long as you can tweak it to work the way you want it to. With Word 2010, you can easily add your own tabs and tab groups to the Ribbon, streamlining tasks you do regularly and making it easy for you to find the tools you need and use most often. To customize the Ribbon, follow these steps:

1. On the File tab, choose Options, and then click the Customize Ribbon tab in the Word Options dialog box.

2. In the Customize The Ribbon column on the right, click New Tab. A new tab and new tab group is added to the diagram on the right.

3. Click to select the new tab and click Rename. The Rename dialog box appears (see Figure 2-25).

4. Type a name for the tab then click OK. Repeat steps 4 and 5 to rename the tab group as well.

5. In the list on the left, click one of the tools you want to include in the new tab group then click Add. The tool is added to the tab group on the right.

6. Continue adding tools as desired until your new tab group includes all the tools you want to display.

7. Click OK to save the changes you made to the Ribbon.

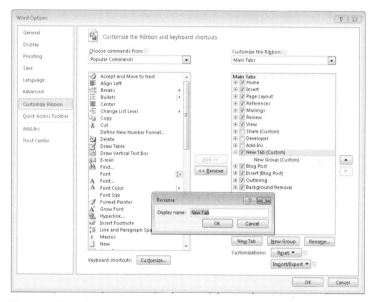

Figure 2-25 Add your own tabs and tab groups to the Ribbon using the Customize Ribbon category in the Word Options dialog box.

Tip

If you later want to return the Ribbon to normal display, on the File tab, choose Options to display the Word Options dialog box. Click Options and choose Customize Ribbon. In the Customizations area, click the Reset arrow, choose Reset All Customizations, and then click OK.

Chapter 2

Setting Up the Microsoft Word Trust Center

The Microsoft Word Trust Center provides enhanced privacy and security options when you are working with files from other sources or sharing the files you create. To display the Trust Center, on the File tab, click Options from Backstage view. In the Word Options dialog box, click Trust Center.

The opening screen of the Trust Center provides you with a series of links concerning privacy and security. Click the Trust Center Settings button on this first screen to see the full range of choices available to you (see Figure 2-26). The following list describes the types of items you can set up in each of the Trust Center categories:

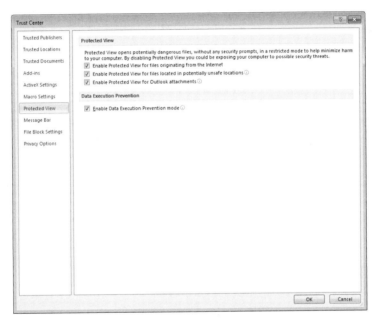

Figure 2-26 The Trust Center provides you with a number of categories you can use to protect your files and your computer system.

- **Trusted Publishers**   With this option, you can specify which publishers of information, add-ins, and more you deem to be trustworthy. Only add people and organizations you know to be secure (it's better to be prompted each time you open a file if there's any chance that a file might be corrupt or have a virus attached). When you specify a publisher as a Trusted Publisher, Word automatically trusts macros in any files from that source.

- **Trusted Locations**   This is a list of acceptable locations and sites you trust. The locations might store documents or templates that include macros. You can add new locations, modify existing locations, and remove locations by using this setting. When you open a document or template from a trusted location, the macros will be enabled automatically; you won't be prompted to enable or disable them.

- **Trusted Documents**   With this option, you can create a list of files that you have determined are safe, from trustworthy sources. You can instruct Word 2010 that all files from a particular server are to be trusted or add individual documents to your Trusted Documents list.

- **Add-Ins**   This option controls the way in which Word treats all third-party add-in utilities. There are three options in this setting: You can insist that all add-ins be digitally signed by the publisher; be prompted when an add-in is unsigned (the code will be blocked); or disallow all add-ins.

- **ActiveX Settings**   You can control how you want Word to handle all Microsoft ActiveX controls that are not recognized as being from a trusted source. Options range from disallowing the ActiveX controls to running in Safe Mode with restrictions.

- **Macro Settings**   This gives you options to control whether the macros you run in a document must be from a trusted source and digitally signed. You also have the option of enabling all macros (which isn't recommended) or disabling all macros.

- **Protected View**   This is a new setting in Word 2010 with which you can open a file in safe mode so that you can see the file contents but not edit what's there. The Protected View message bar enables you to make the call by clicking Enable Editing once you determine that the file is from a trustworthy source.

- **Message Bar**   The Message Bar is where you can specify when you want the Trust Center to display alerts in the Message Bar that appears just below the Ribbon. When you are opening a file from a questionable source, the Message Bar tells you that the source is not trusted and gives you options for proceeding. The Message Bar settings in the Trust Center give you the option of turning this notification off (it is turned on by default). Additionally, the Enable Trust Center Logging check box at the bottom of this screen gives you the choice of logging all notifications you receive in the Message Bar.

- **File Block**   Use these settings to choose which files Word 2010 will open automatically and which you want to block and prompt you for further action. Word developers have found that the file opening process—especially for files opened from the Web or from unrecognized sources—often represent a vulnerability for Word files. To safeguard the files that are opened, Word 2010 blocks the opening of any suspicious files and then prompts you before enabling editing in the file.

Chapter 2

- **Privacy Options**   Provides you with settings with which you to choose whether Word connects to the Internet when you search for help, whether files can be periodically downloaded to log problems with the software, and whether you are signed up for the Customer Experience Improvement Program. Additionally, you can choose document-specific settings (such as whether you are alerted before you send or print a document that has comments and tracking turned on) and translation and research options.

> **Note**
> If you're interested in setting up parental controls for Word, go to the Trust Center, click Privacy Options, and then click Research Options. Parental Control is available in the lower-right corner of the Research Options dialog box.

Customizing Backstage View

As you can see, Backstage view is designed not only to offer you access to the tools that you need to work with your document but also helps you find important information about the preferences you've selected for your file.

The design of Backstage view works similarly to the Ribbon, with tabs, groups, and a variety of techniques for selecting the tools and settings you want to use. Developers can customize Backstage view to incorporate project workflows and display custom information and interactive controls related to specific business tasks.

For more information on extending and customizing the design of Backstage view, see this video produced by the Office Developer Center on extending the functionality of Backstage view: *http://msdn.microsoft.com/en-us/office/ee722027.aspx.*

What's Next?

In this chapter, you learned all about the approach and function of Backstage view, which gives you the tools you need to work with the files you create in Word 2010. You learned how you can display and work with document properties; create, protect, and share files; get help; and set your preferences for the way you want Word 2010 to operate. The next chapter moves into the document creation part of the process by showing you how to design professional-looking documents in Word 2010.

Right Now Document Design with Word 2010

Starting Out with Word 2010 Designs 69

Performing Basic Editing Tasks. 78

Creating Theme-Enabled Documents. 87

Saving Documents 91

Designing Instant Documents 95

What's Next? 100

One of the most exciting things about the changes in Word 2010 is the increased freedom it gives you to create content your way. Whether you want to create a simple mail merge letter, draft a 100-page training manual, produce a four-color annual report, or just post something simple to your blog, creating content is fast, and elegant, and flexible in Word 2010.

As you learned in Chapter 1, "Spotlight on Microsoft Word 2010," a number of the features new to this release are focused on improving your user experience. This means features have been streamlined, flexibility expanded, and new previews and options added so you can make the process more your own. You won't have a lot of decisions to make as you prepare to put your content on the page—you can relax and let the creative process take the lead.

No matter which type of content you are creating, however, it's a good idea to start with the end in mind. And that means having some concept of the design you want to create as you're putting those words and pictures on the page. Word 2010 helps you out in the design department by including themes, building blocks, Quick Style galleries, and more. These elements help you choose the overall look and feel for your content and ensure that the various components you add—pictures, shapes, headlines, and text—are consistent in font, style, and color.

Starting Out with Word 2010 Designs

So what kind of content do you want to create with Word 2010? Chances are that Word has a template for it—whether you are sending a funny greeting card or a sophisticated journal article. From blog posts to annual reports, Word 2010 offers all kinds of tools, options, and styles to support you in creating the layout and look you want to achieve.

Beginning with a Template

If you're like many Word users, you might be comfortable diving right in and starting your document with a blank page. Word 2010 includes more templates than ever—some resident on your computer, and others available on Office Online. And what's more, you can easily access, download, and modify user-generated templates that offer a style or layout that you'd like to use in your own documents.

Templates make great starting points if you are creating a document with a specific layout style. For example, if you want to create a newsletter that includes three columns at the top of the page and two columns in the bottom half of the page, your best bet is to start with a newsletter template and then tweak it to fit the design you're envisioning. Modifying an existing template is much easier than creating a new design from scratch—and you might find that special features like sidebars, picture placeholders, and pull quote boxes add design touches to your documents that you want to keep.

To see which kinds of templates Word 2010 has to offer, click the File tab to display Backstage view and then click New. As you can see in Figure 3-1, the New tab shows you all the templates available on your computer, as well as many different categories for templates that are available on Office Online.

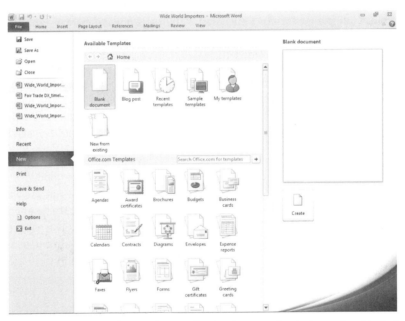

Figure 3-1 The New tab in Backstage view is where you begin to create a blank document or blog post, start a file from an existing file, or choose from a number of template options.

The New tab in Backstage view provides everything you need for the start of a new Word 2010 file. At the top of the center panel you see six choices:

- **Blank Document**   Opens a new document with no specific layout or design options

- **Blog Post**   Displays a new blog post document with space for a post title and content

- **Recent Templates**   Shows you any templates you have recently used in Word 2010

- **Sample Templates**   Displays a selection of templates in different styles and types

- **My Templates**   Opens the New dialog box, showing the Personal Templates tab from which you can choose a template you have added to Word 2010 as the basis for your new document

- **New From Existing**   Opens the New From Existing Document dialog box, in which you can choose the document you want to use as the basis for the new document

In the Office.com Templates area, you see a number of file and folder icons that point you toward additional templates on Office Online. Click the category of template you want to view. Some folders display additional folders offering yet more categories; others display your template choices.

If you don't see a template that offers what you have in mind, you can click in the Search Office.com For Templates box and type a word or phrase describing the kind of template you'd like to find. Figure 3-2 shows the templates displayed when *newsletters* is entered in the search box for Office.com.

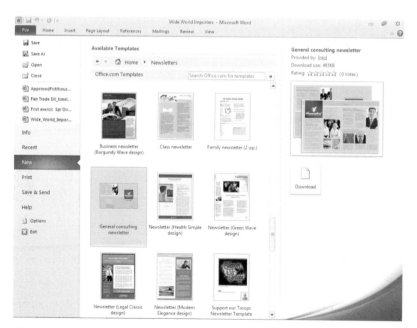

Figure 3-2 You can search for templates available on Office.com.

> **Note**
>
> To remove a template from the Recent Templates view, right-click the template and choose Remove Template. To clear the Recent Templates view, right-click in the area and choose Remove All Recent Templates. Keep in mind that when you remove templates from the Recent Templates area, you are only removing their appearance from that section of the dialog box; you are not permanently removing any templates stored on your computer.

You can preview the different templates available by clicking one and viewing the preview in the right side of the New tab. When you find a template you want to use as the basis for a new document, either double-click the template file icon or select a template icon and click the Create (or Download) button in the panel on the right side of Backstage view.

> **Note**
>
> Only customers running genuine, and properly licensed, Microsoft Office applications can download templates from Microsoft Office Online. For more information about the Microsoft Genuine Advantage, see the Inside Out tip titled "The Microsoft Office Genuine Advantage" in Chapter 4, "Templates and Themes for a Professional Look."

Coordinating Your Document Design

As you begin to explore the templates available in Word 2010, you will notice certain styles used for a variety of document types. For example, you might find the same template design—with colors, fonts, heading style, and backgrounds—used for newsletters, flyers, brochures, and letterhead (see Figure 3-3).

When you choose a consistent look for your documents, you help reinforce a certain image for your organization. The colors might convey a cool, modern tone or a warm, professional feel. Perhaps the fonts are light and playful or traditional and conservative. Whatever look you choose, using the same design on multiple documents helps the people receiving your materials to remember your company or department.

Flyer (Health Modern design, landscape)   Newsletter (Health Modern design)   Envelope (Health Modern design)   Brochure (Health Modern design)

Figure 3-3 You can choose a similar template design for multiple documents to create a consistent design.

Assessing Your Current Design

Every one to two years, it's a good idea to revisit the look and feel of your documents. Do they convey the energy you want them to convey? Do they give readers a positive, professional sense of your company or organization? As you think through the effectiveness of the design of your documents, consider the following questions:

- Have you used a consistent color scheme throughout your documents?

- Does your company or organization have a single logo that is used on all your documents?

- Do you use the same font scheme on all your printed materials?

- Do your business cards, annual report, letterhead, and Web site all have a consistent look and feel?

You can use Word's templates and themes to choose a professional design or a coordinated look, with fonts, colors, and style effects. When you choose a specific style for your document, all elements—from headings and body text to image and shape styles—have an orchestrated look and feel; the entire design works together to reinforce your brand.

Tip

If you are planning a major redesign of your documents, consider pulling together a focus group so you can show a range of design samples to a number of people at once. Invite their feedback about how visually appealing the design seems to them, how easy the text is to read, and how memorable the design is in relation to your company or organizational brand. Be sure to use the feedback participants give you because these folks are representative of the prospective clients and customers you hope will be reading your document in the real world.

Chapter 3

Saving Your Favorite Templates

After you open the template in Word 2010, you might decide that you'd like to save the template to your own templates folder so you can use it again later. To save the template you've just downloaded, follow these steps:

1. Click the File tab to display Backstage view.

2. Click Save As in the Quick Commands list.

3. In the Save As dialog box, scroll to the top of the panel on the left until you see the Templates folder (see Figure 3-4).

4. Click the Templates folder, and type a name for the file in the File Name box.

5. Click the Save As Type arrow and choose Word Template (*.dotx), and then click Save.

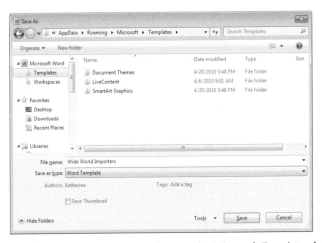

Figure 3-4 Save the new templates to the Microsoft Templates folder.

This saves the template to your My Templates folder so you can access the template easily on the New tab in Backstage view. When you click My Templates in the Available Templates area in the center column on the New tab display, the New dialog box opens, displaying all templates you've saved to your computer (see Figure 3-5). Simply click the template you want to use and click OK to open a new document based on that template.

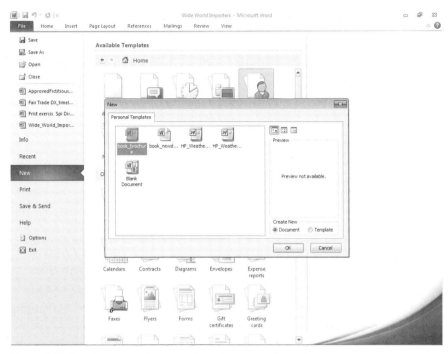

Figure 3-5 Creating a new document based on a saved template.

In Chapter 4, you learn to customize your own templates based on existing templates you've downloaded from Office.com.

Opening Recent Documents

You can display a list of your most recent documents by clicking the Recent tab in Backstage view. This list can show up to 50 of the documents you've most recently opened, which makes it easy to find the file you want even if you can't remember the drive or folder where it's stored.

You can pin a document to the recent documents list by clicking the little pushpin icon to the right of the file name. This pins the document to the top of the recent documents list so it's always there when you need it. (File names will slowly make their way to the bottom of the list as you open additional documents, but a file name will not be removed from the list if it is pinned.) You can change the status of a file on the recent documents list by right-clicking the file and choosing the command you want from the context menu that appears (see Figure 3-6).

Chapter 3

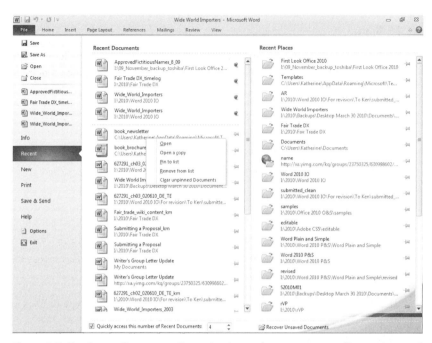

Figure 3-6 The Recent Documents list makes it easy for you to access files you've previously used.

To control how many file names appear in your Recent Documents list, on the File tab, click Options and then click Advanced. On the Advanced tab in the Word Options dialog box, find the Show This Number Of Recent Documents option in the Display section and enter a value for the number of documents you want in the list. Note that although up to 50 recently opened documents can be displayed in the Recent Documents list, your screen size and display resolution might limit the actual number of documents that can be displayed.

Of course, if you aren't sure which file you want to work with or want to choose among multiple files in a folder, you can use the good, old-fashioned Open dialog box. To display the Open dialog box, use one of these techniques:

- Click the File tab to display Backstage view then click Open.

- Click the Open button in your Quick Access Toolbar. (To add the Open button, click the More Commands button in the Customize Quick Access Toolbar list and then click Open in the list on the left, click the Add button, and click OK to add the tool.)

- Press Ctrl+O.

  To use the Open dialog box, navigate to the file you want to open and double-click the file name.

> **Note**
>
> To open multiple files from within the Open dialog box, select files while pressing Shift (for a continuous selection) or Ctrl (for a noncontiguous selection) and then click the Open button.
>
> You might also want to take note of the options available when you click the arrow on the Open button, such as Open And Repair, which can be used to attempt to open a file that's been damaged or corrupted.

Inputting Data

In Chapter 7, "Creating and Reusing Content," you'll learn more about the various ways you can add text, files, pictures, and objects to your Word content. This section touches on the basics, however, so that you can add some of your own data to the new file you create.

The most elementary way of entering content is, of course, to type it. But beyond the simple hunt-and-peck method, you can add content to your Word document using any of the following methods:

- **Insert the contents of another Word document or text file.**   You can insert the contents of another document into the current document without copying and pasting by clicking the Object drop-down arrow in the Text group on the Insert tab and using the Text From File command. The contents of the selected document are inserted into the currently displayed document (and the originating document remains unchanged).

- **Use speech recognition.**   You can use speech recognition to dictate text into your Word documents (see Figure 3-7). Talking into a high-quality microphone—usually part of a headset designed for such purposes—and using a combination of your voice and the mouse, or keyboard, will obtain the best results.

> **Note**
>
> Speech Recognition is available as a part of Windows 7. To begin the process of training Windows 7—and therefore Office 2010 applications—to recognize your voice and receive voice commands, On the Start menu, type **Speech Recognition** in the search box. Click Windows Speech Recognition to get started.

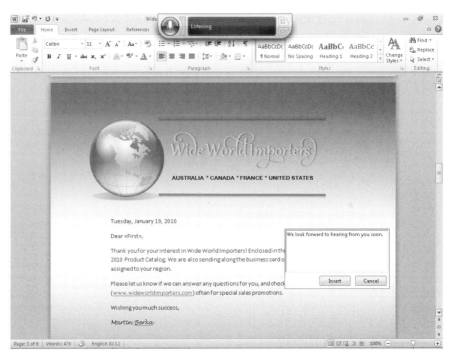

Figure 3-7 You can dictate content by using Windows 7 speech recognition software with Word 2010.

- **Handwrite content using the mouse or a stylus.**   If you have handwriting recognition software installed or if you are using a TabletPC, Word 2010 can recognize handwriting you enter with your mouse or a stylus. When you use handwriting recognition, you can retain your written marks, create drawings, draft equations, or configure Word 2010 to interpret your handwriting and display the information as typed text.

For more information on adding content to Word 2010, see Chapter 7.

Performing Basic Editing Tasks

If you've spent any time working with Word, you know that most documents require some editing. Chances are that your documents are the result of entering information and then editing and formatting the entered text, images, and objects. This section provides information about selecting, copying, cutting, and pasting text; using the Clipboard; and undoing, redoing, and repeating changes—in other words, some of the common tasks you'll perform in Word 2010.

As a more advanced Word user, covering methods of selecting text might seem like old hat to you, but bear with us. A little refresher—especially when some techniques are now easier than ever—is good for the soul.

Selecting Text

Many of the editing tasks you undertake in Word begin with the selection of text. In fact, you can speed up most text modification tasks by mastering precise selection techniques. You can select text in a variety of ways:

- Most commonly, you'll select text by clicking and dragging the mouse (see Table 3-1)

- You also might select text by using keyboard keys (see Table 3-2)

- You can click a style in the Styles pane and select all text in the document that is formatted in the same style

Learn more about selecting text with the purpose of modifying styles in Chapter 11, "Formatting Your Document."

> ### Note
> You can access a couple of key text selection options in Word Options in the Advanced section under Editing Options. You can specify whether to automatically select paragraph marks when you select paragraphs (the Use Smart Paragraph Selection check box) and whether to select entire words when you select part of one word and then part of the next word (the When Selecting, Automatically Select Entire Word check box). Both text selection settings are activated by default.

Table 3-1 Common Methods for Selecting Text Using the Mouse

Selection	Method
Word or single element	Double-click the word.
Sentence	Press Ctrl and click in the sentence.
Paragraph	Triple-click within the paragraph or place your mouse to the far left of the paragraph, (this unmarked area is called the *Selection Bar*) and double-click.
Entire line	In the Selection Bar, point at a line and click once; drag up or down in the Selection Bar to select multiple lines or paragraphs.

Selection	Method
Noncontiguous selection	Select the first item (as described above), hold Ctrl, and then select additional text elsewhere within your document.
Large block of text	Click at the start of the selection, scroll to the end of the selection, and then hold down Shift as you click at the end of the selection.
Vertical block of text	Press Alt and then drag over the text. (Note that this method does not work in Word tables and it might require practice since using Alt+click will trigger the Research task pane.)
Entire document	Triple-click in the Selection Bar or hold Ctrl and click once in the Selection Bar. (Note if using the Ctrl+click method you must first deselect any selected text.)

Table 3-2 **Keyboard Commands for Selecting Text**

Keyboard Command	Selects
F8	Turns on Extend Selection Mode; press twice to select a word, three times to select a sentence, and four times to select the document; press F8 once and then the Enter key to select by paragraph, or press F8 once and then the period (dot) to select by sentence
Ctrl+Shift+F8+arrow keys or mouse button	Vertical or horizontal blocks of text beginning at the insertion point
Esc	Turns off Extend Selection Mode (text will remain selected)
Ctrl+Shift+Left Arrow or Ctrl+Shift+Right Arrow	From the insertion point to the beginning of a word or end of a word, respectively
Shift+Home or Shift+End	From the insertion point to the beginning or end of the current line, respectively
Shift+Page Up or Shift+Page Down	One screen up or down, respectively, beginning from the insertion point
Ctrl+Shift+Home or Ctrl+Shift+End	From the insertion point to the beginning of the document or end of the document, respectively
Ctrl+A	Entire document

Copying, Cutting, and Pasting

No matter what kind of documents you create in Word 2010, copying, cutting, and pasting are probably among the features you use most often. Word 2010 includes a new feature that's tailor-made for people who paste content regularly: *Paste with Live Preview*. Now you'll be able to paste content the way you want it to appear—choosing whether to apply the formatting of the copied text, take on the formatting of the surrounding section, or paste the text as text only.

> **Note**
> The paste options available depend on the type of content you've copied or cut. If you've selected a picture, chart, or diagram, for example, the paste options available for those objects will be different from the paste options available for text.

To use the Copy and Cut functions, select the text you want to manipulate and then choose one of the commands listed in Table 3-3. The table also lists the Paste tools you'll use after you've copied or cut content to the Clipboard.

Table 3-3 **Copy, Cut, and Paste Features**

Keyboard Shortcut	Button	Action
Ctrl+C or Ctrl+Insert		Copy
Ctrl+Shift+C to Paste use Ctrl+Shift+V		Copy Format (Format Painter)
Ctrl+X or Shift+Del		Cut
Ctrl+V or Shift+Insert		Paste
Alt+H+V		Paste Options

Paste Options Buttons

Copying and pasting data has always been an easy way to reuse content you created pre-viously, but one drawback in previous versions of Word was that pasting the content into your document sometimes produced unexpected results. Sometimes the new content appeared in the format you wanted; other times it took on the format of the section you were pasting into.

Paste With Live Preview not only gives you additional controls that help you decide how you want the pasted information to appear but actually enables you to preview the content in the document. This means you can choose paste, point to the paste option you want, and see how the information will look in your document before you click to complete the paste operation.

To use Paste With Live Preview, follow these steps:

1. Copy or cut the information you want to paste into your document.

2. Click to position the cursor at the point you want the content to be pasted.

3. Click Paste, which is in the Clipboard group on the Home tab. The paste options appear.

4. Point to each paste option and preview the information at the cursor position.

5. When you see the paste option you want to use, click it, and the paste operation is completed.

6. You can change the information after you paste it by clicking the Paste Options button that appears beside the pasted content and choosing the option you want (see Figure 3-8).

> ### Note
> To ignore Paste Options after pasting, simply continue to work within your docu-ment or press Esc—the Paste Options button will quietly disappear until the next time you paste content.
>
> To turn off the Paste Options button, on the File tab, click Options and then click Advanced. In the Cut, Copy, And Paste options, clear the Show Paste Options Button When Content Is Pasted check box.

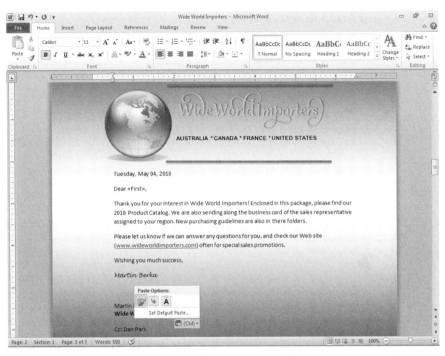

Figure 3-8 By default, the paste options button appears whenever you paste an element in your Word document.

INSIDE OUT   Setting Default Paste Options

The long-awaited options that enable you to choose paste actions are part of Paste With Live Preview in Word 2010. Not only can you choose the setting you want each time you paste content in your document, but you can choose one setting over the others as your default setting. For example, if you want to always paste content as plain text, then set each option to Keep Text Only. You can set the default Paste commands in Word Options on the Advanced tab of the Word Options dialog box or click Paste in the Clipboard group on the Home tab and choose Set Default Paste.

Using the Office Clipboard

There are actually two Clipboards used by Word 2010, the system Clipboard and the Office Clipboard. (For a distinction between the two, see the Inside Out tip entitled "The Office Clipboard and the System Clipboard" on page 85.) The Office Clipboard can store up to 24 items—including text, objects, and graphics—which means you can copy or cut 24 elements from various applications without losing data in the digital abyss.

> **Note**
> Keep in mind that if you copy item 25, the first item you copied to your Office Clipboard is removed.

You can display the Office Clipboard to see all the different items stored there by clicking the dialog launcher in the Clipboard group on the Home tab.

Further, the Office Clipboard task pane provides an easy way to see which Clipboard item contains the information you want to access, as shown in Figure 3-9. You can click an individual item to display a content menu from which you can paste the item into the document or delete the item from the Clipboard.

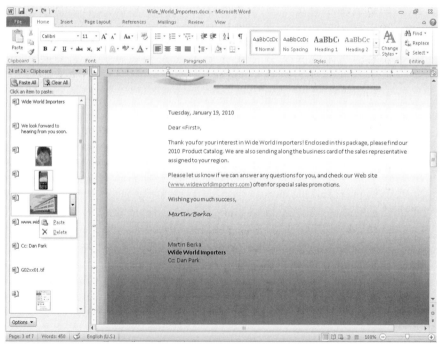

Figure 3-9 The Clipboard holds up to 24 items and displays some of the copied and cut items' contents to help you identify which item you want to paste into a document.

INSIDE OUT   The Office Clipboard and the System Clipboard

You might be wondering how the Office Clipboard relates to the system Clipboard. Here's a quick rundown of how the two relate to one another:

- The last item you copy to the Office Clipboard is stored on the system Clipboard.

- Clearing the Office Clipboard also clears the system Clipboard.

When you click the Paste command on the Home tab, or press Ctrl+V (or any other Paste keyboard command) to paste information, you paste the contents of the system Clipboard (which by default is the last item you added to the Office Clipboard).

Undoing, Redoing, and Repeating

Thank goodness for Undo and Redo in Word 2010. No matter what you're working on in your document, when it comes to editing text, you have ample opportunity to change your mind—not only can you undo edits you've recently made, but you can also redo undone edits and even repeat an action if you need to. Most likely, you'll use the Undo command more frequently than the Redo and Repeat commands, so the next section introduces that feature first.

Using Undo

With the Undo feature, you can undo one or many changes made to a document during the current session—in fact, you can revise up to 1,000 actions in the current file. To undo one or more actions, use any of the following methods:

- Click the Undo button on the Quick Access Toolbar or click the arrow and display the Undo list and click the action you want to undo. (If you don't see the action you're looking for, scroll through the list.) Note when you undo an action in the list, you also undo all the actions that appear above it in the list.

- Press Ctrl+Z or Alt+Backspace to undo the last action.

> **Note**
>
> Though the past 1,000 actions are retained, there might be still be times you encounter a message that you aren't able to undo a current action. If you're a little apprehensive about moving ahead without the Undo safety net, you can take precautionary action. One easy approach is to simply perform the "risky" action last so you won't lose your current Undo list until you're sure you'll no longer need it. Another workaround is to copy the element you want to perform the action on, paste the information into a blank document, perform the desired action on the copied version of your information, and then copy and paste the modified information into the original document. Using this method, you can ensure that if the action doesn't go as planned, your original document remains intact.

Using Redo or Repeat

The default Redo button on the Quick Access Toolbar is a combination of two commands: Redo and Repeat. When you create a new document you will see the Repeat command but as soon as you undo an action, you automatically activate the Redo command. The main role of the Redo command is redo an undone action before you make any further changes. The Repeat feature is fairly self-explanatory—clicking this command repeats the last action you performed. For example, if you applied color or a border to text, you could use the Repeat command to apply the same formatting. To use the Redo or Repeat command you can perform any of the following actions:

- Click Redo on the Quick Access Toolbar immediately after you've undone an action— before you've made any other changes.

- Press Ctrl+Y or Alt+Enter to redo the last undone change.

INSIDE OUT   Where Is the Redo List?

If you miss the Redo button that includes a Redo list, rest assured, it's still available. To add the Redo button that includes a list of Redo actions to your Quick Access Toolbar, click More Commands in the Customize Quick Access Toolbar list. From the Choose Commands From list, select Commands Not In The Ribbon and locate the Redo command (the first Redo command with the icon) that provides a list of Redo actions. Click the command to select it and then click Add to add it to your Quick Access Toolbar. Click OK to save your changes.

You can keep the default Redo button and the Redo button you just added on your Quick Access Toolbar; however, if you are tempted to leave the default Redo button on the Quick Access Toolbar because the Repeat functionality is handy, an alternative option is to remove the default Redo button and use the keyboard shortcut for Repeat (F4) to repeat your last action.

Creating Theme-Enabled Documents

Not everyone is born with design talent. Some of us can easily see how colors and patterns work together. We know how much shadow to use for our pictures. We know which fonts convey the tone we want our text to communicate. But, admittedly, some of us are clueless when it comes to document design.

Knowing how to put together a document that looks good and communicates an air of professionalism and confidence is an important part of making your point, whether you're writing a business plan, sharing a new organizational chart, or putting together a training manual. The look and feel of your document says a lot about its content, and that's where Word 2010 themes come in.

Word 2010 themes offer a coordinated look for your documents that you can apply with a single click. Every document you create in Word 2010 is assigned the Office Theme by default, but you can choose a new theme from the Themes gallery, which assigns a specific color scheme, font collection, and set of styles (which controls shadow, 3-D effects, and more) to your document.

Chapter 3

Tip

Now themes are available throughout Office 2010, which means that you can use the same theme—with the same colors, fonts, and styles—whether you're creating a document, e-mail message, database report, PowerPoint presentation, or Excel worksheet.

Experimenting with Themes

The best way to understand Word 2010 themes is to experiment with them a little bit. You'll find the Themes gallery in the Themes group on the Page Layout tab. When you click the Themes arrow, the Themes gallery appears, offering a collection of looks you can apply to your document (see Figure 3-10).

Figure 3-10 The Themes gallery offers a palette of design choices that you can apply to your Word documents.

You can preview the themes by hovering the mouse over the different selections. You will notice the theme changes in your document clearly if you have headings, body text, pictures, hyperlinks, and perhaps other elements such as lines or shapes. When the theme characteristics are applied to the content of your document, you can easily see the differences from one theme to another.

You can choose a theme from the gallery or modify the settings individually, changing the color, fonts, or effects. The controls for the individual elements are found to the right of the Themes tool in the Themes group:

You'll find various tips throughout this book on how to continue to integrate Theme elements in your documents. For more in-depth information on Themes as well as how to create and customize your document with them, see Chapter 4.

Themes and Colors

The colors that are included as part of the theme you select will show up in various places throughout Word 2010. For example, when you click the Font Color tool in the Font group on the Home tab, the color palette shown in Figure 3-11 appears. As you can see, the colors shown at the top of the palette come directly from the theme you selected. When you choose one of these colors for your text, the color is tied to the theme; if you later change the theme applied to the document, the color of this text will change. You can also choose a color from the Standard Colors section if you want the color to remain the same no matter which theme you choose.

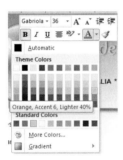

Figure 3-11 As you hover your mouse over the colors in the color palette, a ScreenTip provides more information about the Theme element.

Each color palette has 10 columns of coordinating colors. The first four colors are for text and backgrounds (two dark colors and two light colors), and the additional six colors are for accents. The first row provides the main colors for the Theme; the additional rows provide five variations of the color, starting with the lightest tint and ending with the darkest shade.

> **Note**
> *Tint* is a color mixed with white and *shade* is a color that is mixed with black.

Themes and Fonts

Each theme includes two fonts: one font is used in headings and the other is used for body text. When you click the Font tool in the Fonts group on the Home tab, for example, the theme fonts appear at the top of the fonts list (see Figure 3-12).

Chapter 3

Figure 3-12 The Office Theme uses Cambria for headings and Calibri for body text.

Similar to the way Word handles colors and themes, if you want the font to change when you choose to apply a different theme to the document, use the Theme fonts found in the Theme Fonts section at the top of the font list. If you choose to use a font other than the ones shown in the Theme Fonts list, that font will remain the same if you change the theme at a later time.

Themes and Effects

The theme effects that are applied automatically when you choose a specific theme in Word 2010 control attributes, such as line style, fill, shadow, and three-dimensional effects. If you add pictures, pull quotes, SmartArt, charts, or shapes, the shape effects are added to those elements and change the way they appear on the page. Figure 3-13 shows various effects that go along with the different themes you can apply to your documents.

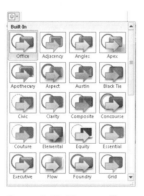

Figure 3-13 Theme effects control line, shadow, and three-dimensional effects for objects like shapes, pictures, and SmartArt.

You'll notice these theme effects when you click an object in your document and choose, for example, Shape Effects on the Drawing Tools Format tab or Picture Effects on the Picture Tools Format tab.

Saving Documents

Years ago I had a sign hanging on my then-cubicle wall: *Save frequently and often*. The publishing company I worked for at the time used a mainframe computer that was almost the size of a small room—and around 3 P.M. every day the server seemed to get sleepy. You never knew when the system would crash and all your work on your current document would be lost.

Thankfully today's technology is more reliable—and smaller—than that. But the warning still holds. Saving your file is as important as it ever was. Nobody wants to lose good thoughts, touching paragraphs, well-phrased copy, or inspiring marketing material. Re-creating documents we've already done once is agony.

Word 2010 helps you out in the Save department, both by preserving files you might have forgotten to save and by making it easy for you to save files where and when you want to save them. Some of the new Save features in Word 2010 include a tool that enables you to recover unsaved files and the ability to save directly to your server, workspace, or SkyDrive account online.

> **Tip**
>
> Before other authors can access and work on the files you save to a shared space, you must have given them the necessary permissions to access the file and have posted the file to a SharePoint Workspace or Windows Live SkyDrive account. You'll find out more about sharing files and co-authoring documents in Part IV, "Word 2010 As a Team Effort, Anywhere, Always."

Performing Simple Saves

Saving your document in the same location with the same name is easy. Simply follow any of these procedures:

- Click the File tab to display Backstage view and then click Save.

- Click the Save button on the Quick Access Toolbar.

- Press Ctrl+S.

Chapter 3

You can take advantage of the simplicity of the Save procedure. Whenever you're about to take a break, press Ctrl+S as you start to roll your chair away from your desk. Or, when your phone rings, click the Save button as you reach for the receiver. Saving your work regularly helps you avoid major data loss headaches when you least expect them (because, as everyone knows, system crashes or disasters usually strike at the most inopportune times).

TROUBLESHOOTING

Pressing Shift and clicking the File tab doesn't change the Save and Close commands to Save All and Close All.

In earlier versions of Word, you can press Shift while opening the File menu, and the Save and Close commands would change to Save All and Close All. This capability isn't included in Word 2010. However, it is easily resolved by adding the Save All and Close All commands to your Quick Access Toolbar (using the More Commands option).

Saving Files with the Save As Dialog Box

The Save As dialog box appears whenever you save a new document or when you choose Save As in Backstage view or press F12. This makes it possible for you to save an existing document as a new file or in another location.

Figure 3-14 shows the Save As dialog box in Windows 7. Note that you can add tags and author names as well as save a thumbnail with the file.

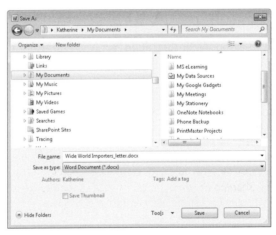

Figure 3-14 You can use the Save As dialog box to add tags and authors to the documents you save.

CAUTION

Keep in mind that including a thumbnail image when you save a document in Word 97-2003 format increases the file size and has been known to cause instabilities in a document.

You also have the option of saving your file to your Windows Live SkyDrive or SharePoint account when you click Save & Send in Backstage view. On the Save & Send tab, you can select where you want to save the file, as shown in Figure 3-15.

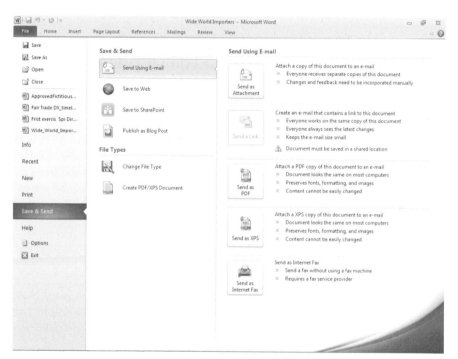

Figure 3-15 On the Save & Send tab in Backstage view, you can choose where you want to save the file you create in Word 2010.

Depending on the location you select, you might be asked to sign in with your Windows Live account, log on to the SharePoint Server, or take further action to prepare and post your file.

> **Note**
>
> At times, you'll want to set up a folder to contain a newly created file. You can easily create a new folder during the Save procedure by clicking New Folder on the toolbar of the Save As dialog box, or right-clicking an empty area of the file list and choosing the New, Folder command.

You can save Word 2010 documents in a variety of file types, which can be convenient if you're saving a file for someone who is using an application other than Word or if you're creating HTML, Portable Document Format (PDF), XML Paper Specification (XPS), or XML documents.

> ### Obtaining Additional File Format Converters
>
> At some point, you might face the task of converting a document for which Word has not supplied a converter. When this situation arises, you'll have to install another converter. In some cases, you can easily obtain a converter from Microsoft Office Online or in the Office Resource Kit. If neither the Web site nor the Office Resource Kit provides what you're looking for, your next step should be to search online for a third-party solution. Be sure to read user reviews and check out the company before you buy and download the utility. In addition, you can search for file conversion programs on shareware sites, using your favorite search engine.

Saving to a SharePoint Site

With the co-authoring and SharePoint Workspace integration in Word 2010, you can set up your SharePoint sites to work just like another folder on your system. That way you can seamlessly save and open files from the SharePoint folder as you would any other folder you regularly use.

If you currently have access to a SharePoint site, you can select the site in the Save As dialog box and save the file directly to that location. Click File to display Backstage view, and then click Save As. On the list at the left side of the dialog box, scroll down to SharePoint Sites. Click it, and then click the site in the right pane that reflects where you want to save the file (see Figure 3-16). Choose the file type, enter a file name, and fill in the tag and author information as needed; then click Save. The file is saved to your SharePoint site.

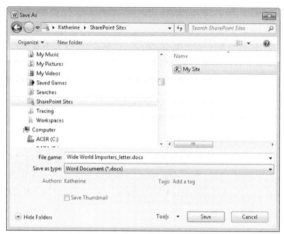

Figure 3-16 If you currently have access to a SharePoint site, the site will appear as a folder choice in the Save As dialog box.

> **Tip**
>
> You can also set up Word 2010 to save directly to your SharePoint Workspace and Windows Live SkyDrive accounts. You'll find more information about this in Chapter 21, "Sharing Your Documents."

Designing Instant Documents

Of course, not all documents you create will require a lot of time and effort in the design department. The trick is to make sure the look and feel reflects what you want people reading your documents to remember about your company, department, project, or team.

Each aspect of your document communicates something unique and hopefully complementary to the whole, giving the document a consistent, effective look. For example, a well-designed document has the following characteristics:

- The colors all work together well in a coordinated scheme that might communicate professionalism, creativity, energy, or dependability.

- The font says something about the tone of your document—and by extension—your company. A light, playful font will communicate a light-hearted approach; a traditional font gives a business-like feel.

- Headings in your document stand out from the text and help readers focus on the most important elements in the design.

- Images should be high quality and large enough to break up the flow of text and provide visual interest.

- If you use a multicolumn design, balance the columns and arrange the layout so the reader always knows where to look next; the design should help guide the reader's eye down the page.

Each of the sections that follow provide examples of documents you can easily produce using templates available to you through Office.com. Once you create the documents, you can customize them with your own content and add quick styles, picture effects, and more to make the documents really shine.

An Annual Report

Your company's annual report is an important communication that lets those interested in your organization—perhaps shareholders, constituents, customers, or the general public—learn what your company accomplished in the previous year and how you are well-positioned to meet the challenges in the future. The annual report you design might be a substantial document—25 pages or more—that might include the following major sections:

- Cover

- Introduction

- Mission Statement

- Letter to Stockholders

- History of Company

- Management Report

- Financial Summary

- Year in Review

- Projections for the Future

- Financial Statements

- Appendices

The design of an annual report is an important consideration because you want to convey excellence, professionalism, and clarity as you tell the story of your previous year. A well-designed annual report can give staff and stakeholders a boost of confidence in your organization and provide a sense of accomplishment for those who helped make the past year a success.

Word 2010 includes a number of report templates you can customize to use as the basis for your annual report. Figure 3-17 shows the Oriel report template. As you can see, the cover page design and the interior page have a different look but share similar colors, fonts, and style.

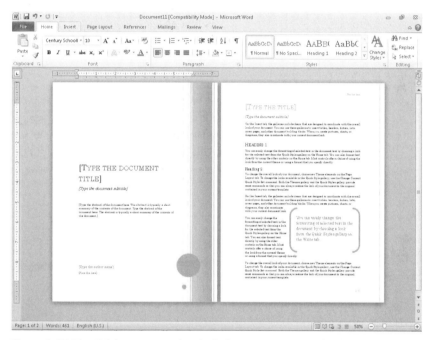

Figure 3-17 The Oriel report template includes a cover page and interior page design you can use for an annual report.

Business Letterhead

Your business letterhead says a lot about your organization through the colors, fonts, and layout you choose. Important elements on letterhead include:

- Your company logo

- A motto or tag line

- Your company address, including your e-mail address and Web site

- Graphic elements such as lines or background images

- Extras such as quotes or a board of directors listing

The main idea for the design of your letterhead, of course, is to provide a sense of company identity while allowing the maximum amount of space on the page for the body of the business letter.

You can find letterhead templates in Word 2010 by following these steps:

1. Click the File tab to display Backstage view.

2. In the Office.com area on the New tab, scroll down to the Stationery icon and click it.

3. Click the Letterhead folder.

4. Click the letterhead template you want to open and then click Download.

Figure 3-18 shows the Oriel letterhead style that corresponds to the annual report style shown in Figure 3-16. As you can see, this letterhead offers a distinctive approach with the company name stretching down the right side of the page. The letter area is open and uncluttered, and the font is a traditional and professional style.

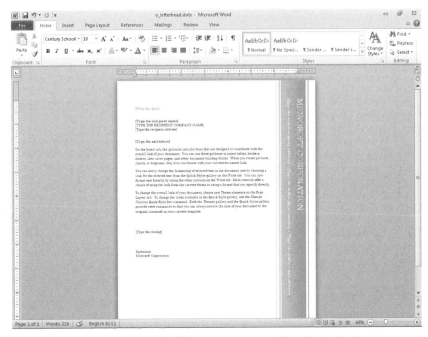

Figure 3-18 The Oriel letterhead offers an open page with a distinctive banner.

A Newsletter

Another popular type of document you might need to create in Word 2010 can call for a slightly more sophisticated design. Newsletters typically include a multicolumn format, stretched over multiple document pages. A well-designed newsletter has the following design characteristics:

- A recognizable and inviting masthead

- Several short stories flowing across multiple pages

- Alternative or mirroring page layouts

- Multiple columns

- Graphic elements such as shaded boxes, backgrounds, or borders to help readers see clearly where one story ends and another begins

- Clear headings to help readers navigate through the document

- A table of contents so readers can see clearly where to find various newsletter elements

- Photos, pictures, or clip art to help add visual interest and break up text

- An inviting and coordinating color scheme

- A font that is easy to read and works well for the layout, not crowding too much text into a small space

Word 2010 includes a number of newsletter templates that offer you a variety of styles. You can choose from two, three, or four-column layouts. The newsletter templates include multiple pages to provide a variety of layouts you can customize with your own images and content. For example, the newsletter template shown in Figure 3-19 includes a two-column format with a table of contents, headlines, sidebars, photos, and more.

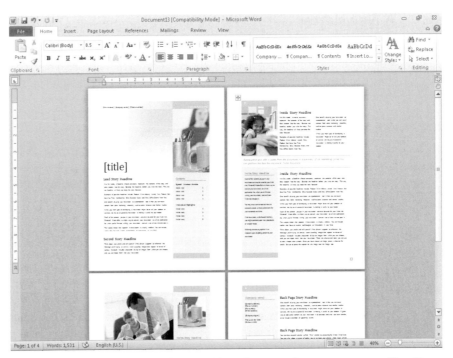

Figure 3-19 This newsletter template provides a four-page layout you can modify with your own text and images.

What's Next?

This chapter walked you through the early choices you'll make as you create a new document, select a theme, and work your new document in various ways. You also found out about the changes to common procedures you'll use when you are selecting, copying, and pasting content or opening and saving files. The next chapter does a deep dive into templates—what goes into them, how you can build documents based on them, and how you can customize templates to fit your own special tasks in Word 2010.

Templates and Themes for a Professional Look

Where Does Your Document Get Its Design? 102

Templates 101: Behind the Scenes.................. 102

Creating Custom Templates 112

Modifying Existing Templates 122

Using the Organizer to Rename, Delete,
and Copy Styles.................................. 123

Applying Themes in Word 2010 126

Changing a Theme............................... 130

Creating a Custom Theme........................ 134

What's Next?.................................... 137

Why make your documents look good?

If you are sharing data with your team, writing copy for a new product brochure, or creating a draft of a new training manual, what's the big deal about design? Thinking through the whys and wherefores of page layout, color schemes, and font choice seems like a lot of trouble when an eye-catching, coordinated design isn't really your main goal.

That's a valid argument if you just want to focus only on the content of your document. But we know that people receiving your message take in more than the characters on the page when they are interpreting the information you're sharing with them. They also notice—perhaps unconsciously—the shape of the letters. They are aware of the colors on the page. They may feel an inner tension if the words are too close together or there are too many of them without a picture to break up the long blocks of text.

And what that means to you, ultimately, is that if your readers don't feel drawn to your document because of its design, your work may never get a good reading. And that could mean all the effort you put into creating great-sounding text could go to waste simply because the right design wasn't used to present it to the reader.

This chapter is all about ways you can apply and customize templates and themes to help you reach and connect with your reader in a way that gets your message read. Both templates and themes move you toward a similar goal—efficiently producing documents that look and sound professional. Whether you are delivering a simple thank-you note or drafting a grant proposal asking for millions of dollars, putting your ideas in an appealing design that helps the reader easily understand what you're trying to say can only help your purpose in the long run.

Where Does Your Document Get Its Design?

Word 2010 includes a number of features that are ready and willing to help you create the kind of design you want for your documents; you just need know which to use, and when to use them. Here's a list of the various features that help you control the look of your documents:

- Document templates contain the whole range of elements that contribute to the format of your document.

- Themes provide a coordinated set of formatting choices that affect the color scheme, font choices, and effects applied to shapes and objects in your document.

- Quick Styles offer a variety of different looks you can apply to the document (for example, Distinctive, Elegant, and Traditional are the names of three Quick Style sets).

- Building blocks are ready-made text segments with formatting you can customize and insert in your document at the appropriate point.

> **Tip**
>
> In addition to these tools that help you apply coordinated effects throughout your document, you can also change the format of individual elements by using the Fonts, Effects, and various style and spacing tools to make changes on the current page. You'll find out more about formatting specific content items—creating lists, applying typographic features, and more—in Chapter 11, "Formatting Your Document."

Templates 101: Behind the Scenes

Whenever you create a new document in Word 2010, your document is based on a template that provides default document creation settings. Every Word document uses a template by default. You may have seen Normal.dotx appearing in a message box somewhere along the line. The Normal.dotx template is a global template that includes default settings for headings, body text, quotes, text boxes, and much more. All templates you work with in Word 2010 will be in one of two formats:

- .dotx is the traditional Word 2010 template

- .dotm is a Word 2010 template with macros enabled

Templates are stored on your computer and are available online at Office.com (as you saw in Chapter 3, "Right Now Document Design with Word 2010"). When you open a new document based on a template, you are creating a new file that includes all the elements included in the template file—basic content elements like text and heading styles, column layout, color scheme, and page margins, as well as more specialized controls like building blocks, content controls, and macros.

Templates can be as complex or as simple as you choose, but their primary purpose is to streamline your document design and save it in such a way that you can use it consistently in other documents you create. For example, you might create a simple template for your business letterhead that includes the address block, space for the recipient name, the date, boilerplate text, and your signature. You can use the letterhead template over and over again for sales or prospect letters. Instead of creating a new document each time and choosing all the formatting settings—margins, fonts, colors, and so forth—you can base your new document on the template and all the formats are applied automatically for you. Simple, effective, and efficient. Nice.

Templates can also contain complex elements and operations, including macros that automate specific functions in the document; content controls that gather data from end users (or merge data from a data source); sophisticated formats; and much more. For example, you might include multicolumn designs, alternating page formats, sections, header and footer specifications, and styles for footnotes, endnotes, citations, and more.

INSIDE OUT   Creating Documents Programmatically

Word 2007 and Word 2010 documents use a different file format than files created in earlier versions of Word. Beginning with Word 2007, the software moved to Ecma Office Open XML format, an efficient means of data storage that separates content from format and enables you to use and share your content easily in a variety of forms. Although it seems as though you open, edit, and close a singular document, the Word 2010 document you modify is actually a collection of files, zipped together and presented to you as a single document. The ZIP package contains document parts, such as individual XML files, graphics, charts, and embedded objects. Viewing the internal components of the ZIP package is simply a matter of renaming the file with a .zip file extension and opening it in any tool that functions on ZIP technology. The following figure shows a view of a template opened in Windows Explorer along with the contents of the Word folder.

Chapter 4

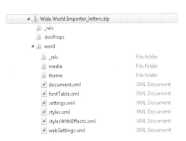

The _rels folder contains information about the relationship between the various elements in the file; each of the xml files contains information that tells Word 2010 how to create the document on the screen.

A document is now stored in individual document parts, such as headers, footers, endnotes, styles, and media. This new functionality gives developers the ability to create new Word documents as well as access and alter data without going through the Word application. For example, if an address or logo stored in the header of several documents changes, the headers can be updated without the need to open each document in Word to make the modification. What this means to you as a Word 2010 user is that the content you create and edit in your Word 2010 documents can be used in a variety of ways. In addition, elements such as templates and themes that you apply to your content can be changed easily to meet different goals.

An Update on Office Open XML

Word 2007 included a Custom XML feature that stirred up a legal challenge for Microsoft, and as a result of a court ruling (which as of this writing is being appealed), Microsoft has opted to remove the Custom XML feature from outstanding Word 2007 versions. The Custom XML feature is not part of Word 2010.

Word 2007 users can install a patch that renders the software unable to read any Custom XML elements within .docx, .docm, or .xml files. This change will not affect the majority of Word users; the feature is used primarily in server-based word processing tasks. To get the patch, find "2007 Microsoft Office Supplement Release (October 2009)" at the Microsoft OEM Partner Center (*http://oem.microsoft.com/Script/ContentPage.aspx?pageid=563214*).

For a more in-depth look at creating and editing documents in the Office Open XML Format, see *Advanced Microsoft Office Documents 2007 Edition Inside Out* by Stephanie Krieger (Microsoft Press, 2007).

Note

You can still use templates created and saved in the Word 97-2003 Document file format (.dot) in Compatibility Mode in Word 2010. Not all program functionality will be available to you—for example, themes work only in Word 2007 or Word 2010—but if you want (or need) to preserve continuity with an older template, you can do so. You will need to remember to use the Save As dialog box to save your document in the earlier template format (.dot) using the Word 97-2003 Document file format.

Understanding How Templates Work

So every document you create is based on a template that contains the structure and tools for shaping the style, formatting, content, and page layout of finished files. Most templates on Office.com include visual elements such as graphics, Content Controls, and custom Building Blocks that are associated with the template. In contrast, Word 2010 bases new, blank documents on the Normal template which, by default, contains no visual elements. The Normal template is discussed in more detail in the next section.

The main purpose of templates is to make formatting and inserting information into documents as efficient, error-free, and automatic as possible. The fewer formatting and typing tasks you have to perform, the better. In addition to speeding up document creation, you can provide custom editing environments for particular projects and clients because templates can also include interface tools (such as a customized Quick Access Toolbar or a customized Ribbon) as well as the previous list of content and layout settings.

Regardless of the information included in templates or whether your template includes macros, you can use two main types of templates when you work in Word:

- **Global templates**   These templates (most notably the Normal and Building Blocks templates) contain settings that are available to all documents regardless of the template used to create the document.

- **Document templates**   Examples include letterhead and those from Office.com, which contain settings that are available only to documents based on that template.

When a document is based on a template, the template is attached, or linked, to the document, and the settings stored in the document template are made available through this link. Having the ability to choose the type of template changes you want to apply gives you the flexibility to affect changes in the current document alone or to create changes that affect all documents you create in Word 2010.

Chapter 4

Getting the Scoop on the Normal Template

The Normal.dotm template is a global template that is always open and working behind the scenes, no matter which template you use to format a specific document. Whenever you start Word, the program automatically looks for the Normal template in the User Template location specified in the File Locations dialog box. In both Windows 7 and Windows Vista, the default location of the User Templates (or Templates) folder is

```
C:\Users\user name\AppData\Roaming\Microsoft\Templates
```

To access the File Locations dialog box, click File, select Options, choose Advanced, scroll to the bottom of the Advanced options window, and click File Locations near the bottom of the Advanced tab, as shown in Figure 4-1.

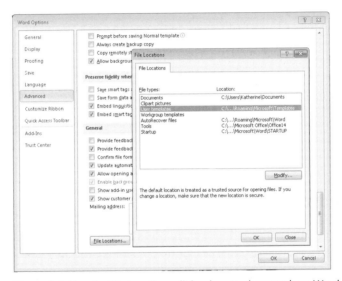

Figure 4-1 Use the File Locations dialog box to change where Word 2010 stores and accesses the templates for your documents.

TROUBLESHOOTING

I don't see the AppData folder in Windows Vista and Windows 7.

By design, the AppData folder in Windows Vista is a hidden folder. If you do not see the AppData folder in your User Profile folder, you need to configure Windows to display hidden files and folders. To do this, click the Start button and choose My Computer (or simply Computer in Windows 7), and then on the Tools menu click Folder Options. In the Folder Options dialog box, on the View tab, select the Show Hidden

Files And Folders option in the Advanced Settings area, and click OK. Note that hidden folders in Windows 7 do appear in Windows Explorer, but they appear to be "dimmed" or not selectable. You can search the contents of hidden folders and view folder properties as needed.

What's in Normal.dotx?

The Normal template uses the Office Theme and contains default styles (but no boilerplate text) that are automatically available whenever you create new, blank documents. As you work in a document, any styles, macros, or other customizations that you save are stored in the Normal template unless you specify otherwise. In addition, you can modify the Normal template to change the default document formatting in Word. As you can imagine, the longer you work with Word, the more customized your Normal.dotm file can become.

Replacing a Damaged Normal.dotx   If the Normal template is damaged, moved, missing, or renamed, Word creates a new Normal template the next time you start the application. The new template is based on the default settings. This automatically generated Normal template won't include any customizations that you've made to a previous version of Normal.dotm.

> **Tip**
>
> If you work with a highly customized Normal template, back up your system's Normal.dotm file every few weeks for safekeeping.

Renaming Normal.dotx   You can also intentionally rename your Normal template and force Word to create a new Normal template. You might want to do this, for example, when you want to preserve the customizations you've added to Normal.dotx but no longer want to use that template with new files you create. If you create a new Normal.dotx, Word creates a fresh Normal template, and then you can copy any selected components you want from the renamed template into the newly generated Normal template by using the Organizer, as described in "Using the Organizer to Rename, Delete, and Copy Styles," on page 123.

To rename the Normal template, follow these steps:

1. Close Word and then display Normal.dotm in your Templates folder.

2. Right-click the Normal template then click Rename.

3. Type a new name for the template.

The next time you open a new, blank document in Word, the document will be based on the standard Normal template without any custom settings.

TROUBLESHOOTING

Word crashes during startup—could the Normal template be corrupt?

If Word crashes during startup, you can quickly determine whether the problem is due to a damaged Registry entry, an add-in, or a corrupt Normal.dotm file. To get to the root of the problem, try starting Word in Safe Mode. When you start Word in Safe Mode, it opens but prevents add-ins and global templates (including Normal.dotm) from loading automatically. To start in Safe Mode, simply hold the Ctrl key while launching Word. Note that you need to continue holding the Ctrl key until you are prompted to start Word in Safe Mode.

If Word opens properly when this method is used but crashes when you try to open it normally, you can deduce that the error doesn't lie in the Word installation. Instead, the error is caused by a damaged Normal template, third-party add-in, or Registry corruption.

To test whether the Normal.dotm file is the culprit, rename the Normal.dotm file and then attempt to start Word normally. If Word starts successfully, a new Normal.dotm file will be created, and you can use the Organizer to copy any components you need from the renamed file into the newly created Normal.dotm file. (To find out more about using the Organizer to work with files, see the section, "Using the Organizer to Rename, Delete, and Copy Styles," on page 123.

If Word still doesn't start properly after you rename your existing Normal.dotm file, the next likely culprit is a third-party add-in followed by Registry corruption.

For additional information on troubleshooting third-party add-ins and Registry corruption, refer to the Troubleshooting guide included on the companion CD to this book.

CAUTION

Because the Normal template is so necessary and so widely used, it's often the first target of macro virus creators. Third-party add-ins that aren't developed properly can display virus-like qualities that can lead to the corruption of your Normal template. Word automatically saves any changes made to your Normal template during the current session when you exit the program, so one way you can protect yourself against viruses and corruption is to change the automatic behavior to instead prompt you before Word automatically saves changes to your Normal template. To do so, click File and then select Options. In the Advanced area under the Save options, turn on Prompt Before Saving Normal Template.

Using Templates from the New Documents Dialog Box

As explained in Chapter 3, Word provides easy access to a number of built-in templates that you can use to create new documents. To access Word templates, click File to display Back-stage view and then choose New. Figure 4-2 displays the New tab.

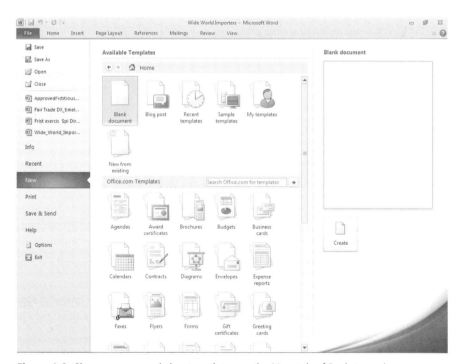

Figure 4-2 Choose new or existing templates on the New tab of Backstage view.

Note

The location for Workgroup Templates is not set by default. Typically, this location is a shared folder on your network. You can set the Workgroup Templates location in the File Locations dialog box, which is available when you click the Advanced tab in the Word Options dialog box.

Once you set a location for Workgroup Templates, you will no longer be able to remove the Workgroup Templates location without editing the Registry. If you find that you prefer not to map Workgroup Templates to a folder after you've added a location, simply map the Workgroup Templates option to the Templates folder. By doing this, you basically instruct Word to show the templates in your Templates folder for both User Templates and Workgroup Templates. If you map the Workgroup Templates option to any other location, your My Templates tab on the New tab will contain files that you would probably prefer not to include.

The following list is a summary of the template options found on the New tab:

- **Blank**   Opens a new document based on the standard blank document template (Normal.dotm)

- **Blog Post**   Displays a new blank document formatted for a blog entry

- **Recent Templates**   Displays a list of templates you have recently used

- **Sample Templates**   Offers a collection of sample templates for different styles and document types

- **My Templates**   Opens the New dialog box and displays templates that you have saved to your computer

- **New From Existing**   Opens the New From Existing Document dialog box and enables you to create a new document based on another document (regardless of whether the document is a template)

Office.com Templates gives you access to a large collection of templates you can download from Office.com. You will find dozens of template styles for all kinds of documents—ranging from marketing and business forms, letters and contracts, to stationery, calendars, certificates, and flyers. To create a new document using a template available on the New tab, follow these steps:

1. Click File to display Backstage view, and then click New.

2. In the Available Templates area, choose the type of template you want to use.

3. If you are using a template from the Sample Templates or My Templates categories, verify the Document option is selected in the Create New area and then click Create or OK (depending on whether the New dialog box is displayed).

If you're opening a template that's installed on your computer, Word immediately creates a new document based on the selected template. If the template isn't installed on your computer, the template is downloaded to your system and displayed in Word. You can then type the contents of the new document and save the document locally or store it on the server, just as you would any other document.

Templates with Text You Can Use

D o you have an idea about the type of document you'd like to create but aren't sure what kind of template you need? In Word 2010, you can easily find templates with boilerplate text you can replace with your own; click in the Office.com search box located at the right side of the center column of the New tab and type a word or phrase that describes the type of template you'd like to find. For example, you might want to send a thank you note and find that you are struggling with those perfect words to properly convey your thoughts. If you type *thank you* in the Search text box and then click the Start Searching arrow, the search results will display templates that include text relating to content commonly found in thank you notes. All you need to do is fill in the names and addresses, and you're good to go.

In addition to retrieving templates from your own computer and Office.com, you can access templates stored on a network, FTP site, document server, or Microsoft SharePoint site. Workgroups frequently need to share templates, so storing templates online provides an ideal way to share templates and ensure that the most up-to-date templates are readily available to team members. In Word, you can easily create new documents based on templates that are stored on networks or the Internet. For more information about sharing documents and using workgroup templates, see Chapter 21, "Sharing Your Documents."

Chapter 4

Creating Custom Templates

When you're familiar with how templates work and how to use existing templates, you're ready to start creating your own. In Word, you can create templates in three ways. You can base a new template on an existing document, an existing template, or create a template from scratch. The method that you use depends on the resources you have on hand, for example:

- **Create a template based on an existing document.** You have a document that contains most or all of the settings you want to use in your new template. When you base a template on an existing document, you create a template that contains the same document Theme as well as all of the styles, macros, and other settings in the document. Most likely, you'll want to modify the document's settings slightly to fine-tune your template.

- **Create a template based on an existing template.** You have a template that contains many of the settings you want to use in your new template, but you want to add or change a few settings without affecting the existing template. The main procedural difference is that you open a template file (.dot, .dotx, or .dotm) instead of a document file (.doc or .docx).

- **Create a template from scratch.** You have no model to use as a starting point for your template or just want to start from the ground up. Building a template from scratch is similar to creating a document from scratch.

When you create custom templates, save them in the Templates folder. Doing so makes them easily accessible via the New tab. Otherwise, you need to either locate the template in Windows Explorer and double-click the template to create a new document based on the template, or locate the template on the New tab by using the New From Existing command and navigate to the location of your template.

> **Note**
>
> When you save a file as a Word template file, you will notice a small change in the file icon—for *.dotx templates, a small gold edge appears along the top of the document icon. For *.dotm files, the gold edge, along with an exclamation point appears. These small visual cues help you to determine whether you've saved the template as a regular template or a macro-enabled template, which will make a difference in the processing of the file.

> **Tip**
> If you don't see the file extensions by default and would like to display them, click Start in Windows 7, choose Computer, and then click Organize. Click Folder and Search Options and choose View. Clear the check box beside Hide Extensions For Known File Types, and then click OK. The file extensions will appear on your files.

Thinking Through Your Template Design

The best time to design a template is before you begin creating one. Yes, you can easily adapt an existing template or change a document you particularly like to work as a template for future documents, but carefully considering what you'd like to accomplish with a template before you start it is the best way to meet your document goals.

- **Watch your document workflow.**   Whether you work as part of a large business or a small team, pay attention to where documents begin—and where they end—in your particular organization. Do documents tend to stay within departments? Do documents find their way out to the public with a variety of looks and logos? Does one person shepherd the creation of all new documents to ensure that everything you create has a consistent look and feel?

- **Keep an eye on the design.**   Chances are that you already have some kind of design at work in your traditional documents. Maybe that design is nothing more than simple black text on a white page; or you might have a color logo, a distinctive font, or other design elements that you use regularly on your business cards, newsletters, and more. Revisit your design with an artist's eye and ask yourself how well the colors, font, and style fits your business today. Is it time for a makeover? If so, gather a sample of each type of document you'd like to include in the new design (the more comprehensive the change, the better), and consider all the documents you want to change as you begin to think through what you'd like to include in a template.

- **Consider your assets.**   In some businesses or organizations, including graphics— photos, diagrams, charts, clip art, and more—is an important part of the document creation. Do you use many photos in your documents? Do your documents regularly feature product images, staff photos, or project diagrams?

- **Think about how you use data.**   Will the people who read your documents be asked to provide information in fields or forms? Will you incorporate data from a data source (such as your Outlook contacts list) as part of a larger mail merge project? If you regularly incorporate data from outside sources in your documents, you can include content controls in your template to help accommodate that need.

Chapter 4

- **Share and share alike.** Consider the final form for the documents you create. Are many of your creations finalized in print, presented on the Web, sent through e-mail, or distributed in PDF format?

Template Elements

Some of the elements you might want to incorporate in your template include:

Banner or masthead	Pictures	Captions
Theme selection	Lines	Columns
Headings	Shaded boxes	Boilerplate text
Body text	Content controls	Macros
Address block	Tables	

Creating a Template Based on an Existing Document

1. Click File and then Open.

2. In the Open dialog box, open the document that contains the formatting and/or text that you want to include in your template.

3. Remove the content you don't want to include in the template.

4. Add any other items—pictures, logos, headings, and more—that you want to include in the template.

Creating a Template Based on an Existing Template

1. Click File and then New.

2. On the New tab, click My Templates to display the New dialog box.

3. Select a template similar to the one you want to create. In the Create New options, click the Template option and then click OK.

Creating a Template Based on a New, Blank Template

Click File, New, and then double-click Blank Document.

Saving Your Template

Once your template has been created, save it by performing the following steps:

1. Click File and then choose Save As.

2. In the Save As dialog box, select the Templates folder by scrolling up to the top folder, which is located in the top-left of the dialog box.

3. In the File Name box, type a name for the new template.

4. In the Save As Type text box, ensure that Word Template (*.dotx) is shown or, if you intend to include macros in your template, click Word Macro-Enabled Template (*.dotm).

5. In Windows 7 or Windows Vista, you can also take the following actions:

    ○ Edit information in the Authors and Tags fields, if desired, by clicking the place-holder text and replacing it. If you are using Windows Vista you can also enter information in the Properties field.

    ○ Select the Save Thumbnail check box if you want to save a thumbnail image (a small image of the first page of a document and its contents) of your new template. Saving a thumbnail is a good idea because the image will appear in the New dialog box as well as in the Preview pane on the New tab; this will help you quickly find the correct template.

6. Click the Save button.

By default, a template saved in the Templates folder appears on the Personal Templates tab in the New dialog box or on a custom tab if the template is placed in a subfolder.

INSIDE OUT   Adding and Removing Word Templates and Tabs in the New Dialog Box

You can control which templates and tabs appear in the New dialog box. To do so, you simply add folders and templates to the User Templates or Workgroup Templates folders. Each folder that you place in either of the template folders creates a tab with the same name in the New dialog box. The following image shows two folders stored in the Templates folder—Wide World Importers and Oriel Electronics—that appear as tabs in the New dialog box.

Chapter 4

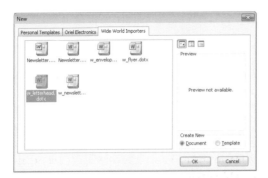

To create a new folder, in the Save As dialog box, click the New Folder button on the toolbar in the Save As dialog box or right-click an empty area of the file list. Select New and then Folder from the context menu.

Once you have added templates and folders, the next time you click My Templates in the New Document dialog box, the tabs and templates you added will be available in the New dialog box. If you want to restore the original tabs and templates, simply delete the templates and folders from the Templates folder. If you prefer, you can right-click and delete templates from within the New dialog box, but you will need to access the contents of the Templates folder to delete the subfolders and remove the tabs from the New dialog box.

You can now modify or add content, styles, boilerplate text, content controls, building blocks, macros, and any other elements you want to include in your template.

Once you have created a new template, test the template to verify that it works by doing the following:

1. Click File to display Backstage view, and then click New.

2. Click My Templates in the New Document task pane, and then select the tab on which the template is located (if necessary).

3. Ensure that the Document option is selected in the Create New area in the Templates dialog box, and then double-click the new template.

The template should open normally in the Word window and you can begin to add your own content as needed in the new document.

INSIDE OUT   Providing Single-Click Access to Templates

If you create a custom document template that you'll access frequently to create new documents, you might consider adding a custom button to the Quick Access Toolbar or creating a desktop shortcut with which you can quickly open a new, blank document based on a particular template. To add a custom button, you first create or record a macro. You then add a button to your Quick Access Toolbar that runs the macro. To learn how to record a macro and add the macro to your Quick Access Toolbar, see Chapter 28, "Working with Macros in Word 2010."

Attaching Templates to Documents

Earlier in this chapter you learned that the global template, Normal.dotx, is attached to all new files you create in Word 2010. When you create a document from an existing template, that document's template is automatically attached to the document. However, you can specify which document template you want to attach to a document, regardless of which template is currently attached. In this circumstance, when you replace the existing document template with a new one, you can choose to automatically update the document's text with the new styles. This makes short work of modifying the formatting throughout the document.

Note

Another method you can use to quickly update a document's styles is to use Quick Style Sets—a new type of formatting template—instead of attaching a new template to your document. For more on creating and working with Quick Style Sets, see Chapter 12, "Applying and Customizing Quick Styles."

Chapter 4

To attach a template to a document and update the document's styles based on the newly attached template, follow these steps:

1. Open your document.

2. Click File to display Backstage view then click Options.

3. In the Word Options dialog box, click Add-Ins.

4. Click the Manage arrow, choose Templates, and then click Go (see Figure 4-3).

5. In the Templates and Add-Ins dialog box, click the Attach button.

6. Navigate to the folder containing the template you want to attach, select the folder, and choose Open.

7. Select the Automatically Update Document Styles check box to apply the template styles to elements in the document (see Figure 4-4).

8. Click OK to complete the process and attach the template.

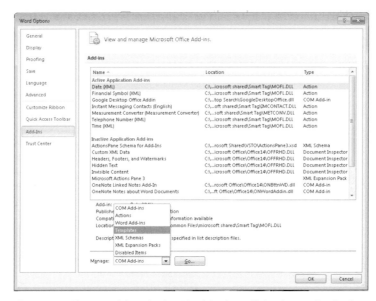

Figure 4-3 Choose Add-Ins in the Word Options dialog box to begin the process of attaching a template to your document.

Tip

If you often attach templates to the documents you create in Word, you can display the Developer tab in the Ribbon so that you can attach templates easily. To display the Developer tab, click File, and then in Backstage view, click Options. Click Customize Ribbon, and in the list on the right side of the window, select the Developer check box and click OK. The Developer tab appears in the Ribbon and you can click Document Template in the Templates group on the Developer tab to display the Templates and Add-Ins dialog box.

Figure 4-4 Select the Automatically Update Document Styles check box to apply styles automatically in your document.

If you configure Word to automatically update styles, keep in mind that the document text must be formatted with styles that have the same style names as those included in the newly attached template. If the style names are the same, Word will update the text formatting to match the newly attached template's style formats. If the document's style names are different from the attached template's style names, you'll need to select and replace instances of each style. If you find that you're faced with changing styles manually, consider using the Select All Instances feature in the Styles And Formatting task pane to choose all instances of an "old" style and then click the new style name in the Styles task pane to replace the styles all at once.

For more information about changing all instances of a style, see Chapter 12.

Working with Global Templates

Up to this point, we've explored ways to create and attach document templates. In addition to the document-specific templates you use to control the formatting and function of individual files, you may in some cases need to work with the global templates Word uses to provide information to your documents. All documents have access to the Normal and Building Blocks global templates, which control features including macros, keyboard shortcuts, and building blocks; these templates are loaded automatically by Word. The main difference between global and document templates is that global templates contain functionality that affects all files you create in Word (for example, macros or keyboard shortcuts you want to be available anytime you use the program) and document templates contain formatting and layout choices that are unique to one or more specific documents.

> **Note**
> Because the Normal and Building Blocks templates are loaded automatically, they do not appear in the Add-Ins list of the Word Options dialog box or in the Templates And Add-Ins dialog box.

Manually Loading Global Templates

After you load global templates, they are listed in the Templates And Add-Ins dialog box. You can specify whether you want to use them on a per-document or per-session basis. To manually load a global template, follow these steps:

1. On the Developer tab in the Templates group, click Document Template.

2. On the Templates tab in the Global Templates And Add-Ins area, click Add to display the Add Template dialog box, which displays the contents of the Templates folder by default.

3. Double-click the name of a template that you want to include in the global template list then click OK to complete the setup.

The template name is added to the list and the check box to the left of the template name is selected by default. This means the template is ready to use in your document. If you do not want to apply the template at this time but leave it loaded with the document so that you can use it later, clear the check box.

Automatically Loading Global Templates

If you often load the same global template, you can configure Word 2010 to load the global template automatically whenever you start the program. The easiest way to accomplish this task is to copy the template into the Word Startup folder. In Windows 7 and Windows Vista, the default location of the Word Startup folder can be found in the following location:

```
C:\Users\user name\AppData\Roaming\Microsoft\Word\STARTUP
```

Be careful when choosing to load global templates automatically. Configuring your system to load global templates each time Word starts consumes system memory and can slow the startup process.

> **Note**
>
> The location of the Word Startup folder can be changed in the File Locations dialog box, which is found in Word Options in the Advanced area.

Unloading Global Templates

By default, global templates are unloaded (but not removed from the list of global templates) when you exit Word. However, if you prefer, you can unload global templates before exiting Word. This means that when you are finished with a global template but wish to continue working in Word, you can unload it or remove a manually loaded global template from the global template list. Note that neither action deletes the template file; unloading and removing a global template from the global template list merely stops the template from serving as a global template. To unload a global template, open the Templates And Add-Ins dialog box (located on the Developer tab), and perform one of the following actions:

- Clear the check box next to the template's name in the Global Templates And Add-Ins list to stop using the global template.

- Select the manually loaded global template in the Global Templates And Add-Ins list and then click Remove to stop using the loaded global template and remove the template from the list.

- If the global template is stored in your Word Startup folder or the Startup folder located in the Office installation path, exit Word and move the template from the respective startup folder to another location. If you have another copy of the template, simply delete the template from the respective Startup folder. Note that the Remove button in the Templates And Add-Ins dialog box will be disabled if the template is located in a Startup folder.

TROUBLESHOOTING

A previously removed global template reappears the next time Word starts.

Some third-party add-ins designed for previous versions of Word load a global template manually each time that Word starts, integrating additional functionality. These templates can be unloaded and removed from the Global Templates And Add-Ins list. However, they will return because they are loaded each time Word starts by a Component Object Model (COM) add-in, which isn't listed in the Templates And Add-Ins dialog box. To resolve this issue, uninstall the add-in using Add Or Remove Programs, which is found in the Control Panel.

Chapter 4

Modifying Existing Templates

Over time, the form and function you need from your templates may change. For example, you may use one template to produce a series of sales literature for a new product, but not long after you begin sharing the literature with customers, you are told that people are having trouble locating some of the content you want them to find. To resolve the problem, you can go back to your template and change the layout, styles, and design elements to fix the issues your readers have pointed out. Modifying an existing template is much easier than creating one from scratch. Now you simply need to make a few changes and apply what you've learned.

> **Tip**
> The changes you make to the existing template will be reflected in all new documents you create in the future that use the template; however, your changes will not affect documents you've created with that template in the past.

Changing the Template File

To change an existing document by working directly in the template, first open the file as a template from the Open dialog box. Here are the steps:

1. Click File and then select Open.

2. Display the contents of the Templates folder (or the folder containing the template you want to modify), and then locate and open the template you want to modify.

3. Change any of the template's text and graphics, styles, formatting, Content Controls, macros, Building Blocks, Quick Access Toolbar, and keyboard shortcuts.

4. On the Quick Access toolbar, click Save.

Remember that whenever you make changes to a document template, you should test the changes by creating a new sample document using the template. To apply any style changes to an existing document to which the template is attached, ensure that the Automatically Update Document Styles check box in the Templates And Add-Ins dialog box is selected after you open the document.

Changing a Template While Working in a Document

If you are working in a document and think of a change you'd like to make to the template, you can do that easily. You might want to add a new style, for example, while you're working on text.

In this case, in the Create New Style dialog box (or in the Modify Style dialog box), select the New Documents Based On This Template option. When you save the document, Word displays a message box that asks whether you want to update the attached document template, as shown in Figure 4-5.

Figure 4-5 You can modify and save changes to an attached document template while you work in a document.

Using the Organizer to Rename, Delete, and Copy Styles

In addition to modifying templates by making changes in template and document files, you can use the Organizer to manage template components. The Organizer dialog box contains tabs for Styles and Macro Project Items, as shown in Figure 4-6.

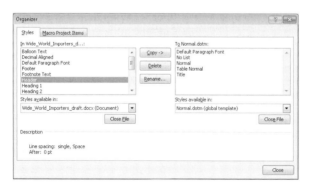

Figure 4-6 You can copy, delete, and rename styles and macros stored in specific documents and templates by using the Organizer.

Chapter 4

To use the Organizer to copy and manage styles and macros in documents and templates, follow these steps:

1. On the Developer tab in the Templates group, click Document Template.

2. In the Templates And Add-Ins dialog box, click Organizer.

3. In the Organizer dialog box, click the Styles or Macro Project Items tab, depending on the element you want to copy, delete, or rename.

4. To copy items to or from templates, or files other than the current file's template and the Normal.dotm template, click the Close File button to close the active document and its attached template or to close the Normal template. Then click Open File and select the template or file you want to open by double-clicking it in the Open dialog box.

5. Select the items you want to copy, delete, or rename. Click Copy, Delete, or Rename as appropriate.

6. Click Close when finished with the Organizer.

TROUBLESHOOTING

I can't copy items to a particular template.

If you try to copy styles or macros to a template that's protected in some way, you might not be able to open the template, accept or reject tracked changes in the template, or save changes to the template. This problem might be due to any of the following reasons:

- The template is protected for tracked changes, comments, or forms.

- The template is encrypted and requires you to enter a password.

- The template is protected by a password. If you don't know the password, you can only open the template as a read-only file.

- The file attributes are set to read-only.

- You don't have access to the server on which the template is stored.

- The template might be open on another computer on your network.

To save changes to a template, the protection settings must be removed, you must gain the proper access permissions, or you must wait until the template is no longer open on another computer on the network.

Protecting Templates

Protecting your template is a good idea, especially if you are creating a template that will be used by others. If you are creating a standard template that everyone in your department will use for any documents that will be sent to customers, putting a few safeguards in place to ensure that template elements aren't overwritten accidentally will help you to ensure the quality of your work and the consistency of your documents. Protecting a template is slightly different from protecting a document, but it's a straightforward process. Here are some ideas you might want to use to protect your templates:

- **Suggest that they be opened as read-only.**   Click File and then select Save As. Click Tools at the bottom of the Save As dialog box and choose General Options. In the General Options dialog box, select the Read-only recommended check box and then click OK. Note that the recommendation to open the template as read-only will be presented each time a new document based on the template is created.

- **Encrypt the document or template.**   Click File and then select Save As. Click Tools at the bottom of the Save As dialog box and choose General Options. In the General Options dialog box (see Figure 4-7), enter a password in the File Encryption Options For This Document text box and then click OK. Note that the password must be entered to create new documents based on the template.

- **Create a file-sharing password.**   Click File and then select Save As. Click Tools at the bottom of the Save As dialog box and choose General Options. In the General Options dialog box, enter a password in the File Sharing options for this document text box and then click OK. Note that a dialog box requesting the password to modify or open as read-only will be presented each time a new document based on the template is created.

- **Protect formatting and editing changes.**   Click Restrict Editing on the Review tab or Developer tab. The Restrict Formatting And Editing Task Pane opens, in which you can specify detailed formatting and editing restrictions. Note that new documents based on the template will contain the same restrictions.

- **Prevent the template from being forwarded, edited, or copied by unauthorized people.**   Apply Windows rights management by clicking the File tab to display Backstage view and then clicking Protect Document in the Permissions area. Click Restrict Permission By People and select Restrict Access to tailor document permissions (based on the roles) to specific people. You can also use the Do Not Reply All to prevent people from inadvertently forwarding the document to a number of people.

Chapter 4

Figure 4-7 Choose General Options on the Tools menu of the Save As dialog box to protect your template.

Applying Themes in Word 2010

If you've ever spent any amount of time painstakingly selecting fonts, coordinating colors, or wishing you had a graphic artist on hand to handle all of the choices you need to make when creating high-impact and persuasive documents, you will love using Themes in Word 2010. With Themes, you can choose a consistent, professional look for your documents—with a single click of the mouse. What's more, you can use the same theme for all sorts of collateral materials so that your annual report has a similar design to your brochures, your organization's stationery, your newsletter, and your Web page.

Word 2010 includes a gallery of dozens of themes that you can use right away in the documents you create. You can also modify existing themes to create new ones or design new themes from scratch. In addition, you can download more themes from Office.com to continually expand and refresh your themes gallery.

> **Note**
>
> Themes became available for the first time in Word 2007; they are not available in versions of Word prior to that release. The settings used to create the theme (fonts, colors, and effects) are converted to styles in previous versions of Word. To obtain the full benefit of themes—which enable you to change the Theme font, color, and effects with a single click of the mouse button—your document needs to be saved in Word 2010 format.

As you learned in Chapter 1, "Spotlight on Word 2010," one of the key design objectives in Word 2010 is to provide you with easy-to-use tools for creating professional, high-quality documents that help bring your ideas to life.

To create the best possible effect for professional documents, most people invest some time in finding and choosing formatting options for headings, body text, captions, borders, and so on. Choosing fonts that seem to go together well by using colors and styles that complement each other typically takes at least a little trial and error, and when you're working under a deadline, that trial and error period uses up precious time.

Word 2010 can help you reduce the time you spend trying different designs by offering sets of options you can use to control the format of your document. By choosing a Theme, you can create professional documents with a coordinated set of colors, fonts, and backgrounds. You'll never again have to wonder about which elements look good together. When you create a new document, you can simply choose the same theme you used for previous documents or choose that theme for a template you create, ensuring that everything you create has the same look and feel, and adding to the consistent way you present your department or company (which helps build recognition). See how the benefit snowballs?

Themes also flow through files you create in other programs in Office 2010. For example, when you create a document using the Opulent Theme in Word, you can also craft a presentation in PowerPoint 2010 that uses the same Theme. And while you're at it, the worksheet in Excel, the data table in Access, and even the e-mail message in Outlook can all use the same theme. This means you can put together a complete package—your monthly newsletter and program literature, your year-end financials and fundraising reports, and a professional presentation for your board—all by using the same theme that can literally be applied with a single click of the mouse.

> **Note**
>
> Before you can change themes with a single click of the mouse, there are a couple of things that you need to be aware of. First, you need to work with a document in Word 2007 or Word 2010 format (Themes are not available in Compatibility Mode). Next, you need to assign styles to the elements in your document (such as Heading 1 or Heading 2 from the Styles group on the Home tab). Themes look for and replace the formats of each of the styles applied to the document elements.

Chapter 4

What's in a Theme?

Themes enable you to change the way that text, tables, and special elements are formatted throughout your document. Figure 4-8 displays a report that uses the Office Theme. The theme settings influence the format of the document in the following ways:

- The font style and color used for the paragraph text

- The font type, style, and color used for the bullet list

- The fonts used in the table headings and row values

- The table style (for example, alternating banded rows) applied to the table

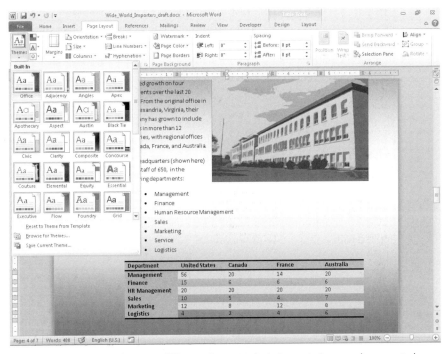

Figure 4-8 When you choose a different theme, styled elements in your document change automatically.

When you choose a theme, the settings are instantly applied to styled elements in your document. You can change themes as often as you like, trying on different looks until you get just the right effect for your document.

Themes, Quick Styles, and Galleries

By default, every document you create is given the Office theme until you choose a different one. The theme coordinates many of the formatting choices that you make throughout the document. For example, suppose that you choose the Flow theme for your current document. A specific set of fonts, colors, and theme effects are applied to the document.

Additionally, the Quick Styles available in the Styles area on the Home tab are coordinated to match the Flow theme as well. Therefore, the fonts available in the Quick Styles are determined by your theme selection. If you choose a different theme, different styles will appear in the Styles gallery to reflect your choice. You can further fine-tune your selection by choosing a particular Quick Style set for your document. When you click the Change Styles arrow (in the Styles group on the Home tab) and choose Style Set, a list of design categories appears (see Figure 4-9). You can choose the category that reflects the style you want to create, and all items—fonts, colors, and effects—consistent with the Theme choices are applied to your document.

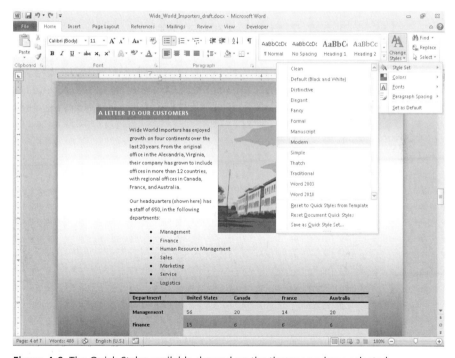

Figure 4-9 The Quick Styles available depend on the theme you have selected.

Learn more about using and customizing Quick Styles in Chapter 12.

Chapter 4

Other galleries offer choices related to the Flow theme selection as well. For example, when you create a table and choose a style in the Table Styles gallery (available on the Design tab of the contextual Table Tools tools), the table styles in that gallery are orchestrated to match the Flow theme, as shown in Figure 4-10.

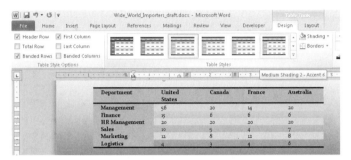

Figure 4-10 The theme you choose for your document coordinates the formatting for various elements in the file, such as tables.

Downloading Themes from Office.com

Microsoft Office Online offers an additional and continually expanding supply of themes and templates you can use with Word 2007 and Word 2010. Visit Office.com (*http://office.microsoft.com/en-us/templates/CT101043291033.aspx*) to browse through the themes selection and download new themes to your computer.

Changing a Theme

When you discover a theme that you like, simply click it to apply it to the selected document; the fonts, colors, and effects that are part of the theme are automatically applied.

Note

If you are creating a new document, the Office theme is applied automatically.

Specifying a theme choice doesn't mean that you give up your right to change your mind. You can further fine-tune your document by changing the fonts, colors, and effects applied when you selected the theme. The next section instructs you how to work with these settings in your documents.

Changing Theme Colors

Chances are that you selected a specific theme because it offers either the font selections or the colors that you want—or both. If you want to change the colors of the selected theme (this does not change the built-in theme itself, but instead modifies the colors already applied to your current document), follow these steps:

1. On the Page Layout tab, in the Themes group, click the Theme Colors button.

   A palette of Theme colors appears, as shown in Figure 4-11.

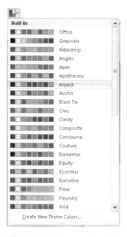

Figure 4-11 Use the Theme Colors button to choose a new color scheme for your document.

2. Position the mouse pointer over a color selection that you'd like to see previewed in your document. (Notice that even though the colors of your document change, the fonts and formats remain the same.)

3. Click the color scheme that you want to apply to your document.

Further possible changes to your document might include applying Quick Styles to your work, creating new styles, or working with style sets.

Choosing a New Font Selection

Each theme that you select contains a set of coordinated fonts that work well together for the various types of content that you might include in your document. Font sets include one font type in two sizes (one for headings and one for body text) or two fonts that complement each other for headings and text.

Chapter 4

You can choose a different font set for the theme applied to your document by following these steps:

1. On the Page Layout tab, click the Theme Fonts button in the Themes group.

   The Theme Fonts gallery appears.

2. Position the pointer on a font set selection to preview the effect in your document, as shown in Figure 4-12.

Figure 4-12 Choose a different font set for your document by clicking the Theme Fonts button.

3. Click the font selection that you want to apply to the theme; the fonts are instantly changed.

Overriding Theme Settings

The theme settings that you choose for your document coordinate various formatting settings used throughout the content. But you don't have to settle for those selections all the way through the document if you want to change things up. You can modify individual sections, headers, or special items (such as captions, quotations, or other elements) by applying different settings directly to those elements. Be aware, however, that when you change a font, color, or effect in this manner (such as changing a heading in your document to Times Roman when the Theme used Calibri), the element is in effect removed from the coordination controlled by the theme. This means the element will no longer change automatically if you choose a different one.

To override the theme's font settings currently applied in your document, simply select the text that you want to change, and then on the Home tab, click the Font arrow. At the top of the Font list, Word shows you the Theme Fonts (the ones that are used in the current theme). If you choose one of these fonts, they will still be changed automatically if you choose a different theme. But you are free to click any font in the list to apply it to the selected text, as shown in the following illustration.

If you want to ensure that all elements in your document can be changed easily when you choose a different theme, consider changing the styles used in individual themes.

Selecting Theme Effects

Theme effects enable you to add an extra touch to your charts, SmartArt graphics, shapes, and pictures. Theme effects control the line thickness, fill color or shade, lighting, and shadow of the selected object. To change the effects selected for your current theme, click the Theme Effects button in the Themes group on the Page Layout tab. The Effects gallery opens, as shown in Figure 4-13.

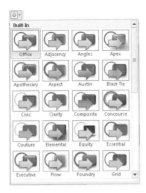

Figure 4-13 Theme effects control the lighting, shadow, and edging of objects in your document.

INSIDE OUT I Can't Tell Which Settings Are in Effect in My Theme

When you first begin creating a new document, you may not have much content to format. That means you may not be sure which settings are in effect for your particular theme. You can see the shadow, lighting, and edging effects that are being used in your document by clicking the Theme Effects button in the Themes group on the Page Layout tab. The Effects gallery opens, and the current effect is highlighted. From the thumbnail of the selected effect, you can view the shadow, lighting, and edging effects that are in use. If you want to change the effects, click a different thumbnail in the gallery, and those settings are applied to your document.

Creating a Custom Theme

Word 2010 themes take the guesswork out of designing professional documents and just generally make life easier. But having themes to rely on shouldn't keep you from creating your own coordinated design efforts. You can easily put together your own themes and save them to the Themes gallery for use in all the documents you create. If you work as part of a team, a department, or a small business, you can create a theme customized to include your own company colors and fonts, and then share the theme with others so all your documents have a similar look and feel.

Creating Your Own Color Scheme

How hard is it to choose a set of colors that really work together? If you're in touch with your creative side, you may feel confident about your ability to mix and match colors. If colors aren't your thing (or you rely on others to tell you whether your clothing choices match), choosing compatible colors may seem like a big chore. No matter where your comfort zone may be, Word can help you put together a theme color set to give your document a professional look. Here's how to do it:

1. On the Page Layout tab, click Theme Colors in the Themes group to display the Theme Colors gallery.

2. Scroll to the bottom of the list and click Create New Theme Colors.

   The Create New Theme Colors dialog box appears, as shown in Figure 4-14.

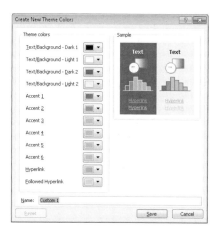

Figure 4-14 Select the colors for a new color scheme in the Create New Theme Colors dialog box.

3. Click the arrow of any element that you want to change.

   A color palette (see the illustration that follows) appears so that you can select the color for that item.

   Continue changing colors until you've made all of the desired changes for the new theme colors. The Sample area displays changes as you make them.

Chapter 4

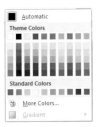

4. When you're satisfied with the colors you've selected, click the Name box and type a name for the new color scheme.

5. Click Save to save your new color scheme.

Apply the new theme colors to your document by clicking the Theme Colors button in the Themes group and choosing the customized theme from the Custom area at the top of the list.

> **Note**
>
> If you add a custom theme element—a font set or color scheme—and then decide that you don't like it after all, you can easily delete it from the list by displaying the gallery (click Theme Colors or Theme Fonts) and right-clicking the item in the Custom area at the top. A list appears, offering three options: Edit, Delete, and Add Gallery To Quick Access Toolbar. Click Delete to remove the custom item.

Customizing Theme Font Sets

You can create your own theme font set by displaying the Theme Fonts gallery (click Theme Fonts in the Themes group on the Page Layout tab), scrolling to the bottom of the list, and clicking Create New Theme Fonts. The Create New Theme Fonts dialog box appears, as shown in Figure 4-15.

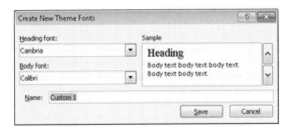

Figure 4-15 Choose a new font for your headings and body text in the Create New Theme Fonts dialog box.

Click the Heading Font arrow to display a list of all fonts available on your system. When you select the font that you want to use for the headings in your document, the Sample area displays the effect of your selection; choose the Body Font in the same way. Enter a name for your new Theme font by typing it in the Name box, and then click Save to save the selection to the Fonts list. The new set appears at the top of the list in the Custom category.

Saving Your Custom Theme

After you've finished tailoring the theme settings to reflect your particular style, you can save the theme so it is accessible through the Themes gallery in the Themes group of the Page Layout tab.

Begin by displaying a document that contains all of the settings that you want to use in your new theme. On the Page Layout tab, click the Themes button in the Themes group. Scroll down to the bottom of the Themes gallery and choose Save Current Theme. The Save Current Theme dialog box appears.

Type a descriptive name for the theme and click Save. The new theme is now available when you click Themes in the Themes group.

CAUTION

Because Word 2010 looks in a specific folder to find the Themes for your documents, it's important that you leave the default folder (Document Themes) selected when you save your theme. Otherwise, the theme will not be displayed in the Themes list by default, and you will need to use Browse For Themes (also in the Themes list) to find your customized theme.

Chapter 4

What's Next?

This chapter introduced two key Word 2010 features that help you coordinate and apply various design elements in your files. You can use Word templates to quickly create professional documents based on existing document settings and use global templates to share functionality among the documents you create. You also learned how themes enable you to apply a consistent look—with specific colors, fonts, and effects—throughout your document and enable you to switch it all out easily if you decide later to choose a different theme. The next chapter helps you put all this design wisdom in the context of your page design by showing you how to control page setup and pagination in your Word 2010 documents.

CHAPTER 5

Customizing Page Setup and Controlling Pagination

Basic Page Setup Options 139

Planning Your Document 142

Simple Margins and Orientations 145

Selecting Paper Size and Source 148

Working in Sections. 151

Adding Page Numbers 159

Adding Headers and Footers 160

Saving Page Setup Defaults to the Current Template. . 168

Adding and Controlling Line Numbers. 170

What's Next? 172

S TARTING with the end in mind is a good idea, whether you're planning documents or planning your life. But what happens when your project seems to mushroom beyond your original expectations? Perhaps the simple four-page report you planned has grown into a multi-section project with high quality photos and fancy layouts. Now you need headers and footers that need to be numbered differently, depending on the section in which they fall. Maybe what you thought was going to be a simple promotional piece has morphed into a four-color booklet with a table of contents and an index. Although it might seem like a big job to adjust your plans and learn how to adapt your pages appropriately, Word 2010 includes a number of features to help you get control of your pages and create the types of documents you want to create.

This chapter helps you think through the basic layout of your document and make decisions about the structure that underlies the content you'll put on the page. Along the way, you'll discover how to set up the page the way you want it and control the way page breaks are used in your document.

Basic Page Setup Options

Whether you successfully plan your work in advance or change strategies midstream, the page setup features of Word 2010 help you control page layout basics. Specifically, when you plan or redesign your pages, you can make choices about the following page setup specifications and options:

- Headers, footers, and page number settings

- Top, bottom, left, and right margin sizes

- Document orientation

- Paper size and tray or cartridge to use when printing

- Whether to print one or two pages per sheet

- Page and text breaks

- Header and footer content and positioning

- Text flow and spacing for languages that use vertical orientation

INSIDE OUT   Planning Page Setup

Although you can select your page settings at any point during the creation or editing of your document, taking time up front to plan basic document settings can save you time, trouble, and corrections later. In addition, if you're creating a standard document for others in your department to use or that you will use repeatedly, setting the basics early can ensure that you don't have to open multiple documents to readjust margin settings, page size, and more. In those cases, you can use an existing document as a guide or create a template with your settings to simplify applying current settings and making future changes.

Planning up front is usually best; however, Word enables you to change direction whenever you want. Keep in mind that when you make drastic changes to an existing document's setup—such as changing the page from portrait to landscape orientation—the content of your page will be dramatically affected. For instance, if you switch to landscape orientation after you've entered text and graphics, set headers and footers, and created section divisions in portrait orientation, you'll most likely have to adjust a few settings to display your information properly on the shorter, wider page.

For additional information on formatting complex documents and planning strategies, see Chapter 6, "Setting Up Your Layout with Page Backgrounds and Columns."

The Page Setup options appear on the Page Layout tab on the Word 2010 Ribbon (see Figure 5-1). Other groups on the Page Layout Ribbon include Themes, Page Background, Paragraph, and Arrange. An easy way to see all page setup options together (and set multiple options at once) is to display the Page Setup dialog box (see Figure 5-2). You do this by clicking the dialog launcher in the lower-right corner of the Page Setup group or by double-clicking in the horizontal or vertical ruler.

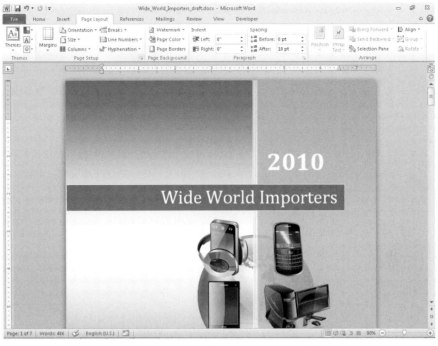

Figure 5-1 The Page Setup group on the Page Layout tab contains the tools you need for setting up the page.

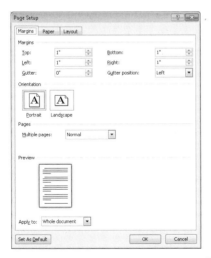

Figure 5-2 The Page Setup dialog box offers a variety of options for setting up your page.

The Page Setup dialog box packs a number of different setup options into one small space. It includes three tabs with which you can make choices for your documents as described here:

- The Margins tab includes all the settings you need to set the outer margins of the document (top, left, bottom, and right) as well as the size of the gutter if you plan to bind the document. Also in the Margins tab, you can choose the orientation of the page (portrait or landscape); select how you want multiple pages to be treated (Normal, Mirror Margins, Two Pages Per Sheet, or Book Fold); and indicate whether you want the settings on the tab to be applied to the selected text only (if you selected text before choosing this option) or to the entire document.

- On the Paper tab, you can choose the size of the page you want to use for your document. You can choose from many different page sizes, set the printer source for the cover page and secondary pages, set print options, and choose whether you want the settings applied to the entire document or the selected text.

- The Layout tab includes the tools you need to create new sections, add and control headers and footers, set text alignment, add line numbers, and add borders to the pages.

> **Tip**
>
> Word 2010 offers you a variety of ways to set and work with the settings for the layout of your pages. For example, you can add and format headers and footers by clicking at the top of bottom of the document page to open the Header or Footer area. You can change orientation, margins, and more by choosing the tool you want in the Page Setup group on the Page Layout tab or, if you choose, you can enter a number of settings at once in the Page Setup dialog box.

Planning Your Document

The length, complexity, and type of your document will determine how many different types of page settings you need to use in order to get your document to look and print the way you want. For a routine letter, a simple blog post, or a memo you share with colleagues, page setup issues might not be important. But if you're using Word 2010 to create and publish an entire book, the tasks you need to accomplish will be much more involved.

For a short document—perhaps two or three pages—you will likely only need to think about with the following page setup options:

- The orientation of the document (portrait or landscape)

- The margins for the page

- The overall size of the page, if you're printing irregular pages

A long document—such as a report with content from different departments, a book project, or a grant proposal with a number of sections—can be a completely different ball-game, altogether. For this longer document, you might be concerned with learning how to set your pages up to accommodate the following scenarios:

- A cover page that doesn't print footers or page numbers

- Footers that include a page number that prints in the outside corners of the page, alternatively right and left

- Section titles that change in the header area

- Changes in layout from one column to multiple columns and back again

- A possible change in orientation if you need to show a large table or worksheet (perhaps in your grant proposal or report)

The following table presents several types of documents along with the page setup elements they typically use and some variations you might encounter.

Image	Document Type	Page Setup Features	Page Setting
	Letter	• Single page • Traditional margins • No page numbering • No headers or footers	Normal
	Short document	• Several pages • Footers with page numbers • Possible title page • Page numbers in same place on every page • Single or multiple column format • Might include high-quality photos, diagrams, or tables	Normal

Chapter 5

Image	Document Type	Page Setup Features	Page Setting
	Report	• Cover page • Multiple pages • Sections with customized headers • Footers • Different odd and even pages • Larger inner margin (for binding) • Could include landscape orientation pages	Mirror margins
	Business Plan	• Cover page • Numerous pages • Sections with customized headers • Footers • Different odd and even pages • Larger inner margin (for binding) • Could include landscape orientation pages • Charts and worksheets • High quality photos • Captions • Could include columnar layout	Mirror margins
	Booklet	• Cover page • Smaller paper size • Larger inner margin • Could include sections with section-based numbering • Landscape orientation • Page numbers • Limited room for photos • Table of contents • Pull quotes and sidebars	Book fold
	Grant proposal	• Cover/title page • Multiple sections • Alternating odd and even page margins • Alternating odd and even page numbering • Headers and footers • Could use numbered headings • Can include high-quality photos • Portrait orientation • Could include landscape orientation for table or worksheet printing • Table of contents	Mirror margins

Simple Margins and Orientations

The page setup items that you'll adjust most often are likely to be margins and page orientation. Word makes accessing these settings simple by including the Margins and Orientation galleries on the Page Layout tab. The margins of your document control the amount of white space at the top, bottom, right, and left edges of the document. You can also control the amount of space used for the gutter; this is the space on the inside edges of facing pages that is reserved for binding. You can customize the gutter setting along the left or top margin of the page, depending on whether you're binding the document in portrait or landscape orientation.

Changing Margin Settings

When you begin working with a new Word document, the left, right, top, and bottom margins are set to 1 inch (or 2.54 centimeters, depending on your preferred unit of measurement). Note that this default setting is different than the default margin settings in previous versions of Word. In Word 2010, you can change margin settings in three basic ways.

- **Use the Margins gallery.**   Choose a margin setting from the Margins gallery on the Page Layout tab, as shown in Figure 5-3.

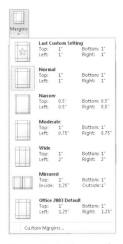

Figure 5-3 Choose the margin setting you want from the Margins gallery.

- **Create a custom margin.**   At the bottom of the Margins gallery, click Custom Margins to open the Page Setup dialog box. Type your preferred settings in the text boxes provided for the top, bottom, left, and right margins.

Chapter 5

> **Tip**
>
> The next time you open the Margins gallery, your custom settings will be listed at the top as Last Custom Setting. If you want new documents to default to your custom settings, see the section titled "Saving Page Setup Defaults to the Current Template," on page 168.

- **Drag the margin marker on the ruler.**   If you are working in Print Layout view, you can choose new margin settings by dragging the edge of the shaded area on the horizontal or vertical ruler to the margin setting you want, as shown here:

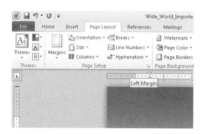

INSIDE OUT   Display Precise Measurements on the Ruler

If you need to set the margins to a specific measurement but don't want to work in the Page Setup dialog box, you can make precise margin adjustments on the ruler as well. Display the ruler by clicking View and selecting the Ruler check box in the Show group. Then simply press and hold the Alt key while dragging the margin marker, or press and hold both the left and right mouse buttons while you drag the marker in the direction you want to increase or decrease the margin. Measurements appear in both the ruler and the margin area to show you precisely the width of the print area and margins.

Tip

To change the default setting for measurement units shown in Word, click File, then in Backstage view, click Options. In the Advanced area, scroll to the Display options, and select a measurement unit from the Show Measurements In Units Of list box. You can choose to work with Inches, Centimeters, Millimeters, Points, or Picas. In case you are unfamiliar with the two last terms, *points* and *picas* are standard print and graphics industry measurements in which 6 points equals one pica, and 72 points equals one inch.

Binding Documents

If you'll be binding the document you create, be sure to specify a gutter margin large enough to accommodate the binding. If your document is to be printed single-sided, every gutter margin will show the spacing you enter along the left margin. If your document is to be printed double-sided, on the Page Layout tab, click the Page Setup dialog launcher. On the Margins tab, click the Multiple Pages arrow, and then choose Mirror Margins to make sure that the margin settings are applied to the left and right interior margins. If you select any option other than Normal on the Multiple Pages list in the Pages area of the Page Setup dialog box, Word disables the Gutter Position option and adds the gutter setting to the appropriate margin, such as applying the gutter setting to the inside margins for book fold documents.

For more information about printing, see Chapter 14, "Printing Documents Professionally."

Choosing Orientation

A document's orientation affects the way content is printed on a page. Typically, letters, invoices, reports, and newsletters use portrait orientation, which prints the page in standard 8.5 × 11-inch format so the page is taller than it is wide. Charts, calendars, and brochures typically use landscape orientation, which prints the page in 11 × 8.5-inch format, resulting in a page that is wider than it is tall.

To change the orientation of a document, on the Page Layout tab on the Ribbon, click the Orientation tool in the Page Setup group. Click Landscape to change the orientation so that the document is printed with the long edge of the paper serving as the top of the page, or click Portrait to print the document with the short edge of the paper serving as the top of the page. Note that page orientation can also be found in the Page Setup dialog box, which you can display by clicking the Page Setup dialog launcher.

Selecting Paper Size and Source

The page size you choose for your document has a lot to do with the overall layout—limiting, for example, how much content you can put on the page. For this reason, setting the page size is one of the tasks you'll want to complete first when you start a new document. Word 2010 supports a large list of paper sizes, ranging from the usual paper sizes to envelope, executive, index card, photo, panorama, banner, and custom sizes.

Once you choose the page size, you'll also need to let Word know where to locate the paper for printing—this is known as identifying the paper source. You might want to specify two different paper sources—one for the cover page which can include letterhead, and one for subsequent pages.

Choosing a Paper Size

To select a standard paper size, click the Size button on the Page Layout tab and select a paper size option in the Size gallery, as shown in Figure 5-4.

Figure 5-4 Choose from standard paper sizes in the Size gallery.

> **Note**
>
> To select a paper size beyond the standard fare, click More Paper Sizes in the Size gallery to open the Page Setup dialog box. Select the Paper tab to access additional paper sizes from the Paper Size list or use the Height and Width text boxes to enter custom settings.

Selecting the Paper Source

Paper source refers to the specific tray on your printer that might contain the paper, envelopes, or other medium that you'll use when you print a document. If you're working with a printer that supports multiple trays, you can customize the settings for the documents you print. For example, you can print one page on letterhead from one tray, or source, and print subsequent pages on blank stock from another tray.

To select a paper source, click the Page Setup dialog launcher on the Page Layout tab, and then click the Paper tab. In the Paper Source area, click the paper tray you want to use as the source for your document's first page, and then click the tray you want to use as the source for all other pages.

Because so many Page Setup options overlap the Print Options settings, Word makes it easy to access Print Options on the Paper tab in the Page Setup dialog box. When you're working with Page Setup options, take a moment to check your print options by clicking the Print Options button in the lower-right corner on the Paper tab. The Print Options button opens the Word Options dialog box, which includes Print options on both the Display and Advanced screens. Coordinating print and page setup options might come in handy, for instance, if you want to use A4 or legal paper sizes or you plan to use duplex printing. In those cases, you can set your print and page setup options at the same time, thereby avoiding having to remember to set appropriate print options when you print the document.

For more information about printing in Word, see Chapter 14.

> **Tip**
>
> **Document Grid**   The Document Grid is available with some Language Settings configurations. This tab enables you to control the horizontal and vertical text flow as well as line and character spacing in documents that use East Asian languages. By using this tab, you can also specify Drawing Grid settings (click Drawing Grid), which give you control over the grid display and other grid settings. You can also access the Font dialog box by clicking Set Font.

Chapter 5

Multiple Page Settings

When you are creating a long document, you might need to use different page settings to accommodate the various elements in your project. For example, if you plan to have your annual report professionally printed, you might want to set up mirrored margins so the inner margin of the page is larger than the outer margin. This enables you to have the report bound and ensure that none of the text disappears into the binding of the page.

You can use the Multiple Pages settings in the Page Setup dialog box to choose the different types of layouts that control the page setup options for your document. Using this control you can choose whether your document should include mirror margins, two pages per sheet, book fold, or reverse book fold. To change the page settings for a multiple-page document, follow these steps:

1. On the Page Layout tab, in the Page Setup group, click the Page Setup dialog launcher to display the Page Setup dialog box.

2. Enter the Margins, Paper, and Layout settings on their respective tabs as you normally would.

3. On the Margins tab, in the Pages area, click the Multiple Pages arrow.

    Table 5-1 explains the effects of the Multiple Pages choices.

4. Click your Multiple Pages choice and then specify the Apply To arrow and choose whether the setting should be applied to the whole document or to the selected text.

    If you selected Book Fold, Apply To is not available because this setting applies to the whole document, but you can specify how many sheets are contained in each booklet.

> **Note**
>
> If your document has more pages than the number of pages you selected for a booklet, Word prints the document as multiple booklets.

Table 5-1 **Choosing Page Settings for Multiple Pages**

Setting	Description
Normal	Used for single-sided printing. Each page has a specific left and right margin.
Mirror Margins	Used for duplex printing in which the margins mirror each other. The left and right margins become the inside and outside margins, respectively.
2 Pages Per Sheet	Divides the current page into two pages.
Book Fold	Treats each left and right page as a spread, using a gutter and mirroring margins as applicable.
Reverse Book Fold	Enables you to create a booklet written in a right-to-left text orientation, such as one written in Arabic or Hebrew, or in an East Asian language that has vertical text (this option is available only when a relevant language is enabled in the Microsoft Office 2010 Language Settings).

Working in Sections

Simple documents are great—you can just open the new document, enter your content, maybe make a few margin adjustments, print, or e-mail the file, and you're done!

Longer, more complex documents involve a bit more thought and planning. Luckily, Word 2010 includes many features that will help you control special considerations in your longer documents. Using sections, for instance, you can make layout and formatting changes while limiting those changes to specific pages in your document. For example, adding section breaks enables you to make the following enhancements in your document:

- Create sections in your document so that you can vary the headers and footers

- Change the margins or layouts within a specific range of pages

- Create layouts that look different on odd and even pages

- Change the document orientation within a specific section

- Set up a section of columns within a longer mostly single-column document

Chapter 5

Working with sections does take a little know-how, however, because much of the formatting goes on behind the scenes and you can end up with unexpected results if you don't understand how sections work.

In Word, as odd as it might sound, the last paragraph mark of a document contains the formatting codes necessary for formatting the content. When you create sections, the section break contains the information for the section that *precedes* it.

Suppose that you have a two-column report that includes a narrative summary of your department's activities on the right, along with photos and statistics on the left. In the next section of your report, you want to show several tables that offer departmental costs and comparisons. These tables are wider than a traditional page, so you want to insert a section break and set those pages to a single-column format with a landscape orientation. Fine, you insert a break and add the tables as needed.

Now if you delete the break you added, you might expect the document to reformat so that the landscape orientation pages change to portrait orientation and your tables are truncated. In fact, what happens—because the section break contains the information for the section that precedes it—is that the entire document is reformatted in landscape orientation.

This is just one example of the ways sections can throw little surprises into your work. So two tips are in order as you begin to work with sections:

- Always turn on paragraph marks by clicking Show/Hide in the Paragraph group on the Home tab so that you can clearly see the breaks you include.

- Only use sections when you need them to change the flow of text, control formatting in parts of your document, or start a new numbering sequence.

CAUTION

Not all long documents require section breaks, and inserting breaks can sometimes make your documents more complex than they need to be. So unless you have a specific reason to create a section break—for example, you want to change the orientation of the next page or apply a page border to only a portion of your document—you might want to avoid using breaks. If you get into trouble later and are experiencing strange formatting issues, turn on paragraph marks by clicking Show/Hide to see whether an oddly placed section break is the culprit.

Creating a Section

Adding a section is an easy task. You can begin a new section anywhere—in the middle of a page or at the beginning of a new one. To insert a section break, follow these steps:

1. Place the insertion point where you want to start the new section.

2. On the Page Layout tab, click Breaks in the Page Setup group to display the Breaks gallery (see Figure 5-5).

3. Click one of the section break types (further described in Table 5-2) then click OK.

   The section is created, and the text flows accordingly.

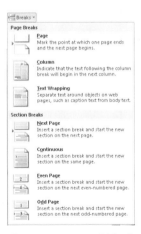

Figure 5-5 From within the Page Breaks gallery, you can view the type of break you are creating before you create it.

Table 5-2 **A Quick Look at Section Types**

Section type	Description	Use
Page	Inserts a page break at the cursor position and creates a new page	You want to begin a new page in the document
Column	Inserts a column break so the text at the cursor position is moved to the top of the new column	You want to control the placement of text among columns
Text Wrapping	Enables you to control text flow around objects in your document	You want to set off special text, titles, or captions
Next Page	Creates a new section at the top of the next page	You want to start a new section with different formatting speci- fications on the next page in the document
Continuous	Creates a new section beginning at the document insertion point	You want to begin a new section in the middle of the current page
Even Page	Creates a new section beginning on an even page; if the current page is an even page, an odd page is inserted and left blank	You want to create a new section with a format used uniquely for even pages
Odd Page	Creates a new section beginning on an odd page; if the current page is an odd page, an even page is inserted and left blank	You want to create a section for odd pages only

Note

If you prefer to use a dialog box to set up your sections, you can click the dialog launcher in the Page Setup group (on the Layout tab) to display the Page Setup dialog box. The first group of settings in the Page Setup dialog box deals with sections. You can choose Continuous, New Column, New Page, Even Page, or Odd Page in the Sec- tion Start list, just as you can in the Breaks gallery. As always, you can change any of your selections at any time, and making changes in the Breaks gallery later will carry through to the settings you entered in the Page Setup dialog box.

Tip

To change page layout settings and insert a section break at the same time, either place your insertion point at the location where you wish to start the new settings or select the portion of the document that will contain the settings, and then display the Page Setup dialog box. From the Apply To list at the bottom of any tab in the dialog box, select This Point Forward, Selected Text (if you had previously selected text in your document), or Whole Document, accordingly. After you make your modifications and click OK, section breaks will be inserted into your document as needed and your page layout settings will be applied to that section.

Inserting Text Wrapping Breaks

Most of the section breaks you add in Word 2010 are pretty straightforward; you position the cursor where you want the break and choose the type of break you want. This section explores text wrapping breaks because they behave a little differently by adjusting the flow of your text.

When you add a text wrapping break, Word forces a text break for layout reasons without starting a new paragraph. For example, you might want to break text at a particular position to appear before and after an inline table, graphic, or object, or you might want to present lines of poetry without applying the document's paragraph style (including paragraph spacing) to each line of text. The Text Wrapping Break option is similar to inserting a manual line break in your document, which you can add by pressing Shift+Enter. Frequently, text wrapping breaks are used to separate text from Web page objects or other text and are the equivalent of inserting a **
** tag in XHTML code.

Saving Formats as Your Own Templates

A reminder: Whenever you go to any significant trouble to create your own format, especially if there's a chance you'll use the format again, consider saving the format you've created as a template that you can use again as the basis for other documents.

To create a template from a document you've made, follow these steps:

1. Click File to display Backstage view.

2. Point to Save As and in the Save As Type field of the Save As dialog box, click Word Template.

3. Type a name for the template in the File Name box.

4. Click Save to save the template file.

Chapter 5

Controlling Page Breaks

As you add content to your Word document, the program automatically adds page breaks for you when you fill a page. In Print Layout and Full Screen Reading views, an automatic page break looks truly like an actual space between pages—you can see where one page ends and another begins. In Draft view, page breaks appear as dotted lines.

In some cases, you might want to add page breaks manually. In Word, you can easily add manual breaks to control pages, sections, and columns. For example, you might want to insert a manual page break in the following instances:

- To create a page containing minimal information, such as a cover page or acknowledgments page

- To separate document content

- To ensure that a figure or table and its caption begin on a new page

- To begin a new section with a heading at the top of a page

- To end a section when you don't want anything else printed on the current page

To create a manual page break, place the insertion point where you want to insert the break. On the Page Layout tab, click Breaks and choose Page. If you prefer to use a shortcut key, you can create the break by positioning the cursor and pressing Ctrl+Enter.

> **Tip**
>
> Do you have a headline style (such as Heading 1) that always begins at the top of a new page? If so, you can instruct Word to handle the page break and the format together in one step by choosing Page Break Before in the Paragraph dialog box. Choose either the Home or Page Layout tab and then click the dialog launcher in the Paragraph group. Click the Line and Page Breaks tab, and in the Pagination area, select the Page break before check box. Click OK to save and apply your change.

> **Note**
>
> If you see a solid line instead of the white space allocated to the page margins in Print Layout view, place your mouse pointer on the solid line and double-click the left mouse button to show the white space. Notice that the Show White Space Between Pages In Print Layout View option can also be found in Word Options in the Display area.

Aligning Content Vertically Between Margins

If you are creating a page—perhaps a cover page—that doesn't have a lot of content, and you want that content to be vertically aligned in a specific way on the page, you can let Word help you with the positioning.

To control the vertical alignment of your content, display the Page Setup dialog box, then on the Layout tab, click the Vertical Alignment arrow and select an alignment option. By default, the vertical alignment is set to Top. You can choose among Top, Center, Justified, or Bottom.

Word aligns the page content based on your selection. For example, if you click Center, Word centers the contents of the page between the top and bottom margins. If you choose Bottom, Word aligns the page contents with the bottom margin and places any extra space at the top of the page, above the content. This little trick can help you create cover pages, section dividers, and posters that always have content positioned no matter how many words—or how few—you include on the page.

TROUBLESHOOTING

My document includes unwanted breaks.

If your document is breaking at odd places or including unwanted blank pages, chances are that the underlying problem lies with your printer. What looks perfect on one computer might look much different when viewed on another computer or if you print the document using a printer other than the one you normally use. Perhaps you inserted manual page breaks to control document pagination—for example, inserting a manual page break to keep paragraphs together on the same page or keep a table or figure together with its caption. If you've ever used this method, then chances are you've encountered the ongoing battle of deleting and reinserting manual page breaks.

Instead of using manual page breaks, you can use pagination formatting instead. Pagination formatting allows you to specify which paragraphs need to stay together on the same page or whether all lines of a paragraph need to remain on the same page. By using pagination formatting, you can make sure the pages break just where you want them to without a lot of fuss and bother.

So to resolve this problem, first locate and delete the unwanted manual page or section breaks. You might need to turn on the formatting marks view to see where these breaks are located. To do so, on the Home tab, in the Paragraph group, click Show/Hide in the Paragraph group.

Chapter 5

Place your insertion point in the paragraph you want to format. Then, on either the Page Layout or Home tab, in the Paragraph group, click the dialog launcher to open the Paragraph dialog box. On the Line And Page Breaks tab, select the Keep lines together check box to keep all lines of a paragraph on the same page. Use the Keep With Next option to force a paragraph to stay on the same page as the following paragraph.

Creating a Page or Section Border

If you want to set up page and section borders for your document while taking care of the rest of your page settings, you can do so by using the Page Setup dialog box or Page Layout tab. To access border settings, click the Page Borders tool, which is located in the Page Background group on the Page Layout tab, or open the Page Setup dialog box and, on the Layout tab, click Borders. The Borders and Shading dialog box appears. Similar to the Page Setup dialog box, the Borders and Shading dialog box includes an Apply to list box. Using the Apply to options, you can add borders to selected pages, text and paragraphs, sections, first page of a section, every page except the first page of a section, and the entire document.

For a more complete discussion about adding page borders, see Chapter 19, "Command Attention with Borders and Shading."

Removing Page and Section Breaks

You can remove the breaks in your Word document in the same way you delete content—simply select them and press Delete. Remember, however, that this can be tricky business because the settings for the *preceding* section are contained in the break; deleting a page or section break reformats the preceding section with the formats that were applied to the document (or section) that follows the deleted break.

Be sure to display the formatting marks in your document by clicking the Show/Hide button, which is in the Paragraph group on the Home tab. With the paragraph, spacing, and section markers visible, as shown in Figure 5-6, you can select and delete the section break like you would any other text. Just in case, you might want to be ready to press Ctrl+Z to undo your action if it doesn't work out the way you expect it to.

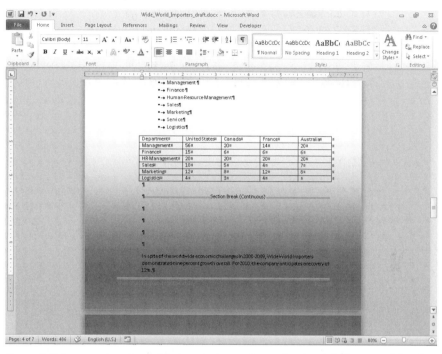

Figure 5-6 You can show formatting marks to see the section break before you delete it.

Adding Page Numbers

Page numbers provide your readers with an easy—and necessary—way to navigate through your document. Whether you are pointing out a specific section in a meeting ("Please turn to page 12") or answering a question your manager has about a chart on page 29, knowing how to get to where you need to be in a document is important.

Word makes adding and formatting page numbers a pretty simple task. You can do it two ways: by using the Page Numbers gallery on the Insert tab or by adding the page numbers within a header or footer you are adding. To display the Page Number gallery, go on the Insert tab and click Page Number in the Header & Footer group. The gallery shown in Figure 5-7 appears.

Chapter 5

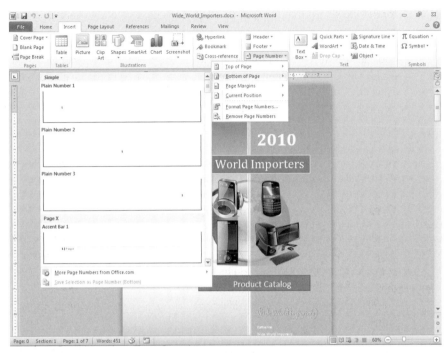

Figure 5-7 Use the Page Number gallery to add a page number to your document.

When you insert a page number by using the Page Number gallery, Word automatically inserts the selected page number and opens the header and footer layer in your document for additional editing. If you want to add more complex page numbering as well as additional information, you can add headers and footers, as described in the next section.

Adding Headers and Footers

Once you've created sections in your document, you might want to add headers and footers. Keep in mind, however, that it's not necessary to have sections in a document in order to add headers and footers—in fact, it's best if you don't add any more sections than you really need. If you have a straightforward document with page numbers in one place and the document title in another, you might be able to keep your headers and footers simple. And of course, when productivity is the bottom line, simple is good.

Adding text to the header (top) and footer (bottom) areas in a Word document serves a number of purposes, but headers and footers are used primarily to present information at the top or bottom of each page that help the reader to determine where they are in a document. You can easily insert page numbers, text, pictures, and clip art in document headers and footers. This section shows you how to add headers and footers and avoid formatting snafus that can pop up when you're trying to get everything arranged perfectly on the page.

You can add headers and footers in Word 2010 by choosing either Header or Footer in the Header & Footer group on the Insert tab or by clicking in the header or footer area of the page and typing the header or footer you want to include. If you choose to create a header or footer using one of the galleries in Word 2010, the available choices provide you with built-in examples that you can insert into your document and modify as needed to suit your content. Whether you use the galleries or enter a header or footer on your own, you can use the tools in the Header & Footer Tools Design tab to format, customize, and align the text you want to include.

Creating Headers and Footers

Headers and footers can provide special information on each page to give your readers information they need about your document. Not all projects need headers and footers, of course, and the information you include is up to you. People often use headers and footers to provide information about the publication, which could include the title, author, page number, creation date, last modified date, confidentiality statements, graphics, and other items.

You can control whether headers and footers differ on odd and even pages, whether the first page has a different header or footer, and where headers and footers are placed relative to the edge of a printed page. You can also change the header or footer from section to section if necessary to give readers the information they need to comfortably navigate your document. Word offers four different types of headers and footers:

- A regular header or footer that appears on the pages of your document

- The First Page header or footer that appears only on—wait for it…you guessed it— the first page of your document

- Odd Page headers or footers, which appear only on the odd pages in your document

- Even Page headers or footers, which appear only on the even pages in your document

So why do we need four different types of headers and footers? Having this variety gives you a range of options for the way headers and footers appear in your project. In one project (see Figure 5-8), you might want to:

- Hide the display of the header and footer on the first page

- Create a regular header that prints the document title centered at the top of each page

- Add an Odd Page footer that puts the page number in the bottom-right corner of odd-numbered pages

- Add an Even Page footer that puts the page number in the bottom-left corner of even-numbered pages

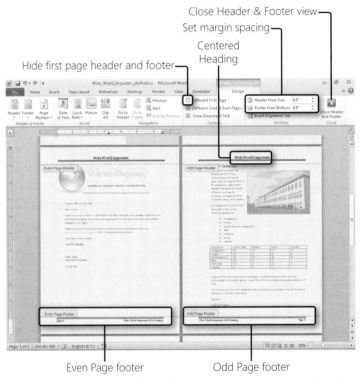

Figure 5-8 Choose the header and footer types you want to achieve the effect you need in your project.

> **Note**
>
> Your document's headers and footers appear in Print Layout view (if the white space between pages isn't hidden), Full Screen Reading view (if the Show Printed Page option is selected). You can also see headers and footers when you're previewing the document on the Print tab of Backstage view. You will not be able to see the headers or footers in your document in Web Layout, Online, or Draft views.

To add a header or footer in your document, follow these steps:

1. On the Insert tab, click either Header or Footer in the Header & Footer group.

2. Scroll through the gallery to find a header or footer style you want to add to your document. Click your choice, and the item is added.

> **Note**
>
> If the desired Header or Footer selection doesn't use your preferred fonts or colors, then modify or change your document Theme, found on the Page Layout tab in the Themes group, before manually making formatting changes. The fonts and colors shown in the Header and Footer galleries are linked to the document Theme and update if the document Theme is changed. For more information about using Themes, see Chapter 4, "Templates and Themes for a Professional Look."

Editing Headers and Footers

When you insert a header or footer, the Header and Footer Tools contextual tab and the header and footer area become available. The content area of the document becomes dimmed, meaning that it is temporarily unavailable. You can enter, edit, and format headers and footers by typing in the areas at the top or bottom of the page or control settings for the header and footer on the Header & Footer Tools Design tab (see Figure 5-9).

Figure 5-9 On the Header & Footer Tools Design tab, you can create, position, and edit headers and footers.

The Header & Footer Tools Design tab contains a variety of tools with which you to add, edit, position, and enhance the headers and footers you create:

- **Header**   This is where you edit or remove a header. It also enables you to select a header's contents and save the selection to the Header gallery so you can use it in other documents.

- **Footer**   With this tool, you can edit or remove a footer. As with Header, you can select the contents of a footer and save the selection to the Footer gallery so you can use it in other documents.

- **Page Number Gallery** Inserts a page number field, such as {PAGE}. You can use this option to add a page number to the top of the page, bottom of the page, in the page margins, or at the current position. This button also includes the Remove Page Numbers option and the Format Page Numbers option, which opens the Page Number Format dialog box in which you apply number formatting, such as add chapter numbers, continue numbering from prior pages, or start numbering at a specified page number.

> **Note**
>
> The Header, Footer, and Page Number galleries are comprised of built-in building blocks (or those downloaded from Office.com). You can also add your own custom building blocks to the galleries.
>
> If you discover that your galleries are empty, you might need to either enable the Building Blocks.dotx template or recreate it. See the Troubleshooting tip titled "My Building Blocks galleries are missing or Building Blocks.dotx is corrupt" in Chapter 10, "Editing, Proofing, and Using Reference Tools."

- **Date & Time** Opens the Date and Time dialog box, in which you insert the current date and time or update the information automatically, insert date fields such as {DATE \@ "M/d/yyyy"}, and insert time fields such as {TIME \@ "h:mm"ss am/pm"}.

- **Quick Parts** Displays a gallery of tools that you can use to add AutoText, document properties, fields, or Building Blocks to your header or footer.

- **Picture** Opens the Insert Picture dialog box and displays the images in your Pictures folder by default.

- **Clip Art** Opens and closes the Clip Art task pane with which you can search and insert clip art items into your header or footer.

- **Go To Header** Jumps to the header section if you are working in the footer section, so you can jump quickly from the footer to the header.

- **Go To Footer** Jumps to the footer section if you are working in the header section, so you can jump quickly from the header to the footer.

- **Previous** Displays the header or footer used in the previous section based on the current location of your cursor. If you click Previous Section while in the footer area, the cursor jumps to the footer area in the preceding section of your document. Note that you must have section breaks, different first page, or different odd and even headers and footers in your document to use this feature.

- **Next**   Displays the header or footer used in the next section based on the current location of your cursor. If you click Next Section while in the header area, the cursor jumps to the header area in the next section of your document. Note that you must have section breaks, different first page, or different odd and even headers and footers in your document to use this feature.

- **Link To Previous**   Links the headers and footers in the current section to the preceding section. Using this option, you can create a continuous flow from section to section. You can also click in the header or footer area and click Ctrl+Shift+R to link the header or footer area to the preceding section. Note that you must have additional sections in your document to use this feature.

- **Different First Page**   Specifies that you want to format the first page's headers and footers differently. For example, you might prefer to omit the page number on a cover page. This option is also available in the Page Setup dialog box.

- **Different Odd & Even Pages**   With this tool you can format headers and footers separately for odd and even pages. For example, you might choose to have the left page headers display your book's title while the right page headers display the chapter title. This option is also available in the Page Setup dialog box.

- **Show Document Text**   Toggles the display of the document's contents. You can hide document text to simplify your view as you create and edit headers and footers.

- **Header From Top**   Controls where the header is positioned from the top edge of the page. This option is also available in the Page Setup dialog box.

- **Footer From Bottom**   Controls where the footer is positioned from the bottom edge of the page. This option is also available in the Page Setup dialog box.

- **Insert Alignment Tab**   Opens the Alignment Tab dialog box to insert a tab relative to the margin or indent. See the following Inside Out tip titled "Alignment Tabs: The 'Relative' Scoop" for more information on this new feature.

- **Close Header And Footer**   Closes the header and footer areas as well as the Header & Footer Tools.

> **Tip**
>
> To manually add or edit a document's header and footer, simply double-click in the header or footer area and type the text you want to add or select text to edit it normally.

Chapter 5

INSIDE OUT Alignment Tabs: The "Relative" Scoop

When you want to align content in the header or footer on the same line, such as a left-aligned company name and right-aligned date, a common method used for mixed alignment is to set tabs manually. The problem with using manual tabs is that if the left or right margins change, the alignment of the content will not change and the manual tabs need to be adjusted accordingly. More often than not, adjusting the tabs is over-looked, and the header or footer content does not line up with the rest of the document.

The answer to this problem is the new Alignment Tab functionality. An Alignment Tab aligns data relative to the margin or indent, whereas a manual tab is set in a fixed position and does not automatically change position if the margins change. To view the Alignment Tab settings, double-click a header or footer in the document. On the Design tab, click Insert Alignment Tab to open the Alignment Tab dialog box, as shown in the following image.

There is a small caveat to using an alignment tab—the ruler doesn't display a visual indication that an alignment tab being used, the way it does with a left, center, or deci-mal tab. When you use an alignment tab to align data in the header or footer, remove any unused tabs from the ruler to help clarify the formatting. To remove a manual tab, simply drag it off the ruler.

Tip

The Alignment Tab dialog box is accessible only when you are viewing the Header & Footer Tools, but you can add alignment tabs anywhere in your document by adding Insert Alignment Tab to your Quick Access Toolbar. To do so, right-click Insert Align-ment Tab on the Header & Footer Tools contextual tab and then click Add To Quick Access Toolbar.

Working with Field Codes in Headers and Footers

When you use the Header & Footer Tools and the Design tab to add elements to headers and footers (such as page numbers, dates, and times), Word often accomplishes the task by inserting field codes. You can control field codes in a number of ways, including the following:

- You can edit a field code by right-clicking it and then choosing Edit Field. The Field dialog box appears, in which you can select from various formats that you can use to display the field's data.

- You can toggle the display between field data and field codes by right-clicking a field and choosing Toggle Field Codes.

- To update a field, select the field and press F9. Alternatively, right-click the field and choose Update Field. You can also click a field, such as a date that updates automatically, and choose the Update command that appears above the field in a new type of container called a Content Control.

- To control whether fields appear with or without gray backgrounds online, click File to display Backstage view, click Options, and on the Advanced tab, scroll to the Show Document Content area, and select an option in the Field Shading list. Available options include Never, Always, or When Selected.

To create different headers and footers for part of a document, you must divide the document into sections and then create headers and footers for each section. If you are working in a document divided into sections but want to continue using the same headers and footers from section to section, click in a section and then, on the Design tab, in the Navigation group, make sure Link To Previous is selected.

Deleting Headers and Footers

To delete a header or footer from a document or section, simply open the header and footer areas (double-click in a header or footer area, or right-click a header or footer area and choose Edit Header or Edit Footer) to display the Header & Footer Tools. Or, on the Design tab, click Remove Header or Remove Footer from the respective Header or Footer gallery. You can also select and delete header and footer content in the same way you select and delete any other content.

CAUTION

If your document contains multiple sections, before you remove or edit headers and footers in your document, remember to turn off the Link To Previous option in following sections to avoid inadvertently changing or deleting headers and footers in the those following sections.

Saving Page Setup Defaults to the Current Template

After establishing the page settings the way you want them in your document, you can save the specifications as your default settings in the document's template (for a more in-depth look at working with templates, see Chapter 4). When you save page setup settings as your default, Word saves the settings to the current template. If your document isn't based on a custom template, the changes are applied to the Normal template (by default, all new Word documents use the Normal template if they aren't based on another template). When you create default page setup settings, they will be applied to all new documents that are created based on the template you are currently using.

To save your settings as the default, follow these steps:

1. Click to place the insertion point at the place in the document where you want to make the changes.

2. Open the Page Setup dialog box by clicking the dialog launcher in the Page Setup group.

3. Specify the margin and page changes you want to make.

4. In the lower-left corner of the Page Setup dialog box, click Set As Default.

   A message box, as shown in Figure 5-10, asks whether you'd like to change the default settings in the current template and indicates which template you are updating. To apply the page settings to the current template, click Yes. If you decide not to alter the template settings, click No.

Figure 5-10 Making the current page setup settings the new default settings alters the template attached to the current document.

CAUTION

Carefully consider whether you should change the default settings for your Normal template (and make those changes sparingly) because the Normal template takes on all settings found in the Page Setup dialog box. First determine which settings the majority of your documents use and set them accordingly. If you need particular specifications for certain documents, it might be best to create a new template for those settings rather than modifying your Normal template.

For more information on creating your own templates see Chapter 4.

Backing Up Your Customizations

For best results when backing up templates and restoring the default Normal template, always keep a clean backup copy of your standard template in a directory other than the Template directory on your hard disk or server. In that way, if you need to return to earlier default specifications, you can do so by simply copying your backup file into the Template directory.

If you are using the Windows 7 or Windows Vista operating system, you can restore templates to earlier versions by replacing an existing template with a shadow copy. A shadow copy of a file is a backup file the operating system saves when you use the Back Up Files Wizard or have System Protection turned on, which is scheduled to run once a day by default. To access a list of shadow copies, right-click the template you want to restore and choose Restore Previous Versions.

Finally, to restore your Normal template to the default settings, you can have Word rebuild the Normal template the next time you start the software. To do this, simply exit Word, rename the Normal template file (choose an easy-to-recognize name, such as Normal_old), and then restart Word. Word automatically builds a new Normal template based on the default settings.

For more information about working with templates and the default location of your Normal template, see Chapter 4.

Chapter 5

Adding and Controlling Line Numbers

If you're working on a document that requires line numbering, such as a legal document or an article you want to submit to a professional journal, line numbers can serve as useful references. Line numbers are placed in the margin next to each line in a document. They allow readers to refer easily to specific lines in a document.

To add line numbers, you can select an option from Line Numbers on the Page Layout tab or choose settings from the Line Numbers dialog box, which can be accessed from the Layout tab in the Page Setup dialog box. Figure 5-11 shows both the Line Number options and the Line Numbers dialog box. By using these tools, you can choose whether to number an entire document continuously, restart numbering on each page, restart numbering in each section, or stop numbering for specific paragraphs. In addition, you can use the Page Setup dialog box to apply numbering to selected parts of a document in the same way that you control margins and other page setup options.

Figure 5-11   The Line Numbers dialog box is how you add and control line numbering for a section, selected text, or the entire document.

To use the Line Numbers on the Page Layout tab to control line numbering, follow these steps:

1. Position your cursor in the document or section in which you want to add line numbers.

2. On the Page Layout tab, click the Line Numbers button and choose an option.

To use the Line Numbers dialog box (accessible from the Layout tab in the Page Layout dialog box) to control line numbering, follow these steps:

1. Click anywhere in a document (or in a section) you want to number that you want to number.

2. On the Page Layout tab, click Line Numbers and choose Line Numbering Options, or on the Page Layout tab, click the Page Setup dialog launcher.

3. On the Layout tab in the Page Setup dialog box, click Line Numbers.

    The Line Numbers dialog box appears, as shown in Figure 5-11.

4. Select the Add Line Numbering check box. In the Start At box, type the number with which you want numbering to begin.

5. In the From Text box, specify number placement by using the up or down arrows, typing a number (by default, the From Text spacing is measured in inches), or accept Auto (the default setting).

6. In the Count By box, enter a value to specify which lines should be accompanied by numbers.

    For instance, if you want to show a number next to every other line, you would enter 2 in the Count By box. To display a number next to each line, retain the default Count By setting of **1**.

7. In the Numbering area, choose the Restart Each Page option if you want each page to be individually numbered; select Restart Each Section if you want the numbering to begin again with each subsequent section; or choose Continuous if you want numbers to increase throughout the document.

8. Click OK to close the Line Numbers dialog box and return to the Page Setup dialog box. Click OK to close the Page Setup dialog box.

TROUBLESHOOTING

I don't have enough room for line numbers.

If you've created heading styles that extend all the way to the left margin of your page, you might find them truncated when you add line numbering. You can fix this by displaying the Line Numbers dialog box and changing the From Text setting. By default, From Text is set to Auto, but by decreasing the amount of space between numbering and text, you can usually make room for both line numbering and headings.

Deleting Line Numbers

You might want to use line numbering only when you are creating, reviewing, and editing your document. In that case, when you're getting close to final preparations for your document, you can remove line numbers by selecting Line Numbering in the Page Setup group on the Page Layout tab. Choose None to remove the line numbers.

What's Next?

This chapter covered Word 2010 page setup features and looked at various methods that you can use to master document layout, sections, and pagination. The next chapter takes you deeper into the realm of page layouts by showing you how to tailor your page backgrounds and set up different column specifications for your project.

Setting Up Your Layout with Page Backgrounds and Columns

The Nature of Complex Documents 173

Layout and Design Fundamentals 175

Designing Backgrounds and Watermarks. 178

Adding Columns. 187

What's Next? 197

W HETHER you ever had to create documents on a Smith-Corona typewriter—or worse, a typesetting system!—or you started using word processing on the PC, chances are that you take some of the benefits of electronic documents for granted. When you open a new file, you can just begin typing, letting the ideas flow as they will. The basic function of the program lays out the text for you and, later, reformats it according to your wishes as you choose bullet lists, numbered lists, and columns to display your text.

This chapter takes a closer look at some of the layout fundamentals that occur at the basic level of formatting in your document. We'll consider layout options, page background and design, watermarks, and columns. Along the way, you'll get a chance to think through how some of these cornerstones of document design will be reflected in the projects you create.

The Nature of Complex Documents

Not all long documents are complex, and not all complex documents are long. But whenever you think about putting together either a project that has a number of different parts or a document that includes many pages and special formats, you've got a number of issues to consider. Which elements should you include? How will you handle them? In what formats should you save the content so that it can be used again later? Will you work on the project by yourself or with a team?

The following ideas help you envision the document project that stretches before you. Whether ultimately you're planning for print or PDF, solo or on a team, thinking through the end result now is a good way to ensure you'll actually get there.

- **Get a clear vision of the project.** If the document you're in charge of preparing is an elaborate annual report, a training manual, a corporate policy statement, or something similar that requires the input of many people, most likely everyone involved will have an opinion about the way it should look and what it should contain. Establishing early on what message you want to communicate in the document, what you want to leave the reader thinking at the end, and what kind of impression you want to make will be critical to ending up at the right place—and on speaking terms with the entire team.

- **Organize the vision and assign tasks.**   Once you have an idea of where you're headed, you need to determine the scope of the project. How many pages? How many colors? Who will do what? These are all important questions that need to be answered right up front when you're working with a large and potentially very expensive project. You might want to write up a vision statement for the document in Word 2010 or OneNote 2010 and share the file with all those involved in the project.

- **Evaluate costs, set a budget, and determine deadlines.**   Connecting numbers and facts to the vision isn't an easy step. Especially if you are preparing this document with the help of a committee or team, you need to carefully weigh the cost, time, and effort requirements. Seemingly small considerations—such as paper weight, page size, and colors used—can make a huge difference in the costs of the project. Create a table in Word 2010 or Excel 2010 to track and compile costs you think will be attached to the creation of the document.

- **Stay in touch with the document team.**   If you have assigned different sections of a document to different people on the team, how do you ensure each person is on track to make his or her goal? Communicating is important, as is ensuring that everyone is on the same page—literally—by working with the same style, theme, or XML schema. If you work together using SharePoint Workspace 2010, you can assign and report on tasks, communicate in real time, and post drafts and other file assets in a shared space that you can synchronize with the SharePoint server.

- **Create and compile content.**   Think about what a nightmare footnotes and endnotes can be when you have 15 different people creating their own individual parts of a document. Luckily, Word 2010 can make coordinating elements, such as citations, footnotes, and endnotes easier because it does quite a bit of the work for you. You can also use master and subdocuments to carve up your long document and put it back together (see Chapter 24, "Special Features for Long Documents," for more about that). And when you need to put together multiple versions of a file you can also fall back on the Compare and Combine features, which help you see what's what, and make changes accordingly.

- **Format the document with the end in mind.**   As you envision the type of document you and your team are creating as well as the way you want to share it, design will play a big part of your considerations. If you are creating something that matches other publications your company has produced, you will already have a set of design specifications to use. If you are creating something new that isn't tied to other formatting considerations, you will need to consider the type of design your audience will respond to. It's a big job—and each person will have his or her own opinion. You can use templates, themes, and Quick Styles in Word to simplify the process of developing a look that hits the mark.

- **Edit and review the first draft.**   Depending on the number of people on your team and the number of review cycles your document will go through, reviewing and editing your document might require you to send various sections in a variety of directions. Be sure to leave time in your schedule so that others have the time they need to review and respond to the sections you send.

- **Incorporate changes and proofread the document.**   Whether you've been using the co-authoring features in Word 2010 or sharing the document by passing it around the team, you need to resolve all the issues and accept revisions (or reject them) as you finalize the document. You'll also want to run the spelling and grammar checker, and double-check any citations before you finalize the document.

- **Prepare for final production.**   The choices you make about the final production of your document will depend on your budget, your audience, and the overall goals of your publication. A four-color, commercial printing process will cost more than something you print on your desktop printer, obviously, but some projects (especially complex ones) just can't be finished any other way. Perhaps you'll be able to share your document as a PDF to save trees as well as production costs. Word includes a number of features to help you prepare to finalize your document. One important feature is Inspect Document (available on the Info tab when you click File), with which you can search for and remove any hidden or personal information left in the file.

- **Finish and distribute the document.**   The last step in preparing your complex document is to save it in the final format appropriate to your purposes—for example, PDF, XPS, or as a final (read-only) document. You can then send the document to others on your team, publish it to your SharePoint site or Windows Live SkyDrive account, or print and distribute it as needed.

Layout and Design Fundamentals

Whether you're designing content that will be read on a page, a screen, or a mobile phone, certain design principles apply. By incorporating some basic ideas into your document design, you can ensure that your document meets its goals, which is for people to read it and take the action you're hoping they'll take.

You might have several goals for the content you produce:

- You want to inform others about a product, service, program, or idea.

- You might want to inspire readers to take action (support your cause, join your group, be glad they bought your product, come to your Web site).

- You want to reinforce your brand so the reader remembers you. You can do this through your visual presentation—the logo, colors, fonts, and pictures you use—and you can post your mission and "Who We Are" statement on your site or in your longer document.

> **Tip**
> For more about choosing a professional design for your publication that offers a good balance of color and layout, see Chapter 4, "Templates and Themes for a Professional Look."

The first objective in any publication is to get the reader's attention. You can produce the most wonderful, inspiring content possible, but if no one gives your document a second look, the content isn't going to have a chance to fulfill its mission. How can your document capture the reader's attention?

- Use an inviting design that is pleasing to the eye and connects with your content.

- Show the reader clearly that the document, site, or file is easy to navigate and understand.

- Demonstrate the value for the reader ("This document shows you clearly").

Once you've got the readers' attention, your design can help ensure that people keep reading. If you think back to your experiences in school, remember how your heart sank when you were assigned a lot of reading in a long, boring book. Nobody wants to read page after page of uninterrupted text—it just looks overwhelming, and even if the subject is one we're fascinated in, we're likely to tune out after just a few pages. To keep people reading, make your pages easy to read by employing the following suggestions:

- Include headings to break up the text and give the reader places to catch his or her breath.

- Insert photos, charts, diagrams, and drawings wherever appropriate.

- Use plenty of white space on the page—don't fill the page with text. This gives the reader's eye a rest.

Some documents you create might simply educate your readers about a specific topic, product, or service. But many documents include—either covertly or overtly—a call to action. What do you want readers to do after they read your document? Perhaps you hope they will side with you on an important issue; maybe you want them to come to your Web site and buy your product; or you might just hope to reinforce your relationship with the reader and affirm their good choices of doing business with you. You can inspire readers to take the action you want them to take by incorporating the following ideas:

- Say explicitly what you hope readers will do after reading your document.

- Make it easy for readers to take the next step (including your Web address, for example, or providing a link readers can go to and purchase your product).

- Provide a mechanism—or at least information and an invitation—that enables readers to follow up with you with any questions or comments about your document.

- Make the call-to-action plain, with a headline ("How You Can Get Involved" or "What To Do Next").

For example, Figure 6-1 shows a report that uses a Word 2010 template. In this design, you can see that white space is used generously to help guide the reader's eye down the page. Titles, headings, and the quote on page 2 all help the reader know what the important pieces of information are and where he or she should read next. When the reader sees instinctively how to manage the flow of information, he or she can relax and take in the meaning of your message.

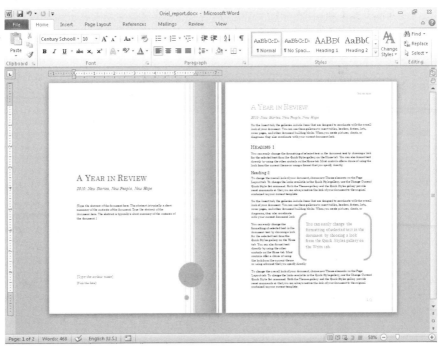

Figure 6-1 White space, titles, clear headings, and pull quotes help readers see what's most important on a page.

Considering Content Delivery

As the capabilities of our programs change, we are able to share files in new ways and easier than ever before. Just a few years ago, your three main choices for sharing a file were to print it, e-mail it, or put it on a disk (remember those?) and handing it to someone.

Today there are many different methods and formats you can use to share the content you create. Some examples include the following:

- Prepare a document that you only intend to print (for example, invitations, postcards, or bookmarks).

- Print a document but also preserve it as a PDF file readers can download from your Web site.

- Send a file by e-mail and also post it to a Windows Live SkyDrive account.

- Save your file directly to a SharePoint Workspace where others on your team can work in it as well.

- Save the file to your OneNote workbook.

- Post content directly to your blog or Web site from your Word document.

- Use the content in a presentation or worksheet.

Each of these avenues might cause you to rethink your design slightly. You might want to format pull quotes as body text if you're posting to a blog, for example, or remove links from a document that will be distributed only in print.

> **Tip**
> One great way to learn more about effective document design is to notice what you like about the documents you receive. When do you feel drawn into reading a document and when does a document leave you cold? Knowing what captures your attention—especially if you read the document all the way to the end—is a key part of connecting with what will work for your audience.

Designing Backgrounds and Watermarks

The background of your document is, well...*background*, and as such it can sometimes be overlooked when we consider document design. However, the background you choose can gracefully support the text your document presents, helping the reader see the important points clearly and framing your ideas in the best possible light. But it can also overpower your text, making it difficult for readers to understand your points and generally detracting from the overall effect of your document. This section explores how to design effective backgrounds that are subtle and add to the overall design of your project.

This section also discusses watermarks. These are typically discreet text elements that you can include on the background of your pages that are often used when information is confidential or proprietary. In this capacity, they inform the reader that the information is not meant to be shared or that it belongs to your company alone. But watermarks are not limited to legal notices; some groups also use watermarks as a kind of brand booster. For example, you can include a shadowy picture of your product behind the text of your sales report.

Adding and Customizing a Page Background

The background you choose for your document should add to the readability of your text and not detract from it. Word 2010 gives you the choice of choosing a specific page color, adding a pattern, or selecting a texture for the pages you create. You can also apply a photo to the background of the page if you choose or apply a custom pattern to the page. This section introduces you to the various ways you can add a touch of design to your page background.

> **Tip**
>
> If the background does not appear on printed pages, you might need to change your print options. Click File to display Backstage view and then click Options. Then on the Display tab, in the Printing Options area, select the Print Background Colors and Images check box then click OK.

Applying Colors and Gradients

To add a color background to your document, on the Page Layout tab, click Page Color in the Page Background group, and then perform any of the following actions (see Figure 6-2):

- Click a color in the Theme Colors area of the palette to choose a color that will be changed if you later choose a different theme.

- Click a color in the Standard Colors area to choose a traditional color that will not be changed if you change the theme.

- Click More Colors to access additional colors that you can apply to your background. You can then click your choice and click OK to add a color to the page.

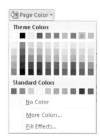

Figure 6-2 Choose a color for the page background from the Theme Colors or Standard Colors area, or click More Colors to see additional choices.

INSIDE OUT   Matching Colors

If you want your page background to match a specific color that is part of a professional palette you use for printing, you can enter the RGB or HSL values to specify the exact hue you want to use. Click Page Color in the Page Background group on the Page Layout tab and choose More Colors. On the Custom tab, choose the color model you want to use. For RBG, enter the Red, Green, and Blue values in the respective fields; for HSL, type the Hue, Saturation, and Luminosity values that reflect your selected colors.

Tip
Notice that when you apply a page background color the hue flows throughout your document. If you want to limit the background color change to a specific page or pages, create a section and choose one page color for the section and another page color for the rest of your document. To learn how to create sections in your document, see Chapter 5, "Customizing Page Setup and Controlling Pagination."

Using Fill Effects and Custom Backgrounds

Word 2010 lets you do more than simply add a color to your page background. You can also choose a special treatment for that color such as a gradient—one color gradually fades into another in the pattern you specify. In addition to gradients, you can add a pattern, texture, or even a custom picture to the background of your page.

To create a gradient for the colors on your page background, follow these steps:

1. On the Page Layout tab, choose Page Color in the Page Background group.

2. Click Fill Effects to display the Fill Effects dialog box.

3. In the Fill Effects dialog box, the Gradient tab is selected (see Figure 6-3). Select the following options:

   - In the Colors area, choose whether you want to use one color, two colors, or one of Word 2010's preset color combinations for the gradient background. If you choose One Color or Two Colors, click the Color arrow and choose the color you want to apply. If you choose Preset, you can choose the preset you want to use.

   - In the Transparency area, use the sliders to set the density range of the color effect. The From value sets the beginning density level (percent); the To value sets the darkest level for the gradient.

   - In the Shading Styles area, choose the direction in which you want the gradient to flow on the page. The Sample display shows you the effect of your choice.

4. Click OK to apply the gradient effect to the current section in your document.

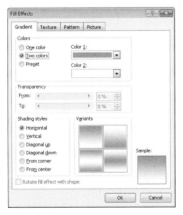

Figure 6-3 The Fill Effects dialog box gives you a number of ways to change the look of the page background.

For special pages, such as a cover page or a section divider, you might want to do something special like apply a texture effect to a background page. The Texture tab in Word 2010 presents you with a variety of interesting textures that you can apply to the page (see Figure 6-4). Click the texture you want to use and the image appears in the Sample display. Click the OK button to add the texture.

Chapter 6

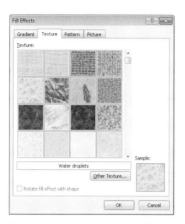

Figure 6-4 Choose a texture for your page background to create a stylized look for a special page.

Tip

You can apply your own files as textures by clicking the Other Texture button and choosing the graphic file in the Select Texture dialog box. Click OK to add the texture to the Texture gallery, and then select it and click OK to add it to the page.

Similarly, the Pattern and Picture tabs in the Fill Effects dialog box is where you can choose a specific pattern for the background or add a photo of your own to the page. On the Pattern tab, you can choose which color you'd like to make the foreground and which you want to apply to the background of the pattern (see Figure 6-5). On the Picture tab you can click Select Picture to choose the photo you want to use for the background of the page (Figure 6-6).

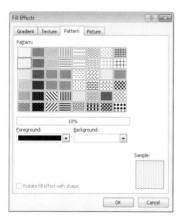

Figure 6-5 Select colors for the foreground and background of the pattern you select.

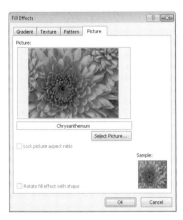

Figure 6-6 Add your own pictures for a special look on the page background.

After you select a color or create a fill effect, Word automatically applies the background to the current document. You can see the background in all views except the Normal and Outline views.

> **Note**
>
> You can quickly check whether Word is configured to print background colors and images by previewing a document that contains background formatting. On the File tab, click Backstage view then click Print to preview the document.
>
> If you later decide you want to remove the page background—whether it is a full page color, a gradient, pattern, texture, or picture—you can do so by clicking Page Color in the Page Background group on the Page Layout tab then clicking No Color.

Adding Watermarks to Printed Documents

Whether you want to identify your document as confidential, add your company name behind the scenes of your text, or add a logo to help reinforce your brand, you can add a watermark to a printed document by choosing the Watermark tool in the Page Background group on the Page Layout tab. The watermark is added as WordArt on the header and footer layer of your document, so you can edit the watermark easily after you place it, changing the content of the text or the style in which it is displayed.

When you click Watermark, the Watermark gallery appears, as shown in Figure 6-7. Scroll through the list to see the various styles. When you see a style you want to add, simply click it, or if you want to create your own, click Custom Watermark.

Figure 6-7 Choose from ready-made watermark styles or create your own in the Watermark gallery.

You can also create a custom watermark using a picture or text by clicking Custom Watermark at the bottom of the Watermark gallery and configuring your settings in the Printed Watermark dialog box (shown in Figure 6-8), such as adding a picture watermark or customizing your own text.

Figure 6-8 You can use the Printed Watermark dialog box to add picture and text watermarks to your documents.

If you later want to remove the watermark you have added, simply choose Watermark in the Page Background group and click Remove Watermark.

Editing a Watermark

If you need to edit your watermark after you add it to your page, you can select it by first double-clicking in a header or footer area to activate the header and footer layer of your document. When the header area is active and the Header & Footer Tools tab is visible on the Ribbon, you can click the watermark. The WordArt tools tab appears on the Ribbon.

Now you can edit the watermark as needed, using any of the WordArt tools that are available to you. You can change the style or direction; modify the fill or outline color; set shadow effects and direction; and much more (see Figure 6-9).

Figure 6-9 You can edit a watermark by selecting it on the header and footer layer and using the WordArt Tools to make your changes.

You can insert a custom picture or text watermark by configuring the settings in the Printed Watermark dialog box. To display the dialog box, click Watermark in the Page Background group on the Page Layout tab and then click Custom Watermark. In the Printed Watermark dialog box, choose one of the following:

- **Picture Watermark**   To insert a picture watermark, click the Picture Watermark option and then click the Select Picture button to choose a picture for the watermark. You can use color or grayscale pictures for watermarks. The Scale option lets you specify a size for the watermark picture. In most cases, you should select the Washout check box (which is selected by default) so that the watermark is unobtrusive and doesn't interfere with your document's readability.

- **Text Watermark**   To insert a text watermark, click the Text Watermark option and then type custom text in the Text box or choose from text in the Text list. Next, configure the Text, Font, Size, Color, and Layout settings. You can display the water-mark text diagonally or horizontally. In most cases, you should select the Semitrans-parent check box so that the watermark doesn't interfere with your document's readability.

TROUBLESHOOTING

My watermark prints every other letter.

Your watermark might display correctly in Print Preview or Print Layout view but only print every other letter. To correct this issue, on the Page Layout tab, click Watermark and then click Custom Watermark. In the Printed Watermark dialog box, clear the Semitransparent option. The underlying cause of this issue is that your printer does not fully understand the Semitransparent option. If you need to use this option, then obtain an updated printer driver from the manufacturer's Web site, which might resolve the issue. As a workaround or until you obtain a driver that supports the Semi-transparent option, you can set the watermark color to a lighter shade to emulate transparency.

Once you configure your picture or text watermark settings, click Apply to preview the watermark without closing the dialog box in case you need to make additional modifica-tions. If you like the results, click Close.

Tweak Word 2010 Layout Options

As you think through your variety of page layout choices in Word 2010, you might want to take a quick look at Word's layout options, which are available on the Advanced tab of the Word Options dialog box. To display Layout Options, click File then Options in Backstage view. On the Advanced tab, scroll down to the bottom of the list and click Layout Options. A long list of very specific choices appears; you can click selections within this list to turn on or off the various features that impact the layout you want to create.

Many of your choices in Layout Options have to do with setting up your tables to behave the way you want them to, but you'll also find settings for line and character spacing, word wrap, bullet and numbered list formatting, and compatibility issues. Read through the options to see if you need any of the features and click the ones you want to add. Click OK to save your changes and close the Word Options dialog box.

Adding Columns

Columns are another big-impact item that influences the overall look and layout of your document. It seems like just a few years ago business documents were pretty ho-hum, single column affairs. Today with the advent of feature-full programs like Word, design has made its way into even the most traditional business reports. We've discovered that in some situations columns not only *look* good, but they also help you communicate your information in a more effective way. For example, you might use columns to:

- Use the space in your document most effectively and fit more text on the page.

- Group similar ideas together in one part of a page so readers can see comparisons easily.

- Provide readers with a feeling that the small chunks of text are easy to read and understand. This enhances readability and signals that readers won't have to work too hard to get your meaning.

- Vary the page layout and increase reader interest.

- Allow for flexibility around graphics, tables, and pictures on your page.

Planning Your Columns

When you begin to plan your project—especially if you're planning a fairly complex document—it's a good idea to start out not at the computer keyboard but at the drawing board, sketching out how you want your pages to look. Will you use two columns or three? Do you want the columns to have equal widths, or will one be narrow and the other two wide? If you use two columns on the first page will you want three on the next? Thinking carefully about your document's final appearance will go a long way toward helping you create it the way you want.

Word gives you the option of creating more than a dozen columns, but in all but the rarest circumstances (such as a simple word or number list), you won't use that many columns— the width of each column would be a scant 0.5 inch! Most traditional documents use one, two, or three columns. In some instances, you might use four, but even those columns will provide little room for more than a few words on a line.

As you prepare your column layout, consider these questions.

- How many columns do you want? Table 6-1 lists the column widths Word uses by default for a table with one to six columns on an 8.5 × 11-inch portrait page with the Equal Column Width option selected.

- Will you include graphics around which your columns need to flow?

- How much space do you want to leave between columns?

- Do you want your columns to be of equal widths or varied widths?

- Will you include a table of contents column that might require more space than a traditional text column?

- Do you want the column settings to extend the full length of the page, or do you want to include a section at the top or bottom of the page that is only a single column?

Table 6-1 **Default Column Widths in Word 2010**

Number of Columns	Width of Each Column (Inches)	Width of Each Column (Centimeters)
1	6 inches	15.24 cm
2	2.75 inches with 0.5-inch spacing	6.98 cm
3	1.67 inches with 0.5-inch spacing	4.23 cm
4	1.13 inches with 0.5-inch spacing	2.86 cm
5	0.8 inches with 0.5-inch spacing	2.03 cm
6	0.58 inches with 0.5-inch spacing	1.48 cm

Tip

If you know you're going to create a multicolumn document, the easiest way to begin is by looking through the Word templates. Word gives you access to a huge collection of template styles from which you can likely find a ready-made column arrangement that fits your needs.

Creating a Multicolumn Document

Creating columns is really a simple task, but it does require a little forethought. First, do you plan to create multiple columns for the entire document or for a section, page, or paragraph? The following sections show you how to create columns first for the full document, then for parts of a document, and finally for selected text only.

You can create columns several different ways. The easiest method is to simply click the Columns button in the Page Setup group on the Page Layout tab and choose the number of columns you want to create. If you have certain specifications—for example, exact column measurements, a spacing requirement of a certain size, or more than four columns—use the Columns dialog box to choose those settings.

> **Tip**
> Be sure to display your document in Print Layout view before you begin working with columns. In Draft view, Web Layout view, and Outline view, you won't see the columns as they will appear in print. Click the view control you want to use on the right side of the status bar to change the view.

Using the Columns Tool

The easiest way to create a multicolumn document is to click Columns in the Page Setup group on the Page Layout tab. When you click the button, the choice of one to three columns is presented, as shown in Figure 6-10. In addition to the choice of one to three columns, you can choose a column style (narrow column on the left or right) from the available choices. Click the column setting you want, and Word will automatically update the layout in your document.

> **Tip**
> If you want to create columns for only a portion of a document, select the text to which you want to apply the column format before you click the Columns button.

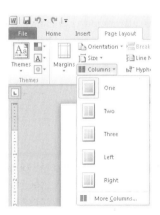

Figure 6-10 Using the Columns gallery, you can select up to three columns from the Standard toolbar.

Choosing Column Specs in the Columns Dialog Box

If you want to create your columns to meet certain specifications—for example, you're creating a follow-up report using a style your department has adopted as its report format of choice—you can create and work with columns settings by using the Columns dialog box. Here's how:

1. On the Page Layout tab, click Columns in the Page Setup group.

2. Click More Columns at the bottom of the Columns gallery to display the Columns dialog box.

3. Click the column format you want to use.

   The Preview section shows you the format you've selected, as shown in Figure 6-11.

4. Enter the new values for the column.

   After you click outside the box, the Preview window updates to reflect your changes.

5. Continue changing columns and any other settings as needed in the Columns dialog box.

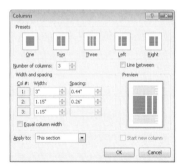

Figure 6-11 You can enter specific column settings in the Columns dialog box.

6. Click OK to apply your formatting.

By default, Word assumes that you want your columns to be of equal widths (unless you choose either the Left or Right preset selection) and that you don't want a line to be placed between the columns you create. If you want to add a line between columns, select the Line Between check box; Word will add the appropriate line.

Creating Columns for Part of a Document

The column settings that you choose will extend by default from the current cursor position through the end of the document (or the end of the current section). But Word also makes it easy for you to vary the way columns are used in your document without tying the settings to a specific section. You might want, for example, to open your document with a paragraph in single-column format and then break up the rest of the document into two columns, as shown in Figure 6-12.

> **Note**
>
> If you add one or more section breaks to your document, you'll find that this section becomes one of your choices in the Apply To box in the Columns dialog box. It also becomes the default choice by Word as to where to apply the columns.

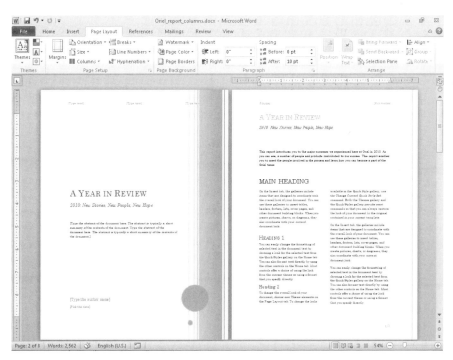

Figure 6-12 You can mix column formats easily in the same document.

Chapter 6

To create a mixed format, follow these steps:

1. Type the opening paragraph with the document set to single-column format.

2. Click to position the pointer where you want to create columns. On the Page Layout tab, click Columns in the Page Setup group.

3. Click More Columns to display the Columns dialog box.

4. Choose the number of columns you want and enter any spacing specifications as needed.

5. Select the Line Between check box if you want a line to be displayed between columns.

6. Click the Apply To arrow and choose This Point Forward, then click OK to close the Columns dialog box and return to the document.

Creating Unequal Column Widths

Although Word automatically sets a number of options for you in the Columns dialog box, you can change those options to create columns that suit your exact document specifica-tions. By choosing the Left or Right preset format, you can tell Word to create columns of unequal width. When you choose the Left preset format, the column to the left will be smaller than the one to the right; when you choose the Right preset, the right column will be the smaller one.

To customize column widths using the Columns dialog box, follow these steps:

1. Choose Columns in the Page Setup group on the Page Layout tab and then click More Columns to display the Columns dialog box.

2. Click in the Number Of Columns box and type the number of columns you want to create.

3. Clear the Equal Column Width check box; the Width settings will become available so that you can customize the settings, as shown in Figure 6-13.

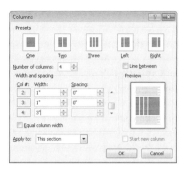

Figure 6-13 Use the Columns dialog box to specify the width and spacing for unequal columns.

4. Modify the Width And Spacing settings for your columns to get the effect you want. The Preview section shows the result of your choices.

5. Click OK to save your choices and return to the document.

Changing Column Width on the Ruler

You can also change the width of columns by dragging the column margins on the ruler at the top of your work area. If you want to keep the spacing the same between columns, position the pointer at the center of the spacing bar. When the pointer changes to a double-headed arrow, move the spacing bar in the direction you want to change the column. For example, to make the left column narrower, drag the spacing bar to the left. To make the left column wider, drag the spacing bar to the right. If you want to resize the columns to a precise measurement, press and hold the Alt key while you drag the spacing bar (see Figure 6-14).

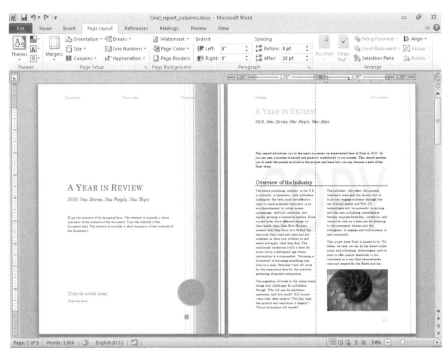

Figure 6-14 You can easily change the width of a column by dragging the spacing bar on the ruler.

You can also increase or decrease the amount of spacing between columns by dragging the edge of the spacing bar to the right or left. For example, to extend the spacing into the right column, drag the right edge of the spacing bar to the right. The size of the right column is reduced by the same amount of space you added to the spacing bar. Note that if the Equal Column Widths check box is selected in the Columns dialog box, all columns will be resized when you click and drag one column edge.

Flowing Text into a Column Layout

Everything in Word should be as simple as putting text into a column layout. When you're turning a single-column document into a multiple-column document, Word does all the work for you. You simply display the Columns dialog box, choose the number of columns you want, specify any width and spacing settings, choose whether you want a line divider, and click OK. Word then formats the document as you selected, whether you already have a document full of text or an empty page.

If you're entering text into columns as you go, no text will appear in the second column until the first column has been filled. That is, if you intend to have only headings in the left column and flow your text into the right column of a two-column format, you'll need to fill the left column with line spaces between headings until you get to the end of the column and Word wraps back up to the top of the right column. In the example shown in Figure 6-15, you can see the paragraph marks showing the line spacing that was inserted to cause the text to flow to the next column.

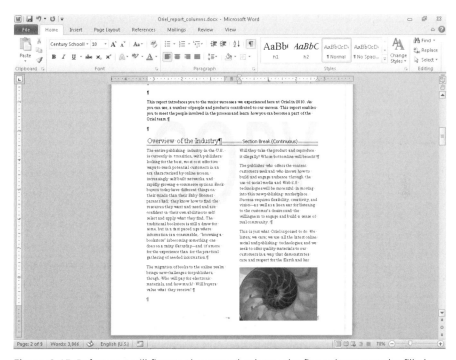

Figure 6-15 Before text will flow to the second column, the first column must be filled.

> **Note**
> There *is* a more efficient way to do this, if your left column is going to be blank except for perhaps a heading at the top. When you know you've entered all you want in a column, you should add a column break instead of using empty paragraphs. You'll learn how to do this in the section titled "Inserting Column Breaks," on page 196.

Beginning a New Column Layout

Longer documents often require a number of different general layouts. For example, the introduction and summary of your report might read better in a single-column format. When you begin to talk about the specifications of your new product line, however, you might go to a multicolumn format that shows photos of your products on the left and descriptions on the right. You might also want to incorporate graphs and tables in the body of those columns.

How can you easily switch between column layouts without disturbing the way text flows in your document? The easiest way to change to a multicolumn format is to place the insertion point where you want to start the new column layout and then follow these steps.

1. On the Page Layout tab, choose Columns in the Page Setup group.

2. Click the More Columns option in the Columns gallery.

3. In the Columns dialog box, select the number of columns you want to include and then add width and spacing settings, if necessary.

    Select the Line Between check box if you want a line separating the columns.

4. In the Apply To box, click the arrow then choose This Point Forward.

5. Select the Start New Column check box.

6. Click OK to return to the document.

    Word moves to the top of the next column, and your column settings are in effect.

Inserting Column Breaks

When you've entered everything you want in a specific column, you can add a column break to force the text flow to the top of the next column. To add a column break, follow these steps.

1. Place the insertion point where you want to insert the column break.

2. On the Page Layout tab, click Breaks.

    The Breaks gallery appears, as shown in Figure 6-16.

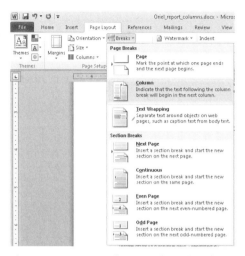

Figure 6-16 You can force a column break to begin entering text at the top of the next column.

3. In the Page Breaks section, click Column.

You are returned to the document, and Word adds a Column break at the insertion point. The text in the column past that point will be wrapped to the top of the next column.

Removing Column Breaks

In Word, you can delete columns as easily as you add them. They can be removed simply by removing a character—just position the insertion point immediately following a break and press Backspace (or select the break itself and press Delete). The column break is removed and the text is flowed back into the previous column.

What's Next?

This chapter covered some of the basics you need to consider as you begin to design your document. Thinking through your design, setting up the background, and choosing the column format you want to use are fundamental for the design of the rest of your document. In the next chapter, you focus on adding, importing, and leveraging the content you add to your Word 2010 documents.

Chapter 6

PART 2

Creating Global Content: From Research to Review

CHAPTER 7

Creating and Reusing Content 201

CHAPTER 8

Navigating Your Document 245

CHAPTER 9

**Translating Text and Working
with Languages** 267

CHAPTER 10

**Editing, Proofing, and Using
Reference Tools** 289

CHAPTER 11

Formatting Your Document 331

CHAPTER 12

**Applying and Customizing
Quick Styles** 379

CHAPTER 13

Working with Outlines 413

CHAPTER 14

Printing Documents Professionally 435

Creating and Reusing Content

Creating Content Today. 201

Entering Text. 203

Creating a Cover Page. 208

Formatting Text as You Go 210

Positioning Your Text. 223

Inserting Symbols and Special Characters 224

Inserting Date and Time Elements. 228

Creating and Using Building Blocks 230

Creating Catalogs of Content. 240

What's Next? 243

At some point in the process, you need to begin to think about how to get the words on the page—which is really the whole point, right? In the last chapter, you learned how to make design decisions that affect the way your document will look, how the content is structured, and whether you want to use columns (and how many) or watermarks in your file. But whether you love to write, or use just about any reason you can think of to avoid it, sooner or later you need to get the content into the document. That's what this chapter is all about.

Creating Content Today

Today we live and work in a content-rich marketplace. With a wide range of publishing options available to you, both online and in print, you have a number of channels ready to distribute what you create, whether you're working for yourself, for a company, or for a volunteer group. What do you plan to do with the content you create? You might:

- Print and share a document

- E-mail the document to clients

- Post the document on the Web

- Turn the document into a Web page or blog post

- Use the content as part of a PowerPoint presentation

- Post some of the content—or links back to the entire document—on Twitter or Facebook

- Split up the content and save it as building blocks that you can use in other documents you create

- Use the content as the narration for a presentation, podcast, or video you create

The list of possible output goes on, limited only by your creativity and the needs of your audience or company. The great thing about having this level of flexibility in the content you create is that you can create a document once and use it many times. And because we're all about content consumption right now—meaning organizations and businesses need to continually update content to stay relevant—being able to share your message in a variety of ways (without having to go back to the drawing board each time) is a great way to keep your message consistent and fresh.

What Does It Mean to Reuse Content?

Word 2010 makes it easier than ever for you to add content to your file and save it in such a way that it can be accessed by others on your team. You can also create building blocks that can be used in a virtually unlimited number of documents, and save the material you create in ways that can be seamlessly pulled into other formats as you need them. This is what we mean by *reusing*—being able to use content you create in multiple ways and for multiple purposes.

For example, suppose that you are working on a training manual for new sales associates that includes general information—perhaps the history of your company and the biographies of key staff members—as well as specific procedures related to your company's sales protocol. First, you might be able to use existing documents to give you some basic content to work with:

- Your company annual report

- Sales letters written in the past

- Company biographies posted on your Web site

- Historical documents that tell the story of your company

- Past training materials

- Marketing materials used to educate the public about who you are and what you do

When you work with content your organization has already created and edited, you are cutting back on the amount of time it takes to prepare the information and have it approved. If an editor on staff has already corrected your punctuation, for example, or a department manager has signed off on the way you describe the newest product, you know that the content is ready to share. Now it's just up to you to put it in the right form—such as a brochure, newsletter, annual report, or blog post—and share it with your constituents.

Ways You Can Reuse Content in Word 2010

Word 2010 is designed to help you create, share, and repurpose your content easily, no matter which type of output you want to produce. Here are a few of the features that help you reuse content you create:

- Templates offer you a wide range of professionally-designed formats to apply.

- Building blocks enable you to save and build your own galleries of reusable content.

- You can publish your documents easily to your SharePoint or Windows Live account so that others with the necessary permissions can access and use the content.

- You can attach an XML schema and use XML tags in your file to mark specific content blocks for easy use in other XML-based formats.

- You can easily share content from your document as a blog post, in your OneNote notebooks, and in social media sites.

In addition to all these ways of using content, you can also produce multiple documents and share them by e-mail, in shared server space, face-to-face via printouts, and as downloads on your Web site. If you can envision it, chances are that you can create it and share it using tools already available to you in Word 2010.

Entering Text

The easiest—but perhaps not the most efficient—way to add content to your new Word document is to type it on the blank page. Depending on your typing skills and how much you have to say, typing can take a little or a lot of your time. And once you type the content, you need to do things such as run the spelling checker, check the grammar, add in any necessary translations, check the punctuation, and pass it around for review.

And that's just the beginning.

But still, original content is a valuable commodity, and if you have the time to create something from scratch, that's great. But think in terms of reusability—how many different ways can this content be used? You should consider every document you create to be recyclable for maximum benefit and efficiency.

With Word 2010, you can drag content directly into your document from other files you're working on. For example, you might:

- Highlight catalog copy from another document and drag that content into your existing document

- Select a range of cells in a worksheet and drag them into your Word file

- Choose slide text on a PowerPoint slide and drag it into your Word document

- Drag highlighted text from an Outlook e-mail message into your open Word file

You can, of course, simply copy and paste information from any number of programs and Web pages into your Word files as well. (Just ensure that you either revise the content to reflect your own words or you have the necessary permissions from the copyright holders before you make that document publicly available.)

Ink for Everyone

If you've been using a Tablet PC or have a drawing tablet (like the Wacom Bamboo), you might enjoy going back and forth between keyboard and tablet. Word 2010 includes improvements in the ink department; now you can choose from a greater number of pens and enjoy more support for a variety of ink functions.

But will you want to use ink to add content to your Word documents? Absolutely! If you think better with a pen in your hand, you can write out your ideas in long-hand, and Word 2010 will translate them into text you can use on your page (see Figure 7-1). You can then copy, paste, format, and edit as normal.

Importing Documents

One easy way to add volumes of content to your new document is to use the Text From File command in Word 2010. You'll find it in the Text group on the Insert tab. The process goes like this:

1. Click to position the cursor at the point where you want to insert the text file.

2. On the Insert tab, click Object in the Text group.

3. Choose Text From File.

4. In the Insert File dialog box, navigate to the file you want to add, click it, and then click Insert (see Figure 7-2). The file is added in the document at the cursor position.

Chapter 7

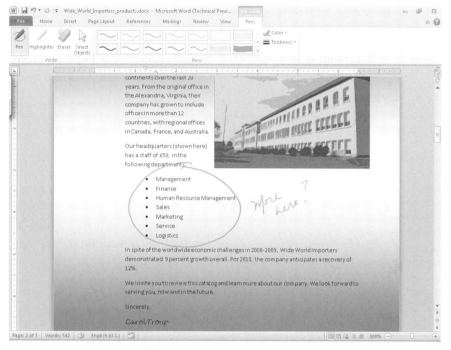

Figure 7-1 You can use the inking capability in Word 2010 to write your documents out in long-hand if that's the way you compose best.

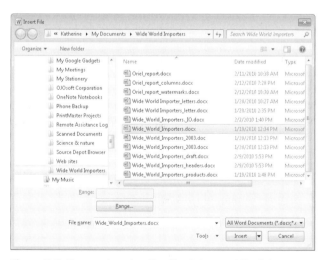

Figure 7-2 You can insert entire files into your Word document to cut down on the amount of text you need to type.

Tip

Word 2010 or Word 2007 documents aren't the only ones you can insert directly into your files; you can also add Word 97-2003 documents, Web page content, template content, files in Rich Text Format (*.rtf), straight text files (*.txt), and OpenDocument text (*.odt).

Note

What's OpenDocument format? The OpenDocument format (*.odt) was developed by the OASIS (Organization for the Advancement of Structured Information Standards) consortium to provide an XML format that promotes easy file exchange for both free and purchased office software. Google Docs and OpenOffice are two examples of software that produces OpenDocument files.

Master Documents and Subdocuments

Inserting one text file into another isn't a far cry from a larger operation that enables you to put together multiple documents—and pull them apart again—when the need arises. Using master and subdocuments, you can organize and share work on a huge project—for example, a multichapter technical book like this one—so that each person on your team can do his or her part, and then compile the whole project in a nice organic whole for finishing and distributing.

The master document contains links to the various subdocuments, but individual authors can work on their documents as needed, making changes, updating content, and reformatting to their hearts' content. Then when the document is pulled together and finished, styles are consistent, page numbers are in place, and the whole document has a consistent look and feel. Nice.

To find out more about working with master and subdocuments for longer projects, see Chapter 24, "Special Features for Long Documents."

Placing Objects

Although this chapter focuses predominantly on ways to add text content to your document (pictures, diagrams, and screenshots are covered in Chapters 16 through 18), there's no denying that the pictures, tables, diagrams, and objects you add to your pages add a lot. Depending on the type of content object you want to add, you will use one of the following procedures to add content to your document:

- Copy and paste a picture, chart, or diagram from another document

- Choose one of the tools in the Illustrations group on the Insert tab to add the object of your choice

- Select Object in the Text group on the Insert tab to create or insert images, charts, worksheets, slides, and more

Tip

When you are adding content to your pages, it's a good idea to keep in mind where you want some of those key elements to go. You might, for example, just add the line "INSERT TABLE" at a point in the document where you want to create a table to illustrate important concepts. You might add little notes to yourself about where you want screenshots to go, how you hope to illustrate a story, and where you want to do some research and add links that might be relevant to the document section. You can create a new style to make your "notes to self" stand out (see Chapter 12, "Applying and Customizing Quick Styles," for more about styles) or add a comment (on the Review tab, choose New Comment in the Comments group) to create a reminder.

Things to Consider for Long Documents

As you're adding content to your document—or planning the content you want to create—you might discover that the document is outgrowing your original vision. If the file will contain sections, illustrations, tables, citations, and more, you might want to consider some of the features Word 2010 includes to help you ensure that your long document is easy to navigate, edit, and share:

- Add a table of contents to help readers find the sections they are most interested in. See Chapter 23, "Preparing Tables of Contents and Indexes," for details.

- Use headers and footers to help readers determine where they are in the file. Chapter 5, "Customizing Page Setup and Controlling Pagination," introduced you to the process for adding headers and footers.

- Use citations, footnotes, and endnotes to give readers additional information or links to relevant sources. See Chapter 10, "Editing, Proofing, and Using Reference Tools," to learn how to use these reference tools.

- Add bookmarks to help readers easily move to key points in your document. Chapter 8, "Navigating Your Document," includes information on bookmarking your file.

- Generate an index to give readers a detailed way to find specific words and phrases in your document. Chapter 23 covers the ins and outs of indexing.

Inserting Building Blocks

Another smart way to add content to your Word document is to create and insert building blocks. A *bulding block* is a segment of ready-made content that you can add to your file at any point you choose. Word 2010 includes a number of predesigned building blocks, but the beauty of this tool is that you can create your own and build an extensive custom library of content. You might, for example, create a building block of content that tells the story of your company's founding, shares your mission statement, or introduces a program or service.

You'll learn more about building blocks in, "Creating and Using Building Blocks," on page 230.

Creating a Cover Page

Not all documents need to start with a cover page, but if you're putting together a multi-page report, designing a manual, or writing a script or proposal, a cover page gives your reader important information about the document to come. Typically, a cover page includes the document title, lists the authors of the project, and can include a description, logo, or creation date.

Most important, the cover page provides the reader with the first impression of your document. If your cover page is vibrant, with engaging pictures and fonts, the reader will be expecting a creative, high-energy document. If the cover page is traditional, with standard fonts and no-nonsense color, the reader will buckle in for some fairly dry (but factual) exposition. Whatever atmosphere you want to create with your cover page, Word 2010 is likely to have a sample that will get you halfway there.

To add a cover page to your document, follow these steps.

1. Open the document to which you want to add the cover page.

2. On the Insert tab, in the Pages group, click Cover Page.

    The Cover Page gallery opens, as you see in Figure 7-3.

Figure 7-3 You can add a predesigned cover page to give readers a professional introduction to your long document.

3. Scroll through the list and click the cover page style you like. You can preview the different choices by hovering the mouse over a style. Click the sample of your preferred cover page to apply it to the document.

4. Click in the text box and type the information you want to add to the page (see Figure 7-4), and then press Ctrl+S to save the document.

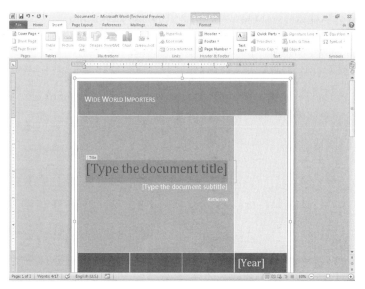

Figure 7-4 Click in a text box on the cover page and replace the placeholder text with your own information.

INSIDE OUT   Creating Your Own Cover Page

You can easily create your own custom cover page and then save it to the Cover Page gallery. On the Insert tab, choose Cover Page then click Save Selection To Cover Page Gallery, which is at the bottom of the Cover Page Gallery. In the Create New Building Block dialog box, type a name for the cover page and add a description, if desired. Click OK to save the cover page to the gallery. The next time you click Cover Page on the Insert tab, you will see your custom cover page in the gallery of available styles.

Formatting Text As You Go

In the last chapter you learned how to set up your document so some of the basic design choices—whether to use columns, for example—are already made when you begin entering text. The themes you choose (covered in Chapter 4, "Templates and Themes for a Professional Look") also help add a layer of formatting controls which ensures that the text you add has a consistent look and feel.

Some of the basic formatting choices you make—for example, should every paragraph begin with an indent?—you can set up as you begin, and then all the text you add

Chapter 7

throughout the document will appear with the format you want. Similarly, you can make choices about things such as the look and spacing of bulleted and numbered lists and special elements like quotes, tables, and more.

Later in this book we'll take a close look at paragraph and list formatting (Chapter 11, "Formatting Your Document") and adding and creating Quick Styles (Chapter 12), but knowing where to find some of the common tools is a good idea right off the bat. This enables you to format your document text as you go along—which can save you time reformatting later.

> **Tip**
>
> Remember that the formats in your document are coordinated according to the theme that you choose for the document. This means that the fonts, colors, and effects (shadows and rules) are all orchestrated so that if you want to change a theme later, you can change the whole look with a click of the mouse. Bear in mind though that elements that you format directly on the page—that is, when you change the theme formatting for a specific element—won't be reflected in the larger theme change if you choose one later on.

Formatting document content is one of the principal tasks undertaken in Office Word 2010, and you'll find formatting commands readily available on the Home tab that you'll use regularly while you're creating your document, as shown in Figure 7-5.

Figure 7-5 The Home tab houses common formatting tools you'll use as you're adding document content.

> **Note**
>
> Word 2010 comes with a set of preconfigured Quick Style Sets. These sets apply the fonts that are part of the theme you select, which helps you speed up the formatting process in your documents. The Quick Style Sets include font families, sizes, and color settings that you can apply easily to your content. You can modify the theme fonts, create custom Quick Style Sets, and even add them to the Ribbon if you like. For more information about working with themes, see Chapter 4. For more information about Quick Styles, see Chapter 12.

While you're working in your document, you'll find that any time you select text, the Mini Toolbar hovers nearby, offering you a floating palette of formatting commands (see Table 7-1). The Mini Toolbar is designed to be convenient and available but not intrusive: if you move your mouse away from the Mini Toolbar, it disappears; but if you move your mouse toward it, it becomes available so that you can choose the tools you want to use (see Figure 7-6).

Figure 7-6 The Mini Toolbar displays next to selected text and when you right-click text in a document.

Table 7-1 Tools on the Mini Toolbar

Tool	Name	Use to
 Calibri (E ▾	Font	Change font of selected text
11 ▾	Font Size	Change the size of selected text
A˄	Grow Font	Increase font size one step
A˅	Shrink Font	Decrease font size one step
律	Decrease Indent	Reduce the left margin
律	Increase Indent	Increase the left margin
B	Bold	Apply boldface to selected text
I	Italic	Italicize selected text
U	Underline	Underline selected text
≣	Center	Center selected text
ab ▾	Text Highlight	Apply highlight
A ▾	Font Color	Change the color of selected text
⬦	Format Painter	Copy formatting settings for selected text

INSIDE OUT   I Don't See a Mini Toolbar

If the Mini Toolbar doesn't appear automatically when you highlight text in your document, it's possible that the feature has been disabled. To display the Mini Toolbar, click the File tab to display Backstage view, and then select Options. In the Word Options dialog box, click Show Mini Toolbar on Selection in the General tab, and click OK. The next time you select text, the Mini Toolbar should appear.

Specifying Fonts and Sizes

Font, fonts, font, *fonts*. Just a decade ago, this word was used mainly by eggheads like me and people who worked with type for a living. But the increasing flexibility and growing feature set of Word has enabled us over the years to choose the type and style we like from a continually growing list of typefaces.

Now in Word 2010, you not only have the ability to choose from a huge slate of font options, but you can easily add your favorite fonts and take advantage of high-end typography features that are available with some OpenType fonts. You'll learn more about OpenType and find out how to use ligatures, stylistic sets, and more, in the section, "High-End Typography in Word 2010," on page 216.

When you're entering or importing content, the quickest way to apply a font is to click at the point you want the font to begin, choose the font, and then type your text. If you've already typed or pasted the text into the document, select the text to which you want to apply the font and then click the Font arrow in the Font group on the Home tab. The list of fonts available on your system appears, as you can see in Figure 7-7.

Figure 7-7 The Font list displays the various fonts available on your system.

At the top of the font list, you see the fonts used for headings and body text, according to the theme you've chosen for your document. Below the Theme Fonts, you see the names of Recently Used Fonts you've applied.

The Font list contains all the currently available fonts. You can temporarily increase or decrease the height of the font list using the sizing handle found at the bottom of the dialog box. You can also press Ctrl+D to open the Font dialog box.

Note

As mentioned in Chapter 4, if you want the font to follow the Theme, use the Theme fonts found in the Theme Fonts section of the Font list. Otherwise, the fonts will not change if your Theme Fonts change. If viewing the Font dialog box, the Theme fonts are identified as +Body and +Headings. In the Font list on the Home tab, they are identified as (Body) and (Headings).

After you choose the font for your text, you might want to select a size. The quickest way to choose a size for your text is to use the Font Size list, located just to the right of the Font list in the Font group on the Home tab. The size of the text is measured in *points*; but be aware that the point unit used to define a font size is not the same as the unit of measure used in the graphics and printing industries. For example, with the unit of measure, 72 points equals one inch; however, a 72-point letter is not 1 inch tall (depending on the font, it's actually a little under three quarters of an inch tall). When you click the Size arrow, you see a list of all sizes available for the selected font. Simply click the size you want to apply to the selected text or at the cursor position.

Tip

If the text size you want to use isn't displayed in the Font Size list, you can click in the Font Size text box and type the specific size you want.

Note

You can enter half-point values in the Font Size text box by using decimal notation (for example, 10.5), and you can specify sizes as tiny as 1 point and as large as 1,638 points (which is approximately two feet high). If you type four-digit numbers in the Font Size text box, don't include a comma separator—use numbers only.

You can also increase or decrease the size of text in increments by using the Grow Font and Shrink Font commands, which are in the Font group on the Home tab. Or, you can use the keyboard shortcuts listed in Table 7-2. When you use the Grow Font or Shrink Font commands on text that contains mixed font sizes, the font size will grow or shrink relative to its original size.

Table 7-2 Keyboard Shortcuts for Incrementally Sizing Text

Keyboard Shortcut	Sizing Effect
Ctrl+]	Enlarges font by 1 point
Ctrl+[	Reduces font by 1 point
Ctrl+Shift+>	Increases font to the next larger size in the Size list
Ctrl+Shift+<	Decreases font to the next smaller size in the Size list

Applying Text Attributes

In addition to selecting fonts and resizing text, you can apply formatting attributes, including boldfacing, italics, and underlining. You can also set various underline styles and underline colors, which are made available by clicking the arrow next to the Underline button, as shown in Figure 7-8. Table 7-3 shows you the tools you will use to apply basic text attributes and effects.

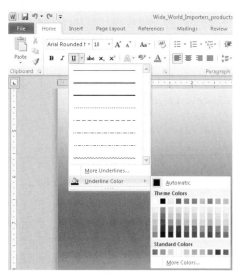

Figure 7-8 Word 2010 provides a variety of underline styles and colors that you can now easily access from the Underline button on the Home tab.

Table 7-3 **Text Attributes and Effects Commands**

Format	Home Tab Command	Keyboard Shortcut
Bold	**B**	Ctrl+B
Italic	*I*	Ctrl+I
Underline	<u>U</u>	Ctrl+U
		Underline Words Only: Ctrl+Shift+W
		Double Underline: Ctrl+Shift+D
Strikethrough	abc	(No built-in keyboard shortcut)
Subscript	x_2	Ctrl+=
Superscript	x^2	Ctrl+Shift+=

Note

The majority of keyboard shortcuts for text attributes and effects as well as Ribbon commands are *toggle commands*, which means that you perform the same action both to apply and to remove a formatting attribute. The exception to this is the keyboard shortcut for the Underline command, Ctrl+U. If an underline style other than the single underline is applied, then press Ctrl+U once to change the underline to a single underline or twice to remove all underlining. Note that the Underline command on the Ribbon will remove all underlining in one action.

High-End Typography in Word 2010

Depending on the nature of the documents you create and the audience who reads them, working with the specific characteristics of the fonts you choose can be an important part of what you do. In Word 2010, you now have the ability to take advantage of specific font qualities available with some OpenType fonts—things like ligatures, stylistic sets, number styles, and more.

OpenType fonts were originally a shared venture between Microsoft and Adobe. Today, they are an open format font specification that supports a wide range of fonts in numerous languages around the globe. OpenType fonts often support additional typography features that other fonts do not—such as ligatures, which treat two characters as a single serif (the letters *fi* are one example of a ligature that is commonly used), and stylistic sets, which offer a range of styles based on a single font choice.

In Word 2010, Gabriola is an example of an OpenType font that you can use to experiment with the typography features. And you can search the Web, buy, and download other OpenType fonts that fit your projects. To take advantage of these OpenType features in your document, follow these steps:

1. Select text that is formatted in an OpenType font.

2. Click the Font group dialog launcher.

3. On the Advanced tab (see Figure 7-9), select OpenType Features, and then enter your choices for the following settings:

    - **Ligatures**   Choose from among None (the default), Standard (industry stan-dard ligatures), Standard and Contextual (which include some contemporary ligatures selected by designers), and All (which reflects all possible ligatures).

    - **Number Spacing**   Select from among Default (the default value specified by each font designer), Proportional (which spaces numbers based on the charac-ter widths), or Tabular, which assigns each number the same width.

    - **Number Forms**   Choose Lining, which gives all numbers the same height and depth, or Old-style, which extends the numbers far above and below the baseline.

    - **Stylistic Sets**   Choose any of the available stylistic sets to apply a new look—perhaps heightened extenders or blockier serifs—to the OpenType text you've selected.

4. Select the Use Contextual Alternates check box if you want the letters in the font to be adjusted based on the context of nearby characters. This feature can smooth the text where special features have been applied.

5. Preview your changes in the Preview window, and when you're happy with the look of the text, click OK to return to your document.

Figure 7-9 Choose an OpenType font and use the Advanced tab to set special typography features for your text.

> **Note**
> Your document must be saved in Word 2010 in order to take advantage of the Open-Type features. Otherwise the settings for the Advanced tab will be unavailable for selection.

Text Effects to Really Wow 'Em

Now in Word 2010 you can also apply real text effects—glows, reflections, shadows, and more—to your document. In previous versions of Word, the phrase *text effect* referred to some pretty ho-hum effects: strikethrough, superscript, and subscript. You can still apply all those effects by selecting your text and clicking the tool you want to use in the Font group on the Home tab, but now you can add to the wow factor by clicking the Text Effects tool and choosing the look you want from the list that appears (see Figure 7-10).

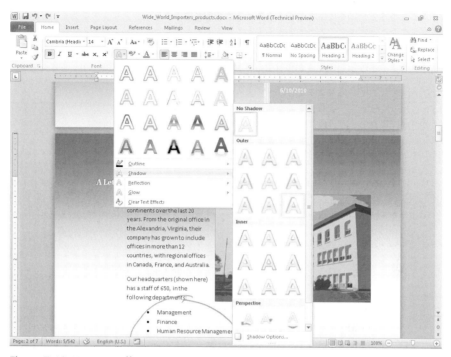

Figure 7-10 New text effects in Word 2010 enable you to add graphical touches to the text in your document.

Here's how to apply text effects to your document:

1. Select the text to which you want to apply the effect.

2. On the Home tab, click Text Effects in the Font group.

3. Point to a style from the Text Effects gallery or select from the four effect styles to apply the desired effect to your text:

    •   **Outline**   Enables you to choose the color, weight, and style of the outline used for the text.

    •   **Shadow**   Enables you to set the shadow settings for the inner, outer, and per-spective shadow of the text. You can also set shadow options.

    •   **Reflection**   Offers the choice of setting a variety of reflection options; you can set the size and distance of the reflection.

    •   **Glow**   Provides a variety of glow colors and styles. You can also set glow options for the text.

> **TIP**
> If you add a special effect to text and decide you don't want to use it after all, you can remove the effect by clicking Clear Formatting in the top-right corner of the Font group.

Additional Text Formats

In addition to basic formatting, Word provides a number of other text formats that can be found in the Font dialog box. To access the Font dialog box, click the dialog launcher in the Font group or press Ctrl+D. Here is a list of additional text effects you'll find in the dialog box:

- Double Strikethrough
- Shadow
- Outline
- Emboss
- Engrave
- Small Caps (Ctrl+Shift+K)
- All Caps (Ctrl+Shift+A)
- Hidden (Ctrl+Shift+H)

Changing Case

Occasionally, you might want to change lowercase text to all caps; all caps to lowercase; mixed-case text to title case; and so forth. Fortunately, you can perform these potentially tedious maneuvers without retyping text. In fact, all you need to do is use the Change Case command on the Home tab. The Change Case command provides the following options:

- Sentence case.
- lowercase
- UPPERCASE
- Capitalize Each Word (Title Case)
- tOGGLE cASE

You can also use Shift+F3 to change the case of text. This keyboard shortcut will cycle through the Change Case options; the outcome depends on what you have selected in your document. If you select a paragraph or sentence, provided the period is selected, Shift+F3 will cycle through UPPERCASE, lowercase, and Sentence case, as opposed to UPPERCASE, lowercase, and Capitalize Each Word.

INSIDE OUT   All Caps vs. Change Case

Though there isn't a visual difference between using the All Caps Font effect (Ctrl+Shift+A) and the UPPERCASE option of Change Case, there is a distinct difference between the two. All Caps is a format that is stored with the text, similar to Bold or Underline, and the Change Case function simply changes the case of the text as if it were originally typed that way in the document. For example, if you use the Clear Formats command (discussed later in this section on page 223), text that you format using All Caps will revert to the case you originally used when you typed it; whereas, with Change Case the case of the text is remains as is when you use the Clear Formats command.

Using the Highlight Tool

The main idea behind highlighting is to call attention to selected text in documents. When reviewing documents, highlight colors can be used to indicate a particular issue (for example, turquoise highlight might specify that a page reference needs to be completed, bright green highlight could be used to draw attention to repeated information, and so forth). Highlighting parts of a document works best when the document is viewed on the screen, although you can use highlighting in printed documents if necessary.

To apply a single instance of highlight, select the text or object and then click the Text Highlight Color command in the Font group on the Home tab. For multiple highlights, click the Text Highlight Color command without selecting any text or objects. The mouse pointer will display as a Highlighter with an I-beam, which you can then drag through text you wish to highlight. To quickly turn off highlighting, click the Text Highlight Color button again, or press Esc.

To change the Highlight color, click the arrow next to the Text Highlight Color command to display the Highlight color palette. To turn off the Highlight feature, click the No Color option.

> **Note**
> You can display or hide text highlighting (but not the highlighted text itself) on the screen and in the printed document without permanently removing the highlighting. Click File to display Backstage view, and then click Options. In the Display section, clear the Show Highlighter Marks check box (the option is selected by default) and then click OK.

Changing Text Color

Applying color gives you another way to customize the look of your text. For example, you might choose the font color for your document headings so that they match a specific color in your company logo. Or you might add color to text when you're creating a brochure, a newsletter, or any other document in which you want a specific headline or product name to stand out. Here's the quickest way to apply color to your document text:

1. Select the text you want to color. Alternatively, position your cursor where you want the text color to begin when you type.

2. Click the Font Color arrow in the Font group on the Home tab.

3. Select a color from the color palette, as shown in Figure 7-11.

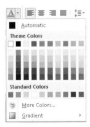

Figure 7-11 Use the color palette to specify the color you want to apply to selected text.

After you've applied color to some text, the Font Color button retains that color setting for the rest of your current session (or until you select another color in the color palette). The color under the *A* on the Font Color button reflects the most recently selected color. You can select other text and simply click the Font Color button to apply the same color to the text; you don't have to repeatedly select the same color in the color palette each time you want to apply the color. By default, the Font Color button is set to Automatic (which generally equates to black).

> **Note**
>
> Again, as described in Chapter 4, if you want the Font Color to change along with the Theme if it is changed, use the colors found in the Theme Colors section of the color palette. If you want the color to remain the same regardless of what Theme is applied, select a color from the Standard Colors section or use More Colors.

Clearing Formatting Attributes

Up to now, we've been looking at adding font formatting attributes, but at times you might want to remove all formatting attributes in a paragraph or selected text. To do so, Word provides the Clear Formatting command on the Home tab (Alt+H+E). To clear all formatting from a selected text or a paragraph, select the text or click in the paragraph and then click the Clear Formatting tool in the Font group on the Home tab. Note that the Clear Formatting command does not remove any highlighting you added using the Text Highlight Color.

> **Note**
>
> To reset font formats to only font formatting defined in the Style, press Ctrl+Spacebar. Alternatively, to reset paragraph formats to only the paragraph formatting defined in the Style, press Ctrl+Q.

Positioning Your Text

The way your text looks—and how readable your readers think it is—has a lot to do with the alignment you choose for the text. Traditional document alignment is often left-aligned, in which the text is aligned along the left margin of the page only. Other alignments include centered, which is often used for headings, and right-aligned, which aligns text along the right margin, but this is rarely used for traditional documents. Another alignment, justified, or fully-aligned text, aligns text along both the left and right margins. This is done by adding and/or removing space between words as needed to spread out or squeeze the text enough to make alignment on both edges possible. Table 7-4 gives you a look at alignment differences.

Table 7-4 **Text Alignment Options**

Setting	Home Tab Command	Keyboard Shortcut	Description
Left	▤	Ctrl+L	Aligns text and other elements (such as graphics and tables) along the left margin, or paragraph indent, leaving a ragged right edge. Left alignment is the default setting.
Center	▤	Ctrl+E	Aligns the midpoint of the selected element with the center point between the page's margins or paragraph indents.
Right	▤	Ctrl+R	Aligns text and other elements along the document's right margin, or paragraph indent, leaving the left margin ragged.
Justified	▤	Ctrl+J	Creates straight (or flush) left and right edges by adding white space between words to force the text to align with the left and right margins or paragraph indents.

Tip

If you want the text in your justified document to be formatted more tightly, click File to display Backstage view, click Options, then on the Advanced tab, click the Layout Options and select the Do Full Justification The Way WordPerfect 6.x For Windows Does check box.

Inserting Symbols and Special Characters

Depending on the nature of the document you create, you might occasionally need to insert characters and symbols that aren't normally available on your keyboard. Perhaps you need to insert a copyright symbol, for example, or add words with accent marks. Word 2010 provides a library of special characters to help you in these circumstances.

Inserting Symbols

The Symbol list and the Symbol dialog box, both found in the Symbols group on the Insert tab, work together to take care of your symbol and special character needs. The dynamic Symbol list updates as you use symbols in the list or from the Symbol dialog box; the last symbol you insert is first in the list. That way, symbols you use frequently are available to you in the Symbols list.

When you want to add a symbol to your document, follow these steps:

1. Click to position the insertion point at the place you want to add the symbol.

2. On the Insert tab, click the Symbol tool in the Symbols group.

3. Click the symbol you want to add. If you don't see the symbol you need, click More Symbols at the bottom of the Symbol list.

4. In the Symbol dialog box (see Figure 7-12), click the Font arrow to choose the font you want to use.

5. Click the symbol you want in the displayed gallery and click Insert.

Figure 7-12 The symbols for the selected font appear in the gallery.

INSIDE OUT   Using the Keyboard to Insert Symbols

You can also insert symbols directly from the keyboard. You can use built-in keyboard commands, assign your own keyboard shortcuts, or create AutoCorrect entries to insert symbols. To find the keyboard command for a symbol, display the Symbol dialog box, click a symbol, and view the Shortcut key, shown at the bottom of the dialog box.

Using the keyboard to insert symbols is a little different from other keyboard shortcuts. You might need to hold Alt and simultaneously press the numbers provided (ASCII character code) on the numeric keypad; other symbols might use two consecutive key board commands, which are identified with a comma separation. For example, to insert a copyright symbol, you need to press Alt+Ctrl+C. In some cases, you might need to type the number and letter combination provided (Unicode hexadecimal value) in the document followed by Alt+X, or press two separate keyboard shortcuts consecutively.

To assign your own keyboard shortcut or create an AutoCorrect entry for symbols you commonly use, select the symbol and then click the respective button at the bottom of the Symbol dialog box.

When you're inserting symbols from within the Symbol dialog box, keep in mind that you can insert multiple symbols at one time. Unlike most dialog boxes, the Symbol dialog box is modeless, which means you can leave the dialog box open and click back into the document to reposition your cursor for the next insertion.

Inserting Symbols Automatically

In addition to inserting symbols manually and using keyboard shortcuts, Word enables you to automatically create symbols as you're typing, without the need to display the Symbol dialog box. The magic behind this trick is the AutoCorrect feature. When the AutoCorrect feature is turned on, Word will automatically insert symbols that are included in the built-in list of AutoCorrect entries when you type their corresponding letters. Table 7-5 lists some of the symbols you can create using the AutoCorrect feature.

When symbols are inserted automatically, Word 2010 displays the AutoCorrect Options button beneath the symbol. (If the button doesn't appear immediately, position the pointer over the symbol until it appears.) Figure 7-13 shows the AutoCorrect Options available after you type ==> to insert a bold right arrow symbol.

Figure 7-13 The AutoCorrect Options enable you to control whether automatically generated symbols should replace typed text.

Table 7-5 **AutoCorrect Symbols**

Symbol	Typed Characters
©	(c)
®	(r)
™	(tm)
…	…
☺	:) or :-)
☺	:| or :-|
☹	:(or :-(
→	-->
←	<--
→	==>
←	<==
⇔	<=>

If an AutoCorrect symbol is inserted but you would prefer to display the text that typed, simply press the Backspace key once after you type the text. For example, if you want to display (c) instead of ©, type an opening parenthesis, c, and then a closing parenthesis. The text changes to the copyright symbol automatically. To revert back to the originally typed text, press the Backspace key, which will remove the copyright symbol and redisplay the (c).

Tip

If you find yourself repeatedly undoing a symbol Word 2010 inserts automatically, you can turn off the feature. Click the File tab, click Options to display the Word Options dialog box, then click AutoCorrect Options in the Proofing category and choose Stop Automatically Correcting.

Inserting Special Characters

Inserting special characters is similar to inserting symbols. You'll find the characters you want to insert on the Special Characters tab in the Symbol dialog box, as shown in Figure 7-14. Most of the special characters are typesetting characters that you use when refining document text. For example, when you want to prevent a first and last name from separating and wrapping to the next line, you might insert a nonbreaking space between them, or if you want to keep a telephone number together, you can use a nonbreaking hyphen.

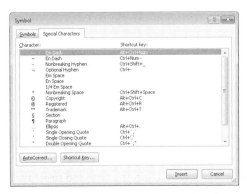

Figure 7-14 The Special Characters tab in the Symbol dialog box provides quick access to special characters.

You can insert special characters by using the Special Characters tab in the Symbol dialog box or pressing keyboard shortcuts. Note that special characters are not added to the Symbol list after you add them to your document.

> To find out how to add sophisticated mathematical equations to your Word 2010 documents, see Chapter 18, "Adding the Extras: Equations, Text Boxes, and Objects."

Inserting Date and Time Elements

Word offers a variety of features you can use to insert dates and times into your documents—those that automatically update as well as static (non-changing) dates and times. You might want to date and timestamp an important proposal, for example. You can click the Date & Time tool in the Text group on the Insert tab to display the Date And Time dialog box, as shown in Figure 7-15. The Date And Time dialog box gives you a quick and easy way to insert dates and times into your documents.

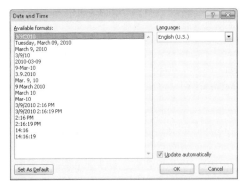

Figure 7-15 The Date And Time dialog box enables you to insert either static dates and times, or those that will update automatically.

> **Note**
>
> The Set As Default button in the Date And Time dialog box sets the default format for dates and times used in Word fields (those that update automatically), such as the *Date* field, which can be inserted by pressing Alt+Shift+D, or the *Time* field, which can be inserted by pressing Alt+Shift+T. The last default that is set will also be selected by default the first time you access the dialog box during your current Word session.

When you use the Date And Time dialog box to insert a date and select the Update Automatically option, the *Date* field will be used. This causes an automatic update to the current system date and time each time you open the document or update the fields. Should the date fail to update (for example, if the document is left open overnight), then place your cursor in the date and click the Update option found above the *Date* field in the Content Control to make the date current. If you do not want a date in a document to update automatically, see the following Troubleshooting tip.

TROUBLESHOOTING

Dates in my document keep updating automatically.

The *Date* field can be used in a document template as a method to automatically insert the current system date in new documents based on the template. The problem with using this method is that more often than not, the date the document was created—not the current system date—is the desired date.

To resolve this issue, you can select the date and press Ctrl+Shift+F9 to convert it to static text or use the *CreateDate* field in the template instead of the *Date* field. When a new document based on the template is created, the *CreateDate* field in the document will update to the current system date, rather than inheriting the creation date of the template, because the document is newly created.

Making this correction in either the template or documents based on the template is a fairly simple process. First, open the document or template, then press Alt+F9 to toggle on the view of Field Codes. The date will look something like:

```
{DATE \@ "d MMMM yyyy"}
```

Place the cursor in front of *Date* and type **CREATE**. The date field should now look something like:

```
{CREATEDATE \@ "d MMMM yyyy"}
```

Press Alt+F9 to toggle off the view of Field Codes and if necessary, place the cursor in the field and then press F9 to update the field. The date the document was created should now display.

If you prefer to use the Field dialog box to insert the *CreateDate* field or other date and time fields, it can be accessed on the Insert tab, near the bottom of the Quick Parts gallery.

Creating and Using Building Blocks

Throughout Word 2010, you find galleries that offer all kinds of choices for the design of elements you add to your pages. For example, you can view and choose headers, footers, page numbers, text boxes, quick tables, and more by displaying a gallery and clicking the item you want. Each of the items in those galleries are actually building blocks—sample elements you can insert into your document in the style you like best. Table 7-6 introduces you to the existing building blocks and indicates on which tab you'll find them.

Table 7-6 **Building Blocks in Word 2010**

Tab	Building Block	Use To
Insert	Cover Pages	Add a predesigned cover page to your document that you can customize as you like
	Headers	Choose a header style to add to your document
	Footers	Select a footer style for your document
	Page Numbers	Choose the style and placement for page numbers
	Text Boxes	Add pull quotes, sidebars, and notes to your document
	Quick Parts	Add AutoText, Document Properties, or Building Blocks
	Equations	Create sophisticated equations with accurate math symbols
Reference	Table of Contents	Choose a table of contents style to add at the cursor position
	Bibliography	Select a preformatted bibliography for the document
Page Layout	Watermark	Select a watermark style for your document

You can easily use existing building blocks to add content to your document and then customize the content to meet the needs of your document. You can also create items you use regularly—and customize them just the way you want—and then save them to a building block gallery so that you can use them again later. For example, you might create a building block that includes your company's mission statement, or prepare a header and footer that are used on all standard business reports.

You can take a look at all the building blocks already included in Word 2010 by displaying the Building Blocks Organizer. On the Insert tab, choose Quick Parts in the Text group, and click Building Blocks Organizer to display the dialog box (see Figure 7-16).

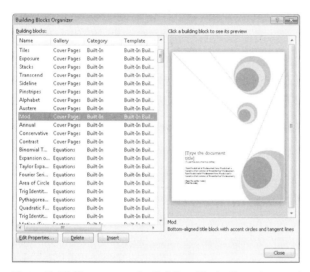

Figure 7-16 You can use the Building Blocks Organizer to view and modify building blocks.

The built-in building blocks in Word 2010 are stored in a template in your computer's Application Data folder. This template is loaded as a global template the first time you access a gallery or display the Building Blocks Organizer in your current Word session, so it's not uncommon to initially experience a slight delay while the building blocks load.

TROUBLESHOOTING

Building Blocks.dotx is corrupt.

If you encounter a message stating that Building Blocks.dotx is corrupt, use your operating system to move Building Blocks.dotx to a new folder or delete the file. A new version of the file will be created the next time you access a Building Block gallery or display the Building Blocks Organizer, but it won't include any customized building blocks you created. For that reason, you may want to save a copy of your Building Blocks.dotx file in another folder on your hard drive, in case your first file becomes corrupt.

Note that Building Blocks.dotx cannot be renamed. It must be moved out of the Document Building Blocks folder or deleted; otherwise, it will continue to load. If you are running Windows 7 or Windows Vista, and you locate Building Blocks.dotx by searching for it, be sure not to delete the version in your Office installation files. Word 2010 stores two Building Blocks.dotx files—one is the master version (kept in the installation files) and the other is your personal copy that is modified as you create and add new building blocks.

To familiarize yourself with the various built-in building blocks, scroll through the Building Blocks Organizer. You can click any entry to preview the building block in the organizer's preview pane. Note that, unlike the building block galleries, the preview does not automatically update to the current document Theme. The list of building blocks in the organizer is sorted by the name of the gallery by default. You can sort building blocks by Name, Gallery, Category, Template, Behavior, or Description by clicking a column heading in the organizer. If you are unable to see all of the columns, use the scroll bar at the bottom to view them.

Tip

While viewing a building block gallery, you can quickly locate a building blocks entry in the Building Blocks Organizer by right-clicking a building block, such as a Cover Page or a Header, and then clicking Organize And Delete. The Building Blocks Organizer opens with the entry selected automatically.

Inserting Existing Building Blocks

You can insert a building block in a document simply by opening a gallery (for example, Text Box on the Insert tab) and clicking the gallery entry you like (see Figure 7-17). The building block is inserted at the cursor position. You can then update the building block and save it back to the gallery to create your own new building block.

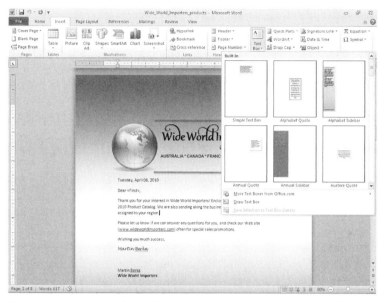

Figure 7-17 Insert a building block by clicking the item you like in the displayed gallery.

> **Tip**
>
> If you want to insert building blocks by using the keyboard, click on the page to position the insertion point where you want to add the content, type the building block name, and then press F3.

Some building block galleries, such as the Cover Page, Table of Contents, and Quick Table galleries, give you additional choices. For example, if you right-click a building block in the Cover Pages gallery, you'll find the following selections:

- Insert At Beginning Of Document

- Insert At Current Document Position

- Insert At Beginning Of Section

- Insert At End Of Section

- Insert At End Of Document

If you right-click an entry in the Quick Tables gallery (displayed when you click Tables on the Insert tab and then point to Quick Tables), you'll also find Insert At Page Header (beginning of the current page) and Insert At Page Footer (end of the current page), as shown in Figure 7-18.

Figure 7-18 Right-click a building block entry to obtain additional options.

After you insert a building block, you can freely customize the building block's formatting and properties without affecting the building block stored in the template.

INSIDE OUT   Building Blocks and Content Controls

You'll notice after inserting one or two building blocks that Word 2010 builds *content controls* into the element that is inserted. For example, when you choose a cover page building block and click in one of the text boxes, you notice that the text item is actually a content control field. This makes life easier for you because your content will remain the same no matter what you choose to do with the building block format later.

For example, when you click and type in the Title area on your new cover page, the information you add is mapped to the Title document property. If you update the content later—perhaps applying a different look or changing the title slightly—all other content that refers to that property will change too. To learn more about content controls in Word 2010, see Chapter 27, "Customizing Documents with Content Controls."

Creating Building Blocks

You can easily turn content you regularly use—for example, a paragraph (or several) of data, logos, graphics, specifically formatted headers or footers, standard tables, or equations—into building blocks. It doesn't matter whether the content is new or old (even from previous Word versions); you can create your own building block by following these steps:

1. Choose the content you want to save as a building block

2. On the Insert tab, click Quick Parts

3. Choose Save Selection To Quick Part Gallery (or press F3)

The Create New Building Block dialog box appears in which you can enter the various specifications for the new block (see Figure 7-19).

Figure 7-19 Use the Create New Building Block dialog box to enter the settings for your new addition.

> ## Tip
>
> If you want to include all paragraph formatting, such as style, line spacing, indentation, alignment, and so forth, select the paragraph mark (¶) along with your content. If you aren't already viewing formatting marks, navigate to the Home tab and click the Show/Hide ¶ button located in the Paragraph group to toggle the formatting marks so you can verify that you included the paragraph mark in your selection. If you do not include the paragraph mark, the inserted building block will match the formatting of the current paragraph.
>
> If you want your building blocks to be theme enabled so that the formats update automatically if changes are made to a theme, then use theme fonts and colors from the Theme Color section of the color palettes.

The Create New Building Block dialog box contains the following options:

- **Name**   Enter a unique name for the building block. If you are creating a set of related building blocks, consider starting all of the names with the same first word so the pieces appear together in the Building Blocks Organizer list: for example, Annual Report Cover, Annual Report Header, and Annual Report Table.

- **Gallery**   Choose the specific gallery where you want the building block to be displayed, such as Cover Pages, Page Numbers, Headers, Footers, Quick Tables, Watermarks, and so on. If your building block isn't related to an existing gallery, choose Quick Parts so that it will appear in the Quick Parts gallery. To use the Custom galleries or the AutoText gallery, see the Inside Out tip titled "Using Custom Galleries and the AutoText Gallery," on page 242.

- **Category**   Choose a category for the building block so that it will be appropriately sorted in the Building Blocks Organizer. Consider creating a new category for your company or department so that all of the associated building blocks are placed in the same category and you can find them easily when you need them.

> **Tip**
> Display your building blocks at the top of the various building block galleries by creating a Category name that starts with a symbol, such as an asterisk, or place the name in parentheses.

- **Description**   Provide a brief description that explains the main purpose of the building block. Descriptions appear as enhanced ScreenTips in the building block gallery and also appear below the preview pane when you select a building block in the Building Blocks Organizer.

- **Save In**   Building blocks can only be saved in templates. You can save building blocks in Building Blocks.dotx (selected by default), Normal.dotm, or a global template so that they are available to all open documents. They can also be saved in a document template that makes the building blocks available only to documents using that template. The Save In list contains Building Blocks.dotx; Normal.dotm; loaded global templates; the attached document template for the active document if it's a template other than Normal.dotm; and any saved template, provided that it is open and the current file. If you are creating building blocks to share with others, you want to save your building blocks in a separate template so you can distribute them. For more information on templates, see Chapter 4. For more information on sharing Building Blocks, see the Inside Out tip titled "Sharing Custom Building Blocks," on page 237.

> **Tip**
> If you don't see the description of the building block appearing in the preview pane or as a ScreenTip, check your Word Options to make sure the Show Feature Descriptions In ScreenTips feature is selected. On the File tab, display Backstage view and then click Options. Click the ScreenTip Style arrow and select the setting.

Note

If you save or modify a building block in Building Blocks.dotx, Normal.dotx (provided that the Prompt Before Saving Normal Template option is turned on in the Advanced area of Word Options), or a global template, you are prompted to save changes to the template when you exit Word. For attached document templates, you are prompted to save changes to the template on closing the document.

- **Options**   Specify whether the building block should be Inserted As Content only at the location of the cursor (such as an equation), Inserted In Its Own Paragraph (such as a heading), or Inserted In Its Own Page (inserts a page break before and after the building block).

Tip

Use the Save Selection To *Gallery Name* gallery found at the bottom of the various building block galleries to quickly access the Create New Building Block dialog box and automatically select the corresponding gallery in the dialog box.

INSIDE OUT   Sharing Custom Building Blocks

If you want to share custom building blocks, save them in a template other than Building Blocks.dotx or Normal.dotm so they can be easily distributed. If you have a set of company or department building blocks you want to share with a number of people, you'll be pleased to know that each person does not need their own personal copy. Two primary locations are recognized by Word for building block files:

- **The Document Building Blocks folder.**   This is used for personal building blocks and makes building blocks available to all documents. In Windows 7 and Windows Vista, you'll find the Building Blocks.dotx here: C:\Users*user name*\ AppData\Roaming\Microsoft\Document Building Blocks\1033

- **Your Word Startup folder.** This is the best spot for company or workgroup building blocks. Templates placed in the Word Startup folder automatically load as a global template when Word starts, and the building blocks are available to all documents. The location of the Word Startup folder can be determined—or modified and pointed to in a shared network location—in Word Options at the bottom of the Advanced area by clicking the File Locations button. The location of the Word Startup folder can also be set during installation by your network administrator.

After the template is placed in the appropriate folder, you need to exit and restart Word for the templates to load and make the building blocks available.

Note

If the building blocks you create are specific to a certain type of document, save them in a document template instead of placing them in a file in the Document Building Blocks or Word Startup folders.

Tip

If you add a number of custom building blocks to the Building Blocks template, remember to back up the template and store your backup copy in a separate location. Like the Normal.dotm template, the Building Blocks.dotx template could potentially become corrupt and you could lose your custom building blocks.

Modifying Building Block Properties

You can modify the properties of a building block—including changing the Save In template setting—by changing the information in the Modify Building Block dialog box (which looks very similar to the Create New Building Block dialog box, as shown in Figure 7-19). To modify building block properties, access the Modify Building Block dialog box by taking either of the following actions:

- Right-click a gallery item and choose Edit Properties.

- Click Quick Parts on the Insert tab, click Building Blocks Organizer, select the name of the Building Block in the organizer list, and click the Edit Properties button.

After you open the Modify Building Block dialog box, make any desired changes and click OK to close the dialog box. A message box displays asking whether you want to redefine the Building Block entry as shown in Figure 7-20. If you click Yes, the changes are effective immediately.

Figure 7-20 When you modify a building block entry, you are asked to confirm your modifications.

You can also redefine a building block, such as changing the content or formatting by simply making your modifications and selecting the content. To do so, on the Insert tab, click Quick Parts, and then click Save Selection To Quick Parts Gallery, or press Alt+F3. In the Create New Building Block dialog box, type the same name as the building block that you want to redefine and make any other necessary changes, such as changing the gallery or category. After you click OK, click Yes when you are asked to confirm the change.

> ### Tip
> If you download building blocks from Microsoft Office Online, a template containing the building blocks is placed in your Document Building Blocks folder. It's recommended that you move the downloaded building blocks to Building Blocks.dotx by editing the properties and changing the Save In location. Otherwise, several templates will load the first time you access a Building Block gallery or the Building Blocks Organizer, which might cause an increase in the initial delay. After the building blocks are moved, you might want to delete the downloaded templates from the Document Building Blocks folder to keep the file sizes as small as possible.

Deleting Building Blocks

To remove the content created when you insert a building block, simply delete it as you would any other content. To delete a building block entry from the gallery in which it appears, select the building block in the Building Blocks Organizer and then click Delete.

A message box appears, asking you to confirm the deletion. If you are sure, click Yes. As with new building blocks and modifications, you are prompted to save changes to the template accordingly; this gives you one last chance to change your mind before permanently deleting a building block from a template.

Creating Catalogs of Content

So as you can see, building blocks provide you with many different ways to save, categorize, and reuse content that you use regularly in the documents you create. You might create a building block that reflects a specific format you like for your pull quotes, add a new building block with a fancy table of contents format, or design a cover page that can be used by everyone writing proposals in your department.

Depending on the types of documents you create, you can have different types of building blocks that save you time and trouble as you create new projects. The following list offers ideas for the types of content you might want to create:

Marketing Materials

- Your mission statement

- Your company history

- Biographies of key staff members

- Headers and footers reflecting your company logo colors

- Pull quotes showing customer feedback blurbs

Sales Reports

- Report introduction

- Your mission statement

- Basic reporting procedures

- Instructions on how to file sales data

- Table styles used for sales reporting

- Explanation of report elements

Fundraising Materials

- Your vision or mission statement

- A listing of board members

- Quotes from happy donors

- Description of upcoming special event

- Headers and footers

- "How to Get Involved" information

Reports and Long Documents

- A cover page used throughout your department

- A listing of managers who need to review the document

- Pull quote or sidebar styles that fit the design

- Headers, footers, and page numbers in the style you want

- Your mission or objective for the document

- Contact information for the co-authors

- Copyright and Library of Congress information

- Table styles

For best results, create the building blocks and save them to a custom gallery (for example, choose Custom 1 in the Gallery field in the Create Building Block dialog box). You can make the custom gallery easy to find by creating a new group in the Ribbon. That way you can easily find the building blocks you want to use in the documents you create. Here are the steps for adding your new gallery to the Ribbon:

1. On the File tab, choose Options.

2. Click Customize Ribbon.

3. In the Customize The Ribbon list on the right, select the tab for which you want to add a new group then click the New Group button.

4. Click the Rename button and enter a name for the group.

5. Click the Choose Commands From arrow and select Commands Not In The Ribbon.

6. Scroll down to the Custom *galleryname* item, click it, and click Add (see Figure 7-21).

7. Click OK to save your changes and view the new entry on the Ribbon.

Chapter 7

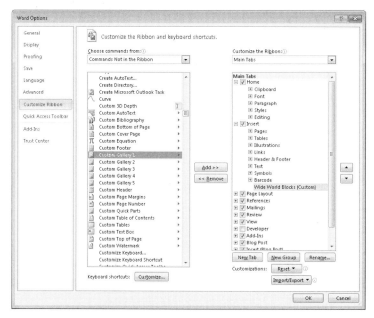

Figure 7-21 You can create a new group and add a custom gallery to the Ribbon so that you can access it easily.

INSIDE OUT   Using Custom Galleries and the AutoText Gallery

When you create or modify a building block, you can select a custom gallery or the AutoText gallery for your entries; however, by default, they appear only in the Building Blocks Organizer. You can add the Custom and AutoText galleries to your Quick Access Toolbar so that you can access the building blocks easily.

1. Right-click the Quick Access Toolbar and then click Customize Quick Access Toolbar.

2. In the Choose Commands From list, select Commands Not In The Ribbon.

3. Locate AutoText or Custom *Gallery Name*, select the AutoText gallery or your desired custom gallery, and then click Add to add it to your Quick Access Toolbar.

4. Click OK to accept your changes and close Word Options.

Tip
Basically any content you create in Word 2010 can be saved as a building block for documents you create in the future. Be creative and have fun with the possibilities. Even if you choose to modify the content after you insert it later, you'll still save yourself the time and trouble of creating it from scratch.

What's Next?

In this chapter you learned about the various ways you can add content to your Word 2010 documents. Whether you want to type the text by hand, copy and paste it from another document, add objects from other programs, or add it using the ink capabilities of Word 2010, Word's features give you the flexibility you need to be creative. You can also be smart about the content you add, and create building blocks to help you standardize the look of your documents and reduce the amount of effort it takes to create similar projects later on. The next chapter shows you the ins and outs of finding your place in your growing document by using the new Navigation Pane in Word 2010.

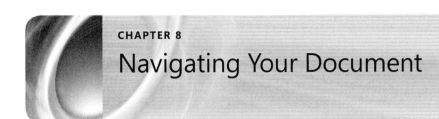

A Quick Look at Navigation in Word 2010. 245

Finding Content with the Navigation Pane 246

Navigating with Browse Object 252

Finding Text and Elements
Within the Current Document 253

Moving through the Document with Go To 259

Creating Bookmarks for Document Navigation 260

Changing the View. 261

Navigating Using Shortcut and Function Keys 264

What's Next? 266

W HETHER you create simple or complex, short or long documents, being able to quickly find what you need is an important part of working efficiently and effectively. When a sales manager calls and asks a question about a new product you're offering, it's important that you be able to find the information you need to answer the question directly. When you are looking for a specific diagram you want to include in another document, you don't want to browse through your manual one page at a time searching for it. You want to be able to move right to the diagram, copy it, and paste it into the right spot in the new document with no hassle and the fewest possible number of steps.

If you've been using Microsoft Word for a while, you probably have favorite ways to get around in the document. You might use Go To, which you can display by pressing F5. Or perhaps you might simply press Page Down until you find the spot you want. This chapter focuses on showing you a variety of ways to find—and bookmark, if you like—the content you need in your Word 2010 documents. The big story here is the addition of the Navigation Pane, which combines several of the navigation features that were available in previous versions of Word and offers them to you in one convenient panel.

A Quick Look at Navigation in Word 2010

The big story in Word 2010 is the addition of the Navigation Pane, which builds on the Document Map feature and enables you to move through the document by using headings, thumbnails, or search phrases. With Word 2010, you can also use the following techniques to get around in your document:

- You can click the Page number in the status bar to display the Go To tab of the Find and Replace dialog box. You can then enter the page you want to find and click Next.

- You can use the Browse Object feature (available both at the bottom of the horizontal scroll bar and in the Navigation Pane) to look for specific elements in your document—headings, tables, graphics, footnotes, and more.

- You can create and use bookmarks to mark a key spot in a document that you or others can then move to easily.

Each of these techniques gives you a different way to find the content you want in your Word 2010 document. Once you locate what you're looking for, you can expand, format, and edit the text to your heart's content.

Finding Content with the Navigation Pane

If you've used previous versions of Word, you might be familiar with the Document Map. Using this feature, you could move around in your document by clicking a section heading or a thumbnail representation of your document pages. The Navigation pane renames and expands the functionality of the document map by adding a live search feature, incorporating access to Find and Browse Object commands, and providing a one-stop-shop for all navigation techniques.

To display the Navigation pane, select the Navigation Pane check box located in the Show group on the View tab (see Figure 8-1).

Figure 8-1 Display the Navigation pane by selecting the check box in the Show group on the View tab.

The Navigation pane appears along the left side of the Word window (see Figure 8-2). The pane offers you three methods to navigate the pages in your document:

- **Browse the headings in your document.** Lists the content you've formatted using the Heading styles and enables you to move to a different part of your document by clicking the heading of the section you want to display.

- **Browse the pages in your document.** Displays images of individual pages in your document. You can move directly to the page you want by clicking the image.

- **Browse the results from your current search.** Displays and highlights all places in your document where the search word or phrase you enter appears. You can move to the location of the phrase by clicking the entry you want.

Browse the headings in your document

Browse the pages in your document

Browse the results from your current search

Figure 8-2 The Navigation pane helps you to find your content in the way that suits you best.

Depending on how you want to move through the document, you can display a different view by simply clicking the tab of the view you want to see. Clicking the second tab in the Navigation pane displays page thumbnails; clicking the third tab displays the search results listing.

> **Note**
>
> If you have not yet searched for information by typing a word or phrase in the search box, the search panel in the Navigation pane displays instructions about how to use this feature.

Chapter 8

You can also use the Navigation pane to make some big changes to your document—it's not just for navigation alone—by moving sections from one place to another; deleting or adding sections and pages; or changing the heading levels to better fit your content needs.

10 Ways to Use the Navigation Pane

The Navigation pane enables you to easily move from one point to another in your document, but you can also use it to perform the following tasks:

- Ensure your headings are parallel in structure (your editor will love you)

- Double-check that you've covered all the sections you wanted to include

- Review the way your document is organized

- Eyeball the layout of your pages to ensure the look is inviting an easy to read

- Ensure you're working with the right version of the document (by scanning for late changes or remaining review comments)

- Search for phrases to ensure that you've spelled product names correctly

- Ensure that you haven't overused a term or phrase

- Do a quick inventory of all the images you've used in your document

- Ensure that your table styles are consistent throughout the document

- Highlight all occurrences of a specific item you want to check

Browsing by Headings

The first tab, which displays the name *Browse The Headings In Your Document* when you hover the mouse over it, displays all the headings that you've formatted using the Heading styles in your document. This display appears by default when you first open the Navigation pane.

For more information about working with styles, see Chapter 12, "Applying and Customizing Quick Styles."

By default, all levels of headings are visible. To change the level of headings that are shown, right-click a heading, point to Show Heading Levels, and click the heading level you want to display, as shown in Figure 8-3.

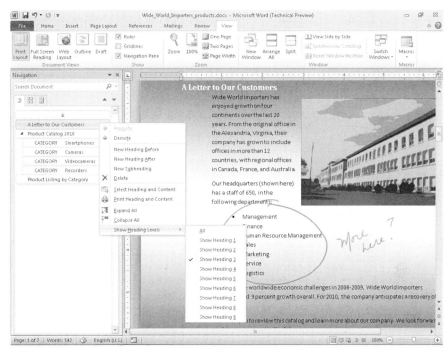

Figure 8-3 Choose the heading levels you want to display in the Navigation pane.

You can also click the arrow symbol to the left of headings in the Navigation pane to expand or collapse sections. To jump to a section in your document, click the section's heading. The heading of the section currently shown in your workspace is highlighted in the Document Map so you can quickly see the current position of the insertion point within the document.

You can also use the controls in contextual menu of the first panel of the Navigation pane to add new headings and subheadings, to change the heading level of a particular heading, or to select or print selected content.

Browse by Page

The second tab in the Navigation Pane, *Browse The Pages In Your Document*, shows you miniature representations of individual pages—complete with tables, backgrounds, images, and more. As you can see in Figure 8-4, even ink appears in the thumbnail image.

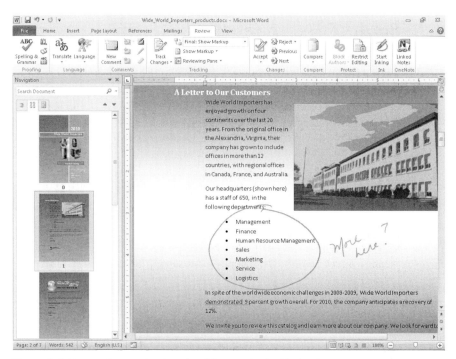

Figure 8-4 You can browse by thumbnail images in the Navigation pane.

> **Tip**
>
> If you are working with tracked changes turned on, the edits will appear in second-color text when you view thumbnails in the Navigation pane, even if Word is currently configured to display as Final text in the Display For Review setting on the Review tab.

Using Browse Pages view, you can quickly scan the document to look for things that leap out at you visually. For example, if you're wondering whether you used the most current table in a specific place or you used the right set of data from an Excel worksheet, you can display thumbnails and move through the document to see whether the information looks the way you expect it to look.

You can also use Browse Pages to check your layout. If you've used too many tables on too many pages in a row, for example, or you have too many pages of text with no visual break, such as a picture or chart, you'll be able to see that by reviewing the pages in the Navigation pane.

Browse by Search Results

The third tab, *Browse The Results From Your Current Search*, lists all the places in your document where the word or phrase you entered in the Search Document box appears. Word 2010 highlights the text everywhere in your document it is found, and the results provide links you can use to move directly to that spot in the file (see Figure 8-5).

And you're not limited to searching by phrase, page, or heading—you can click the Search Document arrow to display a list of additional search choices (see Figure 8-6). You can search for graphics, tables, equations, or footnotes or endnotes by clicking the item you want to look for. Word then moves directly to the first occurrence of the item you specify.

> **Tip**
> The technique for searching for objects in the Navigation pane is similar to the process you'll learn about in "Navigating with Browse Object," which is the subject of the next section.

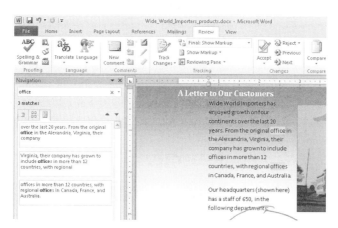

Figure 8-5 Use Browse By Search Results to see where in your document specific words or phrases appear.

Chapter 8

Figure 8-6 You can display additional choices for the type of content you want to find.

Navigating with Browse Object

You can bypass the Navigation pane, if you choose, and use tools handy in the Word window to find specific items in your document. The Browse Object feature enables you to search for specific elements in your document. For example, suppose that you are looking for a specific footnote and want to see only the footnotes you've added so far. You can use the Browse Object tool to move from footnote to footnote until you find the information you seek.

You'll find the Browse Object tool at the bottom of the vertical scroll bar, on the right side of the Word window. Browse Object includes three buttons: Previous Find/Go To, Select Browse Object, and Next Find/Go To. When you click Select Browse Object, a gallery of browse tools appears as shown here:

To use the Browse Object tool to move through your document, follow these steps:

1. Display the Select Browse Object menu by pressing Ctrl+Alt+Home or by clicking the Select Browse Object button (it has a small round icon) toward the bottom of the vertical scroll bar.

2. Select the type of object you want to browse for (for example, Browse By Heading). See Table 8-1 for available options.

3. Click the Previous and Next buttons (above and below the Select Browse Object button in the vertical scroll bar) to navigate from one browse object to the next. Alternately, you can press Ctrl+Page Up to move to the previous object or Ctrl+Page Down to move to the next browse object.

Table 8-1 **Browse Object Tools**

Button	Description
→	Browses by using the Go To tab in the Find And Replace dialog box
🔍	Browses by using the Find tab in the Find And Replace dialog box
📝	Browses by moving between the last three edits
📋	Browses by moving from heading to heading
🖼	Browses by moving from graphic to graphic
▦	Browses by moving from table to table
{a}	Browses by moving from field to field
📑	Browses by moving from endnote to endnote
📄	Browses by moving from footnote to footnote
💬	Browses by moving from comment to comment
🔀	Browses by moving from section to section
📄	Browses by moving from page to page

Finding Text and Elements Within the Current Document

You probably already know that you can find characters, words, phrases, and text elements by typing a search string in the Find And Replace dialog box and then clicking Find Next to move from one instance of the search string to the next. And now you know you can use the Browse search results tab in the Navigation pane to do the same thing.

Chapter 8

But if you prefer to use the Find And Replace dialog box (see Figure 8-7), you can still open it and use it easily, however, now you have three ways to get there:

- On the Home tab, choose Find in the Editing group.

- Display the Navigation Pane and click the arrow to the right of the Search Document box then click Find.

- Press Ctrl+H and click the Find tab.

In many cases, conducting a simple text search using the Find tab might get you where you want to go. But sometimes, you'll want to further refine your search parameters. Click the More button to see additional options.

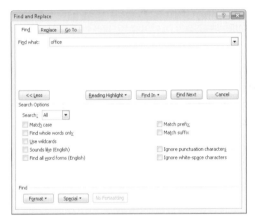

Figure 8-7 You can use the Find and Replace dialog box to locate specific content and add parameters to your search.

The following list gives you a quick look at the search parameters you can use in the Find and Replace dialog box, and Table 8-2 provides you with a list of wildcard characters you can use to streamline your search as you move through your documents:

- **Search**   Specifies whether to search Down, Up, or through All of the document. Note that Word does not search headers, footers, footnotes, or comments.

- **Match Case**   Searches for text in upper or lowercase, exactly as you've entered it. This option is unavailable when you select the Use wildcards, Sounds Like, or Find All word forms check box.

- **Find Whole Words Only**   Searches only for whole words, not parts of longer words. This option also is unavailable when you select the Use wildcards, Sounds like, or Find all word forms check box.

- **Use Wildcards**   Enables you to use wildcard characters in place of text to expand and refine your searches. If you enter wildcard characters in the Find What box without selecting the Use Wildcards option, Word will treat the those characters as plain text. When the Use Wildcards check box is selected and you want to search for a character that is also a wildcard, precede the character with a backslash (\). For example, to search for an asterisk, you must enter *. The wildcards you can use here are: ?. *. @. < >, [ ], and [!].

- **Sounds Like (English)**   Searches for terms that sound like the word or words entered in the Find What box. For example, if you enter **eight**, and then select the Sounds Like check box, Word will find all instances of *eight* as well as *ate*. This feature works only with legitimate words—entering the number **8** and selecting the Sounds Like check box won't return *eight*, *ate*, or *8*, and entering **u r** won't return *you are*.

- **Find All Word Forms (English)**   Searches for all forms of the word entered in the Find What box. For example, if you enter **speak**, Word will find *speak*, *speaking*, *spoke*, *spoken*, *speaks*, and so forth.

- **Match Prefix**   Searches for all words that begin with the text entered in the Find What box. For example, if you enter **ed** and select the Match Prefix check box, Word will find and select the prefix ed in words, such as educate, edition, and editing.

- **Match suffix**   Searches for all words that end with the text entered in the Find What box. For example, if you enter **ed** and select the Match Suffix check box, Word will find and select the suffix ed in words, such as mentioned, moved, named, and happened.

> **Note**
>
> Word does not find words that match both the prefix and suffix to text in the Find What box when you use the check box options. For example, if you enter **ed** in the Find What box and select both the Match prefix and Match suffix check boxes, Word does not find words such as educated or edited. To conduct a search that specifies both the prefix and suffix of the words included in your search results, you would need to use wildcards, such as <(ed)*(ed)>, as described in Table 8-2.

- **Ignore Punctuation Characters**   Searches for matching text regardless of punctuation. Keep in mind that this option ignores added punctuation shown in the text, not punctuation included in the Find What box.

- **Ignore White-Space Characters**   Searches for matching text regardless of the number of spaces between search string letters or words.

Chapter 8

> **Tip**
>
> Look for text directly below the Find What box to see whether any search options are being applied to the current search. For example, if Down is selected in the Search List box and the Match Case check box is selected, the text Search Down, Match case will appear below the Find What text box and the options will be applied to the current search.

Table 8-2 **Using Wildcards in the Find And Replace Dialog Box**

Wildcard	Specifies	Example
?	Any single character	**p?t** finds *pet, pat, pit*
*	Any string of characters	**p*t** finds *pest, parrot, pit*
<	Finds the text at the beginning of a word	**<mark** finds *market* but not *demark*
>	Finds the text at the end of a word	**ter>** finds *winter* but not *terrain*
[ ]	Finds one of the enclosed characters	**t[oa]n** finds *ton* and *tan*
[-]	Finds any character within the specified range	**[r-t]ight** finds *right, sight*, and *tight*
[!x-z]	Finds any single character except characters in the range inside the brackets	**cl[!a]ck** finds *clock* and *cluck* but not *clack*
{n}	Finds exactly *n* occurrences of the preceding character or expression	**ble{2}d** finds *bleed* but not *bled*.
{n,}	Finds at least *n* occurrences of the preceding character or expression	**fe{1,}d** finds *fed* and *feed*
{n,m}	Finds from *n* to *m* occurrences of the preceding character or expression	**10{1,3}** finds *10, 100*, and *1000*
@	Finds one or more occurrences of the preceding character	**mo@d** finds *mod* and *mood*

Finding Instances of Formatting

In addition to finding text strings, you can find (and replace, if you'd like) various formatting settings. To view the available formatting parameters in the expanded Find tab of the Find and Replace dialog box, click the Format button in the lower-left corner. Choosing Font, Paragraph, Tabs, Language, Frame, or Style from the Format menu displays the corresponding formatting dialog box. For example, choosing Font displays a dialog box named Find Font, which looks very similar to the Font dialog box. Choosing the Highlight option lets you specify highlighted or unhighlighted text in the Find What box. For example, choose Highlight once to find highlighted text, choose Highlight again to indicate that you want to find text that is not highlighted, and choose Highlight a third time to find all instances of the search text, regardless of whether highlighting is applied.

> **Tip**
> You can also control basic character formatting by using keyboard shortcuts. To do so, click in the Find What box and press keyboard shortcuts such as Ctrl+B (bold), Ctrl+I (italic), and Ctrl+U (underline) to toggle among applied, not applied, and neither (which equates to no formatting) settings.

You can find instances of formatting without entering text in the Find What box. For example, you could search for highlighted text that isn't italic in the current document by clicking in the Find What text box and applying the Format settings without typing any text. You can, of course, specify text in combination with formatting settings if that's what you need to find.

To clear all formatting commands in the Find What box, click the No Formatting button (if no formatting commands are applied, the Formatting button appears dim). Generally, you'll want to clear formatting when you complete one Find operation and are ready to conduct another.

Finding Special Characters Using Codes

Word further expands your search capabilities by providing special codes that you can use to find document elements, such as paragraph marks, tab characters, endnote marks, and so forth. To view the available special characters, click the Special button in the bottom of the Find and Replace dialog box.

When you choose an option from the Special menu, a code is inserted in the Find What box. If you'd prefer, you can enter a code directly in the Find What box. Table 8-3 lists some commonly used special character codes. Notice that some codes can be used only in the Find what or Replace with box; the Use wildcards option must be turned on or off in certain instances.

> **Note**
> Word can't find floating objects, WordArt, watermarks, or drawing objects. However, if you change a floating object into an inline object, Word can then find the object.

Table 8-3 **Using Special Character Codes in the Find And Replace Dialog Box**

Special Character	Code	Find and Replace Box
ANSI characters	^0*nnn* (where *0* is zero and *nnn* is the character code)	Find What, Replace With
ASCII characters	^nnn (where *nnn* is the character code)	Find What, Replace With
Any Character	^?	Find What (with the Use Wildcards check box cleared)
Any Digit	^#	Find What (with the Use Wildcards check box cleared)
Any Letter	^$	Find What (with the Use Wildcards check box cleared)
Caret Character	^^	Find What, Replace With
Clipboard Contents	^c	Replace With
Closing Field Brace (when field codes are visible)	^21	Find What (with the Use Wildcards check box cleared)
Column Break	^n or ^14	Find What, Replace With
Comment	^a or ^5	Find What (with the Use Wildcards check box cleared)
Em Dash	^+	Find What, Replace With
Em Space (Unicode)	^8195	Find What (with the Use Wildcards check box cleared)
En Dash	^=	Find What, Replace With
En Space (Unicode)	^8194	Find What (with the Use Wildcards check box cleared)
Endnote Mark	^e	Find What (with the Use Wildcards check box cleared)
Field	^d	Find What (with the Use Wildcards check box cleared)
Find What Text	^&	Replace With
Footnote Mark	^f or ^2	Find What (with the Use Wildcards check box cleared)
Graphic or Picture (inline only)	^g	Find What (with the Use Wildcards check box selected)
Graphic or Picture (inline only)	^1	Find What (with the Use Wildcards check box cleared)
Manual Line Break	^| or ^11	Find What, Replace With
Manual Page Break	^m	Replace With
Nonbreaking Hyphen	^~	Find What, Replace With

Special Character	Code	Find and Replace Box
Nonbreaking Space	^s	Find What, Replace With
Opening Field Brace (when field codes are visible)	^19	Find What (with Use Wildcards check box cleared)
Optional Hyphen	^-	Find What, Replace With
Page or Section Break	^12	Fine What, Replace With
Paragraph Character	^v	Find What, Replace With
Paragraph Mark	^p or ^13	Find What (with the Use Wildcards check box cleared), Replace With
Section Break	^b	Find What (with the Use Wildcards check box cleared)
Section Character	^%	Find What, Replace With
Tab Character	^t or ^9	Find What, Replace With
Unicode Character	^Unnnn (were *nnnn* is the character code)	Find What (with the Use Wildcards check box cleared)
White Space	^w	Find What (with the Use Wildcards check box cleared)

Chapter 8

Moving Through the Document with Go To

The Find and Replace dialog box includes another unsung feature that can come in handy when you are navigating through your document. Using Go To, you can move to a specific page easily. You can also use the feature to locate specific elements like comments, bookmarks, and more.

You can display the Go To tab in the Find and Replace dialog box several different ways (see Figure 8-8):

- Press F5 or Ctrl+G.

- Click the Find arrow in the Editing group on the Home tab and click Go To.

- Click the Go To button in the Select Browse Object menu. (To display the Select Browse Object menu, click the Select Browse Object button toward the bottom of the vertical scroll bar.)

- In the Navigation pane, click the arrow at the right of the Search Document box and click Go To.

Figure 8-8 You can use the Go To tab in the Find And Replace dialog box to locate specific items and indicate how many occurrences you want to find.

To use the Go To tab, select a component in the Go To What list box, enter the appropriate value or parameter in the box to the right, and then click Go To (or click Previous or Next if no value or parameter is specified). Here are two examples of uses for the Go To feature:

- To display a particular page in the document, select Page in the Go To What list box, type the page number in the Enter Page Number box, and then click Go To.

- To display the next bookmark in the document, select Bookmark in the Go To What list box, select the bookmark name in the list box, and then click Go To.

Creating Bookmarks for Document Navigation

Bookmarks are a great feature if you find that you often need to return to a particular point in a document. They work in just the way you'd imagine they would—similar to a bookmark you place between pages in a novel. You can set multiple bookmarks in Word and give each bookmark a unique name so that you can return to your place (and remember the topic at hand) easily. Here are the steps for inserting and naming a bookmark:

1. Position the insertion point where you want to insert a bookmark, and then click Bookmark in the Links group on the Insert tab. The Bookmark dialog box appears, as you see in Figure 8-9.

2. In the Bookmark dialog box, type a name for the bookmark then click Add.

Figure 8-9 Create bookmarks to identify places in the document you will return to later.

After you insert a bookmark, you can use the Go To tab to find the bookmarked area as described in the preceding section, or you can click Bookmark on the Insert tab to open the Bookmark dialog box, select the bookmark's name, and then click Go To to move to that point in your document.

Changing the View

Another way to get a quick glimpse of the layout of your document and navigate quickly through the pages involves changing the size and format of the display. You can use the tools in the Zoom group on the View tab to change the way your documents appear so that you can navigate through (and between) them as easily as possible.

- **Zoom** Displays the Zoom dialog box, in which you can choose from among pre-set zoom percentages (or select your own in the Percent box). Additionally, you can choose whether you want to display multiple pages and determine the width of the page as it is displayed.

- **100%** Shows the document at 100 percent size, no matter which previous view was used. This means that if you have enlarged the document to 125%, clicking this tool will take the document display down to 100%; but if you were viewing the document at 50%, clicking it will increase the magnification to 100%.

- **One Page** Displays the current page of the current document as one complete page in the display.

  Depending on whether the document is in portrait or landscape orientation, this results in 62% and 68% zoom, respectively.

- **Two Pages** Displays two pages side by side in the display. This view is helpful if you are checking the continuity of items in your document and want to be able to scan more than one page at a time.

- **Page Width** Displays the page according to the width of the text margins on the page. This view won't give you a sense of the full layout of the page (use One Page or Two Pages for that), but it does give you a quick way to display your content in a way that's easy to read.

Chapter 8

Displaying and Arranging Windows

In addition to changing views by using the Zoom tools, you might want to work with multiple windows as you review and work with different portions of your document. You might,
for example, want to display two sections of the same document in windows side by side so
that you can compare the terminology you used to describe a particular product. You'll find
the commands for creating and working with document windows in the Window group on
the View tab.

Splitting the Document Window

You can divide your document window in two using the Split tool in the Window group. By
splitting the window, you can compare portions of your document easily, without having to
open two separate copies and switch back and forth between them. Follow these steps to
split the document view:

1. On the View tab, choose Split in the Window group. A gray line appears across the
    center of your document.

2. Drag the line to the position on the screen where you want the split to occur.

3. Click the mouse button.

The document is divided into two windows, and the horizontal ruler appears at the dividing point in the document (see Figure 8-10). To select the pane of the window you want to
navigate, simply click in the document in that portion of the window and edit normally.

> **Tip**
> You can also split the window easily by using the splitter, which is the dash symbol
> located just above the View Ruler button at the top of the vertical scroll bar. Position-
> ing the pointer over the tool causes the cursor to change to a double-headed arrow.
> Click and drag the tool downward; the current window splits and you can navigate
> through each pane independently.

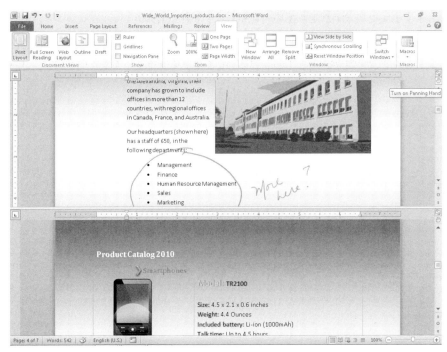

Figure 8-10 You can split one document into two windows to view different sections at the same time.

By default, the document windows scroll together, which means that if you click in either of the windows and press Page Up or Page Down, both windows scroll the same way. If you want to scroll the content in one window while the other remains static, click Synchronous Scrolling in the Window group to turn the feature off. Now you'll be able to move the display in the two windows independently.

To return the split window to a single display, use one of the following methods:

- On the View tab, choose Split in the Window group a second time.

- Double-click the splitter bar.

- Drag the splitter back to its home position.

Viewing Pages Side by Side

Being able to display pages side by side is very helpful when you are working with multiple documents. Suppose, for example, that you're referencing a larger document in a short report you're writing. You can easily find the text you want to use and insert it at the right point in your document when you can see both documents open on the screen at the same time.

Chapter 8

Begin by opening both documents in Word. Then, on the View tab, choose View Side By Side in the Window group. The Compare Side By Side dialog box appears, providing a list of open documents. Click the document you want to display beside the current one and click OK. If you want to scroll the documents independently, click Synchronous Scrolling to turn the feature off.

When you are ready to return to single document display, click the Window group in one of the documents and select View Side By Side again. The original document is returned to your display.

Switching Among Multiple Windows

If you tend to work with many different Word documents at once, you will like the Switch Windows command in the Window group. You can move among open Word documents by clicking Switch Windows in the Window group and selecting the document you'd like to display (see Figure 8-11).

Figure 8-11 Use Switch Windows to move among open Word documents.

This technique is easier than minimizing a window and then looking for the documents you want as you need them—and it's more direct than cycling through open documents using Alt+Tab. Try it—simplicity is good.

Navigating Using Shortcut and Function Keys

If you are an experienced Word user, you probably have a set of shortcut keys you use to move through documents quickly. Happily, the same shortcut keys that have been available in the last several versions of the program are still there. Table 8-4 offers a refresher of the most common keyboard shortcuts and function key combinations.

Table 8-4 **Navigation Shortcuts**

Keyboard Shortcut	Action
Alt+Down Arrow	Moves to the next object
Alt+End	Moves to the end of the row
Alt+F1 (or F11)	Moves to the next field
Alt+F4 (or Ctrl+ F4 or Ctrl+W)	Closes the active document
Alt+F6 (or Ctrl+F6)	Moves to the next window
Alt+Home	Moves to the start of a row
Alt+Page Down	Moves to the end of the current column
Alt+Page Up	Moves to the top of the current column
Alt+Shift+C	Closes the open pane
Alt+Shift+F6 (or Ctrl+Shift+F6)	Displays the previous window
Alt+Up Arrow	Moves to the previous object
Arrow keys	Move the insertion point left, right, up, or down
Ctrl+Alt+Page Down	Moves the insertion point to the bottom of the window
Ctrl+Alt+Page Up	Moves the cursor to the top of the window
Ctrl+Alt+S	Splits the window view
Ctrl+Alt+Y (or Shift+F4)	Finds the next instance of a search term
Ctrl+Alt+Z (or Shift+F5)	Moves to the previous location of the insertion point (even if the insertion point was in a different Word document)
Ctrl+Down Arrow	Moves to the next paragraph or next table cell
Ctrl+End	Moves to the end of the document
Ctrl+F	Displays the Navigation pane
Ctrl+F4 (or Alt+F4 or Ctrl+W)	Closes the active document
Ctrl+F6 (or Alt+F6)	Displays the next window
Ctrl+F7	Activates the window so you can move it using the arrow keys
Ctrl+F8	Activates the window so you can resize the window height and width using the arrow keys
Ctrl+F10	Maximizes the document window
Ctrl+G (or F5)	Displays the Go To tab in the Find And Replace dialog box
Ctrl+Home	Moves to the beginning of the document
Ctrl+Left Arrow	Moves one word to the left

Chapter 8

Keyboard Shortcut	Action
Ctrl+O (or Ctrl+Alt+F2 or Ctrl+F12)	Displays the Open dialog box
Ctrl+Page Down	Browses to the next item (based on the current Browse Object setting)
Ctrl+Page Up	Browses to the previous item (based on the current Browse Object setting)
Ctrl+Right Arrow	Moves one word to the right
Ctrl+Shift+F6 (or Alt+Shift+F6)	Displays the previous window
Ctrl+Up Arrow	Moves to the previous paragraph
Ctrl+W (or Ctrl+F4)	Closes the active document
End	Moves to the end of the current line
Esc	Closes an open gallery or cancels the current action
F6	Moves to the next pane or frame
F11 (or Alt+F1)	Moves to the next field
Home	Moves to the beginning of the current line
PageDown	Displays the next screen
PageUp	Displays the previous screen

What's Next?

Now that you know how to add content to your document and move through the files you create in a number of different ways, you're ready to begin working with some of the more specialized techniques Word 2010 has to offer. The next chapter introduces you to the ways in which you can work with other languages in your text, whether that means translating items on the fly, converting entire documents to a new language, or customizing document information so your colleagues in other areas of the world can use the files you create.

Translating Text and Working with Languages

Translating Content in Word 2010. 268

Setting Up Languages 269

Using the Mini Translator 274

Translating Selected Text. 277

Translating Entire Documents 278

Changing and Adding Translation Services 279

Using Bidirectional Text. 282

Working with the Document Grid. 283

Working with Other Translation Tools 285

What's Next? 287

The content you create in Word 2010 is probably not for your eyes alone. Chances are, the files you create will be shared with many colleagues—perhaps both in your country and around the world. Today our growing global marketplace offers us opportunities to work with teams, vendors, and clients almost any place in the world. Past limitations like geography, time, and access don't hold us back anymore—now we can send files by e-mail or over the Web and translate our text into almost any language imaginable.

Part of the design strategy of Word 2010 is to make it easier for users like you to share your files and collaborate with colleagues no matter where in the world they are located. The translation tools in Word 2010 build on this sharing strategy by offering you a variety of ways with which you can translate words, phrases, or even entire documents. What's more, you can customize the help information and ScreenTips in Word so that users accustomed to other languages can find their way around in the documents you create and share.

In this chapter, you learn how to use Word 2010 to communicate with others who might be using other languages. You also find out how to use the Mini Translator and other translation tools to convert content on the fly. Finally, you discover how to choose the translation services you use and find out about other translation tools available to help you and the colleagues you share documents with around the world.

Translating Content in Word 2010

Word 2010 offers you a variety of flexible translation options you can use to translate content and change the language displayed in the Word window, including the following:

- Translate selected words, phrases, or sections

- Translate entire documents

- Research translation options

- Change the language used in Word help screens

- Provide ScreenTips in another language

So whether you are preparing a document you plan to translate and share with others, translating a document from another language you will use yourself, or changing the Word window to help those who use another language find their way around, Word 2010 has language features to help you complete your translation tasks.

> ### Tip
> By default you can use translation features installed with your version of Microsoft Word 2010 when you translate words and phrases on the fly. You can choose from WorldLingo, an online translation utility, and Microsoft Translator, for translation options. To learn more about your choices, see the section titled "Changing and Adding Translation Services," on page 279.

> ### Note
> Displaying the Word 2010 ScreenTips in a different language requires that you download and install Microsoft Office ScreenTip Language. You can download the utility in 32-bit or 64-bit versions (download the version that corresponds with your version of Word 2010), to display ScreenTips in any of the following languages: Chinese, French, German, Japanese, Russian, and Spanish. Microsoft Office ScreenTip Language is available for Word 2010, Excel 2010, OneNote 2010, Outlook 2010, PowerPoint 2010, Publisher 2010, and Visio Professional 2010. You can download additional languages from the Microsoft Download Center.

Setting Up Languages

The process of adding and setting up languages to work with the translation features in Word 2010 is fairly simple, but there are a few steps you need to complete:

- Choose the language you want to add.

- Download the Microsoft Office 2010 Language Pack if necessary.

- Enable the language.

- Choose whether you want the language to be used in the user interface and help windows and in ScreenTips.

> **Tip**
> Another option you can choose when working with languages in Word 2010 involves setting up the keyboard to reflect the language you are using. This enables you to use characters, accents, and punctuation that are a part of that particular language.

Adding a Language

Your first step in preparing Word 2010 to work with the languages you want involves telling it what those languages are. You use Word Options to install the languages so that they will be available when you're working on your document. Here are the steps for adding an editing language to Word 2010:

1. Open the document you want to use.

2. On the Review tab, click Language in the Language group.

3. Click Language Preferences.

   The Language page of the Word Options dialog box appears, as Figure 9-1 shows.

4. Click the Add Additional Editing Languages arrow, select the language from the list, and then click Add.

The language appears in the Choose Editing Language list. Note that you can click Not Installed to download and install the Microsoft Office 2010 Language Pack if necessary.

Chapter 9

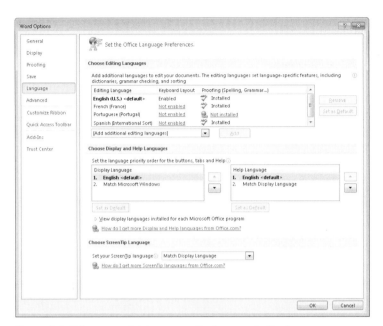

Figure 9-1 When you click Language Preferences in the Language group on the Review tab, Word Options opens so you can add and configure language choices.

Setting a Proofing Language

Word 2010 automatically uses the spelling dictionary of the selected language when you translate or enter content in another language. You can change the language used or choose not to check the spelling in the language if that's your preference. Here are the steps for indicating your choice:

1. On the Review tab, click Language in the Language group.

2. Click Set Proofing Language. The Language dialog box appears (see Figure 9-2).

3. Check the languages in use with the proofing tools.

4. If you want to bypass using the language to check spelling and grammar, select the Do Not Check Spelling Or Grammar check box.

5. Click OK to save your settings.

Figure 9-2 Let Word 2010 know whether you want to use the additional languages to check spelling and grammar in your document.

Tip

In the Languages dialog box you can also set up Word to automatically detect the language you type. This comes in handy, for example, when you use more than one language in a single document. Word can change the language (and the accompanying spelling and grammar dictionaries) when it sees that you have begun entering content in a different language.

Adding Keyboards for Languages

Of course working with files sent to you in other languages involves more than simply *reading* them—you might need to edit, revise, or add to those documents as well. For this reason you might want to customize your keyboard to suit the language you are using. This enables you to work with what might be a familiar key layout and have access to characters unique to the alphabet and language you are using.

Tip

If you want to see what other keyboards look like before you add them to your system, use the Windows Keyboard Layouts tool from MSDN's Go Global Developer Center (*http://msdn.microsoft.com/en-us/goglobal/bb964651.aspx*). Select the keyboard of the country you want to see and click Go; the site displays the keyboard for that language in a popup window.

You can make different keyboards available through Word Options, although this feature is really an aspect of the Windows 7 or Windows Vista operating system. Begin by display-ing Word Options (either by clicking File and choosing Options or by clicking Language

Preferences in the Language group on the Review tab). Then follow these steps to add a keyboard for your particular language:

1. Click the Language category in the Word Options dialog box if necessary.

2. In the box at the top of the window, click the Not Enabled link in the Keyboard Layout column for the language keyboard you want to add.

    The Text Services and Input Languages dialog box appears (see Figure 9-3).

3. Click the Add button.

4. In the Add Input Languages dialog box, scroll to the language you want to add and click the + sign (the plus symbol) to display additional options.

5. Click the + sign next to Keyboard to expand the options then select the check boxes of the items you want to add.

6. Click Other and select the check box of any additional items you want to add—for example, Ink support, as shown in Figure 9-4.

7. Click OK twice to return to the document.

Now you can choose different keyboards as you work, which, coincidentally enough, is the subject of the next section.

Figure 9-3 Choose a new keyboard for an added language in the Text Services And Input Languages dialog box.

Figure 9-4 If your system has Ink support, you can add Ink capability for the added language as well.

Changing Languages As You Type

Once you've installed and enabled the language keyboards you want to use in Word 2010, you can switch among them by clicking the language indicator in the status bar, to the right of the Word Count indicator.

You can also display the Windows Language Bar by clicking the language indicator in the system tray and choosing Show The Language Bar. This positions the Language Bar at the top of your document.

You can now change the language in use by clicking the language selection in the Language Bar. Select the new language from the list that appears (see Figure 9-5).

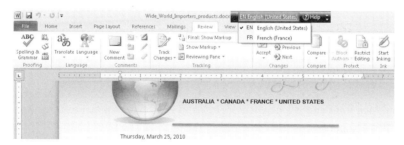

Figure 9-5 You can choose the language you want to use in the Language bar or let Word detect the language automatically.

Tip

If you want to take a look at the keyboard you're currently using, click the Start button, point to All Programs, choose Accessories, click Ease Of Access, and then On-Screen Keyboard. Your current keyboard is displayed on the screen so that you can see the key configuration. You can also type characters by clicking the keys on the on-screen keyboard if you choose.

Changing the Language Bar

When you add new languages and keyboard configurations to Word 2010, the Language Bar includes those options so that you can switch among your choices easily. The Language Bar is actually part of your Windows operating system, so the changes you make will be reflected in all the Office 2010 programs you use.

You can change the Language Bar settings by right-clicking the bar and choosing Settings from the displayed list (as shown in the following illustration). There, you can change the way items are displayed, alter the configuration of the Language Bar, or close the bar if you no longer need it.

Using the Mini Translator

The Mini Translator is a new feature in Word 2010 that makes it easy for you to translate words and phrases as you work in your documents. The Mini Translator comes in handy, for example, when you want to include select phrases in a second language or you want to include a note to a client or colleague in his or her native language. You can easily translate text in your document, copy and paste the selected text, or even have the text read aloud for you so that you know how to pronounce it.

Your first step involves choosing the language you want to use with the Mini Translator. On the Review tab, click Translate in the Language group. Click Choose Translation Language. The Choose Translation Language dialog box appears (see Figure 9-6); click the Translate To arrow, choose the language you want to use from the list that appears, and then click OK.

Figure 9-6 Choose the language you want to use for the translation.

Now you are ready to use the Mini Translator tool. Click the Translate tool in the Language group a second time then click Mini Translator. The Mini Translator pops up over the document window, offering a translation of the text you've selected (if you didn't select any text before choosing Mini Translator, it translates the word at the cursor position). The translation appears in the window at the top of the box; a set of tools beneath the translation offers ways to find out more about the translated content or copy it so that you can use it in your document (see Figure 9-7). Table 9-1 lists the various tools you'll find in the Mini Translator.

Figure 9-7 The Mini Translator pops up in your document window with a translation of the word at the cursor position or the text you've selected.

Table 9-1 **Mini Translator Tools**

Icon	Name	Description
	Expand	Displays more translation options in the Research task pane
	Copy	Copies the selected text to the Office Clipboard
	Play	Pronounces the selected text in the translated language
	Stop	Stops the pronunciation
	Help	Displays Help topics so you can search for more information

When you click the Expand tool, Word 2010 opens the Research task pane, providing additional information about the translation you've selected (see Figure 9-8). Also in the Research task pane, you can choose to set translation options, translate to a different language, and choose the references you want to use to find more information.

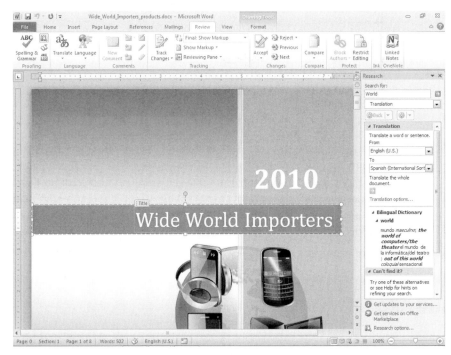

Figure 9-8 Use the Research task pane to find out more about the text you're translating.

INSIDE OUT   Get Real-Time Definitions as You Work

If translating text isn't a big need for you right now, you can still use the Mini Translator to your advantage. You can use the Mini Translator to display definitions and usage information from the Encarta Dictionary.

To change the content of the Mini Translator, click Translate in the Language group on the Review tab. Click Choose Translation Language, and in the Translation Language

Options dialog box, click the Translate To arrow and scroll all the way down to the bottom of the list. Click Encarta Dictionary then click OK. Now the Mini Translator displays information about the word at the cursor position, as shown in the following:

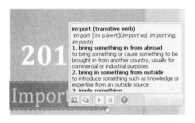

Tip

If you use the Mini Translator often, consider adding it to the Quick Access Toolbar so that you can turn it on and off easily. On the Review tab, click Translate in the Language group, and then right-click Mini Translator. Choose Add To Quick Access Toolbar, and the tool appears at the right end of the toolbar in the top-left corner of the screen.

Chapter 9

Translating Selected Text

Depending on the nature of your document, you might want to change only a selected section or two. Perhaps you're creating a product catalog for prospective clients in another culture. You might want to include a paragraph that tells a little bit about your company in the clients' native language. You can translate those opening paragraphs by using the Mini Translator tool (which is fine for small amounts of text), or you can use the Translate Selected Text tool in the Translate list to make the translation for you and display additional resources about the translated content.

The great thing about using Translate Selected Text is that it gives you additional options that might weigh into the final translation you ultimately use in your document. When you select the text you want to translate, choose Translate Selected Text on the Review tab; the Research task pane appears, in which you can click Insert to add the translation directly to your document. The Research task pane also contains links to additional resources you can use to research further (see Figure 9-9).

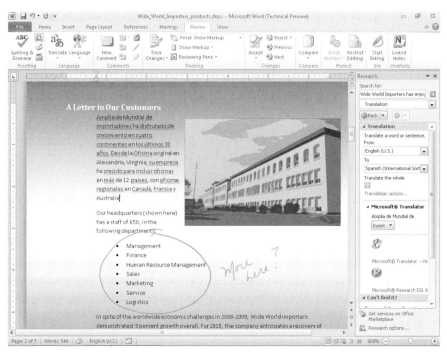

Figure 9-9 You can choose Translate Selected Text to display the Research pane and complete the translation for text sections.

Translating Entire Documents

If you're putting together a document that will be shared with colleagues in another coun-try—or you've received a proposal in a different language that you need to translate—you can use Word's Translate Document tool to translate the entire document. By default this service uses the WorldLingo translation tool and shows both versions of the document—the original language and the translated version you specify—in your browser window. If you click the link that lets you know translation updates are available, the system will update to Microsoft Translator, which is a comprehensive online translation tool being offered by Microsoft.

CAUTION

Be aware that when you translate the entire document using WorldLingo, you are sending the document to an online service. For this reason, avoid sending information that might be considered confidential in your company and, if you're in doubt about the security needed for a specific document, be sure to ask your administrator before translating the file using this option.

Begin by opening the document you want to translate. Then on the Review tab, click Translate in the Language group. Choose Translate Document. (If you want to change the translation language, click Choose Translation Language before you select Translate Document.)

Word alerts you that in order to complete the translation, your document will be sent to an online service. Click Send to continue. The document appears in your browser window, translated into the language you selected (see Figure 9-10).

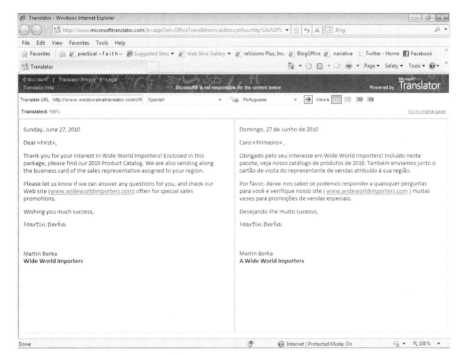

Figure 9-10 When you translate an entire document, the document is displayed as a Web page, showing both the original language (on the left) and the translation (on the right).

Changing and Adding Translation Services

When you first install Word 2010, you'll discover that WorldLingo and Microsoft Translation are the two translation services that are used to translate words, phrases, and documents as you work. You can select the translation service the program uses or choose one that is not listed by default. This means you can add custom services or even create your own dictionary or online translation utility to meet your particular document translation needs. You can customize the translation services in all core Office 2010 applications.

Choosing a Different Service

To change the Word 2010 translation service, follow these steps:

1. On the Review tab, in the Proofing group, click Research.

   The Research task pane appears (if it wasn't already displayed).

2. Click the arrow to the right of the reference field then choose Translation (see Figure 9-11).

3. Click Translation Options in the list area.

   The Translation Options dialog box appears, offering two lists of translation choices. The top of the dialog box lists translations used in the bilingual dictionary resident on your computer, and the second list suggests language pairs available through the machine translation service you select.

4. Select the check box of each language pair you want to translate.

5. For each of the selected language pairs, click the arrow and choose the translation service you want to use (see Figure 9-12).

6. After you've made all your selections, click OK to save your changes.

Figure 9-11 Click Translation options in the Research task pane to make choices about translation services.

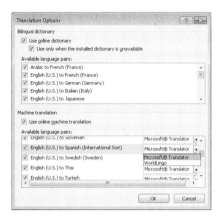

Figure 9-12 Click the arrow to choose a translation service for a particular language pair.

Creating Custom Translations

Of course, translating text is a challenging task, given the complexities and subtle usage considerations of dozens of different languages and cultures. Grammar, sentence structure, and pronoun use vary greatly among languages, and in some cases you might find that the translation offered is close but not exactly accurate for the task at hand.

Although the translations available through various online services are continually being improved, developers might decide to create a set of custom translations for specific words that are used often in common documents. For example, if you regularly work with a team in China, you might want to create a set of common terms your department uses regularly in communications with the Chinese team. You can then share a custom bilingual dictionary with your team that includes your custom translations so that they are available to everyone in your department.

You can create a bilingual translation dictionary by using the Translation Dictionaries Content Development Kit. Find out more about how to develop this custom solution by reading the article, "Creating a Custom Service for Office 2010 Mini Translator," available on *http://blogs.technet.com*.

Adding a New Translation Service

You can add a new translation service to those available in the Translation Options dialog box by displaying the Research task pane and clicking Research Options at the bottom of the pane. In the Research options dialog box, you can review all the research services currently being used by your version of Word. At the bottom of the dialog box, click Add Services (see Figure 9-13).

In the Add Services dialog box, click in the Address box and type the Web address of the service you'd like to use. This could be another subscription translation service available online or a service you've created and posted on your company intranet.

Click Add to include the service in the list of providers available in the Translation Options dialog box. Now you will be able to choose the new service from the list when you make translation choices for language pairs. When you choose a language by using Choose Translation Language in the Translate list, Word will automatically use the service you've assigned to the language pair you want to translate.

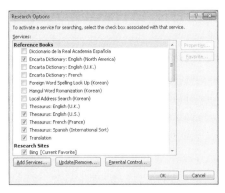

Figure 9-13 You can add your favorite translation service to the list by clicking Add Services.

Using Bidirectional Text

As you begin to expand the number of languages you use to relate with clients and colleagues around the world, it is likely that at some point you'll need to explore working with bidirectional text. A number of languages—most notably, Arabic, Persian, and Hebrew—begin writing at the right side of the page and move to the left. This is known as RTL (right-to-left); languages like English are known as LTR (left-to-right).

When you are creating a document that includes both RTL and LTR text, you need to be able to make choices about the direction of the text. When you install Arabic, Persian, or Hebrew in Word 2010, additional bidirectional features become available that you can use to control the way the text is displayed in the document. Here are some of the features you might want to change if you work with bidirectional text:

- **Change paragraph flow.**   New tools appear in the Paragraph group on the Home tab, with which you can change the direction of paragraph text. The tools appear as paragraph marks with small arrows, indicating text direction.

- **Add color to diacritics.**   On the Advanced tab of the Word Options dialog box, you can apply color to diacritics. Diacritics are the small marks that accent a character in an alphabet. You can instruct Word 2010 to add color to the diacritical marks by selecting the Diacritics check box and choosing the color you want to apply.

- **Document view.**   Also on the Advanced tab of the Word Options dialog box, you can set the Document View setting to control whether the text is displayed from left-to-right (LTR) or right-to-left (RTL).

- **Section direction.**   You can set the text direction in the current section. Choose Layout in the Page Setup group on the Page Layout tab then choose Section Direction.

- **Table properties.**   You can change the direction of text in table cells by right-clicking the table and choosing Table Properties. Change the Table Direction field at the bottom of the dialog box to change the flow of table text.

Working with the Document Grid

If you regularly work with Chinese, Japanese, or Korean, you can use Word's Document Grid to help you control line and character placement in your documents. You can work with Document Grid settings in the Page Setup dialog box. Begin on the Page Layout tab and click the dialog launcher in the bottom-right corner of the Page Setup group. In the Page Setup dialog box, select the Document Grid tab (see Figure 9-14). Note that the Document Grid will appear only if you have installed one of these languages.

Figure 9-14 Use the Document Grid to control line and character spacing for East Asian text.

Chapter 9

Specifying Document Grid Settings

The Document Grid tab is where you control the text flow, number of columns, number of characters per line, character pitch (which is the spacing between characters), number of lines per page, and line pitch. To use the Document Grid features, follow these steps:

1. On the Page Layout tab, click the Page Setup dialog launcher to open the Page Setup dialog box, and then select the Document Grid tab.

2. If you want the text to be shown vertically (appearing top to bottom as you type), in the Text Flow area, click Vertical. Otherwise, for traditional right-to-left text display, leave Horizontal selected.

   You can enter a number of columns in the Columns box if you are working with a multicolumn document. Notice that the Preview image adjusts to display your page setup settings while you work.

3. To turn on the Grid feature, select one of the following options:

   - **Specify Line Grid Only**   Makes only the settings in the Lines area on the Document Grid tab available so that you can choose the amount of space between lines (by selecting the number of lines you want to appear on the page) and the pitch, or spacing, between lines.

   - **Specify Line And Character Grid**   Makes all settings in both Character and Lines areas available. This setting enables you to choose both the number of characters per line and the number of lines per page. You can also choose the pitch of both characters and lines.

   - **Text Snaps To Character Grid**   Disables the Pitch settings and gives you the means to choose the number of characters per line and lines per page.

4. Click the Apply To arrow, choose the option that specifies the portion of the document to which you want to apply the grid, and then click OK.

If you changed the text direction on the Document Grid tab for the entire document, Word automatically updates any existing content after you click OK. If you retained the original text direction prior to the cursor and applied the This Point Forward setting, Word applies the grid effects for existing and new content from the point of the cursor's location forward. If necessary, Word begins a new page to separate content with different formats.

Displaying the Drawing Grid

You can display the drawing grid on your page to help you align objects and text, regardless of your language settings. To toggle the display of gridlines, simply navigate to the View tab and, in the Show group, click Gridlines.

If you installed support for East Asian languages, click the Drawing Grid button on the Document Grid tab in the Page Setup dialog box to access the drawing grid settings. Or on the Page Layout tab, in the Arrange group, click Align then click Grid Settings. Figure 9-15 displays the Drawing Grid dialog box.

Figure 9-15 You can customize the display of the document grid by modifying the Drawing Grid dialog box settings.

> **Note**
> You must be working in Print Layout view to see the document grid. It is not visible in any other view.

Working with Other Translation Tools

Because of our growing global economy and the reach of the World Wide Web, translation tools are more in demand than ever, and this means that new tools are being developed all the time. When you are working with others who are translating to English, they can use the Microsoft Research ESL Assistant to ensure that their English translation is as accurate and understandable as possible. You'll find Microsoft Research ESL Assistant at *www.eslassistant.com* (see Figure 9-16). The service looks for common translation mistakes (such as pronouns and prepositions) and suggests corrections.

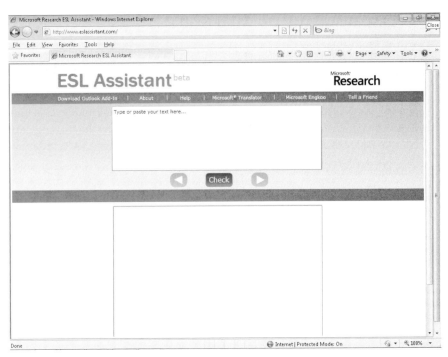

Figure 9-16 Microsoft Research ESL Assistant helps you weed out translation mistakes before you share your document with others.

> **Tip**
>
> You can also access the Microsoft Research ESL Assistant and Microsoft Engkoo through the Research task pane when you have selected Translate options.

Microsoft Engkoo is a research tool provided by Microsoft Research Asia that enables you to search and translate words and phrases in Asian languages. Go to *www.engkoo.com* to use the Web-based tool to search, translate, and correct your text (see Figure 9-17).

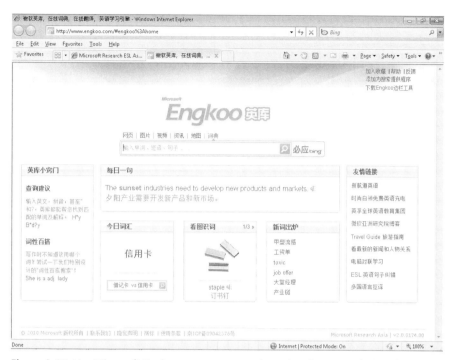

Figure 9-17 Use Microsoft Engkoo to convert, search, and evaluate translations for Asian languages.

What's Next?

Now that you know how to translate the text you receive and share with colleagues and clients in other cultures, you're ready to dive deeper into the accuracy of the documents you create. The next chapter shows you how to use a variety of proofing tools to make sure that your document is in great shape—whether you want to want to run the spelling checker, assess your grammar, or expand your word use with the Word thesaurus. Along the way, you'll also find out how to incorporate references and bibliographies to provide even more resources for interested readers.

Chapter 9

Editing, Proofing, and Using Reference Tools

Editing Tools in Word 2010. 289

Spell It Right!. 290

Proofing Your Document 295

Judging Your Document's Readability Level 306

AutoCorrecting Your Document 307

Adding References in Word 2010 312

Adding and Managing Sources 315

Inserting a Citation. 317

Generating a Bibliography 319

Adding Footnotes and Endnotes 320

Inserting Cross-References 325

What's Next? 329

A dding content to your document is one thing, and translating it so that colleagues all around the world can read it is another. But as you put together a major project— perhaps a slick new 100-page catalog, a compelling grant proposal, or an annual report that you hope will inspire your top stakeholders—getting things right is a major concern. A few easily missed typos can make the whole report look bad; a style or tone that speaks over the head of your audience will leave your message misunderstood; and research without the appropriate footnotes can make you look like you don't know what you're talking about after all.

Luckily, the proofing tools in Microsoft Word 2010 can help you safeguard against these kinds of errors. By running a series of checks—for example, a simple spell check and a grammar check—you can make sure your document is as accurate as it can be. And by using Word's built-in AutoCorrect feature, you can help the program learn where you need a little extra support (and provide it seamlessly) as you're busy crafting the content you want to share. Finally, Word includes a number of tools you can use to add references of all kinds—citations, footnotes, bibliographies, and more—to the projects you create. This chapter introduces you to these proofing tools and methods and helps you make sure the content you produce really shines.

Editing Tools in Word 2010

All of the tools in this chapter play key roles in helping to ensure that your document is the best it can be. And in many cases, they can help you increase your productivity and get your document ready faster by automating common tasks. Here's a list of some of the editing and proofing tools you are likely to use in Word 2010:

- **Spell Checker** Checks the spelling of your document as you add content and flags words that are spelled incorrectly or are unrecognized. You can add your own custom dictionaries with Word 2010 to allow for specialized terminology related to your particular industry or area of expertise.

- **Grammar Checker**   Evaluates your written text to ensure that it is grammatically correct and identifies stylistic or usage problems. You can also use the grammar checker to assess the readability of your document.

- **Thesaurus**   Provides a list of synonyms and antonyms of selected words in your document so that you can vary your word choice and enhance reader interest and the readability of your content.

- **AutoCorrect**   Automatically corrects typos as you enter new content. You can teach AutoCorrect how to work with your particular style, so you can also use it as a short-hand method for entering repeat phrases.

Other Checks Worth Doing

In this chapter you learn about various tools you can use to make sure your content is as accurate as you can make it, but there are other checks you'll want to do before you share your document with others. After you use the editing and proofing tools described in this chapter, you'll want to you use the following quality-control tools to ensure that your document is in good enough shape to share:

- **Inspect Document**   This evaluates your content to verify that it doesn't contain any personal or sensitive information

- **Check Accessibility**   Assesses your file to make sure that people with differing ability levels will be able to read, hear, and understand what you've included

- **Check Compatibility**   This tool tests the document to ensure that others who might be using previous versions of Word will be able to open and view it

To find out more about these types of quality-control checks, see Chapter 20, "Securing Your Word Documents."

Spell It Right!

It's unfortunate that a tiny, easy-to-make mistake like a simple typo can have such an impact on the overall impression your document makes; but it's a fact of life in the business world. If you want to hold on to your credibility with respect to the documents you share with others, spell things right.

Word has always had a spell check tool, and in each version of the program, the spelling checker becomes more powerful and more flexible. In Word 2010 you can easily choose the language for the dictionary you use, and you can create and add custom dictionaries so that you are always using the most recent, approved terminology for your particular industry area. In addition to setting your spelling options and exceptions, you can also have Word evaluate the use of your words in context, which is a big plus when you need to make sure you have the right word in the right spot.

Looking at Error Notifications

Word automatically checks for proofing errors whenever you open a document or type content in your document. By default, Word flags the errors it finds using the following system:

- Spelling errors are underlined with red

- Grammar errors are underlined with green

- Contextual spelling errors are underlined with blue

> **Note**
>
> A blue wavy line is also used for the Mark Formatting Inconsistencies option, which is found in the Advanced section of Word Options and turned off by default. If both options are enabled, a quick way to way to distinguish which type of error is being identified is to right-click the word, or words, and note the offered suggestion.
>
> Suggestions for contextual spelling errors will be alternate word choices; suggestions for formatting inconsistencies will offer to replace the direct formatting with a defined style.

Word also displays Proofing Status in the status bar (see Figure 10-1). The icon indicates whether your document contains any potential errors. If errors are detected, the icon contains an X mark; if no errors are found, the icon contains a check mark. When you hover over the icon with your cursor, the ScreenTip will tell you whether you have errors to correct. Click the Message box to display a list of potential suggestions for the error found.

Figure 10-1 Word lets you know about any errors by showing a notification icon in the status bar.

> **Tip**
> If you do not see the Proofing Status indicator in the status bar, right-click the status
> bar to display the Customizable Status Bar list. Select Spelling And Grammar Check to
> turn on the display.

Fixing Flagged Errors Quickly, Case by Case

After Word marks potential proofing errors, you can resolve each issue on a case-by-case
basis. To access options for fixing a potential error, you can right-click text that has a wavy
underline or click Proofing Status in the status bar to select the next instance of a potential
error. Both techniques display a shortcut menu containing error-fixing options. Different
options are available depending on whether the potential error is a spelling issue, a grammar issue, or a contextual spelling issue. The shortcut menu for a contextual spelling issue is
shown in Figure 10-2.

Figure 10-2 When an error is found, Word provides a suggestion and offers other options for
further research.

Based on the type of error Word flags and whether or not you think the word is used incorrectly, you can choose from among a number of possible responses displayed at the top of
the context menu. Depending on whether you want to correct the word, ignore it, choose a
different language, or look up the word online, Word provides you with a context menu of
choices. Table 10-1 lists the different options you have for working with the potential error.

Table 10-1 **Responding to Proofing Notifications**

Proofing Option	Description
List of Suggestions	For potential spelling or contextual spelling errors, provides one or more words that might represent the correctly spelled version of the word in your text.
	For potential grammar errors, provides a brief description of the problem or possible replacement text.
Ignore	Instructs Word to ignore only the flagged proofing error.
Ignore All	Instructs Word to ignore all instances of the flagged proofing error in the current document.
Add To Dictionary (Spelling only)	Adds the word as it's spelled in your document to your custom dictionary, which ensures that the term won't be flagged as a potential error in the future. (Custom dictionaries are discussed in detail in the section titled "Managing Custom Dictionaries," on page <OV>.)
AutoCorrect (Spelling only)	Use this to add an AutoCorrect entry for the misspelled word. You can have the misspelled word automatically replaced with the correctly spelled word by clicking the correctly spelled word in the AutoCorrect menu, as shown in Figure 10-2. Alternatively, you can manually add an AutoCorrect entry. For more information on AutoCorrect, see page 307.
Language	Specifies that a particular word or phrase is written in another language. If proofreading tools are installed for that language, Word uses the appropriate language dictionary to check the text. If a corresponding language dictionary is not installed, Word will skip the specified words without marking them as potential errors
Spelling or Grammar	Displays the Spelling or Grammar dialog box, which provides access to additional proofing options. These dialog boxes are similar to the Spelling And Grammar dialog box, which you can access on the Review tab in the Proofing group or by pressing F7.
About This Sentence (Grammar only)	Provides additional information about the potential error flagged by Word.
Look Up	Displays the Research pane and presents information from reference sources about the flagged text. If your computer is online, you can find additional information about the term by using other research services and resources such as encyclopedias and Web sites. Note that this option provides information about the flagged text but doesn't necessarily present a grammatical fix.

Chapter 10

If Word flags a spelling error, the AutoCorrect option will also appear in the contextual menu. When you click AutoCorrect, a list of possible spellings appears. You can click one of the displayed words to replace the flagged word with the correct one (see Figure 10-3).

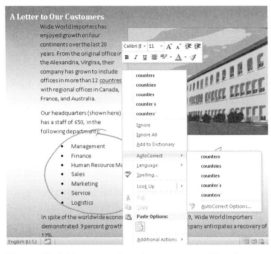

Figure 10-3 You can select the correct spelling for a word in the AutoCorrect menu, and if you make the same mistake in the future, it will be automatically replaced with the correctly spelled word.

CAUTION

To create a case-insensitive AutoCorrect entry, the replace characters must be lower-case. If the entry you wish to add contains uppercase characters, you must manually create the AutoCorrect entry. Otherwise, the case must be identical in order for it to be corrected.

You can also resolve spelling and grammar issues by correcting your text without accessing the shortcut menus. When you manually correct a proofing error, Word automatically removes the wavy underline.

Tip
To use the keyboard to jump to the next proofing error, press Alt+F7.

Proofing Your Document

At times, you might prefer to check your spelling and grammar all at once instead of right-clicking every instance of a potential error. In those cases, you can use the Spelling And Grammar dialog box (Figure 10-4) to work through your document or a block of selected text. To access the Spelling And Grammar dialog box, on the Review tab, click Spelling & Grammar or press F7.

Figure 10-4 You can click Spelling & Grammar on the Review tab to open the Spelling And Grammar dialog box.

You can click in the upper portion of the Spelling And Grammar dialog box and make editing changes. This dialog box is also modeless, which means you can leave the dialog box open, click in the document, make modifications, and then resume the proofing check.

Tip

To check only a portion of your document, select the desired text and then click the Spelling & Grammar button on the Review tab to display the Spelling And Grammar dialog box. When the end of the selected text is reached, Word displays a message stating that it has finished checking the selected text and asking whether you'd like to continue checking the remainder of the document.

INSIDE OUT   Activating the Grammar Checker

You can control whether the grammar checker is activated by selecting or clearing the Check Grammar check box in the Spelling And Grammar dialog box, but to access this particular check box only, click Spelling & Grammar on the Review tab or press F7. If you display the Spelling dialog box or the Grammar dialog box by right-clicking an underlined potential error, the Check Grammar check box will not be available.

Chapter 10

Controlling Proofing Display and Exceptions

In general, while you are creating and editing a document, keeping an eye on spelling and grammatical errors is a must. And using the automated proofing tools is an efficient way to find your potential proofing errors quickly. However, certain types of documents, or portions of documents, can be difficult to read due to the red and green wavy lines that might appear throughout the content. This might not be the result strictly of spelling or grammatical errors either; some documents might contain a lot of abbreviations, slang, and words that aren't in the standard dictionary. Or in the case of technical documents, they might contain fragmented sentences, blocks of programming code, and words that aren't usually capitalized. So in these situations, the content is correct but the proofing marks detract from the document's readability. The following provides a few options that you can use to suppress the display of proofing marks and to specify that perceived spelling and grammar errors should be ignored by all proofing tools. We also have recommendations for using each option:

- **Check Spelling As You Type** and **Mark Grammar As You Type**   These options are found in Word Options in the Proofing section. If you clear the option for Check Spelling As You Type, the display of the red and blue wavy lines will be suppressed when viewing a document. If you clear the option for Mark Grammar As You Type, green wavy lines will be suppressed when you view a document. However, you can still use the Spelling & Grammar feature to check the document for proofing errors. These are application options which means they are specific to your Word installation and apply to all documents. It's recommended that they be used for your personal use only because they will not change the way others view your documents.

- **Hide Spelling Errors In This Document Only** and **Hide Grammar Errors In This Document Only**   These options are also found in Word Options in the Proofing section. Their effect is similar to disabling the Check Spelling As You Type and Mark Grammar As You Type; however, they are saved with the document, as opposed to application options. Spelling errors or grammar errors are not completely ignored—you can still use the Spelling & Grammar feature—but all red and blue wavy lines (if you select the Hide Spelling Errors In This Document Only option) and green wavy lines (if you select the Hide Grammar Errors In This Document Only option) are suppressed when you view the document. If others will be viewing the document, it's recommend that these options be used only after a document has been finalized.

CAUTION

If the document is still in the editing stages and will be edited by others, selecting Hide Spelling Errors In This Document Only and Hide Grammar Errors In This Document Only could result in documents that contain legitimate proofing errors. Many Word users have grown accustomed to Word automatically proofing their documents as they type. If they are not familiar with the proofing options—and if they do not see the red, green, or blue wavy lines—then proofing errors can be inadvertently overlooked.

- **Mark As Final**   You can find this option on the File tab by clicking Protect Document on the Info tab. When a document is marked as final, it cannot be edited, and proofing errors are suppressed from view. It's recommended that this option be used when working in a collaborative environment to let others know the document has been finalized. Note that Mark As Final is not intended to be used for document security because other users can turn off this option and edit the document. Additionally, proofing errors will return to view when Mark As Final is turned off.

- **Do Not Check Spelling Or Grammar**   To display this option, on the Review tab, click Language to select Set Proofing Language. You can select the Do Not Check Spelling Or Grammar check box to turn off the spelling and grammar checker. You might want to reserve this option for those times when you want to suppress proofing in only portions of a document, as opposed to the entire document, such as for blocks of programming code or medical terminology.

Tip

Even though the spelling and grammar tools in Word are effective and helpful, they shouldn't replace proofreading by a real person. These features can't definitively correct your text in all instances. Instead of thinking of the spelling and grammar checking tools as a teacher correcting your work, visualize an assistant who taps you on the shoulder whenever your text seems to go astray and then offers advice on how to fix the problem. Ultimately, you'll need to read through your document carefully to ensure its accuracy.

Chapter 10

Configuring Spelling and Grammar Options

You can control a few spelling options by configuring the Proofing settings in Word Options, as shown in Figure 10-5. On the File tab, click Options, and then click the Proofing category. Table 10-2 provides a description of each of the proofing options. As you can see, some options apply to all Microsoft Office programs, and others relate only to your Word document. By configuring these spelling checker options, you can customize spelling tasks to be as streamlined as possible for the particular types of documents you create.

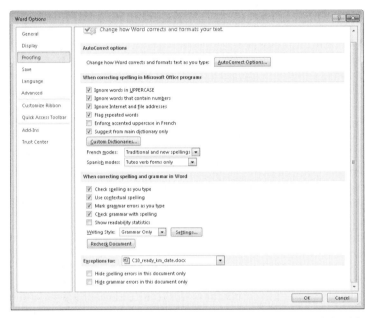

Figure 10-5 The Proofing options allow you to specify how Word should proof your documents.

Table 10-2 Spelling Options for Microsoft Office

Spelling Option	Description
Ignore Words In UPPERCASE	Excludes words in all uppercase from spelling checks. The spelling checker would be hard pressed to understand all acronyms, so this check box is selected by default. If you use a number of acronyms—and you'd like to check them—you can add the acronyms to your custom dictionary and clear the Ignore Words In UPPERCASE check box.
Ignore Words That Contain Numbers	By default, any words that contain numbers are ignored by the spelling checker. You'll especially appreciate this option if you're proofreading documents such as catalogs or price lists in which product codes are combinations of numbers and letters.

Spelling Option	Description
Ignore Internet And File Addresses	By default, the spelling checker ignores Internet addresses, file path names, and e-mail addresses. For example, text such as *C:\clients\microsoft* and *www.microsoft.com* is automatically ignored by the spelling checker. If you prefer to check these types of elements, clear the Ignore Internet And File Addresses check box.
Flag Repeated Words	Ignores repeated words. For example, if you select this option, the spelling checker does not flag *Walla Walla* as a mistake. (Interestingly, if you use *WallaWalla*, it is flagged as a spelling error and the proposed suggestion is *Walla Walla*. Keep in mind that you are your own best proofreader.)
Enforce Accented Uppercase In French	Used with the French (Canada) proofing language. French words that contain uppercase letters that are missing an accent mark are identified.
Suggest From Main Dictionary Only	Word checks all open dictionaries during its spelling check, including the main dictionary and your custom dictionaries. Use this option if you prefer to use only the main dictionary.
French Modes	Used with the French language. Enables spelling rules that predate the French Academy of Language spelling reform of 1990 and those that are recommended by the spelling reform.
Spanish Modes	Used with the Spanish language. Enables you to choose the verb forms you want to use in Spanish translations.
Check Spelling as You Type	Turns on the spell check feature so that Word flags potentially misspelled words as you add content.
Use Contextual Spelling	Enables the contextual spelling check so that Word evaluates context when flagging unrecognized words.
Mark Grammar Errors As You Type	Turns on the grammar checker so that potential grammar problems are flagged as you enter content.
Show Readability Statistics	Evaluates and displays the readability of the document.
Writing Style	Enables you to choose whether to check grammar only or the grammar and style of your document. Click Settings to indicate what you want Word to check.

Chapter 10

Tip

The Recheck Document button under the heading, When Correcting Spelling And Grammar In Word, gives you the opportunity to recheck a document for words and grammar you previously chose to ignore. This feature is also useful for rechecking a document after you've modified your spelling options.

Setting Grammar Rules

You can easily change the rules used when Word checks the grammar in your document. For example, you might want to use passive voice or start a sentence with *And*. You might also want Word to check for punctuation errors, such as two spaces after a period.

> **Note**
> According to the Chicago Manual of Style, typing two spaces between sentences when using a word processing program is no longer necessary.

You can specify your preferred grammar settings in Word Options by using the following steps:

1. On the File tab, click Options, click Proofing, and then specify whether you want the grammar checker to check grammar only or grammar and style by selecting the appropriate option in the Writing Style list.

2. Click Settings. The Grammar Settings dialog box appears, as shown in Figure 10-6.

Figure 10-6 You can choose which grammar and style rules you want Word to use when it searches for potential grammatical errors.

3. Click the arrow in the Require area to instruct Word whether to check for the potential errors.

4. Select or clear the check boxes in the Grammar area to specify whether Word checks each of the characteristics in the document.

5. Scroll down the list and set the Style characteristics you want Word to check, and then click OK to save your changes.

> **Note**
>
> Grammar Only is the default setting. Grammar Style—such as passive voice or start-
> ing a sentence with a conjunction (for example, starting a sentence with *And*)—is not
> checked by default.

An important aspect to keep in mind is that the grammar settings are application specific;
this means they are not stored in the document and the rules will apply to all documents. If
you are sharing your documents with others, and if they do not use the same settings, they
might see different grammatical errors when they view the document.

> **Tip**
>
> When viewing the Grammar Settings dialog box, click the Help button (?) to quickly
> display Help content that provides brief descriptions of the grammar and writing style
> options found in the dialog box.

Managing Custom Dictionaries

When you install Word, you also install a main dictionary. The spelling checker uses the
main dictionary whenever it checks your document for spelling errors. However, you can
also add words to your custom dictionary or add existing dictionaries to the list of dictionaries Word uses to check documents.

When you click Add To Dictionary in the Spelling And Grammar dialog box, Word adds the
selected term to your custom dictionary. After you add terms to your custom dictionary,
Word checks both the main dictionary and your custom dictionary (named CUSTOM.DIC by
default) whenever you run the spelling checker. You can also edit and delete terms in your
custom dictionary as well as create additional custom dictionaries that you can use whenever necessary.

Modifying Custom Dictionaries

As mentioned, you can add terms to your default custom dictionary by clicking Add To
Dictionary in the Spelling And Grammar dialog box. You can also add terms to your custom
dictionary by right-clicking words that are flagged by a red wavy underline and choosing
Add To Dictionary from the shortcut menu. Because adding terms to the custom dictionary is so easy, words that shouldn't be included, such as words or abbreviations that should
be ignored in one document but might be incorrect in other documents might need to be

removed. For example, you might want to allow the word *lite* in a marketing piece but have Word catch the misspelling in other documents. If you regularly add terms to your custom dictionary, or if you suspect that incorrect terms have been added, you should review and manually correct your dictionary to ensure accuracy.

To access and modify your custom dictionary, follow these steps:

1. On the File tab, click Options and then click Proofing. (Alternatively, click the Options button in the Spelling And Grammar dialog box.)

2. Click the Custom Dictionaries button.

    The Custom Dictionaries dialog box appears, as shown in Figure 10-7. Notice that the CUSTOM.DIC dictionary is selected by default.

Figure 10-7 The Custom Dictionaries dialog box provides options for creating and modifying custom dictionaries that Word uses in conjunction with the main dictionary.

3. Select a dictionary in the Dictionary List and then click Edit Word List to display a dictionary editing dialog box, as shown in Figure 10-8.

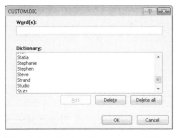

Figure 10-8 The dictionary editing dialog box provides an easy way to create and modify custom dictionaries.

4. Within this dialog box, you can perform the following actions:

    *   **Add a term to a custom dictionary.**   Enter a term in the Word box and then click Add or press Enter. The terms are automatically arranged alphabetically.

- **Delete a term included in a custom dictionary.**   Select a word in the Dictionary list and then click Delete. Or, if you want to remove all words in the list, click Delete All.

5. Click OK twice when you have finished modifying your custom dictionary.

When you add terms to a custom dictionary, keep the following points in mind:

- Words cannot be more than 64 characters and cannot contain spaces.

- The custom dictionary is limited to 5,000 words and cannot be larger than 64 kilobytes (KB).

- Dictionaries are American National Standards Institute (ANSI) text files. This means they can only contain characters that conform to the ANSI encoding standard.

With careful maintenance of your custom dictionary, including adding frequently used terms, you can keep your spelling checker working at peak performance and increase your efficiency. With a well-maintained custom dictionary, you'll avoid having to continually dismiss terms that appear regularly in your documents but aren't included in the main dictionary.

Creating New Custom Dictionaries

At times, you might work on jargon-laden documents that use very specific terminology. For example, if you occasionally work on medical documents that contain terms such as *brachytherapy, echography,* and *osteotomy,* you could create a custom dictionary named Medical that you could activate whenever you're using medical terminology. To create a custom dictionary that you can use in addition to CUSTOM.DIC, follow these steps:

1. Display Word Options and the Proofing options. (Alternatively, click the Options button in the Spelling And Grammar dialog box.) Then click the Custom Dictionaries button.

2. In the Custom Dictionaries dialog box, click New.

    The Create Custom Dictionary dialog box appears. This dialog box displays a list of the custom dictionaries currently available to Word in the UProof folder.

3. Type a name for the new custom dictionary in the File Name box then click Save.

    When you create a custom dictionary, the file is saved with the .dic extension in the UProof folder, along with the CUSTOM.DIC file and any other custom dictionaries you've created.

Chapter 10

After you create a new dictionary, it is added to the Dictionary List in the Custom Dictionaries dialog box and its check box is selected. When the spelling checker runs, it refers to the main dictionary and all custom dictionaries that are selected in the Dictionary List.

> ## Tip
> **When you want to use your custom dictionaries, make sure that the Suggest From Main Dictionary Only option is cleared (the default setting) in the Proofing section of Word Options. If this check box is selected, Word won't refer to your custom dictionaries when the spelling checker is started.**

To add terms to a new custom dictionary, select the dictionary in the Custom Dictionaries dialog box, click Edit Word List, and then manually enter terms. You can also add terms to the dictionary as you work, as described in the section titled "Choosing a Default Dictionary," on page 305.

Adding Custom Dictionaries

Most of the time, you'll either use the CUSTOM.DIC dictionary or create a new custom dictionary. However, you can also add existing dictionaries to the Dictionary List in the Custom Dictionaries dialog box. For example, if you have *Stedman's Medical Dictionary* on your computer, you can add it to the list of custom dictionaries. Adding an existing dictionary is similar to creating a new custom dictionary. To do so, follow these steps:

1. Display Word Options and the Proofing options. (Alternatively, click the Options button in the Spelling And Grammar dialog box.) Then click the Custom Dictionaries button.

2. In the Custom Dictionaries dialog box, click Add to display the Add Custom Dictionary dialog box, which looks almost identical to the Create Custom Dictionaries dialog box.

3. Navigate to the desired dictionary file (you might need to consult your documentation for the custom dictionary to determine the location) and double-click the dictionary's file name.

   The dictionary will appear in the Dictionary List, and its check box will be selected.

By default, custom dictionaries are stored in the folder C:\Users*user name*\AppData\Roaming\Microsoft\UProof. If you have a custom dictionary file (with a .dic extension), you can store the file in the UProof folder. You can then access it from the Custom Dictionaries dialog box.

Converting an Existing List of Terms to a Custom Dictionary

If you have an existing list of terms or a style sheet containing terms you frequently use, you can quickly create a custom dictionary without having to retype or copy all the terms in the dictionary editing dialog box. To convert a list to a custom dictionary, follow these steps:

1.   Verify that each term appears on a separate line with no blank lines inserted between terms. Then save your document as a plain text (.txt) file and close the file.

2.   Right-click the file name in Windows Explorer and rename the file to include the .dic extension. (You must be viewing file extensions when renaming the file.)

3.   After you rename the file, store it in your UProof folder.

The next time you display the Add Custom Dictionary dialog box, you'll see your newly created dictionary listed among the available custom dictionaries. Double-click the newly added dictionary to add it to the Dictionary List in the Custom Dictionaries dialog box.

Choosing a Default Dictionary

By default, all terms you add to a dictionary while running a spelling check are added to the CUSTOM.DIC dictionary. You can change the custom dictionary in which added words are stored by changing the default custom dictionary. By reconfiguring your default dictionary, you can quickly build very specific custom dictionaries without having to enter terms manually.

Let's return to the medical dictionary example. While you're working on a medical document, you could specify the medical dictionary as your default custom dictionary. Then whenever you click Add To Dictionary, the specified term would be added to the medical dictionary instead of CUSTOM.DIC. Configuring Word in this way would serve two purposes: It would avoid adding unnecessary terms to the CUSTOM.DIC dictionary, and it would save you from manually typing terms in the medical dictionary.

To specify which custom dictionary serves as the default file, perform the following actions:

1.   Display Word Options, click Proofing, and then click the Custom Dictionaries button to display the Custom Dictionaries dialog box.

2.   Select the custom dictionary you want to be the default in the Dictionary List.

3.   Click Change Default.

The default custom dictionary will appear at the top of the list with *(Default)* after its name. Now when you add a word to your custom dictionary (by clicking Add To Dictionary in the Spelling And Grammar dialog box or right-clicking a word with a red wavy underline and then clicking Add To Dictionary in the shortcut menu), the term will be added to the new default custom dictionary.

> **Tip**
>
> Most of the time, you won't need to have Word check all your custom dictionaries every time you're working on a document. Therefore, you might want to disable some custom dictionaries until you need them. Other times, you might want to remove a custom dictionary from your Dictionary list altogether. You can do this without deleting the dictionary file. In some cases, you might want to delete a dictionary file because you no longer use it. In the Custom Dictionaries dialog box, disable, remove, or delete a dictionary by clicking the button appropriate to the task you want to complete.

Judging Your Document's Readability Level

You can configure Word to display a readability level for a document after you finish checking spelling and grammar. Word determines readability levels by assigning Flesch Reading Ease scores and Flesch-Kincaid Grade Level scores to documents. These scores are obtained by rating the average number of syllables per word and average number of words per sentence. The Flesch Reading Ease score is based on a 100-point scale, in which a higher score means that a document is easier to read. Scores ranging from 60 to 70 are a good fit for most general purpose documents. The Flesch-Kincaid Grade Level score rates text based on U.S. school grade level. For example, a score of 8.0 means that an eighth grader should be able to understand the text. Most documents intended for the general public should score near the 7.0 or 8.0 level.

To display reading statistics, select the Show Readability Statistics option and completely check your document's spelling and grammar as follows:

1. On the File tab, click Options.

2. Click Proofing, select the Show Readability Statistics check box then click OK.

3. Run a complete spelling and grammar check by clicking Spelling & Grammar on the Review tab, or pressing F7.

   When the check is complete, Word automatically displays information about the reading level of the document, as shown in Figure 10-9.

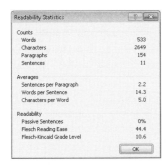

Figure 10-9 The Readability Statistics dialog box shows readability levels in addition to other details such as word count and average words per sentence.

AutoCorrecting Your Document

AutoCorrect is a helpful Word feature that corrects your errors—almost before you know you've made them. AutoCorrect comes with a library of more than one thousand different AutoCorrect entries that is shared across the family of Office 2010 applications, and you can train it to learn new corrections as you work. For example, if you type **yuor** when you mean to type **your**, AutoCorrect automatically reverses the characters in words that it recognizes without any further action from you. You can also use the AutoCorrect functionality as a shorthand method to quickly insert common text and phrases.

AutoCorrect options can be found in Word Options in the Proofing section by clicking the AutoCorrect Options button or by pressing Alt+T+A. The AutoCorrect tab of the Auto-Correct dialog box is shown in Figure 10-10; a description of the options is contained in Table 10-3. All AutoCorrect options are turned on by default, so you should turn off any unwanted options to prevent the correction from occurring while you work.

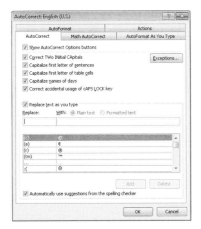

Figure 10-10 Use the AutoCorrect Options dialog box to specify which items you want corrected automatically.

Chapter 10

Table 10-3 **Setting Autocorrect Options**

AutoCorrect Option	Description
Show AutoCorrect Options Buttons	Displays an AutoCorrect Options button when a change is automatically made in your document
Correct TWo INitial CApitals	Converts the second uppercase character to lowercase
Capitalize First Letter Of Sentences	Capitalizes the first letter of the first word in a new sentence; also applies to the first letter you type after pressing Enter
Capitalize First Letter Of Table Cells	Capitalizes the first letter of the first word entered in the cell of a table
Capitalize Names Of Days	Capitalizes the first letter of days of the week
Correct Accidental Usage Of cAPS LOCK Key	Catches the accidental pressing of the Caps Lock key, releases it, and toggles the case of typed characters
Replace Text As You Type	Enables AutoCorrect to make changes to text as you type; if you disable this option then common misspelled words will not be automatically corrected
Replace and With text boxes	Enables you to add your own AutoCorrect entries to the AutoCorrect library
Automatically Use Suggestions From The Spelling Checker	Automatically corrects misspelled words that are similar to words in the main dictionary used by Spell Check
Exceptions	Enables you to specify which items *not* to correct automatically; for more information, see the section titled "Entering Exceptions," on page <OV>

Controlling AutoCorrect Changes

When AutoCorrect makes a change in your document, an AutoCorrect Options button enables you to change the correction if you want to. To view the AutoCorrect Options button, position the mouse pointer over the change that was made. A blue line displays below the change, and the AutoCorrect Options button appears. If you see only the blue line, place your mouse pointer below the change on the blue line and click. The AutoCorrect options will appear, as shown in Figure 10-11.

Figure 10-11 After AutoCorrect makes a change, you can click the options to change or undo it.

Click the AutoCorrect Options button, and then click the Undo or Change option to revert to the previously typed data in the single instance only (you can also press Ctrl+Z or Undo to obtain the same result). Use the Stop option to always prevent the change, or click Control AutoCorrect Options to display the AutoCorrect dialog box. Note that the text of the Undo and Stop options varies depending on the correction made.

Adding AutoCorrect Entries

You can add new AutoCorrect entries three ways:

- If you find a misspelled word that is not automatically corrected and Word provides a list of suggestions for the spelling error, you can easily add the misspelled word as an AutoCorrect entry at the same time that you correct the misspelled word in your document.

- If you are using the Check Spelling As You Type feature, after you right-click the misspelled word to view suggestions, use the AutoCorrect menu and select the correct word to both add the entry to AutoCorrect and correct the spelling error in your document.

- If you are using the Spelling And Grammar dialog box, select the correct suggestion on the Suggestion list and then click the AutoCorrect button that displays for spelling errors.

> **Note**
> AutoCorrect entries are case sensitive. For example, if your misspelled word starts with a capital letter, then the only time that AutoCorrect makes the correction is when it is typed in the exact same case as the AutoCorrect entry. To avoid this situation, use the AutoCorrect dialog box to add your entry as described in the following section.

Chapter 10

You can also use the AutoCorrect dialog box to add new AutoCorrect entries. This method is useful if you have several entries to add, if you need to control the case of the AutoCorrect entry as described in the previous cautionary note, or if you want to use AutoCorrect to replace lengthy words or phrases. For example, if you include your organization's detailed legal copyright statement on everything you print, you can create an AutoCorrect entry that inserts the entire mission statement when you type the letters **lgco.**

> **Note**
>
> AutoCorrect entries are stored in .acl files and are language specific. If you work with multiple languages, verify your current proofing language before creating new Auto-Correct entries.
>
> Additionally, AutoCorrect entries cannot exceed 255 characters. If your AutoCorrect replacement text exceeds the limitation, then create a building block instead. You learn more about building blocks in Chapter 7, "Creating and Reusing Content."

To add new entries by using the AutoCorrect dialog box, use the following steps:

1. On the File tab, click Options, navigate to the Proofing area, and then click the AutoCorrect Options button or press Alt+T+A.

2. In the Replace text box, type the characters that you want to use for your AutoCorrect entry. To make the entry case insensitive, use lowercase letters.

> **CAUTION**
>
> Do not use characters that form a word or acronym that you need to use in your Word documents or other Office 2010 applications; they will always be corrected automatically.
>
> Furthermore, playing tricks on your co-workers, such as changing 2007 to 2006, is strongly discouraged.

3. In the With text box, type the word or phrase that you want replaced automatically in your document as you type. Include any desired capitalization and punctuation.

4. Click Add. Word then adds the new AutoCorrect entry to the list.

> **Tip**
> To use the Formatted Text option, you need to select the formatted data in a document and then display the AutoCorrect dialog box. However, depending on the formatting, you might want to create a building block instead.
>
> Formatted AutoCorrect entries (rich text entries) are not shared with other Office 2010 programs; they are stored in your Normal template.

Replacing and Deleting AutoCorrect Entries

You can edit AutoCorrect entries in the AutoCorrect dialog box by modifying the text in the With text box. The button beneath the list then changes from Add to Replace. When you use the Replace button, Word displays a message box asking you to confirm the action.

You can delete entries in a similar way. Display the AutoCorrect dialog box and, on the AutoCorrect tab, scroll or type the first few characters of the entry in the Replace text box to quickly navigate to the entry. Select the desired entry and click the Delete button. Unlike replacing entries, Word does not display a confirmation for deleting AutoCorrect entries. If the deletion is accidental, you can immediately click the Add button to add the entry back.

Entering Exceptions

Although AutoCorrect is extremely helpful, there are times when you might not want it interfering with what you're trying to do. For example, you might be typing a document full of chemical compounds or creating a list of access codes for the new server. You don't want AutoCorrect to get in there and change the capitalization while you type. In this case, you have two options: you can disable AutoCorrect while you're working on the document, or you can create an exception to specify what you don't want AutoCorrect to change. To add an exception, display the AutoCorrect dialog box, click the Exception button, and add your exception to the respective tab in the AutoCorrect Exceptions dialog box, as shown in Figure 10-12.

Figure 10-12 You can use exceptions to prevent AutoCorrect from making specific corrections.

Chapter 10

To enter AutoCorrect exceptions, click Exceptions on the AutoCorrect tab in the AutoCorrect dialog box, and you can add the following three types of exceptions:

- **First Letter**   This form of capitalization controls the words immediately following abbreviations. (For example, you might have a phrase such as after the merging of Lake Ltd. and Smith Co., in which the word "and" should not be capitalized.)

- **INitial CAps**   Use this tab to enter words and phrases with unusual capitalization that you don't want changed. This might include company names or abbreviations or terms peculiar to your business or industry.

- **Other Corrections**   Enter additional items that you don't want AutoCorrect to change. This might include names, locations, unusual spellings, and phrases that reflect terminology particular to your work.

> **Tip**
> The Automatically Add Words To List option in the AutoCorrect Exceptions dialog box enables you to add exceptions as you work by clicking Undo or pressing Ctrl+Z immediately after an undesired correction is made. Note that this only applies to case changes and not to the Replace Text As You Type option.

Adding References in Word 2010

When you use a variety of sources to prepare a complex document, compiling, organizing, and adding all the references can be a big job. You have magazines and books piled high on your desk, report pages are folded open so you can type in the quotations you want to include, and which citation style is the right one to use? It's hard to remember if you don't create these kinds of documents very often.

Fortunately, Word 2010 includes flexible reference features that help you cut down on the amount of time and effort you spend adding references to your document. When you add citations from books, articles, reports, presentations, or online sources, Source Manager in Word 2010 helps you enter and organize the citations you need so that they appear consistently—in the style you want—throughout your document. Additionally, adding footnotes, endnotes, and cross-references is much easier with the help of the groups on the References tab (see Figure 10-13).

Figure 10-13 The References tab includes all the tools you need to add and manage references in your document.

The different groups on the References tab provide you with the tools you need to add and edit various tables of references.

- The Table Of Contents group includes the commands you'll use to mark items in the document as entries for your table of contents. In addition, there are commands to compile and insert a table based on those entries and update the table after you change it.

- The Footnotes group is where you insert footnotes and endnotes in your document. You can also hide the notes from view if you choose.

- With the Citations & Bibliography group, you can select a style to be used in the current document, add citations, select a bibliography style, and manage the sources you've used in the document.

- Use the Captions group to add captions to diagrams and illustrations in your document. You can also create and update a table of figures and add cross-references to give your readers additional resources to which to refer.

- The Index group includes everything you need to mark index entries and compile and update an index.

- The Table Of Authorities includes the commands for marking legal cases and statutes within a document. After you mark the citations, you can insert and update a table of authorities to display all references to authorities in the document.

In addition to using the References tab to easily insert references, you can also apply styles to the citations, footnotes, and references so they appear in the format you want. The Bibliography command in the Citations & Bibliography group includes a gallery of styles you can apply to the bibliography you create.

Chapter 10

Know Your References

Here's a quick list of the various items you can create using the commands on the References tab:

- **Footnotes** You can add, edit, and manage footnotes by using the Footnotes group. A footnote is a note displayed at the bottom of the printed or displayed page that adds to the information in the text. For example, you might add a footnote citing a resource for a quotation or providing some background information about a statistic you've included.

- **Endnotes** You can add an endnote by clicking Insert Endnote in the Footnotes group. An endnote is a note placed at the end of a chapter, article, report, or essay. Similar to a footnote, the item might provide additional information, a resource citation, or a Web link for further study.

- **Citations** Use the Citations & Bibliography group when you want to refer to print or electronic documents as sources in your work. A citation is typically a quoted or referenced selection from a source and it may or may not reference specific page ranges. When you use Insert Citation to create a reference, you can choose from a source list you've already created. This helps you keep references consistent throughout the document and add them easily to your document as you write.

- **Sources** A source can be almost anything—book, article, conference presentation, Web site, audio recording, TV show or report—that you are using as a source of information for the document you are creating. You add and manage your sources by clicking Manage Sources in the Citations & Bibliography group.

- **Bibliography** After you have inserted all the references you need in your document, you can easily create a bibliography by choosing Bibliography in the Citations & Bibliography group. A bibliography provides a listing of all cited sources. (For more information, see the section titled "Generating a Bibliography," on page 319.)

Other items on the References tab are beyond the scope of this chapter. See Chapter 23, "Preparing Tables of Contents and Indexes," for details about creating a table of contents and an index; see Chapters 16 and 17 to find out about adding pictures and diagrams to your pages.

Referencing in Style

One of the first choices you'll make as you prepare to add references to your document involves selecting the bibliography style you want to use. The bibliography style controls the way in which citations are listed (for example, name first or title first) and which information items are included in the reference.

To choose the style for your document, on the References tab, click the arrow in the Style setting in the Citations & Bibliography group. A list of styles appears, as shown in Figure 10-14 from which you can select the one you want to use. The most common styles are APA, Chicago, and MLA. The Turabian style is often used in academic settings.

Figure 10-14 The style determines the way in which your references are displayed.

When you add sources to your document, the style you select determines the types of information you enter for each source. You'll learn more about this in the next section.

Adding and Managing Sources

To add a source, follow these steps:

1. On the References tab, select Manage Sources in the Citations & Bibliography group.

2. In the Source Manager dialog box, click New.

3. In the Create Source dialog box, click the Type Of Source arrow and choose the type of item you're referencing (see Figure 10-15).

   The fields shown in the dialog box might change depending on the type of item you select. For example, when you choose Article In A Periodical, Periodical Title, Month, Day, and Pages fields are added to the list.

Figure 10-15 Select the type of source you're referencing.

4. Enter the appropriate source information and press Tab to move to the next field or Shift+Tab to move to the previous field.

5. Click OK to save the source information.

   The Create Source dialog box closes, and the item is displayed in both the Master List and the Current List in the Source Manager, as shown in Figure 10-16.

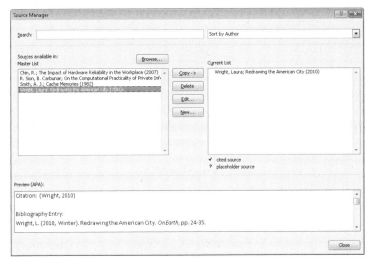

Figure 10-16 The new source is added to the Source Manager dialog box.

> **Tip**
>
> The sources you added to the Source Manager will be available to other documents you create in Word 2010. Whenever you click Manage Sources on the References tab, you will see all the sources you compiled in the Master List in the Source Manager. To add sources from the Master List to the Current List for the

document, display the Source Manager, click the source you want to use, and click Copy. Add the sources you want to the Current List and click Close to close the Source Manager. Those sources will now be available when you choose Insert Citation from the Citations & Bibliography group.

Incorporating Other Source Lists

If you are collaborating on a document, you might need to share your resources with others or work with the sources others have compiled. You can add other source lists to your Master List by following these steps:

1. On the References tab, click Manage Sources to display the Source Manager.

2. In the Source Manager, click Browse.

3. The Open Source List dialog box appears, with the Bibliography folder selected. If necessary, navigate to the folder containing the source list you want to add to the current document.

4. Select the file and click OK to add the sources to the Master List.

Inserting a Citation

Now that you've selected the style and added the sources you will be referencing in your document, inserting a citation is simple.

1. Click where you want to add the citation.

2. On the References tab, click Insert Citation in the Citations & Bibliography group.

3. A list of available sources appears, as shown in Figure 10-17. Click the source you want to add. The reference is inserted at the cursor position.

Figure 10-17 After you create sources, you can add citations easily with Insert Citation.

Editing Citation and Sources

After you insert a citation, you might decide that you want to change the way the item is referenced or modify the information in the citation. To edit the citation, right-click it and choose Edit Citation. The small Edit Citation dialog box appears, in which you can enter different values for the citation fields or suppress their display. Type the new information and click OK to save your changes.

> **Note**
>
> If you are working with Track Changes on, right-clicking displays the Accept/Reject Changes options. If you are using Track Changes and want to edit a citation, click the arrow on the bounding box around the citation to open the correct menu.

When you need to change information in the source reference itself, right-click the citation in the document and choose Edit Source. (If Track Changes is enabled, click the arrow that appears when you point to the citation in order to display your options.) In the Edit Source dialog box, make the necessary changes and click OK to save the edits. The citations in the document are changed to reflect the modifications.

> ### Adding and Using Placeholders
>
> If you are working on the draft of your document and find that you don't have all the sources you need, don't worry—you can insert placeholders for the citations and then add the data when you finally have it. For example, suppose that you are writing an article for your organization's newsletter and want to reference a research study on volunteers and Internet use that you recently read in a professional journal. Instead of interrupting your writing and looking for the source, you can insert a placeholder where you want to incorporate the information. Here's how to do it:
>
> 1. Click where you want to add the placeholder.
>
> 2. On the References tab, click the Insert Citation arrow and choose Add New Placeholder.
>
>   The Placeholder Name dialog box appears so that you can enter a name for the placeholder. Type the name and click OK.
>
> 3. When you're ready to replace the placeholder with citation data, click Manage Sources and click the placeholder you want to replace. (Placeholders are preceded by a question mark.)
>
> 4. Type the citation information in the Edit Source dialog box and click OK to save your changes. The citation is updated in the document automatically.

> **Tip**
> Punctuation characters and spaces aren't accepted in placeholder names. So when you're entering a placeholder name, use only letters, numbers, and the underscore character.

Generating a Bibliography

A good bibliography is a great reader service, providing others with full references they can use to find more information on the topics introduced in your document. After you add citations to your document, you can easily create a professional bibliography by using the Bibliography command in the Citations & Bibliography group.

Begin by positioning the cursor at the point in the document where you want to insert the bibliography. Then click the Bibliography command. A gallery of bibliography styles opens, offering you the option of creating a bibliography or a works cited list (see Figure 10-18). Click the style you want or click Insert Bibliography. The bibliography is then inserted in your document.

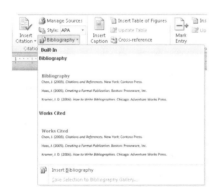

Figure 10-18 Select a bibliography style from the gallery.

You can also create and save your own style of bibliography to the Bibliography gallery. Create a listing of sources and add the heading you want to use. Then select the list and heading and click Bibliography in the Citations & Bibliography group. In the Bibliography gallery, click Save Selection To Bibliography Gallery. The next time you open the gallery to display bibliography options, your new style will appear.

Adding Footnotes and Endnotes

Another way to reference sources in your documents is by adding footnotes and endnotes. In some views, footnotes appear in an area at the bottom of your page, with a separator line and a note reference mark to identify the note. (See Figure 10-19 for an example.) A matching note reference mark appears in the text at the place you create the footnote. By default, the reference marks are numbers, but you can change the referencing style to letters, symbols, or other characters of your choosing.

Figure 10-19 Footnotes appear at the bottom of the page and include a separator line and a note reference mark.

Endnotes are similar to footnotes, except they're placed at the end of a document. Only one separator line separates the text and the endnotes.

> **Note**
> You can enter footnotes of any length, but because the notes are displayed in a small typeface, and they take up room on the document page, it's best to use endnotes when you want to include notes with a lot of commentary.

Inserting Footnotes and Endnotes

When you're ready to insert a footnote or endnote in your document, follow these steps:

1. Click where you want to add the footnote or endnote.

2. On the References tab, in the Footnotes group, click either the Insert Footnote or Insert Endnote command.

   The reference marker is added (to the bottom of the current page, for a footnote, or on the last page of the document, for an endnote). Default values are used to determine the reference marker, the format, and the numbering sequence of the notes.

3. Type the text for the note.

Customizing Footnotes and Endnotes

You can modify a number of footnote and endnote settings to customize the way the notes appear. For example, you might want to use letters instead of numbers as the reference marks; or perhaps you would like to insert a symbol to indicate a footnote or endnote instead of using traditional numbers or letters.

Another change you might want to make involves the sequencing of the notes. If you are working on a collaborative document and have divided a master document into subdocuments for assignment to different team members, you might want to start the footnote numbering at a number other than 1. You can do this by changing the Start At value in the Footnote And Endnote dialog box (see Figure 10-20).

Figure 10-20 Customize settings in the Footnote and Endnote dialog box.

Chapter 10

Display the Footnote And Endnote dialog box by clicking the dialog launcher in the lower-right corner of the Footnotes group on the References tab. Then follow these steps to customize the default settings:

1. In the Location section of the Footnote And Endnote dialog box, click either the Footnotes or Endnotes option.

2. In the Format section, click the Number Format arrow and then choose the numbering scheme you want to use for the note reference marks that identify your footnotes or endnotes (depending on which item you selected).

   You'll find all the traditional choices—numeric, alphabetic, and roman numerals—plus something different: a collection of special symbols. You can choose your own special symbol by clicking Symbol and choosing the symbol you want to use from the displayed gallery in the Symbol dialog box.

3. If you want to start the footnote or endnote with a number other than 1, click in the Start At box and then type the number you want.

4. To indicate that you want footnote and endnote numbering to restart at the beginning of each new section, choose Restart Each Section in the Numbering box.

5. If you have divided your document into sections, you can change the default value in the Apply Changes option.

   Click the arrow to display your choices—you can leave the default setting of Whole Document or choose This Section.

6. Click Insert to add the note with your customized settings.

> **Note**
> The complete footnote and endnote references are visible only in Print Layout and Full Screen Reading view by default. If you want to display and perhaps edit a footnote while working in Web Layout, Outline, or Draft view, simply double-click the reference marker. This opens the Footnotes pane at the bottom of the Word window where you can view and edit the note as needed.

TROUBLESHOOTING

My footnotes disappear on my Web page.

If you created a document, complete with footnotes and endnotes, and then saved it as a Web page, your footnotes haven't disappeared completely—they've simply been moved to the end of the Web document. The footnote reference marks are turned into hyperlinks so that you can access the footnotes easily from any point within the page. Just click the hyperlinked reference mark to bring you directly to the footnote. To return to the previous page, click your browser's Back button.

Moving and Copying Footnotes and Endnotes

If you want to move a footnote or endnote from one position to another, drag the footnote or endnote marker in the text to the new location. If you want to move the mark to a location that's too far away to drag, you can cut and paste the mark by using Ctrl+X to cut and Ctrl+V to paste.

Note

If the position to which you move the footnote precedes another footnote, Word changes the numbering automatically.

If you have a footnote or endnote you plan to use more than once, you can copy a note reference mark instead of typing a duplicate entry. Simply select the note reference mark and then press and hold Ctrl while dragging the mark to the new place in the document.

Deleting Footnotes and Endnotes

When you want to remove a footnote or endnote from your document, go to the place in the document where the note reference mark appears and delete it. Simply removing the text in the Footnotes or Endnotes pane doesn't remove the note itself—Word will still keep the note reference mark in place and reserve the space at the bottom or end of your document for the note content.

Chapter 10

TROUBLESHOOTING

Deleted footnotes won't go away.

If you've deleted a footnote or endnote, but it keeps reappearing, chances are that a portion of formatting for the note has been left behind (a paragraph mark, likely). To find the culprit character, click the Show/Hide command in the Paragraph group on the Home tab. All the paragraph marks will appear, and you can move to the footnote area and delete the stray paragraph mark. The reference in the text will then be deleted.

Creating a New Separator Line

The separator line Word uses to show where the document text ends and the footnote text begins is a fairly nondescript line that extends a short distance across the page. If you want to change the separator line—perhaps to add color or choose a different line style or thickness—use the Borders And Shading dialog box to make the change. To do this, follow these steps:

1. View the document in Draft view.

2. Double-click the footnote or endnote reference mark in your document to open the Footnotes or Endnotes pane at the bottom of the Word window.

3. Click the Footnotes arrow and then select Footnote Separator in the Footnotes list.

4. Delete the existing separator line by clicking it and then pressing Delete.

5. On the Home tab, click the Border command arrow in the Paragraph group.

6. Click Borders And Shading at the bottom of the gallery. The Borders And Shading dialog box appears.

7. On the Borders tab, in the Style list, select the border style you want.

8. Click the bottom and side segments in the Preview section to remove them, leaving only the top line, then click OK to add the new separator line to the document.

TROUBLESHOOTING

My footnote is split across two pages.

Sometimes getting footnotes to print just where you'd intended can be a bit tricky. You might wind up with too many additional blank lines on the page after the footnote, or you could find that your footnote has been divided, with one line appearing on the first page and a second line printing on the next page.

If you find that part of your footnote has moved to the next page, look at the margin settings for the page. The text on the page, the margins, and the footnote length all play a role in the amount of space reserved for your footnote area. On the Page Layout tab, click the Margins down-arrow. Note the space allowed for the margins. Try clicking Custom Margins and reducing the bottom margin setting to allow more room for the footnote. Then click OK to return to the document.

Note

If you do customize the margins of your page in order to adjust the amount of space allowed for footnotes, be sure to preview your page and output a test print before printing your final document.

For best results, try to keep your footnotes short—one or two lines if possible. If you need to insert a long footnote, consider converting it to an endnote so that it can be placed at the end of the document.

Chapter 10

Inserting Cross-References

When you're working on a long document in which you want to refer to other parts of the document, you can use cross-references to help readers find the information they seek. Word lets you add cross-references to a number of different elements in your document, including captions, headings, footnotes and endnotes, and bookmarks.

Tip

You can create cross-references only within the current document. You might create a reference at the beginning of a long report, for example, that points readers to a table in a later section that lists statistics related to a new study. However, you can't create a cross-reference to a table in another document.

Adding a Cross-Reference

If you're working with master documents and subdocuments, be sure to maximize the master document by clicking Expand Subdocuments in the Master Documents group on the Outlining tab. This makes all text accessible before you enter cross-references.

When you're ready to create a cross-reference, start by placing the insertion point where you want the cross-reference to appear in your document. Then follow these steps:

1. Add the text that refers to the cross-reference (for example, you might use a phrase such as "To review the results of our survey, see").

2. On the References tab, click Cross-reference in the Captions group. The Cross-reference dialog box appears, as shown in Figure 10-21.

Figure 10-21 Cross-references enable you to point readers to different elements in your document.

3. Click the Reference type arrow and then make your selection. You can choose from the following document elements:

   - **Numbered Item**   Lists all the text entries beginning with a number

   - **Heading**   Shows all headings based on Word's outline levels or Heading 1, 2, or 3 styles

   - **Bookmark**   Displays all the bookmarks currently listed in the document

   - **Footnote**   Shows all the footnotes inserted in the document

   - **Endnote**   Lists the endnotes you have created

   - **Equation**   Shows any equations you've inserted in the document

- **Figure**   Lists all figure references

- **Table**   Shows all available tables in the document

4. Click the Insert Reference To arrow and then choose the element you want Word to insert in the document.

This item will be inserted at the insertion point.

5. Select the item to which you want to refer by clicking it in the For Which list box, and then click Insert

Word adds the cross-reference to your document as you directed.

6. Click Close to return to your document.

INSIDE OUT   Create Links for a Web Page

If you plan to save your document as a Web page or make it available as an electronic file, you can have Word turn your cross-references into hyperlinks so that readers can easily move from one page to another. To create links for cross-references, select the cross-reference you've created and then display the Cross-reference dialog box by clicking Cross-reference in the Captions group on the References tab. In the Cross-reference dialog box, select the Insert as hyperlink check box and then click Insert. The inserted cross-reference is created as a link to the other location in the document.

Chapter 10

Modifying, Moving, and Updating Cross-References

You can edit and delete the text that introduces a cross-reference the same way you would modify any other text in your document. If you want to modify the item to which a reference refers, you need to make a different kind of change. Here are the steps:

1. Select the item inserted as the cross-reference (for example, you might select *Table 1-1*).

2. Display the Cross-reference dialog box by clicking Cross-reference in the Captions group on the References tab.

3. In the For Which list in the Cross-reference dialog box, click the new item to which you want the cross-reference to refer.

4. Click Insert, and then click the Close button to close the Cross-reference dialog box.

INSIDE OUT Make a Reference Relative

By selecting the Include Above/Below check box in the Cross-reference dialog box, you can have Word create a relative reference to a cross-reference you enter. Create your cross-reference as usual. Then, in the Insert reference to list box, after selecting the item you want inserted, select the Include Above/Below check box. If the insertion point is on the same page as the section or item referenced, Word will insert "above" or "below," based on the position of the reference. If you want to move a cross-reference, simply select the reference in your document and then cut and paste it as you would normally. Once you have the reference in the location you want, press F9. Word updates the reference and makes the connection to the new location. If you want to update all references in a document, select the entire document before pressing F9.

Note

When you want to delete a cross-reference, simply select the reference and then delete it as you would any other text.

TROUBLESHOOTING

Cross-referencing in my document produces an error message.

If you go through the steps to create a cross-reference and instead of the reference you expect, you get an error message saying, "Error! Reference source not found," check to make sure that the information you're referring to hasn't been removed from your document. If the item is still in your document, but the reference still displays an error message, try fixing the problem by selecting the cross-reference and pressing F9 to update the reference. If the problem is caused by a broken link or a moved reference, the item should now be displayed properly.

What's Next?

In this chapter you learned about the many ways you can edit and extend the content in your document. From the basics of using the spelling checker and customizing dictionaries to the ins and outs of the grammar checker and AutoCorrect features, this chapter showed you how Word 2010 helps you make sure your content is as accurate as possible. The second half of this chapter focused on the ways in which you can add references of all types to the documents you create. Whether you plan on using footnotes, endnotes, cross-references, or adding a bibliography to your document, you can easily add, edit, and control the format of your references so they add to the impact of your work and give your readers the information they need.

Formatting Your Document

Paragraph Basics in Word 332

Managing AutoFormat Effectively. 334

Formatting Paragraphs by Aligning
and Indenting Text. 338

Addressing Spacing Issues 343

Controlling Alignment by Using Tabs. 347

Controlling Line and Page Breaks 353

Taking Control of Hyphenation 354

Creating Drop Caps in Existing Paragraphs 357

Creating Effective Lists. 358

Creating a Quick List 361

Enhancing Bulleted Lists 364

Improving Numbered Lists. 367

Changing List Indents 372

Creating and Using Multilevel Lists. 373

What's Next? 378

THERE'S no big secret to making a document look good. Basically you want the look and feel of your pages to fit the style your audience is expecting, leave plenty of white space to give the reader's eye a rest, include interesting visuals, such as photos, tables, or diagrams where they fit, and use colors that are easy on the eye.

Simple, right?

Well, as any professional designer will tell you, there's quite a bit of work behind what appears to be a simple design. Efficiency, consistency, and connection are all important if you want your design to help readers get the message you're trying to convey in your document. And if you want to inspire your readers to a particular action—inviting them to make a donation to your fundraising campaign, for example, or deciding to order your product online—you need to make sure you've considered the format and presentation of your document from a number of important angles.

The last chapter focused on proofing the content you've added to your document and extending it by adding references to your work. This chapter helps you improve the way your content looks by working with all kinds of formatting controls at the paragraph level.

Tip

As you've probably noticed, Word 2010 offers all kinds of tools for formatting at various levels. You can format the entire page; arrange specific sections; change the look of paragraphs, words, and headings; and format individual words. This chapter focuses on working with formats at the paragraph level, which includes formats for lists, alignments, spacing, and hyphenation.

Paragraph Basics in Word 2010

When you think of the word *paragraph*, is a block of text the first thing that comes to mind? Actually, the paragraph mark at the end of a paragraph is the primary component—the text is secondary. It's the paragraph mark (¶) that holds formatting information, such as the style, alignment, and indents. When it comes to formatting and editing documents, the more you understand the role of the paragraph mark, the more control you will have over your Word documents.

Each time you press Enter after a character, heading, graphic, table, chart, list item, or any other element, you create a paragraph. If you press Enter to create a blank "line" between paragraphs, you insert a paragraph mark and create what is considered an empty paragraph because it does not contain text or any other element. You can display paragraph marks (along with other hidden text) in your documents by clicking Show/ Hide on the Home tab, in the Paragraph group, shown here.

——Show/Hide tool

Figure 11-1 illustrates the concept of various paragraph elements in Word. Notice the paragraph mark after each bulleted list item, each paragraph of, each heading, and the empty paragraph toward the top of the page.

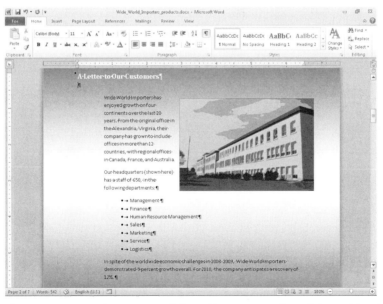

Figure 11-1 In Word, any content followed by a paragraph mark is considered a paragraph, even if it does not contain content.

INSIDE OUT
Showing Specific Formatting Marks

The Show/Hide button in the Paragraph group provides a quick way to display all formatting marks, such as paragraph marks, spaces, tab characters, and other marks that indicate special formatting. In some cases, you might find you want to display only specific formatting marks. You can easily alter your display to show specific formatting marks as follows:

1. On the File tab, click Options and then click Display.

2. Under the heading titled Always Show These Formatting Marks On The Screen, select the formatting marks you want to display. For example, select only Paragraph Marks to show only paragraph marks. Click OK to close Word Options.

After you specify which formatting marks you want to display, those marks will appear in your document, regardless of whether you click Show/Hide. (Note that Show/Hide continues to show all formatting marks when you toggle the button on, regardless of your Display settings.) To hide formatting marks activated using the Display settings, you'll need to revisit Word Options to reconfigure the formatting marks.

Before you begin changing the formats in your document, let's review an important consideration—the efficiency of your formatting. In Word 2010, you can format paragraphs by setting the following paragraph formatting parameters:

- Paragraph alignment

- Indentation

- Spacing between lines

- Spacing before and after paragraphs

- Tabs

- Line and page breaks

- Hyphenation

You can apply these formats to every single instance that you want them to appear, but if you find you need to change an indent throughout your document, do you want to painstakingly select every instance of the indent and change it? Or would you rather specify your preferred indent setting in a single change and have the indents update automatically throughout the document?

If the latter sounds more appealing, then for primary formats—such as the main formatting of individual paragraphs—consider using styles. Styles provide flexibility not only by enabling you to modify document formats simply by modifying the style (covered in Chapter 12, "Applying and Customizing Quick Styles"), but they also enable you to format content more efficiently by applying many formats to text with a single click of the mouse. Whether your formatting plan is to create or modify styles for your formatting needs (which can be accomplished by picking up formats already in use in your document), or to apply direct formatting throughout your document without implementing styles, paragraph formatting will be fundamentally the same.

Managing AutoFormat Effectively

Word includes a number of automatic formatting features that are meant to make your life easier. But sometimes instead of streamlining formatting tasks, the automatic features confuse things by indenting lists you don't want indented or inserting numbers in places you'd rather not have them.

But the good news is that you have control over these automatic features. You can turn each feature on and off and control the items you want Word to change on the fly. This section explores the ins and outs of AutoFormat and shows you how to master the various settings so that it behaves the way you want it to—as a help and not a hindrance.

One of the first confusing aspects is that you actually control AutoFormat choices in two different places in Word. The AutoFormat tab of the AutoCorrect dialog box (see Figure 11-2) contains the commands that AutoFormat corrects by default while you're using the program. The AutoFormat As You Type tab (see Figure 11-3) shows you the elements that will be corrected automatically as you type new content. For users who are having a difficult time getting the format just the way they want it in their documents, it's the settings in the AutoFormat As You Type tab that confound them.

> **Note**
> If you have other languages and/or keyboards installed on your system, you might see additional choices displayed in the AutoFormat dialog box.

Figure 11-2 You'll find the settings for AutoFormat in the AutoCorrect dialog box.

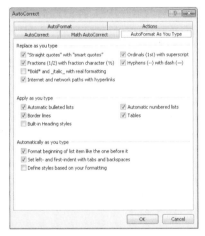

Figure 11-3 AutoFormat As You Type shows you the elements that are adjusted as you enter content on the page.

> ## Note
> Like AutoCorrect, when Word automatically makes a formatting change, an AutoCorrect Options button displays and provides the Undo and Stop options. If the AutoCorrect Options button does not disappear, press Esc to dismiss it.

Chapter 11

Adjusting AutoFormat Choices

To display the AutoFormat settings, on the File tab, click Options and choose Proofing in the Word Options dialog box. Next, click the AutoCorrect Options button (the AutoCorrect dialog box appears) then click AutoFormat.

The settings in this dialog box enable you to choose the elements Word 2010 will change as a matter of course in your documents. Depending on the settings that are selected, Word will automatically perform for the following:

- Apply built-in heading styles, list styles, automatic bulleted lists, and other paragraph styles

- Replace straight quotes with smart quotes, ordinals with superscript, fractions with actual fraction characters, hyphens with dashes, *bold* and _italic_ with real formatting, web links with hyperlinks

- Preserve the styles in your document

- AutoFormat plain text e-mail documents

If you want to turn off the AutoFormat feature for any of these items, simply clear the check box for the option you want to remove. Note however that if you clear the setting (for example "Fractions (1/2) with fraction characters (½)") in the AutoFormat tab, it will not be reformatted in the document, even if you click the option in the AutoFormat As You Type tab.

Changing Options for AutoFormat As You Type

The AutoFormat As You Type tab is also found in the AutoCorrect dialog box (Alt+T+A). You'll notice that many of the settings are the same or similar to the ones available in the AutoFormat tab. The difference here is that you're controlling which of the elements will be changed as you enter content in the document. Table 11-1 provides a description of each setting in the AutoFormat As You Type tab of the AutoCorrect dialog box.

Table 11-1 AutoFormat As You Type Settings

AutoFormat Setting	Description and Use
"Straight Quotes" With "Smart Quotes"	Converts typed quotes and apostrophes to smart, or *curly*, quotes
Fractions (1/2) With Fraction Character (½)	Replaces full-sized typed fractions, such as 1/2, with the fraction symbol; this only works for common fractions such as ¼, ½, and ¾

AutoFormat Setting	Description and Use
Bold And _Italic_ With Real Formatting	A word surrounded by asterisks or underscores is formatted as bold and italic, respectively; the asterisks and underscores are removed
Internet And Network Paths With Hyperlinks	Automatically converts recognized URLs, network paths, and e-mail addresses to hyperlinks
Ordinals (1st) With Superscript	Inserts ordinals (such as 1st, 2nd, 3rd) when you type full-sized ordinals
Hyphens (--) With Dash (—)	Replaces two consecutive hyphens (--) with an em dash (—); for an en dash (–), type a space before and after two consecutive hyphens (--)
Automatic Bulleted Lists	An asterisk (*) followed by a tab at the beginning of a line is converted to a bulleted list
Border Lines	Three consecutive symbols, such as ~,#,*, -,_,= at the beginning of a line are converted to borders
Built-In Heading Styles	Automatically formats short paragraphs (without a period) with Heading styles after pressing Enter twice; a short paragraph at the beginning of the line is formatted with Heading 1, a tab preceding a short paragraph is formatted with Heading 2, two tabs followed by a short paragraph is formatted with Heading 3, and so on
Automatic Numbered Lists	A number followed by a period and a tab or space at the beginning of a line is converted to a numbered list; numbers not followed by a period, along with a tab or at least two spaces, can be converted to a numbered list after pressing Enter
Tables	A series of vertical bars (|) and underscores (_) are converted to tables after pressing Enter; entry must start and end with a vertical bar
Format Beginning Of List Item Like The One Before It	Applies identical formatting to the second and consecutive items in a list; formatting of last character, even a space, determines format
Set Left And First Indent With Tabs And Backspace	Pressing Tab at the beginning of a previously typed paragraph formats the paragraph with a First Line Indent; pressing Backspace after Tab formats the paragraph with a Left Indent
Define Styles Based On Your Formatting	Applies built-in styles that match paragraph formatting; it is recommended that this option be left turned off because it doesn't always function and, when it does, you have no control over which style is applied

Chapter 11

Adding AutoFormat to the Ribbon

If you find that you are using AutoFormat quite a bit, you might want to add the tool to the Ribbon so that you can access it easily. Here are the steps for customizing the Ribbon and adding the AutoFormat tool:

1. On the File tab, click Options.

2. Click Customize Ribbon.

3. In the right side of the dialog box, click the name of the tab in which you want to create the new group (for example, Home).

4. Click New Group.

5. Click Rename and type a name for the new group (perhaps "AutoFormat") then click OK.

6. Click the Choose Commands From arrow and select Commands Not On The Ribbon.

7. Scroll down the list on the left and find AutoFormat.

8. Drag AutoFormat to the new group you created or click the tool and click Add to include it in the selected group. Repeat by dragging or clicking AutoFormat As You Type if you like, and then click OK to save your changes.

Now the AutoFormat tools will appear in the new group in the tab you specified. When you click the tool in the new group, the AutoCorrect dialog box will open, displaying the tab you indicated.

Formatting Paragraphs by Aligning and Indenting Text

One of the most common paragraph-level formatting tasks is aligning paragraphs within a document. But alignment matters don't stop with setting line ending attributes, such as left, center, right, and justified—you can also specify paragraph alignment and indentation as well. Table 11-2 lists the various tools and shortcuts you can use to align and format paragraphs.

Table 11-2 **Paragraph Align and Formatting Tools**

Format	Button	Keyboard shortcut	Description
Align Left		Ctrl+L	Aligns text and other elements along the left margin of the page or specified area, with a ragged right (non-aligned) edge
Align Center		Ctrl+E	Aligns the midpoint of each line with the horizontal center of the page or area
Align Right		Ctrl+R	Aligns text and other elements along the right margin of the page or specified area, with a ragged left edge
Justify		Ctrl+J	Aligns text flush with both the left and right margins of the page or specified area
Decrease Indent		Ctrl+Shift+M	Decreases a paragraph's indent by one tab stop. By default, automatic tab stops are set every 0.5 inch
Increase Indent		Ctrl+M	Increases a paragraph's indent by one tab stop. By default, automatic tab stops are set every 0.5 inch

To apply these paragraph alignments and formats, simply click in the paragraph you want to change and click the tool to apply the setting. Note that you can use the alignment tools together with the Decrease Indent and Increase Indent tools to achieve the effect you want for the selected paragraph.

Using the Ruler to Align Paragraphs

It's easy to align paragraphs and set indent levels using the tools on the Home tab, but when you want to be precise about the way your text aligns, you can use the ruler to set format rules. To display the ruler, on the View tab, select the Ruler check box. You can also display the ruler by clicking the View Ruler button at the top of the vertical scrollbar. After you choose to display the ruler, you'll be able to see it in Draft, Web Layout, and Print Layout views. Note that the *0* (zero) mark on the ruler corresponds to the left margin setting, as shown in Figure 11-4. By default, the left and right margins are set to 1 inch, or 2.54 centimeters, for Letter paper size. Thus, the default setup provides 6.5 inches, or 16.51 centimeters, between the margins for content.

Chapter 11

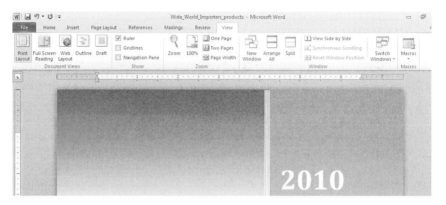

Figure 11-4 The left margin sets the beginning point for ruler measurement.

> **Note**
> To change the unit of measure displayed on your ruler, click Options on the File tab then click Advanced. In the Display area, change the unit in the Show Measurements In Units Of list.

Adjusting Left and Right Indents

To use the ruler to adjust left and right indents, click within the paragraph or select the paragraphs you want to adjust then drag the Left Indent or Right Indent marker on the ruler. If you find that the divisions and tick marks on the ruler are difficult to use when you need precise alignment, you can obtain more accuracy by holding Alt (or press and hold both mouse buttons) as you as drag the indent marks as shown here:

Note that when you drag the Left Indent marker, the First Line Indent and Hanging Indent marker will also move.

INSIDE OUT   Overriding the Drawing Grid

When you use the ruler, if object snapping is enabled, the Drawing Grid is also in effect. By default, the horizontal grid is 0.13 inches, or 0.33 centimeters, which means when you drag the indent markers or other elements, such as a manual tab, they will snap to these increments (note that this does not apply when you initially add a manual tab). When you hold the Alt key, you override the object snapping, which enables you to align content to any measurement, not just to the points on the Drawing Grid. To view the Drawing Grid settings, click Align in the Arrange group on the Page Layout tab then click Grid Settings.

Creating First Line and Hanging Indents

You can use the ruler to create a hanging indent or a first line indent, as illustrated below. To do so, click in the paragraph you want to format (or select multiple paragraphs) and then drag the First Line Indent marker (the one on top) left or right to the desired location, as shown here:

Tip

You can press Ctrl+T to create a hanging indent that aligns body text with the first tab marker. (By default, tabs are set every 0.5 inch, or 1.27 centimeters.) To "unhang" an indent, you can press Ctrl+Shift+T, regardless of how the hanging indent was created. If the paragraph contains a first line indent, pressing Ctrl+T will create a Left Indent.

Aligning Paragraphs by Using the Paragraph Dialog Box

Another way you can align the paragraphs in your document is to use the Paragraph dialog box, which offers its own set of advantages. For example, as shown in Figure 11-5, because the Paragraph box provides a number of settings in one convenient place, you can set multiple paragraph formatting options easily at one time.

To display the Paragraph dialog box, on the Home tab, click the dialog launcher in the lower-right corner of the Paragraph group. Alternatively, you can right-click a paragraph (or selected paragraphs) then click Paragraph.

Chapter 11

Tip
You can also display the Paragraph dialog box by using the dialog launcher found in the Paragraph group on the Page Layout tab.

Figure 11-5 The Paragraph dialog box provides precise and complete control of paragraph formatting.

The Indents And Spacing tab offers the following paragraph alignment options:

- **Alignment** Sets the position of paragraph contents relative to the margins. Available alignment options are Left, Centered, Right, and Justified. The options in this list correspond to the alignment buttons on the Ribbon.

- **Outline level** Sets the level of the paragraph (for example, Heading 1, Heading 2, or Body Text), which might change the indent of the text at the cursor position.

- **Left Indentation** Indents the paragraph from the left by the amount you specify. To display text or graphics within the left margin, enter a negative number in the Left text box.

- **Right Indentation** Indents the paragraph from the right margin by the amount you specify. To display text or graphics within the right margin, enter a negative number in the Right text box.

- **Special** and **By**   Controls the paragraph's first line and hanging indentation. The Special list box has three options: (None), First Line, and Hanging. The (None) option is selected by default. To specify the first line indent, enter a value in the By text box. The Special list box changes to display First Line automatically. For a hanging indent, select Hanging from the Special list and enter a value in the By text box.

You can configure other paragraph settings in the Paragraph dialog box, including paragraph spacing parameters, as you'll see next.

Addressing Spacing Issues

The default spacing in Word 2010 uses 10 points of space after each paragraph and 1.15 lines of space between the lines of a paragraph. This spacing makes documents easier to read online. Interestingly, if you are accustomed to using single spacing and adding an empty paragraph mark to create space between paragraphs, if you use the new defaults instead of single spacing and empty paragraphs, approximately three additional lines are added per page.

> **Note**
>
> If your documents aren't required to follow a specific standard, consider giving the new spacing defaults a few days prior to deciding if you prefer them or not. You might find that you prefer the extra space once you get used to it—and giving readers' eyes a break on a text-filled page is always a good way to encourage them to keep reading.

Additionally, using empty paragraphs to create empty lines can end up causing you more work in the end—especially when you are sorting, copying, and pasting content. When you sort multiple paragraphs, the empty paragraph marks are sorted to the top of your sorted paragraphs, and you need to delete them and manually add them back. And when you copy and paste paragraphs, you might need to manually add and remove the empty paragraph marks.

Long gone are the days when you had to press Enter twice at the end of each paragraph or use tricks such as selecting a paragraph mark and changing the font size to add or increase the space between paragraphs. As you will see in the section "Adjusting Spacing Above and Below Paragraphs" on page 346, adding paragraph spacing is a simple matter of configuring paragraph settings the way you want them. You can easily adjust paragraph spacing at any time in your documents—before, during, or after you enter text—to help improve readability. In particular, you can control line spacing within paragraphs as well as specify the amount of space above and below paragraphs.

If you want to omit space between some paragraphs—such as for an address block—insert a manual line break by pressing Shift+Enter after each line in the address block instead of pressing Enter to begin a new paragraph.

> **Note**
>
> If you want to change the new default spacing for the entire document, or for all new documents based on the Normal template, you can use styles to do the trick. See Chapter 12 for more about creating and working with styles.

INSIDE OUT   Cleaning Up Empty Paragraph Marks

If you previously used empty paragraphs to create space between paragraphs and now prefer to use formatted space instead, you can easily clean up documents that have empty paragraph marks by using the Find And Replace tool. When you press Enter twice, you create a pattern of two paragraph marks in sequence. Using Find And Replace, you can find each occurrence of two paragraph marks and replace each set with a single paragraph mark. To do so, follow these steps:

1. On the Home tab, click Replace in the Editing group and then click More.

2. Place your cursor in the Find What text box, click the Special button, and then click Paragraph Mark. You should see ^*p* in the Find What text box. Click the Special button again and click Paragraph Mark. You should now see ^*p*^*p* in the Find What text box.

3. Place your cursor in the Replace With text box, click the Special button, and then click Paragraph Mark. (Alternatively, type ^**p**.)

4. Click Replace All and confirm the replacement. (You might need to click Replace All multiple times until you have replaced all occurrences of multiple paragraph marks because in the case where several paragraph marks appear together, Word will replace only one in the series at a time.)

5. Click Close to close the Find And Replace dialog box.

After you have removed multiple paragraph marks, you can use formatted space between paragraphs to format your document.

> **Tip**
> If you have several documents in which you need to clean up multiple paragraph marks, consider recording a macro using your Find And Replace steps. For more on how to record macros and add them to your Quick Access Toolbar or assign a keyboard shortcut, see Chapter 28, "Working with Macros in Word 2010."

Specifying Line Spacing

In Word, you can adjust line spacing in several ways, including using the Ribbon, keyboard shortcuts, and the Paragraph dialog box. One quick way to configure a paragraph's line spacing is to click in the paragraph you want to configure (or select multiple paragraphs) and then click the Line Spacing tool (on the Home tab, in the Paragraph group). Line Spacing offers the following options: 1.0, 1.5, 2.0, 2.5, and 3.0. Selecting a number instantly adjusts the selected paragraphs' line spacing. If you select Line Spacing Options, the Paragraph dialog box appears.

You can use the Paragraph dialog box to adjust paragraph line spacing to a precise 1/10 of a point by using the Line Spacing option in conjunction with the At text box on the Indents And Spacing tab (shown previously in Figure 11-5). The Line Spacing list box provides the following options:

- **Single**   Accommodates the largest font per line plus a small amount of extra space to create the appearance of a single-spaced paragraph.

- **1.5 Lines**   Inserts 1.5 times the space allotted for a single line space to the selected paragraph(s).

- **Double**   Inserts twice the space allotted for a single line space to the selected paragraph(s).

- **At Least**   Sets a minimum amount of space for each line as specified in the At text box. When Word encounters a larger font size or a graphic that won't fit in the minimum space, it increases that line's spacing to accommodate the text or graphic.

- **Exactly**   Forces Word to apply an exact line spacing, as specified in the At text box, regardless of what size text or graphics Word encounters. (Otherwise, Word accommodates the largest text or graphic in a line by default.) If Word encounters text or graphics too large to fit in the allotted line space, the text or graphics will appear cut off in your document.

- **Multiple**   Enables you to use the At text box to specify a line spacing setting from 0.06 through 132 lines, in increments of 1/100 of a line. This option provides extra-fine control over line spacing.

Chapter 11

Last but not least, you can quickly adjust a paragraph's line spacing by clicking in a paragraph or selecting multiple paragraphs and then pressing any of the following keyboard shortcuts:

- Ctrl+1 applies single-line spacing to selected paragraphs.

- Ctrl+2 applies double-line spacing to selected paragraphs.

- Ctrl+5 applies 1.5-line spacing to selected paragraphs.

Adjusting Spacing Above and Below Paragraphs

In addition to adjusting spacing between lines within paragraphs, you can configure the space displayed above and below paragraphs instead of adding an empty paragraph mark. By using this method to add space, you're not limited to separating paragraphs by one or two lines; you can separate paragraphs by 0.5 inch, 3 points, and so forth. In addition, if you use spacing consistently within your document, and you find that your document (or a section within your document) runs a little long or comes up a little short, you can select the entire document, a section, or a few paragraphs, and adjust the paragraph spacing options by using the Paragraph dialog box to tighten up or lengthen your document in just a few steps. For additional tips on fitting text, see Chapter 14, "Printing Documents Professionally."

To add spacing above and below selected paragraphs, follow these steps:

1. Click in the paragraph you want to configure, or select multiple paragraphs.

2. On the Home tab, in the Paragraph group, click the dialog launcher then click Indents And Spacing.

3. Enter values in the Before and After text boxes in the Spacing section then click OK. The Before and After spacing options require you to specify in points how much space to insert before and after paragraphs. Keep in mind that 72 points equals 1 inch.

> **Note**
> You can also type other units of measure after the value, and they will be converted to points. Use *cm* for centimeters, *in* for inches, and *li* for line. For example, *.6 li* will be converted to 7.2 points.

If you create styles for your documents, you'll want to consider configuring the Before and After settings when you create paragraph styles. When you add before and after spacing to paragraph styles, you help to ensure that spacing will be applied consistently and automatically throughout your document.

> **Tip**
>
> You can instantly add 12 points of space before a paragraph by selecting the paragraph(s) you want to format and pressing Ctrl+0 (zero). Press Ctrl+0 again to remove the space.

Controlling Alignment by Using Tabs

Back in the days of the typewriter, tabs were used for all types of alignment such as tabbed tables, charts, and columns. Word offers a variety of text alignment tools with which you can create columns, Word tables (instead of tabbed tables), and even charts and diagrams. And yet, with all the advanced formatting features Word 2010 offers, tabs continue to play a key role in aligning text and performing other tab-related activities. You'll use tabs for all sorts of things—from positioning content on a line where you want it, to adding prices in a column on the right side of the page, to centering a heading on a page. Figure 11-6 shows a variety of tab types in action. When you have formatting marks turned on in your document, the tab characters appear as right pointing arrows.

> **Tip**
>
> Instead of using a tabbed table to separate data in your document, you can use a borderless Word table instead. This will provide the appearance of a tabbed table but give you more control over the alignment of your information. Creating a table in this way also helps keep your table from getting bumped out of alignment when an extra space or tab is added. In a table, you can see and fix formatting mistakes easily. For more on Word tables, see Chapter 15, "Clarify Your Concepts in Professional Tables."

Chapter 11

Left tab   Center tab   Right tab

Tabs with leaders:

    Dotted line leader...

    Dashed line leader--

    Solid leader_____

Decimal tabs:

                1.025

          100.25

              .0025

         25

Figure 11-6 You can use a variety of tabs to align content in your Word document.

New documents based on the default Normal template include automatic tab stops every 0.5 inch, or 1.27 centimeters, but these tab stops don't appear in the ruler. You can adjust the default tab stop setting, add custom tabs, clear all tabs, and create tabs with leader lines. To adjust tabs, use the ruler or Tabs dialog box, as discussed in the following sections.

TROUBLESHOOTING

My text keeps shifting to the next tab stop.

If you have used tabs to align text and have needed to add a few more text characters within the tabbed text, you might find that the text shifts to the next tab stop even though there appears to be ample room. The underlying issue is too many automatic tabs or a combination of spaces and tabs to align the text. An example of text aligned at the 3-inch mark on the ruler using automatic tabs is shown here:

Note the 6 tab characters preceding the text (spaces weren't added for this example). Each time the default automatic tabs are set and you press the Tab key, 0.5 inch of space will be reserved for each tab character. If you add text at the beginning of the line, and if it exceeds 0.5 inch, then the text following the tab, or tabs, will shift as shown here:

To resolve this issue, use a manual tab instead of multiple automatic tabs. In this example, a manual Left tab has been set at 3 inches on the ruler:

As a result, there is a total of 3 inches of space available for text between the left margin and the manual tab stop. This space can be used before the text will shift to the next tab stop. In addition, pressing Tab once is far easier than adding multiple tabs and multiple spaces to align text. For more on setting manual tabs, see the next section.

Using the Ruler to Set Tabs

You can set manual tabs by using the horizontal ruler in Word. Using the ruler has a couple of advantages: You get visual feedback as soon as you set the tabs, and you can drag the ruler tabs to the left or right until you're satisfied with their positions. (You can even drag tabs off the ruler to delete them.) As soon as you set a manual tab on the ruler, selected text preceded by a tab character moves to reflect the setting. To use the ruler to add manual tabs, complete the following steps:

1. Click in the paragraph(s) in which you want to set tabs, or position the insertion point at the location where you want to create a new paragraph containing the tab settings.

2. Select the tab type you want to add by clicking the button in the top-left corner of the work area; this is called the *tab selector*. Each click of your mouse will cycle through the available tab types. Table 11-3 shows how each of the tab types appear in the tab selector and other available indent markers. Figure 11-6 (shown previously) shows the various tab types in action.

3. After you select a tab type, click in the lower portion of the ruler (in the white space below the numbers) to insert a manual tab. If you position a manual tab incorrectly, you can drag it off the ruler to delete it or drag it left or right to reposition it.

Chapter 11

Table 11-3 **Tab and Indent Types**

Button	Name	Description
⬜	Left Tab	Text begins at the tab stop and continues right. This is the most commonly used tab type.
⬜	Center Tab	Text is centered on the tab stop.
⬜	Right Tab	Text aligns at the tab stop and moves left.
⬜	Decimal Tab	Aligns a number on the decimal point, or where the decimal point would appear if the number does not show a decimal. When used in a Word table, numbers do not need to be preceded by a Tab character.
⬜	Bar Tab	Creates a vertical line. With this setting, you can draw vertical lines that span any number of horizontal lines of text. This tab type is not used for aligning text in a document.
⬜	First Line Indent	Activates the First Line Indent feature. Allows you to create a first line indent with a single click instead of dragging the indent marker.
⬜	Hanging Indent	Activates the Hanging Indent feature. Using this method, you can create a hanging indent with a single click instead of dragging the indent marker.

INSIDE OUT   Carrying Tabs from One Paragraph to the Next

If you set tabs in a paragraph, those tab settings will automatically carry over into the next paragraph you create when you use the Enter key to start a new paragraph. So, when you press Enter at the end of the paragraph in which you defined tab settings, the new paragraph have the your tab settings as well. On the other hand, if you format tabs in a paragraph that's already embedded among other paragraphs, the tab settings will not automatically extend to the existing paragraphs that follow.

If you want to extend tab formatting to existing paragraphs, you need to select all the paragraphs you want to format before you set the tabs.

Note that if the paragraph contains multiple lines, you'll see the manual tab when your cursor is in any line of the paragraph. However, the manual tab belongs to the paragraph, rather than to each line. For example, deleting the manual tab will affect all lines of the paragraph.

Finally, if you want to set tabs throughout an entire document, press Ctrl+A to select the document and then set your tabs on the ruler. Be aware that setting tabs for an entire document might affect existing tabs, so be sure to review your document after you make wide-ranging changes such as this. In addition, you might want to clear any existing tabs before inserting your new global tabs. The process of deleting tabs is described in the section titled "Clearing Manual Tabs," on page 352.

Creating Tabs by Using the Tabs Dialog Box

In addition to using the ruler to create tabs, you can use the Tabs dialog box, which you display by clicking the Tabs button in the Indents And Spacing tab of the Paragraph dialog box. The Tabs dialog box enables you to use precise measurements to set tabs. You can also create tabs that use leader lines. *Leaders* insert characters—such as dots or dashes (see Figure 11-6 for examples)—in the space before the tab stop; they act as a visual guide, leading the eye to the tabbed text.

Neither of these tasks can be accomplished using the ruler. The main drawback of creating tabs by using the Tabs dialog box is that you won't be able to see how your tabs affect your text until after you close the dialog box and view your document. To display the Tabs dialog box, perform any of the following actions:

- Press Alt+O+T.

- Double-click an existing tab in the horizontal ruler.

- Click Tabs in the Paragraph dialog box.

Figure 11-7 shows the Tabs dialog box. If the currently selected paragraph contains manual tabs, when you display the Tabs dialog box, the tab positions will be listed in the Tab Stop Position list box. Notice that the Default Tab Stops option is set to *0.5 inches* (or 1.27 if your preferred unit of measure is centimeters) by default.

Figure 11-7 Set, move, and modify tabs in the Tabs dialog box.

To use the Tabs dialog box to set manual tabs, follow these steps:

1. Click in the paragraph(s) in which you want to set tabs, or position your insertion point at the location where you want to create a new paragraph containing the tab settings.

2. Display the Tabs dialog box (press Alt+O+T or double-click an existing manual tab on the ruler).

3. Type a tab location—such as **1.75** (inches) or **4.45** (centimeters)—in the Tab Stop Position text box.

4. In the Alignment section, specify whether you want to create a left, center, right, decimal, or bar tab by choosing the respective option.

5. Select a leader line style, if desired, and then click Set. The manual tab will be listed in the Tab Stop Position list box.

6. Add more manual tabs, if desired, by repeating steps 3–5. Then click OK to close the Tabs dialog box when you've finished.

To change the default tab and indent setting (used when you click Increase Indent or Decrease Indent on the Home tab), you can type a new setting in the Default Tab Stops text box in the Tabs dialog box. For example, you could change the default 0.5-inch setting to 0.75 inch. The default setting is used if manual tabs aren't set when you press Tab or click the Increase Indent and Decrease Indent buttons.

Clearing Manual Tabs

Just as you can add manual tabs using the horizontal ruler and the Tabs dialog box, you can also clear manual tabs using these same tools. You can even clear all tabs at one time if you want to remove all the tabs you've set previously and start again. To remove tabs, select the paragraph(s) you want to modify, and then perform one of the following procedures:

- Drag the tab markers off the ruler. (Simply click a tab marker and drag it down into the document area.)

- Display the Tabs dialog box (press Alt+O+T or double-click an existing tab marker in the Ruler), select the tab you want to delete, and then click Clear.

- Display the Tabs dialog box and click Clear All.

TROUBLESHOOTING

Ruler options are unavailable when multiple paragraphs are selected.

In some instances, you might want to modify several paragraphs that have different tab settings so that they all have consistent tab settings. You can do so using both the horizontal ruler and the Tab dialog box. The easiest way to accomplish this task is by performing the following steps:

1. Select the paragraph(s) you want to format. If the tab markers in the horizontal ruler appear shaded or dimmed, the tab settings aren't currently applied to the entire selection. (You probably already know this, so the dimmed tab markers shouldn't faze you.)

2. Double-click a dimmed tab marker (or press Alt+O+T) to display the Tabs dialog box.

3. Click Clear All, click OK, and then click the horizontal ruler to define tab settings that will apply to the entire selection.

Controlling Line and Page Breaks

In Chapter 5, "Customizing Page Setup and Controlling Pagination," you learned about working with pages and sections, and you discovered that Word 2010 can help you keep important paragraphs and lists together on the same page. You control these types of paragraph considerations using the Line And Page Breaks tab in the Paragraph dialog box, shown in Figure 11-8.

Figure 11-8 Use the Line And Page Breaks tab of the Paragraph dialog box to instruct Word to keep specific paragraphs together on a page.

To apply the line and page break settings, select the text you want to format, display the Line And Page Breaks tab, and then select the appropriate check boxes. The following line and page break options are available:

- **Widow/Orphan Control** Ensures that the last line of a paragraph doesn't appear by itself at the top of a new page (a widow) or that the first line of a paragraph doesn't appear by itself at the bottom of a page (an orphan). Widow/Orphan Control is selected by default.

- **Keep Lines Together** Prevents page breaks from occurring within a paragraph. If a page break is needed, Word moves the entire paragraph to the next page.

- **Keep With Next** Prevents a page break from occurring between the selected paragraph and the following paragraph. This feature can be useful when you're using paragraphs that work together to create a single element, such as a table and a table caption or a heading and the following paragraph. (Note that the Heading styles use this format by default.)

> **Note**
>
> If you want to keep a group of paragraphs or rows in a Word table together, omit the last element in the group when using the Keep With Next pagination format.

- **Page Break Before** Inserts a page break before the selected paragraph. Typically this format is used in a style, such as Heading 1, used for chapter headings so that each chapter will automatically start on a new page when the Heading 1 style is applied. For more on styles, see Chapter 12.

The Tight Wrap option affects the way in which paragraphs wrap around text boxes. When you select a text box in your document, the Tight Wrap list offers choices you use to control the way the text wraps around the box:

You can experiment with the text flows around the selected text box to see the effects of the different choices. You can also select Tight Wrap options in addition to the other settings on the Line And Page Breaks tab to keep important information together.

Taking Control of Hyphenation

Once upon a time, long before Word 2010 was a glimmer in anyone's eye, writers and editors had to insert hyphens at the appropriate points when words broke from one line to the next in a document. Thank goodness that for several Word incarnations now, hyphenation has been handled automatically for us. However, there might be times when you want to control whether—and how—hyphenation is used in your document. You might need to decide, for example, whether you're going to hyphenate words at the ends of lines to create an evenly aligned right edge, or you want to bump the whole word to the next line, producing a more ragged look.

If you prefer, you can activate Word's built-in Hyphenation feature to eliminate white space and gaps along the edges of your text. When you use the Hyphenation feature, you can opt to apply hyphenation manually or automatically, as follows:

- **Automatic hyphenation.**   Word automatically hyphenates an entire document. If you later change the document's contents, Word rehyphenates the document as needed, while you work.

- **Manual hyphenation.**   Word searches for instances in which hyphenation is needed; you then manually decide whether to add a hyphen at each instance. If you later modify the document, Word displays and prints only the hyphens that fall at the ends of lines. To rehyphenate the document, repeat the manual hyphenation process.

> **Note**
>
> If you want to apply hyphenation to text that's written in a language other than the Microsoft Office default language, you need to ensure that the language is enabled for editing (through the Microsoft Office 2010 Language Settings), and you need to use Set Proofing Language (go to the Language tab on the Review tab) to set up the proofing tools for that language. You can learn more about translation features and setting up languages in Chapter 9, "Translating Text and Working with Languages."
>
> Either way, the process of adding hyphenation begins with Hyphenation on the Page Layout tab, as shown here:
>
>

Hyphenate an Entire Document Automatically

To automatically hyphenate an entire document, on the Page Layout tab, in the Page Setup group, click Hyphenation and then click Automatic. To configure the automatic hyphenation settings, click Hyphenation Options to display the Hyphenation dialog box, shown in Figure 11-9.

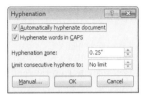

Figure 11-9 Use the Hyphenation dialog box to control hyphenation settings for automatic or manual hyphenation.

> **Tip**
> You can format nonbreaking hyphens to prevent a hyphenated word, number, or phrase from breaking if it falls at the end of a line. For example, you might not want to break a phone number at the end of a line. To insert a nonbreaking hyphen, on the Insert Tab, click Symbol, click More Symbols, and then click Special Characters. Alternatively, press Ctrl+Shift+Hyphen.

In the Hyphenation Zone text box, enter the amount of acceptable white space to leave between the end of the last word in a line and the right margin. If you want fewer hyphens, make the Hyphenation Zone value larger. If you want to reduce ragged edges, make the value smaller.

In the Limit Consecutive Hyphens To text box, type the maximum number of consecutive lines that can end with a hyphen and then click OK.

If you want to turn off the automatic hyphenation feature as well as remove automatically inserted hyphens, on the Page Layout tab, click Hyphenation and then click None.

Hyphenating All or Part of a Document Manually

When you hyphenate a document manually, you can hyphenate the entire document, or you can select part of the document before you display the Hyphenation dialog box. To hyphenate text manually, either select the text you want to hyphenate or ensure that no text is selected if you want to hyphenate the entire document. On the Page Layout tab, click Hyphenation and then click Manual.

When Word identifies a word or phrase that should be hyphenated, the Manual Hyphenation dialog box appears, as shown in Figure 11-10. You can click Yes to insert the suggested hyphen; use the arrow keys or mouse to reposition the hyphen location and then click Yes; click No to ignore the suggestion and move to the next word; or click Cancel to end the hyphenation process.

Figure 11-10 When you choose manual mode, Word prompts you to make a choice about hyphenation.

> **Note**
>
> If hyphenation is not enabled in the selected portion of the document, the Manual Hyphenation dialog box will not be displayed.

Creating Drop Caps in Existing Paragraphs

A popular design feature frequently associated with introductory paragraphs is drop caps. *Drop caps* are the large letters that appear at the very beginning of chapters or sections, and they can give the opening of your document a creative, stylized look.

Word 2010 provides an easy way for you to add drop caps to paragraphs. When you use the Drop Cap feature, Word increases the font size of the first letter of a paragraph and places it in a frame. After the drop cap is automatically created and situated, you can further modify it. To create a drop cap, follow these steps:

1. Click in the paragraph that you want to customize with a drop cap, or, if you want to enlarge more than just the first letter in the paragraph, select the letters or word(s) you want to format as drop caps.

2. On the Insert tab, in the Text group, click Drop Cap to display the Drop Cap gallery (see Figure 11-11).

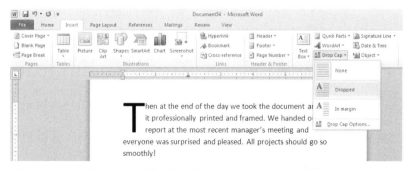

Figure 11-11 A drop cap adds a bit of drama to the opening of your paragraph.

3. Select Dropped or In Margin to add the drop cap to your paragraph. To control drop cap settings, click Drop Cap Options to display the Drop Cap dialog box, as shown in Figure 11-12.

Figure 11-12 Set parameters for the drop cap in the paragraph using the Drop Cap dialog box.

If you decide not to display a drop cap in your paragraph, you can easily remove the formatting. To do so, click in the paragraph containing the drop cap, display the Drop Cap gallery, and then click None.

Finally, note that drop caps appear above your paragraph in Normal view and Outline view. To see the drop cap effect on the screen as it actually appears, view documents in Web Page Layout, Print Layout, or Reading Layout views.

Creating Effective Lists

In our time-pressured work world, everybody loves lists. Lists give people reading your document an easy way to understand what you think are the most important points to remember. A list might outline key thoughts, reinforce main topics, describe a process, or capsulize memorable concepts. Adding bulleted and numbered lists to your document can go a long way toward making your document more readable, which is something for which your readers will be grateful.

Throughout this book, both bulleted and numbered lists are referred to simply as lists because they behave the same way. When you choose a bullet, of course, you're using a special symbol, character, or graphic to start a line. When you use a number, you're selecting the font, size, and color of the numeral you want to use. In addition, you can use roman numerals, letters, and other line identifiers in numbered lists.

When Bullets Work

Word gives you the capacity to create bulleted lists with a number of looks. For instance, you can select bullet characters, colors, and indents. Further, you can place bulleted lists side by side in a multicolumn format. Here are some guidelines to remember when you create bulleted lists:

- **Be concise.**   Fewer words make a larger impact. Unless you must include paragraphs of text for each bullet item, pare your prose down to fewer than three sentences, if you can.

- **Stick to the point.**   A general rule is one point, one bullet. Don't try to cram more than one idea into each bullet item.

- **Be clear.**   Flowery language isn't necessary—clear and simple is best.

- **Don't overdo it.**   Bullets can be so much fun (and easier to write than big blocks of text) that you might be tempted to use them liberally throughout your document. Resist the temptation to overuse bullets in your work and use them only when they bring clarity to your content.

- **Choose a bullet that makes sense.**   If your report is about a new drive train your company is manufacturing, would baby-bottle bullet characters really make sense? Probably not. Be sure to fit the bullet characters you choose to the style and expectations of your audience.

- **Don't use too many at once.**   Don't make your lists burdensome for your readers. If possible, say what you need to say in five to seven bullet points and move back to paragraph style.

Tip
Bullets are ideal for those times when you want to convey short, to-the-point pieces of information. The fact that you use bullets instead of numbers implies to your reader that the points can be read and applied in any order; there's no specific sequence in a bulleted list.

When Numbers Matter

The type of content you include determines whether you need numbered lists in your documents. If you're writing a how-to manual about fly-fishing, you might have quite a few numbered steps, explaining important procedures for preparing equipment, finding the right spot, and setting up for your first cast. If you're creating a marketing plan with a timeline and an action sequence, your steps will define a process that builds a bigger promotions system. Whatever the purpose of your numbered list, you can make sure it's most effective in these ways:

- **Use numbers that fit your tone.** In an upbeat publication, you might want to use specialty numbers or a casual font with oversized numbers. In a more serious piece, you'll want the numbers you select to carry a more purposeful tone.

- **Keep steps clear.** Most often, numbered steps are used to describe a process. Conveniently enough, steps can add clarity to a complex procedure. Therefore, don't muddy the waters by overburdening a numbered step with too much information. Include one or two instructions per step and then move on to the next numbered step.

- **Remember the white space.** Whether you're working with bulleted or numbered lists, the white space in your document is as important as the text on the page—it might be a humbling statement, but it's true. White space gives your readers' eyes a rest, so space list items and avoid crowding steps too closely.

- **Align by design.** As with spacing for bulleted and numbered lists, the alignment of lists matters. Make sure the indents in the second line of the list item align with the first character of text, and ensure that all of the lists throughout your document present a consistent alignment pattern.

> **Tip**
> A numbered list communicates a sequence: First, we have the team meeting; next, we implement the plan; then, we write the report; and finally, we present our results. These items, in a list, would be numbered because they show a definite order and a logical process.

INSIDE OUT   Controlling Automatic Lists

If you want full control over your lists, you need to make sure that you have the Auto-Format options turned off for numbering and bullets. The rationale behind this is that automatic formatting options for list features can conflict with numbered and bulleted lists. If you want to manually add the number and bullet formatting, clear these options before you begin list-making. To do so, follow these steps:

1. On the File tab, click Options and then click Proofing.

2. Click the AutoCorrect Options button and then click the AutoFormat As You Type tab.

3. In the Apply As You Type section, make sure Automatic Bulleted Lists and Automatic Numbered Lists are cleared. (Note that these options are selected by default.)

For more on the AutoFormat As You Type options, see the section, "Managing AutoFormat Effectively," on page 334.

Creating a Quick List

Word makes it easy for you to create both numbered and bulleted lists from existing text and as you type. To create a list from existing text, select the text and then click either Bullets or Numbering on the Home tab in the Paragraph group. Each selected paragraph will be formatted as a single numbered or bulleted list item. As mentioned, you can also create lists while you type. To create a quick list while you type, follow these steps:

1. Place the insertion point where you want to add the list.

2. Click the Numbering button if you want to create a numbered list, or click Bullets if you want to create a bulleted list. Both are shown in Figure 11-13.

3. The list item is added. Type your first item then press Enter. The next bullet or number is added automatically.

Chapter 11

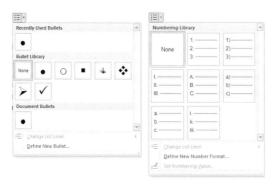

Figure 11-13 The Bullet and Numbering galleries offer various list styles from which you can choose.

4.   Continue entering your list items, pressing Enter after each item.

If you are using a numbered list, when you add or delete an item in the list, the list items will automatically renumber accordingly.

> **Tip**
>
> If you want to start a new paragraph within a bulleted or numbered list, but you're not yet ready for the next bullet or number, press Shift+Enter instead of just Enter. Pressing Shift+Enter ensures that the added information appears as a paragraph but will still be part of the current bulleted or numbered item. When you press Enter later to continue your list, a bullet or number will appear.

Creating Lists While You Type

You can also create lists while you type by using the AutoFormat As You Type features found in the AutoCorrect dialog box. These options are turned on by default, but to verify them, display Word Options, click Proofing, and then click the AutoCorrect Options button. (Alternatively, press Alt+T+A to display the AutoCorrect dialog box.) On the AutoFormat As You Type tab, verify Automatic Bulleted Lists and Automatic Numbered Lists are selected.

If you are creating complex numbering schemes or using multiple numbered lists in a document, this method is not recommended due to the lack of control you have over lists that are automatically generated by Word. With this in mind, you can use the following to create bulleted or numbered lists as you type.

To create a bulleted list in Word, type an asterisk (*), press Tab, type a list entry, and then press Enter. By default, Word will change the asterisk to a bullet and the AutoCorrect

Options button will appear, enabling you to control the automatic bulleted list feature. If you want to create the bulleted list, simply continue to type, and the AutoCorrect Options button will disappear.

Similarly, if you have Automatic Numbered Lists selected in your AutoFormat options, to create a numbered list while you type, enter a number (you can enter any number, but generally, you'd probably want to start with the number 1), press Tab, enter text, and press Enter. Word will format the entry as a numbered list item and display the AutoCorrect Options button with which you can control the creation of the list. Again, to continue creating the numbered list, simply continue to type the next numbered list entry.

Tip

If you want space added between the list items, rather than pressing Enter twice to add an empty paragraph between the list items, use formatted space before or after each paragraph, as described in the section titled "Adjusting Spacing Above and Below Paragraphs," on page 346.

TROUBLESHOOTING

A number is bold or is not formatted like the other numbers in the list.

If your numbers are formatted differently from other numbers in the list, the likely cause is the paragraph mark at the end contains the undesired format.

To resolve this issue, turn on the display of formatting marks (on the Home tab, in the Paragraph group, click Show/Hide), select the paragraph mark, and then clear the formatting. For example, if the number is bold, click Bold to remove the format.

Ending a List the Way You Want

One of the challenges users often face with bulleted and numbered lists is that the lists seem to want to go on forever. After you press Enter on your last list entry, yet another bullet (or number) shows up. Get rid of the extra bullet or number by doing one of three things:

- Click the Bullets or Numbering button to turn off the feature.

- Press Backspace twice to delete the number or bullet and place your cursor at the left margin. The first time you press Backspace, the cursor will line up below the text of the previous list item (as opposed to lining up under the number in previous versions of Word). If your list is indented, continue to press Backspace until your cursor reaches the desired position.

- Press Enter twice after the last item, instead of once.

See the section titled "Creating and Using Multilevel Lists" on page 373 to see how Word 2010 responds when you use Enter and Backspace in a multilevel list.

Enhancing Bulleted Lists

The default Word settings for bulleted and numbered lists are fine when you're creating a quick, simple document that will be passed around the office and eventually end up in the dumpster. But what about those special reports you create or the procedure manuals that others rely on? Those need to have a more professional look and feel; the treatment of lists in your document suddenly become more important.

You can improve a basic bulleted list in several ways. You might want to customize your list by choosing your bullet from the Bullet gallery, selecting a picture bullet, creating your own bullets, or changing indents and spacing for your bullet items.

Choosing a New Bullet from the Bullet Library

Word provides a gallery of preset bullet styles to choose from and a virtually unlimited supply of bullet options that you can pull from symbol typefaces, graphics libraries, and more. To choose a new bullet character for a list, follow these steps:

1. Select the list items with the bullets you want to change or position your cursor where you want to add a list.

2. On the Home tab, click the arrow next to Bullets to display the Bullet gallery, as shown previously in Figure 11-13.

3. Browse the gallery and select another symbol or picture to use as a bullet.

A quick way to access the Bullet gallery is to select your list, right-click, point at Bullets, and then select a new bullet from the gallery.

Using a Custom Bullet

If you don't like any of the bullets in the Bullet gallery, you can select a new bullet by clicking Define New Bullet. The Define New Bullet dialog box appears (see Figure 11-4). If you like to be creative in your documents, you'll enjoy this feature—just a small and subtle change can make a big different in how your content looks on the page.

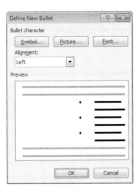

Figure 11-14 The Define New Bullet dialog box gives you the means to change the font and character you use for bullets. You can also change bullet position here.

Click the Symbol and Picture buttons to access additional bullets; use the Font button to modify the font formatting of your bullet. You learn more about these options in the sections that follow.

Changing the Bullet Font

When you click Font in the Define New Bullet dialog box, the Font dialog box appears, as shown in Figure 11-15. Here you can select a typeface and change font settings for bullet characters. Symbol is the default font selected for bullets, which offers you a variety of shapes and symbols you can apply as a bullet character. You might want to choose one of the Wingdings fonts or another symbols font you have installed on your computer. This enables you to select the bullet character you want to use from the variety of symbols included in the font.

Figure 11-15 The Font dialog box enables you to change a bullet character's typeface, style, color, and text effects.

In addition to selecting a bullet font, you can also choose the size, color, and effects of the font you define. Click your options in the various setting boxes and preview the selection in the Preview box at the bottom of the dialog box. You can click OK to save your settings and return to the Define New Bullet dialog box. You'll be able to see the effects of your changes in the preview window there.

Changing a Bullet Symbol

An easy way to customize the look and feel of your document involves changing the symbol used for the bullets in your lists. To customize bullets, click Symbol in the Define New Bullet dialog box to display the Symbol dialog box, as shown in Figure 11-16.

Figure 11-16 Click the symbol you want to select as a new bullet character. If you need to be consistent with lists in other documents, make note of the character code of the item you select.

The Symbol dialog box displays the available characters for the selected font. You can scroll through the list using the vertical scroll bar to find a symbol you want to add or click the symbol you like from the Recently Used Symbols row. Click OK to add the symbol.

If you don't see the bullet symbol you were looking for, you can choose a different font by clicking the Font arrow and selecting a new symbol font from the list. Now scroll through the new symbols to find the one you want.

Notice that you can see the numeric character code in either decimal or hexadecimal format for each character you select in the Symbol dialog box. This enables you to be sure you've used the same bullet throughout this document and in other documents that need a consistent style.

> **Tip**
> You can resize the Symbol dialog box to view additional rows and columns of symbols at a time. To maximize or restore the dialog box, double-click the title bar.

Using a Picture Bullet

For documents that can be a little more creative than your run-of-the-mill business prospectus, who wouldn't love picture bullets? A good picture bullet that fits your document can add a splash of visual interest that might help to keep your reader reading.

What is a picture bullet? It's a graphic image that's small enough to use as a bullet character. Word offers a range of picture bullet styles and shapes, including animated bullets that you can use in documents that will be used online. To display the Picture Bullet dialog box and see the available offerings, click the arrow next to Bullet on the Home tab, click Define New Bullet, and then click Picture. The Picture Bullet dialog box appears, as shown in Figure 11-17.

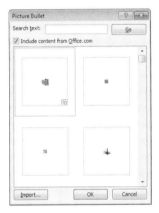

Figure 11-17 Picture bullet options appear in a dialog box that includes a Search Text option.

To select a picture bullet, you simply click the one you want and click OK. Word adds the picture bullet to the Bullet gallery.

If you don't see a picture bullet that you want to use in the Picture Bullet dialog box, enter text in the Search Text box and click Go. Word will search clip art and online files. Online bullet options appear with an image of the world in the lower-left corner of the preview picture. Further, animated bullets (bullets that have small movements, size changes, or color changes when the bullet is viewed online on a Web page) appear with a star in the lower-right corner of a preview picture, as you see in the top-left bullet in Figure 11-17.

Improving Numbered Lists

Like bulleted lists, numbered lists enable you to make your own choices about the look and format of the numerals used. Many procedures you use to customize bulleted lists can also be used to fine-tune numbered lists. Most notably, in numbered lists, you can make modifications by specifying a font, selecting the number style you want, and choosing the number and text position of the items in your list.

Choosing a Numbering Scheme

The style of your numbers can add character to numbered lists. Depending on the nature of your publication, you might use simple traditional characters or larger, colorful characters. Begin by selecting the numbered list you want to change, or position your cursor in an empty paragraph in which you want to start your list, and on the Home tab, click the arrow next to Numbering, and then click a numbering format. Figure 11-18 shows the Numbering gallery.

Figure 11-18 Choose the numbering style you like or create a new one.

Modifying the Numbering Style

If you aren't particularly happy with the available numbering styles, you can define a new number format or choose from one of the styles not displayed in the gallery. To create a new number format, display the Numbering gallery and then click Define New Number Format. The Define New Number Format dialog box appears, providing formatting options for numbered lists (see Figure 11-19).

Figure 11-19 The Define New Number Format dialog box gives you the means to create a new number format and change number position.

To select a new number style, click the Number Style list to see the available style choices. Depending on the nature of your document, you might want to select roman numeral style, alphanumeric characters, or even numbers that are spelled out as text. Here is the range of choices for the number styles you can select:

1, 2, 3

I, II, III

i, ii, iii

A, B, C

a, b, c

1st, 2nd, 3rd

One, Two Three

First, Second, Third

01, 02, 03

001, 002, 003

0001, 0002, 0003

00001, 00002, 00003

After you select the number style you want, you can determine at which number you want the list to begin by clicking in the Start At text box and then typing the number for the starting point. If you prefer, you can use the up or down arrows on the Start At text box to increase or decrease the number by one.

Chapter 11

Tip

If you want to create a list that includes multiple levels, you might find that using a multilevel list instead of a numbered list better fits your content needs. See the section, "Creating and Using Multilevel Lists,"on page 373 for specific directions.

Note

When you use Numbering, you are using a single style called List Paragraph. If you are using complex numbering or using multiple unique lists in a document, then create a new list style instead. The Define New List Style command is found on the Home tab in the Paragraph group, at the bottom of the Multilevel List gallery.

This method will create a style for each new list and provide more control over editing the list and applying the correct list to the related paragraphs. For more information on creating list styles, see the section titled "Creating a New List Style," on page 375.

Continuing Numbering

Some of your numbered list items might be separated by elements such as charts, explanatory paragraphs, or sidebars. When you click the Numbering button, if Word doesn't automatically continue with the next numbered step in your process, you can continue numbers in an existing numbered list in several ways:

- If the AutoCorrect Options button appears in the document, click it and click Continue Numbering.

- Display the Numbering gallery and then click Set Numbering Value. In the Set Numbering Value dialog box, shown in Figure 11-20, select Continue From Previous List. (This option is also available when you right-click a list item.)

Figure 11-20 Use the Set Numbering Value dialog box to continue a numbered list or skip numbers.

- Right-click the first incorrect number in a numbered list and then click Continue Numbering.

Restarting Numbering

Restarting numbered lists is similar to continuing numbered lists. The main difference is that you'll choose the Restart Numbering option instead of the Continue Numbering option. To restart a numbered list with the number 1, take any of the following actions:

- Click the AutoCorrect Options button and then click Restart Numbering. (If available.)

- Display the Numbering gallery and then click Set Numbering Value. In the dialog box, select Start New List and type **1** (one) in the Set Value To text box. (This option is also available when you right-click a list item.)

- In a numbered list, right-click the number that you want to change to the number 1 and click Restart At 1.

If you want to restart a list with a number other than 1 (but you don't want to continue the preceding list), select Set Numbering Value from the Numbering gallery. Enter a number in the Set Value To text box and then click OK.

Converting a Bulleted List to a Numbered List (or Vice Versa)

You can easily convert bulleted lists to numbered lists and vice versa. To do so, simply select the list and then click either the Bullets button or the Numbering button on the Home tab. After you convert a list, you can tweak the list's appearance and settings while the list is selected by using the methods previously described in this chapter.

Chapter 11

TROUBLESHOOTING

My numbered list will not continue from the previous list.

If you attempt to continue numbering from a previous list, and each time you select Continue Numbering the list still starts at 1, the underlying problem is that a new list has been defined in the document. This can occur if you modify the indents by using the ruler or Paragraph dialog box, or if you change to another list in the Numbering gallery.

To resolve this issue, select the last correctly numbered list item, be sure to include the paragraph mark in your selection since it holds the number format, then on the Home tab, in the Clipboard group, click the Format Painter to copy the correct list format. Select the incorrectly numbered list item and be sure to include the paragraph mark in your selection. The correct number format should be applied.

To permanently resolve the issue, or if you need to change the list indents or adjust the formatting of the list, create and use a list style, described in the section titled "Creating a New List Style," on page 375.

Changing List Indents

Use the Adjust List Indents dialog box to modify the number position, text indent, or change the character that follows a number or bullet. To display the dialog box, right-click a list item and click Adjust List Indents. Figure 11-21 displays the Adjust List Indents dialog box.

Figure 11-21 The Adjust List Indents dialog box is where you modify the number position, indent, and change the character following a number or bullet.

The Adjust List Indents dialog box includes the following options:

- **Number Position**   Changes the position of the number or bullet's indent from the left margin

- **Text Indent**   Changes the amount of space between the number or bullet and the beginning of the text

- **Follow Number With**   Changes the default Tab character following the number to a space or nothing

- **Add Tab Stop At**   If using a Tab character following the bullet or number, this option adds a manual tab stop at the selected position

CAUTION

When you change list indents by using the Adjust List Indents dialog box or using the indent methods described previously in this chapter, such as using the ruler or Paragraph dialog box, you apply direct formatting on top of the list, which can result in list instabilities. Consider creating a list style instead of using direct formatting, which is discussed in the section titled "Creating a New List Style," on page 375.

Creating and Using Multilevel Lists

Some of your documents might require more than a simple bulleted or numbered list. Perhaps you want to incorporate a fairly sophisticated outline in your document, or you want to spell out a technique process that essentially nests lists within lists. Word 2010 includes a feature known as multilevel lists that enable you to define up to nine numbering levels. You can mix numerals and letters, uppercase and lowercase letters, and a variety of styles to create the type of list that best fits the needs of your document. If you don't see a multilevel list style in the gallery that fits what you're looking for, you can create a new list style that directly maps to the requirements of your content.

Applying a Multilevel List

You access the Multilevel List gallery by clicking the Multilevel List tool to the right of the Numbering tool in the Paragraph group of the Home tab. The Multilevel List gallery is shown in Figure 11-22.

Chapter 11

Figure 11-22 The Multilevel List gallery offers a variety of list options.

You create a multilevel list using the same methods as you would to add bullets or numbering. The main difference is that you are working with multiple list levels, as opposed to a single list level. When using a multilevel list, you can change the list level by using any of the following methods:

- To promote a list level, press Enter. Continuing to press Enter will promote the list item to the highest level, at which point the list will end.

- Press Tab to demote the list level, which moved the text at the cursor position to the right, Shift+Tab to promote the list level, which moves the text out toward the left margin.

> **Note**
>
> To use Tab and Shift+Tab, the option Set Left And First Indent With Tabs And Backspace must be selected in the AutoCorrect dialog box on the AutoFormat As You Type tab. To display the AutoCorrect dialog box, on the File tab, click Options, click Proofing, and then click AutoCorrect Options.

- On the Home tab, in the Paragraph group, click Increase Indent to demote the list level, or Decrease Indent to promote the list level.

- Right-click the list item then click Increase Indent to demote the list level, or Decrease Indent to promote the list level.

- Click Multilevel List, then at the bottom of the gallery, point at Change List Level, and then click the correct list level from the list of choices.

The Multilevel List gallery includes two options for creating a new multilevel list: Define New Multilevel List and Define New List Style. The Define New Multilevel List command is for creating a list that you won't ever change. The Define New List Style command essentially provides "packaging" for a multilevel list that can be easily modified and shared with other documents. Thus, the best practice is to define a new list style as opposed to defining a new multilevel list.

When you create a new list style, you have more control over the list. For example, you can apply the correct list to related list items; format the list style, such as modifying indents; and delete unneeded list styles from your document.

In the next two sections, you learn more about creating list styles.

Creating a New List Style

When you're looking for a specific type of list that doesn't appear in the Multilevel List gallery, Word 2010 gives you the option of creating the new list yourself. To Begin the process of creating a new list style, on the Home tab, click the arrow to the right of Multilevel List in the Paragraph group. At the bottom of the gallery, click Define New List Style. The Define New List Style dialog box will appear, as you see in Figure 11-23.

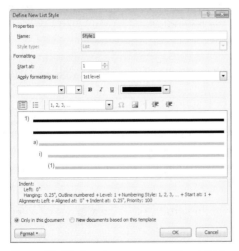

Figure 11-23 Creating a new multilevel list begins in the Define New List Style dialog box.

To complete your new list style, follow these steps:

1. In the Name text box, type a name for your style.

2. For a simple list, use the formatting options provided in the Define New List Style dialog box.

   For example, select a number format or bullet for each level of your list. For a more complex list, or to adjust the list indents, click the Format button at the bottom of the dialog box and then click Numbering. The Modify Multilevel list dialog box is shown in Figure 11-24.

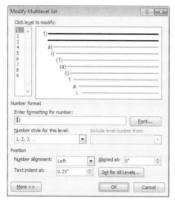

Figure 11-24 Set new styles and formatting for the list in the Modify Multilevel list dialog box.

3. In Click Level To Modify, verify level 1 is selected and then set the following options in the order provided here (the order provided is based on the best method to follow, not the order the options appear in the dialog box):

   - **Number Format**   Select a Number Style from the Number Style For This Level list. If creating a multilevel list style using bullets, scroll to the bottom of the list to view bullet and picture options.

   - **Enter Formatting For Number**   Modify the character preceding or following the previously selected number or bullet. For example, replace a parenthesis with a period, or add text preceding the number, such as Chapter or Heading.

CAUTION

If you modify the shaded value (the number or character selected by using the Number Style For This Level list), the value will not dynamically update.

- **Font**   Click the Font button to change the font formatting for the list number or character.

- **Include level number from**   This option is enabled for levels 2 through 9. It provides the ability to include the number from the previous level, such as 2a), a format that is often used in technical documents.

Note

To use legal style numbering, such as 2.1.1, click More and select the Legal Style Numbering option. The Number list will be disabled, and each level will use legal style numbering. In the Include Level Number From list, select each level of numbering you want to include. For example, for Level 3, select Level 1 and then select Level 2.

If you want periods to appear between the numbers, type them in the Enter formatting for number text box after you select each level from the Include level number from list.

- **Position**   Change the Number Alignment, if necessary. In the Aligned At text box, type a value for the space between the left margin and the number (Left Indent). In the Text Indent At text box, type a value for the space between the number and list text (Hanging Indent).

Tip

To set consistent spacing for each list level so that the next level begins below the text position of the previous level, click Set for all levels and modify the settings accordingly. A standard offset is 0.25 inches, or 0.64 centimeters, between list levels.

---

4. Select the next list level and modify the formatting options using the recommended order provided in step 3. Repeat for any additional list levels.

5. When you are finished defining your list style, click OK to close the Multilevel List Style dialog box. Then click OK to close the Define New List Style dialog box and create your new list style.

After you have created your list style, you can use it as you would any other list in the Multilevel List gallery. Your new list style will appear in the section titled List Styles.

Chapter 11

What's Next?

This chapter was all about formatting paragraphs, whether you're interested in aligning, spacing, or hyphenating them or arranging them in all sorts of lists. The next chapter looks closely at the ways you can use all this formatting power to your advantage by creating, modifying, and applying Quick Styles in your Word 2010 documents.

Style Design with Users in Mind 379

Exploring the Quick Style Gallery
and Quick Style Sets. 384

Working with the Styles Pane. 390

Creating and Modifying Styles 395

Style Management Tools. 400

What's Next? 411

T he more sophisticated you become with the documents you produce, the more likely you are to want to automate and organize the content you create and use. Word 2010 offers a number of features that help you to work more efficiently and productively. Building blocks, which you learned about in Chapter 7, "Creating and Reusing Content," help you create, save, and reuse content in various ways in all sorts of documents. Styles are to formats what building blocks are to content. With a style, you can use a ready-made set of formatting attributes and apply them consistently to characters, paragraphs, lists, and tables. This helps you build consistency into your document (one of the keystones of effective communication; sudden changes of format can interrupt your reader and cause them to lose the thread of your message).

Word 2010 carries on the Quick Styles approach started in Word 2007 by offering you a gallery of style sets that you can apply to the text in your document. These style sets are tied to the theme you've selected (remember themes? We covered them in Chapter 4, "Templates and Themes for a Professional Look"), so the types of style sets you find in your current document will vary depending on the theme you've selected for your basic document design.

And of course, you can tailor the style sets, create your own, and modify existing styles to your heart's content. These items and more are the focus of this chapter.

Style Design with Users in Mind

In Chapter 11, "Formatting Your Document," you learned about a number of ways Word 2010 helps you automate and control your formatting and apply ready-made formatting choices—such as bulleted, numbered, and multilevel list styles—to your document content. Because there are so many different ways to use styles in Word, developers separated the tools you use to apply text styles, list styles, and table styles. This helps you find and apply just the styles you need for the document element with which you happen to be working.

> ## Tip
> The styles you use for formatting lists and text in your document are found on the Home tab, in the Paragraph and Styles groups. The styles used for formatting tables appear on the Table Tools contextual tab. To learn more about table styles in Word 2010, see Chapter 15, "Clarify Your Concepts in Professional Tables."

Word 2010 also provides the Styles gallery and the Styles pane to help you see which styles are available in your document and choose or modify them to suit your needs.

> ## Watching Styles as You Work
>
> If you want to see which styles are currently in play in the document you're working on, you can display a Style area along the left side of your document. The area lists the various styles connected to paragraphs, headings, images, and more in your document text. To display the Styles area, follow these steps:
>
> 1. On the File tab, click Options.
>
> 2. On the Advanced tab, scroll to Display options.
>
> 3. Increase the Style Area Pane Width in Draft and Outline View value, and then click OK.
>
> 4. Click Draft to see the styles currently in use.

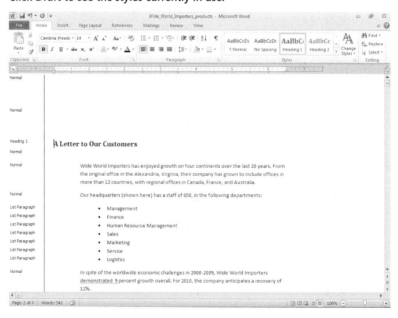

You can leave the Style area displayed while you work if you want to be able to check styles as you move along in your document. You can add content and edit in Page Layout mode, and then click the Draft tool in the lower-right corner of the screen to check your styles periodically. If you want to close the Styles area later, simply redisplay the Advanced tab, scroll to Display options, and return the Style Area Pane Width in Draft and Outline View value to 0.

Style Fundamentals

You'll find the Styles gallery at the right side on the Home tab, in the Styles group. To see all the styles that are currently available based on the theme you've selected, click the Styles More button. The gallery offers a number of styles of different sorts—headline styles, body text styles, quotes, and more (see Figure 12-1).

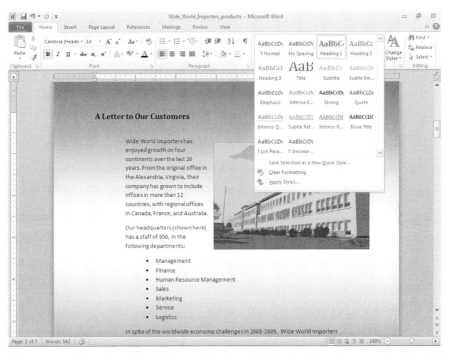

Figure 12-1 The Styles gallery offers a collection of styles based on the currently selected theme that you are likely to want to apply.

You'll notice a couple of things about the styles in the gallery. First, each selection shows a preview of the way the text will look when it's formatted in that particular style. The styles offer different font sizes, styles, and effects (such as underline or font color). Notice also that to the left of some of the styles in the gallery, you see a small paragraph mark. This mark lets you know what kind of style you're selecting. The ones with a paragraph mark are known—not surprisingly—as paragraph styles.

Word has five primary types of styles for formatting specific content, which are described in the following list:

- **Paragraph**   Used for formatting a paragraph as a whole. Attributes for an entire paragraph, such as alignment, line spacing, indents, tabs, paragraph spacing, borders, and shading, can be defined in a paragraph style. Fonts can also be part of a paragraph style. In addition, you can apply character styles locally within a paragraph to add specific formatting attributes to selected words.

> **Note**
> The Default Paragraph Font is used when a paragraph contains no direct font formatting and a character style is not applied.

- **Character**   Character styles are designed to change the format of individual characters, letters, words, or phrases. You might apply a character style, for example, to boldface a particular product name or to make a definition term stand out. Character styles, in effect, layer over paragraph styles so both can be used at once. Additionally, linked styles can be used as both paragraph and character styles.

> **Note**
> Because the bold format is considered a toggle format, if a character style that includes the bold format is used with a paragraph style that is also defined with the bold format, the character style cancels out the bold of the paragraph style, which results in text that is not bold. This is an idiosyncrasy of toggle formats: two "on codes" result in an "off code," so the resulting text will *not* appear in bold.

- **Linked Style**   A linked style is a combination paragraph and character style. Font formats defined in the style can be used as a character style and applied to a portion of a paragraph, or it can be used as a paragraph style with both the font and paragraph formats applied to the entire paragraph. If you select text within a paragraph and apply a style but the entire paragraph is formatted, then you are using a paragraph style rather than a linked style. Note that Word 2010 includes many linked styles.

> **Tip**
> In cases where you want to use linked styles strictly as a paragraph style, you can turn off linking by displaying the Style pane (click the dialog launcher in the Styles group), and clicking Disable Linked Styles.

> **Note**
> Heading 1, for example, is actually a linked style and not a paragraph style. In Style Example 1, because the cursor was placed in the paragraph and no text was selected, Heading 1 acted as a paragraph style and the formats were applied to the entire paragraph. Had you selected a portion of the paragraph, then the font formats of the styles would have been applied to the selected text only.

- **List**   List styles are used for defining multilevel lists. Font formatting can be defined in the style, but the only paragraph formats that can be defined are paragraph indents, which are defined in the numbering format. See Chapter 11 for more information on creating and modifying list styles.

- **Table**   Table styles are used for defining table formatting. Paragraph and font formats can be defined along with table properties. Banding formats (alternating row or column colors) and specific table elements, such as the header row, total row, first column, last column, and so on, can be formatted individually.

Styles are defined and stored with the document, and wherever the document goes, the formatting travels with it. If a built-in style such as Heading 1 is modified in a document, then by default those modifications are only stored in that document and the modification does not change the built-in style. If you make changes to a style that is part of the attached template (for example, Normal.dotm), Word 2010 will ask you when you close the file whether you want to update the current styles. If you want the style changes to be applied to the template (and thus available to other documents that use that same template), click Yes. If you click No, the styles will remain active in the current document only.

> **Note**
> When you create a new document based on the default Normal template, it includes the following defined styles: Normal, Headings 1–3, Default Paragraph Font, Table Normal, and No List. Other styles are available to the document, but they aren't actually defined in your document.

Chapter 12

Exploring the Quick Style Gallery and Quick Style Sets

Quick Styles were introduced in Word 2007; in Word 2010, they continue to offer sets of styles that you can easily apply to your documents—with a single click. Quick Styles are designed to look good together so you can feel confident about the formats you apply. Quick Styles come in a variety of designs, which gives you a wide range of choices for the look and feel of your document.

Distinctive	Modern	Traditional
Elegant	Newsprint	Word 2003
Fancy	Perspective	Word 2010
Formal	Simple	
Manuscript	Thatch	

Quick Styles help to automate the formats you apply to your document and reduce the amount of work you need to do if you decide to change the look and feel of the document or reuse some of the content in another file. Because Quick Styles are tied to themes, when you choose a different theme, the look and feel of the headings, body text, list styles, and more will change automatically. And you can create a completely different look by choosing a different Quick Style set for your document.

> **Note**
>
> If you have created new formats in your document but not applied styles to text elements, those items will not be updated automatically when you change Quick Style sets or themes.

> **Note**
>
> You might have noticed that the term Quick Styles is used in other chapters. It is not used in reference to the Styles group found on the Home tab because the term Quick Styles is not limited to text styles. Quick Styles are galleries of predefined formats found throughout Word 2010, such as the Picture gallery (Picture Quick Styles), the Chart gallery (Chart Quick Styles), and the SmartArt gallery (SmartArt Quick Styles), to name but a few. For a better understanding, if you reduce the width of your Word window small enough, the auto scale functionality of the Ribbon reduces these in-Ribbon galleries to a single button labeled Quick Styles.
>
> For the sake of clarity, in this chapter, the term Quick Styles refers to the Quick Style gallery found on the Home tab.

Applying and Modifying Styles Using the Quick Style Gallery

The process of applying a Quick Style is very simple. Open the document to which you want to apply the style set and follow these steps:

1. Click in the document at the point where you want to apply the style, or select the text you want to format.

2. On the Home tab, click the style you want in the Styles gallery.

   You can display additional styles by clicking the More button in the lower-right corner of the gallery (see Figure 12-2).

3. Hover the mouse over the style set you'd like to see. Your document previews the set at the pointer position.

4. Click the style you want to apply.

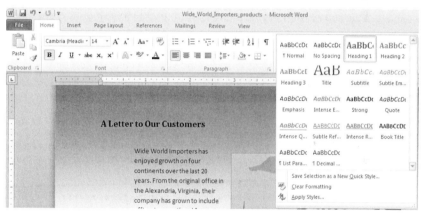

Figure 12-2 Click in the Styles gallery to apply a style to your document.

Note

In order to preview styles by hovering the mouse over gallery items, you must be viewing the document in either Print Layout or Web Layout view.

What if the desired style isn't quite what you are looking for? Perhaps you'd rather see Heading 1 formatted in a different font color instead. You can update a style using the Quick Style gallery by following these simple steps:

1. Select the paragraph you want to change and apply the new setting for the attributes you want to modify (for example, apply the color choice you want).

2. With the text selected, on the Home tab, right-click Heading 1 in the Quick Style gallery. Click Update Heading 1 To Match Selection.

   Heading 1 should now be updated to match the formats specified in the current paragraph.

That's all you need to do to redefine a style. If you want to verify your results, place your cursor in the second paragraph and click the Heading 1 style in the Quick Style gallery.

You might have noticed other options when you right-clicked the style, such as Select All # Instance(s); Rename, which allows you to rename the style; Remove From Quick Style Gallery, which removes the style from the gallery but does not remove the style from the document; and Modify, as shown in the following image.

The Modify option opens the Modify Style dialog box and provides additional options that are not available when updating a style using the Update Style Name To Match Selection method. You can learn more about the Modify Style dialog box in the section titled "Creating and Modifying Styles," on page 395.

Switching and Modifying Quick Style Sets

The 11 different Quick Style Sets give you a wide range to choose from as you're planning the overall design of your document. From traditional to modern, from contemplative to businesslike, the different style sets convey unique senses of tone and format. You can easily switch among the Quick Style Sets in your document, applying new fonts, sizes, and styles for headings, body text, and special text elements in your file—all with a single click. To exchange a Quick Style Set, follow these steps:

1. Open the document you want to change.

2. In the Styles group on the Home tab, click Change Styles.

3. Point to Style Sets and hover your mouse over the Style Set list.

   Note how Live Preview shows you how the formats of the Quick Styles Sets will look in your document.

4. Once you find a Style Set you like, click to exchange the Quick Styles with the new Style Set.

Note

To exchange document formatting in documents you already created using a Quick Style Set, the styles in the document must use the same style names as those used in the new Quick Style Set.

Themes vs. Quick Style Sets

At first glance, applying Themes and Quick Style Sets might seem like a great way to set the stage for formatting conflicts. Actually, these two features work together to define document formatting for Theme-enabled documents, and it is the reason why Theme Colors and Theme Fonts are also accessible in the Change Styles options. To differentiate the roles, Themes control the Theme Fonts and Theme Colors in a document, while Quick Style Sets use Theme Fonts and Theme Colors in their style definitions. When you change the Theme, the fonts and colors used in the Quick Style Sets also change.

Custom Quick Style Sets

Quick Style Sets are stored in external document template (.dotx) files, and you can easily save the set of Quick Styles for any document as a Quick Style Set. You might want to create a custom Quick Style Set, for example, to share with your co-authors who are working on sections of the large project you're creating together.

To create a new, custom Quick Style Set, follow these steps:

1. Open the document you want to use to define the Quick Style Set.

2. Use the styles in the Styles gallery to format the headings, body text, and other text elements in the document as you want them to appear in the new Quick Style Set.

Chapter 12

3. Change the style to reflect the formatting you want to include by making your formatting changes, right-clicking the corresponding style in the Styles gallery, and clicking Update <style> to Match Selection. For example, if you want to update the Heading 1 style, change the format in the text in the document that is assigned to the Heading 1 style, and then right-click Heading 1 in the Style gallery and choose Update Heading 1 To Match Selection. Repeat as needed with other styles in the document.

Note

If you want Theme-enabled Quick Style Sets, then use fonts from the Theme Fonts area of the Font list—use (Headings) or (Body) depending on the type of style you are modifying or creating—and colors from the Theme Colors area in the Font Color palette.

4. If you do not want to include a style in your Quick Style Set, right-click the style and click Remove From Quick Style Gallery.

   Note that this does not delete the style, but only removes it from the gallery.

5. Once you make all of your changes, click Change Styles, point to Style Set, and click Save As Quick Style Set, located at the bottom of the list. The Save Quick Style Set dialog box displays.

CAUTION

In addition to saving the styles listed in the Quick Style Gallery, the Document Defaults are also saved in a Quick Style Set and should be set accordingly, or you might encounter undesired results in other styles when using your custom Quick Style Set in other documents. For more on Document Defaults, see the section titled "Managing Styles," on page 404.

6. In the Save As Quick Style dialog box, do not change the Save In folder. Type a name for your new Quick Style Set in the File Name text box and then click Save.

   Your Quick Style Set is saved in the QuickStyles folder and will now appear in the Quick Style Set list so that you can choose it for future documents.

7. Test your new Quick Style Set by creating a new document and changing the Quick Style Set accordingly.

Note

Any template or document placed in the QuickStyles folder that contains Quick Styles is available in the list of Style Sets. The QuickStyles folder will be the C:\Users*user name*\AppData\Roaming\Microsoft folder for both Windows 7 and Windows Vista.

To delete a custom Quick Style Set, simply delete the Quick Style Set file from the QuickStyles folder. Built-in Quick Style Sets can also be modified and deleted from the QuickStyles folder.

INSIDE OUT   Resetting Quick Styles

When you modify styles that are part of the Quick Style Set or change Quick Style Sets, you have the option to reset the styles. The options for resetting can be found at the bottom of the Quick Style Set list. These two options, Reset To Quick Styles From Template and Reset Document Quick Styles, might appear to provide the same functionality; however, there is a distinct difference between these options.

Reset Document Quick Styles is only available if you change Quick Style Sets or modify styles in the Quick Style gallery. When this option is used, the Quick Styles revert to the formatting of the Quick Style Set saved with the last version of the document. If you are experimenting with Quick Styles, you can always return to the formatting defined in the Quick Styles when the document was first opened. Note that once you have saved and closed the document, any changes you made to Quick Styles become the new document Quick Styles. Additionally, this option only applies to those styles that are part of the Quick Style gallery and does not reset any other styles in the document.

Reset To Quick Styles From *Template* (if the document template is not the Normal template, then the command reads Reset To Quick Styles From *Template Name* Template) resets the Quick Styles to those in the attached document template. This option is similar to using the Automatically Update Document Styles option found in the Templates And Add-Ins dialog box, previously discussed in Chapter 4. However, it only applies to styles in the Quick Style gallery and not to all document styles. If you need to update all styles in a document, use the Automatically Update Document Styles option instead.

To set a Quick Style Set as your default set of styles for all new documents based on the Normal template, use the Set As Default command under Change Styles.

Chapter 12

If the command reads Set Default for *Template Name* Template, then the defaults are set for all documents based on the template indicated in the text of the command.

Working with the Styles Pane

If you are wondering about the other built-in styles not shown by default in the Quick Style gallery, this section of the chapter covers how you can access them.

Along with the Quick Style gallery, there are two additional tools—the Styles pane and the Apply Styles pane—that you can use to access styles as well as another style tool designed specifically for the Quick Access Toolbar (discussed in the Inside Out tip titled "Where is the Old Styles Combo Box?" on page 391). In general, these tools provide the same functionality, and you can use them either in combination or use only the tool that meets your needs. The following list describes the Styles pane and Apply Styles pane and how to access them:

- **Styles pane.** The Styles pane is your primary tool for applying and modifying styles. This pane provides a list of styles and gives you access to style management tools, such as the New Style dialog box, Style Inspector, and Manage Styles dialog box. To access the Styles pane, click the dialog launcher in the Styles group on the Home tab, or press Alt+Ctrl+Shift+S to toggle its view. The Styles pane can float or be docked along the side of your document window.

- **Apply Styles pane.** Smaller than the Styles pane, the Apply Styles pane uses a combo box to access styles. It is intended to be used as a small floating pane, but it can also be docked. To access the Apply Styles pane, click the More button on the Quick Styles gallery and then click Apply Styles below the gallery, or press Ctrl+Shift+S to display the Apply Styles pane shown here:

To apply a style using any of these tools, simply place your cursor in a paragraph—you can also select a portion of a paragraph or select multiple paragraphs—and then click the style to apply it.

INSIDE OUT   Where Is the Old Styles Combo Box?

If you recognized the Ctrl+Shift+S keyboard shortcut from previous versions of Word but didn't see the old familiar Styles combo found previously on the Formatting toolbar, rest assured that you can still use the Styles combo box in Word 2010. Originally, the Apply Styles pane was to be the replacement control, but many Word enthusiasts felt it wasn't quite the same. Microsoft listened to their feedback and created a Styles combo box that can be added to the Quick Access Toolbar—the ability to hold Shift and then click the list arrow to toggle the display of all styles was included as well.

To add the Styles combo box, click the Customize Quick Access Toolbar button at the end of the Quick Access Toolbar and then click More Commands. From the Choose Commands From list, click Commands Not In The Ribbon, locate Style as shown in the following image, and click Add to include it on your Quick Access Toolbar. Now you can choose and apply the styles from the Quick Access Toolbar by simply clicking the Styles arrow and selecting the style you want.

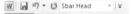

Mastering the Styles Pane

The Styles pane is your central hub for style management. Here you'll find a list of all styles currently in use in your document. You also have the option of displaying all paragraph and linked styles available to you as well as styles displayed in formats that will be used in the document. To open the Styles pane, click the dialog launcher in the Styles group on the Home tab or press Alt+Ctrl+Shift+S. Two examples of the Styles pane (with and without the formatting preview) are shown in Figure 12-3.

Figure 12-3 The Styles pane is shown with the default view on the left and the Show Preview option selected on the right.

When you create a new document based on the Normal template in Word 2010, the Styles pane shows the same styles found in the Quick Style gallery by default. You can display all styles by using the Options link at the bottom of the Styles pane.

Table and list styles are not displayed in the Styles pane. To display list styles, use the Multi-level List tool on the Home tab in the Paragraph group; you can access Table styles in the Table Styles gallery, which is on the contextual Table Tools Design tab (displayed when a table is active). The Apply Styles pane and Styles combo box can list all styles, including table and list styles.

The Styles pane contains the following elements:

- **Styles**   The Styles list shows the name of the style followed by a symbol that identifies the style type: paragraph (¶), character (a), and linked (¶a). If no symbol appears next to a list item, the item represents direct formatting (not shown by default). For any style in the Style list, you can hover the pointer over the style to view a summary of the style's settings (style definition) and access additional options by clicking the arrow that appears to the left (or right-click the style). This includes options that are similar to those you see when you right-click a style in the Quick Style gallery, such as Update Style Name To Match Selection, Select All # Instance(s), Modify, and Add To Quick Style Gallery. It also includes the ability to delete a style and clear the formatting from text that uses the style. For in-depth information on these options, see the next Inside Out tip titled "Clearing and Deleting Styles."

- **Disable Linked Styles**   You can, in effect, "turn off" the linked styles aspect of your styles so that they behave like paragraph styles, applying a style to the entire paragraph and not only selected text.

- **Show Preview**   You can view style formats in the Styles list to help you find styles visually.

- **New Style**   Displays the Create New Style From Formatting dialog box. This is where you can create a new style. Additional details on new styles can be found in the section titled "Creating and Modifying Styles," on page 395.

- **Style Inspector**   Opens the Style Inspector dialog box, which helps you to identify the style and formatting applied to paragraphs and text. Using the Style Inspector, you can open the Reveal Formatting task pane as well as identify and clear styles and formatting, which is discussed in the section titled "Inspecting Styles," on page 401.

- **Manage Styles**   Opens the Manage Styles dialog box, in which you can modify, create, and import/export styles; specify the names and order of the styles that show in the Styles pane and Apply Styles list by default; and restrict availability of styles and the ability to change style sets or Themes. For more information, see the section titled "Style Management Tools," on page 400.

● **Options**   Opens the Style Pane Options dialog box, as shown in Figure 12-4. With Options, you can specify which styles are displayed—such as Recommended, In Use, In Current Document, or All Styles—and how they are sorted. You can also enable the display of direct formatting in the Styles list and Styles combo box. As previously noted, direct formatting does not include a style type symbol to the left of the name.

Figure 12-4 You can set display options for styles using the Style Pane Options dialog box.

INSIDE OUT   Clearing and Deleting Styles

When you delete a style that is currently used in the document, text formatted with the deleted style reverts to the Normal style and text formatted with a character style reverts to direct formatting. If the style is based on another style, the option reads Revert To *Style Name* and reverts to the style identified. However, styles that are linked to additional functionality in Word, such as the Heading styles and the Normal style, cannot be deleted.

Additionally, when you delete a built-in style, it's removed from the document but not necessarily deleted. It remains in the style list and is available for future use; however, if it was previously modified, it reverts to its default settings.

The Clear Formatting Of # Instances option (found when you click the arrow to the left of a style, or right-click a style) in the Styles pane is similar to deleting a style. Text reverts to the Normal style, but all font formatting is cleared and the style itself remains unchanged. Note that you can also use the Clear Formatting option, which can be found on the Home tab in the Font group, and the Clear All option in the Styles pane to accomplish the same result on selected text.

TROUBLESHOOTING

I can't use the Select All or Clear All options in the Styles pane.

If you find that the Select All or Clear Formatting options are disabled when you click the arrow to the left of a style in the Styles pane and the style is in use (even if the disabled text indicates it isn't), this typically occurs because the Keep Track Of Formatting option is not selected in the Word Options dialog box. To locate this option, display Word Options and click Advanced. The Keep Track Of Formatting option can be found in the Editing Options area.

Note

The Hide Built-in Name When Alternate Name Exists option is used when an alias, or another name, is assigned to a style. They are created by typing a comma after the style name when creating, modifying, or renaming a style and then typing the alias. If you see a style name such as Heading 1, H1, H1 is the alias. The primary purpose of an alias is to facilitate quick navigation to the style when using the keyboard method to apply styles using either the Apply Styles pane or Styles combo box.

INSIDE OUT   Selecting and Changing All Instances of a Style

Once you apply styles to your text, changing the look of your document becomes much easier. With styles applied, you can easily select all instances of a style which can speed up a number of tasks related to consistent formatting of similar elements. For example, you might want to select all instances of styled text because you want to replace one style with another. You might want to delete all text that appears in a particular style (such as all paragraphs formatted as Production Notes within a working document), or you might want to copy all similarly styled elements to a new document (such as all headlines from a newsletter to create a promotional piece). Regardless of your reasons, the Select All # Instances of *Style Name* can make short work of what could otherwise be cumbersome tasks. To access Select All # Instances of *Style Name*, right-click a style in the Quick Style gallery or on the options displayed when clicking the arrow to the left of a style on the Styles pane.

Creating and Modifying Styles

With all the different styles and style sets Word 2010 offers, you might never need to create unique styles of your own. But if you want to create a specific effect—suppose, for example, that you want to match the font and style in other documents your company has produced—you can create your own styles to fit the format you're envisioning.

Many complex documents, such as the manuscript used to create this book, might use a set of styles to format specific document components. For example, there are three primary styles used for an Inside Out tip: a style for the title, a style for the text in the tip, and a style to denote the end of the tip. These types of situations call for creating custom styles. This section covers creating new styles and explains how to modify styles by using the Modify Style dialog box.

One of the easiest ways to create a style is to format existing text and then define a style based on the formatted text. Here are the steps to get you started:

1. Begin by formatting the text you want to save as a style.

2. Click the dialog launcher in the Styles group to display the Styles pane.

3. Click the New Style button. The Create New Style from Formatting dialog box appears (see Figure 12-5).

Figure 12-5 Select settings for the new style in the Create New Style From Formatting dialog box.

The Create New Style From Formatting dialog box offers options specific to the type of style you're creating (character, paragraph, linked [paragraph and character], table, or list), as well as access to formatting options found throughout Word. You'll find that the options in the Formatting area change depending on the type of style you are creating; the Format button at the bottom provides access to the various dialog boxes if you are looking for a specific formatting option that isn't available in the main dialog box. Depending on the style type, some dialog boxes are inaccessible if the formats are not supported.

After you customize your formats in a document and display the Create New Style From Formatting dialog box, finish creating your new style by following these steps:

1. In the dialog box, type a name for your new style in the Name box.

   Think carefully when you consider names to associate with styles—the more descriptive your style names are, the easier it is for you (and others) to identify each style's purpose and apply the proper style within documents.

2. In the Style Type list box, specify whether your style is a paragraph, character, linked (paragraph and character), table, or list style. Most styles are paragraph or linked styles.

3. Specify a style on which to base your new style. (See the section titled "Additional Style Options" on page 398 for more information on this option.)

4. Set the style for the following paragraph.

5. In the Formatting area, configure any additional properties for your style using the Font and Size options, as well as color selection, alignment, line spacing, above and below spacing, and indents.

6. If necessary, click Format to access additional formatting options (see Figure 12-6).

Figure 12-6 Click Format to set additional options in key formatting areas.

7. When you finish configuring formatting options, click OK.

> **Tip**
> To quickly create a new style based on your formatting and add it to the Quick Style gallery, right-click the text, point to Styles, and then click Save Selection As New Quick Style. Alternatively, click the More button on the Quick Style gallery and then click Save Selection As New Quick Style.

The newly-created style appears in the Styles pane as well as in the Quick Styles gallery. You can use and modify your new styles just as if they were built-in styles. The next few sections address some of the additional configuration options found in the Create New Style From Formatting dialog box, such as the Style Based On and Style For Following Paragraph options.

Modifying Existing Styles

Modifying a style is just as easy as creating a style. The main difference between creating and modifying styles is that you use the Modify Style dialog box instead of the Create New Style From Formatting dialog box. The following list provides the most common methods used for accessing the Modify Style dialog box:

- **Apply Styles dialog box**   Select a style in the Style Name list and click Modify.

- **Quick Styles gallery**   Right-click the style and choose Modify. If you simply want to change a style's name, right-click a style and click Rename to open the Rename Style dialog box.

- **Styles pane**   Hover the pointer over a style name, click the arrow, and choose Modify, or right-click a style name and click Modify.

The Modify Style dialog box looks very similar to its counterpart, the Create New Style From Formatting dialog box. It contains the same options with which you can configure most of the same settings that are available when you create a new style.

INSIDE OUT   Displaying Only the Styles Currently in Use in Your Document

The Styles pane shows a mix of styles available in your document—both those in use and those not used. You can change this option to show only those styles that have been put into play in your current document. This helps you check the consistency of styles you've used and make choices about where to remove or consolidate styles you no longer need.

To display only the styles in use in the current document, click the dialog launcher in the Styles group to display the Styles pane. Click Options at the bottom of the pane and, in the Style Pane Options dialog box, click the Select Styles To Show arrow, and then click In Use. Click OK to save your changes and return to the Styles pane.

Additional Style Options

The additional options in the Create New Style From Formatting dialog box can take you even further into automating the formatting of your documents. It doesn't matter if you want to add styles to the Quick Style gallery as you go, update styles automatically when you make formatting changes on the fly, or opt to modify the document template that's keeping track of your current Quick Styles, you can use these options to customize the way Word uses Quick Styles to streamline your document formatting tasks.

Basing Styles on Existing Styles

By default, the styles you create in the Create New Styles From Formatting dialog box are based on whichever style was in use when you accessed the dialog box. A good way to understand a based-on style is to think of it as a parent style. When you base a style on another style, it means that your style uses all of the settings of the based-on style plus whatever modifications you make to the style, unless you explicitly define the settings. This provides you with the capability to link or "chain" styles together.

For example, if you create a new style based on Heading 1, and your new style is defined with only the Center paragraph alignment format, your new style inherits any changes made to Heading 1 but always maintains the Center format—even if Heading 1 uses the Left alignment format. Although this maintains consistency in related styles, this option can also create a mess if you're not careful. It's for this reason that many people use Normal or (No Style) as their based-on style. If you want more insight into the difference between basing a style on the Normal style or (No Style), see the section titled "The Relationship Between Document Defaults, the Normal Style, and (No Style)," on page 408.

> **Note**
>
> When a style is based on another style, the Delete *Style Name* option in the Styles pane reads Revert To *Style Name*. When the Revert command is used, the style is deleted and all paragraphs formatted with the style revert to the base style, as opposed to the Normal style.

Specifying Styles for Following Paragraphs

Some styles are predictable—you can predict which style elements are likely to precede or follow them 99 percent of the time. For example, most of the headings in your documents are probably followed by Normal text, or perhaps your documents use a figure number element that is almost always followed or preceded by a figure caption. You can take advantage of style predictability and save yourself many unnecessary formatting steps by configuring settings for paragraphs that follow specific elements.

When you specify a style to be applied automatically to a paragraph following a paragraph that itself has a particular style, you specify that you want to apply that style after you press Enter at the end of the current style (paragraph). You can easily specify a style for a subsequent paragraph as you're creating a new style. To do so, select a style in the Style For Following Paragraph list box in the Create New Style From Formatting dialog box.

If you don't specify a subsequent paragraph style, Word continues to use the current style for subsequent paragraphs until you choose another one.

Allowing Styles to Automatically Update

The Automatically Update option can be one of the most dangerous options in the dialog box if used incorrectly or the most beneficial if used correctly. When you allow a style to automatically update, every formatting change you make to text to which the style is applied automatically changes the style definition, and all text formatted with the style updates before your eyes. While this sounds like a marvelous idea and one that could help tremendously with formatting tasks, consider applying the bold format to a portion of a paragraph and finding other paragraphs in your document have also changed to bold. Better yet, if another group of styles is using that style as their based-on style, a good portion of your document could end up bold as well—except, of course, those words that are already bold. They will no longer be bold because bold is a toggle format and, as previously noted in the section titled "Style Fundamentals" (on page 381), two bold formats result in a not-bold format. (You might encounter similar results if you do not use a little thought when setting the Style Based On option.)

Chapter 12

Modifying the Document Template

By default, when you create a new style in Word, it is added only to the current document. Similarly, if you modify a built-in style, that modification applies only to the existing document. But you have the option to add the style, or modifications, to the template attached to the current document if you choose. You can easily add a new style to a template by selecting the New Documents Based On This Template option (in the Create New Style From Formatting dialog box or the Modify Style dialog box) before you click OK.

Keep in mind that when you add a style to a template, you add the style to the template that's attached to the current document. Because Normal.dotm is the default template in Word, the Normal template is used for a great number of documents. If the style you are adding is not a style you commonly use, consider creating either a Quick Style Set or, depending on your needs, a custom template instead, as described in Chapter 4.

> **Note**
>
> If you add to or modify a style in the document template, you are prompted to save changes when closing the file. However, if the document template is the Normal template, you are prompted to save changes to the Normal template only when you exit Word if the Prompt Before Saving Normal Template option is turned on in the Save section on the Advanced tab in Word Options.
>
> If you inadvertently add a style to a template, including the Normal template, you must open the template to delete the style or use the Import/Export button in the Manage Styles dialog box to display the Organizer and use it to delete the style. For more information on the Organizer, see Chapter 4.

Style Management Tools

So now that you've got all these styles in various Quick Style Sets and templates, what will you do with them all? Knowing how to manage the styles you use is an important part of keeping your documents efficient and extensible. You can inspect your formatting using the Style Inspector and the Reveal Formatting task pane. In addition, you can use Manage Styles to coordinate the management of your styles by setting defaults, editing style settings, choosing recommended styles, and restricting the ways in which styles can be changed in your document. The following sections provide detailed descriptions of all these tools.

Inspecting Styles

To open the Style Inspector, click the Style Inspector button in the Styles pane (press Ctrl+Shift+Alt+S to open the Styles pane). You can keep the Styles Inspector open even if you close the Styles pane or change views. Figure 12-7 shows the Style Inspector.

Figure 12-7 Use the Style Inspector to ensure that your styles are applied properly.

The Style Inspector distinguishes Paragraph Formatting and Text Level Formatting along with any additional direct formats that might be applied. It also provides four buttons for clearing formats. Each button uses the same icon, but they each serve a different purpose as described in the following list:

- **Reset To Normal Paragraph Style**   Resets the paragraph to the Normal style but leaves any character styles or direct font formatting.

- **Clear Paragraph Formatting** (Ctrl+Q)   Clears any direct paragraph formats listed in the Plus area, such as an indent that is not defined in the style.

- **Clear Character Style**   Clears a character style and resets font formatting to the Default Paragraph Font but leaves any direct font formatting.

- **Clear Character Formatting** (Ctrl+Spacebar)   Clears any direct font formatting listed in the Plus area, such as a font that is not defined in the style.

Reveal Formatting Task Pane

If you like to see all the different settings that go into a style you've selected, you'll like using the Reveal Formatting pane. You can display the pane by clicking the Reveal Formatting button in the Style Inspector or by clicking text in the style you want to inspect and pressing Shift+F1. Figure 12-8 shows the Reveal Formatting pane.

Figure 12-8 The Reveal Formatting pane lists the format settings for the text at the insertion point.

The Reveal Formatting pane lists all of the format specifications for the selected text. The format items are grouped into three basic categories:

- **Font**   This group includes format settings that apply to the characters used in the document, including the font type and size, as well as the proofing language for the selected text.

- **Paragraph**   This group contains format settings for aspects of the paragraph, such as the selected paragraph style, text alignment, indentation settings, and paragraph spacing (before and after spacing, as well as line spacing).

- **Section**   This group includes the format settings you use to control larger portions of the document, including overall margin settings, page layout choices, and paper selections.

> **Note**
> Depending on the selected text, other areas display in the Reveal Formatting pane. For example, a table includes Table and Cell areas, and a numbered or bulleted list has a Bullets and Numbering area.

You can make formatting changes to the text at the insertion point directly from the Reveal Formatting pane by simply clicking the blue underlined link to open the relevant dialog box.

Comparing to Other Text Formats

Another great time-saving option available to you in the Reveal Formatting pane is the ability to compare and contrast similar text styles with subtle differences. Have you ever studied a heading and wondered why it doesn't look quite right when compared with another heading in your document? You can use Reveal Formatting to compare the formatting differences for you, as shown in the following graphic.

To display this type of comparison, follow these steps:

1. Select the first text selection and press Shift+F1 to display the Reveal Formatting pane.

2. Select the Compare to another selection check box.

3. Choose the second selection. The Reveal Formatting pane shows every formatting difference between the selections.

4. If you want to modify either of the formats, click the blue underlined links in the task pane to open the relevant dialog box.

Tip
To access additional options for the compared text, click in one of the Selected Text boxes and click the arrow to the right of the compared text. Options include Select All Text With Similar Formatting, Apply Formatting Of Original Selection, and Clear Formatting.

Chapter 12

Tracking Inconsistent Formatting

Another way to keep an eye on styles while you work is to enable the option to track inconsistent formatting. When this option is turned on, a blue wavy line appears under text that uses direct formatting similar to a style used in your document.

Use Word Options to turn this feature on or off. On the File tab, click Options then click Advanced. In the Editing Options area, select the Keep Track Of Formatting check box. Select the Mark Formatting Inconsistencies check box, and then click OK.

> **Note**
>
> The contextual spelling feature also uses a blue wavy line to identify possible contextual spelling errors. For more on this feature, see Chapter 10, "Editing, Proofing, and Using Reference Tools."

INSIDE OUT   Where Did that Style Come from?

One final offering in the Reveal Formatting pane that's worth a mention: you can find the source of a particular style by selecting the Distinguish Style Source check box at the bottom of the Reveal Formatting pane.

Selecting this check box causes Word to display the style from which the new style was created. For example, if a Note style applied to a segment of text in your document was created based on your Body Text style, the task pane shows you that information. That's helpful to know if you're planning to change the Body Text style at some point—you'll be able to see at a glance which other items in your document will be affected by the change.

Managing Styles

If you want a kind of one-stop shop for the various decisions you need to make as you manage the styles in your documents, the Manage Styles dialog box is that place. You use the Manage Styles dialog box to limit style formatting; choose the styles you want to be displayed in the Styles pane and Apply Styles dialog box; edit styles; and more.

You display the Manage Styles dialog box by clicking the Manage Styles button at the bottom of the Styles pane. The dialog box (see Figure 12-9) offers four different tabs and an array of options you can use to fine-tune the way styles operate in your current document. The four tabs you'll work with in the Manage Styles dialog box are described in the following list:

- **Edit**   The Edit tab, shown in the following graphic, is where you can modify all styles—even those that are not currently displayed in the Styles pane—and allows for the creation of new styles. Additionally, the Sort Order option includes the ability to list styles By Type and Based On style.

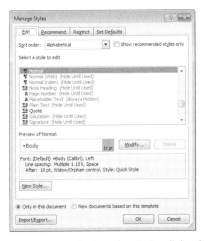

Figure 12-9 The Manage Styles dialog box is where you can make a variety of choices about the way styles operate in your document.

> **Note**
> The Import/Export button opens the Organizer, which allows you to copy styles between documents and templates, rename, and delete styles. For more information on using the Organizer to copy styles and between templates and documents, see Chapter 4.

- **Recommend** The Recommend tab, shown in the following graphic, is where you can create a recommended list of styles that are used when displaying recommended styles in the Styles pane. This tab allows you to specify the sort order of recommended styles, hide styles from view until they are used, or always hide the styles. Those assigned with the same priority will sort alphabetically.

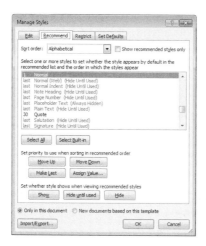

- **Restrict** Using the Restrict tab (shown in the following image), you can restrict specific styles as well as block Theme switching and Quick Style Set switching. For example, if a document must be limited to include only the styles for Headings 1 through 3, then you can restrict all other heading styles. The Limit Formatting To Permitted Styles option restricts formatting to only those styles that are marked as restricted and disables direct formatting, which includes font formatting such as Bold, Italic, and Underline; a character style must be used instead. This option can also be password protected and is the same as using the Limit Formatting Styles To A Selection Of Styles option found on the Restrict Formatting And Editing pane, which can be displayed using the Protect Document button on the Review tab.

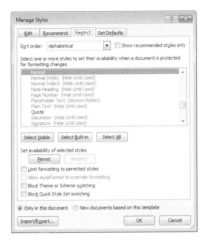

> ### Note
> In the option labeled Block Theme Or Scheme Switching, both terms refer to Themes. There isn't a separate Scheme functionality.

● **Set Defaults**   The settings on the Set Defaults tab, shown in the following image, control the Document Defaults for font and paragraph formatting in a document. If you do not explicitly define a format in a style, the Document Defaults are used. For example, assume that you create a new style and do not change the default font. If you later change the font for the Document Defaults, your style also uses the newly defined font. Additionally, when you save a Quick Style Set, the current Document Defaults are also saved and defined as the Document Defaults for the Quick Style Set. For more information about this feature, see the next section, titled "The Relationship Between Document Defaults, the Normal Style, and (No Style)."

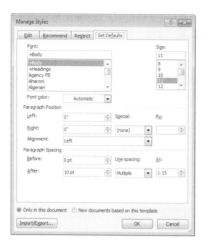

Tip

You can set additional font and paragraph formats for the Document Defaults that are not displayed on the Set Defaults tab. To set additional font defaults, click the dialog launcher in the Font group on the Home tab to display the Font dialog box. To set additional paragraph defaults, click the dialog launcher in the Paragraph group on the Home tab to display the Paragraph dialog box.

For either dialog box, set your desired formats, click the Default button at the bottom of the dialog box, and confirm the changes when prompted.

The Relationship Between Document Defaults, the Normal Style, and (No Style)

In versions of Word prior to 2007, the Document Defaults were hard-wired into the application and could not be changed. Word 2007 brought the switch to Office Open XML formats, which paved the way for one of the biggest advancements in styles: the Document Defaults in Word 2007 and Word 2010 are now stored in the documents (and templates) themselves and can be modified easily. Understanding the role that Document Defaults play is crucial in creating well-behaved documents. It can help you determine what you should use for your based-on style and perhaps help you avoid certain style nuances that can occur if your styles are not set correctly.

An interesting style aspect that many Word veterans might never have realized is if you do not modify the Normal style in a document or if the formats for the Normal style match those of the Document Defaults, the Normal style isn't actually defined—it's an "empty" style and the Document Defaults are used instead. That being the case, in Word 2010, if you do not modify your Normal style and if you base your styles on the Normal style, essentially you are using the Document Defaults, and changes made to the Document Defaults are reflected in the Normal style.

The exposure of Document Defaults also changes the behavior of using (No Style) as your base style from previous versions. Like the Normal style, (No Style) also looks to the Document Defaults to obtain base formats. If your formats are not explicitly defined in your style, then those from the Document Defaults are used.

For example, assume that you base a style on (No Style) and do not use a font that is different from the font defined in the Document Defaults. If you later change the font in the Document Defaults, that change is also reflected in the style. It might be interesting to note that the behavior of (No Style) hasn't actually changed from previous versions; previously you simply did not have access to the Document Defaults and were unable to make formatting modifications.

At this point, you might be wondering whether you should ever modify the Normal style if you are using it as your based-on style. This answer depends on the complexity of your document. If it is a simple letter, memo, or small report, modifying the Normal style should not be an issue. However, you might find it easier to leave the Normal style unmodified, use it as your based-on style, and then set the base formats using the Document Defaults. If your document or template maximizes the power of styles, it's better to leave the Normal style untouched. You should modify the Document Defaults instead.

Keyboard Shortcuts for Styles

Keyboard shortcuts give you an easy way to apply the styles you want while you're creating your document. This means that you don't have to go from keyboard to mouse and back again; you can simply keep your hands on the keyboard and style away to your heart's content. You can use a built-in shortcut or create a keyboard shortcut that you can press whenever you need a particular style. Table 12-1 lists commonly used keyboard shortcuts for a few built-in styles.

Table 12-1 Keyboard Shortcuts for Built-in Styles

Style	Keyboard shortcut
Normal	Ctrl+Shift+N
Heading 1	Ctrl+Alt+1
Heading 2	Ctrl+Alt+2
Heading 3	Ctrl+Alt+3
Demote Heading Level	Alt+Shift+Right Arrow
Promote Heading Level	Alt+Shift+Left Arrow

Chapter 12

To create your own keyboard shortcut, follow these steps:

1. Click the dialog box launcher in the Styles group to display the Styles pane.

2. Click the arrow of the style to which you want to assign a keyboard shortcut.

3. Click Modify.

4. In the Modify Style dialog box, click the Format button and then click Shortcut Key. The Customize Keyboard dialog box appears, as shown in Figure 12-10.

Figure 12-10 You can use the Customize Keyboard dialog box to create keyboard shortcuts for styles.

5. Press the keyboard shortcut you want to use. If the combination is already in use, the dialog box indicates which feature uses the keyboard shortcut. If the combination is available, the Currently Assigned To label (displayed below the Current Keys list after the keys are pressed) indicates that the keyboard command is unassigned.

CAUTION

If the keyboard shortcut is currently assigned and is noted below the Current Keys list after the keys are pressed, clicking the Assign button in the Customize Keyboard dialog box will cause the new custom keyboard shortcut to override the built-in keyboard shortcut.

6. In the Save Changes In list box, specify whether you want to save the keyboard shortcut in the global Normal template, in another template, or in the active document only (thereby not adding the shortcut to any template).

> ### Note
> If you save a keyboard shortcut in a template, make sure you also have the New Documents Based On This Template option selected in the Modify Or Create Style dialog box. Otherwise, you could inadvertently create a keyboard shortcut in the template that does include the style.

7. Click Assign, Close, and OK to close the Modify Style dialog box.

8. Test your keyboard shortcut to confirm your results.

To remove the keyboard shortcut, follow the same steps for adding a shortcut to open the Customize Keyboard dialog box. In the Customize Keyboard dialog box, select the shortcut in the Current Keys area, use the Save Changes In list to specify where to implement the removal, and then click Remove.

What's Next?

This chapter showed you how you can use Word 2010 styles to control the formatting in your documents and introduced you to the tools you can use to manage your styles and inspect text formatting. The next chapter offers another way to view and organize your document content—using Outline view to review and arrange sections in a way that best fits the information you're sharing.

Chapter 12

Working with Outlines

Getting Started Outlining in Word 2010 413

The Basics of a Good Outline 414

Eleven Reasons to Outline Your Next
Complex Project 415

Viewing a Document in Outline View 417

Creating a New Outline 421

Choosing Outline Display 422

Working with Headings in Outline View 426

Displaying Outline and Print Layout View at the
Same Time 428

Changing Your Outline 429

Printing Your Outline 431

The Navigation Pane vs. Using Outline View 433

What's Next? 434

A re you a collector of good content? If you're like me, you might keep a notes file open alongside your Word document (or a OneNote side note, poised and ready for good ideas you find) so that you can copy and paste or snip the content and tuck it away for later. In this age of reusable content, being able to work with the "big picture" of your ideas, assigning them specific tags or themes, and categorizing them into sections or larger frameworks of content seems like a smart way to manage the volumes of information that pour your way.

You can use the Outline view in Microsoft Word 2010 to work specifically with the big picture of your document, no matter if you are working on a 20-page annual report, a 500-page book project, or something in-between. Whether you collaborate or work solo, whether you incorporate diagrams and sophisticated charts or stick with text, Outline view can help you organize your thoughts and your words as you move your project toward the finish line.

This chapter introduces you to the various outlining capabilities of Word 2010. Along the way you'll learn about all the different tools designed to help you take the big picture and relate it to the smaller details that are so important to the overall flow of your larger project.

Getting Started Outlining in Word 2010

Word 2010—like its predecessors—includes an Outline view that enables you to focus on managing the sections in your document. When you display Outline view by clicking the Outline view tool in the lower-right corner of the screen or clicking Outline on the View tab, the Outlining tab offers just what you need to control the display of your outline and modify the headings to fit your needs. Simply point and click to set the level of display that you want to show in your outline, turn formatting on and off, and tweak the outline as your document needs demand (see Figure 13-1).

Figure 13-1 The new Outlining tab includes all of the tools you need for working with outlines in Word 2010.

The Basics of a Good Outline

Although many of us learned about outlines for the first time in elementary school, the outlines you use in the business world might not conform exactly to the rigid rules you remember from the classroom. Generally a good outline does strive to meet the following goals:

- Be logical in sequence

- Next subordinate headings within higher level heads

- Include two subheads within each subsection

- Try to be parallel in language and tone

- Deal with topics of comparable depth (for example, all level-1 headings have the same relative importance; level-2 Headings less so, and so on)

The way in which you create your outline, however, should really have more to do with the needs of your document and the desires of your audience than it should be forced to conform to rules that don't fit your project.

When it comes to the creative process, the idea of using an outline is simply to get your ideas down in a way that provides you with a structure for your document and helps ensure that you're covering the major points necessary to include. If you find yourself stuck in the planning stage, try some of the following techniques to get the ideas flowing:

- **The process outline.**   Does your document lend itself to a series of steps? For example, if you're writing an article about managing an international project, plan out what you want to say as a series of steps. Perhaps the first thing you do in managing a global initiative is to determine the scope of the project. That's step 1. Next, you take a look at the resources you have available. There's your second heading. Third, who are the members of your team? Continue until you have completed the process and then review your major steps. Your outline headings can evolve directly from those steps that you've identified.

- **The question outline.**   You can also use a series of questions to help you identify the important sections of your outline. Basic questions might include the following: What is this document about? (This would be your "Overview" or "Introduction" section.) Who is this document for? What is the mission of our company? Who are our department managers? Where is our facility? What types of services and products do we offer? Who are our customers? How have we improved since last year? What's new and exciting about us? What will we focus on next year?

  Each of these questions gives you a different vantage point from which to consider the content for your document. Put yourself in your readers' shoes. What do they want to see? What do they want to know about you? Questions can help you make sure that you are providing the information that will best connect with the readers of your document.

- **The big-to-small outline.**   Another way to approach a writing task is to move from the big picture to the individual point of view. This works well in documents that you hope will influence others—for example, sales documents, annual reports, grant proposals, or fundraising materials. Your document starts with the big picture—the statement of a problem, concern, or desire that is common to most of us—and then moves toward the specific (how your company or organization uniquely meets the need you established in the big picture). For example, suppose that you are writing an annual report for Coral Reef Divers. Using the big perspective, you would talk about the environmental threats to the coral reef and the important role that the coral reef serves in balancing the ecosystem. You could then zoom in to talk about the specific factors that your organization identifies as most important and, finally, fully explore the services and options that your organization provides as a response.

Eleven Reasons to Outline Your Next Complex Project

Even if you're a stream-of-consciousness writer, you'll find some benefit in outlining your long or complex documents. Once you create an outline in Word, you've got something to start with—something you can use to build your document, edit it, and organize (or reorganize) and share it. With that outline, you can also move seamlessly to and from a table of contents that's linked to the work in progress.

If you do not typically use outlining (and you're not alone), consider these reasons for outlining long documents in Word:

- **You're more likely to meet your goals.**   If your job involves writing grant proposals, producing product evaluations, writing annual reports, or composing print publications, you know that your document must reach a particular goal. You need to know where you're going, why you're going there, and who you're trying to take with you. When you first type document headings in Word, you're defining the steps that take you to the goal of your document. Your headings reflect the major categories of information that your audience wants to know. As you create the outline, you can make sure you're covering all of the topics necessary to reach your goal.

- **You can create an organized, thoughtful document.** Your outline lists not only the major categories but also smaller subtopics within each category. The multilevel capabilities offered by Word outlines (up to nine levels) enable you to organize your thoughts to the smallest detail.

- **The headings remind you where you're going.** Once you've produced an outline that you're happy with, you're free to write the document as your muse strikes. If you tend to write as inspiration leads, you can simply go with the flow and let the words fly—in the appropriate sections, of course. (If you change your mind, you can always move the sections later if you choose.) If you're more of a left brain, analytical writer, you can craft your sentences within the structured topics, making sure you've got the requisite topic sentence, supporting sentences, and closing or transition sentence.

- **You can easily reorganize your document at any time.** Word gives you the means to move parts of your document easily, even after your long document is filled with text. You can collapse topics to their headings and move them around as you like. And of course, Undo usually reverses your most recent action if you decide it was a bad move.

- **You can expand and collapse topics.** The expand and collapse outline features of Word 2010 enable you to change what you're viewing in the document. A fully expanded outline shows everything entered thus far—therefore, all of the text you've written, subheadings you've added, and notes you've inserted are visible in a fully expanded outline view. If you want to limit the display to only headings and sub-headings, you can collapse the outline to show only those items. This enables you to check that your organization is logical, you've covered everything you want to cover, and your topics are in the right order.

- **You can divide long documents into subdocuments or merge subdocuments into one long document.** Using the Word 2010 Master Document feature, you can divide long documents into smaller chunks so that you can work with them more easily. When you pull the document back together, all of the pieces can be merged into one coherent whole. Using the outlining feature enables you to see at a glance the most logical places for divisions.

For more information about creating and working with Master Documents, see Chapter 24, "Special Features for Long Documents."

- **You can see what doesn't fit.**   Outlining also gives you a way to see what doesn't work in your document. If there's a topic that really needs to be a separate document or a heading that is begging for a rewrite, it stands out. Of course, you can edit, move, and enter text in Outline view, so making those changes is a simple matter.

- **You can easily change heading levels.**   The outlining feature of Word comes on its own tab, complete with commands, giving you the means to promote or demote headings and text. For example, if you want to change a level-1 heading to a level-2 heading, you can do so with the click of a button. This also works for text that you want to raise to a heading or headings that you want to drop to body text.

- **You can work seamlessly with the table of contents.**   If you've created a table of contents (TOC) for your document, you can update it on the fly and move directly to it to make changes, if needed. This saves you the hassle—and potential error—of creating a document with a separate TOC that might not be updated when the document is updated.

- **You can easily divide your document by sections when you're working with a team.**   If your company or organization is like many others, producing the annual report is a big deal. Many people—from a variety of departments—might be involved in the creation, editing, design, and review of the document. When you work from an outline, you can easily assign specific sections to people in various departments—the finance manager writes the financial narrative, the operations manager drafts the section about the building expansion. You get the idea. You can then put the document back together and use the outline to organize the document exactly the way you want it before beginning the final review stage.

- **You can print your outline for handouts, reviews, or talking points.**   Word gives you the option of printing only the outline of your document, which is a nice feature when you want to show others the key points in a document or presentation but don't want them reading along word for word. Whether you do this in the review stage, as part of a collaborative effort, or to condense your finished document to a printable outline, you can display and print only the headings that you want your readers to see.

Viewing a Document in Outline View

Being able to view the outline of your document is helpful whether you're starting a document from scratch or working with an existing file with text and headings already entered and formatted. You can display Outline view in several different ways: on the View tab, choose Outline in the Document Views group; by pressing Ctrl+Alt+O; or by clicking Outline in the View tools in the bottom right corner of the Word window.

If you enter headings in your document and format them with one of heading styles (Heading 1, Heading 2, or Heading 3) provided by Word, they appear as headings in Outline view, as shown in Figure 13-2. The basic text styles applied to your document are reflected in the outline, but all paragraph formatting (indents, before and after spacing, and line spacing) is suppressed. When you return to Print Layout or Web Layout view, the paragraph formatting is visible again.

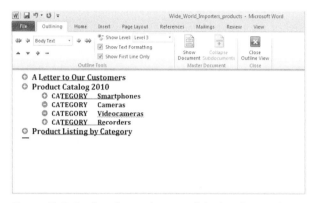

Figure 13-2 Outline view makes use of the headings styles you apply in your document.

TROUBLESHOOTING

Headings don't show up in Outline view.

When you switch to Outline view, why don't any of your headings appear? If you didn't use the built-in heading styles that Word offers—Heading 1, Heading 2, or Heading 3—Word won't automatically recognize the headings as outline levels. To correct the problem, click the headings in the outline one by one, click the Outline Level arrow in the Outline Tools group, and choose the heading level you want in the list. If you want to change all of the headings at once, select all of your headings (press and hold Ctrl while you click to the left of the headings you want to select), click the Outline Level arrow, and choose the level you want to apply to the headings.

Several different types of symbols appear in Outline view, as shown in Table 13-1. They let you know what action to take while you are working in an outline.

Table 13-1 **Outline Symbols**

Symbol	Description
○	If double-clicked, alternately displays and hides subordinate headings and text paragraphs
○	Indicates that there are no subordinate headings or text paragraphs
○ <u>Product Listing by Category</u>	Shows that the topic includes body text or subheadings
● Carol Troup, CEO ● Wide World Importers	Topic marker; indicates that the lowest-level outline entry is formatted as body text

Exploring Outlining Tools

When you display your document in Outline view, the Outlining tools appear automatically in the Ribbon. The Outlining tab provides two different groups: Outline Tools and Master Document. The Outline Tools group includes everything you need to work with the various levels in your outline and tailor the display of the outline to show only what you want to see. The Master Document group offers two tools that come in handy when you create and work with subdocuments. Table 13-2 lists and describes the Outlining Tools.

Table 13-2 **Outlining Tools**

Tool	Name	Description
⇤	Promote To Heading 1	Raises the outline level of the selection to the highest outline level, Heading 1
←	Promote	Raises the outline level of the selection by one level
Body Text ▾	Outline Level	Enables you to view and change the outline level of the selection
→	Demote	Lowers the outline level of the selection by one level
⇥	Demote To Body Text	Lowers the outline level of the selection to the lowest outline level, body text
▲	Move Up	Moves the selection up one level in the outline
▼	Move Down	Moves the selection down one level in the outline
✛	Expand	Expands the outline heading to show subheadings and text
━	Collapse	Reduces selection to top-level headings, hiding subordinate headings and text

Chapter 13

INSIDE OUT   Using the Snipping Tool and Outline View

You can use the Windows Snipping Tool, available in Windows Vista, Windows 7, and as a downloadable add-on to Windows XP, to grab content from your intranet, public Web sites, or other projects and post them in your Word documents. To turn it on, click the Start button and select Snipping Tool. With the document or page you want to snip displayed on the screen, drag the area of the display you want to capture. When the Snipping Tool window appears, click Edit and click Copy.

Ues Alt+Tab to display your Word document, and if necessary, click the Outline view button to display Outline view. Right-click at the point you want to add the information and click Paste. The snipped content is pasted at the cursor position. You will need to assign heading levels as appropriate to integrate the new content to the outline.

If you've snipped an image, however, you will notice that a blank space appears in the outline but no picture appears. If you display Page Layout view, you'll see that the image was included in the snipped content. At this point the only way to get an image to appear in Outline view is to save the file in Word 97-2003 format. There's a trade-off here, however, because you lose the capabilities of some of the other important features the Word 2010 offers. If you simply must have access to those images alongside your Word document, one other option is available: paste the content into a OneNote 2010 side note using Word's Linked Notes feature in the Review tab. As you see in the following image, the content appears in the OneNote page to the right of your Word 2010 document.

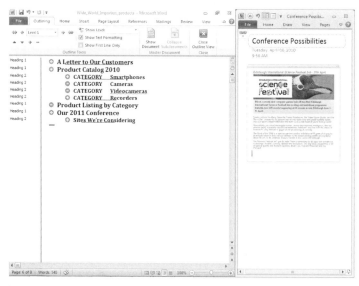

Creating a New Outline

Creating a new outline in Word is simple. If you're just starting a document, simply click the Outline button in the View tools in the lower-right corner of the Word window. Follow these steps to start the new outline:

1. Type the text for your heading. The heading is automatically formatted in the Heading 1 style.

2. Press Enter. The insertion point moves to the next line in the outline.

3. To create a sublevel, click Demote on the Outlining toolbar or press Tab.

   Word indents the insertion point and changes the first outline symbol (−) to a plus (+) symbol, indicating that the heading now has a subordinate entry.

4. Type the text for that entry.

5. Press Enter to move to the next line in your outline.

   By default, Word creates the next heading at the same level as the heading you last entered.

   If you want to create another sublevel, click Demote or press Tab. To raise an entry one heading level, click the Promote button or press Shift+Tab. If you want to move all the way out to the left margin and create a Heading 1 outline level when you have created multiple sublevels, click the Promote To Heading 1 button.

6. Continue typing entries until your outline is completed. Figure 13-3 displays a sample outline with multiple outline levels.

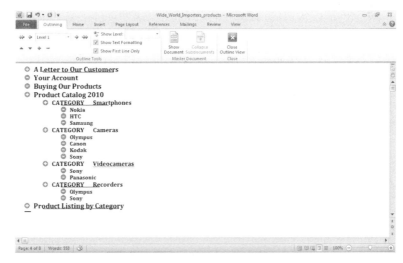

Figure 13-3 Outlining is a simple matter of identifying key topics in your document, naming them, and ordering them the way you want.

Remember that in order for headings to act and display properly in the Outline window, you must format them in the styles that Word will recognize—Heading 1, Heading 2, or Heading 3; however, you can modify the styles any way you like for those headings. You can use the Styles gallery to change the formatting choices for those styles and save the changes in the current document. Word can also make the changes to all similar heading styles in your document automatically. For more information on using Styles to format headings easily, see Chapter 12, "Applying and Customizing Quick Styles."

Note

In some instances, you might want to use the Tab key to actually insert a Tab character between words and not to demote a heading level in your outline. When you want to insert an actual tab in your outline, press Ctrl+Tab instead of simply pressing the Tab key.

Tip

Got a great idea for a new project? Use Outline view to brainstorm the main points of the idea and then switch to Normal or Page Layout view to flesh out the details.

Choosing Outline Display

When working in Word's Outline view, you can customize the display so that you see only the heading levels you want to view. For example, you might want to see only the first-level heads in your outline so you can ensure that all of your most important topics are covered. Or you might want to see every level to check the completeness of the subtopics. You can easily move back and forth between various outline displays by using the Outline Tools.

TROUBLESHOOTING

Outline view is displaying pasted content incorrectly.

Depending on where you copied your content originally, you might be working with hidden codes in the document that are fouling up your format in Outline view. In Web copy, text can include soft returns instead of hard returns between paragraphs, which can leave Word not knowing where to break lines and sections.

You can solve this problem by displaying non-printing characters and deleting any unwanted elements before you display the document in Outline view. To display hidden characters, click the Show/Hide tool in the Paragraph group of the Home tab (alternately, press Ctrl+*).

Displaying Different Levels of Text

To limit the display of your outline to only level-1 headings, for example, click the Show Level arrow to display the list of levels. Click Level 1 to display only the first level, as shown in Figure 13-4.

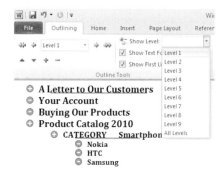

Figure 13-4 In the Show Level list box, you can control the levels displayed in Outline view by choosing what you want to see.

INSIDE OUT   Copy Document Headings Without All of the Text

Being able to collapse the outline display to headings only provides you with a quick look at the overall organization of your document. If only you could copy and paste only the headings of your outline as well. Unfortunately, when you highlight the entire outline, copy it, and paste it into another document, the whole thing—headings and subordinate text—goes along for the ride. One workaround is to create a table of contents (TOC) to the appropriate level (Chapter 23, "Preparing Tables of Contents and Indexes," tells you how to do this) and then convert the TOC to regular text. You can then copy the headings and paste them into a document.

Note
Other methods of changing which heading levels appear can be used. You can click the Expand or Collapse button on the Outlining toolbar, or you can double-click the Plus (+) symbol to the left of a heading to display subordinate items.

Showing the First Line of Text

When you want to see the paragraph text you enter, you can have Word display only the first line of text so that you can see the content of the paragraph without displaying it entirely. Why might you want to display only the first line of text? Here are a few reasons:

- To check the order in which you discuss topics

- To decide whether to move text to a different part of the document

- To review the primary points you've covered under subheadings

When all levels in your outline are displayed, you can specify first line text display by selecting the Show First Line Only check box in the Outline Tools group on the Outlining tab. The display changes to show the first text lines, as shown in Figure 13-5. To restore full paragraphs again, clear the check box.

Figure 13-5 Displaying only the first line of a paragraph lets you see section openings so that you can make informed choices about reordering topics.

> **Tip**
>
> If you want to change the line lengths in Outline view so that the text wraps the way you want it to, on the File tab, choose Options. In the Word Options dialog box, click Advanced, and then in the Show Document Content section, select the Show Text Wrapped within the Document Window check box. When that setting is checked, you can adjust the wrapping of text both in Outline and Draft views by simply changing the width of the document window.

Removing and Showing Formatting

Another quick change that you might want to make is to suppress the display of formatting in your outline. As described earlier in this chapter, when you change to Outline view, the headings are shown with whatever character formatting they're assigned in the other Word views. When you're working in the outline, however, you might find formatting differences distracting while you consider the content and organization of your topics.

To hide the formatting in your outline, select the Show Text Formatting check box in the Outline Tools group on the Outlining tab. This control actually functions as a toggle, meaning that the first click hides the formatting and the second displays it again. Figure 13-6 shows you what a simple outline looks like when all formatting has been suppressed.

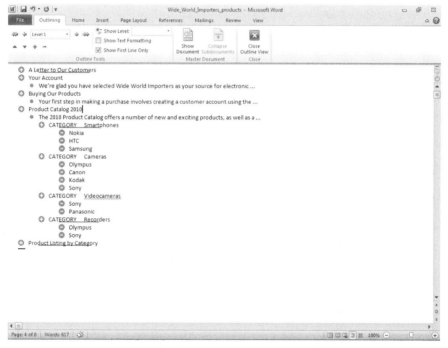

Figure 13-6 When you want to focus on the thoughts in your outline without visual distractions, you can hide the formatting.

Working with Headings in Outline View

Whether you create an outline from scratch or use the outline of an existing document, you'll invariably want to change some headings and insert and delete others. Headings are easy to work with in Outline view—with a simple click of a tool, you can change heading levels, move headings in the outline, and even demote a heading to body text if you like.

Adding a Heading

When you want to insert a heading in an existing outline, in Outline view, find the heading that you want the new heading to follow. Then simply place the cursor after that heading and press Enter. If you want the heading to be at the same level as the heading preceding it, simply type the new heading. If you want to promote or demote the heading level, click the appropriate button before typing your text.

Applying Outline Levels

You can choose the outline level for your heading by using the Outline Level list box on the Outlining toolbar. Click in the heading to which you want to apply the outline level and then click the Outline Level arrow to display the list, as shown in Figure 13-7. Choose the level you want, and the format is applied to the heading.

Figure 13-7 If you know which outline level you want to assign to the new heading, choose it directly from the Outline Level list box.

Promoting and Demoting Headings

Once you have text in your outline, you can change outline levels easily, such as moving a heading from level 1 to level 2 or from body text up to level 3. Promoting a heading takes it one level higher in the outline, and demoting a heading moves it one level down in the outline.

Each time you click the Demote button, Word moves the heading one level down the Outline Level scheme. Outline view shows the change by indenting the heading and changing the formatting. Conversely, the Promote button raises the heading level of the selected text until you reach Level 1, which is the highest outline level available.

When you want to demote and promote in larger increments, such as moving a heading all the way to the topmost level or changing a heading to body text, use the Promote To Heading 1 or Demote To Body Text buttons.

When might you want to promote or demote text? You could be working on a report and realize that a topic you've placed at a Heading 2 level is really part of another topic. You can first change the heading level to reflect the level that the heading should be so as to fit in the outline where you want it to go, and then you can move the selection to that point. You can also drag and drop the selection where you want it to appear in the outline; you might need to adjust the heading level depending on where you drop the section.

> **Tip**
>
> When you change a heading by promoting or demoting it, all subheadings within that section are also promoted or demoted (depending on which action you selected).

INSIDE OUT   Importing an Outline from a Text File

Suppose that you've been planning a large, complicated project for a long time, and after weeks of collaboration with peers and two or three review passes, the outline is finally approved. You've been passing it around as an e-mail message, however, and now you want to bring the outline into Word and start building a document on it. What do you do next?

One way to handle this situation is to simply cut and paste the outline into a new Word document and go through and format the headings appropriately. But if your outline is 20 pages long, you might not relish the busywork. A better way to handle this is to let Search and Replace assign the appropriate heading levels for you. Here's how to do that:

1. With the text file open in Word, press Ctrl+H.

2. In the Find What box, type the characters you've used to identify the first level heading (for example, <1>).

3. In the Replace With box, type ^& and then click Format, choose Style, and in the Replace Style dialog box, click the style you want to apply to the text (such as Heading 1), and then click OK.

4. Back in the Find And Replace dialog box, click Replace All, and Word formats the headings as you've specified.

5. Repeat to format additional headings in your document.

6. Display the finished outline in Outline view to view the outline.

Displaying Outline and Print Layout View at the Same Time

If you want to be able to see how the changes you're making in Outline view are affecting your document as it will appear in print, you can easily view your document in both Outline view and Print Layout view at the same time. Simply drag the split bar (located at the top of the vertical scroll bar) down the screen to open another window displaying the current document.

To change that area to another view, click in it to give it focus and then select the view you want, such as Outline view. Figure 13-8 demonstrates how the document appears when you are viewing a document in both Print Layout and Outline view.

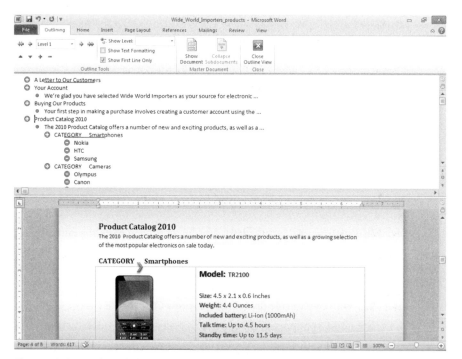

Figure 13-8 Use the split bar to open another window and display the current document using different views.

Changing Your Outline

Once you arrange all heading levels the way you want them, you might decide to move some of your outline topics around. That's one of the biggest benefits of using Outline view—you can easily see which topics fit, which do not fit, or which would work better somewhere else.

Expanding and Collapsing the Outline

The symbols in the Outline window give you clues about what (if anything) is subordinate to the level displayed in the outline. You can use these symbols (introduced in Table 13-1) to alternately display and hide sections and subsections in your document.

You'll find two easy methods for expanding and collapsing the topics in your outline. To expand a topic, you can double-click the plus sign to the left of the target heading, or, if you prefer, you can simply make sure the heading is selected then click Expand.

Collapse works the same way. Simply click in the heading of the topic you want to hide and then double-click the plus sign, or click Collapse on the Outlining toolbar.

Moving Outline Topics

Another benefit to Outline view is that you can move entire topics in your document from place to place. It doesn't matter if you choose to use the Outlining tools, cut and paste text using the Office Clipboard, or drag what you've selected from place to place, as you'll see in the following sections, you can easily move portions of your document around as needed.

Moving Topics Up and Down

When you want to move part of an outline to an earlier point in your document or closer to the end, you can use two of the Outlining tools—Move Up and Move Down—to do the trick. Start by selecting the entire part you want to move and then click Move Up to move the selection up one heading. If you want to move it more than one level up, click Move Up as many times as needed to position the selection in the right place.

Use Move Down in the same way. Select the part of your outline that you want to move and then click Move Down on the Outlining toolbar. If you want to move the selection more than one level down, continue to click Move Down.

If you want to move only a heading and not an entire topic, click in the heading before choosing Move Up or Move Down. Word moves only the selected heading and leaves any subordinate headings and text in place.

Cutting and Pasting Parts of the Outline

You can also cut and paste parts of your documents in Outline view. This procedure is help-ful when you know you want to move a topic but are not exactly sure where you want to put it. You can cut and paste part of an outline by following these steps:

1. Select the portion of the outline you want to move.

2. On the Home tab, click Cut in the Clipboard group. (Alternatively, you can click Ctrl+X if you prefer.)

    The selected portion is removed from the outline and placed on the Office Clipboard.

3. Scroll through the outline until you find the place where you'd like to paste your selection. Click to place the cursor there.

4. Click Paste in the Clipboard group on the Home tab (or use Ctrl+V). The selection is pasted at the new location.

Forget What's on the Clipboard?

The Clipboard keeps track of everything you copy, cut, or paste while you're work-ing. However, when you are moving sections around in your document, you can easily lose track of what you've clipped out of your file. If you need to view the con-tents of the Clipboard, on the Home tab, click the dialog launcher in the Clipboard group.

The Clipboard appears when you click the Clipboard dialog launcher, displaying every-thing you've placed on the Clipboard recently (the Clipboard holds a total of 24 items). To work with the items on the Clipboard, click the item you want to use and select the command you want from the displayed list.

Dragging to a New Location

If the part of your outline you want to move is within dragging distance of the new loca-tion, you can highlight it and drag it to the new position. As you drag, the pointer changes, showing a small box beneath the arrow. A horizontal line moves from line to line, tracking the point at which the selection will be inserted when you release the mouse button.

You might want to display only high-level headings before you move part of your outline. This enables you to see more of your outline on the screen, and you'll have a shorter distance to drag what you're moving. Even if text is not displayed, subordinate headings and body text are moved with the heading.

Restructuring Your Document in Outline View

Outline view makes it easy and fast to move sections around in a very long document. Instead of waiting for the copy-and-paste process (which actually puts all that content on the Clipboard), you can simply select the sections you want to move and drag them to the new location. If you'd rather stick with keyboard shortcuts, use Alt+Shift+up arrow or Alt+Shift+down arrow to move the selected content up or down in the outline list.

You can also select and move multiple headings. For example, suppose that you want to move the last 20 pages of your report to the center of your document; you can simply select all the affected headings and move them together to the new position.

Printing Your Outline

At various stages throughout the process of viewing, editing, arranging, reorganizing, and formatting the headings in your outline, you might want to print a copy to see how things are shaping up. Printing is the same process whether you're printing a long document or just an outline. Here are the steps:

1. Switch to Outline view and then display your outline.

2. Display only those headings you want to print by using the Collapse and Expand buttons and selecting the outline levels you want to see.

3. On the File tab, click Print. In the Print window, select your options then click OK to print as usual.

   The outline is printed as displayed on the screen.

TROUBLESHOOTING

I have too many page breaks in my printed outline.

Suppose that you've finished working on the outline for the Coral Reef Divers report, and the development team is waiting to see what you've come up with. You've gone back over it several times to make sure you have all of the sections organized properly and the outline levels set correctly. Everything looks good.

But when you print the outline, there are big gaps in the center of the pages. In the file, the text looks fine—what's the problem? Chances are the blank spots are due to Word's treatment of manual page breaks. If you've inserted manual page breaks in your document, you need to remove them before printing the outline; otherwise, the blank spots will prevail.

To remove manual page breaks, on the Home tab, click the Show/Hide tool in the Paragraph group to display all formatting marks in your outline. Then move to each page break symbol, double-click it, and press Delete. Save your document and print again. The unwanted breaks should be gone.

INSIDE OUT   When I View My Outline on the Screen in Outline View, the Indents Look Right, but When I Print, the Indents Are Gone

Outline view uses indents to display the subordination level of the various headings in your document. As such, the indents don't actually exist on the document page; instead they are simply used to show you the various outline heading levels.

If you want the indents to be in place when you print the document, you need to use the Outline Numbered tool to set up the spacing. Select the text to which you want to apply the format change, and click the Multilevel List tool in the Paragraph group on the Home tab. Click the style of list you want to apply, and Word reformats your headings accordingly. Now when you view the outline in Outline view or in Page Layout view, you will see the indents for the headings in your document.

If you'd like, you can change the amount of space used in the indent by right-clicking one of the list numerals and choosing Adjust List Indents. Use the Text Indent At setting in the Position area to indicate the amount of space by which you want the text to be indented. Click OK to save your changes.

The Navigation Pane vs. Using Outline View

You learned about the Navigation pane in Chapter 1, "Spotlight on Microsoft Word 2010," and discovered the number of ways you can move through your document and find elements that are important in your work. With the Navigation pane, you can find your way using headings, page thumbnails, or search results. When you use headings to navigate the document, the headings are linked to the document, which means you can click any topic to move easily to that part of the document. To display the Navigation pane, select the Navigation Pane check box in the Show group on the View tab.

The great thing about using the Navigation pane for navigation is that you can view your document in two ways at once: in a pseudo outline format and also in Print Layout view. You can move to the topic you want to see by clicking the heading in the left panel of the work area.

Why have the Navigation pane *and* an outlining feature? First, the Navigation pane is a handy tool when you want to do things such as check the wording of a topic, make sure the text you've added fits the heading, and see at a glance that you've covered all of the topics you intended to cover. But when you want to change the heading levels of text, reorganize parts, or affect the table of contents in any way, the Outlining features area is a better choice. For major structuring changes, text reorganizations, heading modifications, and more, you want to work in Outline view. For simple, lay-of-the-land operations, the Navigation Pane provides you with a clear picture of your document in a form that you can access and navigate quickly. However, for all other outline-related tasks, you can find what you need in Outline view.

INSIDE OUT   Alphabetizing Headings in Outline View

If the document you're working on requires that your content appear in alphabetical order, arranged by headings, you can do the necessary sorting in Outline view. You might want to use this feature, for example, when you're preparing a product catalog to share with clients or preparing a program reference guide for new hires. Here are the steps for alphabetizing your headings:

1. Display Outline view.

2. Select all headings you want to alphabetize.

3. On the Home tab, in the Paragraph group, click the Sort tool.

4. In the Sort Text dialog box, click OK. This keeps the default settings, which instructs Word to sort the content by text paragraphs (which includes headings).

Now your content is alphabetized, and when you expand the Outline view to show subordinate content or change the view to Page Layout view, you'll see that all content traveled with the headings as they were reordered in the document, as demonstrated in the following:

What's Next?

There are a number of benefits to outlining your document—whether you're just getting started brainstorming a new project or reviewing and evaluating one you've been working on for a while. With the outlining features in Word, you can organize, move, adjust, and fine-tune the outline of your document so your content flows smoothly in your document. The next chapter finishes up Part Two of the book by showing you how to master the printing tools available in Word 2010.

CHAPTER 14

Printing Documents Professionally

Printing in a Greener World 435

The (Almost) One-Click Print Process in Word 2010 . . 436

Printing Quickly and Efficiently 443

Canceling a Print Job 446

Setting Print Options 447

Specialized Printing 454

What's Next? 460

W E'VE been hearing about the upcoming "paperless society" for years, and although we can see signs that it is clearly on its way, chances are that you still need to print—and print often—when you create documents in Word. Whether you print and send letters, reports, brochures, booklets, labels, or forms, printing in Word 2010 has just become easier. Now print and print preview are together in one view, so you can review, adjust, and choose print options, all in the same Backstage view. Nice.

This chapter walks you through various print operations in Word 2010 and throws in a number of troubleshooting ideas for good measure. Along the way, you'll find information on setting various options and tailoring your print jobs so that you can finalize and distribute your documents to the people waiting for them.

Printing in a Greener World

Today we are more aware of the cost of our printing than ever before. The paper we consume, the ink cartridges we use, and the electricity that drives it all require resources we try to use wisely. When you're working in Word 2010, this green consciousness might manifest itself in a number of ways:

- Proofing your document electronically and printing only your final version

- Saving the document as a PDF or XPS file and printing only when necessary

- Using double-sided printing instead of printing on one side of the page only or printing multiple pages per sheet

- Sharing printers in a department in lieu of having a printer on every desk

- Designing content that works in print, online, and electronically

When you design content that can be used in print or online, some of the benefits for the online versions are that you can use colorful backgrounds and creative layout elements (without worrying about printing costs), interactive features (such as hyperlinks), and, fundamentally, as many "pages" as you need to get your message across. With that said, online content is limited by the fonts you can use, quality of images, and writing style (online content should be concise and easy to scan), to name just a few constraints. As you might imagine, printed content also has benefits and drawbacks. Two of the main benefits of printed material are that you can precisely control the page layout of printed content, and your audience doesn't need to log on to access your publication.

Often, material is adapted for use in both print and online content. When you are faced with this dual-purpose task, consider setting up some common processes and rules to ensure that your content best serves each desired purpose. For instance:

- Use Web fonts in all online materials, but feel free to use custom fonts for your printed material. Many marketing departments create consistency among materials by pre-establishing two "required" sets of fonts—one set for online content and another set for printed works. An easy way to accommodate both sets is to create Quick Style Sets for each type, as is discussed in Chapter 12, "Applying and Customizing Quick Styles."

- Include color blocks in online materials (such as for backgrounds or navigation bars), but omit large color areas from most printed materials. Word helps in this department by including an option to not print background colors and images by default. In addition, the added benefit of themes (discussed in Chapter 4, "Templates and Themes for a Professional Look") aids in quick color switching.

- Show hyperlinks online, but verify that all links in printed materials show the actual Web address instead of the linked text.

Of course, you won't always be in charge of the content you work with—you might need to print online content or print colorful pages in black and white, for example. In this chapter, all of the primary print options are covered so that you'll be able to control your print jobs, regardless of whether you are printing online content or designing content to be printed.

The (Almost) One-Click Print Process in Word 2010

The new integrated Print view in Backstage view is one of the big new productivity features in Word 2010. Now previewing and printing is easier than ever—you can make print options changes and see those changes reflected in the preview window. To access the integrated Print view, on the File tab, choose Print, as shown in Figure 14-1.

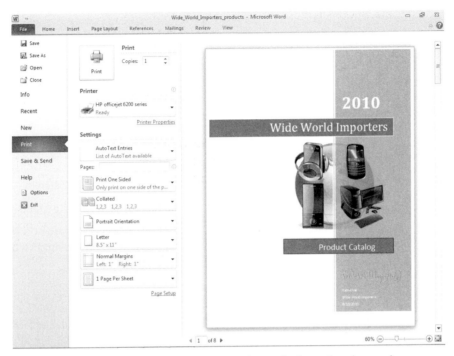

Figure 14-1 The Print window incorporates preview and print options in one view.

One of the most important aspects to keep in mind when preparing your document for printing is that Word is always in contact with your current printer. Word uses the driver for the current printer for various tasks, such as to obtain the available fonts that are displayed on the Font list and for document pagination.

When you view a document in Print Layout view, for example, you are seeing the document as it will look when printed on the currently selected printer. For this reason, if you plan on printing a document, you should make sure the printer you intend to use is set as the current printer prior to setting printing options or making any layout adjustments in your document. To change to a different printer, click Printer on the File tab (see Figure 14-2). You can choose a new printer by clicking the one you want from the list. After you make this change, you might see slight pagination changes in your document.

Chapter 14

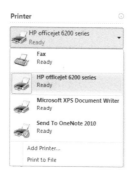

Figure 14-2 Change printers by clicking the one you want from the Printer list.

Because pagination can change when you use another printer, another important aspect to keep in mind is that attempts to control pagination using manual page breaks typically fail and result in empty or partially empty pages when another printer driver is used to print or view the document.

> **Tip**
>
> If you intend to print your document on a printer that is not available, such as when you are working at home and you intend to print the document at your office, you can still install the correct printer driver and use it for document preparation even if the printer is not physically available.

Previewing Your Document

Even though Print view displays your document as it will look when printed, you should make a habit of paging though your entire document before printing. Like a painter stepping back from the canvas, you can use preview to take a big-picture look at a page or series of pages before you commit the information to hard copy. You can examine entire pages at once, checking for obvious page setup errors and oddities and even applying minor fixes to correct some of the errors you discover. For example, in preview, you can quickly see when an image box overlays text (or vice versa), when a single line runs onto the next page, or when indented text is misaligned.

In the Print window you have a chance to view your document from a variety of perspectives before you print. By default, when you click Print in Backstage view (or press either Ctrl+F2 or Ctrl+Alt+I), the current page is shown in the preview window on the right (see Figure 14-3).

Note

You can add Print Preview and Print to your Quick Access Toolbar so that you can display Print view without having to display Backstage view. On the File tab, click Options then click Quick Access Toolbar. In the list on the left, click Print Preview and Print, click Add, and then click OK. The new tool—Print Preview and Print—is added to the right side of the Quick Access Toolbar.

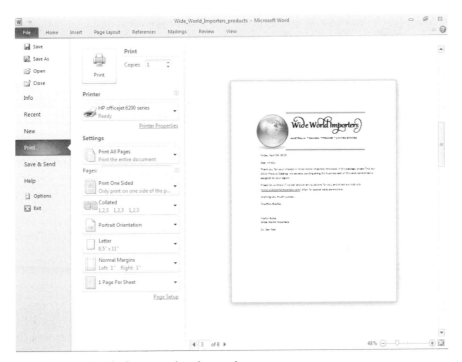

Figure 14-3 A simple document in print preview.

Zooming In on the Details

Using the Zoom tools on the Print Preview tab or the View tab in other views, you can examine your documents by zooming in to see details and zooming out to evaluate the flow of content on multiple pages. You can select a specific section, page, or group of pages on which to focus.

You can change your view by sliding the indicator marker or clicking the minus (–) and plus (+) signs at each end of the spectrum to decrease or increase the current view by 10 percent per click. Using the slider, you can view your document from 10 percent to 500 percent of its normal size. Furthermore, as you change the percentage, Word by default automatically shows the number of pages that fit within the view in the workspace (for example, if you view a multipage document formatted for standard 8.5 × 11-inch paper at 30 percent, you will probably see three pages onscreen simultaneously). You can use the Zoom Slider and Zoom Level in this manner in both Print Preview and Print Layout view. Figure 14-4 shows the preview of multiple pages.

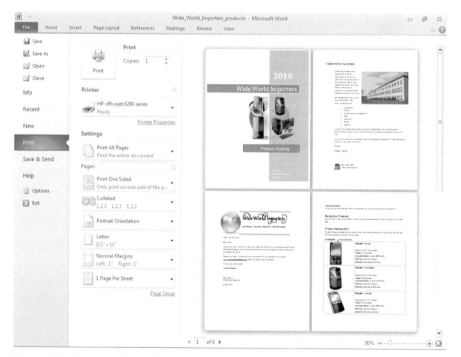

Figure 14-4 Zoom tools enable you to preview several pages of your document at one time, depending on the percentage at which you choose to view them.

> **Note**
>
> In other views, such as Draft and Outline, you can use the Zoom tools but will not see clear page divisions as you see in Figure 14-4. Note that the Zoom Slider and Zoom Level are not available in Full Screen Reading view.

You can also display the Zoom dialog box, shown in Figure 14-5, to further modify your view. To open the Zoom dialog box, double-click the percentage of display, which is to the left of the Zoom slider, as shown in Figure 14-4. A few useful options in the Zoom dialog box are the Many Pages option, which is used to specify how many pages to show, and the Whole Page option, which sets the zoom to the width of the document's text.

Figure 14-5 The Zoom dialog box enables you to configure exact viewing details in Print Preview.

Making Changes While Previewing

As you zoom in, out, and move around while previewing your document, you might see details you want to change. For basic editing tasks—like correcting a typo or changing a format—you need to go on the File tab again to return to your document to fix the problems; you'll be returned to the original location the cursor was positioned when you displayed Backstage view, which means that you might have to search all over for the areas you want to change.

Changes you can make while previewing your document that will be immediately apparent in the preview window are these:

- **Adjusting margins, indents, line numbering, and borders.**   You can choose the margins setting (second from the bottom in the center panel of Print view) to display a list of margin options (see Figure 14-6). Click Custom Margins to display the Page Setup dialog box and change additional options.

- **Change paper size.**   Click the paper size setting (third from the bottom) and choose the paper size you want to view. The preview window changes to reflect the change. Your text will be reflowed automatically but you might need to resize pictures, diagrams, or other added elements.

- **Change document orientation.**   Click the orientation setting (fourth from the bottom) to change from portrait to landscape orientation (or vice versa). Again, the preview changes to reflect your choice and text is reflowed automatically. You might need to exit Backstage view to align pictures and other objects before you print.

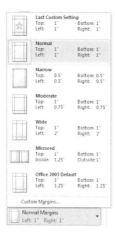

Figure 14-6 You can choose new margins and set other page options from within Print view.

Note

You can also change a number of page specifications using the Page Setup link at the bottom of the center panel in Print view. When you click Page Setup you have the option of changing margins, orientation, line numbering, borders, page size, and layout.

INSIDE OUT "Fitting" Text

If you need to fit text to a specific page or number of pages, you can use several methods to accomplish this task. Reducing the font size or changing the page margins are typically two of the first methods you might try. If those methods don't condense text enough, you might want to try the following techniques:

- **Spacing Before/After Paragraphs.** If you use formatted space between paragraphs as opposed to empty paragraphs, you can adjust the spacing before or after paragraphs. Space between paragraphs rarely needs to be 10 or 12 points, and you can type any amount, even as small as one-tenth of a point. You can also type other units of measure after the value and they will be converted to points. Use cm for centimeters, in for inches, and li for lines. For example, .6 li is converted to 7.2 points. The Spacing Before and Spacing After options can be found in the Paragraph dialog box on the Indents And Spacing tab in the Spacing area. To display the Paragraph dialog box, click the dialog launcher in the Paragraph group on the Home tab.

- **Set Exact Line Height.**   Line spacing, or the amount of space between the lines of a paragraph, is typically more space than necessary. Setting line spacing to an exact line height can reduce the space between lines and allows more text to fit on a page. The line height you need depends on the font size, and it might take some experimentation to find the best height so that the text is still easy to read. To adjust the line spacing, on the Home tab, click the dialog launcher in the Paragraph group. In the Spacing area, change Line Spacing to Exactly, and then start by making the adjustments in 1-point increments using the At text box. Note that you can also use increments of one-tenth of a point by typing directly in the At text box.

- **Condense Character Spacing.**   Condensing the amount of space between characters is a common method used to reduce page count, and the results are hardly noticeable. Condensing your text by even one-tenth of a point makes an impact on page count. To condense spacing between characters, on the Home tab, click the dialog launcher in the Font group to display the Font dialog box. Click the Character Spacing tab, change the Spacing option to Condensed, and modify the points in the By text box.

These methods can be used in combination, or you might find that a single method resolves the issue. And while the methods were presented in the context of reducing page count, you can also use these same tools to increase spacing and page count, if need be.

Chapter 14

Printing Quickly and Efficiently

When you're happy with the preview of your document, you're ready to print. By far, the easiest and most common printing task is printing an entire document. When you want to send the entire document to the current printer, simply click Print, and then click the Print button at the top of the center column of Print view on the File tab.

> **Tip**
> For faster printing, you might want to add Quick Print to your Quick Access Toolbar. To do so, click the More button at the end and then click Quick Print. You can see which printer is the current selection by hovering the mouse over Quick Print.

You can also print a Word document from within Word and in Windows Explorer without opening the file or the Print dialog box by right-clicking a file or group of files in the Open dialog box and then clicking Print from the shortcut menu. Note that you will likely encounter a message box stating that the command cannot be performed because a dialog box is open. Click OK to close the message, and then close the Open dialog box; the document or documents will then be sent to the printer.

> **Tip**
>
> Send to OneNote 2010 is one of the settings available in your Printer selection setting in Print view. This enables you to easily—and instantly—print a copy of your current document directly to your OneNote 2010 workbook.

Printing Selected Text

Perhaps you've been talking with a co-author about a specific section and she's offered to take a look at it for you. You want to print just those two pages so that the two of you can look at it side by side. To print just that portion of the document, follow these steps:

1. Highlight the text you want to print.

2. On the File tab, click Print.

3. In the first option in the Settings area, click Print Selected Text (see Figure 14-7), and then click Print.

   The selected portion is printed on the currently selected printer.

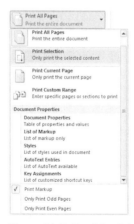

Figure 14-7 Use Print Selected Text to print a portion of a document.

TROUBLESHOOTING

An extra blank page is output when I print.

If an extra blank page prints at the end of your print job, there might be an extra paragraph return or two inserted at the end of your document. To delete the empty paragraphs, display hidden characters in your document (click the Show/Hide button in the Paragraph group on the Home tab, or press Ctrl+Shift+*) and then delete the extra paragraph markers. After you delete the extra paragraph markers, you can verify that the extra blank page has been removed by viewing your document in Print Preview.

If the extra paragraph mark is after a table, then this paragraph mark cannot be deleted. The workaround for this issue is to select the paragraph mark and change the font size to 1 point. You also need to remove any spacing before or after the paragraph and make sure it is formatted with single line spacing.

Chapter 14

Tip

If you and your co-authors have gone through multiple revisions with Tracked Changes turned on and you want to print and discuss a list of all your collective changes, you can have Word print just a list of revisions. On the File tab, click Print then click the top arrow beneath Settings. In the list that appears, click List of Markup and then click Print.

Printing Hidden Text

It's possible that not all text in your document is be meant for all eyes to see. For example, some hidden text is be created by specific Word features, such as index fields and table of contents fields. But other text—perhaps financial forecasts, staff salaries, or other sensitive information—can also be hidden from view for specific projects and audiences.

You can display hidden text on the screen by clicking the Show/Hide tool in the Paragraph group of the Home tab. Alternately, you can press Ctrl+Shift+8 to toggle the display of hidden text on and off. Hidden text appears marked by a dotted underline.

Hidden text does not print by default, regardless of whether it displayed on your screen. If you want to print hidden text, you need to change your Print options. On the File tab, click Options then click Display. Under Printing Options, click the Print Hidden Text check box and click OK to save the change.

> **Note**
>
> This option is an application option as opposed to an option that is stored with the document. It will remain in effect for all documents.

Canceling a Print Job

On occasion, you might decide at the last moment to cancel a print job. The way you cancel a print job depends on whether background printing is turned on. By default, Word activates background printing, which means that you can continue working while you print a document. To change this setting, on the File tab, click Options then click Advanced. Then scroll to the Print area and clear the Print In Background check box. To halt printing from within Word while your computer is sending a document to the printer, follow one of these two procedures:

- If background printing is disabled, click Cancel or press Esc.

- If background printing is enabled, click the Cancel button in the Status bar while the document is being sent to the printer. If you're printing a short document, the Cancel button might not be visible long enough for you to cancel the printing task.

TROUBLESHOOTING

The wrong font appears in my document on the screen or when printed.

In some cases, a font that you're using might not show up in your document. Instead, Word substitutes another font for the unavailable font. You can control which font is used as the substitute font by performing the following steps:

1. On the File tab, click Options then click Advanced. Scroll to the Show Document Content options and click the Font Substitution button. If your document doesn't require font substitution (because all fonts used in the document are available), Word displays a message stating that no font substitution is necessary. If your document does require font substitution, the Font Substitution dialog box opens, listing the affected fonts.

2. Under Font Substitutions, click the missing font name under Missing Document Font and then click a substitute font in the Substituted Font box.

3. Click the Convert Permanently button to permanently convert all of the missing fonts in the current document to their current substitute fonts, which means that the document now uses the substitute fonts; if the document is opened on another computer, the substitute fonts are used instead of the original fonts. Once the missing fonts are converted to the substitute fonts, they cannot be converted back.

Similarly, some fonts might show up on the screen but print differently from the way they are displayed. In these cases, Word might be printing a draft copy (display Word Options, click Advanced, and scroll down to view the Print options) or the font you're using might not be available in your printer. To fix a missing printer font, you should change the offending font to a TrueType font or another font that's supported by your printer.

Chapter 14

Setting Print Options

For some projects, you might need to perform printing tasks that are more complex than merely printing single copies of entire documents, and there might be times when you do not want to use Quick Print and send the entire document to the current printer. For example, you might need to change the printer or print only specific pages. For these tasks, you need to change the default print settings.

Begin by displaying the Print view on the File tab and choosing Print. Alternately, you can press Ctrl+P.

Printing More than One Copy of a Single Document

To print multiple copies of a document, simply click in the Copies box to the right of the Print button and enter the number of copies you want to print. By default, Word collates multiple copies of a print job. Notice the Collate option in the Settings area of the Print view (see Figure 14-8).

Figure 14-8 You can specify the number of copies and choose your collating preference.

When collating is enabled, Word sends one copy of your print job to the printer with the collating instructions. In the long run, this method is probably easier for an end user. But depending on the printer, it might take longer to process if the document is printed, and then the next copy is printed, and so forth. It can also cause bottlenecks in a print queue if the document contains many large graphics or extensive formatting. If you prefer, you can choose Uncollated. On some laser printers, printing without collating might speed the process and avoid bottlenecks in the print queue because the printer won't need to reprocess information for each copy of a page.

> **Note**
> The Print To File option generates a .prn file that can be created using a Printer Command Language (PCL) or PostScript (PS) printer driver. Primarily, these files are used for creating PDF or TIF files. To actually print a .prn file, you need to type a print command at a Command Prompt, such as `COPY /B Filename.prn \\ComputerName\PrinterShareName`.

Printing Ranges

In many cases, you'll want to print a selection of pages instead of an entire document. For example, you might want to select and print a few paragraphs of text, print two or three noncontiguous sections within a long report, or print the cover letter attached to your updated résumé. To print specific pages and sections within a document, use the following options:

- **Print All Pages**   Prints the entire document; the default selection.

- **Print Selection**   Prints selected text starting at the top of the printed page. To use this option, text must be selected in the document prior to displaying the Print dialog box. Note that the selection must be a contiguous text selection.

- **Print Current Page**   Prints the page currently displayed on the screen (even if you have scrolled away from the page containing the cursor) or the selected page in Print Preview (if multiple pages are shown).

- **Print Custom Range**   Prints only the pages, page ranges, and sections you specify. Use commas for individual pages and hyphens for a range of pages. For example, enter **1-5,9,15-18** to print pages 1 through 5, page 9, and pages 15 through 18. If your document contains sections, you must specify which pages and sections to print. Precede the page number with *p* and use *s* for section. For example, type **s2,s4** to print all of sections 2 and 4; type **p3s4-p6s5** to print from page 3, section 4 to page 6, section 5.

> **Tip**
>
> Word uses the formatted page number, as opposed to the physical page number (Page X Of Y shown in the status bar), for printing. To quickly determine the formatted page number and section number, note the Page and Section in your status bar and enter the values in the Print dialog box as you see them. If you do not see the Page and Section, right-click the Customizable Status bar, click Formatted Page Number, and then click Section to add them to your status bar.

Printing Odd and Even Pages

If you want to print using both sides of each sheet of paper, but you don't have a *duplex printer* (a printer that can automatically print on both sides of a sheet), use the Manual Duplex option in the Print Settings area. If this option is selected, Word prints all of the pages that appear on one side of the paper and then prompts you to turn the stack over and feed the pages into the printer again.

Another alternative is to use the options, Only Print Odd Pages and Only Print Even Pages, located in the Print settings (see Figure 14-9). To accomplish this, you can print all of the odd pages first, turn the printed pages over, reinsert the paper into your printer's paper tray, and then print the even pages. You'll probably have to experiment with your printer tray to ensure that you insert the paper properly. To assist in this task, take a few sheets of paper and annotate them with Top, Bottom, Odd, and Even. Print only the same number of pages so you can get a better idea of how your device prints without using a lot of paper.

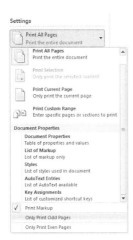

Figure 14-9 Choose Only Print Odd Pages or Only Print Even Pages if you want to print on both sides of the page with a non-duplex printer.

> **Note**
>
> Keep in mind that printing in this way can eventually cause printers to jam as a result of the ink from the already printed pages building up as they pass through your printer. If you do a lot of two-sided printing, you should probably invest in a printer that is designed to handle it.

> **Tip**
>
> If your print margins seem out of whack or your page prints in the wrong orientation, check your printer settings to ensure they aren't overriding Word's print settings. On the File tab, click Print then click Printer Properties. Check the orientation setting on the Layout tab and change it if necessary; click OK to return to the Print window.

Printing Document Elements

As you know, documents consist of much more than just the content that appears on a page. Documents can include document properties, styles, tracked changes, and comments, as well as other elements available to the document such as Building Blocks and keyboard shortcut assignments. In some cases, you might want to print these items instead of the actual document. The Print settings enable you to print common elements by selecting them in the Print What list. Using this technique, you can print the following:

- **Document Properties**   Prints information stored in the File Properties, such as the file name, location, template, title, author, creation date, last saved date, number of words, and so forth. You can view document properties in the Info page of Backstage view (see Figure 14-10).

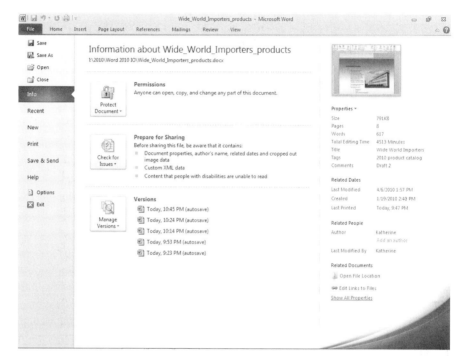

Figure 14-10 You can print all document properties to keep pertinent information with the printed file.

- **List of Markup**   Prints a list of all changes in the document, letting you know what type of change was made and by whom. Word 2010 organizes the changes into the following categories:

  - Main document changes and comments

  - Header and footer changes

  - Header and footer text box changes

  - Footnote changes

  - Endnote changes

- **Styles**   Creates an alphabetical list of styles defined in the current document. Each list entry includes the style definition, such as formatting attributes, style for the following paragraph, based on style, style type, and so forth.

  For more information about creating and using styles, see Chapter 12.

- **AutoText Entries**   Prints a complete alphabetical list of the AutoText entries available to the document that are stored in any global templates or the current document template.

- **Key Assignments**   Prints an alphabetical list of custom shortcut keys created for standard Word commands and other functions such as macros and styles. If no custom shortcut keys or macros are included in the document, the printout includes the document location and the text Global Key Assignments to indicate that only the global shortcuts are in effect for the document.

  For more information about working with macros, see Chapter 28, "Working with Macros in Word 2010."

TROUBLESHOOTING

Printing a markup list for a page range doesn't work.

Unfortunately, you can't print a markup list for a range of pages—you must print either a complete list of all changes made to an entire document or none at all. Luckily, if you're flexible, you can work around this limitation. The easiest approach is to forget about the list and instead print a range of pages using the Document Showing Markup option. You'll be able to see the tracked changes and comments in this view—it just won't be printed in list format (and in many cases, the changes make more sense when you see them in a document instead of listed one after another).

Of course, in some instances you might really need to print a list of markups for a range of pages. Don't worry—there's still hope. One way you can accomplish this is to copy the portion of the document containing the tracked changes to a new document and print the list of markup for the new document instead.

Printing Several Pages per Sheet

In Word, you can print more than one document page on a single sheet of paper. This feature helps you to better see a document's layout and can be used to present information in a visually concise manner (it's not a bad way to save a few sheets of paper, either). You'll find that printing several pages per sheet is similar to previewing multiple pages. (The difference is that the printed pages generally provide a clearer view of the pages' contents.) When you print multiple pages on a single sheet of paper, Word shrinks the pages to the appropriate size for printing purposes. To set up this arrangement, follow these steps:

1. On the File tab, click Print (or press Ctrl+P) to display the Print view.

2. Click the last setting in the Settings area then click the item that represents what you want to print (see Figure 14-11). You can print up to 16 pages per sheet.

Figure 14-11 Choose the number of pages you want to print per sheet.

Note

You must use the values in the Pages Per Sheet list to specify the number of pages to be printed—you can't type a value. In addition, the feature is available only when the Document or Document Showing Markup option is selected in the Print What list.

Scaling Printed Documents

Just as you can reduce and enlarge copies when you use a photocopier, you can reduce and enlarge your print output in Word by using the Scale To Paper Size option at the bottom of the Page Per Sheet setting. Scaling documents can come in handy when you are printing on nonstandard paper sizes or when you want to shrink your output slightly to ensure that information isn't cut off at the margins.

The key to scaling documents is to use the Scale To Paper Size list, which is located at the bottom of the Settings list in Print view. The Scale To Paper Size list includes a variety of sizing options including Letter, Legal, Executive, A4, various envelope sizes, index cards, photo sizes, banners, and so forth. To view the list of options, click the Scale To Paper Size option. By default, the No Scaling option is selected.

> **Note**
> Using Scale To Paper Size scales your document for the current printing session only. Also, it doesn't resize or alter the document's contents.

TROUBLESHOOTING

Characters are cut off in Word 2010.

If your printer is spitting out odd characters or cutting off the bottoms of words, there's a problem somewhere in the way Word is communicating the information to your printer. To ensure Word is sending the information correctly, on the File tab, choose Options, then in the Advanced tab, scroll down to Layout Options, clear the Don't Center Exact Line Height Lines check box, and then click OK.

You can also check your printer properties in the Device and Hardware window to ensure you are using the latest printer driver available for your machine.

Specialized Printing

In addition to the options available in the Print view, Word offers a number of other printing options, some of which were discussed earlier in this chapter. Two sets of primary printing options are found in Word Options. Common print options are found in the Display area; others can be found in the Advanced area, as shown in Figure 14-12.

Figure 14-12 You can set additional print options in the Advanced and Display tabs of the Word Options dialog box.

Some noteworthy printing options are also found in the Compatibility Options as well. Table 14-1 provides the location of each option along with a detailed summary.

> **Tip**
> To view the effect of the majority of printing options on a document prior to printing, preview the document in Print view.

Table 14-1 **Additional Printing Options in Word Options**

Option	Description
Printing Options in the Display Section	
Print Drawings Created In Word	Prints drawing objects, such as shapes and text boxes, as well as floating objects, such as images and embedded objects. If this option is turned off, white space is used in place of inline drawing objects, floating objects are suppressed, and inline objects, such as an embedded Excel workbook, are printed.
Print Background Colors And Images	Prints page colors and other effects, such as images added using the Page Color command on the Page Layout tab.
Print Document Properties	Prints the document properties on a separate page whenever you print the document.
Print Hidden Text	Prints text formatted as hidden text even if it is not currently displayed in the document.
Update Fields Before Printing	Updates all fields—such as cross references, Tables of Contents, calculations, and so on—in a document before printing. This option also updates most fields when switching to Print Preview.
Update Linked Data Before Printing	Updates data linked from other documents such as a linked and embedded Excel workbook before printing.
Printing Options in the Advanced Section	
Use Draft Quality	Prints a document with minimal formatting if your printer supports draft-quality output.
Print In Background	Enables you to continue working while print tasks are being processed (although you might notice a slight slowing in response times as you work).
Print Pages In Reverse Order	Prints a document in reverse order, beginning with the document's last page.
Print XML Tags	Prints the XML tags embedded in the content of a document marked with XML tags provided by the attached schema.
Print Field Codes Instead Of Their Values	Prints the field code, such as {DATE} or {TIME}, in place of the value of the field.
Allow Fields Containing Tracked Changes to Update Before Printing	Prints the most recently updated field contents in a form or document with content controls.

Chapter 14

Option	Description
Print On The Front Of The Sheet For Duplex Printing	Prints the front of each sheet when printing on a printer that does not have duplex capability. Pages print in reverse order so that when you flip the stack to print on the back, the pages print in the proper order.
Print On The Back Of The Sheet For Duplex Printing	Prints the back of each sheet when printing on a printer that does not have duplex capability. Pages print in ascending order so that they correspond to a stack of pages that are printed on the front in reverse order.
Scale Content For A4 Or 8.5 x 11" Paper Sizes	Enables automatic switching between standard 8.5-by-11-inch paper and the narrower, slightly longer A4 paper size used in most countries. This option is selected by default.
Default Tray	Specifies which printer tray should be used by default. For more information about selecting paper sources, see Chapter 3, "Right Now Document Design with Word 2010."
Print Postscript Over Text	Prints PostScript code (such as watermarks or overprinted text) when a document contains PRINT fields.
Print Only the Data From A Form	Prints only the text entered into a document using form fields, relative to their placement in the document. Used for printing on pre-printed forms.
Compatibility Options (Located at the bottom of the Advanced area in the Layout Options)	
Print Body Text Before Header/Footer	Prints the main text layer before the Header/Footer layer, which allows for the process of PostScript codes in the text layer. This functionality is the reverse of the default order.
Print Colors As Black On Noncolor Printers	Prints all colors as black, instead of using grayscale, when using a noncolor printer.
Use Printer Metrics To Lay Out Document	Word uses built-in metrics to lay out the document, as opposed to information from the printer driver. This option allows your document to look the same on the screen no matter what printer driver is installed; however, it still prints using information provided by the printer driver.

Printing Envelopes

On occasion, you might want to print a single envelope or an individual sheet of labels instead of a document. If you have several envelopes or labels to print, you might want to consider using Mail Merge instead. When you want to print a simple envelope or a set of labels, on the Mailings tab, click either Envelopes or Labels to open the Envelopes and Labels dialog box, as shown in Figure 14-13.

For information about conducting mail merges, see Chapter 26, "Creating Mailings Large and Small."

Figure 14-13 The Envelopes And Labels dialog box enables you to complete simple envelope and label print jobs.

> ## Tip
> If the address block is not automatically displayed in the Envelopes And Labels dialog box or if you have multiple address blocks, select the address block prior to displaying the Envelopes And Labels dialog box.

The Envelopes tab includes a number of quick options that you can set before printing an envelope. Here's an overview:

- **Print**   Starts the print process, so make sure to set your other options and load the printer before clicking this button.

- **Add To Document**   Adds the envelope to the current document so that the envelope and document can be printed together.

- **Options**   Displays the Envelope Options dialog box in which you can choose the envelope size, font, and printer feed specifications. You can also click the Preview envelope image or the Feed preview image to access the Envelope Options dialog box.

- **E-Postage Properties**   Enables you to work with an e-postage account if you've previously set up an electronic postage add-in from the Web.

- **Cancel**   Closes the Envelopes and Labels dialog box without saving settings.

To print an envelope, simply follow these steps:

1. On the Mailings tab, click Envelopes.

2. If necessary, type the recipient address in the Delivery Address box or click Insert Address next to the Delivery Address label. If you click Insert Address (above the Delivery Address text box), choose a profile (such as Outlook) and select the recipient in the Select Name dialog box.

3. Type a return address in the Return Address box or click Insert Address next to the Return Address label, and then select the return address you want to use. Or, if you prefer not to include a return address, click the Omit check box.

4. If you want to choose a nonstandard size envelope or change the font used in the address blocks, click Options or click image in the Preview area to display the Envelope Options dialog box. Select the envelope size and font you want to use and click OK.

> **Tip**
> To change the font for individual lines or portions of the address, select the text you wish to format, right-click the selected text, and click Font to display the Font dialog box.

5. If you've subscribed to an e-postage service and want to add electronic postage to the envelope, click E-Postage Properties to set postage options. Select the Add Electronic Postage check box to enable the feature for the current envelope.

6. Ensure that your printer is ready and the envelope is inserted as shown in the Feed area of the dialog box.

7. Click Print. If you want Word to save the created envelope with the document, click Add To Document.

Creating Labels

Instead of printing directly on envelopes, you might want to print mailing labels. Word provides an easy way for you to print labels in a wide range of shapes and sizes. If you want to print a single label or a few labels—not enough to warrant using mail merge—you can use the Labels tab in the Envelopes and Labels dialog box to print labels quickly. Using the options on the Labels tab, you can enter the label information, choose the way you want the label printed (a single label or a whole page of labels), and make selections about the label size and e-postage. Here's how to print labels:

1. On the Mailings tab, click Labels.

    The Envelopes And Labels dialog box opens with the Labels tab displayed, as shown in Figure 14-14.

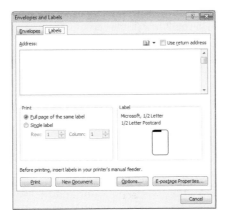

Figure 14-14 The Labels tab in the Envelopes And Labels dialog box enables you to process simple label printing jobs.

2. By default, Word prints a full page of labels. If you want to print only one, click the Single Label option in the Print area.

3. The selected label is shown in the Label area. If you want to select a different label, click the graphic in the Label area or click Options to make a new selection. (Both actions open the Label Options dialog box.) Click OK after you select your label size and feed setting.

4. When you finish entering your choices, ensure that your printer is loaded correctly and click Print, or click New Document to create a full page of labels in a new document.

Chapter 14

> **Tip**
>
> To create a document with blank labels, leave the Address text box blank, select the Full Page Of Same Label option, and then click New Document.
>
> This method also enables you to type several addresses and print them on a sheet of labels instead of printing individual labels one at a time in the Envelopes and Labels dialog box. If you've already used labels on the sheet, simply start your first address in the column and row that corresponds to the next available label. Note that depending on the way your printer feeds a sheet and the type of labels you are using, feeding a label sheet multiple times could result in a printer jam.

What's Next?

This chapter covered the ins and outs of printing your Word 2010 documents, including methods to print selected text, your entire document, or a variety of ranges or document elements. The next chapter shows you how to plan, create, and format tables in Word.

PART 3

Make Your Point, Clearly and Visually

CHAPTER 15

Clarifying Your Concepts in Professional Tables 463

CHAPTER 16

Create Compelling SmartArt Diagrams and Charts. 493

CHAPTER 17

Adding and Editing Pictures and Screenshots. 523

CHAPTER 18

Adding the Extras: Equations, Text Boxes, and Objects 561

CHAPTER 19

Command Attention with Borders and Shading. 587

Clarifying Your Concepts in Professional Tables

Creating Tables Today 463

Choose Your Method: Creating Tables in Word 464

Creating Nested Tables 471

Editing Tables 472

Enhancing Your Tables with Formatting 480

Positioning Tables in Your Document 485

Resizing Tables 487

Working with Functions in Tables 490

What's Next? 491

D ON'T you just love tables? You're reading a long, fairly boring report, when suddenly you come to a table that lists, in simple columns and rows, the data you most most to understand. *Ah*, you think, *now I get it. Time well spent.* And you return to your To Do list, feeling like you've accomplished something.

Tables play a vital role in helping your readers understand the information you're presenting. This chapter shows you a variety of ways to add, enhance, format, streamline, and accessorize the tables you add to your Word 2010 documents. You can apply table styles, customize the look and feel, format the data, rearrange the size, and much, much more. You can also import tables from other programs, flow text around tables, and even design your whole document to fit within a well-ordered, nice-and-neat table frame.

Depending on how fancy and involved you want to get, you might just want to insert one of the Quick Tables that are already available in Word or build your own intricate table from the page up. It's your choice, and this chapter will show you how. We'll start with the easiest approach first—using Quick Tables.

Creating Tables Today

Years ago—if and when you actually used a typewriter to create documents—preparing a table was a bit of a hassle. You had to be very careful with the tab stops (which meant pressing the Tab key at just the right places). You needed plenty of correction fluid, too. In the early days of Microsoft Word, a table was a fairly straightforward tool you could use to create a grid of rows and columns in your document into which you could simply type text. It wasn't particularly pretty, but it worked.

Today, Word 2010 offers tables that do all kinds of things. You can stylize them to match the colors, fonts, and effects used in your documents. You can insert functions, perform math calculations, and add content controls to collect information. You can import tables from other programs or copy and paste tables created in Word into other files. You can add hyperlinks, so clicking a table opens a completely different document or Web page.

One of the biggest considerations in this day of reusable content is that the table you create might be used in other formats in addition to print. Using tables is particularly helpful when you are creating content that might be offered in different mediums. Perhaps you're creating a blog post, a Web page, or a report that you'll share electronically by e-mail.

The table serves as a container for your data, enabling you to control the way that data is presented. You can also easily move data in and out of tables by using Word's Convert to Text and Convert to Table features (which you'll learn more about later in this chapter on page 469).

Creating Well-Formed Tables

The secret to creating an effective table is in the planning. What do you want the table to show? What will your readers be looking for, and how can you best organize that data to help them find what they need? Here are some additional questions to ask as you're thinking about the table you're going to create:

- Do you need to create the table in a limited space in your document?

- Do you want the style of the table to match the styles you've used for other document elements?

- How many rows and columns will you need?

- Will the table content include text, numbers, or both?

- Will you use functions for totaling and averaging columns?

- Will you have other, similar tables in your document?

- Will readers view the table on the printed page, online, or in an e-mail message?

- Do you want readers to *do* anything in the table? (For example, fill in a blank, click a check box, or type a comment?)

Choose Your Method: Creating Tables in Word

Word provides you with a number of ways to create tables for your document, but if you want fast and easy (with the option of customizing it after you create it), start with Quick Tables. With Quick Tables, you can add ready-made, professional tables to your document with the click of the mouse button. Other methods involve drawing a table with the Draw Table tool; using Insert Table to display a dialog box where you can enter the number of rows and columns you want; or importing a table from another program. Each method of adding tables has its own merit. A closer look at your choices shows that you can:

- Add a Quick Table to insert a predesigned table at the cursor position

- Choose the number of rows and columns you want in the Insert Table gallery and let Word create the table for you

- Use the Insert Table dialog box to AutoSize cell content and choose the number of rows and columns you want to create

- Draw a table freehand on the page

- Select text and then choose Convert Text To Table to turn it into a table quickly

- Embed a Microsoft Excel spreadsheet

The method you choose will depend on your data—for example, if you want to take advantage of formula creation in Excel, use the Excel Spreadsheet method; or use the Convert Text To Table method if you are transforming a data list that already exists in your document into a table.

This section introduces you to each of these methods. Let's start with the simplest first: Quick Tables.

Adding a Quick Table

When you simply need to create a table of text and numbers so you can present ideas to your readers clearly, a Quick Table is probably the easiest way to go. These tables are ready-made in Word 2010 and stored as building blocks that you can insert on your page and customize as needed.

To add a Quick Table to your document, follow these steps:

1. Click to position the cursor where you want the table to appear.

2. On the Insert tab, click Table in the Tables group.

3. Point to Quick Tables to view a gallery of available Quick Tables (see Figure 15-1).

4. Scroll through the Quick Tables gallery until you find a table you want to use. Click the format of your choice to add it to your document.

Chapter 15

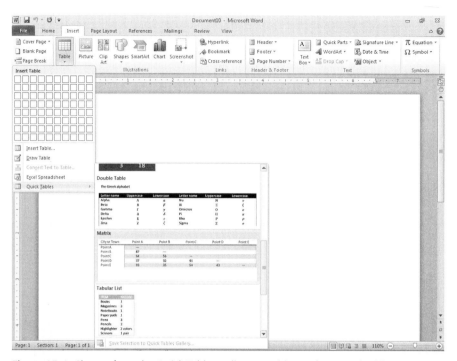

Figure 15-1 Choose from the Quick Tables gallery to add a preformatted table to your document.

> **Note**
>
> Chapter 4, "Templates and Themes for a Professional Look," covers the way in which themes influence formatting options available for various items in your document. A theme includes specific fonts, colors, and effects that are then coordinated with charts, Quick Styles, and even Quick Tables and table styles (more about this on page 482). The content and overall design of the tables you see displayed in the Quick Tables gallery will remain the same no matter which theme you have selected for your document. But if you change the theme, you will notice that the colors, fonts, and shading effects used in the Quick Tables change to match the new theme.

Using the Row and Column Grid to Create a Table

When you click Table in the Tables group on the Insert tab, a mixed list of options appears, as is shown in Figure 15-1. The grid of blank boxes at the top of the Table list is a clickable control that you can use to point and click your way to creating a new table. Here's how to do it:

1. Display the Table list by clicking Table on the Insert tab.

2. Move the pointer down and to the right until the number of rows and columns you want to create in the table is selected (Figure 15-2). Notice that the number of rows and columns is displayed at the top of the list. Additionally, Live Preview shows the table at the cursor position in your document.

3. When the table is the size you want, click the mouse to add it to the document.

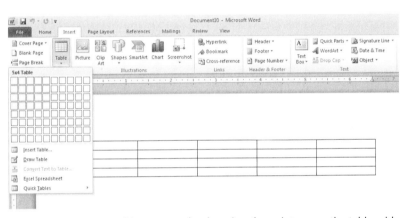

Figure 15-2 Create a table your way by dragging the pointer over the table grid.

Inserting a Table and Specifying AutoFit Options

When you know the number of rows and columns you want to create in a table and you want to control the way the text fits in those cells, you can use the Insert Table dialog box to create the table in the dimensions you want. On the Insert tab, choose Table then click Insert Table. The Insert Table dialog box appears, as you see in Figure 15-3.

Figure 15-3 Use the Insert Table dialog box when you know the number of rows and columns you want your table to have.

Enter the values you want by clicking in the appropriate field and typing (or use the arrows to increase or decrease the numbers displayed in the fields). In the AutoFit behavior area, choose whether you want the columns in the table to be set to a specific width (this is help-ful if you are formatting a table to precise specifications so that it will fit in a particular spot in your document). Additionally, you can click AutoFit To Contents to have Word adjust the size of the table cell to fit the contents of that cell, or choose AutoFit To Window to resize the table to maximize the space available in the document window.

> **Tip**
>
> The AutoFit To Window choice becomes important if you are preparing a document that will be used on the Web. The table will adjust automatically based on the width of the window used to display the document. This means that the entire width of the table will always stay within your reader's viewing area, no matter how wide their browser window is.
>
> If you want Word to remember the settings you've entered in the Insert Table dialog box so they will be applied to other tables you create in the current document, select the Remember Dimensions For New Tables check box and then click OK.

Drawing a Table

If you prefer to draw tables as you go along rather than relying on ready-made tables and tools, then on the Insert tab, click Table and choose Draw Table. The pointer changes to an electronic "pencil" that you can use—by clicking and dragging—to draw the table the way you want it. You can also add lines for rows and columns and make editing changes while you work.

The contextual Table Tools appear on the Ribbon, with Draw Table selected in the Draw Borders group on the Design tab. You can customize the line style, thickness, and color by using the tools in this group (more about this on page 482). If you add a line you want to remove, click the Eraser tool then click the line you want to delete. Figure 15-4 shows columns being added to a drawn table.

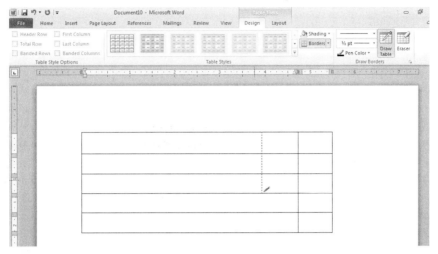

Figure 15-4 You can click and drag the mouse to draw the cell borders which creates rows and columns in a drawn table.

> **Tip**
> If you want to create a table in the middle of a text section and have the text automatically wrap around it, press Ctrl while you draw the table.

Converting Text to a Table

When you have lists of information that you think would look better—or make more sense to your readers—in table format, you can easily convert the text to a table. Select the text in your Word document and then on the Insert tab, click Table. Then choose Convert Text To Table.

The Convert Text To Table dialog box asks for input similar to that requested in the Insert Table dialog box. You specify how many columns and rows you want to use, how you want to use AutoFit, and finally, which characters have been used to delineate the individual text entries. That is, which characters instruct word that the text following the character should be in the next column (a tab character, for example). Click your choices then click OK. Word makes the text into a new table.

Converting Tables to Text

What happens when you don't want a table to be a table anymore? Suppose that you've created a great table for the annual report, but now someone wants it in text form—no tables allowed. How do you preserve the data and lose the grid? You can make the change easily. Click the table then select the Layout tab in the Table Tools. Choose Convert To Text in the Data group. In the Convert Table To Text dialog box, select the character you want Word to insert to mark the beginning and end of individual text entries. You might have Word separate your table entries by inserting commas, paragraph marks, or another character of your choice between them. Click OK to convert the table to text.

Inserting an Excel Spreadsheet

In situations when you're working with a lot of numeric data or you need to be able to perform calculations with that data, you can take advantage of Excel features that are available to you as you work in Word. When you add an Excel spreadsheet as a table in your Word document, you have access to the conditional formatting features in Excel, which include cell styling, table formatting, and more. You can even include the new sparklines feature in Excel 2010 in your Word document. Here are the steps for including an Excel worksheet in your Word document:

1. Position the pointer at the location in the document where you want to create the table.

2. On the Insert tab, choose Table.

3. Click Excel Spreadsheet in the Table list.

   An Excel worksheet window pops up over your Word document. The Ribbon changes to reflect Excel features.

4. Enter your data, create formulas, and apply formats as needed (see Figure 15-5).

5. Return to the Word document by clicking outside the Excel worksheet area.

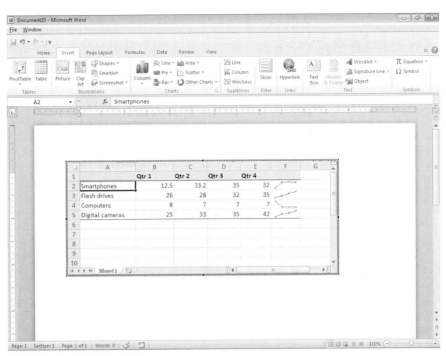

Figure 15-5 Choose the Excel Spreadsheet option from the Table list to use Excel spreadsheet features in your table.

Whenever you want to modify the table, simply double-click it in the Word document, and an Excel window will open. You can then edit the information as needed, apply formatting changes, and more. When you click outside the worksheet, the window closes and the data in your table is updated to reflect your changes.

Creating Nested Tables

With Word 2010, you can create nested tables—tables within tables—in your documents. A nested table makes it possible for you to show readers various elements that go into a particular data item in your table. Suppose, for example, that the Wide World Importers annual report includes a table that shows sales results broken down by quarter. One product in particular offers a greater number of models than the others, and in this case, inserting a table within a table can show readers how each of the different products contribute to the results shown in the cell (see Figure 15-6).

	Qtr 1		Qtr 2	Qtr 4	Qtr 4	
Smartphones		12.5	33.2	35		32
Flash drives						35
	Flash 8G	25				
	Flash 4G	10				
	Pendant Fl	26				
	FOB Flash	33				
		26	28	32		
Computers						7
		8	7	7		
Digital cameras						42
		25	33	35		

Figure 15-6 You can easily create a table within a table to help display your data as completely as possible.

To create a nested table, simply click in the cell in which you want to add the second table and repeat the table creation steps described previously. For example, you can add a Quick Table or choose to draw the table freehand. Either way, you can then use Table Styles to format the table to achieve the look you want.

> **Tip**
>
> For more about formatting your table with Table Styles, see the section titled "Changing Table Format by Using Table Styles," on page 480.

Editing Tables

One of the nice aspects about tables is that once you get the structure in place that you like—which data goes in the rows, and which data goes in the columns—you can easily plug different data sets in to display different results.

Once your data is entered, you might want to reorganize it, edit it, add to it, and delete some of it. That means adding rows and columns—perhaps moving the rows you already have—and deleting others. You might decide to rearrange the order of columns, which means moving data from one side of the table to the other. To do that without any unexpected surprises ("Hey, why did Word paste my whole table in that single cell?!"), you need to understand some of the hidden features behind the table display you see on your screen.

Displaying Table Formatting Marks

One of the secrets in moving and editing table data successfully lies in seeing the unseen. Each cell, row, and column in a table is given a marker that delineates the end of the item. When you move, copy, or paste information, these unseen markers might go along, giving you unexpected results at best or overwriting your existing data at worst. To display the hidden marks in your current Word table, click Show/Hide in the Paragraph group on the Home tab. The various table formatting marks will appear, as shown in Figure 15-7.

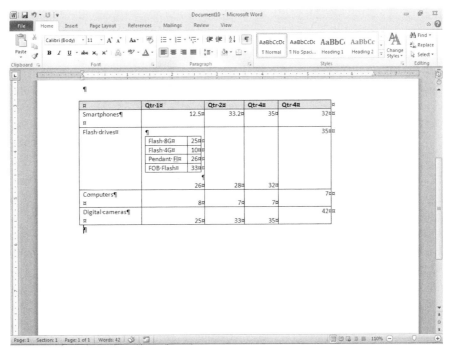

Figure 15-7 Table formatting marks identify the end of individual cells, rows, columns, and the table itself.

When you select table data for moving, copying, or deleting, be sure to turn formatting marks on to avoid inadvertently including hidden formatting codes that can change the look or behavior of your table.

INSIDE OUT   Control the Way Formatting Marks Are Displayed in Your Document

You can change the types of formatting marks that appear in your document window. If you don't see all the formatting marks you expect, someone might have set the View options to limit the ones that are displayed by default. You can turn all the formatting marks back on by clicking Options on the File tab. On the Display tab, select the Show All Formatting Marks check box then click OK to return to your document. Now all of your formatting marks will appear automatically whenever you click Show/Hide.

Selecting Table Cells

To move and copy rows, columns, and cells, start by selecting the ones you want to move or copy; this lets Word know which data you want to work with. As you get comfortable working with tables, you'll discover the tricks to selecting just the data you want for various operations. Table 15-1 lists the different methods you can use to select the content in your tables.

INSIDE OUT   Use Multiple Table Selections

You can select noncontiguous sections of a table by pressing and holding Ctrl while you click additional selections. In a product listing, for example, this capability enables you to choose only the products that you want to include in the catalog you're producing. After you select the products you want, you can copy the information and paste it in a new table, leaving out all products you don't want to use.

Table 15-1 **Selecting Table Segments**

Selection	Method	Use
Entire table	Click the table and then click the table move handle that appears in the upper left corner of the table.	You want to move, copy, format, or delete an entire table.
Single row	Click outside the table to the left of the row.	You want to reorder, format, copy, move, insert, or delete a row.
Single column	Click outside the table just above the column.	You want to move, format, copy, insert, or delete a column.
Single cell	Click to the left of any data entered in the cell.	You want to move, copy, delete, or clear that cell.
Multiple cells, rows, or columns	Drag across the elements you want to select.	You want to move, format, copy, or delete sections of a table.

Copying and Pasting Table Data

Although copying is basically a simple operation, copying table data can be a bit tricky because the pasted data can sometimes go where you're not expecting it to go. For example, if you want to copy all the information into one cell in the new table, the data might instead be spread over the entire row, replacing existing data. If you want to copy multiple cells to multiple cells in the new table, the incoming cells might all be lumped into the cell at the insertion point. Or you can easily—and accidentally—create a nested table in your existing table when you really just meant to copy a few cells. How do you avoid these kinds of copy surprises?

First, know what you're copying. The trick is to select cell data if you want to copy cell data. Likewise, select the cells themselves (or rows or columns) if that's what you want to copy. By capturing the table formatting marks when you highlight the section you want to copy, you can be sure you get the results you expect.

Next, know where you're copying to. If you are copying a row or a column, make sure you've allowed enough room for the incoming data so that important entries won't be overwritten and lost. The new changes to the Paste tool in Word 2010 can help you with this. After you copy the table data you want, click in the table where you want to place the data then right-click. The context menu displays the Paste Options that are appropriate to the type of data you've copied—you might see a Keep Source Formatting option, a Merge Formatting option, or Keep Text Only option (see Figure 15-8).

Figure 15-8 Before you paste table data, right-click in the cell to see your Paste options.

Tip
Paste Options might also include other selections—such as Picture, Use Destination Styles, Link & Keep Source Formatting, and Link & Use Destination Styles, depending on the type of content you've copied in the table cells.

Chapter 15

Inserting Columns and Rows

Some tables seem to take on a life of their own once you begin adding data in the columns and rows. If you want to increase the size of your table by adding a column, you can do it using either method described here:

- Click the column label of the column beside which you want to add the new column. Then click Layout in the contextual Table Tools and choose Insert Left or Insert Right in the Rows & Columns group (see Figure Figure 15-9).

- Right-click the column label of the column, point to Insert, and click Insert Columns To The Left or Insert Columns To The Right.

Figure 15-9 The Layout tab of the contextual Table Tools has what you need to insert columns and rows.

When you manually add data to a table by typing the entry and pressing Tab, Word will continue creating new rows as long as you continue entering data. But when you want to add rows in the middle of a table, for example, or add many rows at once, you can follow the procedures given previously but choose Insert Above or Below instead of Left or Right.

If you want to insert multiple columns or rows, simply highlight the number of columns (or rows) that you want to insert. For example, to add three columns to the left of an existing column, highlight three contiguous columns, beginning with the one beside which you want to insert the new columns. Then right-click the selected columns, point to Insert, and choose Insert Columns To The Left. The three columns are added as you specified.

Inserting Cells

In some circumstances, you might want to insert cells in a table without adding an entire row or column. You might need to do this, for example, when you have overlooked a product name and number in your listing and need to add it without changing the entire table. To insert cells in a table, simply select the cell (or cells) below which you want to insert new cells. Right-click the selected cell, point to Insert, and choose Insert Cells. In the Insert Cells dialog box, click the option you need (as shown in the graphic that follows) then click OK. The cells in the table are changed accordingly.

Deleting Columns, Rows, and Cells

If you decide that you don't need certain rows or columns after all, or if you have empty rows you didn't use, you can easily delete them. Simply highlight the rows or columns and right-click to display the context menu which will display a choice for deletion, depending on what you've selected. If you selected a row, you'll see Delete Row in the context menu; if you selected a single cell, you'll see only Delete Cell.

You can also delete table elements by clicking the table handle in the upper-left corner of the table then click Delete in the Rows & Columns group on the Layout tab. A list of deletion options appears from which you can choose the item you want to delete.

When you choose to delete cells in a table, Word displays the Delete Cells dialog box so that you can identify where you want remaining cells to be shifted. Click your selection and then click OK to return to the document.

Moving Rows and Columns

In some instances, you might want to select parts of your table and move them to other parts of your document—perhaps you want to create a new table, move rows to another position in the table, or divide one large table into two to make them easier to understand. (You can also use the Split Table command, located on the Layout tab of Table Tools, to divide one table into two.)

When you want to move rows or columns, simply select the rows or columns you want to move and drag the selected block to the new location. Be sure to click Show/Hide in the Paragraph group on the Home tab before you select the columns or rows to ensure that you've included the end of row or column markers in your selection. The table rows or columns are relocated as you specified.

Merging Cells

Sometimes tables seem to grow out of proportion. Or perhaps data in one cell is related to data in two or more other cells. For example, you might want to display the text "2010" over four adjacent cells in the next row that contain the text "Q1", "Q2", "Q3", and "Q4", so that these cells appear as a subgroup under "2010". If you're looking for a way to consolidate data, you can use the Merge Cells command to take data from separate cells and combine it in one cell. To merge cells in your table, select the cells—or the rows or columns—you want to merge and select the Layout tab in Table Tools. Then click Merge Cells in the Merge group. The cells you selected are combined into a single cell.

> **Note**
>
> After a merge, you'll probably need to do some editing to get your data looking the way you want. Data takes on the format of the receiving cell; you might wind up with extra lines and odd capitalization as a result.

Splitting Cells

As you might imagine, splitting cells is the opposite of merging them. When you have a collection of data that you want to divide into separate cells, rows, or columns, you can use Split Cells on the Layout tab of the contextual Table Tools. To split cells, begin by selecting the cell, row, or column you want to split. Click Split Cells in the Merge group of the Layout tab. In the Split Cells dialog box, enter the number of columns and rows over which you want to divide the data. If you have previously merged the data you are now splitting, Word "remembers" the original number of columns and rows and suggests those values for the division. To retain the basic format and apply existing row and column formatting to the new columns and rows, leave the Merge Cells Before Split check box selected. Click OK to split the cells.

Adjust Column Sizes After Splits and Merges

After splitting or merging table cells, you'll probably need to redistribute the space in the columns. To resize a column quickly, point to the column border in the top row of the column you want to change. When the pointer changes to a double-headed arrow, drag the column border in the direction you want to resize the column. When the column is at the size you want, release the mouse button.

If you need to apply a more precise measurement to the width of the column, right-click in the column and choose Table Properties. Click the Column tab in the Table Properties dialog box, enter the appropriate column width in the Preferred Width box, and then click OK.

Change Cell Spacing and Alignments

One aspect of working with tables that can be frustrating to new users involves getting the content in the table to look just the way you want. Sometimes the text is too close to the cell border; at other times, a picture aligns oddly in the cell space or changes the look of the overall table.

You can control the amount of spacing in a cell as well as the alignment of the content within the cell by using the tools in the Alignment group on the Table Tools Layout contextual tab. The nine tools on the left side of the group enable you to choose how you want the content to be aligned within the cell.

Clicking the Cell Margins tool displays the Table Options dialog box in which you can enter the amount of space you want to appear along the Top, Bottom, Right, and Left sides of each cell.

When Size Matters

Suppose that your table is growing and growing. How big is too big? When should you divide the table into two smaller tables that readers might be able to absorb more easily?

Your first consideration should be the type of document you are producing. If you are creating a blog post that you want people to be able to read quickly online, don't add enormous tables that require the visitor to scroll down through your web page. Break the large table into several small tables that readers can quickly click and view individually.

In a print document, consider whether the table will continue over several pages. It's not unusual for a table to span more than one page, but if your table is running on for pages and pages, consider breaking the long table into smaller chunks. You can repeat the column labels at the top of each page to refresh your readers' memories.

If your table needs to extend horizontally, you can change the page orientation to landscape mode to accommodate the number of columns printed on the page. Be sure to size the columns so they take only the amount of space they need; cut out extra space and text.

This should help you create effective tables that your readers can navigate without being overwhelmed by the amount of information you're presenting.

Enhancing Your Tables with Formatting

Once upon a time, tables might have been boring columns of text and numbers, but no more. In Word 2010 you can apply any number of styles to your table—or create your own—to add color, typography, pictures, and more to give them just the look you want. You can change basically everything about a table—from the font to the shading to the line style and thickness and the display (or not) of the table grid.

By far, the easiest way to change the format of your table is to apply a table style. This section covers this method and also provides quick steps for customizing specific elements of your table.

TROUBLESHOOTING

Where is the Table AutoFormat feature?

If you are a Word 2003 user, you might wonder where the Table AutoFormat feature went. Table Styles enables you to choose and then change the format of tables you create quickly in your documents. In Word 2010, Table AutoFormat lives on in both of these features.

Changing Table Format by Using Table Styles

Word 2010 gives you a simple and elegant way to control a host of formatting options in your document. The theme you selected controls the formatting choices you'll see for all kinds of elements—your tables included. If you didn't choose a theme for your document, the Office theme is applied by default.

When you add a table to your Word document, the tabs for the contextual Table Tools appear above the Ribbon. On the Design tab, you'll see the Table Styles. Use these styles to change the format of your table with a simple click of the mouse. A table style can add the following formatting elements to your table:

- A new font, size, style, and color for table text

- A different look for gridlines and the table border

- A new style of shading for columns and rows

- A different kind of alignment for table data

Tip

Use the Table Style options on the Design tab of the contextual Table Tools to control the types of styles you see in the Table Styles gallery and to apply quick changes to your selected table. For example, if you want to see styles that include shading behind alternate columns, select the Banded Columns check box.

To apply a style to your table, click in the table, then on the Design tab in the contextual Table Tools, click one of the designs in the Table Styles gallery on the Ribbon.

If you don't see one you like, click the More button in the lower-right corner of the gallery to display a larger selection. As soon as you click a style, it is applied instantly to your table (see Figure 15-10).

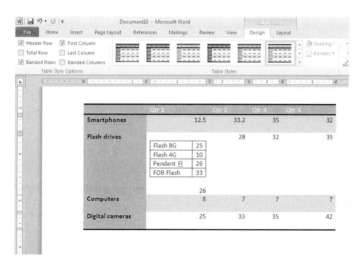

Figure 15-10 Use Table Styles to add a quick, professional look to the tables in your document.

Note

You can also use Live Preview to see how the change will look before you actually select it—just position the mouse pointer over a style you like, and the table will appear with that format. If you want to use that style, click it in the Table Styles gallery.

How Do Themes Affect Table Styles?

When you add a Quick Table to your Word document, the colors, fonts, and effects used in the tables displayed in the Quick Table gallery are preselected to match the document theme in use. The table styles that appear on the Design tab of the contextual Table Tools are also coordinated so that their color schemes, fonts, and line styles all correspond to the design elements in that particular theme.

This means that if at some point you choose a different theme for your document (on the Page Layout tab, choose Themes and make a new choice), the tables in your document will automatically change to reflect the colors, fonts, and line styles used in the new theme.

If you modify some table style elements but do not save your changes as a new table style, those changes will not be updated when the new theme specifications are applied. For example, suppose that you added a yellow highlight to the data in one column of your table. When you apply a new theme, the colors, fonts, and line styles will change, but the yellow highlight remains.

Creating Custom Table Styles

If you have adopted a particular type of table format that you want to use for all your company's documents, you can easily create a table style and save it to the gallery for reuse later. To create a new table style, follow these steps:

1. Create the table as usual and apply any formatting you want to be reflected in the final style.

2. Click in the table to select it.

3. On the Design tab of the contextual Table Tools, click the More button in the lower-right corner of the Table Styles gallery.

4. At the bottom of the gallery, click New Table Style. The Create New Style From Formatting dialog box appears, as Figure 15-11 shows.

5. Make any additional formatting choices (for example, font color, size, and style; line width, style, and color) and enter a name for the style in the Name box.

6. Select whether you want the table style to be available in all documents or only in the current document, and then click OK to save the new table style.

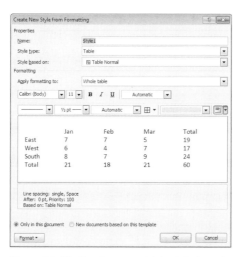

Figure 15-11 Create a new table style based on a table format you want to use regularly in your documents.

Now your new table style is available in the Table Styles gallery. If you decide that you'd like to further modify or delete the style, simply right-click it and choose Modify Table Style or Delete Table Style.

> ## Tip
> If you want to designate one of the table styles in the Table Styles gallery as the default table style used for all the tables you create, simply click it and choose Set As Default.

TROUBLESHOOTING

My table style will not accept my preferred font size.

A longstanding issue when creating table styles has been the inability to set a specific font size for the table style. Various scenarios might occur, but one example is if the font size of the Normal style is 12 points, you cannot set a font size of 10 points in the table style. Another example is if the font size of the Normal style is greater than 12 points; in this case, you cannot specify a font size in the table style. In both examples, the font size for the Normal style is used instead.

The underlying reason for the table style issues is the modification of the Normal style. If the Normal style is the same as the Document Defaults, then the Normal style is empty and the Document Defaults are used. If the Normal style is not empty and a font size is defined, then the font size defined in the Normal style takes precedence over the table style.

Even if you do not completely grasp the underlying rationale—it took working through several scenarios to fully understand this myself—the solution to this issue is simple. All you need to do is modify the formats for the Normal style so that they match those of the Document Defaults. Then modify the Document Defaults and use it as your formatting base instead of the Normal style. If the Normal style is left unchanged, then the longstanding issues involving the Table Style type, as well as some issues involving the List Style type, are circumvented.

Additionally, if you encounter these issues in some documents but not others, this can help to explain why these events occur. Note that the resolution is the same even if the documents were created in a previous version of Word.

More Formatting Fun

As mentioned earlier in this chapter, the simplest and most convenient way to format your tables involves using the table styles that come with Word because they are predesigned to coordinate with the overall theme selected for your document. When you use one of them, you know they're going to look good with the other formatting in your document. But if you really want to break out of the mold and make some customizations of your own, you might want to use the following table formatting tools to do it:

- Experiment with custom borders on your table by selecting the table and choosing Borders on the Design tab of the contextual Table Tools (see the graphic that follows). Use the Line Weight, Line Style, and Pen Color tools in the Draw Borders group to help get the style just right. And of course, if you don't like what you see, use the Eraser tool to remove it.

- Put your own shading behind table data by using the Shading tool on the Design tab of Table Tools. When you click Shading, a color palette appears, displaying choices that are in line with the selected theme. The palette also gives you the option of choosing custom colors. Again, have fun and experiment, but if things go horribly wrong, choose No Color or press Ctrl+Z to undo your creative catastrophe.

Positioning Tables in Your Document

In some cases, you might be perfectly happy creating a table at the cursor position and leaving it at that. In other cases, you might want to position the table more intentionally. You can use the options on the Table tab of the Table Properties dialog box to control the way in which your table is positioned. Display the dialog box by right-clicking in your table and choosing Table Properties. Click Table then click Left, Center, or Right alignment to specify whether you want your table to be positioned on the left margin of the document, centered between the margins, or aligned on the right.

> **Tip**
> You can have Word indent the table by a specific amount of space by using the Indent From Left option on the Table tab of the Table Properties dialog box. The default setting is zero, but you can increase the indent by clicking the up arrow.

Flowing Text Around Tables

Text wrap becomes an important consideration when you're working with multiple tables in a long document. Two options are available: None, which means text will not wrap around the table at all but appear above and below it, or Around, which flows text up to and around the table. Choose how you want text to flow by clicking the Table tab in the Table Properties dialog box.

When you click Around, the Positioning button becomes available. Click Positioning to display the Table Positioning dialog box (shown in Figure 15-12) in which you make choices that control where the table is positioned in your document by default.

Figure 15-12 The Table Positioning dialog box enables you to control the default table position for your document.

These choices include the following:

- The horizontal and vertical positioning of the table (choose Left, Right, Center, Inside, or Outside)

- The element to which the table position is relative (choose Margin, Page, Column for the horizontal position and Margin, Page, Paragraph for the vertical position)

- The space you want to leave between the table and surrounding text

- Whether you want to allow the text to overlap the table boundary and whether you want the table to stay fixed in place or move with text if it is reformatted

> **Note**
> Different tables require different settings. Take the time to experiment with the best effects for your particular table.

Sorting Table Data

One of the great features of Word tables is that they provide more than a clear way of organizing data—they also give you a means of *reorganizing* data. Word includes a Sort function so that you can easily reorder the information in your table by searching and sorting on certain key words or phrases. You might, for example, want to organize a conference registration list by sorting first according to state and then alphabetically by last name.

To use the Sort feature, select the table data you want to sort and click Sort in the Data group on the Layout tab. In the Sort dialog box, enter your preferences for the sort procedure and click OK to complete it.

INSIDE OUT   I Want to Print Formatted Table Content Without Row and Column Lines

If you want to remove all formatting in the table before printing, you can press Ctrl+Alt+U; however, if you want to keep shading intact, for example, and remove only the gridlines in the table, follow these steps:

1. Right-click the table.

2. Click Borders And Shading. In the Borders And Shading dialog box, click None then click OK.

The borders are removed from the cells in the table and you can now print normally.

Resizing Tables

It's not unusual to need to resize a table either while you're creating it or soon after. When you begin to create a table, you don't always know how large it will be. Perhaps you add more columns, include more information, or incorporate another set of data. Making the change to a new size—larger or smaller—is straightforward. Word gives you options for controlling the size of the table and offers flexibility for resizing your table exactly the way you want. This section explains how you can work with Word to best handle table-sizing issues.

Understanding AutoFit

Remember that when you create a table using the Insert Table dialog box, AutoFit is one of the setup options available to you. With AutoFit you can automatically resize your window as needed, and it is actually already working, by default, to create fixed column widths in your table. AutoFit offers three options:

- **Fixed Column Width**   With this option, you can choose a specific width for the columns you create.

- **AutoFit To Contents**   This adjusts the width of columns to accommodate the data you enter.

- **AutoFit To Window**   Choosing this option sizes a table so that it fits within a document or Web browser window. This size changes depending on the size of the window, which means that the table will be automatically redrawn as the user resizes the window.

INSIDE OUT   Test AutoFit To Window

If you want to see how resizing your table will affect the rest of the text displayed in your document, you can easily test AutoFit To Window by creating your table, choosing AutoFit To Window (you can do this before you create the table or afterward), and then displaying the table in Web Layout view. While the table is displayed, resize your document window. Notice how the table is automatically reformatted so that it always fits within the borders of the window.

Resizing an Entire Table

Although AutoFit does a good job of keeping on top of the way your table needs to grow (or shrink), there will be times when you want to make those changes yourself. The easiest way to resize a table is to drag a table corner. Here's the process in a nutshell: click the table resize handle in the lower-right corner of the table and drag it in the direction you want the table to be resized. The cells are redrawn to reflect the new size of the table.

Note

You can resize tables only in Print Layout and Web Layout views. Although you can see a table in Draft view, the table resize handle is not available.

Setting Preset and Percent Table Sizes

The Table Properties dialog box gives you two very different sizing options. To open it, right-click in your table, and then choose Table Properties. To create a table based on a fixed measurement, click the Table tab and in the Size section, select the Preferred Width check box and enter the width for the table you're going to create. Click the Measure In arrow and select Inches, then click OK.

The best use of this feature, however, is in creating a table that reformats automatically, based on the size of the browser window. In other words, if you're viewing your table as part of a Web page, and you reduce the size of your browser window, the table will refor-mat so that it will stay entirely visible, even in the smaller window. This is a great feature if you're often switching back and forth between applications and want to keep your infor-mation open on the screen. To create a table whose dimensions are based on a percentage of screen display, click the Measure In arrow, select Percent, and then click OK. The table will be reformatted as needed to stay within the size of the Web browser window.

Changing Column Width and Row Height

The fastest way to change the width and height of columns and rows is also the easiest. You simply position the pointer over the dividing line of the column or row you want to change and, when the pointer changes to a double-headed arrow, drag the border in the desired direction. Be sure that you've grabbed the border for the entire column or row, however, because it's possible to move the border for a single cell, which won't help if you want to adjust an entire column or row. (Make sure all cells are deselected if you want to resize the entire column.)

Distributing Data Evenly in Rows and Columns

Distributing your data refers to the process of spacing and aligning data within cells. By default, when you create a basic table and enter text, the text aligns along the left border of the cell, placed in the first line of the cell. To distribute your data evenly in the rows and columns of your table (spacing it evenly between the top and bottom margins of the row and in the center of the column), right-click in the column or row you want to change, choose Cell Alignment and then select one of the Align Center commands. Or you can also use the Alignment group on the Layout tab.

Changing Text Direction

While we're talking about distributing data, let's also discuss rotating the text in your table cells. You can orient your horizontal text on a vertical axis, which gives you the means to create interesting column headings for your tables.

To change the display of existing text, start by selecting it and then clicking Text Direction in the Alignment group on the Layout tab. Here's what you can expect to happen:

- On the first click, the Text Direction tool displays the text vertically, with the start of the text at the top of the page, extending down toward the table.

- Click again and the Text Direction tool displays the text vertically, with the start of the text at the top of the table, extending upward toward the top of the page.

- Click a third time and the Text Direction tool puts your text back to normal.

Using Tables as Page Layout Tools

If you are using Word to create a Web page that will include columns or other elements you want to hold in position in the page, you can use a table to contain the content so it displays properly in the reader's Web browser.

You might, for example, create a table that contains three columns and five to seven rows, and then place the content in each of those cells relevant to where you want the text and pictures to appear on the page. Use the rulers if necessarily to position the information precisely, and increase your cell margins to adjust the amount of space between the content and the border of the cell. When you have the content positioned the way you want it, make the table grid invisible by clicking the table. To do this, on the Table Tools Design tab, click Borders and choose No Border. If the table has shading, click the Shading tool in the Table Styles group and click No Color. Preview the table in Web Layout to see how it will appear in the browser window.

Working with Functions in Tables

Although Word is happy to leave the truly complicated calculations to its companion, Excel, the program includes support for working with a number of functions in your tables. Some of the Word tables you create will no doubt include numbers—and some of those columns will require totals, averages, and more. You can create a number of calculations, depending on what you want the data in your tables to do. You can create your own formulas and work with other Word functions by using the Formula dialog box, shown in Figure 15-13.

Figure 15-13 You can create your own formulas in the Formula dialog box.

To create a formula in a table, follow these steps:

1. Click in the cell where you want to add the formula.

2. Choose the Layout tab in the contextual Table Tools. Click Formula in the Data Group to display the Formula dialog box.

    Word might insert the function it expects you to use based on the cell you selected in the table.

3. You can use the displayed formula as is or highlight and erase the existing formula, type = in the Formula box, and click the Paste function arrow. Choose the function you want to use. The function is added to the Formula box, and parentheses are supplied.

4. Click OK to close the Formula dialog box. Word will then calculate the answer and display it in the table cell.

> ## Controlling Table Breaks
>
> If you are working on a large table and know that the table will be divided among several pages, you have some additional choices to make. If you want to specify that your table breaks at a particular point, click in that row to position the cursor and then display the Table Properties dialog box (alternatively, right-click the table and choose Table Properties). Click the Row tab. Next, select the Allow Row To Break Across Pages check box to instruct Word to insert the page break at that point in the table. If you want that row to be repeated as the header row on subsequent pages, click Repeat As Header Row At Top Of Each Page.

What's Next?

This chapter showed you how to quickly add, edit, and format professional looking tables in Word. The next chapter enables you to display your ideas more visually, using SmartArt diagrams and charts.

CHAPTER 16

Create Compelling SmartArt Diagrams and Charts

Adding SmartArt Diagrams 493

Creative Charting 499

Introducing Word 2010 Chart Types 499

Creating a Basic Chart 501

Entering Chart Data 506

Editing and Enhancing Chart Information 509

Formatting Charts 518

What's Next? 522

DEPENDING on the nature of the document you're creating, it might be important to both show and tell readers the points you most want them to remember. You can illustrate your most important ideas—showcasing comparisons, depicting processes, and portraying important relationships among departments, vendors, sales data, and more. And in addition to the functional nature of the illustrations you can add in Word 2010, they just look nice; they add color, special effects, dimension, and more to your two-dimensional page.

In this chapter you learn about SmartArt, the diagramming tool that is included as part of Word 2010, and find out how to add and enhance charts in your Word document. What's more, the charts you add interact easily with Excel 2010, so you can use simple worksheet sections or complex calculations as part of the charts you create.

Adding SmartArt Diagrams

The name *SmartArt* says much about the functionality of this feature, which was first made available in Word 2007. SmartArt enables you to diagram your ideas easily—in a wide variety of ways—and enhance those diagrams by adding special effects, such as shadows, 3-D effects, styles, color schemes, and more.

SmartArt simplifies the process of creating diagrams of all sorts. When you need to create any kind of diagram that illustrates a process, a workflow, a listing, or the way things work together, you can do it quickly with just a few clicks of the mouse using SmartArt.

SmartArt is an interactive diagramming tool that is a dramatic improvement over the diagram feature available in versions prior to Word 2007. With earlier tools, you were limited to six diagram types, and your formatting options were also limited. With SmartArt, you can choose from a large collection of diagram styles, customize them to your heart's content, and include your own pictures within the body of the diagram. What's more, you can apply a variety of design styles to add depth, shadow, shine, and perspective.

Creating the SmartArt Diagram

When you're in the document, begin by positioning the cursor where you want the diagram to appear. Then on the Insert tab, in the Illustrations group, click SmartArt. The Choose A SmartArt Graphic dialog box appears, as shown in Figure 16-1.

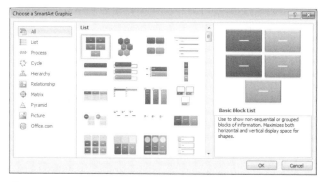

Figure 16-1 Start your SmartArt graphic by choosing the type of diagram you want to create.

The Choose A SmartArt Graphic dialog box presents several different types of diagrams from which you can choose, each designed to convey a specific type of information.

- A list diagram displays a nonsequential series of items. You might use a list diagram to introduce a series of new products in your spring catalog.

- A process diagram can show a step-by-step process. For example, you might use a process diagram to show a new trainee how to log on to your computer system.

- A cycle diagram can show the workflow of a particular operation, typically something that is repeated in a cyclical process.

- A hierarchy diagram shows levels, so it is a logical candidate for organization charts.

- A relationship diagram shows how various items relate to each other. You might use a relationship diagram, for example, to show how different roles in a volunteer work group complement each other to provide specific services to the organization.

- A matrix diagram is helpful when you want to compare four items in a format that is easy for viewers to understand. You might use a matrix diagram to explain the research focus for each quarter of the next fiscal year.

- A pyramid diagram shows items in relationship that typically build from the bottom up. A good example of a pyramid diagram is a fundraising chart in which the bottom level represents the largest number of beginning level donors who contribute to the organization, and the top level represents the smaller percentage of major donors.

- A picture diagram enables you to create a diagram in which the photos are the main point. You might use a picture diagram, for example, to show range of products in your product line and who manages the various divisions.

- The Office.com selection provides you with additional SmartArt choices you can use in a number of different diagram styles.

Begin the process of creating your SmartArt diagram by choosing the diagram type you want from the left panel of the Choose A SmartArt Graphic dialog box. Notice that when you click a diagram type, styles for that particular diagram appear in the center of the dialog box. Click the style you like, and you'll see an illustration and detailed description of the type of diagram you've selected displayed on the right (see Figure 16-2). Click OK to create the diagram.

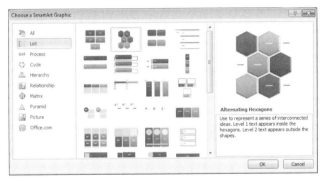

Figure 16-2 The SmartArt graphic style you select is displayed and described in the right side of the dialog box.

The diagram appears at the cursor position. Figure 16-3 shows a picture diagram as it first appears. Notice that SmartArt Tools contextual tabs appear automatically in the Ribbon as soon as you create the diagram. You will use the tools on the SmartArt Tools Design tab to edit and enhance the diagram by adding text boxes and pictures, changing the diagrams colors, and applying styles. Use the tools in the SmartArt Tools Format tab to change the appearance of text and shapes in the diagram.

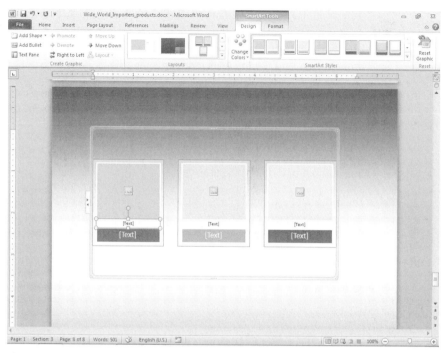

Figure 16-3 Use the SmartArt Tools Design tab to choose the layout, style, and color for your diagram.

Adding and Formatting Diagram Text

Adding text to your diagram is simple: just click in the first text box and type the text you want to display in the box. Press Tab to move to the next text box. Repeat as needed until the text boxes are filled. If you run out of text shapes and need to add a new one, click the Add Shape down arrow in the Create Graphics group on the SmartArt Tools Design tab and choose whether you want to add a shape after, before, above, or below the current shape.

If you prefer to enter all text at once rather than clicking individual shapes and typing text entries, you can display the SmartArt text pane. On the SmartArt Tools Design tab, click Text Pane in the Create Graphic group, then in the Text Pane, click in the item you want to change and type your text.

You can format the text in the diagram by highlighting the text and choosing the text options from the Mini Toolbar that appears above the selection. You can also apply text styles by highlighting the text, clicking the Format tab, and choosing the setting you want to apply in the WordArt Styles group. Text Effects is a new tool in Word 2010 with which you can apply special treatments—Shadow, Reflection, Glow, Bevel, 3-D Rotation, and Transform—to the text you select (see Figure 16-4).

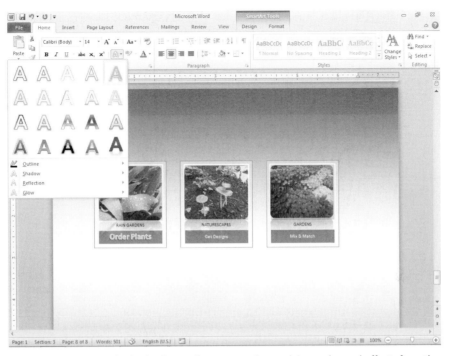

Figure 16-4 Change the look of your diagram text by applying styles and effects from the WordArt Styles group on the SmartArt Tools Format tab.

Making Formatting Changes in the Diagram

You can apply special formats to give your diagrams a professional look while carrying over the design of your publication in terms of color scheme, fonts, and more. Similar to the chart options available with traditional charting in Word, SmartArt diagrams also offer you a variety of layouts and styles that you can apply directly to the diagrams in your documents. To change the layout of the diagram, click it and select the Design tab on the SmartArt Tools contextual tab. Then click the More button in the Layouts gallery to display the full range of layout possibilities. Depending on the type of diagram you've created, you will see a variety of layout options. Click the one that best fits the data concepts you're trying to convey.

Like other objects in Word 2010, the available formatting settings that you can apply to your SmartArt are influenced by the theme selected for the document. You can change the colors in your SmartArt diagram by selecting a preset color palette with the Change Colors tool, which is available in the SmartArt Styles group on the SmartArt Tools Design tab. When you choose Change Colors, a palette of choices appears. The colors that correspond to the selected theme appear in the top portion of the palette. Point to the one you want to preview then click your final choice to apply it to the diagram in your document.

Chapter 16

SmartArt Quick Styles offer you a gallery of ready-made styles (complete with 3-D settings, shadows, rotation, lighting, and more) that you can apply to your diagram with a click of the mouse. Click the More button to display all the choices and select the one you want (see Figure 16-5).

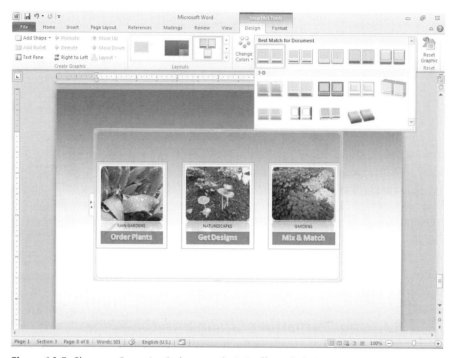

Figure 16-5 Choose a SmartArt Style to apply 3-D effects, lighting, and more.

Note

You might start out with rectangles in a list diagram or circles in a relationship diagram, but that doesn't mean you have to stick with those shapes. You can replace a traditional shape with a unique one of your choosing by selecting the traditional shape and clicking Change Shape in the Shapes group of the SmartArt Tools Format. Click the Change Shape down arrow and select a shape from the displayed list. The shape in your diagram is replaced with the new shape. This can be done for any part of the graphic that can be selected as a separate shape (for example, one rectangle in a list).

Creative Charting

Charts can dramatically enhance the information you're sharing with others in the documents you create. A chart can show a reader at a glance what percentage of sales a particular product comprises. A bar chart quickly shows which division is outselling all the others. An area chart can show the results of tracking over time. The charts you include in your documents give you a way to visually showcase important data that others will understand easily. You might use a chart to:

- Announce a new sales competition for your staff.

- Show the number of volunteers each of your regional sites has trained in the previous quarter using a pie chart.

- Show the staff how the new construction on your building is coming along by placing a bar chart over a photo of the building as it's being constructed.

- Point out which sites are recruiting the greatest number of volunteers using textured columns.

> **Note**
> What's the difference between a chart and a graph? Nothing, really. The terms are often used interchangeably to describe the graphical depiction of data—early on, the term *charting* referred to a type of mapmaking. *Graphing*, on the other hand, involved plotting data points and discerning trends and relationships. Today, the terms mean essentially the same thing; charts and graphs help you illustrate trends and relationships in your data. *Diagramming* usually refers to the process of using a specific model to generate flowcharts or diagrams.

Chapter 16

Introducing Word 2010 Chart Types

Charts are often used to illustrate relationships—how one item relates to another, how an item this year relates to the same item last year, how a product is selling over time. Eleven different chart types are available:

- **Column**   A column chart is used to show data comparisons. You might show, for example, how two data series "stack up" against each other for the first quarter.

- **Line**   A line chart plots data points over time or by category. You might use a line chart to show a trend in product returns over a six-month period.

- **Pie** A pie chart shows the relationship of different data items to the whole. Each pie comprises 100 percent of the series being graphed, and each slice is shown as a percentage of the pie. You might use a pie chart to show the relative size of individual departments in the northeastern sales division of your company.

- **Bar** Word shows a bar chart as horizontal bars, graphing data items over time (or other categories). You might use a bar chart to compare the stages of different products in a production cycle.

- **Area** An area chart gives you the means to compare data two different ways: you can show the accumulated result of the data items, and you can show how the data (and their relationship to one another) change over time. For example, you might use an area chart to show how many students took each module of the exam at two different universities.

- **XY (Scatter)** With an XY chart, you can plot pairs of data points over time. You might use an XY chart to contrast the test scores from a battery of exams given at two different universities.

- **Stock** A stock chart displays four values for a single item—open, high, low, close—and is designed to show the variance in a particular item within a specific period of time.

- **Surface** A surface chart is a great way to compare the change of three data items over time. Through the use of colored levels, a surface chart shows in three-dimension form where the data in a particular series leads (see Figure 16-6).

- **Doughnut** A doughnut chart is similar to a pie chart in that it shows the relationship between data items. Doughnut charts enable you to compare two sets of data and the way in which they relate to the whole and to each other. You might use a doughnut chart to portray two different sales campaigns. The sections of the doughnut could represent the different sales channels, and you could compare and contrast the different effects of each channel.

- **Bubble** With a bubble chart, you can plot three different data series. Each item is plotted at a particular point in time and shows the data value as a bubble. You can see, for example, which accounts had the highest charges during the second quarter.

- **Radar** A radar chart plots multiple data points and shows their relation to a center point. You might use a radar chart to show how each regional sales division fared in a recent sales competition.

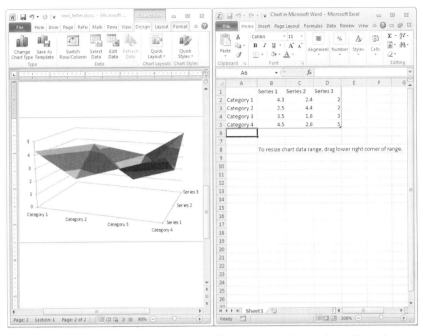

Figure 16-6 With a surface chart, you can illustrate series data in three dimensions.

Creating a Basic Chart

The process of creating a chart in Word is simple. First click to position the cursor wherever you want the chart to appear (you can move the chart later if you choose) then follow these steps:

1. On the Insert tab (on the Ribbon), click Chart in the Illustrations group.

    The Insert Chart dialog box appears, as shown in Figure 16-7.

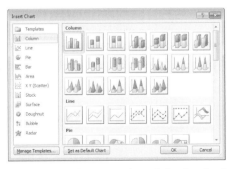

Figure 16-7 The Insert Chart dialog box is where you can view and choose the type of chart that meets your needs.

2. Choose the chart type you want to create by clicking it in the left pane of the Insert Chart dialog box.

The gallery area on the right shows the various styles available for the chart type you selected. Click OK to create the chart.

The default chart in the type you selected appears in the document on the left side of the Word window; on the right side of the window, Excel displays a datasheet that includes placeholder data (see Figure 16-8). You can now modify the data so it is relevant to your document.

3. Click the close box to close the datasheet, and the chart in your document is updated accordingly.

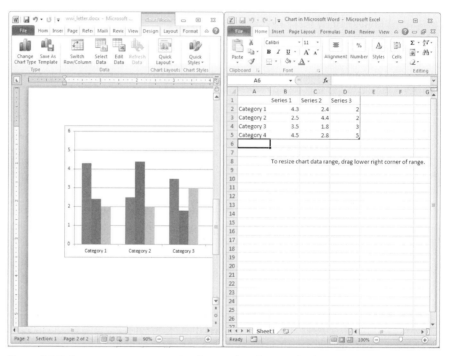

Figure 16-8 As soon as you create the chart, a datasheet with placeholder data appears. Replace the data with your own, and the chart is updated automatically.

That's all there is to adding your first chart to a Word document. But now comes the fun part—enhancing the chart with the Word Chart Tools.

> **Note**
>
> The gallery area of the Insert Chart dialog box contains all the chart types available to you, so if you prefer, you can simply use the vertical scroll bar in the dialog box to view all the different chart styles. That way, if you really aren't sure what the type of chart you want to create is called—but you know it when you see it—you can look over all the styles quickly and make your selection by double-clicking it.

Changing the Chart Type

Making sure you have the right chart for the data you're displaying is an important part of communicating your concepts most effectively. Some charts, such as bar and column charts, are best for comparing data items—for example, tracking the sales of apples compared to oranges. Other charts, such as pie charts, are better for showing the relation of individual items to a whole—such as the fundraising totals of your two top volunteer groups as they compare to total fundraising dollars in August 2010.

Word makes it simple for you to select and change chart types. Start by creating a new chart or by displaying the chart you've already created. Click the chart (if necessary) so that the contextual Chart Tools are displayed on the Ribbon. On the Design tab, click Change Chart Type in the Type group (on the far left side of the Ribbon). The Change Chart Type dialog box (which you saw earlier as the Insert Chart dialog box) opens, offering you the range of chart types that were available to you when you initially created the chart. Simply click the chart type you want, click OK, and Word changes the display of the chart in your document and modifies the datasheet if needed.

> **Note**
>
> If you really like the chart type you've selected, you can make it the default chart that is used automatically whenever you create a new one. Simply click Set As Default Chart in the Insert Chart (or Change Chart Type) dialog box. Each time you create a new chart, the chart type you selected will be used by default.

Creating a Chart Template

Word offers so many ways to enhance the design of your charts that you might want to create your own templates so the charts you create are consistent in all of your documents. If you work for a company that standardizes its published materials, creating and using a custom template gives you the means to make your charts distinctive while keeping them professionally appealing and consistent with your overall brand.

After you've created, enhanced, and saved your chart (which you learn how to do on page 506), you can save it as a template. It will then be available to you in the Templates folder that appears in the left pane of the Insert Chart dialog box.

To create a template based on an existing chart, simply select the chart and then select the Design tab in the contextual Chart Tools. In the Type group, click the Save As Template option. In the Save Chart Template dialog box, enter a name for the new chart and click Save (see Figure 16-9). Word saves the chart by default in the Templates folder, making it available to all your other Office applications as well. The next time you open the Insert Chart dialog box, the template you saved will be available in the Chart Templates folder.

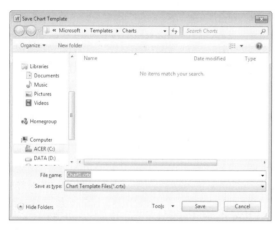

Figure 16-9 Save a customized chart as a template so that you can use it in other documents you create.

> **Note**
>
> If you change the theme selected for your document, any charts you create using a chart template will not update to reflect the new theme. To update the format of your chart, click the edge of the chart frame to select it, and then click Reset To Match Style in the Current Selection group on the Format tab of the contextual Chart Tools.

Understanding the Chart Tools

As soon as you create a chart, Word displays the contextual Chart Tools, which offers you a collection of specialized tools you'll use to design, enhance, format, and save the chart you create (see Figure 16-10).

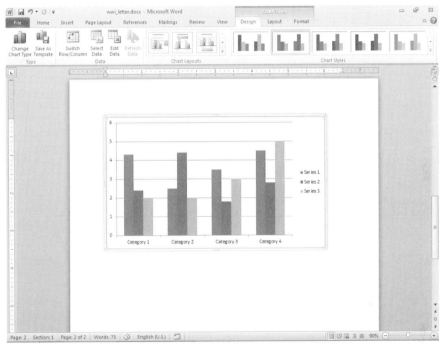

Figure 16-10 The contextual Chart Tools enable you to change the design, layout, and format of your chart.

The contextual Chart Tools offer three tabs with different sets of tools for different types of tasks.

- **Design** With the Design tab, you can change the type of your chart, work with chart data, select a chart layout, and choose the style and color for the chart you want to create.

- **Layout** This tab lets you focus on specific chart elements. With the Layout tools, you can add pictures, shapes, and more; add and format labels; modify the axes in the chart; add color, pictures, or 3-D effects to the background; and insert elements like trend lines, markers, and more that help readers analyze the data they are reviewing.

- **Format** The Format tab includes tools that let you enhance the look of your chart by choosing the size of shapes on the chart; adding shadows, fills, and outlines; changing the size of the chart; and selecting text wrapping and positioning options.

Throughout the rest of this chapter, you'll learn more about when to use each of the tabs in Chart Tools to change, enhance, and finalize the charts in your Word documents.

Entering Chart Data

When you first create a new chart, Word inserts a default set of dummy data into the datasheet and displays the datasheet in Excel. You use the datasheet to enter, arrange, and select the data you want to include in your chart. Throughout the life of your Word document, you can add to and update the information in the datasheet as needed, ensuring that your chart always stays fresh and reflects your most current data.

> **Note**
> You can choose to link or embed chart data in a Word document. If you link a chart in your Word document to an external source, it will be updated whenever the source document changes. If you embed a chart in your document, you'll be able to edit the chart as you would normally, by double-clicking it in the hosting document.

You will use the Data group (available on the Chart Tools Design tab) to work with your chart's datasheet (see Figure 16-11). Here's a quick look at the tools in that group:

- **Switch Row/Column** With this tool, you can swap rows and columns to create a different display of the data in your datasheet.

- **Select Data** Displays the Select Data Source dialog box, in which you can choose the data range you want to use for the chart. Additionally, you can choose the series and category items you want to include or hide from display.

- **Edit Data** Displays the datasheet so that you can change, add to, or delete information on the datasheet.

Figure 16-11 Use the Data group on the Chart Tools Design tab to work with the data in your chart's datasheet.

Working with the Datasheet

Figure 16-12 shows the datasheet that appears when you create a new pie chart in Word. As you can see, the series names (Series 1, Series 2, and Series 3) and the category names are all generic. The data in the datasheet doesn't mean anything at this point—it simply provides the chart engine with something to display in the sample chart.

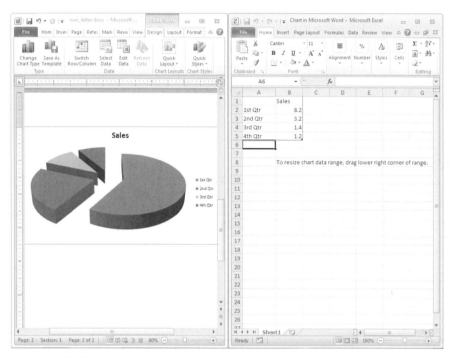

Figure 16-12 The datasheet displays the data values and labels used to create your chart.

> ### Note
> If you close the datasheet by clicking the Excel close button, you can redisplay it while you edit the chart by clicking Edit Data in the Data group on the Design tab of the contextual Chart Tools.

The datasheet is actually an Excel worksheet, so the tools on the Ribbon might look familiar to you. Changing the data in the datasheet is a simple matter of clicking in the cell you want to change and typing the new information. You'll find the following items on the datasheet.

- **Categories** The items in the columns are the categories placed along the horizontal axis of the chart. Categories might include months, quarters, stages of a project, or some other unit by which the value can be measured.

- **Data Series** The data series show the items that are being graphed, according to the categories selected.

- **Values** The data entered in the cells of the datasheet are scaled against the value axis, which is the vertical axis.

> **Note**
> By default, the datasheet includes data used to display the chart you add to your page. The first thing you will most likely do when you open the datasheet will be to delete the existing data so that you can enter your own. You can type the values directly into the cells or copy and paste the information into the datasheet from another source.

Changing the Data Arrangement

By default, the new Word chart displays the categories along the horizontal axis and the values along the vertical axis, but if you choose, you can flip that configuration to display your data differently.

To change the arrangement of the data in your chart, follow these steps:

1. Select the chart you want to change.

   The Chart Tools tabs appear.

2. On the Design tab, in the Data group, click Switch Row/Column.

   The chart is redrawn automatically.

> **Tip**
> Although you're creating a chart for use in your Word document, you might want to use data from other programs to create the chart. Because the chart datasheet is actually an Excel worksheet, you can link to external data sources supported by Excel. To display your choices for using external data in your Excel datasheet, click the Data tab in the datasheet and choose the option in the Get External Data group that best reflects the type of data you want to use. For more about working with Excel 2010, see *Microsoft Excel 2010 Inside Out*, by Mark Dodge and Craig Stinson (Microsoft Press, 2010).

Editing and Enhancing Chart Information

The chart that Word 2010 adds to your document will be fairly straightforward, without much formatting or color. After you create the basic chart, you can add to, edit, and enhance your chart in a number of different ways. Begin by clicking the chart you want to change; the contextual Chart Tools appears automatically along the top of the Ribbon. You use the Chart Tools, shown in Figure 16-13, to change the chart layout, choose a chart style (including colors and shadow effects), add titles and labels, change the look of the background and axes, and much more. The sections that follow show you how to add specific items to your charts to make them easier for readers to understand.

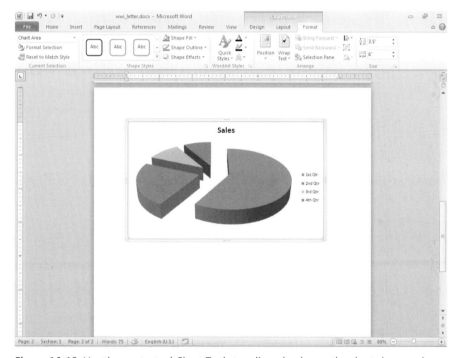

Figure 16-13 Use the contextual Chart Tools to edit and enhance the charts in your document.

> **Note**
> Although many of the elements you'll find on the Chart Tools tab relate to all the different chart types, some controls are disabled for certain charts. For example, the tools in the Axes group on the Layout tab are disabled when a pie chart is selected because they don't apply to that type of chart.

Chapter 16

Choosing a New Chart Layout

If you spend some time working on a chart and just don't feel it portrays what you want to convey, you can easily switch chart types by applying a new layout to the chart. A chart layout is like a template—complete with a legend style, data labels, and more—that you apply to the chart you've already created. You can choose a layout for your chart when you want to save yourself the time and trouble of choosing a number of chart options individually.

To apply a chart layout, click the chart to select it, and then on the Chart Tools Design tab, click the More button in the lower-right corner of the Chart Layouts gallery to display the whole collection of layouts (see Figure 16-14). Simply click the layout to apply it to your chart.

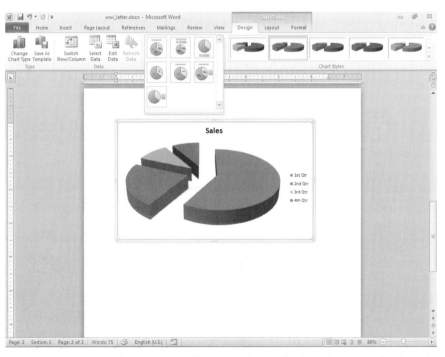

Figure 16-14 Use the Chart Layouts gallery to apply specific chart formats to the charts in your document.

Applying a Chart Style

Word includes another design feature that makes creating a professional chart much easier. The Chart Style gallery includes dozens of visual styles that you can apply to a chart in your document. Chart Styles include:

- Color selection

- 3-D effects

- Shadow effects

- Outline style and color

- Background effects

To apply a chart style, select the chart, and then on the Chart Tools Design tab, click the More button in the lower-right corner of the Chart Styles gallery and then choose the style you want from the displayed collection (see Figure 16-15).

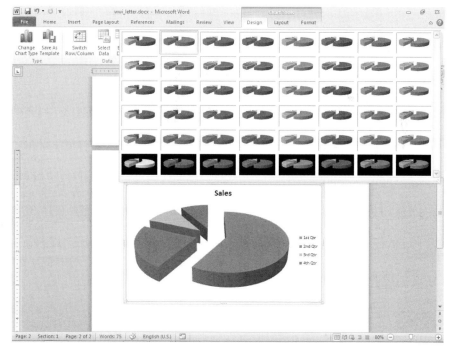

Figure 16-15 The Chart Styles gallery gives your chart a professional look with the click of a button.

Chapter 16

Change Fonts with the Mini Toolbar

By now you've probably noticed that Word 2010 is all about context. Whatever project you're working on, Word offers you just the tools you need to complete it. When you want to change the font used in a chart, simply highlight the text you want to change. The Mini Toolbar appears over the text with which you can easily choose a new font, change the size, make the font larger or smaller, change the color, and more. Simply click your choice and the text is changed. All things should be so simple.

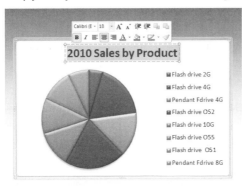

Adding a Chart Title

Not all charts need titles, but a chart title can help readers understand the "big picture" you're trying to communicate. To add a title to your chart, click Chart Title in the Labels group on the Layout tab of the contextual Chart Tools. In the gallery, choose whether you want the title to be centered on the chart or placed above the chart. (If you decide later that you want to move the title, you can simply drag it to the point on the chart where you want it to appear.) Centered Overlay Title enables the chart to be displayed at maximum size (which is important if you have a fairly complex chart), while Above Chart reduces the chart size slightly to make room for the title. Experiment with each choice to find the one that's right for your chart.

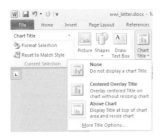

> **Note**
>
> Chances are that you won't have a lot of room in your document for lengthy chart titles. A good title pulls out key words that reflect what the chart portrays. If you're comparing volunteer recruitment methods, "Recruitment Methods Comparison" works. Not exciting, but accurate. If you can think of something exciting too, all the better.

Working with Axes

The axes of your chart are important in that they set up the structure for the way in which data is displayed. You can use two different tools in the contextual Chart Tools to work with axes. Both are found on the Layout tab.

If you want to instruct Word to display the title of an axis, click Axis Titles in the Labels group. To add an axis title to your chart, begin by clicking Axis Titles and pointing to the axis you want to change (Primary Horizontal Axis or Primary Vertical Axis). When you point to the Horizontal Axis selection, choose Show Title Below Axis to add the title text box to the chart. (You can click and drag the title box anywhere on the chart you'd like it to appear—but be sure to keep it close to the axis so your readers will understand what it refers to.) If you select Primary Vertical Axis, you will see three choices: Rotated Title, Vertical Title, and Horizontal Title. Select your display choice, and then simply click in the text box and type the text for your axis title.

If you want to change the way in which information is displayed along the axis, you can choose Axes in the Axes group. When you click the Axes tool, a list appears, offering Primary Horizontal Axis and Primary Vertical Axis as options. Choose the axis you want to change, and another set of choices appears (see Figure 16-16). For the horizontal axis, your choices involve whether the axis runs right to left (or vice versa) and where the data labels appear. For the vertical axis, you can choose the value increments you want to appear on the axis (thousands, millions, or billions).

Chapter 16

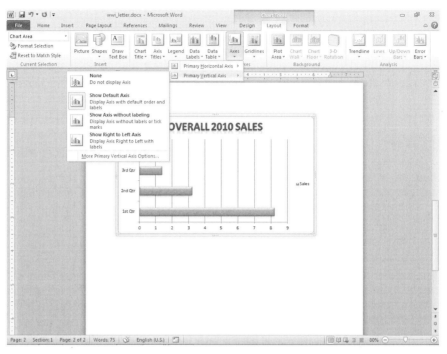

Figure 16-16 Choose the axis you want to change and make your selection from the gallery.

If you want to further control the axes in your chart, you can choose More Primary Vertical Axis Options or More Primary Horizontal Axis Options at the bottom of each of the respective galleries. To further refine how your axes appear, you need to display the Format Axis dialog box, as shown in Figure 16-17. In this dialog box, you can choose the increments for the values on the vertical axis, set the tick mark type, and determine the placement of the chart floor. In the Format Axis dialog box for the horizontal axis, you can also set axis type and tick mark settings, and choose where the vertical axis crosses the horizontal axis. Additionally, in both dialog boxes, you can choose line color and fill, shadow, and 3-D effects for the axes.

> **Note**
> You will be able to choose settings for the chart floor only when you are working with a 3-D chart.

Figure 16-17 You can choose additional options for the axes in your chart by using the Format Axis dialog box.

> **Note**
>
> To hide or display axis tick marks, display the Format Axis dialog box and clear or select the Major Tick Mark Type and Minor Tick Mark Type options, as appropriate. Click Close to save your settings.

Add Gridlines and Trendlines

If you're working with complicated charts that have multiple data series, gridlines can help clarify the comparisons and conclusions you want readers to draw from your chart. Select the Gridlines tool in the Axes group on the Chart Tools Layout tab. Then click either Primary Horizontal Gridlines or Primary Vertical Gridlines. Both choices give you the option of selecting major gridlines, minor gridlines, or major and minor gridlines.

> **Note**
>
> You can be creative with the gridlines in your chart if you want to shake things up a little bit. Word 2010 enables you to choose new gradients for your gridlines and add shadows and arrows. Simply right-click the gridline you want to change in the chart and select Format Gridlines. The dialog box that appears will be either Format Major Gridlines or Format Minor Gridlines, depending on which set of gridlines you selected.

Chapter 16

Choose Line Color, Line Style, Shadow, or Glow and Soft Edges in the left panel and then select the options you want to apply to your chart. Click Close to save your settings and apply them to your chart.

Be forewarned, however: with gridlines, a little goes a long way, so be sure to add only what your reader needs to understand your data. Too many lines will clutter up your chart and make it more difficult for readers to decipher; they can even render the chart unreadable if there are too many too close together.

Displaying and Positioning a Legend

Word assumes that you want a legend for your chart when you first create it. If you don't feel the legend is needed and want to have more space for your chart, you can remove the legend by clicking Legend in the Labels group on the Layout tab (available in the Chart Tools). When you choose None (the first option on the list), the legend is hidden. The chart is enlarged to fill the space the legend previously occupied.

You can also control where the legend is placed in the chart by clicking the Legend tool in the Labels group. A range of options appears from which you can choose, as shown in Figure 16-18.

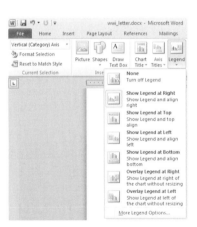

Figure 16-18 With the Legend tool in the Labels group, you can control the placement of your chart legend.

> ## Tip
> You can further change and enhance the legend you add to your chart by clicking More Legend Options at the bottom of the options list that appears when you click Legends in the Labels group.

Working with Data Labels

Data labels are helpful when you need to give the reader further clues about which data items go with which series or category. Word gives you the ability to add several different kinds of data labels to your charts. You might want to add percentages to pie slices, for example, or category labels to stacked bars. Click Data Labels in the Labels group to display a list of placement choices for the data labels on your chart.

By default, Word displays data values in the pie slices or bars of your chart. You can change the type of information displayed and add special features such as color, shadows, outlines, and 3-D options by choosing Data Labels in the Labels group and clicking More Data Label Options. In the Format Data Labels dialog box (see Figure 16-19), you can choose the label contents you want to display (series name, category name, value, or percentage).

Figure 16-19 Display and enhance data labels on your chart using options in the Format Data Labels dialog box.

> **Note**
>
> You can choose to display more than one type of label. For example, you might want to display both percentages and category names on a pie chart. If you select more than one label type, use a separator to distinguish the labels. Click the Separator arrow to display a list of choices and then click the one you want to use.

One more way to ensure that readers get the connection between your data trends and the categories being plotted: you can use the Legend Key feature to add small legend tags to the left of each data label. Readers will be able to see at a glance which items relate to the categories in your chart legend.

> **Note**
>
> The data labels Word uses are taken directly from your datasheet. If you want to change a data label on the chart, it's best to go back to the datasheet and make the change there. Otherwise, the label change might not "stick," and you might see the same old label displayed the next time you view your chart.

TROUBLESHOOTING

I can't see axis titles in my chart.

If you're having trouble seeing the axis titles along the Category and Values axes on your chart, the chart area might be too small to display all the chart information successfully. Try enlarging the chart by clicking it and then dragging one of the resize handles outward. If that doesn't do the trick, right-click the axis title while editing the chart and then choose a different font or font size on the Mini Toolbar.

Formatting Charts

Word gives you the ability to format all the different elements included in your chart. You might want to change the font of a title, resize the labels, change the background color, change the line thickness, apply a pattern, or perform any number of other tricks—including adding drop shadows, glow effects, or 3-D enhancements.

To choose the chart object you want to work with, click the chart, choose the Layout tab on the Chart Tools, and then click the Chart Elements arrow in the Current Selection group. A list of possible objects appears, as shown in Figure 16-20. When you click your choice, Word selects that item in the chart. You can then right-click the item to display a format choice—for example, right-clicking a legend displays a shortcut menu including the Format Legend command. When you select that command, a formatting dialog box appears in which you can select the colors, styles, and placement for the legend.

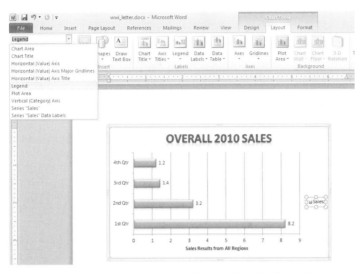

Figure 16-20 Use the Chart Elements list to select the chart element you want to change.

The formatting commands available vary depending on the type of chart you're creating and the chart element you've selected. You'll see a different set of options, for example, when you right-click a chart axis than you will when you right-click the legend.

Changing the Format of Your Chart Elements

Word includes a Ribbon full of formatting choices that enable you to add color and texture to the shapes of the elements in your chart. Additionally, you can use the Format options to apply special effects to your text by changing color, adding mirroring, shadowing, glow effects, and more. Here are a few possibilities to consider as you think about the ways you want to enhance your chart.

- Do you want a border around your chart? If so, what kind? You make those choices on the Format tab of the Chart Tools.

- Do you want to choose a different color or line thickness for the border of your chart? Look in the Shape Styles group on the Format tab for the choices you need.

- Would you like to add a drop shadow to the chart? Click the Shape Effects down arrow, point to Shadow, and then choose the style you want.

- Do you want to apply a special text effect to your title or axes titles? Choose a Word-Art style that reflects the way you want the text in your chart to appear.

You can change each of these items by first selecting the chart you want to change and then by selecting the Format tab on the Chart Tools. Figure 16-21 shows the commands that are available when the Format tab is selected.

Figure 16-21 The Format tab includes tools for changing colors, shapes, shadows, and more in your charts.

Formatting Shapes

Word provides you with an almost unlimited number of ways to enhance charts in your documents. One way you can make a big visual difference is by applying formats to the shapes that make up the chart. For example, consider the chart title in Figure 16-22. The 3-D style applied to the title is one of many available in the Shape Styles gallery (on the Chart Tools Format tab).

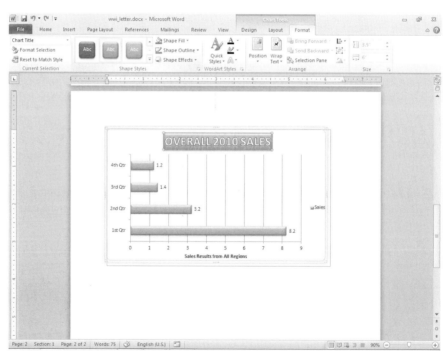

Figure 16-22 You can add special styles to the shapes in your chart by using the Shape Styles gallery.

Begin by selecting the object in your chart that you want to change. Anything that you can click qualifies—you can change the title, the label area, the individual data series, the axes, and more. When you select an element, Word automatically updates the Shape Styles to show the styles available for that chart element. You can click the More button to see the entire gallery of styles available for the selected element. Click your selection to apply it to the chart.

Adding Shadows, Glows, and More

You can make further changes to the shape you've selected using the additional choices in the Shape Styles group on the Format tab.

- **Shape Fill**   This option displays a palette in which you can change the color, gradient, pattern, or texture of the selected shape.

- **Shape Outline**   This choice includes color selections as well as line width and style choices that change the outline of the shape.

- **Shape Effects**   Select Shape Effects to display a gallery of style choices with which you can add shadows, make the shape glow, soften the edges, rotate the shape in 3-D, and much more (see Figure 16-23).

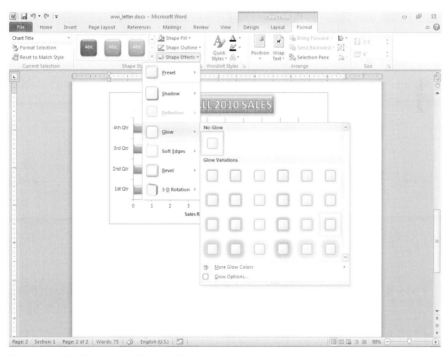

Figure 16-23 The Shape Effects gallery gives you options to dramatically change the look of shapes in your chart.

What's Next?

This chapter showed you how the SmartArt and chart features in Word 2010 make it easy to create, modify, and enhance diagrams and charts in your Word documents. The next chapter continues this creative focus by showing you how to make the most of Word's ability to add impact with pictures and objects. Additionally, you'll find out how to arrange art objects on the page to help give your document that finished, professional look.

CHAPTER 17

Adding and Editing Pictures and Screenshots

Adding Art to Your Word Documents. 523

Editing Pictures. 532

Removing Picture Backgrounds. 539

Enhancing Pictures. 541

Modifying Shapes and Lines 544

Adding Screenshots and Clippings 553

Arranging Art on the Page 553

What's Next?. 559

P ICTURE editing is one of the big stories in Word 2010. Now you can place, edit, enhance, and arrange your pictures—which might include clip art, photos, drawings, and even screen captures—easily and with style on your document pages.

With literally just a few clicks of the mouse, you can add, edit, and stylize images in your document in a variety of ways: adding shadows and frames, applying three-dimensional (3-D) styles, changing colors, angles, and much more. And new artistic effects give you a great range of special filters you can apply to your art; an ordinary, everyday photo can become a pencil sketch, a watercolor painting, or look as though it's wrapped in plastic! This gives you a tremendous amount of flexibility for the art you use on your pages, which, in turn, helps you capture and keep the reader's attention while creating the professional effect you want.

Of all the things you can do in Word 2010 to make your documents look inviting and professional, the features covered in this chapter are second only to the ability to add Themes (which, as you learned in Chapter 4, "Templates and Themes for a Professional Look," provide you with the ability to stylize your entire document—heads, text, and more—with a single click of the mouse button). So have fun, experiment, and get creative!

Adding Art to Your Word Documents

Word 2010 makes it easy to illustrate the concepts in your documents, no matter what your objective might be; for example, to show off a new product, entice people to subscribe to your blog, encourage folks to daydream a little, or just give your readers' eyes a rest. As shown in the graphic that follows, you'll find an Illustrations group (on the Insert tab on the Ribbon) containing all the tools you need to create various types of images.

For example, you can add:

- Photos, logos, and graphics files by using the Picture tool

- Clip art (including photos and audio and video clips) by choosing Clip Art

- Shapes for quick drawings, lines, simple diagrams, and more by clicking Shapes

- Pictures of your computer screen by clicking Screenshot

This section shows you how to add, edit, and enhance illustrations in your document via the tools in the Illustrations group.

To find out more about adding SmartArt diagrams to your document or creating custom charts to display data, see Chapter 16, "Create Compelling SmartArt Diagrams and Charts."

Inserting Pictures

If you have already created and saved illustrations or pictures that you want to use in your document, the easiest way to place those images into your document is to click the Picture tool in the Illustrations group on the Insert tab. The Insert Picture dialog box appears, in which you navigate to the location of the image you want to add. Select the picture and then click Insert to add it to your document (see Figure 17-1).

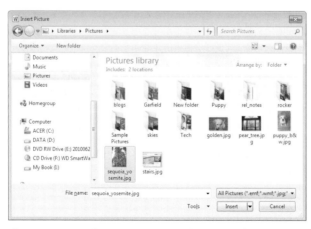

Figure 17-1 Use the Insert Picture dialog box to find and select the file you want to add to your page.

Word 2010 accepts graphics files in a number of popular formats, as Table 17-1 shows. By default, All Pictures is selected in the File Type list (located toward the lower-right of the Insert Picture dialog box). If you want to see only files of a certain format, click the All Pictures arrow and choose the format you want to display from the list.

Table 17-1 Picture Files Supported in Word 2010

Supported Format	File Extension
Windows Enhanced Metafile	.emf
Windows Metafile	.wmf
JPEG File Interchange Format	.jpg
Portable Network Graphic	.png
Windows Bitmap	.bmp
Graphics Interchange Format	.gif
Compressed Windows Enhanced Metafile	.emz
Compressed Windows Metafile	.wmz
Compressed Macintosh PICT	.pict
Tagged Image File Format	.tiff
WordPerfect Graphics	.wpg
Computer Graphics Metafile	.cgm
Encapsulated Postscript	.eps
Macintosh PICT	.pict

INSIDE OUT   Add Multiple Images

You can add more than one picture at once while using the Insert Picture dialog box. Simply click the first image you want to add then press and hold Ctrl while you click additional images, or press and hold Shift while clicking the last image in a list of images you want to select. When everything you want is selected, click Insert. Word then imports all selected images at once into the current document.

Chapter 17

Add Now, Edit Later

In some situations you might want to add a photo, logo, or drawing that is not quite finished to your document. If your group is designing a new logo, for example, you might want to insert the logo in your document while it is going through the review process, with the idea that you will update the logo with the finalized version after it's finished.

When you use Insert Picture to add the image to your Word page, you can maintain a link to the original file so that when the image is updated (in the case of our example, the logo graphic), the changes are reflected in your Word document as well. To maintain this link, select the file in the Insert Picture dialog box then click the arrow to the right of the Insert button. Click Insert and Link from the list that appears.

Adding Clip Art

You probably already know that Word includes a collection of clip art you can use in your own documents. You'll find all sorts of different topics represented, from animals to transportation to people and holidays. In addition to the clip art images available in your version of Word, you can also include Office.com content to expand the number of results presented to you when you're on the hunt for just the right illustration. When you want to insert a piece of clip art in a document, click Clip Art in the Illustrations group. The Clip Art task pane appears along the right edge of the document window (see Figure 17-2).

In the Clip Art task pane, type what you're looking for in the Search for box and then click the Go button. You don't need to know the name of a specific category—simply enter a word that describes the kinds of images you want to display: for example, *people*. A selection of clips related to the word or phrase you entered appears in the task pane. If you want to include clip art from Office.com, select the Include Office.com Content check box. The results of the search appear in the task pane display area.

Figure 17-2 Use the Clip Art task pane to find and add images that illustrate ideas in your document.

Adding Art and Entering Keywords

When you find the clip art you want, click it to have Word add it to your document. If you want to display additional choices, however, hover the mouse over the selection, and an arrow becomes available on the right side of the clip. Click it to see a contextual menu that offers additional ways you can fine-tune and work with the image (see Figure 17-3).

Figure 17-3 Use the contextual menu to customize the image for your use.

You can choose to use Insert to place the image, which is just like clicking it in the results panel; Word inserts it at the cursor position on your page. Or, you might want to use Copy To so you can use it in another document. The option Make Available Offline appears in the contextual menu when you click a clip that is currently stored on Office.com. Clicking the option displays the Copy To Collection dialog box in which you can choose where in the Microsoft Office Clip Organizer you'd like to save the file.

Edit Keywords is an important selection if you are preparing an online document because search engines will read the keywords you use and perhaps display your Web page in someone's search results list. When you click Edit Keywords, the Keywords dialog box appears (see Figure 17-4). You can review the existing keywords or add keywords of your own by clicking in the Keyword box, typing the word, and then clicking the Add button. Click Close when you are finished entering keywords.

Figure 17-4 Keywords help your online document show up in search results.

Narrowing Your Art Search

By default, the Clip Art task pane searches for all kinds of potential art files—everything from cartoon-like drawings that relate to the word or phrase you entered to photographs, movies, and even sounds. You might love it that you have such a sweeping choice—or you might want to narrow the results so that you can find what you want in a more focused manner. Word makes it easy for you to search for a particular file type for your document. For example, suppose that you need to find the best photographs you can for use in an annual report. You can narrow your search so that only photographs related to your search phrase are displayed, which makes finding what you need much easier. Here's how to do it:

1. Click Clip Art in the Illustrations group on the Insert tab to display the Clip Art task pane.

2. In the Search For box, enter a word or phrase that describes the types of images you'd like to see.

3. Click the Results Should Be arrow to display the list of media types.

4. Select the Photographs check box (see Figure 17-5) then click the Go button.

Figure 17-5 Limit your search to a specific file type to focus your results.

The Clip Art task pane displays only photographs that reflect the topic you entered at the top of the pane. Click the image that you want to add to your document.

Manage Your Images and Clips

The Microsoft Clip Organizer enables you to keep all your image, sound, and motion files in one place, arranged according to category. To start the Microsoft Clip Organizer, click the Start button, point to All Programs, click Microsoft Office, and then click the program name in the Microsoft Office 2010 Tools. To choose clip art from the Microsoft Clip Organizer, simply navigate to the image you want and select it in the view window. Here's a quick look at some of the tasks you might want to use the Clip Organizer to accomplish:

- Save your favorite images and media clips by dragging the item to your Favorites folder.

- Add your own images to the Clip Organizer by selecting Add Clips To Organizer from the File menu and clicking Automatically.

- Create a new collection in the Clip Organizer by choosing New Collection in the File menu. You can then name the collection and add your own clips.

- Review the properties of a specific image or media clip by selecting the item and then choosing Preview/Properties from the clip's contextual menu.

- Add or edit clip keywords by selecting the clip and choosing Edit Keywords. Use the Add, Modify, or Delete buttons to change the keywords as needed.

- Remove clips you no longer need by deleting them from the existing category or deleting them from the Clip Organizer. Select the item you want to remove then choose the Delete option that reflects the type of deletion you want.

Chapter 17

Adding Shapes and Lines

Do you like to create your own illustrations using the various shape tools in Word? If so, you'll find the shape tools in the Illustrations group on the Insert tab. When you want to draw any configuration of shapes or lines, you'll begin with the Shapes tool. When you click Shapes, a gallery full of shapes and lines appears (see Figure 17-6).

Figure 17-6 The Shapes gallery offers you a large selection of shapes and tools to use.

To draw a shape or line, simply click the tool you want and use the pointer to draw the object on the screen. If you plan to use multiple shapes and lines—perhaps to create a simple diagram or flowchart—working on the drawing canvas helps you to keep all items together and work with them as a group. Using the drawing canvas is optional, however— you can choose to simply draw the shapes and lines directly on the document page. The next section gives you more detail on using the drawing canvas when you're working with shapes.

Working with the Drawing Canvas

You'll find the New Drawing Canvas option at the bottom of the Shapes gallery. Although it's not required that you use it to create all your drawings and shapes, the drawing canvas does make it easier when you need to draw and work with multiple shapes in one area. When a drawing's shapes are contained in a drawing canvas, you can move and resize the drawing as a unit as well as position the drawing relative to surrounding text and graphics.

When you choose New Drawing Canvas from the Shapes gallery, a new canvas appears, displaying a frame-like boundary. You can drag the sides and corners to resize the canvas as needed. Although the drawing canvas doesn't have borders or background formatting, you can add formatting features to it just as you can customize any other drawing object. You might want to add color and shading, resize the frame, or add 3-D effects.

Using the Drawing Grid

When you're using shapes and lines, the drawing grid is another handy tool that can help you to align items in the drawing as you create them. The drawing grid is available whether you're using the drawing canvas or not.

To display the drawing grid, on the View tab, click Gridlines in the Show group. A grid appears on the work area of your document, as Figure 17-7 shows. Notice that the margins of the document are left blank.

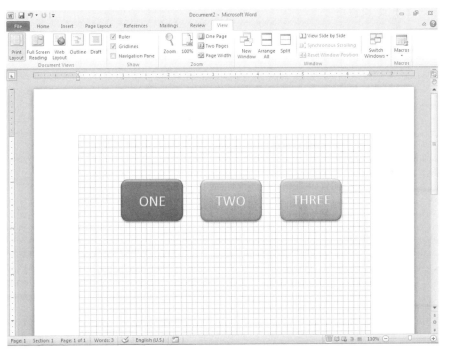

Figure 17-7 Display the drawing grid when you need to precisely align shapes and lines.

Now when you draw a shape or line, the object automatically snaps to a line on the grid. If you are displaying inches as your unit of measurement, the gridlines appear at intervals of 1/8 of an inch. If your unit of measurement is set to centimeters, the grid marks off 1/3 of a centimeter with each block. And if you are using picas, each grid block is equal to 1/8 of a pica.

Chapter 17

To change the unit of measurement displayed in the grid, on the File tab, click Options then select the Advanced tab and scroll down to the Display options. Click the Show Measurements in Units Of arrow and choose the measurement setting you prefer. You can choose from Inches, Centimeters, Millimeters, Points, and Picas.

> **Tip**
> If you want to position an object in such a way that it doesn't align to the grid (even though the grid is still enabled), click the shape and hold the mouse button down for a moment, then press Alt and drag the shape or line to the position where you want it to appear. When you release the mouse button, the object will remain where you placed it, whether or not it is aligned with the grid.

Editing Pictures

Today, it is easy to grab your own digital photos and include them in documents you create. But what will you do for important documents you'll be sharing with your public? Do you need to buy professional photos for high-quality work, or is there something you can do in Word to make your images really pop?

Word 2010 includes a number of enhancements when it comes to picture editing, and the program also adds a valuable feature known as Artistic Effects, with which you can apply all sorts of filters to your images to give them a special artistic look. So the answer can be good both for your budget and your audience—Word 2010 picture editing tools can help you make ho-hum images look great.

Applying Artistic Effects

Now when you work with pictures in Word you can transform ordinary photos using a variety of available filters. The new Artistic Effects enable you to turn an everyday image into a stylized graphic that looks like a pencil drawing, a chalk sketch, a watercolor painting, or even a picture set in cement, viewed through a screen, or wrapped in plastic! To apply Artistic Effects to a picture on your page, simply click the picture and then select the Picture Tools Format tab. In the Adjust group, click Artistic Effects. A gallery of filters appears; you can preview the different effects by pointing to them with the mouse. Figure 17-8 shows the Texturize effect being applied to a picture.

Figure 17-8 With Artistic Effects, you can apply stylized looks to your everyday pictures.

The styles of the Artistic Effects vary widely, so you can find styles that range from conservative and understated (Line Drawing, for example) to abstract (Plastic Wrap). Here are the various effects you can apply:

Chalk Sketch	Photocopy	Mosaic Bubbles
Light Screen	Pencil Grayscale	Pastels Smooth
Cement	Paint Brush	Line Drawing
Cutout	Film Grain	Blur
Marker	Crisscross Etching	Glass
Paint Strokes	Glow Edges	Plastic Wrap
Watercolor Sponge	Pencil Sketch	
Texturizer	Glow Diffused	

You can tailor the look of individual Artistic Effects by clicking the Artistic Effects Options item at the bottom of the Artistic Effects gallery. In the Format Picture dialog box, choose the Artistic Effect you want to change, adjust the settings to reflect what you'd like to see, and click OK to save your changes.

Chapter 17

Although Artistic Effects are fun and interesting, use them sparingly in your document (for example, choose one style and stick with it) and don't overdo the artistic flair. A little "artsy" goes a long way, so make sure your products are recognizable, images of people are clear, and your pictures support the overall goal of your document, whatever that might be.

Editing and Adjusting Images

Word includes a number of image adjustment tools that you can use to bring out the best in your images. You'll find the whole set located in the Adjustment group of the contextual Picture Tools. To display the tools, click on the picture you want to change. The Picture Tools appear on the Ribbon. The Format tab is automatically selected.

The Adjustment group is located on the far left. Depending on the type of change you want to make to your picture, click one of the following tools:

- **Corrections**   With this tool, you can sharpen and soften the image and adjust brightness and contrast. These settings change the intensity of the outlines in the picture as well as the amount of light included in an image. You can easily review the different choices in the gallery (which are applied to the actual picture you have selected in your document) and click the item that reflects the effect you'd like to create (see Figure 17-9).

- **Color**   This control helps you make color adjustments to the color saturation of the image (ranging from no color to high color), the tone of the color used (from cool to warm), and the colors you might use to recolor an image. Again, click the gallery item that matches the way you'd like the picture to look.

> **Tip**
> Recoloring an image enables you to apply a color wash to your picture that might, for instance, give it an old-fashioned feel (like a sepia-toned image) or make it blend naturally with the color scheme in the Theme applied to your document.

- **Compress Pictures**   This reduces the file size of the image (not the actual dimensions of the image in the document) so that when you save the file, it will be as compact as possible. When Word displays the Compress Pictures dialog box, click OK to compress all images in the document. If you want to compress only the selected image(s), choose the Apply To Selected Pictures Only check box before you click OK.

- **Change Picture**   Change Picture displays the Insert Picture dialog box so that you can replace the selected photo with a new one.

- **Reset Picture**   The Reset Picture tool reverses any modifications you've made to the original photo, returning it to its original size, shape, and coloring. You can click the arrow to the right of the tool to reset the picture effects only or to return the picture to its earlier display and size.

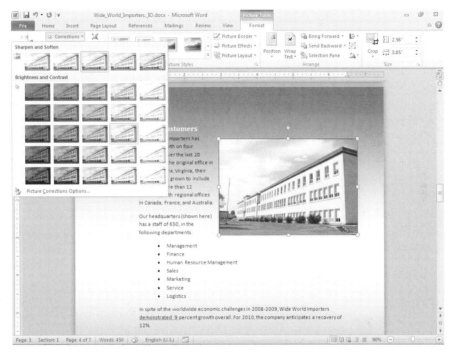

Figure 17-9 Click Corrections to change the sharpness, brightness, and contrast of your picture.

Cropping Pictures

Cropping images is a simple process, but it can dramatically improve the look of your photo by removing unnecessary elements from the image. For example, suppose that a diver's swim fin appears in the corner of an underwater photo you want to use for the Coral Reef Divers annual report. You can easily crop the photo to remove the unwanted fin and help your readers focus on the important part of the photo.

To crop your photo, follow these steps:

1. Insert the photo in your document and then select to display the Picture Tools.

2. Click Crop in the Size group. The pointer changes to a cropping tool.

3. Position the tool on the edge or corner of the image where you want to begin cropping, then drag the side or corner of the image inward until the portion of the picture you want to remove has been cropped out (see Figure 17-10).

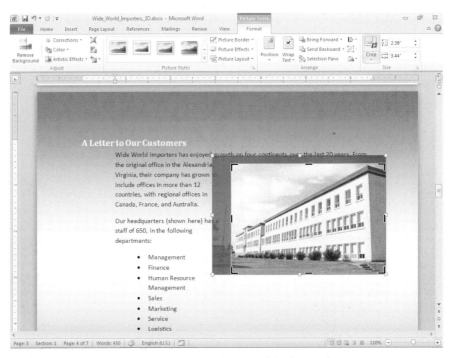

Figure 17-10 Crop a photo to display only the part of the image that you want.

> **Tip**
>
> When you crop a photo, the rest of the image isn't actually gone; its display is merely blocked from view beyond the boundary of the crop area. This means that if you decide to move the photo to another part of the document and redisplay the hidden part of the image, you can do that. Just select the Crop tool again and this time, drag the corner or side outward to reveal the rest of the hidden image. Note, however, that if you have selected the Delete Cropped Areas Of Pictures check box in the Compression Settings dialog box, the cropped portions of the image will in fact be deleted when you save the document.

Now in Word 2010, you can do even more with the Crop tool. You can click Crop and use the tool as just described, or if you want, you can crop the image to a specific shape. To do so, click the Crop arrow and choose Crop To Shape then click the shape you want to use from the gallery that appears. The shape is applied to the selected image. You can also use the Fill and Fit options to change the way the picture appears after the crop. When you choose Fill, the cropped picture fills the resulting picture frame and any portions of the picture outside the frame are cropped. When you choose Fit, the picture is fitted to the new frame and the aspect ratio is preserved.

You can also adjust the aspect ratio of the picture you crop by clicking Aspect Ratio in the Crop list and then clicking the aspect setting you want to use. If you are unsure about what will look best on your page, click a size and preview it on the page. If you want to undo the change, simply press Ctrl+Z.

Using a Picture as a Page Background

You can turn a picture you like into a background for your Word document. On the Page Layout tab, click in the Page Background group then click Page Color. Choose Fill Effects from the list that appears.

In the Fill Effects dialog box, choose the Picture tab. Then choose Select Picture and choose the picture you want to use for your background from the Select Picture dialog box. Click Insert to add the picture to the Fill Effects dialog box then click OK. The image is added to the background of your document. Note that if the image size is smaller than the length and width of your page, it will be repeated, or tiled, as needed to fill the space.

If you want to remove the picture, on the Page Layout tab, click Page Color, and then click No Color. The background picture is removed because the new selection overrides any previous Page Color selection.

Resizing Pictures

An operation that goes hand-in-hand with cropping is resizing the images you import. This is one technique you'll use all the time—pictures rarely come into your documents at just the right size.

Resizing a picture in Word is similar to resizing any object. To begin, click the image to select it. Handles appear around the edges of the object. If you want to enlarge the image, click in one corner of the picture and drag the handle outward. When the image is the size you want, release the mouse button.

Chapter 17

If resizing your picture to a precise measurement is important, use the Size command, available in the picture's options. Here's how:

1. Right-click the image in your document.

2. Choose Size and Position from the options that appear.

3. On the Size tab of the Layout dialog box, choose whether you want the Height and Width of the image to be relative to the page or set using absolute values (see Figure 17-11).

   Additionally, you can enter other positioning and size values, such as Rotation and Scale.

Figure 17-11 Use the Size tab of the Layout dialog box when you want to enter a specific size for an image.

4. Click OK to save your settings, and Word resizes the image according to your specifications.

Rotating Pictures

Some of your documents are likely to be fairly straightforward and won't require a lot of special picture techniques. But once in a while you will have a reason to do something fun like rotating pictures. With the Rotate control in Word you can simply drag a picture in the direction you want to turn it—very simple and easy to use. Instead of moving the image in predesigned increments, the Rotate tool lets you be in control of how far you want the picture to revolve.

Start by clicking the picture in your document. You'll notice that a round green handle appears in the top center of your image. This is the rotate handle. Position the mouse on that handle; note that the pointer changes to a curved arrow, indicating that you can drag the handle in the direction you want to rotate the image (see the graphic that follows). If you prefer, you can alternatively indicate the specific degree by which you want to rotate the image by entering the value in the Rotation box on the Size tab of the Layout dialog box.

> ### Tip
>
> **When you apply shadows or frames or other special picture effects to the image, Word automatically takes the angle into account, with no calculating required. Nice.**

Removing Picture Backgrounds

Have you ever found just the right image for one of your documents but then had a hard time trying to edit out something in the background that you didn't want to include? Now Word 2010 helps you easily lift an object right off a picture background. This gives you more flexibility in creating images that focuses your readers' attention on only that which you want most to illustrate.

Begin by clicking the picture you want to edit. On the Picture Tools Format tab, look for the Remove Background tool, which is located at the far-left end of the Ribbon in the Adjust group. Click this tool and Word automatically selects what it sees as the image background and displays the Background removal tab (see Figure 17-12).

Chapter 17

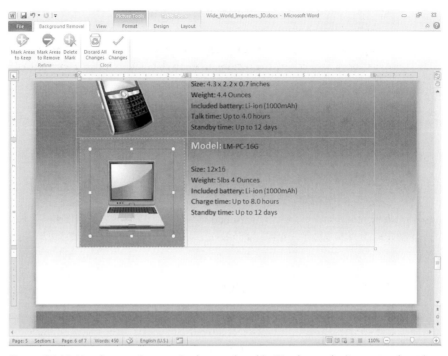

Figure 17-12 Use the new Remove Background tool in Word to make items stand out in your pictures.

If Word has done a good job of selecting the background, you can simply click Keep Changes and be done. If you need to tweak the image a bit to include all the background elements in the selection that Word might have missed, you can do so by using the following methods:

- Drag the cropping frame inward or outward to adjust the background selection

- Add or remove individual areas in the picture by clicking Mark Areas To Keep or Mark Areas To Remove

- Remove an area you marked by clicking Delete Mark

- Abandon your changes by clicking Discard All Changes

After you adjust the background to include all elements you want to remove, click Keep Changes. Word removes the background and you have only the element you wanted, ready to use in your document.

> **Tip**
> If you ever want to return the image to full display and restore the background, you
> can do so by clicking the picture, then on the Picture Tools Format tab, click Reset Pic-
> ture in the Adjust group.

Enhancing Pictures

Once you add and edit the pictures in your document, you might want to add some additional stylistic touches that help your pictures look like a part of your overall document
design. Picture Styles are great because they give you the most dramatic enhancements for
the smallest amount of effort. You can also add borders and tweak the effects to change
the look of the images on the page.

Applying Picture Styles to Your Images

Picture styles work similarly to the other quick styles you'll find in strategic places throughout Word 2010. When you select a picture in your document, the contextual Picture Tools
become available on the Ribbon. The Picture Styles have their own group in the middle of
the Format tab, as shown in the following illustration.

The Picture Styles gallery shows the various styles you can apply to the selected image. You
can display the entire selection of styles by clicking the More button in the lower-right corner of the gallery (see Figure 17-13). Preview the various styles by positioning the mouse
pointer over an item in the gallery; when you find one you want to use, click the mouse to
select the picture style.

Chapter 17

Figure 17-13 The Picture Styles gallery provides you with many different ways to display an image.

Adding a Picture Border

When you click Picture Border in the Picture Styles group, a color palette appears from which you can choose the color of the border you want to apply, as well as the weight and style of the line used to create the border (see Figure 17-14). The top portion of the palette lists the colors that match the theme that is currently applied to your document; the Standard Colors area of the palette provides primary colors. If you want to choose a color that does not appear in the palette, click More Outline Colors and then select the color from either the Standard or Custom tab. To apply it to the selected picture, click OK after you choose the color.

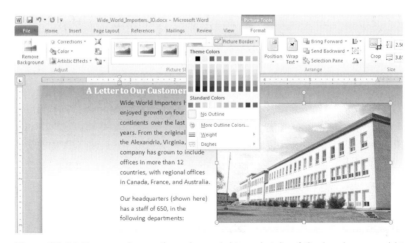

Figure 17-14 You can choose the color, weight, and style of the border you add to your pictures.

Adding a Picture Effect

Picture effects give you a wide range of special formats you can apply to the selected picture. You can choose from among a variety of shadow styles, apply a glow to the outer edges, display a reflection of the image, soften the edges, create a beveled effect, and apply 3-D effects and rotation.

To apply a picture effect, select the picture and then click Picture Effects in the Picture Styles group. A palette of choices appears. Point to the effects category you want to apply (Preset, Shadow, Reflection, Glow, Soft Edges, Bevel, and 3-D Rotation). A palette of effects opens to display your choice. Use Live Preview to see how the different effects will appear in your document (see Figure 17-15).

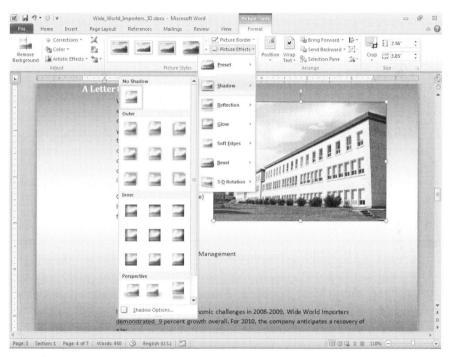

Figure 17-15 Use Picture Effects to enhance your pictures by adding shadows, bevel effects, 3-D effects, and more.

Adding Captions to Pictures

Readers like to know what your images contain, so unless you're certain that readers will understand what your images are showing, you might want to consider adding figure captions.

The process is simple, and you can control the look and placement of the text by following these steps:

1. Right-click the picture to which you want to add the caption.

2. Click Insert Caption to display the Caption dialog box, as Figure 17-16 shows.

Figure 17-16 You can easily add captions to the images in your document by right-clicking a picture and choosing Insert Caption.

3. In the top text box, type the caption you want to appear with the figure.

   You might want to customize the look of the caption by changing one of the following items:

   - If you want to hide the label (for example, Figure), select the Exclude Label From Caption check box.

   - If you want to change the way in which the captions are numbered, click the Numbering button and select your choice.

4. Click OK to save the caption settings and return to the document.

The caption is displayed in a color, font, size, and style that are controlled by the theme selected for your document. If you change the theme later (on the Page Layout tab, select Themes and choose a new theme from the gallery), the captions will be reformatted automatically.

If you prefer to change the format of the captions, you can do so on the Home tab by choosing new settings from your choices in the Font group. Remember, however, that once you change the captions from a theme-supported style, you must reformat them manually if you ever apply a new theme.

Modifying Shapes and Lines

In the preceding section, you learned how to change and enhance the pictures you include in your document. This section focuses on drawings—the shapes and lines you add to help illustrate concepts in your text. Pictures and shapes share some similar techniques because they are both art objects. In that sense, anything you can do to a picture object—move, copy, resize, rotate, or delete—you can also do with a shape or line.

But shapes and lines have some peculiarities that pictures don't. For example, although you can recolor a picture by changing the overall color wash or mode assigned to it, you cannot actually change the picture itself. When you create a shape, on the other hand, you can choose from a wide range of color options to fill the shape—you can blend colors, make them transparent, choose gradients, and even fill them with textures. And what's more, you can add text directly into the shapes so that they are more than just a pretty ornament, they are functional, too.

Applying Shape Styles

When you first add a shape to your document, it might not look like much—perhaps just a simple black outline on a white page. You can change that dramatically with a click of the mouse.

Select the shape or shapes, and the contextual Drawing Tools appears on the Ribbon. Click one of the selections in the Shape Styles palette or click the More button in the lower-right corner of the gallery to display the entire collection, and then click the style you want to apply to the shape. Suddenly it takes on depth, color, and in some cases, lighting qualities (see Figure 17-17).

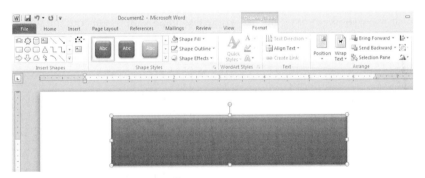

Figure 17-17 Use the Shape Styles to add color, line style, and perspective to your shapes.

> **Note**
> Similar to Picture Styles, some of the settings in the Shape Styles are controlled by the theme currently selected for your document. For example, the colors shown in the Shape Styles gallery correspond to the overall colors used in the theme currently in use.

Chapter 17

Adding and Formatting Shape Text

You can easily add text to some shapes you draw using the Shapes tools. Right-click the shape into which you want to include the text and then choose Add Text if it is available (see Figure 17-18). The cursor is positioned in the shape. Type the text you want to appear in the shape. Notice that the text reformats automatically to accommodate the amount of room in the shape.

Figure 17-18 Choose Add Text to position the cursor inside the shape.

If you want to reformat the text inside the shape, simply highlight the text and choose the formatting you want from the Mini Toolbar that appears above the selection (see Figure 17-19). For best results, keep the text items short and easy to understand.

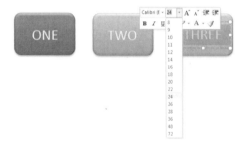

Figure 17-19 Change the format of shape text by using the Mini Toolbar that appears above the added text.

Modifying Lines and Fills

A shape you create in Word has two main areas: the borders (called the shape *outline*) and the interior (called the shape *fill*). With the Shape Fill and Shape Outline tools in the Styles group of the Drawing Tools palette (located just to the right of the Shape Styles gallery), you can choose different settings for the display of those items.

Changing the Shape Fill

You can be really creative with the interior of the shapes you add to Word, displaying them in wild colors (or better yet, colors that correspond to your logo or letterhead), adding special textures, even inserting pictures. Follow these steps to enhance the interior of your shapes:

1. Click the shape you want to change.

2. Click Shape Fill arrow in the Shape Styles group of the Drawing Tools.

3. From the list that appears, choose the type of effect you'd like to apply.

   Figure 17-20 shows the gallery that appears when you choose Textures, and Table 17-2 describes each of the choices.

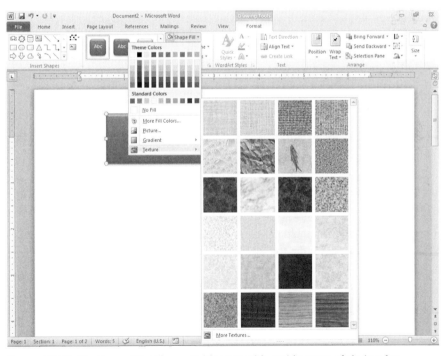

Figure 17-20 The Shape Fill gallery provides you with a wide range of choices for formatting the shapes in your document.

4. Click your choice, and the format is applied to the shape.

Table 17-2 **Shape Fill Options**

Choose	When You Want to
A color	Fill the shape with a color you select
No Fill	Display no fill color or pattern in the shape
More Fill Colors	Choose a color other than the ones shown in the Theme Colors and Standard Colors areas of the palette
Picture	Fill the shape with a photo or other image
Gradient	Give the shape lighting effects and perspective
Texture	Add a textured appearance—such as sand, wood, metal, or fabric—to the selected shape

Choosing a Custom Color

When you click More Colors, the Custom Colors dialog box appears, in which you can choose a specific hue. You can choose a color either by using the crosshair or the slider bar to the right of the display area. Beneath the display area, you see Red, Green, and Blue value boxes that reflect the color values indicated by the crosshair and slider bar. The Red, Green, and Blue value boxes specify exact RGB color values for graphics. If you know the RGB values of a specific color you want to use, you can enter those values in the appropriate boxes, or you can click the up and down arrows to scroll through values. Click OK to save your choice.

Making Shapes Transparent

When you click More Fill Colors, the Custom tab of the Colors dialog box appears. At the bottom of the tab, you see a Transparency slider. You can use the Transparency option to determine the degree to which another shape, text, image, chart, or page background is visible through the shape.

By default, a shape is set to 0% transparency (opaque) when it is created. To increase the transparency, simply drag the slider to the right. When transparency is set to 100%, the background object will be completely visible through the shape. For most purposes, using a setting of 50 to 60% enables you to see the image behind the shape without losing sight of the shape itself.

Formatting Shadows and 3-D Effects

In addition to adding textures and colors, you can apply shadow and three-dimensional (3-D) effects to your shapes and lines in Word 2010. Although some shadow and 3-D effects were available in the previous version of Word, these features have been dramatically improved and are now included as a choice in the Shape Effects gallery. Now you have a broad collection of options at your disposal for tailoring your shapes and lines to get just the look you want.

Adding and Controlling Shadows

You can instantly add depth to your drawings in Word by adding a shadow to the edge of an object. Click Shape Effects in the Shape Styles group on the Drawing Tools Format tab and point to Shadow. The gallery of choices shown in Figure 17-21 appears, from which you can choose the type of shadow you want to apply.

Figure 17-21 You can easily add depth to a shape in your document by adding a shadow effect.

If you later want to remove the shadow, click the shape and choose Shadow Effects again, But this time, click No Shadow (at the top of the gallery).

Changing the Position and Appearance of Shadows

After you apply a shadow, you can adjust the shadow's position relative to the object and control additional settings, such as how transparent the shadow is, what its angle looks like, and how far it extends from the edge of the shape. You can make these changes using the Shadow Options choice (available at the bottom of the Shadow gallery) that appears when you click Shape Effects and point to Shadow.

The Format Shape dialog box appears, as you see in Figure 17-22, in which you can enter your choices for the Transparency, Size, Blur, Angle, and Distance of the shadow.

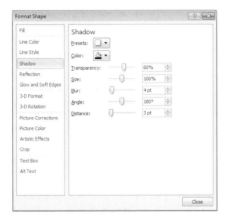

Figure 17-22 You can tailor the appearance of the shadow by using the settings in the Shadow tab of the Format Shape dialog box.

Coloring Shadows

In addition to adjusting a shadow's position and overall appearance, you can also apply a color to a shadow. To do so, follow these steps:

1. Select the shape with the shadow you want to change.

2. Click Shape Effects and point to Shadow to display the Shadow list.

3. Point to Shadow Options. The Format Shape dialog box appears.

4. Click the Color tool. A color palette appears, showing Theme Colors, Standard Colors, and Recent Colors.

   Note that Recent Colors is available only if you have previously made color choices.

5. Click the color you want to use for the shadow, or click More Colors to display the Colors dialog box (then select the color and choose OK to apply it).

INSIDE OUT   My Document Includes Color Images, but I Want Them to Print in Black and White

You can change your images so they print in black and white by recoloring the images. To recolor the images, select all images in the document that you want to change and click Color in the Adjust group. Click Recolor and then click Grayscale in the Recolor gallery.

Applying and Customizing 3-D Effects

You might wonder what else is involved in making a shape appear three-dimensional. Shadows seem to be the most important characteristic, right? Word 2010 makes 3-D easy by offering a number of shape styles that apply the effects for you. But you can further customize the look if you like. For example, you can set the depth and height of an object, apply a special surface covering such as metal or plastic, and choose the way in which you want the light to reflect off the shape's surface.

Changing 3-D Effects

To change or add 3-D effects to the shapes in your document, you can use several of the choices in the Shape Effects gallery. For example, Bevel settings make the shape appear to rise up from the surface of the page; Shadow adds depth and a sense of background. You can also use the 3-D Rotation choices to skew the shape and give it a more three-dimensional feel (see Figure 17-23). Position the pointer over an item to preview how it will look in the document. When you find the one you like, click it to select it.

Chapter 17

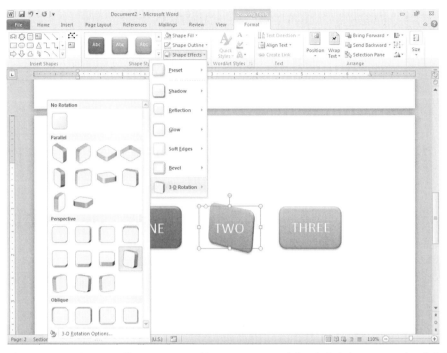

Figure 17-23 The 3-D Effects group enables you to control depth, height, perspective, lighting, and more.

INSIDE OUT   I Want to Add Text to Freehand Drawings

When you create a freehand drawing, you can't right-click the drawing and choose Add Text. To work around this limitation, you can click Text Box in the Text group on the Insert tab and then draw a text box on top of your freehand drawing. Now you can type and format text in the text box. If you want to ensure that the text and drawing aren't separated or layered incorrectly in the future, choose the shape and the text box (by pressing Shift as you click the objects), and then click Group in the Arrange group on the Ribbon.

Adding Screenshots and Clippings

Another new feature in Word 2010 enables you to easily add pictures of your screen for those times when a screen capture will quickly convey what would take you paragraphs of text to explain. You can capture an entire picture of the current screen or grab just the part you need to insert in a document. Here's how it's done:

1. On the Insert tab, click Screenshot in the Illustrations group.

2. A gallery of screenshots appears, showing you the various screens available on your computer at the moment (see Figure 17-24).

3. Click the one you want to insert at the cursor position.

Figure 17-24 You can insert a picture of your screen in your current document.

If you'd rather grab only a portion of a screen, click Screenshot in the Illustrations group and click Screen Clipping. A cross-hair pointer appears, with which you select the area of the screen you want to include. When you release the mouse button, the section of the screen you clipped is inserted on your page.

Arranging Art on the Page

Now that you know how to add and enhance pictures as well as how to create and modify drawings, the final step for working with art in your document involves arranging objects on the page so that everything flows together well. To accomplish this, you need to know how to group and ungroup objects, handle object layering, and set up text flow the way you want it.

Aligning Objects

When you have a number of objects in your document, arranging them so that they fit together well is a big part of making sure your document looks as good as possible. If you've created a drawing that includes a number of shapes and lines, or you've added special elements to offset WordArt titles, or you want to ensure two photos line up on the page, you can use the Align tool in the Arrange group to put things in their proper order.

Here are the steps for aligning objects on your page:

1. Select the objects you want to align by pressing and holding Shift while clicking the objects.

2. Click Align in the Arrange group on the Ribbon. A list of Align choices appears (see Figure 17-25).

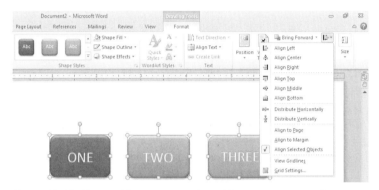

Figure 17-25 Choose Align to ensure that objects on your page line up.

3. Point to a choice you want to preview in your document and then click to select the one you want. All selected items are aligned according to your choice.

TROUBLESHOOTING

I can't select multiple objects.

If you press Shift and click items in your document but they don't become part of your selection, most likely the Wrap Text setting for the items you're trying to select is still set to In Line With Text. To make the object available for selection and alignment, choose Text Wrapping (in the Arrange group) and select In Front Of Text.

Note

You can't select pictures and shapes at the same time; and if the picture is a bitmap, you can't select it with other objects. The workaround for this problem is to place all of the objects in a drawing canvas.

Note
If you have the Snap Objects To Grid feature turned on while you work on the drawing grid, but you want to move objects freely and without being constrained to the grid, you can override the feature by pressing Alt while you drag an object.

Distributing vs. Aligning

When would you want to distribute the objects on your page, as opposed to aligning them? When you are working with multiple objects in a shared space, you can use Distribute to arrange the objects so that they are evenly spaced. Here are a few guidelines for using Distribute to arrange objects on your page:

- Distribute Horizontally and Distribute Vertically are available only when you have selected three or more objects.

- Distributing objects spaces them evenly between the objects on the outer boundary of the space. For example, if you have a set of four buttons on the left side of the page, click all four buttons and then click Distribute Horizontally. The buttons are spaced evenly within the same amount of space they originally occupied.

- By default, the objects you select are distributed relative to each other. To distribute objects relative to the drawing canvas instead, select the items and then choose Align to Canvas.

Grouping and Ungrouping Objects

All art objects you add to your document—pictures, shapes, lines, and WordArt—are individual objects in their own right. If you create a drawing by using a variety of art elements (whether you use a drawing canvas or not), being able to combine those elements into a single group enables you to move, copy, and modify all items at once.

You can also group objects to ensure that certain elements stay together no matter what. Grouping also comes in handy when you want to make sure that layered objects don't inadvertently become incorrectly layered. You can ungroup grouped items at any time, which means that you can edit any part of a grouped object whenever necessary.

To group objects, begin by arranging the objects where you want them to appear in the document. Then select the objects you want to group (press Shift and click each object you want to include). Next, click Group in the Arrange group in the Drawing Tools. The multiple handles that surrounded each item now disappear, and one set of handles appears for the entire group. You can move, copy, and resize the group as needed.

If you want to make a change to any object within the group, you'll need to ungroup it before you can work with it. To ungroup objects, select the group and click Ungroup in the Arrange group on the Ribbon.

Controlling Object Layering

When you create a drawing that contains many objects, you'll need to control which objects are layered in front of and behind other objects. Paying attention to how objects are layered can save you from inadvertently hiding parts of your drawings that should be visible.

Put your objects in the right order on the page by selecting an object and clicking either Bring To Front or Send To Back in the Arrange group. Clicking the selection itself performs the action—in other words, when you click Bring To Front, the selected object moves to the front of any other objects at that point on the page.

Both the Bring To Front and Send To Back tools have their own sets of options. Click the arrow to the left of each selection to see how you can further qualify the selection. Depending on the number of objects you have layered in your drawing, you might want to move the object in front of text, bring it forward one level, or send it backward behind another object. Experiment with these choices to get a feel for them. You will use these tools often if you do a lot of drawing in Word.

> **Tip**
> If you're having trouble selecting an object, it might be positioned behind another object on the page. Press Tab to cycle through the selected objects until the handles of the object you want are displayed, indicating that it is selected.

Choosing Art Position

Depending on how many pictures, drawings, and objects you will be using on your pages, you might want some kind of method of positioning your object that doesn't require clicking and dragging or aligning and distributing. With the Position tool in the Arrange group you can select the position on the page where you want your image(s) to appear, with text automatically flowing around it. Here's how to easily position an image in your document:

1. Select the image you want to position.

2. Click Position in the Arrange group. A gallery of position options appears.

3. Click the position you want to use for the current page.

Now as you add headlines, text, and other objects to the page, the image will be placed in the position you indicated. If you want to fine-tune your selection of the image position, click More Layout Options at the bottom of the Position gallery to display the Advanced Layout dialog box. From there, you can specify your choices related to the horizontal alignment, vertical alignment, and position of the object, as well as the way in which it relates to surrounding text.

Controlling Text Wrapping

If the Position tool helps you determine how the image relates to the entire page (and it does), the Text Wrapping tool determines the relationship between your art and your text. When you choose a Text Wrapping option, you are telling Word how you want the text to flow around (or through or behind) the image you have added. This is a simple and flexible feature that gives you a number of creative ways to create and enhance the layout of your page. Here's how to do it:

1. Click the image you want to use.

2. In the Arrange group on the Ribbon, click the Wrap Text arrow.

   A list of Text Wrapping options appears. By default, In Line With Text might be selected (unless you've changed it previously), which means that the image is treated like text and will move with the paragraph as you add text to the document.

3. Select the Wrap Text choice that you want to apply to the selected image.

   The selection is applied to the image, and the text reflows accordingly. Table 17-3 describes each of the choices in more detail.

Chapter 17

Table 17-3 **Text Wrapping Choices**

Choose	When You Want to
In Line With Text	Keep the image in line with the text so that it moves along with the current paragraph (this is selected by default).
Square	Wrap the text to the left and right of the image.
Tight	Flow the text right up to the edge of the selected object with no outer margin of white space.
Behind Text	Flow the text over the image.
In Front Of Text	Display the text behind the image.
Top And Bottom	Flow the text above and below—but not through—the image. Text does not appear on the sides of the image; this is left blank.
Through	Flow text up to the border of your picture (you can use this with Edit Wrap Points to create a special text flow for your pages).
Edit Wrap Points	Create a new boundary for your image that enables you to design the way the text wraps around it.

TROUBLESHOOTING

My images are only displaying halfway.

If the image is not displaying completely, check your Wrap Text settings. Display the Wrap Text choices (in the Arrange group) and click Top And Bottom or In Front Of Text. If the image still doesn't display properly, check with the manufacturer of your graphics card to see whether an updated driver is available.

Adding and Editing Wrap Points

Most of the Text Wrapping choices are self-explanatory; you can see what they do by experimenting with them in your document. But one item is worth further exploration because it can enable you to create sophisticated layouts easily.

You can use the Edit Wrap Points choice in the Text Wrapping list to create your own boundary for text flow in your document. You do this by simply dragging one of the edit points into a position that shows the text where to flow. Here's how it's done:

1.   Select the image you want to use.

2. Click Wrap Text in the Arrange group and ensure that either Tight or Through is the choice selected. (If you choose any other wrapping style, Edit Wrap Points will not be available.)

3. Choose Edit Wrap Points.

    A red dashed boundary with several black handles appears around your image.

4. Click one of the handles and drag it to create the boundary you want to set for the text flow (see Figure 17-26). The line stays where you put it.

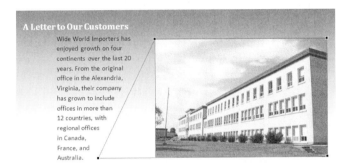

Figure 17-26 You can create your own Edit Wrap Points to customize the text flow on your page.

5. To create another handle (you aren't limited to following the shape of the image—you can stretch and add edit points any place you choose), simply click in the boundary line and drag it out to the point at which you want it.

    This creates another handle at that point and establishes the boundary where you put it.

What's Next?

This chapter introduced you to all things art—now you know how to add, enhance, and arrange pictures, clip art, shapes, and screenshots on your document page. The next chapter takes you into the realm of the exceptions, by introducing you to techniques you can use with Word extras—equations, text boxes, objects, and more.

Chapter 17

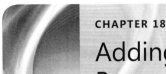

Adding the Extras: Equations, Text Boxes, and Objects

Inserting Mathematical Equations. 561

Using Math AutoCorrect. 568

Adding and Linking Text Boxes 570

Linking Text Boxes to Flow Text. 578

Adding Objects to Your Word Document. 583

What's Next? 585

DEPENDING on the content you're pulling together in your Word documents, you might need to add extra elements from time to time. If you're working on a research document, for example, you might want to create a sophisticated mathematical equation as part of the text. Luckily, Word 2010 includes an enhanced Equation Editor that gives you all the tools you need to create elaborate equations that only a scientist could love. If you want to add special effects like pull-quotes and sidebars to your document, you'll like the text box feature, which makes it easy for you to add, format, and link text boxes in the document. And if you need to insert objects—like worksheets you've already created in Excel, charts you want to update automatically, or slides from a PowerPoint presentation—you can link or embed the object in your document so it is always within reach when you need it.

This chapter shows you how to create and work with each of these Word "extras." Along the way, you'll also find some new ideas for enhancing the content you add to your pages.

Inserting Mathematical Equations

Word 2010 vastly improved your choices for inserting mathematical equations in your documents. The equation capability in Word 2007 was already a considerable improvement over previous versions, but Word 2010 expands the range of tools and flexibility available with the Equation Editor even further. Now you can create sophisticated equations that are capable of reflecting the complexity your calculations need to show. You can easily select an equation from the Equation gallery and modify it to suit your needs or craft an equation from scratch using the many tools and expressions available in the Editor.

You can add equations two ways in Word 2010. The first method is the easiest: you can simply click the Equations arrow (in the Symbols group on the Insert tab) and click the equation you want to add from the gallery that appears (see Figure 18-1). The second method involves actually building the equation yourself—but don't worry; Word makes it easy for you by displaying a range of structure and symbol tools that you can simply click to add the equation elements you want.

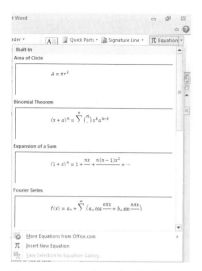

Figure 18-1 The Equation Gallery includes a built-in collection of common equations that you can insert into your documents and modify to meet your needs.

> **Note**
>
> The new Equations functionality is not available in Compatibility Mode; therefore, equations within documents that are opened in previous versions of Word or saved in the Word 97-2003 file format will be converted to images.

Choosing an Equation from the Gallery

To insert a new equation via the Equation gallery, click the Equation button in the Symbol group on the Insert tab, then click the arrow below the Equation button and click an equation in the Equation gallery, or press Alt+=. Once an equation is inserted, the contextual Equation Tools appear, as shown in Figure 18-2. The Design tab contains a large collection of tools, symbols, and mathematical structures you can use to insert and control equations.

Figure 18-2 The contextual Equation Tools provide the tools, options, symbols, and structures necessary to meet most of your equation building needs.

Building an Equation from Scratch

Though Word 2010 provides some common built-in equations, chances are that if your content requires this kind of high-end equation, you will probably need to build many of your own. To help you create your equations, the Design tab offers all sorts of tools you can use to add the various elements to your equation. In the Symbols group, you'll find a large collection of math-related symbols and structures. To access the symbol sets, click the More arrow in the Symbols gallery. To access additional symbol sets, click the arrow next to Symbol Set, as shown in Figure 18-3. For a list of symbol sets and their descriptions, see Table 18-1.

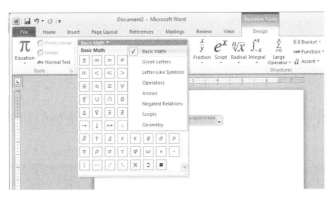

Figure 18-3 Word 2010 offers several symbol sets that you can use to construct your equation.

Table 18-1 **Symbol Sets and Descriptions**

Symbol Set	Description
Basic Math	Commonly used mathematical symbols, such as > and <
Greek Letters	Uppercase and lowercase letters from the Greek alphabet
Letter-Like Symbols	Symbols that resemble letters
Operators	• **Common Binary Operators** Symbols that act on two quantities, such as + and ÷ • **Common Relational Operators** Symbols that express a relationship between two expressions, such as = and ~ • **Basic N-ary Operators** Operators that act across a range of variables or terms • **Advanced Binary Operators** Additional symbols that act on two quantities • **Advanced Relational Operators** Additional symbols that express a relationship between two expressions
Arrows	Symbols that indicate direction
Negated Relations	Symbols that express a negated relationship
Scripts	The mathematical Script, Fraktur, and Double-Struck typefaces
Geometry	Commonly used geometric symbols

In addition to numbers, letters, and symbols, most equations also require mathematical structures. The Structures group on the Design tab provides structures you can insert and then customize if necessary by filling placeholders (small dotted boxes) with values. Available structures are grouped into the following categories: Fraction, Script, Radical, Integral, Large Operator, Bracket, Function, Accent, Limit And Log, Operator, and Matrix. Figure 18-4 shows the gallery that appears when you click the Radical tool.

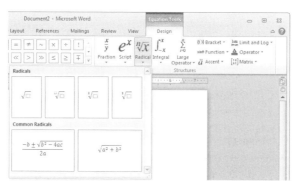

Figure 18-4 Word provides a large collection of mathematical structures that you can use to build equations.

> **Tip**
> Equation placeholders do not appear in Full Screen Reading view, Print Preview, or in printed documents.

The process of constructing your equation is a simple matter of adding the Equation content control, and then typing what you want to add and clicking the structure and symbols you want to use. Word inserts what you type and click as you build the equation, as shown in the following illustration:

Click handle and drag
to a new location

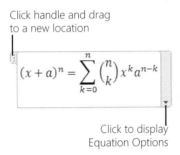

Click to display
Equation Options

Controlling Equation Display

When you insert an equation, it appears in what's called a *content control*, which is a kind of content placeholder for interactive elements on your page. You can use the tools in the Structures and Symbols groups on the Equation Tools Design tab to build your equation, or you can click the Equation Options button on the right side of the equation to change the way the equation is displayed (see Figure 18-5). Here's what you can use the different options to do:

- **Professional** This option converts the selected formula to a two-dimensional display, showing fractions as fractions, for example, with one set of values above another.

- **Linear** Linear converts the equation so that the entire formula is on a single line, which makes the characters easier to edit.

- **Change To Inline/Display** This alters the way the equation appears in your document. Display shows the equation in the center of the line; Inline positions the equation in line with your paragraph text.

Chapter 18

- **Justification** Using Justification, you can choose how the equation will be placed on the page. Choices include Left, Right, or Centered, or leave the default, Centered As a Group, selected.

Figure 18-5 Within Equation options, you can save an equation to the gallery as well as choose the way the equation is displayed.

> ## Tip
> The Normal Text tool, which is available in the Tools group on the Equation Tools Design tab, makes it possible for you to enter non-math text in the middle of your equation. Simply click the equation and then click Normal Text before typing the information you want to add.

Setting Equation Options

There are a number of settings being used behind the scenes to help you construct your equations as easily as possible. You can display and change those settings by displaying and updating the choices in the Equation Options dialog box. To display the dialog box (see Figure 18-6), click the dialog launcher in the lower-right corner of the Tools group on the Equation Tools Design tab.

You can use the options in the Equation Options dialog box to instruct Word which font you want to use for your equations as well as how you want the equations formatted on the page. You can also set AutoCorrect options (more about that in a minute) as well as set the default values you want to be applied to all equations you create. Click the Defaults button to set these values as the default; Word will prompt you to confirm that you really want to apply these settings because all documents that use the Normal.dotx template will be affected by the change. After you're done entering your settings, click OK to return to the document page.

Figure 18-6 Choose your preferences for equations in the Equation Options dialog box.

> **Note**
>
> If you create equations that look fine in Word on the screen but do not print as expected, verify that you have downloaded the most up-to-date drivers from your printer manufacturer's Web site.

Save an Equation to the Gallery

If you are particularly fond of the equation you just created and you think you will use it in other documents you prepare, you can save it to the Equation gallery so it is ready to be inserted on the page whenever you need it. To save the equation you've added, click the Equation and then click the Equation Options arrow in the lower-right corner of the control. From the list that displays, choose Save As New Equation. The Create New Building Block dialog box appears, as you see in Figure 18-7.

Figure 18-7 Add the specifics of your new equation in the Create New Building Block dialog box.

Type a name (choose one that will help you remember the equation content) and then choose a Category for the equation. You can also enter a description if you'd like and click Options to choose whether the content is inserted by itself, or placed in its own paragraph or on its own page. Click OK after you finish entering the information; the equation is added at the top of the Equations gallery.

Using Math AutoCorrect

Similar to the functionality of the AutoCorrect feature, with Math AutoCorrect, you can enter a few characters of a commonly used math function and let the program automatically insert the entire function for you. Math AutoCorrect works only with Linear format (meaning your equation needs to be all on one line), and the feature is only turned on by default in math equations, although you can change the setting so equations are updated anywhere in your document if you choose.

To display the Math AutoCorrect options, go to the Equation Options dialog box by clicking the dialog launcher in the lower-right corner of the Tools group and then click Math Auto-Correct. You can also press Alt+T+A and then click the Math AutoCorrect tab. The Math AutoCorrect dialog box is where you can create the shortcuts you want to use when generating your equations (see Figure 18-8).

Figure 18-8 With Math AutoCorrect, you can use the Linear Format to create equations.

Note

Math AutoCorrect entries are case sensitive. An entry such as \Sigma changes to Σ (the uppercase Greek character) while \sigma changes to σ (the lowercase Greek character).

Note

The Recognized Functions button provides a list of expressions that are not automatically italicized when creating equations. You can add additional expressions to the list.

If you want to use Math AutoCorrect anywhere in your document, select the Use Math Auto-Correct Rules Outside Of Math Regions option. Otherwise, you can only use Math AutoCorrect in an Equation Content Control by inserting a new equation from the Equation gallery on the Insert tab or by pressing Alt+=.

Note

The Equation gallery and the ability to insert new equations are disabled if you are using Word in Compatibility Mode; however, Math AutoCorrect can still be used.

To create new Math AutoCorrect entries, first select the desired symbol or group of symbols in a document and display the AutoCorrect dialog box (Alt+T+A). On the Math Auto-Correct tab, type your replace characters in the Replace text box. Your replace characters do not need to start with a backslash (\), but this syntax is recommended to maintain consistency.

Note

If you have standard equations, consider turning them into Building Blocks and associating them with the Equations gallery to ease insertion.

Chapter 18

INSIDE OUT   Call Attention to Your Equations

You can add emphasis to an equation by adding a rectangle around it. Here's how to do it: create a new equation (Alt+=), click Normal Text in the Tools group of the Equation Tools Design tab, and then type **\rect (\quadratic)**. The spaces here are very important, so be sure to include them. Your equation should look like the following image:

The spaces are important because they trigger Math AutoCorrect to convert the equation as you type. In the example here, once you type the space after \rect, you see a small rectangle. The space after (\quadratic converts to a quadratic formula. After you type the closing parentheses and the space, the rectangle is placed around the equation.

Adding and Linking Text Boxes

Text boxes give you a lot of flexibility in how you add and display text "extras" in your document. You might add a text box with a quote from a happy customer, for example, or provide information on how a prospective member can subscribe to your newsletter. Word 2010 includes a number of features with which you can add, edit, and enhance your text boxes easily. You can assign all sorts of looks to the boxes and use the colors, fonts, and styles associated with the theme you've selected to keep the appearance consistent and professional.

When placing text in Word, you can use either text boxes or shapes that are formatted to contain text. You might use text boxes when you want to position a block of text that stands out and isn't part of the normal flow of column text on your page. Or you might add a text box to contain continuing content from another page—for example, you might create a newsletter in which a story starts on the cover page but concludes on another page, later in the newsletter.

In addition to creating interesting page layouts and continuing a story from one text block to another (also referred to as flowing text in linked text boxes), you might also want to use text boxes to accomplish the following tasks:

- Change the format of selected text

- Rotate or flip text

- Change text orientation

- Group text blocks and change their alignment or distribution as a group

This part of the chapter describes how you can manipulate and control text using text boxes and shapes as text containers. (Once a shape contains text, it is converted to a text box.) Keep in mind that when you're working with text boxes, you must work in Print Layout view to be able to see the text boxes while you work. Figure 18-9 displays a text box (formatted as a shape) on the left as well as two text boxes inserted using the Text Box gallery—all in Print Layout view.

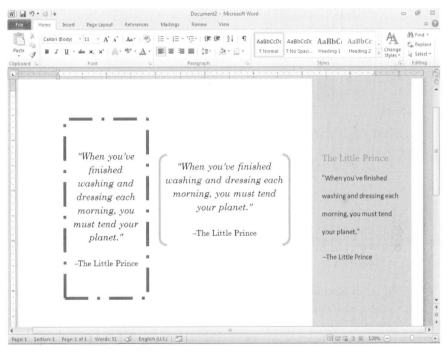

Figure 18-9 Text boxes bring attention to your information and separate related text from other document content.

As you can see, the active text box is shown surrounded by a frame-like border built from dashed lines and sizing handles. This border appears whenever you click a text box, and it serves a number of purposes, including moving and resizing the text box as well as providing access to the text box properties.

Chapter 18

Adding Text Boxes

Word 2010 makes adding text boxes a simple task using the Text Box gallery, which is found on the Insert tab in the Text group. An example of the Text Box gallery is shown in Figure 18-10.

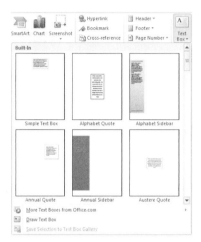

Figure 18-10 The Text Box gallery provides preformatted, theme-enabled text boxes.

The Text Box gallery includes various text box styles. For example, you can use simple text boxes that can be moved and positioned anywhere on a page to create what is called a pull quote (the middle text box in Figure 18-9), or you can choose those that are automatically placed on the edge of the page, to create a sidebar (the text box on the right in Figure 18-9).

You can also use the Draw Text Box command, found toward the bottom of the Text Box gallery, to manually draw and insert text boxes. However, if you need more than a standard text box, you might find that starting with a text box from the gallery and making minor formatting modifications, such as changing it to another shape, achieves faster results.

> **Note**
> To start with a Shape as a text container, use the Shapes gallery found on the Insert tab. To add text, right-click the shape and click Add Text, which converts the shape to a text box. You will see contextual Text Box Tools when the shape is activated instead of contextual Drawing Tools, which do not contain the additional text options described in this chapter.

As you create text boxes in your document, you can move and resize them in the same manner that you move and resize drawing objects—dragging them by their edges and sizing handles. To move a text box, point to the border, watch for the Move mouse pointer (multi-directional arrows), then click and drag the text box to another location. To resize a text box, you can drag the sizing handles (the small blue boxes and circles shown in Figure 18-11) to change the width and height of the text box.

Figure 18-11 Use the blue boxes and circles surrounding text boxes to reshape text into more interesting configurations.

> **Note**
> Use the blue circles on each corner to resize the shape proportionally; the blue boxes resize only the height or width.

If the text box is formatted as a shape, it can be rotated by dragging the green circle (only the shape rotates, the text stays horizontal). Some shapes can be reshaped by dragging the yellow diamond.

> **Note**
> To place existing text into a text box, select the text, then on the Insert tab, display the Text Box gallery and click Draw Text Box at the bottom. The selected text is automatically inserted into a standard text box. Keep in mind that this method does not apply to using shapes.

Inserting Text into Text Boxes

After you create text boxes, you are ready to add text and formatting. You can insert text into containers in a few predictable ways such as typing, pasting copied information, and dragging content into the text box. If you are creating a newsletter-style document that will consist of multiple linked text boxes, see the Inside Out tip titled "Linked Text Boxes: Room to Edit" on page 579 for instructions on creating the content in another document and inserting it into the text boxes.

In addition to inserting text, you can insert graphics, tables, fields, and content controls into text boxes. However, there are items that you cannot include in text boxes, among them are the following:

Columns	Comments
Drop caps	Endnotes
Footnotes	Indexes
Page and column breaks	Tables of Figures

Formatting Text Boxes

By default, when you create a text box as opposed to inserting a text box from the Text Box gallery, it appears as a white (not transparent) box surrounded by thin (0.75 point) black lines. Fortunately, text boxes don't have to be limited to plain white rectangles strategically placed around your document. You can format text boxes in the same manner that you format other drawing objects. For example, by using the formatting options found on the contextual Drawing Tools tab, you can apply fill and line colors by using the Shape Fill and Shape Outline tools; apply Shape Styles; change the text box to another shape; and add effects, glow, and more. To format text boxes using the Format tab (shown in the following image), select the text box you want to format and then click the appropriate tool.

> **Note**
>
> To quickly activate and display the contextual Text Box Tools, double-click the edge of a text box.

In addition to the formatting tools on the Format tab, you can format text boxes using the Text Box options in the Format Shape dialog box. Specifically, you can control the position of text inside text boxes, and you can have Word automatically resize a text box to accommodate the complete text of a story.

Controlling Text in Text Boxes

You can control the distance between the text and the edges of its bounding text box by adjusting the internal margin of the text box, as described in the following steps:

1. Click the text box to active it. On the Format tab, in the Shape Styles group, click the dialog launcher to display the Format Shape dialog box.

2. Click the Text Box tab, as shown in Figure 18-12.

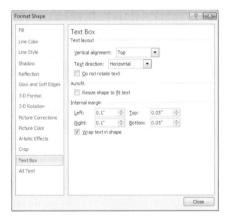

Figure 18-12 You can control the spacing around text in text boxes by configuring the internal margin settings in the Format Shape dialog box.

3. In the Internal Margin area, increase or decrease the left, right, top, and bottom margin measurements to control the distance between the text and the selected object's edges. Click Close to apply the settings.

In addition to controlling internal margins, you can change the direction of text inside text boxes. To do so, click in a text box and then, in the Text group on the Drawing Tools Format tab, click Text Direction. You can continue to click the button to cycle through the available text direction options or click the arrow to display a list of text direction choices.

> **Note**
> When you change the text direction in a linked text box, you change the text direction in all text boxes that are linked to it as well, throughout the story. In other words, you can't change the text direction in a single text box if it's part of a linked series of text boxes. For more information about linked text boxes, see the section titled "Linking Text Boxes to Flow Text," on page 578.

Changing Text Box Shapes

The beauty of using shapes is that you can change your mind regarding which shape you want to use at any time. Changing the shape of a text box is similar to changing shapes that don't contain text. To do so, ensure that you're working in Print Layout view and then follow these simple steps:

1. Click the text box you want to modify. To select multiple text boxes, press and hold Shift while clicking each text box.

2. On the Insert tab, click Shapes then select another shape from the gallery.

All selected text boxes take on the new shape but retain all other format settings, such as color and internal margins.

INSIDE OUT   Set Tight Text Wrapping Around Text in Text Boxes

When a text box is placed in a paragraph and the line color for a text box has been removed, the text surrounding the text box continues to wrap to the boundaries of the text box, as opposed to wrapping to the text inside of the text box. In some instances, you might want to modify this behavior and wrap text around the text shown in the document instead of the invisible boundaries of the text box. In order to achieve the desired results, you can use the new Tight Wrap options for text box, found in the Paragraph dialog box on the Line And Page Breaks tab, shown in the following image:

The Tight Wrap options apply to paragraphs that wrap around a text box, rather than the text inside of the text box.

To effectively use the Tight Wrap options, follow these steps:

1. Click a text box to active it.

2. On the Format tab, in the Shape Styles group, click the dialog launcher. In the Format Shape dialog box, set the following options:

    - On the Fill and Line Color tabs, set Fill Color to No Fill and Line Color to No Line

    - On the Text Box tab, set the Vertical Alignment to Middle

3. On the Home tab, in the Paragraph group, click the dialog launcher. In the Paragraph dialog box, set the following options:

    - On the Indents and Spacing tab, set the Alignment to Center

    - On the Line And Page Breaks tab, set Tight Wrap to All

Depending on the text box placement and the amount of text in the text box, you might need to modify the Internal Margins for the text box (found on the Text Box tab in the Format Text Box dialog box) and experiment with the other Tight Wrap options, such as First And Last Lines, First Line Only, or Last Line Only in order to obtain the best text wrapping results for your specific text box.

Linking Text Boxes to Flow Text

If you've ever created a newsletter or brochure, you know how tricky it can be to fill text areas and properly manage jumps from one page to another. In Word, you can simplify these types of tasks by linking text boxes. When you link text boxes, you indicate that any text you insert into one text box will automatically flow into the next text box when the first text box cannot accommodate all of the inserted text. After you insert text into linked text boxes, you can edit the text to make your story longer or shorter. Word automatically reflows the text throughout the series of linked text boxes.

> **Note**
> The maximum number of linked text boxes allowable in one document is 31, which means that you can have up to 32 linked text containers in one document.

When you want to link text boxes or shapes, you need to keep the following limitations in mind:

- Linked text boxes must be contained in a single document (they cannot be located in different subdocuments of a master document).

- A text box cannot already be linked to another series or story.

Before you flow text into a series of linked text boxes, you should be sure that you've made most of the changes to your text. You can then draw the text boxes you want to link and into which you'll import your story. When your text is ready and your text boxes are drawn, follow these steps to link the text boxes and insert the text:

1. In Print Layout view, click the first text box or shape into which you want to insert text.

2. On the Format tab, click Create Link. The pointer changes to an upright pitcher, as shown in the following example:

3. Move the pointer to the text box to which you want to link the first text box. When you move the upright pitcher pointer over a text box that can receive the link, the pitcher tilts and turns into a pouring pitcher. Click the second text box to link it to the first text box.

4. To link a third text box, click the text box that you just linked to the first text box, click Create Link, and then click the third text box.

You can create a chain of linked text boxes using this method.

> **Note**
>
> If you click Create Link and then decide not to link to another box, press Esc to cancel the linking process.

5. Once you link your text boxes, click in the first text box and insert text by typing or pasting content.

For an efficient method to use for lengthy content, see the following Inside Out tip titled "Linked Text Boxes: Room to Edit."

> **Note**
>
> If you have a complete story that's ready to flow into text boxes, you can insert the story into the text boxes while you link them. To do this, insert your story into the first text box and then link to the next text box as described in Steps 1–3. When you use this approach, the text flows into the text boxes while you link them.

INSIDE OUT   Linked Text Boxes: Room to Edit

If the document you are creating is more of a newsletter-style document that will contain a series of linked text boxes, then consider typing and editing the text content in another Word document so you can format and perform fine-tune tasks in a larger editing area. After your text boxes are created and linked, you can insert the content of the document and populate the linked text boxes. To insert the file content, select the first linked text box and navigate to the Insert tab. Click the arrow next to Object, click the Text From File command, select your document, and then click Insert to insert the contents.

Moving Between Linked Text Boxes

After you link text boxes, you can easily jump from one text box to another. To do so, select a text box that's part of a linked series of text boxes. Position your insertion point at the end of text in a filled text box and then press the right arrow key. You can also jump to the preceding text box by positioning your insertion point at the beginning of the text in a text box and then pressing the left arrow key.

> **Note**
> If you often need to move forward and backward among linked text boxes, you might want to add the Next Text Box and Previous Text Box buttons to the Quick Access Toolbar from Commands Not In The Ribbon.

Copying or Moving Linked Text Boxes

You can copy or move a story (including text boxes and their contents) to another document or another location in the same document. If your story consists of multiple linked text boxes that aren't contained on a single drawing canvas, you must select all of the linked text boxes in the story before you can copy the story and text boxes. If they are on a single drawing canvas, you can select any text box in the series of linked text boxes and copy the entire story and the selected text box to another location. Or, you can select all of the text boxes on the drawing canvas to copy the story and all of the associated text boxes.

> **Note**
> To create a drawing canvas, on the Insert tab, click Shapes, and then click New Drawing Canvas. To automatically insert a drawing canvas by default when you insert a text box or shape, display Word Options, then in the Advanced area, select Automatically Create Drawing Canvas When Inserting AutoShapes.

When you copy one or a few linked text boxes (but not an entire story) that are not on a drawing canvas, you copy only the selected text box or boxes without the content. When you copy a single text box that is part of an entire story that appears in text boxes on a single drawing canvas, you copy the entire story along with the selected text box. This means that when you paste the text box, you will probably need to resize it to see the entire story or will need to add text boxes and link them to the newly inserted text box.

If you want to copy an entire story along with all of the text boxes containing the story, you need to select all of the text boxes before copying them, as described in the following procedure:

1. In Print Layout view, select a text box in the story by clicking the edge of the text box.

> **Note**
>
> You must select the edge of a text box if you want to copy the text box. If you click inside the text box and then click Copy on the Home tab, or press Ctrl+C, Word does not copy anything.
>
> If you want to copy multiple text boxes, you can click anywhere in the text box while you press Shift and click to select additional text boxes.

2. Press Shift and then click the text boxes you want to copy or move.

3. In the Clipboard group on the Home tab, click Copy or Cut (or press Ctrl+C or Ctrl+X).

4. Click where you want to reposition the text boxes, then in the Clipboard group on the Home tab, click Paste (or press Ctrl+V).

To copy or move content that appears within a text box without copying or moving the text box itself, select just the text or content in the same way that you select standard text and content and then copy or move it in the same way you normally copy or move content in Word documents. To select and copy all text in a linked story, click in the story, press Ctrl+A, and either copy and paste or drag the text to the desired location. You can select all of the text in a story by using Ctrl+A regardless of whether the story's text boxes are on a drawing canvas.

INSIDE OUT   Obtaining Word Count Statistics for Text Box Content

In Word 2010, you can include text within text boxes in your document's word count statistic—this ability was not available in versions of Word prior to Word 2007. To control whether to include text inside text boxes in word count statistics, open the Word Count dialog box by clicking Words in the status bar. Select or clear the Include Textboxes, Footnotes And Endnotes check box to count or exclude text inside of text boxes in your word count statistics.

Breaking Text Box Links

You can break links between text boxes just as easily as you create them. When you break a link, you remove only the link between the selected text box and the text box that follows it in the series—you don't remove all of the links in a linked series. Essentially, when you break a link, you divide a story into two series of linked text boxes or segments. By default, the first series of linked text boxes contains the story, and linked text boxes in the second series are empty.

To break a link between text boxes, follow these steps:

1. In Print Layout view, click the edge of the text box from which you want the text to stop flowing.

   The selected text box becomes the last text box in the first linked series of text boxes.

2. On the Drawing Tools Format tab, click Break Link in the Text group.

At this point, text stops flowing in the last text box before the broken link, and the second series of linked text boxes are empty. If the text doesn't fit in the first series of linked text boxes after you break a link, you can create and link additional text boxes or enlarge the existing text boxes to provide enough room to display the entire text.

> **Note**
> You can cut a text box in the middle of a linked series of text boxes without deleting any parts of your story. To do so, simply right-click the edge of a text box and then click Cut. When you cut a linked text box, the story readjusts and the text flows into the next text box.

Deleting Linked Text Boxes Without Losing Text

To delete a text box, you simply select a text box and press Delete or right-click the text box border and click Cut. Normally, performing this action on a nonlinked text box deletes both the text box and its contents. In contrast, when you delete a text box that's part of a linked series of text boxes, the text from the deleted text box automatically flows into the remaining linked text boxes. If the remaining text boxes aren't large enough to properly display the story in its entirety, you must resize the remaining text boxes, create additional text boxes, or edit your story to fit in the existing text boxes. Keep in mind that Word doesn't notify you when text overflows the boundaries of the final text box, so you should always be extra diligent about checking the flow of stories and making sure that no text is hidden.

> **Note**
> To avoid deleting an entire story when you delete a standalone, nonlinked text box,
> click in the text box, press Ctrl+A to select the story, and then either drag or copy the
> selected story into your document before you delete the text box.

Adding Objects to Your Word Document

One of the great things about Word 2010 is that it gets along well with others. When you
have files, charts, presentations, notes, worksheets, and even audio and video clips that
you want to include as part of a document, Word helps you out. To link or embed objects
in your document, you use the Object tool, which is available in the Text group on the
Insert tab.

> **Tip**
> You are likely to see the acronym OLE when you read about objects in Word. This refers
> to Object Linking and Embedding, which is the name of Microsoft's object technology.
> With OLE, you can add objects to your document that maintain a link to the original
> source file so that you can return to it (and the application that created it) for easy
> editing. This way, any changes you make in the source file are reflected in your Word
> document as well.

What's the difference between linking and embedding? When an object is linked to your
file, the object isn't actually stored in the Word document. A link is maintained so that if
the source file for the object changes, the changes will be reflected in your document. You
might use this technique, for example, when you want to include data from a sales report
that your sales manager keeps. When she updates the report, the changes are reflected
automatically in your document.

When you embed an object in your file, the source of the object is stored within your Word
document. You can easily edit the object by double-clicking it; this activates the program
that was used to create the object and you can make your changes and save them to return
to the updated object in your document.

As you can imagine, linking is great when you are working collaboratively on documents in
which the data often changes. It's also helpful when you want to keep the size of the document small (and the source file for the object is stored elsewhere). Embedding your objects

is a good idea if file size is not an issue and you want simply to be able to edit the object on the fly without leaving Word.

Insert an Object

When you're ready to add an object to your Word page, click the Object arrow in the Text group on the Insert tab and choose Object. In the Object dialog box (Figure 18-13), click one of the following tabs:

- **Create New**   Use this if you want to add a new item to your Word page

- **Create From File**   Select this if you want to add an object you've already created in a different document

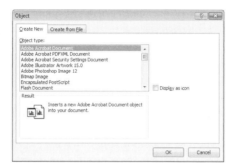

Figure 18-13 You use the Objects dialog box to create or add objects to your Word pages.

Create a New Object

On the Create New tab in the Object dialog box, you can choose the type of object you want to create and Word launches the necessary program so you can do it. You can create a wide range of objects, directly from within Word—Adobe Acrobat PDF files, bitmap images, Excel worksheets and charts, PowerPoint slides and shows, Microsoft Works documents, and more.

Scroll through the list and click the type of object you want to create. Click the file type you want and then, if you want the object to be displayed as an icon in your text (as opposed to appearing as the created object), select the Display as icon check box. (If you select this check box, another option becomes available so that you can choose the icon used to represent the object.) Click OK and Word opens the program needed to create the new object.

Adding an Existing Object

If you want to add an object you've already created to your Word document, click the Create From File tab in the Object dialog box (see Figure 18-14). Click Browse to navigate to the folder containing the file you want to use, select it, and click OK.

Figure 18-14 Use Create From File to add an existing object to your Word pages.

Back in the Object dialog box, select the Link To File check box if you want to maintain a link to the original file. This way, if you make changes to that source file, they will be reflected in your document. Click Open to add the object to your page.

What's Next?

This chapter introduced you to a few of the "extras" you might want to add to your Word pages, such as equations, text boxes, and objects. The next chapter moves into the collaborative realm by helping you explore the ways you can share, review, compare, merge, and edit documents you and your team members make to present to the world.

CHAPTER 19

Command Attention with Borders and Shading

Adding a Simple Border 587

Creating Enhanced Borders 588

Creating Partial Borders 596

Adding a Border to a Page 597

Adding Borders to Sections and Paragraphs 600

Adjusting Border Spacing 601

Inserting Horizontal Lines. 603

Adding Borders to Pictures. 604

Adding Table Borders 605

Applying Shading Behind Content 606

What's Next? 609

B ORDERS and shading are two of those features that are super easy to apply but can make a big difference in the way your document looks to your readers. Adding a border to a sidebar can give the section a professional look it might not achieve just hanging out there in your text. Adding a background shade can help call attention to a particular paragraph or two. And by fine-tuning borders on a table, section, or page, you can add a simple but sophisticated design element that keeps your readers' interest and gives your document that "put together" look.

This chapter shows you how to add and customize the borders and shading in your document, whether you want to apply the features to paragraphs, sections, your whole document, or tables and images on the page.

Some of the reasons you might want to use borders and shading include:

- You want to create a border around a table.

- You want to format a heading that includes white text on a colorful background.

- You need a shaded sidebar for a section of text that accompanies an article.

- You would like to add a border around a table of contents so that readers can find it easily.

Adding a Simple Border

To quickly and easily add a plain border to an item in your document, on the Home tab, in the Paragraph group, click the arrow to the right of the Borders button. A list of border options appears, as shown in Figure 19-1. Click Outside Border to enclose the selected item in a border (or choose another Border option if you prefer). Your most recent selection also becomes the option shown on the face of the button, on the assumption that you might want to use it again soon.

Figure 19-1 Clicking the Borders arrow in the Paragraph group displays a list of border choices.

Note

Keep in mind that the Borders button is a toggle button. This means that with a click of the button, you can add borders at the cursor position if they aren't present or remove borders if they are present.

INSIDE OUT Clear Borders Quickly with No Border

Although you can use the toggle effect of the Borders button to remove border lines, you might want to clear all existing borders before applying new settings. To clear existing borders, highlight the section you want to modify, click No Border in the Borders gallery, and then, while the section is still selected, click the border style you want to use.

Creating Enhanced Borders

A simple one-line border might do the trick when you are interested in only a box that sets off items from surrounding text. But if you want to use the border as a design element on your page, you can use the Borders And Shading dialog box to tailor the selections and create a more sophisticated effect. The Borders And Shading dialog box presents you with a variety of looks for your border (including 3-D and shadow effects). You can also change the style, color, and width of the lines you use or create a partial border by selecting only the line segments you want to display.

To create a customized border, begin by placing the insertion point in the paragraph where you want the border to start or by selecting the data around which you want to create the border. For example, if you want to add a border around a paragraph that lists your corporate Web site and contact information, highlight that paragraph and then display the Borders And Shading dialog box in one of two ways:

- On the Page Layout tab, select the Page Borders tool in the Page Background group. In the Borders And Shading dialog box, select the Borders tab.

- Click the Borders arrow (in the Paragraph group on the Home tab) and select Borders And Shading (the last option on the list).

    The Borders And Shading dialog box appears, as shown in Figure 19-2.

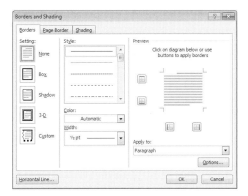

Figure 19-2 Use the Borders And Shading dialog box to choose border style and placement.

You can make all kinds of border changes and tweak attributes in any number of ways by adjusting the style, color, width, line, and shading settings. The Borders And Shading dialog box provides three tabs: Borders, Page Border, and Shading. The following list presents a quick overview of what you can do on each tab:

- **Borders** Contains options for choosing the border style, color, and width, as well as options for choosing partial borders (for example, you can choose to which edges of the selection you want to assign a border).

- **Page Border** Includes the same options you find on the Border tab, with one addition: the Art list at the bottom of the center panel enables you to add special border art to the pages in your document.

- **Shading** On this tab, you can apply a background color or pattern behind selected text.

Dressing Up Your Border

You will probably want to modify the Setting options when you open the Borders And Shading dialog box. These options control the overall look of the border, and they vary depending on whether you're working in a table or with standard text. If you're working with standard text, you can choose from the following Setting options:

- **None**   Shows no border around selected text and objects; this is the default.

- **Box**   Encloses the selection in a simple line box.

- **Shadow**   Outlines the selection with a box and adds a drop shadow below and to the right of the selection.

- **3-D**   Creates a three-dimensional effect for the selected border, making it appear to "stand out" from the page.

- **Custom**   Configures the Preview area so you can choose and customize the line segments you want to include in your border.

If you're working with a table or selected cells, you can choose among the following Setting options:

- **None**   Shows no border around the table or selected cells.

- **Box**   Encloses the table or selected cells in a simple line box without internal lines.

- **All**   Outlines the entire table or selected cells, including borders between cells; this is the default.

- **Grid**   Outlines a table or selected cells with a heavier exterior border and lighter interior borders.

- **Custom**   Configures the Preview area so that you can choose and customize the line segments you want to include in your border.

> **Note**
> You can mix and match border types to achieve the effect you want. For example, you can add borders to part of a table and hide borders in other parts to create the appearance of lines for text on forms that users will fill out. You can further combine border options, such as color and line widths, to make borders visually appealing.

To apply one of the Setting options shown in the Borders And Shading dialog box, click in the paragraph, table, image, or other element that you want to format, or select text or cells. Then display the Borders And Shading dialog box and click the Setting selection on the Borders tab. If you don't want to make any additional changes, you can simply click OK to return to your document.

The border is added to the current text, table, or selected object. If the cursor is positioned in a new blank paragraph before you display the Borders And Shading dialog box, the border appears around the insertion point and expands as you type, including added paragraphs, images, tables, and other elements.

To end the expansion of the border, either click outside the formatted area or press Enter at the end of the formatted area, and then format the new blank paragraph marker by using the No Border setting on the Borders button.

> **Note**
>
> If you add a border and decide that you don't like it, you can do away with it immediately by clicking Undo in the Quick Access Toolbar at the top of the Word window or by pressing Ctrl+Z. You can also click the Borders tool in the Paragraph group and select No Border to clear the border lines.

TROUBLESHOOTING

The changes I made to the borders in my table disappeared.

If you change the border or shading of a table and discover that the changes you specified weren't made when you closed the Borders And Shading dialog box, it could be because the table's formatting marks weren't selected properly before you applied formatting options. To avoid this problem, click Show/Hide in the Paragraph group on the Home tab to display all of the formatting characters in your document before you apply formatting. Then select the table, making sure to include the end-of-row marks at the ends of the rows. Next, right-click the table, choose Borders And Shading to display the Borders And Shading dialog box, and then enter your settings. Because the table formatting marks are included, the changes should stick after you close the Borders And Shading dialog box.

Selecting Line Styles for Borders

Word provides 24 line styles that you can use to create border effects. From simple, straight lines to dotted, double, and triple lines, you can create a variety of looks by changing line styles. Figure 19-3 shows a few examples of borders created with different line styles.

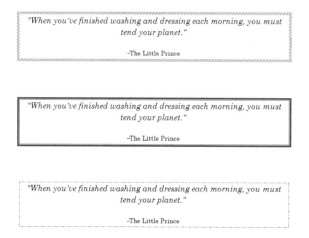

Figure 19-3 The line style you choose has a dramatic effect on the overall look of a border.

To choose a line style for a border, display the Borders And Shading dialog box and select a line style in the Style list on the Borders tab. The Preview area shows the effect of your choices. Set any other border choices you want then click OK. The document is updated with your changes.

TROUBLESHOOTING

There's not enough contrast in my double line.

If you create a double line and can't see enough variation between lines of different weights, you can play around with the line widths to achieve a better contrast. Start by clicking in or selecting the area with the border. Next, display the Borders And Shading dialog box by clicking the Borders button and choosing Borders And Shading at the bottom of the gallery. On the Width list, choose a new line width setting. In the Preview area in the dialog box, click the line you want to change.

Choosing Color

When you begin adding lines and borders to your publication, Word uses the Automatic color by default, which is black if you are using the standard Windows color scheme. However, you have all of the colors offered by Word at your disposal, so you can get as colorful as your document design allows. To choose new border colors, follow these steps:

1. Click in or select the elements you want to format with border colors.

    If the content already has a border and you only want to color the existing lines, you can retain the current border and simply apply a color setting to the existing border settings.

2. On the Home tab, in the Paragraph group, click Borders And Shading. Choose Borders And Shading at the bottom of the list to display the Borders And Shading dialog box.

3. On the Borders tab, select a Setting option and line style if you're creating a new border.

    If you're working with an existing border, you can make changes as desired.

4. Click the Color arrow. The color palette appears, as shown in Figure 19-4.

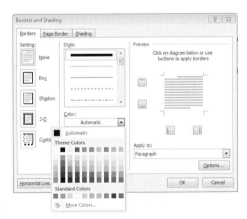

Figure 19-4 You can use the color palette to select a color for lines and shading.

5. Click the color you want to use from the color palette or, if you don't see the color you were hoping for, click More Colors.

    The Colors dialog box appears, in which you can find the color you're looking for. Click the color you want. If you're creating a new border, the color setting is reflected in the Preview area immediately. If you're adjusting the color setting for an existing border, you need to click each line in the Preview area to apply the color setting. In this way, you can control the line color for each border line.

6. Click OK and the color settings are applied in your document.

> **Note**
>
> The Color palette is divided into two areas. The Theme Colors area provides colors from the document theme, and the Standard Colors area offers primary colors. More Colors displays the Colors dialog box so that you can choose from a wide range of colors or create your own custom color. If you choose a color that is not included in the Theme Colors section, it won't be changed automatically if you later choose a different theme for the document. To make sure that colors can be automatically swapped whenever you choose a new theme, select Theme Colors only.

When You Need to Match Colors Exactly

Suppose that you're using Word 2010 to create a Web page or document that must con-form to last year's annual report, right down to the color scheme. When you need to match colors, choosing accurate border colors can become an especially important issue. For times like these, you can use the Custom tab in the Colors dialog box to enter the exact RGB (Red, Green, and Blue) or HSL (Hue, Saturation, and Luminance) values for custom colors. To configure the Custom tab in the Colors dialog box for borders, perform the fol-lowing steps:

1. Click the border for which you want to change the color.

2. On the Page Layout tab, in the Page Background group, choose Page Borders.

3. On the Borders tab in the Borders And Shading dialog box, click the Color down arrow.

4. Click More Colors on the color palette.

5. In the Colors dialog box, click the Custom tab.

6. On the Color Model list, choose RGB, HSL, or another available color scheme (see Figure 19-5).

7. Enter values in the Red, Green, and Blue, or Hue, Sat, and Lum text boxes as appropriate (depending on the color model you choose).

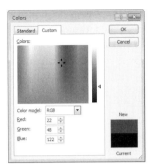

Figure 19-5 You can match border colors exactly in the Colors dialog box.

8. Click OK to close the Colors dialog box.

9. Finish configuring your border settings in the Borders And Shading dialog box then click OK to apply the custom color.

INSIDE OUT   How Do I Choose the Best Colors for Borders?

The easiest way to choose colors for any section of your document is to choose a theme that controls the fonts, colors, and effects used throughout the entire piece. If you don't want to use an existing theme or customize a theme to include the elements you prefer, the question of choosing effective colors for your borders remains.

The trick to selecting effective colors for a document's text, images, table borders, lines, shading, and other components is to work with a color scheme that consists of three or four main colors that complement the document's design and provide appropriate contrast. After you identify a color scheme, you can play with the colors a little to add interest. For instance, if headings are dark blue, you might consider using the same blue or a slightly lighter shade of the same blue for borders and lines. In addition, document design often benefits from a consistent use of color across the board for similar design elements. For instance, in a magazine or newsletter, all sidebars might be placed in a green box while quotations appear in yellow boxes. That way, when readers see green, they know they're about to read a sidebar; when they see yellow, they recognize that they're reading a quotation. Color used wisely can greatly increase the readability and visual appeal of a publication.

You can simplify the task of selecting colors that work well together by using one of the predesigned Word Themes as you create your document. When you use a Word Theme, the colors displayed in the Theme Colors area of the Color palette help you choose colors that are already used consistently in the document color scheme.

Controlling Border Width

When you create a simple border, the default line width is 0.5 point, which is a simple, thin line. If you want to create a more dramatic effect—whether you leave the line black or add color—you can change the width of the line. To change line width, display the Borders And Shading dialog box, click the Width arrow, and then click the width you want. Available point sizes include $^1/_4$, $^1/_2$, $^3/_4$, 1, $1^1/_2$, $2^1/_4$, 3, $4^1/_2$, and 6.

> **Note**
>
> You can use line widths to create a special effect for partial borders. For example, to add a wide line above and below content, select the area you want to enclose between the lines, display the Borders And Shading dialog box, and then on the Borders tab, click the Custom setting. Select a line style, click the Width arrow, and then choose a larger point size, such as 3 point. In the Preview area, click the top-horizontal edge of the preview page. A line is added to the top border. Next, click the bottom-horizontal edge of the preview page then click OK. Word adds the thick line border above and below the selected area.

Creating Partial Borders

Not every paragraph, table, or object you enclose in a border needs four lines surrounding it. You might want to add only two lines—perhaps along the top and right side of a paragraph—to help set it apart from an article that appears beside it. You might use only a top and bottom rule to contain your table of contents. Or you might use a single line to set off a quotation from the main text in a report or to mark the start of a new section.

Creating a partial border is a simple task, and you use the Custom Setting option and the Preview area of the Borders And Shading dialog box to accomplish it. Here are the steps:

1. Click in a table or paragraph, or select the information around which you want to create the border.

2. On the Home tab, in the Paragraph group, click the Borders button.

3. On the Borders tab, click the Custom setting. Specify the border's line style, color, and width.

4. In the Preview area, click each edge of the preview paragraph to indicate where border lines should appear, or click the buttons that correspond to the edge or edges that should have a border line.

> **Note**
> You can toggle border lines on and off by clicking the borders in the Preview area's sample page or by clicking the Preview buttons surrounding the sample page.

Adding a Border to a Page

Many of the techniques you use to add a border to a section, table, or object in a document can be used to add borders to entire pages as well. When might you want to do that? You could add a page border to a special page you want to stand out in a document—perhaps parts pages that mark the beginning of a new section, or an executive summary page to which you want to call attention. Figure 19-6 displays a document with a page border. You can create standard page borders or use Art Border. This section shows you how.

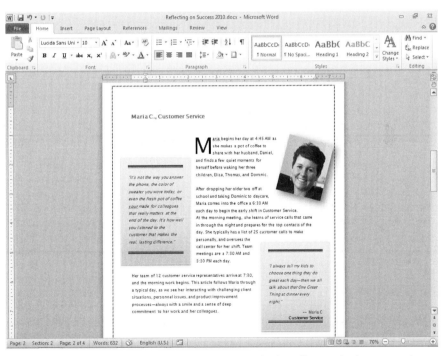

Figure 19-6 By default, page border settings are applied to all pages in the current document.

Creating a Page Border

Begin the process of adding a border to the page by displaying the Borders and Shading dialog box and selecting the Page Border tab. The main visual difference between the Borders tab and the Page Border tab is the addition of the Art list (which is covered on page 599). On the Page Border tab, after you make all of your border choices, the border is applied to an entire page, section, or document. The following procedure describes the process:

1. Click in a page or section to which you want to apply a border.

2. On the Home tab, in the Paragraph group, click the Borders button.

3. In the Borders And Shading dialog box, select the Page Border tab.

4. Click a page border setting (Box, Shadow, 3-D, or Custom).

5. From the Style list, select a line style.

6. On the Color list, select a color if desired.

7. Click the Width arrow and then choose the line width you want.

    The Style, Color, and Width settings are reflected in the Preview area.

8. If desired, use the Preview image to select which edges of the page will have a page border.

9. On the Apply To list, specify where the border should apply.

    Available options are Whole Document, This Section, This Section – First Page Only, and This Section – All Except First Page. By default, Whole Document is selected on the Apply To list; therefore, the border is added to all pages in the current document.

10. Click OK to close the dialog box and apply the page border settings to the current document.

> **Note**
>
> To apply a page border to a single page (other than the first page) or to a few pages in a long document, you must first set off the page or pages by creating a section. To learn more about creating and working with sections, see Chapter 6, "Setting Up Your Layout with Page Backgrounds and Columns."

INSIDE OUT How Do I Change the Border on the First Page Only?

When you add a page border, by default, Word applies the border to all of the pages in your document. What if you want to skip the border on the first page or apply the border only to the first page? You can do either of these things easily by using the Apply To setting on the Page Border tab in the Borders And Shading dialog box. To suppress the display of the border for the first page, on the Page Border tab, click the Apply To arrow then select This Section – All Except First Page. To apply the border to the first page only, choose This Section – First Page Only in the Apply To list on the Page Border tab.

Adding an Artistic Border

The Art Page Border feature, known in earlier versions of Microsoft Office as BorderArt, is where you can add an artistic touch to entire pages in your document. Special graphics are placed in patterns—either in black and white or in color—and used as borders for a page, group of pages, or selected sides of pages. To apply an artistic page border, follow these steps:

1. Click in the document to which you want to add the border.

2. On the Home tab, in the Paragraph group, click the Borders button to display the Borders And Shading dialog box, and then select the Page Border tab.

3. Click the Art arrow then scroll through the art borders. Select an Art option.

   The Preview area displays your change. To control which borders will contain graphics, you can click the border segments to add and remove the images.

4. On the Apply To list, choose which pages should include the border.

   You can include the border on the Whole Document, This Section, This Section – First Page Only, or This Section – All Except First Page.

5. Click OK and the border is added to the document according to your choices.

Artistic borders can be colorful and vibrant, but they can also be a bit much for some professional documents. For that reason, you should use art borders sparingly and use discretion to determine whether they are appropriate on a case-by-case basis.

Adding Borders to Sections and Paragraphs

Borders add emphasis to the page, section, or paragraph to which you want to call the reader's attention. Word 2010 makes it easy to add borders to sections, paragraphs, images, or even words or phrases, if you like. Using the Apply To setting in the Borders And Shading dialog box, you can choose the item you want to change.

- If you want to create a border around a section in your document, use the Page Border tab. On the Apply To list, you can find what you need to specify section bordering options.

- If you want to add a border around a paragraph, text, table, image, selected table cell, or other element in your document, use the Borders tab. The Apply To options on that tab offer choices specific to the item you choose.

INSIDE OUT   My Border Covers Up Part of a Photo in My Document

You might find that the page or section border that you've added overlaps an image in your document. You can fix this (and create a great effect at the same time) by moving the border behind the image. To do so, display the Borders And Shading dialog box (click Borders in the Paragraph group on the Home tab), select the Page Border tab, and then click Options. In the Options section, clear the check box for Always Display In Front.

Bordering Sections

You might want to create a border around a section when you have specific information to highlight or when you want to set a section apart from the main flow of the text. To create a section border, start by placing the insertion point in the section you want to highlight. Display the Borders And Shading dialog box (click Borders in the Paragraph group on the Home tab) and then click the Page Border tab. Next, configure the border effects, including the Setting option and line style, color, and width. Click the Apply To arrow and select your choice: Whole Document, This Section, This Section – First Page Only, or This Section – All Except First Page. Finally, click the OK button to create your border.

If you want to see how the border looks for the entire section, click Print on the File tab. Adjust the Zoom controls so that two pages appear in the preview area. This helps you see the effect of your border selection on more than one page in your document.

INSIDE OUT   Use Border Settings to Add Blank Lines

Here's a great way to add horizontal lines for write-in spaces in your documents. Press Enter to insert a number of blank lines in your document in the area where you want to create horizontal lines. Then select the blank lines, click the arrow on the Borders button, and then click the Inside Horizontal Border option. Evenly spaced lines are added automatically, extending from the left to the right margin.

Adjusting Border Spacing

Word makes a few assumptions about the way borders appear in documents. By default, it sets a small margin to borders applied to a paragraph and a larger margin to borders for sections and pages. When you add a border to a paragraph, Word adds a 1-point margin to the top and bottom and a 4-point margin along the left and right edges of the border. When you add a page or section border, it adds 24-point margins on all four sides, measured from the edge of the page.

To access border options with which you can adjust spacing between borders and content, display the Borders And Shading dialog box (click Borders And Shading in the Paragraph group on the Home tab). Click the Borders tab if you're changing the options for a paragraph border, or click the Page Border tab if you're working with a document or section border. Each of these choices displays different selections in the Border And Shading Options dialog box.

If the Borders tab is displayed when you click Options in the lower-right corner of the dialog box, the Border And Shading Options dialog box appears, as shown in Figure 19-7. If the Page Borders tab is selected, you will see the dialog box shown in Figure 19-8.

Figure 19-7 You control border margins and make choices about border alignment in the Border And Shading Options dialog box.

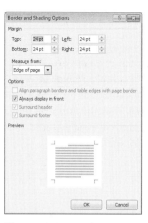

Figure 19-8 Use the Page Border tab to display the options available for spacing the border of an entire page.

To make changes to the border margins, click in the box you want to change and type a new value, or use the up and down arrows to increase or decrease the value shown.

For page borders, Word automatically measures the margin from the edge of the page, but you can change the setting so that the measurement reflects spacing between the text and the surrounding border. To make this change, click the Measure From arrow and choose Text. When working with the Borders tab, the Border And Shading Options dialog box only allows you to configure the space between the border and text.

Other options in the Border And Shading Options dialog box are available only if you're working with a page or section border. By default, Word 2010 includes any headers and footers inside the bordered area and, also by default, enables the Always Display In Front check box, which causes the border to be in front of any text or graphic objects that might overlap it. If you have other borders or tables within the bordered section, the Align Paragraph Borders And Table Edges With Page Border check box is also available to you. If you want Word to align all of these borders, select this check box.

After you finished choosing border options, click OK twice to return to your document.

> **Note**
>
> If you select a table before you display the Borders And Shading dialog box, your options on the Apply To list display Text, Paragraph, Table, and Cell.

TROUBLESHOOTING

My border isn't printing correctly.

If your page border doesn't print along one edge of the page or is positioned too close to an edge, check the border's margin options. To do this, display the Page Border tab of the Borders And Shading dialog box and then click Options. In the Margin area, check your settings. If you set up your border to be measured from Edge Of Page, the space between the text and the border might be pushing the border into the nonprintable area, depending on your printer's specifications. (Most printers do not print in the 0.5-inch area around the perimeter of the page.) Choose the Measure From arrow and select Text. Adjust the margins if necessary and print out a test page to see whether this corrects the problem.

Inserting Horizontal Lines

Word provides a collection of graphical horizontal lines that you can insert in documents to help set off a section, call attention to a special element in text, or set off a sidebar or special element. To add a graphical horizontal line to a document, follow these steps:

1. Place the insertion point where you want to add the line.

2. Display the Borders And Shading dialog box and select any tab.

3. Click the Horizontal Line button in the lower-left corner of the dialog box to display the Horizontal Line dialog box, as shown in Figure 19-9.

Figure 19-9 The Horizontal Line dialog box displays predesigned graphical lines that you can insert in your document.

4. Scroll through the selections and click a line style to add the line.

After you place a horizontal line in a document, you can select, copy, paste, resize, move, and color it as you would other graphical items. To change the format of the line, right-click it, choose Format Horizontal Line, and select the settings you want to change. Furthermore, you can insert additional instances of the line by choosing the Horizontal Line option from the Borders button menu.

> **Tip**
> You can create your own graphical lines in Word or another program (such as Windows Paint or Microsoft PowerPoint 2010) and then add the customized line to your Horizontal Line gallery. To import a custom line, display the Borders And Shading dialog box and click Horizontal Line. In the Horizontal Line dialog box, click Import. Navigate to the file you want to use, click it, and then click Add. The line is added to the gallery and remains selected, ready for you to use.

Adding Borders to Pictures

Adding borders to pictures is a little different than adding borders to text. Instead of using the Borders And Shading dialog box, adding a border to a picture involves changing the formatting settings for that particular object in your document. Here's how it's done:

1. Click the picture or chart to which you want to add the border.

   The contextual Picture Tools appears above the Ribbon.

2. In the Picture Styles group, click Picture Border.

   The Picture Border list appears, as shown in Figure 19-10.

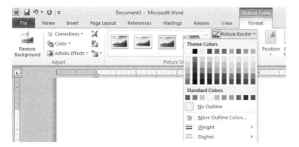

Figure 19-10 In the Picture Styles group of the Picture Tools contextual tab, choose Picture Border to add a border to an image in your document.

3. Click the color you want in the Theme Colors area of the gallery.

It's a good idea to stay with the Theme Colors so that they coordinate with the colors in the rest of your document.

4. Use the Weight And Dashes settings to choose the width and style of the line used for the picture border.

Remember that you can point to a selection to preview it before selecting it.

> **Note**
> You can also spruce up the images in your documents by adding drop shadows, applying 3-D settings, rotating images, and much more. For more about working with pictures in your Word documents, see Chapter 17, "Adding and Editing Pictures and Screenshots."

Adding Table Borders

Word includes an entire set of border options that you can apply to your tables. The tools are easy to use and can help you change a boring table into something that looks professional and really showcases your data effectively. For in-depth coverage of creating and working with tables, be sure to check out Chapter 15, "Clarify Your Concepts in Professional Tables." This section provides the basic steps for adding borders and shades to your tables.

As you know, Word includes a gallery of table styles that you can apply to your tables. The table styles that are available to you depend on the theme you've selected for the document. (For more information about using themes in Word 2010, see Chapter 4, "Templates and Themes for a Professional Look.") The table styles that appear could give you all of the borders you'll ever need. However, if you want to change the borders used in the style, knowing how to customize your table borders comes in handy.

In the Borders And Shading dialog box, you can choose the border setting, style, color, and width, as you learned earlier in this chapter. If you want to experiment with custom lines and mix and match line styles in your table border, use the tools presented on the Design tab, which is available on the Table Tools contextual tab that appear when you select the table. The following procedure shows you how to do it:

1. Begin by selecting the table element to which you want to apply the border.

You might select the entire table or simply a column, row, a single cell, or selection of cells. To select a specific cell, simply click it to position the cursor in that location.

2. On the contextual Table Tools tab, click Design.

3. In the Draw Borders group, click the Line Style arrow to choose the line style you want for the border, as shown in Figure 19-11.

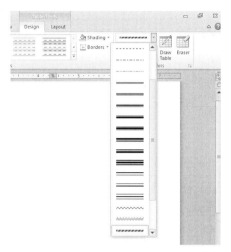

Figure 19-11 Choose the line style and weight before you add a border to table elements.

4. Click the Line Weight arrow to choose the weight (or thickness) you want for the border.

5. In the Table Styles group, click the Borders arrow to display the list of Border options you saw earlier in this chapter.

6. Click your selection to apply the border to the selected table elements.

> **Note**
> If you like the border style you created for a table you've been working with, you can save the style and reuse it. To do so, click the More button in the Table Styles gallery (available when you choose Design on the contextual Table Tools). Choose New Table Style from the bottom of the gallery. Enter a name for the new style and click OK to save it.

Applying Shading Behind Content

You might occasionally want more than a border to make something in your document stand out. Adding shading can help call attention to passages of text that you want to highlight. For example, you might add a shade to highlight a special quotation, draw the reader's eye to an important summary, or make items pop out from the page. When you add a shade to text, you can control the color, transparency, and pattern used to create the shaded effect.

Applying Shades to Tables and Paragraphs

Word's table styles make use of shading in various ways to create professional effects for your tables. You can use one of the preset table styles by selecting the table and then choosing the style you like from the Table Style gallery (available when you choose Design on the contextual Table Tools tab). Chapter 15 includes detailed information on using table styles to format your tables.

When you want to apply custom shading to text, paragraphs, table cells, tables, or headings, you can use the Shading tab in the Borders And Shading dialog box. You can also choose the Shading button in the Paragraph group on the Home tab (when you've selected text) or the Shading button on the Design tab on the contextual Table Tools tab (when you have selected a table). To apply shading effects, follow these steps:

1. Select the item you want to shade.

2. Display the Borders And Shading dialog box then select the Shading tab.

   The Shading tab contains various options that you can use to add and modify shades.

> ### Note
> The borders and shading features of Word work independently, which means that if you add shading without adding a border, the item appears with only the shade behind it—no outer border is added automatically. To add a border to a shaded item, select it and then display the Borders And Shading dialog box. Choose border settings on the Borders tab and then click OK to apply the border to the shaded selection.

3. In the Fill area, click the color you want to apply.

   If you don't see the color you want, you can click More Colors to open the Colors dialog box and choose another. Alternatively, you can click the Custom tab in the Colors dialog box to enter the RGB or HSL values for a custom color (described on page 594).

4. In the Patterns area, click the Style arrow to display your choices for the density or pattern of the color you select. Choose a lower percentage for a lighter shade.

   The Preview area shows the effect of each selection. Check carefully to make sure that the pattern doesn't make your text more difficult to read.

5. Click OK to apply the shading settings.

To remove shading, select the shaded content and then perform one of the following actions:

- Highlight the shaded area then click the Shading arrow in the Paragraph group on the Home tab. Choose No Color.

- Display the Borders And Shading dialog box, click the Shading tab, choose No Color in the Fill area, and then click OK.

- Remove the pattern by displaying the Borders And Shading dialog box, clicking the Shading tab, and then clicking the Style arrow in the Patterns area. Click Clear to remove the pattern and then click OK.

Shading Considerations

As with the caveat given earlier about art borders, remember that a little shading goes a long way. Done thoughtfully and with readers' needs in mind, shading can be effective in calling attention to certain elements and helping special design objects stand out on the page (especially in a complex document). Yet overusing shading or using the wrong mix of colors and patterns can make your document or Web page harder for people to read, which means they'll turn the page or click away from your site—and you'll lose your audience.

To use shading effectively, consider the following guidelines:

- **Use shading on a need-to-use basis.**   Don't sprinkle shades all the way through your document at random. Give a shade a reason, such as, "Every time we mention a new board member, we'll provide a brief biography in a shaded sidebar."

- **Choose intensities carefully.**   A shade that looks light on the screen might be much darker in print. Always look at your document in print form whenever possible, even for online content. You never know when a reader will decide to print an online page for later reference.

- **Check your color choices.** If you lack confidence in your color choices, use the Theme Colors area of the color palette. Apply your color based on the element you are formatting, such as text or background, and let the document Theme handle the contrasts for you.

- **Test your contrasts.** When you add a colored shade behind text, be sure to increase the contrast between the color of the shade and the color of the text. Be careful with using dark backgrounds: select a light (white or yellow) text color to ensure that the text can be easily read. If you choose a dark blue background, black text won't show up clearly.

- **Print test pages on a printer that produces comparable output.** If you're printing colored shades, be sure to print a test page on a color printer.

- **If you're creating a Web page, use Web-safe colors for your shades.** Most Web browsers today can support the standard colors used in the Windows palette. If you choose customized colors, however, some browsers might not display the color accurately. Test the display of the page with different browsers to check the colors you select.

What's Next?

This chapter rounded out Part III of this book, which focused on ways you can communicate your point clearly using all sorts of visual tools that are available in Word 2010. It also focused on adding professional polish to your documents by demonstrating how to add borders and shading to your paragraphs, sections, pages, pictures, and tables. The next chapter introduces the concept of sharing and securing your documents in Word 2010—techniques that come in handy in our increasingly collaborative workplace.

PART 4

Word 2010 As a Team Effort, Anywhere, Always

CHAPTER 20

Securing Your Word Documents 613

CHAPTER 21

Sharing Your Documents 641

CHAPTER 22

**Collaborating and Co-Authoring
in Real Time** 667

Securing Your Word Documents

Protection Features in Word 2010. 614

Working with Protected View 615

Marking a File as Final. 618

Encrypting Documents 620

Applying Editing Restrictions. 622

Removing Personal Information and Hidden Data. . . . 625

Preparing PDF and XPS Files. 626

Signing Your Documents with Digital Signatures
and Stamps 628

Working with the Trust Center. 633

Setting Permission Levels 636

Checking Document Accessibility 638

Ensuring Document Compatibility 639

What's Next? 640

THERE are good reasons today to take file security seriously. Whether you work alone in a home office or trade files and collaborate with colleagues all over the globe, chances are that your documents bump up against security risks all the time. In addition to the anti-virus program running on your computer, Word offers a number of features that help you keep your information private, secure, and safeguarded.

In today's world of always-on, connect-everywhere technology, it's not unusual to be working with teammates across the country while you're sitting at a coffee shop, riding the train, or checking e-mail on your phone. We trade so many files back and forth and we think they go directly to the recipient and back again. But what if a file falls into the wrong hands? Or what if someone hijacks your e-mail account? Microsoft Word 2010 can help you to ensure that only the information you want to share is included in your document. It also makes it easy for you to tailor permissions so you give only those people you want to have access to your document the necessary permissions to work with your content. And the new Protected View feature runs a series of background checks—invisible to you—on a document before you even open it, helping you ensure that you aren't putting your data and your computer in harm's way.

This chapter is all about the features with which Word 2010 can help you secure your files. Most people know the importance of using security measures at the network level or being careful to safeguard files they send as e-mail attachments or post to an online site, but Word provides you with a number of tools you can use to protect your content at the document level as well. For example, you might want to protect your document in the following ways:

- Control who can open, modify, distribute, and print your documents

- Specify the types of changes others can make to your documents

- Remove personal and hidden information

- Save the document in a non-modifiable, fixed format so others can view and print the file but not change it

- Identify yourself as the author of a document (by using digital signatures)

- Protect yourself and others from macro viruses

It's likely that you'll use a number of these features together to provide the best measure of protection for your Word documents. The next section gives you a quick overview of the security features in Word 2010.

Protection Features in Word 2010

Word is designed to meet the reality that our workplace has changed—the global, mobile, and wireless workforce now has security concerns that standalone, desktop PC users did not have in the past. Many of today's users need to be able to access documents in a variety of versions and share them with people all over the world, at a moment's notice. Securing sensitive documents has become more important than ever.

The big change in security in Word 2010—in fact, in all Office 2010 programs—is the addition of Protected View, a new security measure that puts each file you open in a kind of protected "sandbox" until the file is deemed to be a safe for you to use. Developers noticed that there was vulnerability in Word files as they were going through the file open procedure, so they created a way to validate them while they were being opened to lessen the risk that the file would be bringing a virus with it.

When you click Protect Document on the Info tab (click the File tab to display Backstage view), you'll find the following features that are designed to safeguard your documents:.

- **Mark As Final**   Mark As Final saves the document in its final form, as read-only, so others receiving the file will only be able to view and print the file.

- **Encrypt With Password**   With this feature, you can set a password and encrypt your document before sending it to others.

- **Restrict Editing**   This displays the Restrict Formatting And Editing task pane so that you can specify the types of changes you will allow—and by whom.

- **Restrict Permission By People**   Displays a list from which you can choose one of three permission settings: Unrestricted Access, Restricted Access, or Manage Credentials.

- **Add A Digital Signature**   Here, you can authenticate your document for others by adding a digital signature directly in the document file.

Additionally with Word 2010, you can perform a series of checks in the document to con-firm that you are prepared to share it with others. Here are the tools you'll find in the Check For Issues list in the Prepare For Sharing area on the Info tab in Backstage view:

- **Inspect Document**   Launches the Document Inspector, in which you can have Word review your document and point out any sensitive or personal information you might not want to share.

- **Check Accessibility**   Runs a check to ensure that people who are differently abled will be able to read or otherwise use the content in your document.

- **Check Compatibility**   Checks for features that are not supported in an earlier ver-sion of Word. This helps you know that all the content you created will be able to be viewed by others who might not yet have Word 2010.

In addition to the features in the Protect Document list and the evaluation tools you can use before you share the file, Word offers these security features:

- **The Word 2010 Trust Center**   You'll find the Word 2010 Trust Center on the File tab by choosing Options and clicking Trust Center. The Trust Center is where you can disable macros in your Word documents, choose whether Microsoft ActiveX controls are enabled in documents you receive, and create a list of Trusted Publishers, among other tasks.

- **PDF and XPS formats**   Support for saving your documents in PDF and XPS is built right into Word 2010. You can use the Save As command to save the file in PDF or XPS format, or you can choose Create PDF/XPS Document in the Save & Send tab. PDF and XPS formats give you the means to save your Word documents in a plat-form-independent format that others can view but not change.

Working with Protected View

The developers of Office 2010 found that one area vulnerable to attack was the process of opening a file from a previous version of Office. For this reason, they developed a new security approach that operates behind the scenes when you open a new document. The file must pass a series of checks—called a file validation process—before it is considered a safe and allowed to open normally. If the software finds anything suspicious, the document is displayed in Protected View (see Figure 20-1).

Figure 20-1 A document that could be a security risk is flagged in Protected View.

Word 2010 lets you know that a file is in Protected View by displaying a message bar across the top of the work area. If you know the sender of the file or are certain the file is safe, you can click Enable Editing to remove the protection and edit the file normally. You can change which files Word 2010 flags for protection by changing the settings in the Trust Center.

Choosing What's Displayed in Protected View

The Protected View message bar appears whenever you try to open a file that has either been blocked or has been determined to be in a file format flagged for blocking. If you want to see the contents of the file or know the person or company who sent it, you can open the file in Protected View. Protected View is a safe mode in which you can view the file without it potentially impacting your other files. When you know the file is okay, you can click the Enable Editing button to open the file normally.

With Word 2010, you can choose when Protected View is used for your files. By default, all the settings are selected for Protected View, which means that Word displays the Protected View message bar whenever a file fails validation, when it comes from the Internet, when you're downloading it from a potentially unsafe location, or when you're opening an Outlook e-mail attachment. Also by default, Word turns on Data Execution Prevention mode, which ensures that any process that tries to execute when you open the document will be blocked.

You can change these settings on the Protected View tab in the Trust Center. Here are the steps:

1. Click the File tab to display Backstage view then click Options.

2. Click Trust Center, and then click Trust Center Settings.

3. Select Protected View.

4. Clear the check mark of any setting you do not want to keep (see Figure 20-2), then click OK twice to return to the document.

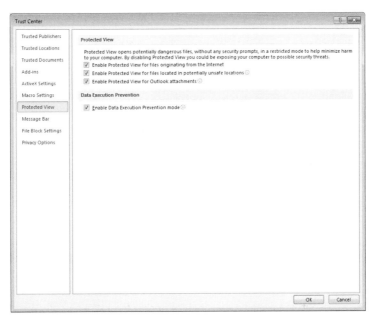

Figure 20-2 You can change when Word uses Protected View to safeguard a document as you open it.

Changing File Validation

Because the internal checks Word performs when determining whether your file is safe have to do with the file format, you can tell Word 2010 which file types you want to validate before opening them. This controls the types of files that trigger validation when Protected View is used to safeguard files that you are opening. You can choose that files be checked when you open a file or save a file, or both. Here's how to review and change the file types Word flags as potential problems:

1. Click the File tab to display Backstage view then click Options.

2. Click Trust Center, and then click the Trust Center Settings button.

3. Click the File Block Settings category (see   for descriptions).

4. Clear the check mark in any file type you don't want to validate.

5. Select those file types that you do want to check in the Open And Save columns (see Figure 20-3).

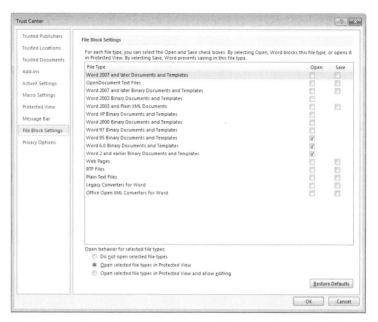

Figure 20-3 You can select which file formats you want Word to validate.

Table 20-1 **File Block Behaviors**

Setting	Description
Do Not Open Selected File Types	The selected files are blocked and will not be opened
Open Selected File Types In Protected View	Opens the selected file in a safe mode that is protected from other files and processes
Open Selected File Types In Protected View And Allow Editing	Opens the selected file type in safe mode but allows the user to edit as normal

Marking a File As Final

Have you ever finished a document and then sent it out to team members or managers, only to receive back a marked up copy with someone's last-minute changes? To avoid this, Word includes the Mark As Final feature with which you can mark a file as final.

When you are finished with a document, double-check it to be sure it's what you want. Then on the File tab, select the Info tab, click Protect Document, and then click Mark As Final. A message box informs you that the document will be marked as final and then saved. Click OK to continue.

After the file is saved, many of the commands on the Ribbon are not available because you can no longer modify the file in any way. A prompt in the message bar lets users know that the file has been marked as final but gives them the option to edit anyway. In addition, a Marked As Final symbol appears in the document's status bar to let you know that the document has been finalized, as shown in Figure 20-4.

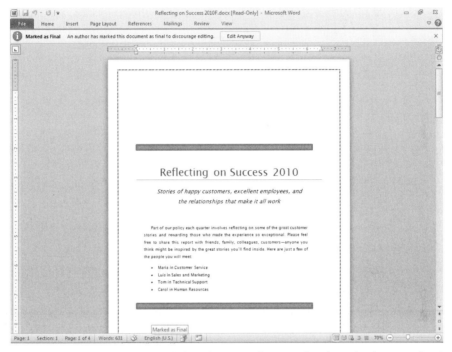

Figure 20-4 The message bar and the indicator in the status bar show the document has been marked as final.

> **Note**
>
> When you use Mark As Final without additional security functionality, such as a digital signature, users can disable the Mark As Final command, edit the document, and turn on Mark As Final again. The only indication that changes have been made is the Save Date. To ensure that the document is secure, be sure to use an additional protection feature such digital signatures.

Encrypting Documents

Another way to restrict which users can open or modify a document is to encrypt the document and use password protection. Encrypting a document encodes it so that it will be unreadable to those who don't have the password. When you encrypt the file, users must enter a password before they can open or change the document. Standard passwords in Word are case-sensitive. They can be up to 15 characters long, and they can contain any combination of letters, numerals, spaces, and symbols. Here's how to encrypt your document:

1. Open the document you want to protect.

2. On the File tab, click Protect Document.

   The Protect Document list appears, as shown in Figure 20-5.

Figure 20-5 On the File tab, click Protect Document to display security options in Word.

3. Click Encrypt With Password.

   The Encrypt Document dialog box appears, as shown in Figure 20-6.

Figure 20-6 The Encrypt Document dialog box is where you can add a password to protect your document

4. Type the password for your document.

After you click OK, Word will prompt you to reenter the password to verify it. After you click OK the second time, password protection and encryption features will be in effect.

CAUTION

It's important that you keep track of the password you assign to your encrypted document because Word has no way to recover it if it is misplaced or forgotten. You might want to keep a backup copy of the document somewhere that is available only to you—just in case.

After you assign a password to open a document, the Password dialog box will appear whenever a user attempts to open the document, as shown in Figure 20-7. To open the document, the user must enter the correct password and click OK. If a user doesn't know the password, she can click Cancel to abort the process.

Figure 20-7 The user must enter the correct password to access an encrypted file.

Removing Protection

You might decide somewhere along the line that you don't need the level of protection you've added to your document after all. If you want to remove permissions or cancel password protection, you can do it easily by performing the following:

- To remove permissions, click Change Permissions in the message bar (below the Ribbon). The Permission dialog box appears. Clear the Restrict Permission To This Document check box then click OK to save your changes. Permissions will no longer be in effect for the current document.

- To cancel password protection, you must first open the document by using the password. On the File tab, display the Info tab in Backstage view, click Protect Document, and then click Encrypt With Password. In the Encrypt Document dialog box, delete the password. Click OK to save the setting, and the password will no longer be used for the document.

> **Note**
>
> In most cases, you'll lose your password protection if you save your document in a format other than Word's native document format. For example, if you save a Word document as a Web page or a PDF file, Word will let you know that password protection will be lost if you continue with the save operation.

Applying Editing Restrictions

You can restrict the available editing and formatting capabilities in a Word document. When you restrict editing, users are able to open the document, but they can't change text beyond how you specify. You can choose to limit formatting changes or editing changes or both. Most of the character formatting tools on the Ribbon, along with other text formatting tools (such as formatting keyboard commands), are inaccessible when a document has formatting restrictions applied. You can control the styles that appear in the Styles gallery and block users' ability to choose different Quick Style sets in the document.

> **Note**
>
> Be aware that even if the document is protected with a password, the Protect Document functionality is intended to be used in a collaborative environment and offers only a limited means of security. For a higher level of security, use encryption, or save the document as a PDF or XPS file.

To restrict formatting and editing, on the File tab, select the Info tab then click Protect Document. Click Restrict Editing. The Restrict Formatting And Editing pane, shown in Figure 20-8, appears along the right side of the Word window.

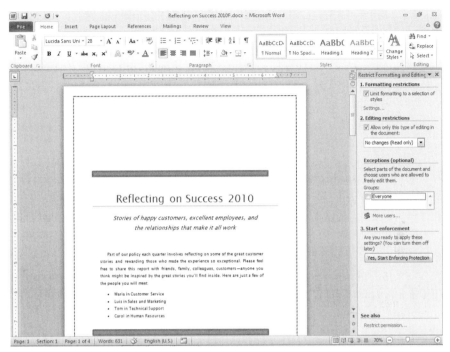

Figure 20-8 You can enable editing restrictions to stop users from making formatting and editing changes in your document.

To set up editing restrictions in the Restrict Formatting And Editing pane, follow these steps:

1. Select the Limit Formatting To A Selection Of Styles check box and then click Settings. The Formatting Restrictions dialog box appears.

2. The Limit Formatting To A Selection Of Styles check box is already selected. Click Settings to go through the list; clear any of the items you want to restrict users from changing in the document.

3. You can take the following actions.

    *   Manually select and clear style check boxes to specify a group of styles that you want to allow users to access.

    *   Select All if you want all styles to be allowed.

    *   Select Recommended Minimum to limit styles to a recommended group of styles.

    *   Select None if you don't want users to have access to any styles.

4. In the Formatting area of the Formatting Restrictions dialog box, choose whether you want to allow AutoFormatting to be applied in spite of formatting restrictions.

    You can also elect to make it impossible for users to change the theme or color scheme, or choose a different Quick Style set. Select the check box of any item you want to apply then click OK.

    If the document contains styles that you didn't select in Step 3, a message box appears, stating that the document contains formatting or styles that aren't allowed and asking whether you would like to remove them.

    Click No to apply the formatting settings without changing the document's current formatting, or click Yes to remove the styles from the document. Keep in mind that if you click None in Step 3 and then click Yes in the message box in this step, your document will be formatted in Normal style throughout. In most cases, you'll probably want to retain the current formatting in the document, so you should click No in the message box.

5. In the Restrict Formatting And Editing pane, select the Allow Only This Type Of Editing In The Document check box, and choose one of the following from the list:

    - **No Changes (Read only)**   Limits all editing changes in the document

    - **Tracked Changes**   Users can make changes but turns on revision marks

    - **Comments**   Limits users to adding comments in the text

    - **Filling In Forms**   Allows users to only add form information

6. In the Exceptions area, you can indicate who (if anyone) you want to be able to be exceptions to the rules you have just added.

    The list of names is extracted from your contacts list. Click More Users to add users to the list. You can click the arrow at the end of the Everyone selection to specify regions of the document where the exceptions will be in effect.

7. Click Yes then click Start Enforcing Protection. The Start Enforcing Protection dialog box opens.

8. In the Start Enforcing Protection dialog box, enter a password in the Enter New Password (Optional) box and then re-enter the password in the Re-enter Password To Confirm box.

    If you don't want to use password protection, leave the password boxes empty. Click OK to complete the procedure.

After formatting restrictions are enforced, users won't be able to apply character formats or use styles that aren't included on the approved list of styles.

To turn off formatting restrictions, click Protect Document again, click Stop Protection at the bottom of the Restrict Formatting And Editing pane, enter a password if required, and then click OK.

Removing Personal Information and Hidden Data

One easy security measure you can take when sharing documents with others is to remove information you don't intend for others to see. For example, you can remove personal information so that people who view your document won't be able to see the names of reviewers, the author of the document, and so forth. If your document contains other hidden information, you'll want to eliminate that as well. If you don't delete hidden information, other people who view your document might see data you'd rather they didn't, especially if they save your Word document in another file format (information hidden in a Word document doesn't remain hidden when a Word document is saved in another format and viewed in another application). This section shows you how to remove personal information from documents before you share the documents with others.

In addition to removing personal information, be sure to remove hidden text and accept or reject any tracked changes before you pass your document to others. For more information about accepting and rejecting tracked changes, see Chapter 22, "Collaborating and Co-Authoring in Real Time."

Removing Personal Information

In Word, you can easily remove the following types of personal information:

- File properties, such as author name, manager name, company name, and last saved by information

- Names associated with comments and revisions (Word will change reviewers' names to *Author* automatically)

- Routing slips

- E-mail message headers generated when you click the E-Mail button

To remove these informational tidbits, run the Document Inspector, which is available in the Check For Issues list on the Info tab in Backstage view. Here are the steps:

1. With your file open, on the File tab, click Check For Issues on the Info tab.

2. Click Inspect Document.

The Document Inspector dialog box appears, as you see in Figure 20-9. All items are selected. This means that all the listed checks will be performed automatically. If you want to skip any of the items in the list, clear the item's check box.

Figure 20-9 The Document Inspector searches the document for sensitive, personal, or hidden information and prompts you to remove it.

3. Click Inspect to evaluate the document. The results show you what the Document Inspector found. If hidden items were discovered, the Inspector alerts you and provides a Remove All button for each inspection type so that you can delete the unwanted information.

4. Click Remove All to clear the unwanted items.

5. Click Reinspect to run the Document Inspector again.

6. When the inspection reveals no more hidden information, click the Close button to complete the process and return to your document.

Preparing PDF and XPS Files

For years, Word users have been asking for PDF support for their Word documents. Now at last in Word 2010, the feature is built into the functioning of the program. You can use two different methods to save your file as a PDF or XPS file: use the Save & Send tab in Backstage view, or use the Save As dialog box.

Understanding PDF and XPS

PDF (Portable Document Format) files are saved in a fixed layout, meaning that although readers can view, print, and share files, they cannot modify the format or content. Users must have a special PDF reader to read PDF files. The most popular PDF reader is Acrobat Reader, a free downloadable utility from Adobe Systems (*www.adobe.com*). Because PDF preserves the format of the final document, this format is often used for submitting final files to commercial printers, to post documents online, and to save and share work that includes highly detailed and colorful graphics.

XPS is a fixed-layout format that has been developed by Microsoft. The format is actually a page-definition format that creates the page electronically in a way that can be read by people, programs, and PCs. Similar to PDF, XPS file format allows users to view, print, and share files but limits others from making changes in the file itself.

To learn more about the XPS format, visit the XPS Web site at *www.microsoft.com/whdc/xps/*.

Saving Your Document As PDF and XPS

The actual process for saving your file in PDF or XPS format is super simple. Just open the document you want to use and click File to display Backstage view. Click the Save & Send tab and then click Create PDF/XPS Document. Click Create a PDF/XPS.

The Publish As PDF or XPS dialog box appears, in which you can navigate to the folder where you want to store the file. Click in the File Name box and type a name for the file, then click Save As Type to choose either PDF or XPS Document.

If you want to view the file after saving it, select the Open File After Publishing check box. In the Optimize For area, choose whether you want to save the file in Standard or Minimum size. Click the Options button to display choices about the page ranges included in the file and the type of information saved with the file (see Figure 20-10).

After you click OK, the file is saved in the format you specified. If you selected the Open After Publishing check box and you have a PDF or XPS reader installed on your computer, the file will open automatically so that you can see your file the way others will view it.

Figure 20-10 Choose Options to enter your preferences for the range of pages and information to be included in the PDF or XPS file.

Signing Your Documents with Digital Signatures and Stamps

Word lets you digitally sign your documents so that others know the file is authentic—and you can add stamp signature lines as well. Word supports digital certificates that are provided by third-party vendors (the program has a built-in link to Office Marketplace where you can evaluate different services easily) as well as digital certificates that you create yourself. There are a couple of items to bear in mind when deciding on what type of signature you want to use:

- When a document is prepared using a third-party digital signature service, the document is authenticated and people who receive your files can be certain they have been authenticated.

- When you create a digital certificate yourself, the item is not authenticated, but it does provide a useful service. A document you digitally sign indicates to the user that they are receiving a document that has not been modified since you created it. (A digital signature becomes invalid if the document is revised after it is signed.)

> **Note**
> Microsoft Excel 2010, Word 2010, and PowerPoint 2010 all support digital signatures.

Getting a Digital ID

To get your own digital ID, on the File tab, click Protect Document and then click Add A Digital Signature. If you don't have a signature of your own, a message box appears explaining the limits and availability of digital signatures. The message box also provides a button you can click to see the signature services that are available from third-party sources on Office Marketplace (see Figure 20-11).

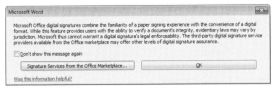

Figure 20-11 You can opt to obtain a digital ID from a vendor or create your own in the Get A Digital ID dialog box.

Chapter 20

> ## Working with Certificate Authorities and Security Administrators
>
> When you obtain a digital certificate from a certification authority, you must submit an application to the authority and pay a fee (which is usually an annual rate based on the type of security you want to obtain). When you receive your digital certificate, the certification authority provides instructions for installation. Similarly, if you work with an in-house security administrator, you'll need to follow your organization's policies regarding how digital certificates are distributed and how they are added to your macros and files.

Creating a Digital ID

When you see the Get A Digital ID dialog box, click Create Your Own Digital ID then click OK; the Create A Digital ID dialog box appears, in which you can fill in your information and click Create to create your own digital certificate. Remember, however, that this type of certification is unauthenticated, so it doesn't provide much security assurance to others outside your local area network. However, it can assure those receiving your files that they have the most recent version of your original work.

When you click OK, the Sign dialog box appears, providing an area for you to enter the reason you are signing the document (see Figure 20-12). Additionally, you can verify that you are the person shown to be signing the document (if others use your computer, be sure to verify that the correct digital ID appears in the Signing As: line). Click the Sign button to add your digital signature to the document.

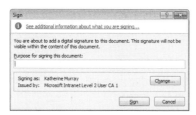

Figure 20-12 Use the Sign dialog box to enter your purpose for signing and complete the process.

The Signature Confirmation dialog box lets you know that your signature has been saved with the document. If the document is changed after this point, the signature will no longer be valid and you will need to re-sign the document.

At this point, you've successfully created an unauthenticated digital certificate that you can use to sign your documents.

Attaching a Digital Signature to a File

After you create or obtain a digital certificate, you can authenticate your files by digitally signing them. Basically, digitally signing a file means that you've attached your digital certificate to the document. In the last section, you saw how Word 2010 automatically applies the newly created digital ID to the currently open document. If you want to attach your digital signature to another file, follow these steps:

1. Open the document you want to digitally sign.

2. On the File tab, click Protect Document on the Info tab and click Add A Digital Signature. Click OK in the message box that appears.

3. The Sign dialog box is displayed. Type the purpose for signing the document and verify that the Signing As value is correct.

4. Click the Sign button to attach your signature to the document.

INSIDE OUT   How Can I Tell that a Document Has Been Digitally Signed?

When a digital signature has been added to a document, a small red symbol appears in the status bar of your Word document. When you position the mouse pointer over the symbol, the ToolTip displays the message, "This document contains signatures." To display information about the signatures, click the symbol once. Signatures are displayed in the Signatures pane along the right side of the Word window.

Adding a Stamp

The stamp signature feature in Word 2010 enables you to use an image, or if you have an inking feature, such as on a Tablet PC—a hand-written signature, as a stamp on your Word documents. (Note that this feature is also available for Excel workbooks.)

You will need a digital ID to add a stamp signature to your documents. The process involves two parts: first you create the stamp signature line in the document, and then you add the image you want to use for the stamp and digitally sign it. (Note that depending on how you will be using the document, you might be creating it and sending it to another person, who then signs the signature line and returns it to you.)

To add the stamp signature line to the document, on the Insert tab, click the Signature Line arrow in the Text group. Select Stamp Signature Line. The Signature Setup dialog box appears, in which you can enter the signer's information and add any instructions you want the signer to see before signing. Click OK to save your changes.

To sign the stamp signature line, double-click it. The Sign dialog box appears. Click Select Image to display a dialog box, in which you can select the image you want to use as your digital signature. Navigate to the file and click Select, then simply click Sign and the stamp signature is added to the document.

Viewing Signatures

When a document has been digitally signed, the View Signatures option automatically displays when you open the document. When you click View Signatures in the message bar at the top of the Word window, the Signatures pane appears along the right side of the signed document by default. A small certificate indicator in the status bar also shows you that the document has signatures, as shown in the following illustration:

Click the File tab to display Backstage view to find out more about the signatures in your document (see Figure 20-13). Click View Signatures to display the signature in the Signatures task pane, along the right side of your document. You can display more information about the signature by clicking the arrow and clicking your choice in the list that appears. After you add the signature to the file, the Info tab lets you know you are working with a signed document and gives you the option of viewing the signatures (see Figure 20-14).

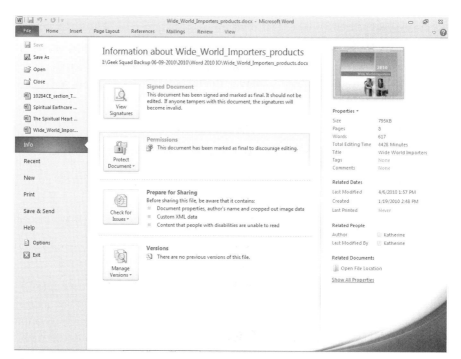

Figure 20-13 Click View Signatures to see the signatures in the Signatures task pane.

Figure 20-14 You can find out more about the signature in the Signatures task pane.

Removing a Signature

After you add a certificate to a document, you can remove it at any time. To do so, click the File tab to display Backstage view, then display the Signatures list by clicking View Signatures on the Info tab. Click the arrow of the signature you want to remove and select Remove Signature. The Remove Signature dialog box appears, asking you to confirm that you want to complete the operation. Click Yes to delete the signature. Note, however, that this action simply removes the signature from the current document—it doesn't delete the certificate.

Checking for the Red X

When you are checking the certificates associated with files you receive, be on the lookout for the red X. A digital certificate displayed with a red X might mean the certificate is unauthenticated or cannot be verified. A red X can also indicate the following security issues associated with a certificate:

- Someone has tampered with the signed file.

- The certificate was not issued by a trusted certification authority.

- The certificate was issued without verification (such as a free certificate authority trial download).

- The certificate was invalid when it was used to sign the file or macros.

When you see a certificate with a red X, proceed with caution. This is a clear sign that something about the certificate is amiss.

Working with the Trust Center

Each of the Microsoft Office 2010 programs includes the Trust Center, a special area within the program options where you to control settings related to security and privacy. Some Trust Center settings you enter in one application flow through to other applications as well.

To display the Word Trust Center, follow these steps.

1. On the File tab, click Options.

2. Click Trust Center, which is located in the navigation pane on the left side of the dialog box, then click the Trust Center Settings button.

   The Trust Center opens, as you see in Figure 20-15.

Chapter 20

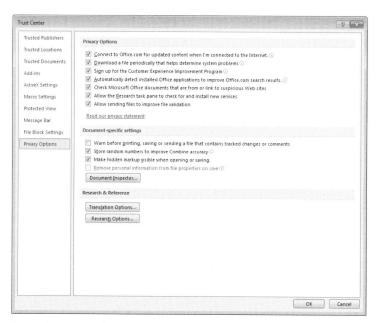

Figure 20-15 Use the Trust Center to set security and privacy options while you work with Word.

The Trust Center includes 10 different categories, each tailored to a specific area of security or privacy. Here's a quick run-down of what you'll find in the various groups.

- **Trusted Publishers**   Displays a list of the digital certificates you've accepted from other individuals or companies. When you open a document that includes a macro, the Message Bar appears alerting you to that fact. If the document is from a trusted source, and if a digital signature has been added, you can choose to add that publisher to your Trusted Publishers list.

- **Trusted Locations**   Shows the locations that you have accepted as safe sources for files you open. You can add new locations, change locations, or remove locations by working with the options on the Trusted Locations screen. Note that the Workgroup Templates folder (found in Word Options/Advanced and File Locations at the bottom) is also considered a trusted location and it does not automatically appear in this list.

- **Trusted Documents**   Specifies documents or network folders that you trust so those files will not cause Protected View to display.

- **Add-ins**   Determines whether you will require the authentication of add-ins (meaning they must be signed by someone in your Trusted Publisher's list before you approve their installation) or whether you choose to disable all add-ins.

- **ActiveX Settings**   Gives you the choice of what to do with ActiveX controls that do not come from a trusted source. Your options range from totally disallowing ActiveX controls to running them after being prompted to openly running all ActiveX controls (which is not recommended for security reasons).

- **Macro Settings**   Offers selections for working with macros that are not authenticated or from a trusted location. You can disallow them, disable macros with notification, allow only macros with digital signatures, or enable all macros unconditionally (again, not recommended).

- **Protected View**   Presents you with the option of changing the items that trigger Word to display Protected View.

- **Message Bar**   Enables you to choose whether you want the message bar to display information when content has been blocked.

- **File Block Settings**   Lets you choose which files are blocked or displayed in Protected View when you first open them.

- **Privacy Options**   Includes several different groups of settings that help you control how much information is shared about your computer use and individual documents. Additionally, you can set your preferences for the Research and Translate tools in Word.

Simply choose the settings that best fit the way you want your version of Word to operate and then click OK to save your settings. The settings you select in the Trust Center are global settings, meaning they are in effect for the entire application. You can at any time return to the Trust Center to check or remove Trusted Publishers, change Trusted Locations, or modify any of the settings you've previously entered.

Viewing and Removing Trusted Sources

When you open a file that includes digitally signed macros (and the signer isn't included on your Trusted Publishers list, as described in this section), you'll be asked whether you want to trust all macros from the signer. If you click Yes, the signer will be added to your list of trusted publishers. Before you add a signer, you should carefully review the publisher's certificate (watch for the red X). You should especially review the certificate's Issued To, Issued By, and Valid From fields. After you add a signer to your Trusted Publishers list, in the future, Word will automatically enable macros signed by the publisher. As you add new trusted sources, they'll be added to the Trusted Publishers list.

Chapter 20

If you later decide that you'd like to remove a signer from your Trusted Publishers list, you can do so at any time, as follows:

1. On the File tab, click Options, then click Trust Center and choose Trust Center Settings.

2. Click Trusted Publishers in the navigation bar in the Trust Center window.

3. Select the publisher you want to remove. Click Remove, and then click OK.

Microsoft digitally signs all add-ins and templates (if they contain macros) that you download from Office Online. After you add Microsoft to your list of trusted publishers for one of these installed files, all subsequent interactions with these files will not generate messages.

Setting Permission Levels

Depending on the suite of Office 2010 you are using, you might also be able to control a variety of permission levels so that those viewing and working with your document are granted only the access that you specify. This feature is known as Information Rights Management (IRM) functionality; it is how you customize the permissions users are given so that they can access and modify your file.

With IRM functionality, you can restrict permission to Word documents and document content so that only those who you want to have access to your files can open them; you can also control whether documents can be forwarded, printed, or accessed after a specified number of days; and, you can specify the following three access levels for Word documents:

- **Read** Allows specified users to read a document but not edit, print, or copy the content.

- **Change** Allows specified users to read, edit, and save changes to a document but not print the document.

- **Full Control** Gives specified users full authoring permissions and the freedom to do anything with a document. (Document authors always have full control.)

To set access levels for specified users, use the Permission dialog box, as shown in Figure 20-16. To open the Permission dialog box, on the File tab, point to Protect Document on the Info tab, point to Restrict Permission By People, and click Restricted Access. After the Permission dialog box appears, select the Restrict Permission To This Document check box to make the Read and Change boxes available.

Figure 20-16 You use the Permission dialog box to grant Read or Change access to users by entering their e-mail addresses in the Read or Change boxes.

Customizing Permissions

Along with access levels, you can set additional permissions and settings using the Permission dialog box. To access the additional permissions and settings options, click the More Options button in the lower-left corner of the Permission dialog box. You can also change a user's access level in the More Options dialog box by clicking the Access Level setting next to the user's e-mail address and selecting a new access level. Additional permissions and settings that you can set for each user include the following:

- **This Document Expires On**   Sets an expiration date for the document, after which the document will be unavailable to selected users.

- **Print Content**   Grants printing capabilities to users with Read or Change access levels.

- **Allow Users With Read Access To Copy Content**   Enables users with Read access to copy the entire or partial document.

- **Access Content Programmatically**   Enables users to use certain Word program features in the document, such as Smart Tags.

- **Users Can Request Additional Permissions From**   Specifies an address that users can send requests to change their permission status.

- **Require A Connection To Verify A User's Permission**   Requires that users connect to the Internet to verify their credentials each time they access the document.

- **Set Defaults**   Sets the current settings as the default for documents with restricted permissions.

Chapter 20

Applying Permissions to Documents

To apply permissions to a document, follow these steps.

1. Open the document you want to protect.

2. On the File tab, click Protect Document on the Info tab.

3. Click Restrict Permission By People then click Restricted Access.

4. In the Permission dialog box, select the Restrict Permission To This Document check box.

5. Click the Change or Read label (hovering the mouse pointer over the label will change the label to a button) to access your address book or enter e-mail addresses in the Read or Change boxes of the users who can access the document.

   If you're entering more than one e-mail address, separate the addresses with a semicolon. If desired, click More Options to further configure user permissions.

6. Click OK to save your settings.

When you open the document in the future, the message bar shows that the document now has restricted access (see Figure 20-17). If you want to change the settings currently in effect for the document, you can click Change Permission to display the Permissions dialog box.

Figure 20-17 The message bar, just below the Ribbon, lets you know that restrictions have been applied to the current document.

Checking Document Accessibility

Another important check for documents that you create to share with others—or post in a public folder or shared drive—concerns the issue of accessibility. More than ever before, all kinds of users are working with Microsoft Office files, no matter what their skills and limitations might be. In order to ensure that differently-abled workers can access the content in your Word file, you can use the Accessibility Checker.

On the File tab, point to Check For Issues on the Info tab. Click Check Accessibility. The Accessibility Checker task pane appears along the right side of your Word window, showing the results of the test (see Figure 20-18). In the top half of the pane, you can view the Inspection Results, which lists all the issues Word found in your document. In the lower portion of the pane, you see Additional Information, which tells you why it is important to fix the selected issue and provides suggestions for the ways in which you can do so.

Work one by one through the various items and when you've completed the changes, save the document and run the Accessibility Checker once more to ensure that your file is ready to share.

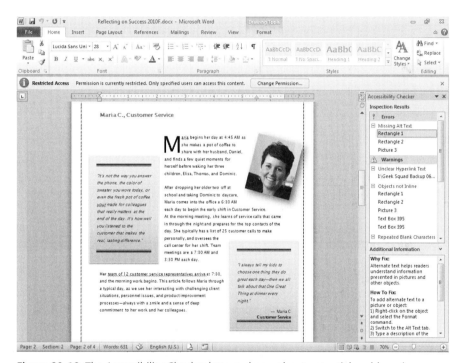

Figure 20-18 The Accessibility Checker lets you know about potential problems in your document that might hinder others who need to access it.

Ensuring Document Compatibility

When your work requires that you share your Word 2010 document with others who are using previous versions of Word, you might not think anything about the different file formats until one of your peers lets you know that your Word 2010 document can't be opened in Word 2003.

There are two workarounds for this. First, your peer can download the Microsoft Office Compatibility Pack from Microsoft at *www.microsoft.com/downloads* and run the utility so that she can open Word 2010 files. Second, you can run the Compatibility Checker to see which features, if any, might be unavailable if you save your file in an earlier version of Word.

To run the Compatibility Checker, on the File tab, click Check For Issues on the Info tab. Click Check Compatibility. The Microsoft Word Compatibility Checker dialog box appears, listing any features that might be unavailable and giving you a description of what the difference means (see Figure 20-19). You can click the arrow to choose the versions of Word you want to check against. Click OK when you're done.

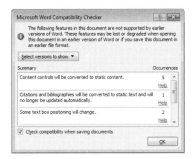

Figure 20-19 The Microsoft Word Compatibility Checker lets you to see which features will be unavailable to peers using a previous version of Word.

What's Next?

This chapter has introduced you to the far-reaching security and privacy features in Word 2010. Now that you know how to manage the access to your files, you can prepare to share, edit, review, and compare collaborative documents, which just happens to be what the next chapter is all about.

Sharing Your Documents

Sharing Documents in Word 641

Word 2010 New Sharing Options 644

A Closer Look at SharePoint Workspace 2010 646

Setting Up and Using Windows Live SkyDrive. 651

Working with Network Locations 654

Using Workgroup Templates 656

Sharing Word Documents via E-Mail 658

Using Word to Send Faxes 663

What's Next? 666

ONCE upon a time, we typed our documents in our ho-hum word-processing programs, sent the file to the printer, carried the printed pages down the hall, and handed them to a colleague for review. Projects were completed in a linear, assembly-line fashion; one person finished a section, another created the design, a layout person assembled the document, and a proofreader looked it all over.

Today things happen much faster and much more collaboratively than that. You might be part of a team—with colleagues on different continents—and you could all be working simultaneously to complete a document within a specific timeframe. You're working on the executive summary while she writes the financial narrative. He's putting together the charts, and she's gathering the list of bios for your board members.

When the draft is done you all need to review it, make comments and changes, tweak the almost-done piece, and finalize your work. How can you do this as a team? How do you share files easily (perhaps across long distances) and not override each other's work? Word 2010 includes a number of features that make collaborating easier than ever. In fact, collaboration was one of the banner design elements as Word 2010 was in development. In this chapter you learn about the various ways in which you can share your documents with your colleagues. (In the next chapter, you find out how to use revision marks, compare and merge, and the new co-authoring tools to fine-tune your shared document.)

Sharing Documents in Word

The developers of Word 2010 realize that you don't work in a vacuum and that you need to collaborate—easily—on the documents you create. They know this, at least in part, because they work the same way. In today's highly connected and accelerated workplace, projects need to be progressing in many areas all at once—businesses can't afford to take months preparing a document while one colleague after another has her turn with a revision.

Word 2010 includes a number of features that make collaboration easier—and more secure—than ever. With the addition of SharePoint Workspaces 2010 in the Microsoft Office Professional Plus 2010 suite, Word users who work with SharePoint Server can easily move their documents to and from the server. If you work at home or at the office using one of the other Office 2010 suites, you can use your Windows Live SkyDrive account with Office 2010 Web Apps to post your content online and share the files with colleagues.

In addition to these online possibilities, Word 2010 includes a number of tools in the Save & Share tab of Backstage view that you can use to share files in a variety of ways. Whether you're sending a file as an XML Paper Specification (XPS) or Portable Document Format (PDF) attachment, posting it on a document server or SharePoint site, or sending the file as an Internet fax, when you click the Microsoft Office Button, you'll find commands to help you accomplish your objectives.

- If you want to send your document as an e-mail message or as an attachment to a message in either PDF or XPS format, you'll find the options you want by clicking the File tab to display Backstage view then clicking Save & Send (see Figure 21-1). This is also where you'll go if you want to send an Internet fax.

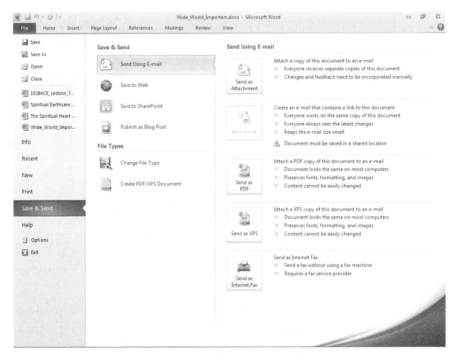

Figure 21-1 Use the tools in the Save & Send tab to send a document as an e-mail message, as an attachment, or as a fax.

- If you want to post the document to a document server or create a document work-space by using Windows SharePoint Services, click Save to Web or Save to SharePoint to see the choices that appear in the rightmost column (see Figure 21-2).

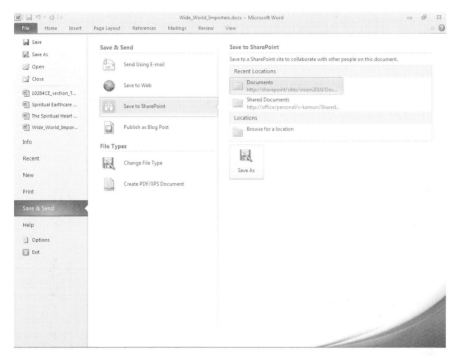

Figure 21-2 You can also save the document to a document server or to your Windows Live SkyDrive account using the tools in the Save & Send tab.

In addition to these sharing techniques, you might want to collaborate with team members using any (or all!) of the following methods:

- Sending files back and forth while you're instant messaging with group members

- Posting updated files directly to network server space

- Creating shared files and folders that others on your team can access

- Creating and sharing workgroup templates

- Sharing information via fax and e-mail

- Creating a dynamic shared workspace with Microsoft SharePoint Workspace 2010

Throughout this chapter, you learn more about using these features. The world is getting smaller by the minute! The techniques in this chapter show you how to increase your effectiveness and share-ability in Word 2010.

Word 2010 New Sharing Options

The developers of Word 2010 understood and took seriously the fact that the world is rapidly becoming smaller at the same time that our workplace is expanding. We often work collaboratively with colleagues who could be just about anywhere—down the hall, in another state, or living and working on another continent. What's more, the colleague may be sitting at his desk, working on a remote laptop, or simply checking documents as he carries his cell phone around with him during the day.

How does Word 2010 accommodate all these possible work styles? Two key tools help you organize, share, and work on your documents in a way that supports all kinds of configurations:

- Microsoft SharePoint Workspace 2010 is part of the Microsoft Office Professional Plus 2010 suite; it enables enterprise workers who have access to Microsoft SharePoint 2010 to create a shared workspace, in which they can organize, upload, download, and check in or check out files the team will use. SharePoint Workspace also includes the ability to create Groove workspaces, in which you can hold meetings, chat in real time, share screens, assign tasks, and more (see Figure 21-3).

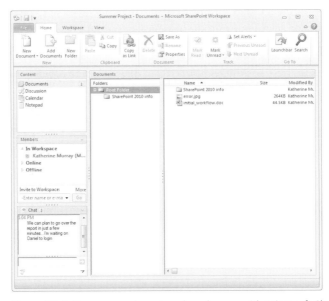

Figure 21-3 You can create a shared workspace with Microsoft SharePoint Workspace 2010, where you can share and organize files easily.

- If you are using one of the other Office 2010 suites, you can post your files and share them online using Windows Live SkyDrive (see Figure 21-4). This seamless file posting and sharing is part of the access and support for Office Web Apps, which include the Word Web App, PowerPoint Web App, OneNote Web App, and Excel Web App. Using Windows Live SkyDrive you can post files, set permissions, and check files in and out. Using the Word Web App, you can edit the document online—alone or with co-authors—and control the way the document is shared.

Figure 21-4 Windows Live SkyDrive is a free online account that you can use to post, share, create, organize, and co-author files, presentations, notebooks, and workbooks.

Tip

You learn more about editing and co-authoring shared files in the Word Web App in Chapter 22, "Collaborating and Co-Authoring in Real Time."

A Closer Look at SharePoint Workspace 2010

SharePoint Workspace 2010 is part of Microsoft Office Professional Plus 2010, and its primary purpose is to enable you to easily move files from the server to your computer so that you can work with them offline. After you complete your work, you can seamlessly sync the file back to the server, where others can check it out and work with it.

You can also create Groove workspaces, which add more than document and file management features. When you create a Groove workspace in SharePoint Workspace 2010, you can chat in real time with your workspace colleagues, add tasks and actions, hold discussions, and much more.

Creating a New Workspace

If SharePoint Workspace 2010 is part of your Office 2010 suite, you can launch the software by clicking the Start button on the taskbar, pointing to All Programs, clicking Microsoft Office, and choosing Microsoft SharePoint Workspace 2010. You are asked to create an account, and then the program's Launchbar appears, showing any SharePoint workspaces or Groove workspaces you currently have permissions to use (see Figure 21-5).

Figure 21-5 The SharePoint Workspace 2010 Launchbar lists all your workspaces and is where you can get in touch with contacts.

To add a new workspace to SharePoint Workspaces, click the New arrow and choose one of the following options:

- **SharePoint Workspace**   This creates a workspace in which you can synchronize files with files on your server.

- **Groove Workspace**   This option creates a workspace that includes tools like chat, lists, a sketchpad, and more.

- **Shared Folder**   Specifies one of the folders on your computer that you can share with users who have the necessary permissions.

You can also create a new SharePoint Workspace while you're working on the SharePoint Server site. When you click Site Actions in the SharePoint Server site and choose Sync to SharePoint Workspace from the list (see Figure 21-6), SharePoint will prompt you to download the files you need. When the download is complete, SharePoint lets you know (see Figure 21-7).

Figure 21-6 You can create a new SharePoint Workspace from the SharePoint Server by clicking Site Actions and choosing Sync to SharePoint Workspace.

Chapter 21

Figure 21-7 SharePoint creates the workspace for you; when the process is complete, click Open Workspace.

After you click the Open Workspace button, SharePoint Workspace 2010 launches (if it isn't already open), displaying the new workspace. Click the Documents folder then double-click the file you'd like to open. The document opens in the familiar Word window.

Collaborating with Groove Workspaces

If you used Office Groove 2007 previously—which was available in Microsoft Office Ultimate 2007 and Microsoft Office Enterprise 2007—you'll be pleased to know it is now a part of SharePoint Workspace 2010. Where SharePoint Workspace helps you take files offline and work on them, Groove workspaces give you the means to connect and bring small teams together in a virtual workspace.

Groove really shines for collaborative projects, offering instant chat features, shared calendars, discussion groups, file sharing, alerts, whiteboards for group presentations, and more. And Groove syncs easily both with your individual computer (you can work on projects offline and then update files when you log in) and with SharePoint, so you can update lists and download information seamlessly.

Groove is ideal for creating, managing, and sharing libraries of Word documents related to a specific project or workgroup. Together, SharePoint Workspace 2010 and Groove give you the means to organize, protect, share, and brainstorm all that's needed to get your projects done.

Chapter 21

Checking Out and Checking In a Document

When you open a document you've saved to SharePoint Workspace 2010, the message bar lets you know the status of the document. If the document is currently checked in to the server, it will be unavailable for you to edit. You can click Check Out in the message bar to check the file out of the server site and open it in SharePoint Workspace 2010 (see Figure 21-8). While the file is checked out to you, no one else will be able to edit it.

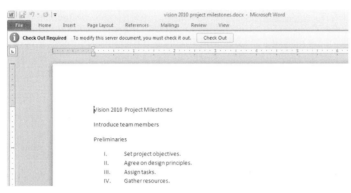

Figure 21-8 Use the message bar to check out a file and open it in SharePoint Workspace 2010.

You can edit the file normally, applying formats, adding content, including all the elements, styles, diagrams, and more that you would include in any Word document. When you are ready to save the file back to the server, click the File tab to display Backstage view. The Check In area on the Info tab lets you know the status of the file (see Figure 21-9). You can click Check In to sync the file with the server and return it to checked in status, or, if you didn't make changes to the file or want to abandon what you've done, you can click Discard Check Out.

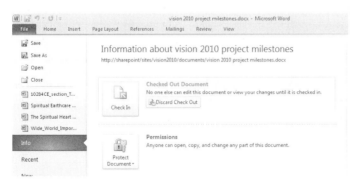

Figure 21-9 Click Check In to check the file back in to the server or click Discard Check Out to abandon your changes.

Create and Save a New Document

You can create a new document in SharePoint Workspace 2010 and post it to the server as needed. Begin in SharePoint Workspace 2010, and open the workspace you want to use. In the Documents list, click the folder in which you want to store the new file. Then, on the Home tab, click New Document. Word opens a new document and displays file properties at the top of the file. You can click in the fields to type the document name as well as the start date and end date.

When you are ready to save the file to the server, click the Save icon in the Quick Access Toolbar. The Save As dialog box opens, showing the server location area in the Look In field at the top of the dialog box (see Figure 21-10). Enter additional file information (such as adding tags to aid in searching) and click Save. After the file is saved to the server, the server location appears in the top-right of the document (see Figure 21-11).

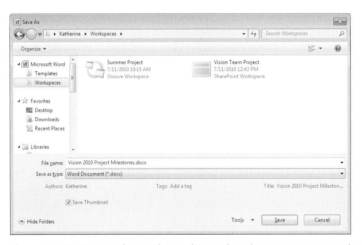

Figure 21-10 You can choose the workspace location you want to use in the Save As dialog box.

Figure 21-11 The location of the document appears in the top right corner.

Setting Up and Using Windows Live SkyDrive

If you are using an Office 2010 suite that doesn't include SharePoint Workspace 2010, another method of sharing files online is available to you. Using Windows Live SkyDrive, you can post and share folders and files from Word, Excel, PowerPoint, and more. All you need to log in to your SkyDrive account is your Windows Live ID. Here are the steps for logging in and displaying your SkyDrive account:

1. Open your Web browser and go to *www.windowslive.com*.

2. Log in with your Windows Live ID and password.

3. In the window that opens, click Office at the top of the screen.

4. A list of files (if any) you've previously posted to the site are displayed (see Figure 21-12).

5. Add files by clicking the Add Files link.

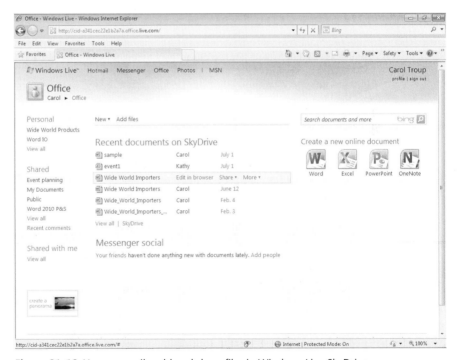

Figure 21-12 You can easily add and share files in Windows Live SkyDrive.

Sharing a File

In order to share the files you post in Windows Live SkyDrive with others, you need to give permissions to the individuals with whom you want to work so they can access the account and the files. To set the necessary permissions and share the file, display your Windows Live SkyDrive account and hover the mouse over the file you want to share. Links will appear at the mouse position. Click Share then choose Edit Permissions (see Figure 21-13).

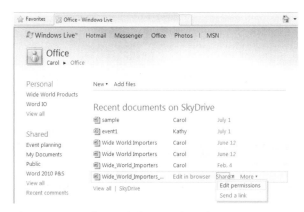

Figure 21-13 Edit permissions to give others access to your files.

In the Permissions window, click the Documents link, and in the Information area, click People I Selected. Next, click Edit Permissions and, in the Add Specific People line, type the e-mail addresses of those with whom you want to share the files in your My Documents folder. Windows Live adds each person to the list at the bottom of the window.

Set the permissions level for each person by clicking the permissions arrow for each contact and choosing one of the following options:

- **Can View Files**   This option limits the recipient to read-only permissions; they won't be able to change the content of the file.

- **Can Add, Edit Details, And Delete Files**   This option assigns the necessary permission to edit, reformat, and even delete the files in the folder.

After you set permissions, click Save. In the Send A Notification window, you can add a message explaining what the link is for, and then click Send to send the message.

Save Your Document to a Shared Space

Word 2010 makes the process of saving files to your Windows Live SkyDrive as seamless as possible. In fact, you can create an account and post files to SkyDrive in one smooth step from within Word. Here's how to do it:

1.   Open the document you want to save online.

2.   Click the File tab to display Backstage view.

3.   On the Save & Send tab, click Save to Web; the options in the right panel change to reflect your choice.

4.   Click one of the folders shown or click New to sign in and create a new folder.

Word 2010 also gives you the option of switching users (in Figure 21-14, notice that the option is "Not Carol?"). Word 2010 also gives you the option of signing in, if you haven't already done that. And if you haven't previously created a Windows Live account, a button will appear so you can do that from within Word.

To complete the save, simply click the folder you want to use or click New and follow the on-screen prompts to save the file.

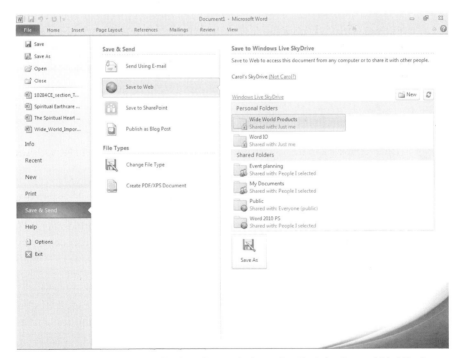

Figure 21-14 You can save a file directly to Windows Live SkyDrive from within Word.

Chapter 21

> **Tip**
> Windows Live also includes a Windows Live Sign-In Assistant that you can install so that you don't need to sign in to Windows Live in the future when you save a document to your online account.

Working with Network Locations

In the true spirit of Web and desktop integration, you can use Word to create, copy, save, and manage folders and files that reside on a network, the Web, File Transfer Protocol (FTP) servers, or in a shared workspace. After you create shortcuts to online folders (and if you have the proper permissions), you can work with online files and folders as though they were on your local computer. Of course, taking advantage of working with networks and the Web implies that you are connected to a network or have a connection to the Internet. The first order of business when you're working with online documents involves configuring your system so that you can access network places and FTP sites.

Creating a Network Location

Your first step involves mapping the network drive to specify to Windows the location of the folder that will store the files. Although you can access documents and folders in existing Network Places from within Word, you need to set up links to new network places by using the Add Network Location Wizard.

To create a network place in Windows Vista or Windows 7, follow these steps:

1. Click the Start button then click Computer.

2. Right-click in the Computer window and then click Add A Network Location.

3. Follow the steps on the Add Network Location Wizard pages to create a link to the network place.

After you add a network location, you can access documents and folders on the network place from within Word.

Linking to FTP Sites

In the same way that you access other network places, you can add FTP sites to your list of Internet sites, if you have access to a network or the Internet. You can also add FTP sites to your list of network places while you're working in Word. To create shortcuts to FTP sites, follow these steps:

1. Click the Start button then click Computer.

2. Right-click in the window and choose Add A Network Location to start the wizard.

3. Click Next, then click Choose A Custom Network Location. Click Next again.

4. Enter the FTP address in the form **ftp://ftp.address.com**. Click Next.

5. Enter your login information for the FTP site or leave Log On Anonymously checked. Click Next.

6. Type a name for the connection, click Next, and then click Finish.

The FTP site will be available in the Computer area of the Open and Save As dialog boxes. You can now choose that location as needed for opening and saving your files.

Accessing Resources Stored in Network Locations

You access network locations in the same way that you access local files and folders—simply navigate to the online file and folder locations in the Open dialog box and then create a local shortcut to the document, if desired. To open an online folder or file by using the Open dialog box, follow these steps:

1. On the File tab, click Open.

2. In the Open dialog box, scroll down the list on the left. Click the FTP site or network folder you added.

3. Navigate to the file you want to open, select it, and click Open to begin working with the file.

Saving Documents to a Network Location

In addition to opening files from network locations, you'll probably want to save files to online locations. The process of saving files to online locations is similar to saving files locally. To save a newly-created file to an online location, follow these steps:

1. On the File tab, click Save As.

2. In the Save As dialog box, click the name of the network location or FTP site you added. (Double-click any subfolders you want to access as well.)

3. In the File Name box, type a name for the file (or retain the current name) then click Save.

> **Note**
> If you open a document from a network location, you can save your changes to the online document by pressing Ctrl+S. To save the document locally, you must first use the Save As command to save the document to a location on your computer.

Using Workgroup Templates

A convenient way to keep a group supplied with the most up-to-date templates is to store common templates centrally on a network server. (These shared templates are generally referred to as *workgroup templates*.) By doing so, you can ensure that everyone working on similar projects can access the same versions of templates at any time. A central repository for workgroup templates also saves everyone the headache of distributing and obtaining individual copies of the latest templates, and it can help to standardize documents across the board.

You create workgroup templates in the same way you create other templates. You then designate a folder as the workgroup template container and make sure that everyone's computer is configured to point to that file. Generally speaking, you'll want to make workgroup templates read-only files so that no one accidentally changes the template information. If you want to ensure that only certain people can access the files, you might want to assign passwords or designate the network share as read-only.

For more information about creating templates, see Chapter 4 "Templates and Themes for a Professional Look." For information about making documents read-only and password-protected, see Chapter 20, "Securing Your Word Documents."

To specify the location of workgroup templates on an individual computer, follow these steps:

1. Click the File tab to display Backstage view, and then click Options.

2. Click Advanced then scroll down to the General settings. Click File Locations.

3. In the File Types list, select Workgroup Templates, as shown in Figure 21-15.

Figure 21-15 Click File Locations on the Advanced page of the Word Options dialog box to specify locations for a number of file types, including workgroup templates.

4. Click Modify to open the Modify Location dialog box.

5. Create a new folder or navigate to and select the folder that contains the workgroup templates, click OK to close the Modify Location dialog box, and then click OK to close the Word Options dialog box.

To access templates stored in the workgroup templates folder, users can click the My Templates link, which is located in the Templates list in the New Document window. The templates appear on the My Templates tab. If workgroup templates are stored in a sub-folder in the workgroup templates folder, the New dialog box includes a tab with the same name as the subfolder, and the templates stored within the subfolder appear on that tab (see Figure 21-16).

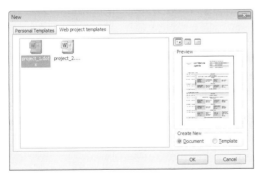

Figure 21-16 The workgroup templates are available in the New dialog box.

INSIDE OUT   Store Workgroup Templates in a Web Folder

You can't indicate an Internet location for your workgroup templates on the File Locations tab in the Options dialog box—the workgroup templates folder must be stored in a location on your computer or network. If you want to store templates in a Web folder, you need to create a network locations link. You can use the template by clicking New in Backstage view, choosing New From Existing, and choosing the network location in the New From Existing Document dialog box.

Sharing Word Documents via E-Mail

Many people e-mail documents back and forth, and for those projects that are linear in nature—for example, I finish a chapter and send it on to my editor—e-mail may be good enough. (When you need to collaborate on a piece, however, consider using file sharing in Windows Live SkyDrive or your SharePoint Workspace.)

When you e-mail a document to another person, your colleague can make a few changes, and send it back if necessary (or simply send you an e-mail message, saying "Perfect!").

Securely Sending Documents via E-Mail

If others won't need to make changes in the document, and you want to send it in the most secure form possible, consider saving the file as a PDF or XPS file before you send it. PDF and XPS formats save your document as a paginated, noneditable file that you can share with others for review.

To save the file in PDF/XPS format, on the File tab, click Save & Send. Click Create PDF/XPS Document at the bottom of the center column, and then click the Create PDF/XPS button. In the Publisher As PDF Or XPS dialog box, choose the folder where you want to store the file and select the File Type you want to create, then click Publish.

For more about working with PDF and XPS formats, see Chapter 20.

When you want to send your Word document directly to others on your team, follow these steps:

1. Start with your Word document open on the screen.

2. On the File tab, click Save & Send.

3. Click Send As Attachment.

If you have set up an e-mail client (as opposed to using only Web-based e-mail), a new e-mail message window appears; your current document shows up as an attachment (see Figure 21-17).

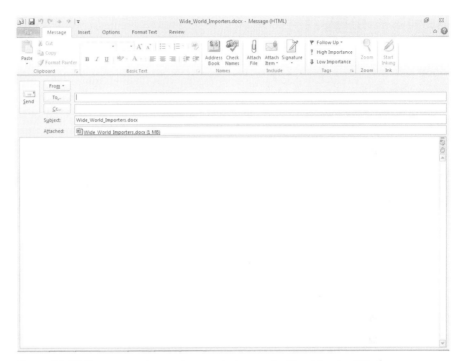

Figure 21-17 You can send your document via e-mail without leaving Word.

You will notice that the new message window Word opens is actually the Outlook 2010 new message window. You can specify the recipient information and send the message as usual. The rest of this section explores some of the e-mail features you might want to add when you are sharing your Word documents with your colleagues.

Setting E-Mail Priority

Depending on the nature of the document you're sharing with others, you might want to mark e-mail messages as urgent or not-at-all urgent (also known as *high-priority* and *low-priority messages)*. Marking your messages lets recipients know at a glance whether they should give special attention to a message.

To set e-mail priority for a message, click either High Importance or Low Importance in the Options command set on the Message tab, as shown in the image that follows:

Clicking High Importance adds a red exclamation mark to the e-mail so that when it arrives in the recipient's Inbox, it's clear that the message is one of priority. For best results, only use High Importance when the message really does have some urgency attached to it—otherwise, your recipients might begin to disregard the important messages you send. Conversely, clicking Low Importance adds a blue down-arrow to the message, letting the recipient know that the message is not an urgent matter.

Flagging a Message for Follow-Up

You can add flags to e-mail messages to indicate that some sort of follow-up action needs to be taken after the message is read. When you add a flag to a message, the recipient sees the flag in Outlook when the message arrives in the Inbox. To add a flag, click Follow Up in the Tags group on the Message tab. A list of options appears from which you can choose when the follow-up action is to take place, as shown in the following image:

Requesting Receipts

We've all had the experience of sending a particularly important document by e-mail and then eagerly awaiting to hear what the recipient thought of the draft. By using the Receipts feature when you e-mail Word 2010 documents, you can make sure that you know when the document has been received and read.

On the Options tab in the message window, choose either Request Delivery Receipt or Request Read Receipt (or both) in the Tracking command set. When you select Request Delivery Receipt, an e-mail message is sent to you automatically when the message is delivered to the recipient. When you click Request Read Receipt, you are notified by e-mail when the file has been opened.

> **Note**
> The Delivery Receipt options are only as reliable as the recipient wants them to be. In most cases the recipient is required to allow a receipt to be sent to the original sender. If the recipient doesn't allow this, then the sender won't be notified.

Delaying Delivery

If you want to make sure that your recipients receive the document to review at a specific time—perhaps at the start of a fundraising drive or the public release of software—you can delay its delivery using the Do Not Deliver Before option. You can also use this feature to create a number of different e-mail messages and set them all to be delivered at the same time.

On the Options tab in the message window, click Delay Delivery in the More Options group. The Properties dialog box appears, in which you can specify when you want the message to go out (see Figure 21-18).

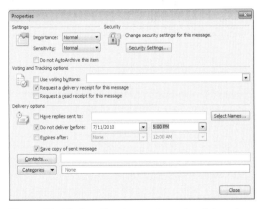

Figure 21-18 Specify when you want a delayed message to be delivered by setting options in the Message Options dialog box.

In the Delivery Options area of the Message Options dialog box, click the Do Not Deliver Before arrow and choose the date on which you want the message to be delivered. Next, click the time field and choose the appropriate time from the list. Click Close to save your settings; if Outlook 2010 is running when the message is scheduled to be sent, the message will be delivered after the date and time you specified.

Chapter 21

Include Voting Buttons

Another interesting e-mail feature that might be helpful when you're working on collaborative documents is the voting function. When you send your document attached to a message from Word, you can use Voting buttons to give recipients a say, for example, in whether to keep an attached document as your final report or go back for another draft.

To use the voting feature, display the message as usual and then click the Options tab. In the Tracking command set, click Use Voting Buttons. A list of voting options appears, as shown in Figure 21-19. Click the voting type you want to include and then send the message as usual.

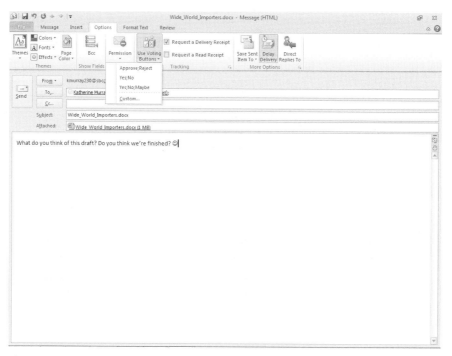

Figure 21-19 Choose the type of voting options you want to include and then send the message.

When the message arrives in the recipient's Inbox (in Outlook), a prompt instructs the user to cast their vote in the Respond group on the Ribbon. When the recipient clicks the Vote button, the voting options appear (see Figure 21-20).

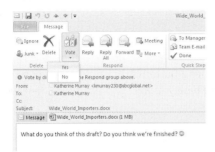

Figure 21-20 Recipients can easily vote when they receive the message in Outlook.

Using Word to Send Faxes

Faxing is yet another fast, convenient way to get information from your office or home computer to other people around the country or around the world. With Word 2010, you can use an online service to send your document via fax.

Creating and Sending a Fax

When you want to send your document as an Internet fax, click the File tab to display Backstage view then choose Save & Send. Click Send As Internet Fax, which is located at the bottom of the options in the right panel. The document is prepared as a fax, as you see in Figure 21-21. You can then add the recipient information, change the style of the fax by clicking the various styles in the Fax Service task pane. You can also click Preview to see how your fax will appear, and then, when you're ready, click Send to send the fax.

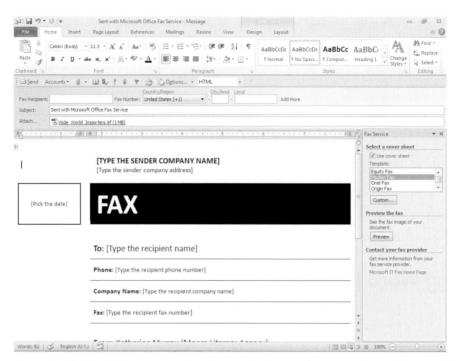

Figure 21-21 Word includes a number of templates that you can use as the basis for your fax.

Choosing a Fax Service

If you don't have a fax modem installed on your computer, but you'd like to take advantage of features provided with online faxing, you can sign up to use an Internet fax service. Word now works seamlessly with Internet fax services, and you'll find that you have quite a bit of control over faxes you send using this method.

To sign up with a fax service, on the File tab, point to Send, and then click Internet Fax. When you choose this option for the first time, you'll see a message box indicating that you must sign up with a fax service provider before you can send faxes. Click OK to go to the Fax Services page of Microsoft Office Online, where you'll find a selection of available fax services.

INSIDE OUT   I Can't Use the Internet Fax Service to Send a Fax

When you use an Internet fax service to send a fax, you basically convert your document into a TIFF file and attach it to an e-mail message, which is then sent to the recipient's fax machine or fax modem. The body of the e-mail message contains the cover sheet, and the attached TIFF file is the fax document. By default, to use an Internet fax service, you must have both Outlook and Word installed and configured on your system. If your fax isn't being sent, or if you're not sure whether your fax was sent, you can perform the following checks:

- Verify that Outlook sent your fax. To do this, open Outlook and then look in the Sent Items folder. Your fax will appear as an e-mail message with an attachment. If your fax message is waiting in the Outbox folder, click Send/Receive to send the fax.

- Check the Outlook Inbox to see whether you received a message from your Internet fax service provider that states whether your fax transmission succeeded or failed. Generally, Internet fax services send confirmation messages to your Outlook inbox whenever you attempt to send a fax.

- Ensure that the Microsoft Office Document Image Writer print driver is installed in your Printers And Faxes folder. If it is missing, you can install it using Microsoft Office Setup. To do so, click the Start button, then click Control Panel, Programs, Programs And Features, Microsoft Office 2010, and then click the Change button. Select Add Or Remove Features, click Continue, expand Office Tools, expand Microsoft Office Document Imaging, click Microsoft Office Document Image Writer, click Run From My Computer, click Update, and then click OK after the update completes.

- Ensure that your Internet fax service is properly activated. If you're unsure, visit your Internet fax service provider's online help pages or contact their support group. Usually, after you sign up with an Internet fax service provider, you'll receive a welcome e-mail message verifying your status, user information, and login parameters.

> **Tip**
> Use the Mail Merge Wizard to send multiple faxes that you create. Start by opening the document you want to fax. Then choose Tools, Letters And Mailings, and then Mail Merge. The Mail Merge task pane opens. When the Mail Merge Wizard asks you to specify a print option, choose your fax application in the Name list in the Print dialog box. For more information about creating and working with mail-merged documents, see Chapter 26, "Creating Mailings Large and Small."

What's Next?

This chapter provided in-depth information on how you can use Word 2010 to share your documents with colleagues, whether you're using Microsoft SharePoint Workspace 2010, Windows Live SkyDrive, or any number of other options available in the Save & Send tab in Backstage view. The next chapter builds on this idea of file sharing by showing you how to add comments, track changes, and combine or compare multiple versions of a document. You also learn about the new co-authoring possibilities in Word 2010 and find out how to communicate in real time with your colleagues as you all work collaboratively on the file.

CHAPTER 22

Collaborating and Co-Authoring in Real Time

Benefits of an Organized Revision Process. 667

Familiarizing Yourself with Markup Tools. 668

Setting Reviewer Name 671

Viewing Comments and Revisions. 673

Adding and Managing Comments Effectively. 675

Tracking Changes 677

Configuring Balloon and Reviewing Pane Options. . . . 680

Printing Comments and Tracked Changes 684

Reviewing Comments and Tracked Changes 685

Comparing or Combining Documents 693

Co-Authoring Documents in Word 2010 697

What's Next? 702

MOST of the larger projects you create in Word—annual reports, sales catalogs, brochures, mass mailings, and more—are likely to require the input of a team. Often many colleagues work together to design, draft, edit, revise, and finalize a document, and this means that being able to collaborate effectively and efficiently is one of the key ingredients of a successful project.

Word 2010 includes a number of markup tools that enable you to see the changes your teammates are proposing, accept or reject the changes, add and review comments, compare and merge documents, and more. An important new feature in Word 2010 is the co-authoring capability, with which you and your co-authors can simultaneously edit a document on SharePoint Workspaces or your Windows Live SkyDrive site. What's more, if you're using Office Communicator, you can interact with your co-authors in real time by sending instant messages, e-mail, or making a voice or video call. This chapter walks you through these various ways to collaborate using Word 2010 so that you can complete your project—successfully and on time.

Benefits of an Organized Revision Process

Any time you're managing a large project, it's important to keep all the pieces straight. This is especially true if you're working with multiple versions of files—sending one copy to marketing for approval, another to sales, and yet another to the communications department—you need to be certain that you have the latest version of a file when you go to compile results and finalize the document.

The markup tools in Word 2010 have been around for a couple of versions now, and they provide you with the tools you need to easily track changes and merge feedback into one cohesive whole. Using markup tools, coworkers can collaborate on publications without losing ideas along the way; educators can require students to track and show changes while the class works through the writing process; and you can keep an eye on personal document changes, such as changes to legal agreements or contracts in negotiation.

No matter how many people you have on your team, everyone can review the same document and incorporate changes and comments with those made by others. After colleagues make their modifications, others in the group can insert responses directly into the document. Throughout the process, Word meticulously tracks and color-codes everyone's comments and changes—as long as you configure the markup features properly.

Familiarizing Yourself with Markup Tools

To help streamline the revision process, the proofing, commenting, tracking, comparison, and document protection tools are grouped on the Review tab (Figure 22-1). Although you can track changes for your own purposes, the true strength of Word's revision tools becomes clear when you work with others. When you collaborate on a document, you can use Word to track and merge the changes and comments made by other contributors, highlight information to draw attention to selected text and graphics, and add ink and voice comments. Specifically, Word provides the following reviewing and markup tools:

- **Comments.** Use comments to annotate a document with suggestions and queries without actually changing the document. In Word 2010, you can add text, ink, and voice comments to documents. Comments are identified by comment markers in the text, which can be displayed as balloons in the margin or as ScreenTips along with the commenter's initials, as described in the section titled "Adding and Managing Comments Effectively," on page 675.

- **Track Changes feature.** Records editing changes, including deletions, added content, and formatting changes made to a document. Word can track and color-code changes from multiple reviewers, and the changes can later be evaluated and accepted or rejected on a case-by-case or global basis. For more information about the Track Changes feature, see the section titled "Tracking Changes," on page 677.

- **Compare (Legal Blackline) and Combine.** Use this tool to compare the differences between two documents and all revisions that are attributed to a single author. Combine is used for merging two or more documents along with identifying who changed what in the document. For more on these features, see the section titled "Comparing or Combining Documents," on page 693.

- **Ink support for Tablet PCs.** Use this feature to draw and write on documents directly by using a stylus or other drawing device. Using ink on a Tablet PC is discussed in the section titled "Inserting Voice and Handwritten Comments," on page 676.

- **Protect Document options.**   With these options, you can restrict formatting and editing capabilities for reviewers.

  For more information about document protection, see Chapter 20, "Securing Your Word Documents."

- **Voice comment.**   Inserts Voice comments into a document, as described in the section titled "Inserting Voice and Handwritten Comments," on page 676.

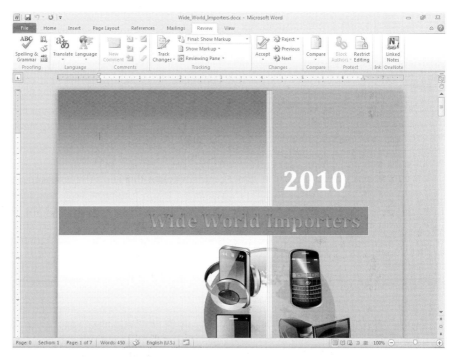

Figure 22-1 The Review tab provides tools that you can use to work with comments, tracked changes, proofing, document comparison, and document protection.

As you can see in Figure 22-1, the Review tab contains everything you need for checking, translating, adding comments to, tracking changes in, comparing, and safeguarding your document. You can also link directly to a OneNote notebook so that you can keep your notes and resources organized as you work. Table 22-1 introduces you to some of the key markup tools you're likely to use on the Review tab.

Table 22-1 **Markup Features on the Review Tab**

Button	Name	Description
New Comment	New Comment	Inserts a new comment balloon that you can use to enter a text comment.
	Delete Comment	Deletes a selected comment. You can delete only shown comments (when selected reviewer comments are shown or hidden), or delete all comments at once.
	Previous Comment	Jumps to the previous comment in the current document relative to the insertion point.
	Next Comment	Jumps to the next comment in the current document relative to the insertion point.
	Ink Comment	If you have a Tablet PC or drawing pad, opens an ink comment window.
	Pen	Selects the pen so you can write an ink comment.
	Ink Comment Eraser	Selects the eraser so you can erase ink comments.
Track Changes	Track Changes	Controls whether the Track Changes feature is turned off or on and provides access to Tracking options and user name settings.
Final: Show Markup	Display For Review	Controls how Word displays revisions and comments in the current document; available options are Final Show Markup, Final, Original Showing Markup, and Original.
Show Markup	Show Markup	Provides options with which you can show or hide Comments, Ink Annotations, Insertions And Deletions, Formatting, and Reviewers.
Reviewing Pane	Reviewing Pane	Shows or hides the Reviewing pane, which displays the complete text of tracked changes and comments. This can be opened in vertical or horizontal position.
Accept	Accept And Move To Next	Options include: accepts a selected tracked change in the document and moves to the next; accepts a change without moving to the next change; accepts all changes shown (when selected reviewer revisions are shown or hidden); or accepts all changes in the document at once.

Button	Name	Description
Reject ▾	Reject And Move To Next	Options include: rejects a change (which returns the text to its original state) and moves to the next change; rejects a change without moving to the next change; rejects all changes shown (when selected reviewer revisions are shown or hidden); or rejects all changes in the document at once.
Previous	Previous Change	Jumps to the previous tracked change or comment in the current document relative to the insertion point.
Next	Next Change	Jumps to the next tracked change or comment in the current document relative to the insertion point.
Compare	Compare	Provides access to the Compare (legal blackline) and the Combine (merge revisions) functions.
Block Authors ▾	Block Authors	Blocks authors from changing a shared document.
Restrict Editing	Restrict Editing	Sets your preferences for the types of changes that can be made to the document.

Chapter 22

Setting Reviewer Name

If you are the only one commenting in the current document, you can click Track Changes and jump right in with your review. But if you will be sharing a review with a number of people, you might want to take a moment and make sure that those reading your comments will know who inserted them. Here's the process for updating your user name and initials:

1. On the Review tab, click the arrow below Track Changes then click Change User Name.

    The General area in Word Options appears.

2. Click in the User Name text box and type the name you want to use to identify your comments; enter your initials in the Initials text box (see Figure 22-2).

Figure 22-2 Word uses the User Name and Initials entered in Word Options to identify comments and tracked changes in documents.

3. Click OK to close Word Options.

Keep in mind that the information you enter in Word Options is used by all of the programs in the Office 2010 programs.

Configuring Colors Associated with Reviewers

By default, Word automatically uses a different color for each reviewer's comments and tracked changes in a document. If you prefer all comments and tracked changes to be displayed in a single color, or you want to change the way color is used for tracked changes, you can change the default setting by clicking the Track Changes arrow on the Review tab, and then clicking Change Tracking Options. The Track Changes Options dialog box opens, as shown in Figure 22-3.

Figure 22-3 By default, comments, insertions, deletions, and formatting changes are displayed in a different color for each reviewer.

Use the Track Changes Options dialog box to specify a color for all comments, insertions, deletions, and formatting changes by selecting a color on the Color lists. By default, By Author is selected for Insertions, Deletions, and Comments, which means that Word automatically assigns a different color to each person who inserts comments or tracked changes. Keep in mind that this setting doesn't always color-code each person's changes with the same color every time. Instead, the By Author option simply guarantees that every person's marks appear in a distinct color—the color for each person will most likely change each time Word is restarted and the document is reopened.

If you're viewing a document that's color-coded for a number of reviewers, you can quickly see which colors are currently assigned to which reviewers. To do so, click Show Markup on the Review tab then point at Reviewers. You'll see a list of reviewer names accompanied by color-coded check boxes, as shown in Figure 22-4. In addition to seeing the reviewer color assignments, you can use the Reviewer options (found on the Review tab under Show Markup) to specify whose comments and tracked changes are displayed in the current document by selecting and clearing the check boxes next to each reviewer's name. When you clear a check box while in Print Layout, Full Screen Reading, or Web Layout view, that reviewer's comment and tracked change balloons are hidden, and text inserted by the reviewer appears as regular body text. To redisplay a reviewer's comments and changes, reselect the reviewer's check box.

Figure 22-4 The Reviewers control is where you choose which reviewer's comments you want to see.

Viewing Comments and Revisions

Depending on how you like to work in Word, you might prefer to see revision marks and questions in balloons, along the right or left sides of the document, or in the Reviewing pane, which appears either along the left side or across the bottom of the document window.

If you choose to work in the Reviewing pane, you will be able to see it in Print Layout, Web Layout, Outline, and Draft views. If you switch to Full Screen Reading view while you're reviewing comments, the changes will appear in balloons alongside your text. Figure 22-5 shows a screen in which the Reviewing pane is open on the left, in the vertical position.

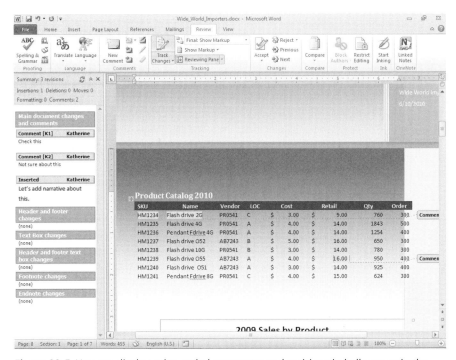

Figure 22-5 You can display color-coded comments and revisions in balloons or in the Reviewing pane.

Word gives you many visual cues to help you understand the changes included in comments and revisions. For example, notice in Figure 22-5 that in both the balloons and the Reviewing pane (in the shaded heading), the word *Comment* identifies the information as a comment.

> **Note**
> Deletions, formatting changes, and moves display in balloons and the Reviewing pane; insertions display in the document and Reviewing pane but not in balloons.

You can color code balloons and headings in the Reviewing pane to associate them with particular users, and each heading in the Reviewing pane displays the user name of the person who inserted the comment or made the revision. In addition, comments include the reviewer's initials and are automatically numbered sequentially throughout the document. When viewing comments in balloons, the content associated with comments is highlighted in the document to help visually link commented areas to corresponding comments. The highlighting of each instance of commented content matches the corresponding comment's balloon color, which simplifies identifying who created which comments. The combination of user initials, comment numbering, and color-coded content highlighting makes identifying and referring to comments easy in Word 2010.

> **Note**
>
> The highlight used in the document for comments and revisions is not the same as the Text Highlight Color found on the Home tab in the Font group. When comments and revisions are removed, the highlight on the text is also removed. Many reviewers use the Highlight tool to annotate content in the document; however, if you highlighted text by using the Text Highlight Color tool, you need to remove the highlight manually by selecting the text, clicking Text Highlight Color, and choosing No Color.

Adding and Managing Comments Effectively

When you or your reviewers add comments to a document, those comments might include questions, comments, suggestions, or even content to be added into the document. Comments give other users a means to call your attention to something without altering the text itself. Adding comments is a simple task, and managing and resolving them involves only reading the comment, making the call, and clicking Accept or Reject.

Inserting Comments

Things don't get much easier in Word than inserting a comment. When you're reviewing a document and see something you want to comment on, simply click in that paragraph (or select the text to which you want the comment to refer), then on the Review tab, click New Comment in the Comments group. A comment balloon appears, extending from the place where you positioned the cursor or your text selection (as demonstrated in the image that follows). Add your comment by simply typing text, then click outside the comment balloon. That's all there is to it!

> **Tip**
>
> If you press Enter while typing a comment, a line will be added in the comment balloon. To end the comment, click outside the balloon or press Esc.

You can edit comments you add just as you would edit standard text. If a comment is long and its contents aren't entirely displayed in a balloon, click the ellipsis in the balloon to open the Reviewing pane. If the Reviewing pane isn't visible, you can toggle it on by clicking Reviewing Pane on the Review tab.

> **Tip**
>
> You can use the keyboard to close the Reviewing pane by pressing Alt+Shift+C.

INSIDE OUT Editing Text in the Reviewing Pane

You can select text and press Backspace to delete it in the Reviewing pane. You can also press Ctrl+Backspace or Ctrl+Delete to delete entire words at one time.

> **Tip**
>
> You aren't limited to inserting only text in the comments you add. If you want to paste an image, insert a screenshot, or add a logo in a comment balloon, you can do that, as well. Simply copy the item you want to include, click in the comment balloon, and press Ctrl+V.

Inserting Voice and Handwritten Comments

If you use a Tablet PC or drawing tablet, you can include voice comments and handwritten comments in your documents. Basically, voice comments are sound objects added inside comment balloons. Before you can add a voice comment, you need to add the Insert Voice button to the Quick Access Toolbar. You can find this button under Commands Not In The Ribbon. To create ink comments, simply activate your ink features by moving the pen or clicking the drawing surface. Then click the New Comment button on the Review tab and write your comment in the comment bubble.

Tracking Changes

Adding comments is great when you want reviewers to give you feedback based on the overall content or direction of your document. But what about those times when you want someone to add their own text, edit what you've written, or otherwise enhance your first draft? When you're sharing the document creation tasks with colleagues, you can help keep all the changes straight and see what your coworkers have done in the file by using Tracked Changes.

Track Changes is available in the Tracking group on the Review tab. When you click Track Changes to enable the feature, Word records the deletions, insertions, and formatting changes made by each reviewer who modifies the document. By default, Word displays each reviewer's changes in a different color so that you can easily identify the sources of changes within your document. When you work with a document that has been modified by reviewers, you can use the Display For Review list on the Review tab to display the changed document in four views, as described here:

- **Final Show Markup**   This is the default display view. This view displays the final document showing deletions, comments, formatting changes, and moved content. Insertions are displayed in the document content, and deletions are displayed in balloons by default.

- **Final**   Hides the tracked changes and shows how the document would appear if you accepted all the changes. Comments are also suppressed in this view.

- **Original Show Markup**   Displays the original document and shows deletions, comments, formatting changes, and moved content. Insertions are shown in balloons, and deleted content is displayed in the document.

- **Original**   Hides the tracked changes and shows the original, unchanged document so that you can see how the document would look if you rejected all changes. Comments are also suppressed in this view.

Being able to display your document in these various ways can help as you add, accept, and reject tracked changes. Note, however, that Word doesn't track some changes when you modify a document, including changes you make involving the following list:

- Background colors

- Embedded fonts

- Some types of mail merge information, such as whether a file is a main document or data file

- Some table modifications

Chapter 22

You probably won't find that these limitations interfere with tasks involving tracked changes, but you should be aware of the exceptions just in case. In addition, you might sometimes see a message box warning that an action will not be marked as a change—such as modifying a table. In these cases, you have the option of clicking OK to proceed or Cancel to avoid making a change that won't be tracked.

Tracking Changes While You Edit

When you track changes in a document, you can opt to display or hide the tracking marks while you work. Generally, it's easier to hide tracked changes if you're editing and writing text, and it's better to view tracking marks when you're reviewing a document's changes. When Word 2010 tracks changes, it automatically records insertions or deletions in balloons (depending on your view, as described in the preceding section), which you can view in Print Layout, Full Screen Reading, or Web Layout view. Word marks tracked changes in a document as follows:

- **Added text.**   Appears in the reviewer's color with underlining.

- **Deleted text.**   Displays in the reviewer's color in a balloon. If the inline option is chosen, deleted text shows in the content area with a strikethrough line indicating the deletion.

- **Moved text.**   Shows text moved within a document automatically marked in green (the default) with double-underlines below the moved text. In addition, the balloons for moved text include a Go button in the lower-right corner that you can click to move from the original location to the new location and vice versa.

> **Note**
> Moved text is unavailable in Compatibility Mode.

- **Text added and then deleted by the reviewer**.   Displays as though the text had never been added. No marks appear in a document in places where a reviewer adds information and then deletes the added information. (Rest assured your typos will not be tracked!)

In addition to these actions, Word automatically inserts a vertical line, called a *changed line* (also known in the publishing industry as *change bars*), along the left margin to indicate that a change has been made. This line appears wherever text or formatting changes are made while the Track Changes feature is turned on. Finally, the Reviewing pane automatically generates a summary of changes including the number of insertions, deletions, moves, formatting changes, and comments, as well as a grand total.

Figure 22-6 shows that the document is displayed in Final Showing Markup view, which presents inserted and deleted text in line and formatting changes in balloons. Notice the changed line in the left margin, which specifies that the text next to the line has been modified in some way. For more information about configuring changed lines, see the section titled "Customizing the Appearance of Changed Lines," on page 680.

You'll also see in Figure 22-6 that the status bar displays *Track Changes: On*. To view this information in your status bar, right-click the status bar and click Track Changes on the Customize Status Bar menu. By doing so, you can simply click Track Changes in the status bar to control whether the feature is turned on or off.

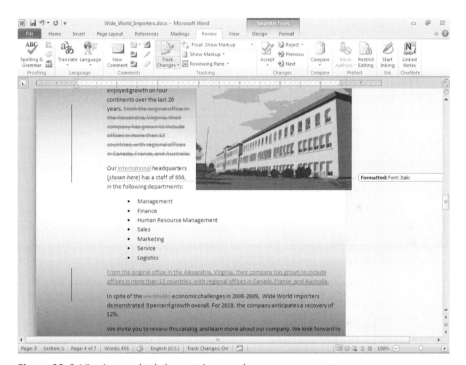

Figure 22-6 Viewing tracked changes in your document.

You turn Track Changes on or off in a document by using one of the following methods:

- On the Review tab, click the top half of the Track Changes button (if you click the bottom half, you display options for Track Changes).

- Press Ctrl+Shift+E.

- If you added Track Changes to your status bar, click Track Changes there.

When Track Changes is turned on, Word monitors your changes regardless of whether your view reflects the tracked changes as marked-up text. You can always tell whether changes are being tracked by looking at the Track Changes button on the status bar because the button indicates On or Off, depending on your current working mode.

> **Note**
> You can control who can make tracked changes to your document by clicking Restrict Editing in the Protect group and using the Restrict Formatting And Editing task pane. For more information about document protection, see Chapter 20.

Customizing the Appearance of Changed Lines

Regardless of your selections for formatting inserted, deleted, moved, and reformatted information, you can still use changed lines to indicate in a general way where changes have occurred in a document. You can specify where changed lines are displayed on the page (along the right, left, or outside borders) and the color in which they are displayed. By default, changed lines are set to Auto, which is typically black. To configure how changed lines are displayed, open the Track Changes Options dialog box and modify the Changed Lines options in the Markup section.

After you configure the changed lines settings, all documents you open that contain tracked changes will use the newly-configured settings. In addition, any currently opened documents that contain tracked changes will be reformatted automatically to reflect the new settings.

> **Note**
> In Draft view, all changed lines appear on the left regardless of the setting you config-ure in the Markup section in the Track Changes Options dialog box. The changed lines color setting applies in all views.

Configuring Balloon and Reviewing Pane Options

When you work with comment and track change balloons, you can control a variety of balloon options. Specifically, you can format balloon and Reviewing pane label text (which is the text displayed on Reviewing pane bars, above each comment or tracked change); specify when balloons are to be displayed; adjust balloon width and placement; and specify whether lines should connect balloons to text.

Balloon and Reviewing Pane Styles

You can modify the font styles of balloon and Reviewing pane text and labels in the same manner you modify other styles in Word documents—by using the Styles task pane. To modify the Balloon Text style that controls the balloon labels (such as Comment, Inserted, Deleted, and Formatted) and to change the Comment Text style (the text typed by reviewers), follow these steps:

1. On the Home tab, click the Styles dialog launcher (or press Ctrl+Alt+Shift+S) to open the Styles task pane.

2. In the Styles pane, click the Manage Styles button.

3. On the Edit tab in the Sort Order list, select Alphabetical, select Balloon Text in the Select A Style To Edit listbox, and then click Modify.

4. In the Modify Style dialog box, select any options you want.

   Choose whether you want to make the changes to the current document only or add the formatting to the document's template (either Normal.dotm or another attached template), and then click OK.

5. In the Manage Styles dialog box, select Comment Text then click Modify.

6. In the Modify Style dialog box, select any options you want.

   Choose whether you want to make the changes to the current document only or add the formatting to the document's template, and then click OK twice to close both dialog boxes.

You can also modify comment text by selecting the text or label in an existing comment in the Reviewing pane or balloon, applying format settings, and then updating the style to match the selected text. For more information about working with styles, see Chapter 12, "Applying and Customizing Quick Styles."

When you modify the Comment Text style, you change the appearance of the text only (not the labels) in the comment balloons and comment entries in the Reviewing pane. You do not modify the inserted or deleted text displayed in tracked-change balloons or labels for Reviewing pane entries.

Showing and Hiding Balloons

If you prefer to work with the Reviewing pane and not with balloons, you can turn them off. If you prefer, you can use balloons only to show comments and formatting changes. To control balloon display (in Print Layout, Full Screen Reading, and Web Layout views), on the Review tab, click Show Markup then click Balloons, or you can configure the Use Balloons option in the Change Tracking Options dialog box. The following describes the options found under Balloons on the Show Markup list.

- **Show Revisions In Balloons**   Shows all changes in balloons (equivalent of Always in the Track Changes Options dialog box).

- **Show All Revisions Inline**   Turns off balloons (equivalent of Never in the Track Changes Options dialog box).

- **Show Only Comments And Formatting In Balloons**   Shows comments and formatting changes in balloons and shows inserted and deleted text inline (equivalent of Only For Comments/Formatting in the Track Changes Options dialog box).

Regardless of whether you hide or show balloons, comments are displayed as ScreenTips when you position your mouse pointer over a comment indicator.

> **Note**
> You can specify whether the lines used to connect balloons to text are displayed or hidden by selecting or clearing the Show Lines Connecting To Text check box on the Track Changes Options dialog box. When you clear this check box, balloons are displayed in the margin without a connector line when they aren't selected. When you select a comment, a solid line appears that connects the balloon to the comment indicator in the text.

Adjusting Balloon Size and Location for Online Viewing

If you are new to balloons, you might find that they take some getting used to, even if you've used comments and tracking tools in the Reviewing pane. To help you customize balloons to suit your working style, Microsoft provides a few options that you can use to control their width and position. In fact, you can control balloon width and location for online viewing as well as for printing purposes. This section addresses configuring the online presentation of balloons. For more information about configuring balloons for printing, see the section titled "Printing Comments and Tracked Changes," on page 684.

To set the balloon width and specify whether balloons are displayed in the right or left margin, you must configure the Track Changes Options dialog box, as follows:

1. On the Review tab, click the Track Changes arrow, and then click Change Tracking Options.

2. In the Track Changes Options dialog box, make sure that the Use Balloons (Print And Web Layout) list box is set to Always or Only For Comments/Formatting.

3. Click the Measure In arrow and select whether you want to measure balloons by using your preferred unit of measure (such as inches or centimeters) or percentage of the page.

    For more information about the Measure In options, see the Inside Out tip titled "Sizing Balloons—Measurement vs. Percentage" in the following sidebar.

4. In the Preferred Width box, enter a percentage or measurement (such as inches or centimeters) for the width of the balloons.

5. In the Margin box, click the Left or Right option to specify on which side of the document text you want balloons to appear.

6. Click OK to apply the balloon settings.

Unfortunately, you can't preview your balloon settings from within the Track Changes Options dialog box. Your best plan when configuring balloons is to try a few settings and see which works best for you on your monitor.

INSIDE OUT   Sizing Balloons—Measurement vs. Percentage

When you size balloons, Word configures them without compromising the document's content area. This is accomplished by expanding the view of your document and not by reducing the document's content area. To clarify, let's look at the two Measure In options.

When you use the unit of measure, you provide a set size in which your balloons appear in your document's margin. For example, if you specify 2 inches or 5.08 centimeters, your page's view expands so that balloons are displayed within an area that's 2 inches (or 5.08 centimeters) wide, starting from the document's margin.

Similarly, if you size balloons using the Percent option, the balloons are displayed as a percentage of the page's size without compromising the document's content area. For example, if you specify balloons to be 100 percent, the balloons are sized equal to 100 percent of the page, and the width of your view is expanded accordingly (doubled, in this case).

You can easily see how balloons are displayed relative to the current document by modifying the balloon size and then viewing your document in Print Preview mode.

Chapter 22

Printing Comments and Tracked Changes

In some situations, you might want to print out the comments and tracked changes that are displayed in your document. Perhaps you want to take the document to share at a meeting, or review the changes while you're on the train tonight going home. When you print a document containing comments and tracked changes, you can configure print settings in two areas: the Track Changes Options dialog box and in the Print window in Backstage view.

On the Review tab, click the Track Changes arrow and select Change Tracking Options to display the Track Changes Options dialog box. In the Use Balloons area, choose how you want Word to adjust the paper orientation to accommodate added balloons. You can select any of the following settings on the Paper Orientation in Printing list:

- **Auto** Specifies that Word can determine the best orientation for your document automatically, based on your margin settings and balloon width settings.

- **Preserve** Prints the document with the orientation specified in the Page Setup dialog box. This is the default setting.

- **Force Landscape** Prints balloons and the document in landscape format to allow the most room for the display of balloons.

After you choose how you want Word to handle page orientation when you print documents with comment balloons, you're ready to configure your Print settings.

Click the File tab to display Backstage view then click Print. In the Print window, you can specify whether to print the document showing markup (the default setting when comments and tracked changes are displayed) or you can opt to print only a list of the markup changes made in a document. If you want to print a document's changes, you typically want to print the document showing changes instead of printing only a list of changes. Depending on the length of the document and number of revisions, when you print a list of changes, the list can become long and confusing.

To efficiently print tracked changes and comments in a document, follow these steps:

1. Display your document in Print Layout view.

2. Display the tracked changes in the manner in which you want them to be printed by using the Show Markup list on the Review tab.

   In addition, you can select specific reviewer's tracked changes and comments by clicking Reviewers (under Show Markup) and specifying which reviewers' revisions and comments should be displayed and subsequently printed.

> ### Tip
> The easiest way to print a document with only its comments is to print the document with comment balloons in the margin and hide the other types of margin balloons (insertions, deletions, and formatting changes).

3. Click the File tab to display Backstage view and then click Print, or press Ctrl+P to display the Print tab.

4. Click the first item under Settings and ensure that Print Markup (under Document Properties) is selected, and then click Print.

The document is printed with balloons in the margin and Word reduces the view of the page to accommodate them. This doesn't affect your document's layout parameters—it's just a temporary modification for the purposes of printing balloons along with a document.

> ### Note
> When you print a document with markup, the Markup Area Highlight shading (the light gray shading behind balloons onscreen) is not printed.

Reviewing Comments and Tracked Changes

Assume that your document has made its rounds, and now it's up to you to review the tracked changes and comments. You can review all tracked changes and comments at the same time, or you can suppress the view of comments or tracked changes and review them individually. Regardless of which method you choose, the process is the same and can be accomplished by using these steps:

1. On the Review tab, ensure that either Final Show Markup or Original Show Markup is selected on the Display For Review list.

2. Click Show Markup on the Review tab and verify that all options are turned on, such as Comments, Ink, Insertions And Deletions, and Formatting, to view all changes and comments.

   You also have the option of turning on only those options that you want to review.

> **Note**
>
> The Markup Area Highlight option in Show Markup controls whether the Markup Area (where the balloons display) appears shaded. By default, Markup Area Highlight is selected and the Markup Area appears light gray.

At this point, you can review the tracked changes and comments manually by scrolling through your document or the Reviewing pane. If you prefer to use the navigation commands on the Review tab to navigate between comments only, use the Previous and Next commands in the Comments group. To navigate between both comments and tracked changes, use the Previous and Next commands in the Changes group.

Navigating Your Comments

You can navigate between comments only by using the Select Browse Object feature (press Ctrl+Alt+Home), which enables you to navigate between comments using Ctrl+Page Up (Previous) and Ctrl+Page Down (Next) in any view.

Another way you can move easily from comment to comment involves using the Navigation pane. Display the pane by selecting the Navigation Pane check box in the Show group on the View tab. Click the Find Options and Additional Search Commands arrow at the top of the box. Click Comments from the list and then choose the reviewer who added the comments you want to find, as shown in the following image:

You can also use the Go To tab in the Find And Replace dialog box (press Ctrl+G). On the Go To tab, you can select Comment on the Go To What list. Then choose to view all reviewers' comments or a selected reviewer's comments by selecting Any Reviewer or a specific name in the Enter Reviewer's Name list. For more information about using the Browse Object feature and the Go To tab, see Chapter 8, "Navigating Your Document."

Depending on the current view, the behavior of either set of Next and Previous commands might vary. The views and variations in behavior are described as follows:

- **Draft view.** Revisions are shown inline; comments can be displayed in the Reviewing pane, or you can view the comment by positioning your cursor over the comment marker and reading the ScreenTip text. When you click either set of Previous or Next commands, the Reviewing pane opens when a comment is encountered (if it isn't open already).

- **Full Screen Reading view without balloons.** Revisions are shown inline; comment indicators are shown, but the Reviewing pane doesn't open. You can view the comment by positioning your cursor over the comment marker and reading the ScreenTip text. (Previous and Next commands are not available in this view.)

- **Outline view.** Revisions are shown inline; comments can be viewed as ScreenTip text or in the Reviewing pane. When you click either set of Previous or Next commands, the Reviewing pane opens when a comment is encountered (if it isn't open already), and the view changes to Draft view automatically.

- **Print Layout, Full Screen Reading, or Web Layout view with balloons.** The active balloon is indicated by a dark outline, darker shading, and solid connector line. As previously noted, Previous and Next commands are not available in Full Screen Reading Layout. You can press the Alt+Up arrow or Alt+Down arrow to move up or down among balloons on a single page. (The Alt+Up and Alt+Down keyboard commands also work in Print Layout and Web Layout views.)

- **Print Layout or Web Layout view without balloons.** Revisions are shown inline; comments can be viewed in the Reviewing pane. When you click either set of Previous or Next commands, the Reviewing pane opens when a comment is encountered (if it isn't open already).

When you view balloons, you might notice that some have an ellipsis in the lower-right corner. This symbol indicates that the entire text doesn't fit in the balloon. To view the remainder of the text, click the ellipsis to open the Reviewing pane, which displays the entire revision or comment.

Responding to Comments

Naturally, as you read through comments, you might want to respond to them. You can do so in the following ways:

- Type directly in a comment, in which case your response won't be color-coded according to your user name. In this scenario, you might want to include your name or initials so others know who is making the additional comment.

- Click in the comment you want to respond to and then click New Comment on the Reviewing toolbar, or press Ctrl+Alt+M. A new balloon opens directly below the balloon you're responding to, or a blank entry opens in the Reviewing pane with the format Comment[initials#R#] in the header. The first number is the number of the comment, and the R# indicates that the comment is a response to the comment number indicated. To add your response, simply add your comment.

> **Note**
> To see when a comment was inserted and who created it, you can hover the mouse pointer over the comment balloon. When you do this, a ScreenTip appears that displays the comment's creation date and time as well as the user name of the person who created the comment. If you're working in the Reviewing pane, each Reviewing pane bar displays the user name and insertion date and time automatically.

Deleting Comments

Generally, comments serve a temporary purpose—reviewers insert comments, someone addresses the comments, and then the comments are removed before the document's final publication (either online or in print). If you work with comments, you need to know how to delete them so you won't unintentionally include them in your final publication. As you might expect, you can delete comments in several ways. You can delete a single comment, delete comments from a specific reviewer (or reviewers), or delete all comments by using the following techniques:

- **Delete a single comment.**   Right-click a comment balloon and then click Delete Comment on the shortcut menu. Or select a comment balloon, and in the Comments group on the Review tab, click Delete.

- **Delete comments from a specific reviewer.**   First, clear the check boxes for all reviewers by clicking Show Markup on the Review tab, clicking Reviewers, and then choosing All Reviewers. Next, display only the comments you want to delete by clicking Show Markup, clicking Reviewers, and then selecting the check box next to the reviewer's name whose comments you want to delete. (You can repeat this process to select additional reviewers as well.) To delete the displayed comments, in the Comments group on the Review tab, click the arrow below Delete, and then click Delete All Comments Shown.

- **Delete all comments in the document.**   Ensure that all reviewers' comments are displayed. (This is the default setting, but if all reviewers' comments aren't displayed, click Show Markup on the Review tab, click Reviewers, and then click All Reviewers.)

In the Comments group on the Review tab, click the arrow below Delete then click Delete All Comments In Document.

CAUTION

Keep in mind that when you delete all comments at once by clicking the Delete All Comments In Document option, you delete all comments in the document, regardless of whether they are visible on the screen.

You can also delete comments one at a time from within the Reviewing pane. To do so, right-click a comment in the Reviewing pane and click Delete Comment on the shortcut menu, or click in a comment and click Delete on the Review tab.

Accepting and Rejecting Proposed Edits

After a document has gone through the review cycle and you receive a file containing a number of tracked changes, you can keep or discard the edits by accepting or rejecting the changes. You can address each edit on a case-by-case basis (generally, this is the recommended practice), or you can accept multiple changes at once. In either case, you can reject and accept proposed changes by using the appropriate buttons on the Review tab or by right-clicking changes (or balloons) then clicking options on the shortcut menu.

Figure 22-7 shows the shortcut menu that you see when you right-click moved text. Notice the new Follow Move option, which you can use to jump to the origin or destination of moved text in relation to the text you right-click. (If you right-click deleted text, you receive the same menu without the Follow Move option; if you right-click inserted text, the Accept Deletion and Reject Deletion options change to Accept Insertion and Reject Insertion.) The next few sections describe ways to accept and reject changes.

Figure 22-7 You can right-click tracked changes to access options you can use to resolve proposed changes, including the option to jump to the origin or destination of moved text.

> **Note**
>
> Before you start accepting and rejecting tracked changes and deleting comments, consider saving a version of the document with all of the tracked changes and comments intact. In that way, you'll have a copy on hand if you want to return to the marked-up version of the document.

Addressing Tracked Changes One at a Time

The key to accessing the changes you want to review is to configure your view properly before you start going through the changes and making choices about them. Here are the settings you want to use as you begin to review tracked changes:

- **Show document markup.**   Show your document in either Final Showing Markup or Original Showing Markup in the Display For Review list in the Tracking group on the Review tab.

- **Specify the type(s) of changes to display.**   Use the Show Markup options on the Review tab to specify which types of changes you want to review. If you want to view revisions only, then make sure Comments is not selected.

- **Display selected user revisions and comments.**   Click Show Markup on the Review tab, click Reviewers to open the list of reviewers, and then choose which reviewers' markup changes you want to resolve. You can resolve all changes at one time (by selecting the All Reviewers option), or you can select any combination of listed reviewers.

> **Note**
>
> You'll notice after the first or second click that the list of Reviewers closes automatically after each change you make to the list. Therefore, if you want to view the revisions and comments of only a few reviewers from a long list, first clear the All Reviewers check box (instead of clearing each reviewer one at a time). Then, click the names of those who made the changes you want to review. This way, you can configure the list with as few clicks as possible and avoid having to reopen the list repeatedly.

INSIDE OUT   Optimizing a Document's Readability when Some Reviewer Marks Are Hidden

When you turn off the display of a reviewer's tracked changes, any text deleted by the reviewer is restored and text inserted by the reviewer appears as regular text. As you can imagine, this can result in some strange mixtures of original and added text. If some text looks particularly confusing, display all reviewers' marks or change the display of revisions to Final before you enter additional (and possibly unnecessary) revisions.

- **Specify how balloons should display.** Click Show Marksup on the Review tab, click Balloons, and then click to show revisions in balloons, all revisions inline, or only comments and formatting in balloons.

- **Show or hide the Reviewing pane.** Decide whether you want the Reviewing pane to be open while you work as well as whether it should appear along the bottom or left side of your window.

After you display the changes you want to work with, you can move from tracked change to tracked change by using the Previous and Next buttons in the Changes group on the Review tab (if comments are displayed, the Previous and Next commands in the Changes group will navigate between both tracked changes and comments). You can also view and click edits in the Reviewing pane, or you can scroll through the document and address edits in a less linear manner. Regardless of how you arrive at a tracked change, you can handle it in either of the following ways:

- Right-click a change (in the document body, in the Reviewing pane, or in a balloon) and choose to accept or reject the change by using the shortcut menu.

- Click in a change and then click the Accept or Reject button on the Review tab to accept or reject the change and move to the next revision. Or, click the Accept or Reject arrow and click Accept Change or Reject Change to accept or reject the change without moving to the next revision.

After you accept or reject a change, Word displays the revised text as standard text. If you change your mind about a change, you can undo your action by clicking Undo on the Quick Access Toolbar or pressing Ctrl+Z.

Chapter 22

Accepting or Rejecting All Tracked Changes at Once

At times, you might want to accept or reject all changes in a document. For example, maybe you've gone through the document carefully, reading and changing the document in Final view. When you're satisfied with the document, you want to simply accept all changes instead of resolving each change individually. You can do so by executing a single command.

To accept or reject all changes in a document, use the Accept All Changes In Document or Reject All Changes In Document commands. To access these commands, click the arrow below Accept or Reject on the Review tab then click the appropriate command, as shown in Figure 22-8.

Figure 22-8 You can accept or reject all changes or only those changes by a particular reviewer by using the Accept and Reject options, which are accessible from the Review tab.

In addition to accepting or rejecting all changes in a document, you can show a subset of reviewers' changes and accept or reject only those changes. To control which changes are displayed in your document, click Show Markup on the Review tab, click Reviewers, and then select which reviewers' changes you want to display and resolve. After you configure your display, click the Accept or Reject arrow, and then click the Accept All Changes Shown or Reject All Changes Shown option.

> **Tip**
>
> Between resolving tracked changes individually and globally accepting or rejecting all changes in an entire document lays the realm of accepting and rejecting edits contained in selected text. In other words, you can resolve editing issues on a piecemeal basis. For example, you might want to select a paragraph or two that you've reviewed. To do so, select the specific text, and then click Accept or Reject on the Review tab to accept or reject the tracked changes contained in the selected text.

INSIDE OUT   Comments, Revisions, and the Document Inspector

You can remove all comments and revisions by using the Document Inspector. To do so, on the File tab, click Check For Issues in the Info tab, and then click Inspect Document. Ensure that the Comments, Revisions, Versions, And Annotations check box is selected, and then click Inspect. If the Document Inspector finds any leftover comments or revisions, you can click Remove All to accept all revision marks and delete all comments.

Keep in mind that when you use the Remove All option in the Document Inspector to delete all revisions and comments, you cannot use the Undo command to retrieve the revisions and comments. If you suddenly realize you do not want to remove the revisions and comments after you click Remove All, your only recourse is to close the document without saving changes. Therefore, always save your documents before you run the Document Inspector!

Comparing or Combining Documents

The Compare feature in Word 2010 can save you a lot of time and trouble when you want to see at a glance what the difference might be between two similar files. Perhaps a colleague reviewed a file and made a few changes, but you aren't sure whether they conflict with changes you've made in the meantime. Compare can help you resolve this.

And when you're finished comparing the documents, you can easily combine them to get the most recent changes all put together in one nice, neat file.

Note

A character-level change occurs when a change is made to a few characters of a word, such as when only the case of the first letter is changed. At the word level, the entire word is shown as a revision; at the character level, only the letter is shown as a revision.

The following section of the chapter describes comparing and combining documents after changes have been made to a document.

Chapter 22

Comparing Two Versions of a Document

Ideally, when you use Compare, the original and the revised document won't both contain tracked changes. If either document contains tracked changes, Word treats the documents as though the changes have been accepted and doesn't display them in the comparison document. Additionally, all revisions in the comparison document are attributed to a single author, and you can see what changes have been made to the original document regardless of whether track changes were turned on when modifications were being made. The changes made in the revised document are shown in the original as tracked changes. To compare two versions of one document and view the differences, follow these steps:

1. On the Review tab, click Compare. Then from the list, click Compare.

   The Compare Documents dialog box opens.

2. In the Original Document area, click the Folder icon to navigate to and select the original document, or select the document from the drop-down list.

3. In the Revised Document area, click the Folder icon to navigate to and select the revised document, or select the document from the drop-down list.

4. Click More to show the Compare Documents options. Verify that New Document is selected in the Show Changes In area (you can also choose to show changes in the original or revised document), as shown in Figure 22-9.

Figure 22-9 Use the Compare Documents dialog box to choose two documents to compare—an original and a revised version.

5. Click OK. The original and revised documents remain unaltered and a new Compared Document is created and shown automatically.

> **Note**
>
> If either (or both) of the documents being compared has tracked changes, you'll see a message box stating that Word will compare the documents as if the tracked changes have been accepted. Click Yes to continue the comparing procedure.

6. To view all three versions of the document at once, click Show Source Documents on the Review tab, and then click Show Both. In this view, the original, revised, and compared documents are displayed in the new tri-pane review panel, as shown in Figure 22-10.

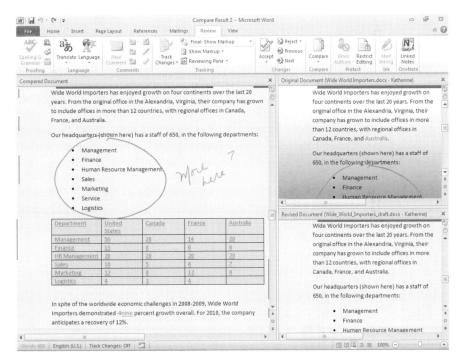

Figure 22-10 The new tri-pane display shows the original, revised, and comparison results on the screen at the same time.

The new Compared Document displays the changed text in an unnamed document file. You need to save and name the file if you want to store it for future use.

INSIDE OUT   Confidential Revisions

The Compare function can also be used as a tool to keep reviewer names, dates, and times of revisions confidential. If you no longer have an original copy of a document containing tracked changes, simply create a copy of the document, reject all changes, and use it as the original. Display the Compare dialog box and select the original and the revised documents. In the Revised area, in the Label Changes With text box, type another name, such as Reviewer. This method does not allow you to change the dates and times of revisions, but all revision dates and times reflect the system date and time when the Compare function was used. Note that this doesn't apply to Comments that might be contained in the documents.

Combining Revisions from Multiple Authors

In contrast, you use Combine to combine, or merge, two or more documents. All modifications made to the original or revised documents become tracked changes. Unlike the Compare feature, if the revised document contains tracked changes, these changes appear as tracked changes in the combined document. All authors are identified and their revisions are combined into one document. To use the Combine function, use the following steps:

1. On the Review tab, click Compare then click Combine. The Combine Documents dialog box opens, which looks similar to the Compare Documents dialog box you saw in Figure 22-9.

2. In the Original Document area, click the Folder icon to navigate to and select the original document, or select the document from the drop-down list.

3. In the Revised Document area, click the Folder icon to navigate to and select the revised document (or select the document from the drop-down list) and then click OK.

> **Note**
> If you do not see the tri-pane review panel, then on the Review tab, click Show Source Documents and then click Show Both.

To combine additional documents, combine the resulting Combined Document with another document containing changes.

> **Note**
> At times, you might want to compare two documents side-by-side without merging them. In those cases, you should adjust your view without using the Compare or Combine features. To learn how to use the View Side By Side feature, see Chapter 8.

TROUBLESHOOTING

What happened to the File Versions feature?

In previous versions of Word, you could save versions of your document and store the information within the document file. You can now review the versions of your document by clicking the File tab and, in the Info tab of Backstage view, review the files listed in the Versions area. If you want to recover a version of the file you didn't save, click Manage Versions and choose Recover Draft Versions. Then, in the Open dialog box, click the file you want and click Open.

Co-Authoring Documents in Word 2010

When you are working with colleagues to produce an important document, being able to work collaboratively—and communicate while you're working—is an important part of keeping the project on track. Word 2010 now includes a co-authoring feature, with which you can edit a document simultaneously—while others are working in the file as well. As each person edits the file, the section being edited is locked so the other person can't change that section. Both you and your co-author can see the changes being made in real time, and contact each other online using the presence features available through Office Communicator. This can help you resolve questions quickly, edit documents concurrently, and finalize your work in a fraction of the time a shared project might have taken previously.

In order to use Word's co-authoring features, you need to save the document to either a SharePoint Workspace 2010 site or your Windows Live SkyDrive account. Set the necessary permissions to give your co-authors access to the document. Then open the document normally, in Windows Live SkyDrive or SharePoint Workspaces.

Chapter 21, "Sharing Your Documents," explains how to set permissions and share documents on SharePoint Workspaces and Windows Live SkyDrive.

When a co-author first logs into the file on which you are both working, Word displays a small alert message in the lower portion of your screen. You can click the message if you want to contact your co-author immediately; otherwise, simply edit the file as normal.

> ## Tip
> If you are using SharePoint Workspace 2010, you can open a Word file and work with your co-authors without any other tools. If you are a home user, you need to post your Word document to your Windows Live SkyDrive account and use the Word Web App to open and edit the document. To find out more about the Word Web App, see Chapter 25, "Blogging and Using the Word Web App."

Editing Simultaneously and Saving Changes

You can edit the document normally as you work alongside your co-authors. The edits appear in balloons, along with your contact name, letting your co-author know where the changes are being made in the document. Word will prompt you to save the file to update all changes so that you will be able to see the changes your co-authors are making as well (see Figure 22-11).

Figure 22-11 The message bar prompts you to save the file to update changes.

The Info tab of Backstage view also provides you with important information about the status of the file, the co-authors currently working on the file, and any version information you need to know. You can click Save to save your file changes and update the screen display. If you are working with Office Communicator, you'll be able to tell whether she is available for contact by the colors displayed to the left of a co-author's name. Green means you can reach the co-author by clicking the contact information and choosing one of the communication options; red means the co-author is busy; and yellow means the person is away (see Figure 22-12).

Chapter 22

Figure 22-12 The Info tab shows how many people are working on the file and lets you know the status of the file.

> **Tip**
> If you want to block a co-author from working on a section of a shared file, select the text you want to protect, click the Review tab, and then click Block Authors in the Protect group.

Contacting Your Co-Author

When you are working simultaneously in a file with a co-author, you can contact her by e-mail, instant message, or phone to ask questions about the file, discuss possibilities, or just generally talk through your plans for the edits. All the tools you need are right there in the document window.

Click the indicator in the status bar showing the number of authors currently working on the document; a popup list displays the names of your co-authors (see Figure 22-13). Click the name of the person you want to contact, and that person's contact card appears (see Figure 22-14).

Figure 22-13 Click the indicator in the status bar to see who else is working in your document.

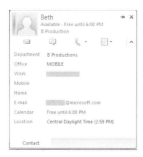

Figure 22-14 Your co-author's contact card offers different ways to communicate.

The contact card provides you with several different ways to contact your co-author. You can choose one of the following options:

- Send an e-mail message to the author

- Start an instant messaging conversation

- Make a phone call

- Schedule a meeting

Troubleshooting Co-Authoring

The new co-authoring features in Word 2010 are great when you need to collaborate in real time using either SharePoint Workspace 2010 or the Word Web App. Not all files make

Chapter 22

good candidates for co-authoring, however. If your file uses any of the following elements, Word developers say co-authoring might not work the way it should:

- The file is checked out by another user.

- The file uses IRM (Information Rights Management) or DRM (Digital Rights Management) to secure the document.

- The document is encrypted.

- The file is saved in an earlier Word file format.

- The file has been marked as final.

- The file includes ActiveX controls.

- The document incorporates objects like SmartArt, a chart, or ink.

- The document is a master document.

If any of these items are currently in use in the document you want to share, you might need to resort to a sequential check-in/check-out process in order to get all the revisions you need in that specific file. Depending on the nature of the file, you might also be able to remove the elements that interfere with co-authoring and then add them after the co-authoring work on the document is done.

What's Next?

This chapter shows you how you can control the editing and commenting that goes on in a collaborative document. Whether you share your document with 1 reviewer or 20, you can keep the comments straight, choose what you want to keep, and discard the rest. You also learned how to compare and merge documents, and you found out about the new co-authoring features available when you work with others who are using SharePoint Workspace 2010 or the Word Web App. The next chapter kicks off the last part of this book by showing you how to create and customize tables of contents and indexes.

Word 2010 Interactive

CHAPTER 23

**Preparing Tables of Contents
and Indexes** 705

CHAPTER 24

Special Features for Long Documents 731

CHAPTER 25

**Blogging and Using the
Word Web App** 747

CHAPTER 26

Creating Mailings Large and Small 761

CHAPTER 27

**Customizing Documents with
Content Controls** 789

CHAPTER 28

Working with Macros in Word 2010 811

Preparing Tables of Contents and Indexes

Creating Effective Reference Tables. 706

Creating a Table of Contents 707

Preparing a TOC for the Web 714

Customizing a TOC. 714

Adding Indexes. 716

Creating Index Entries 718

Generating the Index. 723

Updating an Index 727

AutoMarking Entries with a Concordance File 728

What's Next? 730

WHEN it comes to navigating a document—particularly longer documents—your readers need a clear roadmap that points out how to find the information they are most interested in reading. A good table of contents provides this kind of roadmap, helping the reader see how the document is organized, listing clear headings that reflect the content covered, and perhaps offering main and secondary sections in a way that assists the reader to easily find what he is looking for.

A good index, especially in a long, complex document, gives readers a more detailed way to find the specific item they want to see. Your index should offer a wide range of words and phrases readers might use to look up specific content topics, and it must present the reader with page numbers showing exactly where those topics are found. When they are prepared well, a table of contents and an index provide readers with a sense that they can easily find what they need in your document—both from the big picture and the detailed view—which ensures that your document will be read and used in the way you hope it will.

> ## Note
> Often readers will review a table of contents (or the index) of a document or book before deciding whether to read it. They are wondering (1) Is this worth my time? (2) Will I find what I need in here? and (3) Is this document relevant to me? If you want people to read what you've prepared, create a good table of contents to show them how your document fits what they're looking for. The clearer your table of contents, the better your readers will like it.

This chapter introduces you to creating tables of contents, other reference tables, and indexes in Word 2010. You'll learn how to create, edit, customize, and update your table of contents. You'll also find out how to add entries for the special reference tables that make it easy to locate figures, citations, and more in your long documents. Finally, you'll learn the ins and outs of creating indexes that spotlight the key topics in your document.

Creating Effective Reference Tables

Headings are the real secret to creating a helpful table of contents (TOC). If you've written clear, understandable headings, your readers will know where to turn for the information they want.

The next consideration is the way in which you format these headings—if you don't use styles Word 2010 recognizes, it won't collect the headings the way you want. To create the TOC you want, keep these guidelines in mind.

- **Use Word's built-in heading styles—or create your own custom styles based on them.**   When you're working in Outline view or working with master documents, use Word's built-in heading styles—Heading 1, Heading 2, and Heading 3. Additionally, you are probably familiar with the various outline levels—1 through 9—that you can assign in Outline view. When you use Word to create a table of contents, it uses the built-in heading styles by default. You can teach Word how to use the outline levels or your own custom styles, but it takes a few more steps.

- **Make your headings clear and concise.**   The best headings are short (between four and ten words) and communicate the subject clearly. The headings for your document will vary, of course, depending on content, but if your objective is to help readers find what they want quickly, you'll be closer to meeting your goal if you keep your headings short, sweet, and smart.

- **Avoid confusing headings.**   If the tone of your document is conversationally hip, you might be tempted to throw in little humorous sayings or quips as headings throughout your text. As a wise editor once asked, "Would readers understand what this heading means if they opened the book at this page?" If helping readers understand your message is your main goal, avoid phrases that might confuse them.

You can include literally any text in your document as part of the TOC by selecting entries manually. For more information on manual table of contents entries, see the section titled "Adding TOC Entries Manually," on page 710.

Creating a Table of Contents

Once you've checked your headings to make sure they're clear and concise and that you've assigned a heading style Word will recognize, you can generate the table of contents. You can use two different procedures to do this. The easiest way is to choose a TOC style from the gallery and let Word do the rest. Or, if you prefer, you can use the Table Of Contents dialog box to customize the look of the table in a way that fits your needs. This section takes you through both of these techniques.

Using a TOC Style

Word 2010 includes ready-made TOC styles that you can use to create a stylized, professional looking table of contents. The easiest way to create one is to just click the look you like in the Table Of Contents gallery. Begin by clicking in the document at the point at which you want to add the TOC. Then, on the References tab, click the Table Of Contents arrow to display the styles gallery (see Figure 23-1).

Figure 23-1 The Table Of Contents gallery displays a number of styles you can use to create your TOC.

Click the table style you want to create. Word compiles the TOC and places it at the cursor position, using the headings in your document and indenting the heads based on the headline style they reflect (see Figure 23-2).

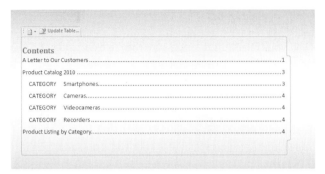

Figure 23-2 Word applies the selected TOC style to the heading styles in your document and compiles the table of contents.

Depending on the style you selected in the Table Of Contents gallery, Word might automatically add the title "Contents" or "Table of Contents." It might also add right-aligned page numbers and dot leaders (the dots spanning the space from the end of the heading text to the page numbers). First-level headings are aligned with the left margin, while second-level headings are indented one tab position to show their subordination.

When you click the table of contents, the table highlights and contextual tools appear above the selected table. You learn more about these tools in the section titled "Editing and Updating a TOC," on page 712.

> **Tip**
> If you click the Table Of Contents tool on the References tab and don't see any sample styles in the gallery, click the Add Text tool then clear the Do Not Show Table Of Contents option.

Creating a Customized TOC

If you want to create a table of contents that meets certain specifications, you can use the Table Of Contents dialog box to enter the values you want to set. To start the process, on the References tab, click the Table Of Contents tool in the Table Of Contents group. Next, click Insert Table Of Contents at the bottom of the Table Of Contents gallery. The Table Of Contents dialog box appears (see Figure 23-3). At the left side of the dialog box, you can see how the default settings will be applied to your table of contents. As you can see, in the Print Preview region, each level of heading is indented one tab position, tab leaders are used, and numbers are aligned along the right margin. In the Web Preview region on the right, no leaders are used, no page numbers are used, and each heading is actually a hyperlink. When users click a link in the TOC, they will be taken to the corresponding section in the Web document.

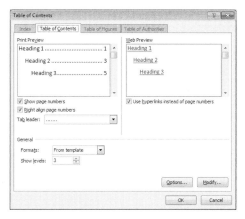

Figure 23-3 You can customize the settings for the table of contents by using the Table Of Contents dialog box.

Using the various settings in the Table Of Contents dialog box, you can customize your table of contents in the following ways:

- Position the page numbers immediately following the headings by clearing the Right Align Page Numbers check box.

- Remove the page numbers altogether by clearing the Show Page Numbers check box.

- Change the tab leader by clicking the Tab Leader arrow and choosing a different line setting.

- Choose a different format set for the heading styles by clicking the Formats arrow then choosing a different set (see Figure 23-4). For more information on working with formats, see the section titled "Choosing a TOC Format," on page 711.

Figure 23-4 Choose a different format to change the heading styles used in the TOC.

Chapter 23

- Change the number of levels that are displayed in your table of contents by clicking the up arrow or the down arrow in the Show Levels field to increase or decrease the value, respectively.

- If you're preparing a Web document and want a traditional TOC to appear instead of links, you can clear the Use Hyperlinks Instead Of Page Numbers check box. This causes page numbers and tab leaders to be displayed in the Web document.

> **Note**
>
> The Options and Modify buttons in the Table Of Contents dialog box display options with which you can choose the headings and styles that are used in your table of contents. For more about customizing the styles of your TOC, see the section titled "Changing TOC Styles," on page 715.

After you select the settings you want to use for your TOC, click OK to save your selections and return to the document. The table of contents is inserted at the cursor position.

Adding TOC Entries Manually

You aren't limited to using only headings in your table of contents. You can select any word or phrase in your document for inclusion in the TOC by selecting the text you want to use in the table of contents and pressing the shortcut key combination Alt+Shift+O. The Mark Table Of Contents Entry dialog box appears, as shown in Figure 23-5, and the entry you highlighted appears in the Entry box.

Figure 23-5 Enter TOC entries manually in the Mark Table Of Contents Entry dialog box.

You can click Mark to add the entry or, if you have more than one table of contents in the current document, click the Table Identifier arrow and choose to which TOC you want to assign this entry. (This step is unnecessary if you're creating only one TOC at a time.)

Another change you can make if you choose, involves the level at which the table of contents entry is displayed. In the Level box, enter the level at which you want the entry to be listed. The first-level entry is the default. This controls the amount of space by which the entry is indented.

The Mark Table Of Contents Entry dialog box remains open on your screen so that you can continue to add table of contents entries as needed. To choose the next entry, simply double-click it in your document. When you click back in the Mark Table Of Contents Entry dialog box, the entry in the first field changes to reflect your choice. Set the options you want and click Mark. When you're finished adding entries, click Close.

Compiling the Manual TOC

When you're ready to generate the table of contents using the entries you've added manually, begin by clicking to position the cursor at the point where you want to add the TOC. On the References tab, click Table Of Contents, and then click Insert Table Of Contents from the gallery that appears. In the Table Of Contents dialog box, click the Options button in the lower-right corner. Now select the Table Entry Fields check box. This adds the TOC entries to the table of contents.

To find out more about the Table Of Contents Options dialog box, see the section titled "Customizing a TOC," on page 714.

Click OK twice to close the dialog boxes. Word adds the new TOC at the insertion point.

INSIDE OUT   Display Only Your Manual Entries

If you want your table of contents to include only the entries you've added manually, display the Table Of Contents dialog box by choosing Insert Table Of Contents from the Table Of Contents gallery. Click the Options button in the lower-right corner of the dialog box. In the Table Of Contents Options dialog box, clear both the Styles and Outline Levels check boxes. Click OK to save your settings and then click OK a second time to return to the document. Press F9 to update the TOC; only your manual entries should appear.

Choosing a TOC Format

When it comes to formatting your tables of content, simplicity is the rule. You want your readers to be able to find the content they need easily, so keeping the design of the TOC as clear as possible is a good idea. The simple table of contents format gives you a standard TOC with right-aligned page numbers, dot leaders, and left-aligned headings. You can choose from a number of specially-designed TOC formats so that your table of contents fits the style of your publication.

The easiest way to apply a table of contents format, of course, is to click the one you like in the Table Of Contents gallery. If you want to see what other formats are available or choose something different, you can use the Format list in the Table Of Contents dialog box. The formats shown there—From Template, Classic, Distinctive, Fancy, Modern, Formal, and Simple—offer different combinations of text styles for your TOC. If you are working with a template, the From Template option might be selected for you by default. Make your choice and click OK; you'll be able to see the results in the Print Preview and Web Preview windows at the top of the dialog box. When you find the format you want to use, click OK. The table of contents is created and formats are assigned as you selected.

> **Note**
>
> If you want to change the format of a table of contents you've already created, select the table before you display the Table Of Contents dialog box. Next, click the Formats arrow, click the style you want, and then click OK. Word displays a message box asking whether you want to replace the selected TOC. Click OK to update the selected TOC with the new format.

TROUBLESHOOTING

Headings are missing in my TOC.

After you generate a table of contents for your Word document, review the document and check your headings carefully. If any headings are missing in the TOC, it might be because you've added the headings in text boxes or shapes.

Word creates your table of contents by gathering all the headings and table of contents entry fields. If you've placed text in objects that you've added to the document, the entries might not be found automatically. To add these items to the TOC, just select the text items, copy them, and paste them on the text layer. Finally, press F9 to update the TOC.

Editing and Updating a TOC

As you work with your document, you are likely to make changes to it, moving sections around and adding and editing headings and text. When you make a heading change, your

TOC consequently becomes obsolete and no longer reflects your most recent changes. To correct this, you can update the table of contents in two different ways:

- Press F9.

- Click Update Table in the contextual tab that appears at the top of the TOC when it is selected (see Figure 23-6).

Figure 23-6 The table of contents object offers an Update Table tool that becomes available when you click it.

Word searches the document and updates the TOC to reflect any changes you've made to headings.

Note

You can use the contextual TOC commands to choose a different style for your TOC as well. To do so, select the table of contents and click the Table Of Contents arrow (just to the left of the Update Table command). The Table Of Contents gallery appears, from which you can choose a different TOC style.

CAUTION

To remove a TOC, use the Remove Table Of Contents, found at the bottom of the Table Of Contents gallery instead of deleting the TOC field. When you manually delete a TOC, hidden bookmarks are left in the document that could later cause incorrect references in the TOC, or if too many bookmarks have been added it can result in document corruption.

Chapter 23

Preparing a TOC for the Web

When you generate a table of contents for your document, a Web Preview appears next to the TOC Print Preview in the Table Of Contents tab in the Table Of Contents dialog box. Try out a Web TOC in your document by placing the insertion point where you want to add the TOC and clicking Insert Table Of Contents in the Table Of Contents gallery. In the Table Of Contents dialog box, ensure that the Use Hyperlinks Instead Of Page Numbers check box is selected and then click OK. The TOC is added at the insertion point. To see the TOC in Web format, choose View then select Web Layout. The TOC appears as a table of active hyperlinks, as shown in Figure 23-7, each of which takes you to the corresponding document section.

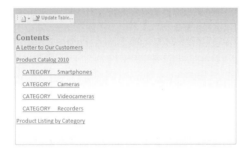

Figure 23-7 When you display Web Layout view, you'll see hyperlinks in your Web TOC.

Customizing a TOC

You can make additional changes to your table of contents by customizing both the elements you include in the TOC and the styles you use to include them. Figure 23-8 shows the Table Of Contents Options dialog box and the features available to you. To display these options, choose Insert Table Of Contents from the Table Of Contents gallery then click Options.

Figure 23-8 Choose the elements you want to use in the Table Of Contents Options dialog box.

Matching Entry Styles to TOC Levels

Part of making sure the right entries show up in your table of contents in the right way involves ensuring that they are mapped to the right TOC levels. The Table Of Contents Options dialog box is where you make that happen. For example, Headings 1, 2, and 3 are assigned to TOC levels 1, 2, and 3. This indicates that Heading 1 is shown as level 1, meaning it will be aligned with the left margin of your document. Level 2 appears indented one tab position, and level 3 is indented two tabs from the left margin. You can set additional levels as well if your document requires that level of detail in the TOC.

To add styles to the TOC, scroll down through the list to find other styles in your document—either styles you've created or existing styles—and then enter a TOC level in the text boxes on the right. The styles you select are included in the TOC when it's generated, appearing according to the level you specify. Click OK to save your changes, and then click Yes when prompted about whether you want to replace the existing table of contents with the updated table.

Changing TOC Styles

When you are working with styles in the Table Of Contents Options dialog box, the styles that are available are taken from the template being used to format your document. If you've selected From Template in the Formats list in the Table Of Contents dialog box, the Modify button is enabled. When you click Modify, the Style dialog box appears, and you're given the choice of adding, deleting, or changing the styles used in the table of contents. When you click Modify in the Style dialog box, the Modify Style dialog box appears, in which you can make font and formatting changes to the selected style (see Figure 23-9).

Figure 23-9 Changing entry style in the Style dialog box.

Select the item you want to change in the Styles list. The specifications used to create the look appear in the description box at the bottom of the dialog box. Preview shows you how that particular item is formatted. Click Modify to make changes to the style.

In the Modify Style dialog box, you can make all kinds of modifications to the style of the table of contents. You've seen this dialog box before—it's the same one you use to change styles throughout the rest of your document. Make any necessary changes and click OK to save the new settings. Click OK in the Style dialog box to save the changes to the style. Finally, click OK once more to return to your document then update the TOC by pressing F9.

For a refresher on creating new style effects in the Modify Style dialog box, see Chapter 12, "Applying and Customizing Quick Styles."

> **Note**
> If you want to undo your selections and reset the options to their default settings, click the Reset button in the Table Of Contents Options dialog box.

Adding Indexes

An index is one of those things that you might not notice until you discover that it's missing. Suppose that you are researching current statistics on Web advertising. Your own startup business will rely on advertising for a revenue stream, and this is an important item to include in a business plan that you hope will attract investors. You have a number of reports that the chief executive officer (CEO) passed along to you about the state of the Web, but none of them includes an index to direct you to the advertising statistics you need. Now you'll need to spend the afternoon skimming the reports to find the data.

A properly prepared index would save a lot of aggravation. An index entry might include the following items to help you get right to the information you're looking for:

- A primary topic (for example, Advertising)

- A subtopic (such as Web)

- Page numbers (inserted automatically by the indexing tool)

- Cross-references (for example, *See also Banner advertising*)

Each of these elements help readers find the topics they want to learn more about. Primary topics and subtopics are both alphabetized; subtopics are indented within primary topics, and cross-references appear in place of page numbers, along the right edge of the index column.

What Makes a Good Index?

Think of the various indexes you've used in the past. No doubt some were better than others. Some left out the main topics you were looking for or seemed disorganized. And some documents might not have had an index at all, which can be really frustrating when you're looking for something specific.

There's a recipe for creating a good index, so if you've never created one before, take heart. Here are some things you should be sure to include in the indexes you create:

- **Usability.**   An index is first and foremost a reader service. Make sure that you've included all major topics, and that you've thought through the alternative ways readers might be looking for those topics. Include topics, subtopics, and references to other topics for related information (for example, *See* Parenting teens).

- **Readability.**   Using terms your readers will recognize—whether or not they're familiar with the content of your document—is important. If you're unsure about the various ways a reader might reference a certain topic, ask others how they would look it up so that you know what kinds of phrasing would be helpful. Talk to others on your team or in your department to make sure you've used words and phrases that will be easily understood.

- **Cross-references.**   Cross-references in an index refer readers to other topics that provide more information.

- **Logical structure**.   One mistake new indexers often make is to include every important-sounding word they think would be helpful. You'll help your readers find what they are looking for if you think through your index carefully. Which topics are most important? How many different ways might a reader refer to them? What are the words that will be used most often in a search?

- **Multiple entries.**   Listing a topic in more than one way helps readers find what they're looking for. For example, someone wanting to know how to choose a background color for a heading might look under *document*, *headings*, *color*, or *background* to find that particular topic.

> **Note**
> After you identify key words and phrases for your index, create a list and send it to others in your department. Ask for their input, additions, and suggestions. Doing this type of phrase testing for your index before you create it can save you editing time later.

> **Note**
> One place you can get clues for important index terms is your table of contents. Which words and phrases are used in your headings? Definitely include those terms in your index and look for plenty of opportunities to create subentries from the topics within those sections.

Indexing with Word

Creating indexes in Word is an interactive process that is partly hands-on and partly automatic. You create a Word index in three basic stages:

1. Mark the index entries in your document.

2. Position the cursor at the point in the document where you want to place the index (typically this is the end of the document).

3. Use the Insert Index command to compile the index from the entries you entered.

> **Tip**
> If there are terms you're sure to include in your index, you can add them to a concordance file. Word will use the file to quickly mark the index entries you want. For more about creating a concordance file, see the section titled "AutoMarking Entries with a Concordance File," on page 728.

Creating Index Entries

The first step in creating your index is to indicate which words and phrases you want to include in the index. Word makes it easy for you to enter index entries as you go. And once you display the Mark Index Entry dialog box, you can mark additional entries, add subentries, and add cross-references and page ranges.

Marking Index Entries

Similar to the process of marking table of contents entries manually, marking an index entry involves selecting a word or phrase you want to use in the index and instructing Word to mark it as an index entry. You can create an index entry in two different ways:

- If you want to begin with text that is already in the document, select and use existing text.

- If you want to add an entry that is not based on an existing word or phrase in your document, click to place the insertion point in the paragraph where you want to add the index entry.

To add index entries using an existing word or phrase, select the text you want to include in the index, then on the Reference tab, click Mark Entry in the Index group. The Mark Index Entry dialog box appears, as shown in Figure 23-10.

Figure 23-10 You use the Mark Index Entry dialog box to enter index entries and subentries.

The selected text appears in the Main Entry box. If necessary, you can edit the text that appears.

If you are not using existing text for your marker, place the insertion point at the location where you want the marker (rather than selecting text), then on the Reference tab, click Mark Entry in the Index group and type the entry you want in the Main Entry box.

Click the Mark button to mark the entry. If you want to add other entries, leave the dialog box open, select the text on the page, and click Mark again. Use this process to include as many additional entries as you need. When you are finished adding entries, click Close to save your changes and return to the document.

> **Tip**
>
> Edit the entry in the Mark Index Entry dialog box to make it as clear as possible. For example, instead of a phrase that appears in your document, such as *served in the state legislature*, you might enter *legislature*, or *government service*.

Creating Subentries

Subentries give your readers additional ways to find the topics you include in your index. You might have both primary topics and subentries that interrelate. For example, *eco-vacations* might be a primary topic at one point in your index, but it might also be a subentry (*tourism, eco-vacations*) in another.

Often subentries are like secondary topics that readers can use to narrow their search on a specific topic. For example, if your report is about a new HR training program that your company offers, one main index entry and the related subentries might look like this:

Human resources 21–32

 Creating a personnel file, 21

 Updating personnel data, 24

 Personnel evaluations, 26

 Training program for, 30

A subentry provides readers with additional references they can look up. Instead of simply reading through the whole *Human resources* section in order to find what they want, they can go right to *Personnel evaluations* on page 26. Subentries also add depth and functionality to your index as a whole, which further assists readers in finding what they're looking for.

Here's a quick way to enter subentries if you want to avoid repeated clicks in the dialog box: simply type the main entry and the subentry in the Mark Index Entry dialog box, separating the entries with a colon. You can use this technique to create up to seven levels of subentries—although an index that complex would probably confuse most readers! For best results, stick to one or perhaps two subentry levels, depending on the complexity of your document.

Tip

If you find yourself entering too many subentries for a particular topic, you might want to create another main entry to divide the list. If your main entry is followed by a whole column of subentries, your readers might become lost in the list and not remember the main entry heading.

Selecting Repeated Entries

When you're putting together a quick index and want to reference all occurrences of a particular word or phrase, you can do that easily using the Mark Index Entry dialog box. Start by selecting the text you want to index and then display the Mark Index Entry dialog box using either method previously provided. Change the Main Entry text to show the entry you want. Enter a subentry, if you want to include one. When your entry text is as you want it, click Mark All; Word searches for the word or phrase throughout the document and applies an index entry to every occurrence.

Note

One of the limitations of Mark All is that the program marks every occurrence as it appears. This means that not only will you have the same index entry for each item (which doesn't give you the flexibility of creating multiple references to the same topic), but also that Word will find only the words or phrases that exactly match the text you've entered. For example, if you enter *composer*, *composers* will be found, but not *composing* or *composition*. So if you feel it's important to reference multiple forms of a particular word, be sure to create index entries for each one so they are all included in the finished index.

INSIDE OUT   Indexing Long Entries

If the entry you are adding actually spans several pages, instead of inserting an entry on every page, you can create a bookmark and then reference that bookmark in your index. Start by highlighting the text passage you want to index. Then, on the Insert tab, click Bookmark in the Links group. Enter a name for the bookmark and then click Add. Next, on the References tab, click Mark Entry in the Index group. In the Mark Index Entry dialog box, click Page Range in the Options area. Click the Bookmark arrow and choose the bookmark you just created. Click Mark to add the bookmark entry to your index.

Formatting Entries

As you add index entries, you can specify formatting for the characters and page numbers, thus cutting down on time spent editing and formatting your index after you create it. Formatting can help you highlight certain words, phrases, or page numbers, so they catch the reader's eye.

Format an index entry by selecting the text you want to include. Display the Mark Index Entry dialog box and edit the text in the Main Entry box as needed. In the Main Entry box, select the text you want to format; press Ctrl+B to apply bold, Ctrl+I for italic, or Ctrl+U for underline styles. You can also right-click the entry, choose Font, and select additional formatting settings for the entry. Finish the entry, making any other changes you want to make, and then click Mark to add the entry.

By selecting or clearing the check boxes in the Page Number Format section of the Mark Index Entry dialog box, you can also control the format of the page numbers Word adds to the index. You might want to use bold or italic to highlight certain entries. For example, a bold page number might indicate the most in-depth coverage of an item, and an italic page number might include biographical information or reference another work.

Adding Cross-References

Although the main purpose of an index is to provide readers with the page numbers they need to find the topics they're interested in, not all of your entries will provide page number references. Some might instead point readers to other topics in your index. A cross-reference acts as a pointer to an entry (or group of entries) containing related information. It helps you to direct readers who might be looking for a specific topic under a different name to the information they want in your document.

To create a cross-reference in your index, select the text for the index entry or position the insertion point in the document and display the Mark Index Entry dialog box. Enter the Main Entry text, if needed, and click the Cross-Reference option.

After the word *See*, type the index entry to which you want to refer readers. For example, you might create cross-references that look like this:

> Training sessions. *See* Retreat sessions.

Specifying Page Ranges

By default, Word assigns the index entry the number of the current page. If you select and create an entry on page 3, for example, Word shows that page number with the index entry. But if you want to direct your readers to the full range of pages on which a specific topic is covered, you can do so by using bookmarks you've already created.

Begin by displaying the Mark Index Entry dialog box. Enter the text you want in the Main Entry and Subentry boxes, if needed, and then click the Page Range option. Click the Bookmark arrow to display the list of bookmarks in the current document then click the bookmark you want to use. Finally, click Mark to add the entry.

If you haven't created bookmarks to mark places in your document and want to find out how to do it, see Chapter 8, "Navigating Your Document."

When you create the index later, Word will insert an en dash (a long dash) between the page numbers in the range. A page range entry looks like this:

Human resources, 21–29

Generating the Index

Once you've marked all the entries you want to include in your index, you're ready for Word to compile the index and place it in your document. When Word compiles the index, it gathers all the entries you've marked, assigns page numbers as you've specified, and alphabetizes the entries. Finally, after you click OK, Word places the index at the insertion point.

INSIDE OUT   Review Your Document

Although you can update an index easily by pressing F9 (you can go back and edit your index entries at this time, if you choose), you'll lose any additional formatting you've added to the index after it is compiled. For example, if you've added alphabetical headings (- A -, - B -, and so forth), when you select the index and press F9, the headings will disappear. So it's worth your time, *before* Word compiles the index, to go back through the document and review your index entries to ensure that you haven't missed anything important.

Page through the document to review important headings, sections, and captions that you want to include in your index. Start the process of creating the index by placing the insertion point where you want to create the index and then, on the References tab, click Insert Index in the Index group. The Index dialog box appears, with the Index tab selected, as shown in Figure 23-11. In this dialog box, you can choose the format for text entries, page numbers, tabs, and leader characters.

Chapter 23

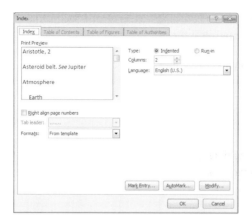

Figure 23-11 The Index tab provides the options and commands you need to create the index.

> **Note**
>
> Notice the Mark Entry button on the Index tab of the Index dialog box. If you begin
> making your formatting choices for the index and suddenly remember a topic you
> want to include in the index, you can click Mark Entry to open the Mark Index Entry
> dialog box. However, be aware that doing so closes the Index dialog box.

Choosing the Index Format

One of the most important choices you'll make in the Index dialog box involves the format
for the compiled index. How do you want the index to look? When you click the Formats
arrow, Word presents the following choices:

- **From Template**   The default; leaves out alphabetical headings that separate sections in the index.

- **Classic**   Centers the alphabetic headings over the index column.

- **Fancy**   Encloses the heading in a shadowed box.

- **Modern**   Italicizes the heading and places a rule above it.

- **Bulleted**   Formats the heading as a block letter and centers it over the index
  column.

- **Formal**   Right-aligns page numbers, adds dot leaders, italicizes the heading, and indents the heading from the left margin.

- **Simple**   Removes all alphabetic headings and special formats.

Each of these options produces a different index format, which is displayed in the Print Preview region of the dialog box. To make your choice, click the Formats arrow and then click the selection you want.

If you later decide to change the default alignment of the numbering or choose a different leader character, those changes will override the settings belonging to the different formats.

> **Tip**
> Experiment with and preview the different formats for your index before selecting the one you want by clicking the choices in the Formats list on the Index tab in the Index dialog box. When you choose a format style, the Print Preview region of the dialog box shows your selection so that you can see the formatting effect of each style.

Choosing Index Alignment

After you create your index, you might want to make changes to the alignment and tab leaders that the format applied. You can change these settings so that page numbers are aligned along the right edge of the index column, and tab leaders are added to help guide the reader to the related page number.

To change the alignment of page numbers in your index, on the References tab, click Insert Index (on the Index tab) to display the Index dialog box. Click the Indented option if necessary and then select the Right Align Page Numbers check box. Click the Tab Leader arrow then select the type of leader you want. Finally, click OK to create the index; the page numbers are formatted as you selected.

Changing the Way Entries Are Displayed

Another choice in the Index dialog box lets you choose whether you want index subentries to be run in with the index main entries or indented below them. Simply click your choice, and Word will format the index accordingly.

Chapter 23

When you choose Indented, your index subentries are indented beneath the main entries, like this:

Human resources

Creating a personnel file, 21

When you choose Run-In, the subentries are placed on the same line with the main entries, like this:

Human resources: Creating a personnel file, 21; Updating personnel data, 24

TROUBLESHOOTING

Error messages appear in my index.

You've marked your index entries and created the index by clicking Insert Index on the Index tab of the References tab. But after Word places the index in your document, you notice that error messages appear instead of the page numbers. The most likely cause is that you created the index in a subdocument rather than in the master document of your publication.

To resolve the problem, close the current document by clicking the File tab and clicking Close. Then open the master document. (For more information on working with master documents, see Chapter 24, "Special Features for Long Documents.") Expand all sub-documents and then press F9 to update your index. The page numbers should display correctly.

Changing Index Columns

Depending on the length of your document, the size of the index you're creating, and the number of pages you have available for the index, you might want to format your index in multiple columns. By default, Word compiles your index in two columns, but you might want to change this setting if you have a short index that will occupy only a partial column, or if you want to run text in the column beside the index you create.

You can create up to four columns on each page of the index. To make a change, display the Index dialog box and click the Columns up arrow or down arrow to increase or decrease the number of columns you want.

TROUBLESHOOTING

My index columns don't line up.

You've finished marking all the entries in your long document. On the References tab, you click Insert Index and select the format you want. You elect to create an indented index that's displayed in three columns. After reviewing your choices, you click OK to have Word compile the index. But when you see the index on the screen, you notice that the middle column is not aligning across the top with the other two columns; it seems to be starting a little lower on the page. What's going on?

Although Word automatically creates a section break both before and after your index, it's possible that an extra line space is preceding the first line in the second column. To confirm this, on the Home tab, click the Show/Hide button in the Paragraph group to display hidden paragraph marks in your document. Then review the top and bottom entries in each column. If you see an unwanted paragraph mark, select it and press Delete to remove it. Then press F9 to have Word update your index and balance the columns.

Updating an Index

You can update an index at any time by clicking anywhere within it and pressing F9. This means that after you look at the compiled index, you can go back into the document and add entries you missed. Word updates the index, and the choices you made in the Index dialog box are preserved.

> **Note**
>
> If you've made any formatting changes, such as selecting a different format style or changing from Indented to Run-In style, Word asks whether you want to replace the existing index with the new one. If you haven't made any editing changes in the current index—or you're willing to re-enter the changes you've made—select Yes. Word replaces the existing index with the new, updated one, and you'll need to re-enter those edits. If you select Cancel, the operation is canceled, and your changes are not made.

AutoMarking Entries with a Concordance File

A concordance file is a simple table you create to track and enter index entries easily. The table you create is a two-column table. In the first column, you enter the text you want Word to mark as the entry. And in the second column, you enter the text for the entry as you want it to appear in the index. Here are the steps to create a concordance file:

1. In a new document, on the Insert tab, click Table in the Tables group.

2. Create a two-column table.

3. In the first column, enter the words or phrases you want Word to mark for the entry.

> **Note**
> The entries in the first column are case sensitive. To create case insensitive entries, use all lowercase characters. Note that AutoCorrect might capitalize the first letter of each word automatically. If this behavior occurs, display the Auto-Correct Options (hover your mouse over the automatic change) and then click Stop Auto-Capitalizing First Letter Of Table Cells.

4. In the second column, type the index entry for the text in the first column. Be sure to type each entry in a separate cell.

5. Save and close the concordance file.

6. Open the file you want to index.

7. On the References tab, click Insert Index to display the Index dialog box.

8. Click the AutoMark button to display the Open Index AutoMark File dialog box (see Figure 23-12).

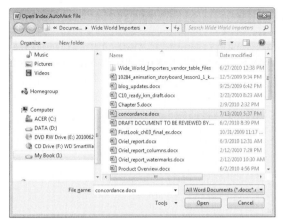

Figure 23-12 Use the Open Index AutoMark File dialog box to choose the concordance file for your index.

9. Navigate to and select the concordance file, and then click Open. Word automatically searches your document and locates each entry with the words you specified in the concordance file. (Word marks only the first occurrence of an entry in any one paragraph.)

> **Tip**
> Indexing in Word is a fairly straightforward process, but it's a good idea to practice working with the indexing features before you use them on a real document.

INSIDE OUT   Creating a Lean and Effective Concordance File

You think you're saving lots of time and trouble by creating a concordance file that lists topics you want to be sure to include in your index. After you finish creating and saving the list, you create the index, but you wind up with all kinds of unnecessary entries. For example, in your publication on contemporary music, you wanted to index references to *jazz*, but when your index is compiled, you see that the word *jazz* appeared in your publication in many different places and contexts. As a result, your index has many more references than you need.

Chapter 23

A workaround for compiling huge indexes full of unnecessary AutoMarked entries is to create the majority of the index entries manually using the Mark Index Entry dialog box (which you display by pressing Alt+Shift+X). Then use the concordance file and AutoMark in the Index dialog box to add to your basic index entries, including only key words or phrases that are used in the sections to which you want to refer your readers.

What's Next?

When you begin creating long or complex projects, it becomes more important than ever to help your readers find just the information they're looking for in your document. The table of contents and the index you produce provide two key ways readers can locate both the big-picture items and the more detailed subtopics in your text. This chapter showed you how to create each of these elements, and we'll continue this long-document theme in the next chapter as you learn about additional features that are helpful to include in your substantial projects.

Special Features for Long Documents

What Goes into a Long Document?. 732

Building a Table of Figures 732

Adding a Table of Authorities. 734

When Master Documents Make Sense 736

What's Next? 745

S OME projects you create in Word 2010 will be short and sweet—a memo, a two-page newsletter, an easy report. But other documents might be huge and require the ongoing work of many people. A book like this one, for example, involved hundreds and hundreds of Word pages, as well as an author, editors, tech reviewers, project managers, and more.

Consistency and continuity is important with any project, but it becomes particularly important when you work on longer documents. You need to ensure that all the parts of your document use the same styles, treat tables and figures the same way, and have consistent headers and footers. You need to be able to check the overall organization of your document, making sure that the topics flow logically, and that you've arranged them in the best possible order.

This is fairly easy to do in a normal document when you're working with 10, 20, or even 30 pages. But what about those large projects, for which various team members are taking a chapter or two, somebody else is plugging in the charts, and yet another person is checking the citations and references? And when you have numerous tables, figures, or lists of references, how do you keep it all organized so readers can find what they need easily in your text?

This chapter focuses on the things you are likely to want to add to long documents—such as a table of figures and table of authorities. You'll also learn about the master documents feature—which can be a bit unpredictable in some situations and more reliable in others—and find out how to use AutoSummarize to create an abstract of your document with just a few clicks of the mouse.

What Goes into a Long Document?

Some long documents are fairly straight-forward, but chances are that the longer your document is, the more you'll need to add features that help your readers find what they need, without difficulty. The following elements might be part of helping your readers navigate your longer documents:

- Headers and footers (with page numbers) help readers to identify which section and chapter they are reading.

- A cover page gives readers the scope and theme of the overall project.

- Citations, footnotes, or endnotes give readers information about the resources and quotes you've cited.

- A bibliography provides a list of resources readers can use to find out more about your topic.

- Line numbers are sometimes used when a document is going through the review process to help all reviewers comment on content, based on the number of the line in which it appears.

In addition to these common elements for longer documents, you might have more specialized needs, such as the table of figures and table of authorities (described in this chapter). These elements can give your readers additional resources for locating the key items in your document they might need to find quickly (like when a board member asks a pointed question about a chart on the annual report).

Building a Table of Figures

When you have Word generate a table of figures to use as a reference tool in your document, it searches for and collects the figure captions you've added. This means that you need to set up your captions before you generate the table.

Adding Captions

Start by adding labels to the items you want to include in your table of figures. You can add captions while you work by using Word's AutoCaption feature. On the References tab, click Insert Caption in the Captions group. The Caption dialog box appears, as you see in Figure 24-1. This is where you enter the text for the caption and choose the way you want it labeled and numbered.

Figure 24-1 Enter the settings for your captions in the Caption dialog box.

Click the AutoCaption button. In the AutoCaption dialog box, select the file type of the object you want to create captions for, as shown in Figure 24-2. In the Options area, click the Use Label arrow and choose whether you want the captions to be added to equations, figures, or tables. Click the Position arrow to choose whether you want the caption to appear above or below the item, and then click OK. The captions are added to your figures using the label and position settings you selected.

Figure 24-2 Use the AutoCaption dialog box to add labels and numbers to your figures automatically.

Controlling Figure Numbering

You can also add figure numbering to your captions in the Caption dialog box. Select the element to which you want to add the numbering (or update your other caption choices) and then click the Numbering button. The Caption Numbering dialog box appears, as shown in Figure 24-3.

Figure 24-3 With the Caption Numbering dialog box, you can choose the format and style of the numbering sequence.

Begin by choosing the format you want to use for the numbering sequence. You can choose the traditional 1, 2, 3 (or A, B, C) or you can choose roman numerals in the Format list box. If you want to include chapter numbers (which Word picks up from the text), select the Include Chapter Number check box. Next, specify the first heading style in the chapter (this shows Word where to begin looking) then select a separator character from the Use Separator list box (Word will place this between the chapter number and the figure number). Click OK to save the settings. When you add your next figure, the caption number will be applied automatically.

Generating a Table of Figures

After you've added captions to your illustrations, you can use those captions to create a table of the figures in your document. A table of figures is a helpful reference in long documents that include important charts, scientific diagrams, or other illustrations that users will want to refer to as they read.

To create a table of figures, begin by clicking at the position in the document where you want to add the table. On the References tab, in the Captions group, click Insert Table Of Figures. The Table Of Figures dialog box appears. The default selections for the table are displayed in the preview boxes (see Figure 24-4). Change the settings as needed then click OK to create the table. The table of figures is placed in the document at the insertion point.

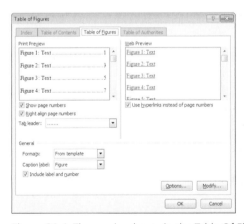

Figure 24-4 The preview boxes in the Table Of Figures dialog box show the default selections.

Adding a Table of Authorities

A table of authorities is a more specialized table reference that helps you track, compile, and display citations in your document. You'll use this feature most often for legal documents that reference cases, rules, treaties, and other documents. Before you can create a table of citations, obviously, you need to have placed those citations within the body of the document.

Adding Citations Manually

In Chapter 10, "Editing, Proofing, and Using Reference Tools," you learned how to use cita-tions to create effective bibliographies. But because you need to have entered citations before you can create a table that lists them, here's a quick summary of the process:

1. Select the citation in the document.

2. Press Alt+Shift+I. The Mark Citation dialog box appears with the selected citation displayed in the Selected Text box, as shown in Figure 24-5.

Figure 24-5 Use the Mark Citation dialog box to include citations in your table of authorities.

3. Click the Category arrow then choose the type of citation you're creating.

4. Edit the citation, if needed, in the Short Citation box, and then click Mark.

    Word adds the necessary codes to your document to identify the citation for inclu-sion in the table of authorities.

5. If you want to continue adding citations, click Next Citation.

6. Click Close to close the dialog box when you're finished adding citations.

> **Note**
>
> You can also add citations directly into the Table Of Authorities dialog box. To do so, click the References tab and select the Insert Table Of Authorities command in the Table Of Authorities group. Click Mark Citation to display the Mark Citation dialog box. Enter your citation as needed then click Mark to complete the entry.

Generating the Table of Authorities

After you've entered the citations you want to reference, you can start the process of creating a table of authorities. On the References tab, Table Of Authorities group, click Insert Table Of Authorities. The Table Of Authorities dialog box appears, as Figure 24-6 shows.

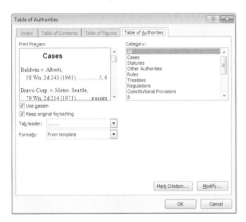

Figure 24-6 The Table Of Authorities dialog box includes everything you need for entering and formatting the table.

Choose the category you want to use from the list on the right. You use the different categories to select the type of element that will comprise the table. Click the Formats arrow and select the formatting style you want; then click OK to create the table of authorities.

> **Note**
> If you've created multiple tables in your document, be sure to update each table independently. To update a table, click in it, and then press F9.

When Master Documents Make Sense

At its most basic level, a master document holds several separate files—called subdocuments—together. You might create a master document to handle the following projects:

- A book-length manuscript in which each team member writes and edits one chapter.

- A grant proposal in which different committee members are responsible for different pieces.

For example, your executive director is writing the executive summary, your financial officer is providing the budget, and your development committee chairperson is writing the objective and evaluation sections.

- Your international company's annual report, which is a compilation of a number of different sections, including the introduction, the program descriptions, the donor thank-you section, sections from each office site, and letters from clients served. Each person on your publications team could research and write a different piece of the report.

- A technical manual that's a collaborative effort between your IT department and a technical illustrator.

  After each chapter is written, you can send it as a subdocument to the illustrator, who can create and place the illustrations and then return the subdocument to be integrated back into the master.

When they work the way they are supposed to, master documents can help you:

- Keep track of disparate sections and open and print them all rather than working with individual files

- Display and collapse subdocuments to switch between views easily

- Coordinate pieces of a project that are distributed to other team members

- Review and easily reorganize a long document

- Control styles, margins, and other formats throughout a long document

- Work with a long document as a whole for operations such as printing, checking spelling, and using the Find and Find And Replace features

Master Document Mayhem and Workarounds

Unfortunately, because of the way master documents work, users occasionally have trouble with this feature. (You can find ample evidence of this by doing an online search.) The problem seems to come from the way information is stored in the master document and subdocuments. Word keeps track of a considerable amount of information for each of the individual files, templates, building block files, sections, and more that you create. In some cases, one or more files can become corrupt due to a conflict in the information tracked for the file.

If the document you are creating really does call for you to use master documents, and nothing else will do, you can do a few things to safeguard your master and subdocuments as much as possible:

- Only include the links to your subdocuments in the master document file. In other words, don't mix content and subdocument links. The master file seems to stay healthier when you keep it clean and simple.

- Keep regular backups of all your files—master and subdocuments. That way if one of the files becomes corrupt, you can substitute your backup copy. This does require more organization and religious follow-through on your part, but it's better than trying to restore a corrupt file.

If you're not so sure you want to continue with your plan to use master documents, you might try one of these workarounds:

- Divide the large file into its individual components and assign each author his or her individual document part. Then add the finalized individual documents into the main document before you begin your review process (on the Insert tab, click Text From File from the Object tool in the Text group).

- You could leave the entire document together, assign editing restrictions so that your team members can edit only their individual sections, and post the document on your SharePoint 2010 server or Windows Live SkyDrive account. Using this method, you can take advantage of Word's co-authoring features to work on the file.

Getting Started with a Master Document

If you decide that you want to try using a master document and subdocuments for your long project, begin in Outline view by clicking the Outline icon in the view tools, which is located in the lower-right corner of the Word 2010 window. In Outline view, the Master Document group contains the tools you need. When you click Show Document, additional tools become available. Figure 24-7 shows a document with a subdocument already defined; the Master Document tools are visible on the Outlining tab. Table 24-1 introduces you to the Master Document tools.

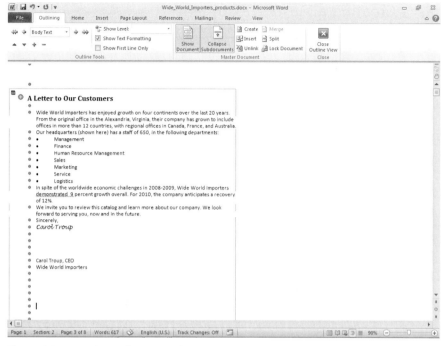

Figure 24-7 Start in Outline view when you want to create master documents and subdocuments.

Table 24-1 Master Document Tools

Tool	Description
Show Document	Switches the display to master document view so that you can see subdocument icons
Collapse Subdocuments	Limits the display of subdocument sections to their heading levels
Create	Creates a subdocument of the current selection
Insert	Inserts an existing document as a subdocument
Unlink	Removes the subdocument designation and returns the selection to being a normal part of the master document
Merge	Puts two or more selected subdocuments together
Split	Divides a subdocument into two subdocuments
Lock Document	Secures the subdocument so that no further changes can be made

Chapter 24

Creating a Master Document

When you are ready to create a master document, you can start with an existing document and turn it into a master document by creating subdocuments within it, or create a master document from scratch, creating the outline headings and subdocuments as you go.

To start fresh, open a new document and display Outline view. Enter the document title and the main headings. Make sure you give each heading that you want to turn into a subdocument the Heading 1 style. Enter any other headings you want to include and give them the appropriate heading levels by using the Outline tools on the Outlining tab. Remember to save the file.

If you already have a document you want to use as a master document, start by opening the file you want to use and displaying it in Outline view. The heading styles you've assigned to the text in your document become the headings in the master document outline.

> **Tip**
>
> If you think you might like to keep a copy of your outline before it's been divided into subdocuments, on the File tab, choose Save As to save a backup copy of the outline file. Although you can easily remove subdocument divisions and integrate subdocuments into the master later, that's a big hassle if you simply want an original version of the outline to refer to later.

TROUBLESHOOTING

My document headings don't appear in Outline view.

When you change to Outline view, you might find that your headings don't look like headings anymore. This can occur if you created your own styles and didn't base them on the Heading 1 or Heading 2 styles in Word, or you simply entered the headings using the Normal style. If this is the case, Word won't recognize your headings.

To fix this easily, click the Promote button in the Outline Tools group to raise the text to Level 1, which also assigns the Heading 1 style. You can easily modify your custom styles and base them on the Heading 1 style so that you can get the look you want and still be able to work with Outline view and Master Documents mode. For more on setting up and working with styles, see Chapter 12, "Applying and Customizing Quick Styles."

Creating Subdocuments

Once you have the basic outline in place, you can instruct Word how you want to divide the master document. Start by making sure that all headings and subheadings you want to include in the subdocument are displayed. Click the Show Level drop-down arrow in the Outline Tools group on the Outlining tab and select All Levels.

Click the plus (+) symbol to the left of the heading for the text you want to use for the subdocument. (When you click the + symbol, the entire topic is selected.) Click Create in the Master Documents group, and the topic is marked as a subdocument (see Figure 24-8). Save the document. Word saves the subdocument as a separate file in the same folder by default. The Heading 1 text at the beginning of the file is used as the file name.

Figure 24-8 Word creates the subdocument.

Importing Data for Subdocuments

You can also create subdocuments by inserting other files into your master document. In this case, you might have a partial outline you're working with, or you might start a new file for your master and then open existing files into it. Regardless of how you get the document pieces together, begin with your master document open on the screen. Display the document in Outline view. Place the insertion point where you want to add the subdocument then click Insert in the Master Document group. This opens the Insert Subdocument dialog box (see Figure 24-9).

Navigate to the file you want to import, select it, and then click Open. The subdocument is added to the master document at the insertion point. Add or create other subdocuments as needed. When you're finished creating subdocuments, save the file. Word saves the master document and the subdocuments in the folder you specify.

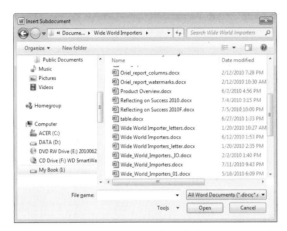

Figure 24-9 Importing an existing file into a master document to use as a subdocument saves you data entry and organizing time.

Working with the Master and Subdocuments

The basic idea behind master documents is that you can have one large file in which all pieces are represented, but for convenience and expediency's sake, each of the pieces can be worked on by different people at the same time. As you begin to work with and edit the text of your document, you'll need to know how to navigate among the files to make any changes.

After you create a master document and subdocuments within it, Word changes the way it saves the file information. No longer is everything stored within the single document. Now the master document contains links to the subdocuments, and when you expand and work with the subdocuments within the master, you are really, through links, working in the individual subdocument files themselves. You can see how this can get complicated as all the changes in the individual files are stores and then reflected in the linked master document.

The following items show you how to do some basic tasks with master documents and subdocuments:

- **Move a document.** To move to the subdocument, simply press Ctrl and click the link. The subdocument file opens in a new Word window on your screen. You can now edit the file as needed.

TROUBLESHOOTING

Word can't find my subdocument files.

If you later reorganize your files and move subdocuments from one place to another—
even if you are moving them within the same directory to new subfolders—Word will
display the message "cannot open the specified file." To re-establish links between your
master document and subdocuments, first delete the broken subdocument link and
then use Insert in the Master Document group on the Outlining tab to relink the document from its new location.

● **Expand subdocuments.**   To expand and display the subdocuments in the master
document, begin by clicking at the beginning of the document. (Change to Outline
view, if necessary.) Click Expand Subdocuments in the Master Document group on
the Outlining tab. All subdocuments in your master document are displayed. The
subdocument icon and any subordinate text and graphics also appear.

Tip

When you expand subdocuments in the master document, you can change to
Print Layout view to see how the sections will look in print form. You can make
formatting changes, check spelling, and use Find and Replace to your heart's
content while you're in Print Layout view so that you can see how the format is
affected. Then return to Outline view to finish working with the master document and to move sections, if needed.

● **Collapse subdocuments.**   Once you've expanded the subdocuments in the master,
the Expand Subdocuments button changes to Collapse Subdocuments so that you
can again suppress the display of the subdocuments. You'll want to do this before
you reorder subdocuments in your master document. To collapse the master display,
click anywhere in the document and select Collapse Subdocuments. The master goes
back to its links-only display.

Note

If you want to collapse only the heading levels within a subdocument, use the
normal Collapse button on the Outline Tools command tab of the Outlining tab
to control that display.

TROUBLESHOOTING

Different styles appear in the master document and subdocuments.

If you notice that the headings in your master document and subdocuments look different, check the template you've applied to them. To do this, on the File tab, choose Options then click Add-Ins. Click the Manage arrow, choose Templates from the list that appears, and then click Go. The Templates And Add-Ins dialog box appears. In the Document Template section, review each file to ensure that both the master and the subdocument have the same template selected and that the Automatically Update Document Styles check box is selected. If necessary, attach a different template by clicking Attach and, in the Attach Template dialog box, navigating to the template file you want. Make your selection then click Open. Click OK to close the Templates And Add-Ins dialog box and return to the document.

- **Merge subdocuments.** To merge subdocuments, display the file into which you want to merge the second file then click Expand Subdocuments. Check to ensure that the subdocuments are included in the correct order. Click Merge in the Master Document group to merge the documents.

> ### Note
> When Word combines subdocuments, the first file "takes on" the new data, and everything is saved into that file.

- **Separate subdocuments.** If you create a new topic or want to divide a subdocument into two, simply create a new heading at the point where you want to make the break (or raise an existing heading to a Heading 1 level), and then in the Master Document group on the Outlining tab, click Split. The subdocument is divided at the insertion point.

- **Convert subdocuments.** To convert subdocuments back into a single document, display the master in Outline view, select all subdocuments you want to merge, and then click Unlink in the Master Document group on the Outlining tab.

TROUBLESHOOTING

The master document is incomplete when printed.

If you find that some sections are missing when you print your master document, return to Outline view and scroll through the document to verify that all sections have been expanded. Anything left collapsed will not be printed, so ensure that you expand the entire document, if that's your intention, before you print.

What's Next?

This chapter showed you how to add tables of figures and tables of authorities to your long documents. It also introduced you to the risks and blessings of using master documents. You can easily create master documents and divide them into subdocuments that you can share with your team—just be sure to keep regular backups of all the files, and do your best to ensure that your master is as simple as possible. The next chapter moves into the online realm by introducing you to Word 2010's blogging tool and the Word Web App.

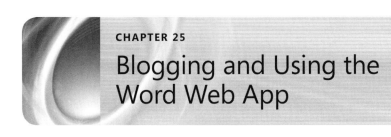

Everybody Blogs. 747

Starting a New Blog Post 750

Configuring Your Blog Account. 755

Using the Word Web App. 757

What's Next? 759

So, do you blog? It's a common question people really are asking each other—and not just at dinner parties, either. When you punch up your resume, add something about your blog. New clients will want to know if you have any blogging experience. If you're in an industry that relates to the public—and most of us are, in one way or another—having blogging experience is like adding a gold star to your personnel file, because today is all about the buzz, and if you can contribute to it, you're in demand.

In case you hadn't noticed, blogging is everywhere on the Web—individuals are doing it, mommies are doing it, businesses are doing it, and news corporations are *certainly* doing it. Let's do it. Let's talk about blogging in Word 2010.

The developers of Word have long been aware of the rise of interest in the blogosphere, and for that reason, for the last couple of incarnations, Word has included blogging as part of the program. You can start a new post using a method similar to starting a new document. And you can post directly to your blog without ever leaving Word. This is especially nice because it keeps a copy of the blog post where you can review it or use it in something else if you like, which is not the case if you simply use an online blogging tool to add your posts.

This chapter introduces you to the blogging features in Word and also opens up the conversation to the new Word Web App, the easy-to-use online version of Word that makes it possible for you to edit your annual report in coffee shops or trade files with colleagues in Tangiers. Very simple and very slick.

Everybody Blogs

Come on, admit it. You've thought about blogging. No, maybe you don't want to blog about your job as a purchaser of widgets for a large thingamabob factory. But you *might* like to blog about your interest in photography; or the fun travels you took last summer; or your interest in rare coins.

Blogging gives everyone a voice, and that's one of the great benefits. It also represents one of the greatest challenges. Because *everyone* can blog, it becomes important to make yours stand out; to say something profound or interesting and somehow distinguish your content, your product, or your company. Blogging started in the mid-1990s, but most of the phenomenal growth in the "blogosphere" has taken place since 2000. Bloggers come from all walks of life, all age groups, and all perspectives—a fact that is both exciting and overwhelming when you begin to browse through the number of blogs available out there for your review.

At its most basic level, blogging is personal (or corporate) web publishing that you can do almost instantly—but it's also more than that. One thing that sets blogs apart from other pages on the Web is their fast-changing nature and the fact that they often include links— links to other blogs, to resource sites, to communities, to media, and more. Links are created when others reference your blog in their own posts (and vice versa). Trackbacks enable people reading blogs to move from one to the next to the next. Bloggers are able to publish the latest news and can, within minutes, reach a worldwide audience, thanks to all the other bloggers who are searching for and linking to posts on that same topic. Combine this with Twitter and you have news unfolding as it happens—literally.

Some people blog for pleasure; they stay in touch with family and friends, or simply share their interests and outlook with the world. Others blog with purpose; they comment on political, corporate, or societal ideas and events, or they highlight stories that the mainstream media misses (or won't spend much time on, such as behind the scenes stories on current events).

Bloggers told it like it was during and after the destruction caused by the earthquake in Haiti, they report on the war in Afghanistan, they help expose corrupt politicians and companies, and they provide a voice—sometimes a very loud and far-reaching voice—that broadcasts a part of the cultural debate that might not be well represented elsewhere.

The first blogging tools were a bit clunky and required users to learn HTML to post. As a result, most of the early bloggers were experts in technology. As blogging caught on, the tools became more user-friendly; even those without any programming experience could simply add their writing and photos to a page without a lot of hassle or technical know-how.

Blogging sites such as Blogger and LiveJournal have had a lot to do with the ever-expanding popularity of blogging. Utilities like blogrolls (a type of free utility that bloggers use to show links to their own favorite blogs) helped to expand the links. Social networking tools, such as Facebook, Twitter, and LinkedIn make it easy for bloggers to share what they post with not just a single community but *communities* of communities.

You might wonder what blogging has to do with professional or corporate communications. Depending on the type of business you have, to a greater or lesser extent, your communication with your customers is important. Letting them know what you're doing by writing about your new products, showing key new features, or introducing them to staff members can help the customer feel he "knows" your company.

Many companies today are encouraging their employees to blog about their projects (within nondisclosure guidelines, of course) to help give potential customers a behind-the-scenes look at the corporate life and mission. Microsoft is one of those companies with a large group of corporate bloggers—in fact, during the beta testing of Microsoft Office 2010, representatives from the different Microsoft Office 2010 program groups blogged for many months before the release. Interested users could go to the blogs to find posts on the latest new features in their favorite applications and find information on new or challenging tools—straight from the horse's mouth.

Microsoft Office Blogs

You'll find a lot of good information on the Microsoft Office 2010 blogs. Typically posts are added on a regular basis, so check the blog of your favorite program to find out tips and tricks that will help you get more out of your application. Here's the list of blogs you might want to check out:

- Office blogs: *http://blogs.office.com/*

- Excel team blog: *http://blogs.msdn.com/b/excel/*

- Word team blog: *http://blogs.office.com/b/microsoft-word/*

- Office Web Apps blog: *http://blogs.msdn.com/b/officewebapps/*

- OneNote blog: *http://blogs.office.com/b/microsoft-onenote/*

- Outlook blog: *http://blogs.msdn.com/b/outlook/*

- PowerPoint blog: *http://blogs.msdn.com/b/powerpoint/*

- Publisher blog: *http://blogs.msdn.com/b/microsoft_office_publisher/*

- Access blog: *http://blogs.msdn.com/b/access/*

Starting a New Blog Post

Basically, creating a blog post is the same as creating any document—you click and type your text as you want it to appear. Follow these steps to start a new blog post:

1. Click the File tab to display Backstage view.

2. Click New, click Blog Post, and then click Create (see Figure 25-1).

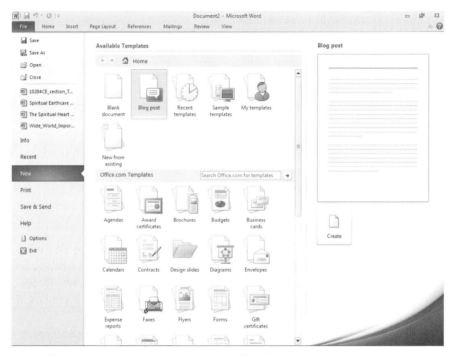

Figure 25-1 Choose Blog Post in the New tab of Backstage view to start the process of creating a blog entry.

3. The Blog Post window opens and a popup dialog box appears, asking you to register your blog account (see the image that follows). For now, click Register Later (you learn how to register your account on page 755) to return to the Blog Post window, as shown in Figure 25-2.

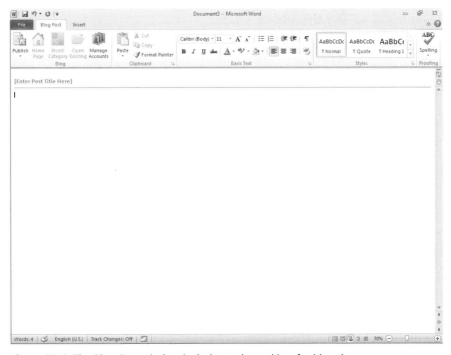

Figure 25-2 The Blog Post window includes tools used just for blogging.

The Blog Post window includes two command tabs: Blog Post and Insert. When the Blog Post tab is selected (as it is in Figure 25-2), the groups provide you with the tools you need for working with your blog, working with the clipboard, entering basic text, applying styles, and proofing your entry. The Insert tab is available only if your blogging service permits you to include photos.

> **Tip**
>
> If you have more than one blog configured to work with Word 2010, a control is available so you can choose the blog to which you want to post.

Entering Text

To begin entering text for your post, click in the [Enter Post Title Here] prompt and type the title for your blog entry (see Figure 25-3).

Figure 25-3 Click the prompt and type your post title.

Click below the line to begin entering the text for the body of your post. After you type the entry, click the Spelling tool to run the spelling checker. You can also change the typeface, size, color, or alignment of the text, just as you would modify the formatting of a traditional document.

If you want to change the style of the text, click one of the styles in the Style gallery or click the More button in the lower-right corner of the gallery. The Styles gallery opens, in which you can review and select the type of text style you want to apply to the post text.

Inserting a Web Link

As mentioned earlier, blogs wouldn't be blogs without the links—they would be static Web pages. To add a hyperlink to your blog post, follow these steps:

1. Highlight the section to which you want to add the link.

2. On the Insert tab, click Hyperlink (see Figure 25-4).

   The Insert Hyperlink dialog box appears.

3. In the Address box, type the URL to which you want to link the selected text.

4. Click OK to save the link.

   The text will appear underlined in a blue font, indicating that it is now a hyperlink. If you want to ensure that you typed the link correctly, hover the pointer over the link. The URL will appear in a pop-up box above the link.

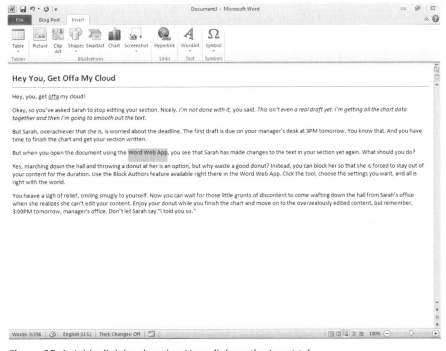

Figure 25-4 Add a link by choosing Hyperlink on the Insert tab.

Adding a Category to Your Post

Categorizing your blog post helps search engines locate what you're blogging about and also gives your regular readers a way to find all posts related to a specific topic. To add a category to your post, click the Insert Category tool in the Blog group on the Blog Post tab. The Category field appears above the body text of your post. Click the arrow to see the list of categories. Click the one you want to apply to the post you created.

> **Note**
> The categories that appear depend on the categories created to work with your blog program. Some programs provide ready-made categories; with others, you can set up and use categories of your own.

What Will You Blog About?

The content of your blog will depend largely on your purpose. If you're just blogging for fun, to keep family apprised of all the happenings in your part of the world, or to share your interest or expertise in a particular topic, the posts will probably include stories, events, photos, and more. If you are blogging to build your expertise in a particular area, you might want to include all the latest news stories related to your area of interest as well as files and presentations you create. If you are hoping to inspire others to join your nonprofit organization, you might include stories of those who have been helped by your organization in the past. If you want to get the word out about your candidacy, share your passion for movies, or share your philosophy with the rest of the world, you might include links, stories, photos, resources, and engaging bits of information in the areas you want to highlight.

Here are some questions to consider as you plan the content for your blog:

- **Who is your "typical reader"?** Getting a clear picture of that person—and that person's expectations—can help you connect with your reader right from the start.

- **What age is the reader?** Knowing the general demographics of your typical reader will be helpful. Chances are that because blogging is a kind of "real voice" medium, you might connect most easily with those close to your own age level. But many people have a knack for speaking to everyone at once. Know the interests, energy level, and passions of the audience you are addressing.

- **What is the reader most interested in?** Is your reader fascinated with technology, passionate about the environment, concerned about the political climate, or focusing on her newborn? Thinking about topics in which your reader might be fascinated right now will help you develop a sense for what others will find interesting on your blog.

- **What do you want the person to do after reading your blog?** If you want the person to come back, subscribe to your newsletter, try your product, sign up for your mailing list, or write to their congressperson, be sure you say so directly somewhere in the body of your blog.

- **Are there any limitations on your subject matter?** If you are writing a corporate blog, there might be definite guidelines for the type of content you can include. Additionally, you need to consider the fact that public blogs can be read by virtually everyone. This means that unless you restrict your blog so that only the people you specify can view it, you might have children as well as adults reading what you write (including your mother and grandmother!). Think through any limitations—and any ramifications of your posting—before you post.

Adding a Picture to Your Post

Most blog posts include a heading and supporting text. Some blog posts include photos, as well. You can add photos to your Word blog post by clicking at the place you want to add the picture and selecting the Insert tab. Click Picture in the Illustrations group.

In the Insert Picture dialog box, navigate to the folder storing the picture you want to include, select the picture, and then click Insert. Once you add the picture to the post, the contextual Picture Tools tab appears. You can edit, resize, or add a style or special effect to the picture, as you normally would.

Configuring Your Blog Account

When you're ready to publish your blog post, on the Blog Post tab, click Publish in the Blog group. If you haven't yet set up your blog account (or if you clicked Register Later in the Blog Post window, as mentioned earlier in this chapter), you will be asked to enter the information for your blog account or sign up for a new one.

Click Manage Accounts in the Blog group to start the process of setting up your new blog account. In the Blog Accounts window, click New. The New Blog Post window appears. Begin by clicking the Blog arrow and choosing your service from the list. Here's a quick introduction to each of the items on the list:

- **Windows Live Spaces**   Windows Live Spaces is a free blogging and social networking service where you can blog, post photos, and connect with friends and family online. To find out more, go to *http://windowslive.com/Online/spaces*.

- **Blogger**   Blogger is one of the largest and oldest blogging services available. Now part of Google, Blogger offers free blogging services without ads. Go to *www.blogger.com* for more information.

- **SharePoint Blog**   To use this feature, you must have access to a company server running Windows SharePoint Services. Ask your system administrator for more information on whether your local server runs Windows SharePoint Services and to find out whether you have the permissions you need to post a blog to that server.

- **Community Server**   Community Server is an online community-building program that is free for personal use but has varying licenses for commercial use. Community Server includes both blogging and forum posting features. For more information, go to *http://Telligent.com*.

- **Other**   Use this if you have a service provider different from those shown in the list. If you have a different provider, click the My Providers Isn't Listed link.

Make your choice and click Next. The New Account Window appears, asking for information about the blog. If you selected Windows Live Spaces, the New Windows Live Spaces Account dialog box appears, as shown in Figure 25-5. If you selected a Blogger account, the New Blogger Account window asks you to enter your user name and password.

Figure 25-5 Setting up an account in the New Windows Live Spaces Account dialog box.

Type your space name and enter the secret word. Select the Remember Secret Word check box if you want Windows Live Spaces to save your secret word and apply it automatically whenever you post. These settings set up the access to your blog.

Now you need to set up the picture options so that you'll be able to include photos, graphics, pictures, diagrams, and charts in your posts. Click the Picture Options button to display the Picture Options dialog box (see Figure 25-6). Here you'll choose the way in which your pictures will be hosted. Click the Picture Provider arrow and choose My Own Server if you have server space in which your images can be housed. If you have your own server space, click that option and enter the upload URL and source URL. Then click OK twice to return to your post.

Figure 25-6 You can choose Picture Options to control the way images are uploaded to your blog.

Using the Word Web App

Imagine how nice it is to not be tied to your computer at work. Using the Word Web App, you can continue working on your Word documents anywhere you have Web access. You can review reports at the coffee shop, log in and edit a letter from home, or even make last-minute changes on a brochure from your Windows-based smartphone.

The Word Web App—and all the Office Web Apps, for that matter—are free for you to use with your copy of Office 2010. The Office Web Apps work seamlessly with Windows Live SkyDrive so that you can easily upload, share, and work on your documents wherever you can get online. Once you upload your documents using Windows Live SkyDrive—or directly from within Word—you can edit them easily using the Word Web App.

Save Your Document to Windows Live SkyDrive

Begin the process by saving your Word document to your Windows Live SkyDrive account. On the File tab, choose Save & Send then click Save To Web. Choose one of the folders or click New to sign in and create a new online folder.

If you don't yet have a Windows Live SkyDrive account, click Sign Up and follow the onscreen prompts to obtain a Windows Live ID.

> **Tip**
> You can invite others to co-author the file you've saved in Windows Live SkyDrive by providing permissions to the users with whom you want to share the file. For more about setting file permissions in Windows Live SkyDrive, see Chapter 21, "Sharing Your Documents."

Open Your Document in the Word Web App

When you're out and about and want to work on your file using the Word Web App, first log in to your Windows Live SkyDrive account, and then click Office at the top of the window. A list of files you've added to the space appears. Hover the mouse over the file you want to see then click Edit In Browser (see Figure 25-7).

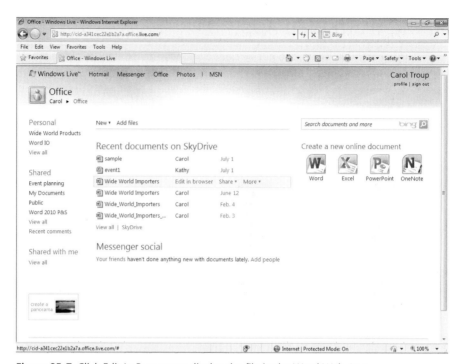

Figure 25-7 Click Edit In Browser to display the file in the Word Web App.

> **Tip**
>
> You can add more files to your Windows Live SkyDrive account by clicking Add Files and then dragging files to the upload space or clicking Select Files From Your Computer and choosing the files you want to add.

You can also open a document in Word 2010, which opens the file on your computer and then synchronizes your changes with the version on the server when you save the file.

Working with the Word Web App

When you open the file in the browser to work on it in the Word Web App, the first thing you'll notice is the familiar Word Ribbon. Not all the tabs are available, but you'll have the tools you need to work with the various elements on your pages and do all you need to do (see Figure 25-8).

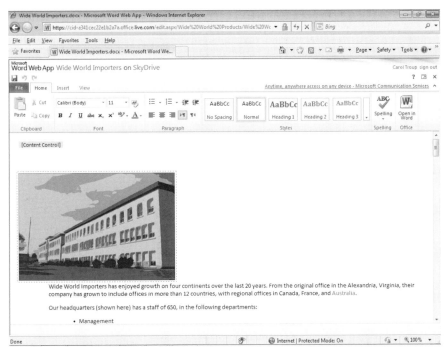

Figure 25-8 The Word Web App includes tools for creating, editing, and sharing your files.

As you can see, you can add content, assign styles, check spelling, and more using the Word Web App. On the Insert tab, you'll find the tools you need to add tables, pictures, clip art, and links. The View tab gives you the choice of moving between Edit view and Reading view.

If you want to open a copy of the file in Word 2010, click Open in Word in the Office group on the Home tab. The file opens in Word but it is still linked to the online file; when you make changes to the file they are synchronized with the server so that the most up-to-date version of the file is available online.

What's Next?

This chapter introduced you to Word's blogging utility and showed you how to access and begin working with the Word Web App. The next chapter offers another way of sharing your documents by showing you how to prepare and send mailings in Word.

CHAPTER 26

Creating Mailings Large and Small

Mail Merge Overview 762

Know Your Merge Terms. 763

Starting the Mail Merge Project. 763

Selecting the Document Type 764

Starting Out with the Main Document. 765

Choosing Your Recipients 768

Choosing and Sorting Recipient Information 771

Adding Merge Fields 774

Previewing the Merge 781

Merging the Documents. 783

Creating a Directory. 784

Printing Envelopes and Labels 785

What's Next? 788

YOUR public awaits. How will you reach them with messages about your products, your programs, your board members, your staff? How do you talk about all the great stuff you do and encourage them to get involved?

Yes, Facebook. Sure, LinkedIn. But don't forget the almighty personalized letter.

When you communicate with your customers, clients, donors, or prospects, you are saying something about your organization and the way in which it values contact. If your letters, postcards, or personalized catalogs are dry, boring, and impersonal, the people reading your information are likely to remember a few of the facts that seem relevant and move on. But if you customize your e-mail, newsletter, or print letter by referring to the contact using their first name, mentioning products and programs the person is interested in, and showing them you remember the last time they bought from your catalog, you've gone a long way toward showing that customer you know what you're doing. You remember them, they're important, and your mailing reflects that.

This is the heart of a good mailing campaign—caring about and connecting with your reader. When you design a mail merge project in Word 2010 (something Word helps you do, by the way), you are in fact merging a letter, e-mail message, newsletter, catalog, or other personalized document with your data list to produce a customized document that appears to have been written just for the person who receives it. Of course, your larger plan is to send out 500 of these personalized documents, so each of those 500 people feels like a valued customer. Simple, right?

This chapter shows you how to create a mail merge project from start to finish. You can easily tweak and customize things along the way, and use (or not) the Step By Step Mail Merge

Wizard to lead you through the process. Like anything else in Word, if you do mailings very rarely, you might need a reminder from time to time about the various steps involved, but for the most part, the process is pretty intuitive.

Mail Merge Overview

Using the mail merge feature in Word, you can create letters, faxes, e-mail messages, envelopes, labels, and directories once and use them many times. The merge process is basically the same for all document types. All the commands you need are on the Mailings tab on the Ribbon, arranged in the order you need them (see Figure 26-1). Here's a quick rundown of the steps involved in the mail merge process:

1. Select the document type you want to create by choosing Envelopes or Labels in the Create group or by clicking Start Mail Merge in the Start Mail Merge group.

    In this step, you determine whether you want Word to create a letter, e-mail message, envelope, labels, or directory.

2. Select the recipients by choosing Select Recipients in the Start Mail Merge group.

    At this point, you can type a new list, choose your data list from an existing file, or select your Outlook Contacts list.

3. Write your letter (or e-mail message) and then add the necessary merge fields by using the commands in the Write & Insert Fields group.

4. Preview the merge operation and make any last minute changes by selecting commands in the Preview Results group.

5. Merge the document and the data source, and print or send the results by using the Finish & Merge command in the Finish group.

Figure 26-1 The Mailings tab contains the commands you will use to create your mailing project.

The next several sections explain more about each of these steps.

INSIDE OUT   Where Is the Mail Merge Wizard?

The Mailings tab is convenient because it provides you with all the commands you'll use for completing a mail merge project. You can see all the commands at once and simply click the one you need. But if you prefer to follow a more directed process for your project, you can use the Mail Merge Wizard that was introduced in Word 2003 and is still available in Word 2010. To start the Mail Merge Wizard, on the Mailings tab, click the Start Mail Merge button. The last command on the list of options that appears is Step By Step Mail Merge Wizard. Click this command to launch the wizard in a task pane on the right side of the Word window. Follow the prompts in the wizard to complete your project.

Know Your Merge Terms

The following terms might be new to you if you are learning about mail merge for the first time.

- **Main document.**   The letter, e-mail, envelope, or label into which the data will be merged.

- **Source file.**   Also known as the source list or recipients list, this is the file from which the merge data is taken.

- **Merge fields.**   Identifiers inserted in the main document that indicate to Word the position and type of data you want inserted at that point in the document.

- **Address block.**   Includes name and address information.

- **Greeting line.**   Adds the opening salutation, along with the name(s) of the recipient(s) you select.

Starting the Mail Merge Project

Whether you plan to save the postage and send it by e-mail or bite the bullet and send it in print, a little forethought is in order when you are organizing any kind of a big mailing project. Depending on the size and type of the mailing, you might begin working on the project weeks (or months!) in advance of your mailing date. Here are some examples of mailing projects, ranging from small to large.

- A follow-up e-mail message to a person who just bought one of your electronic gadgets

- A personalized e-mail newsletter sent to all the donors in your database

- A quick thank you letter to people who recently visited your open house

- A fundraising letter that thanks donors for their contributions last year and asks them to make a pledge for this year

- A customized catalog that includes only products in which the customer has indicated an interest

- A prospectus mailed to a particular client, designed to include the client's personal, business, and purchasing data

Selecting the Document Type

Your first choice in the mail merge process involves selecting the type of document you want to create. Will you be sending a direct mail letter, an e-mail message, or a fax? Perhaps you want to start with envelopes and labels, or create a directory to store listings of data such as customer names and addresses, product information, and personnel contact data. The Start Mail Merge command tab includes the tools you'll use for the first part of preparing your mailing project. Click Start Mail Merge to display the options showing the type of merge document you can create (see Figure 26-2). When you click Letters, E-Mail Messages, or Directory, Word displays the type of document you are creating.

Figure 26-2 Begin the merge process by choosing the type of merge document you want to create.

If you want to simply open a blank Word document, choose Normal Word Document. Additionally, if you prefer to use the Mail Merge Wizard, click Step by Step Mail Merge Wizard. This wizard appears in a task pane on the right side of the window and takes you through the steps involved in the merge process.

> **Note**
>
> Choosing Envelopes or Labels in the Start Mail Merge options displays the Envelope Options or Label Options dialog box, in which you can enter the information to print either of these items. For more about preparing envelopes and labels, see the section titled "Printing Envelopes and Labels," on page 785.

Starting Out with the Main Document

The main document is the document that holds the text that doesn't change—in other words, the boilerplate text that will appear on all the sales letters you send out or all your past due notices (or, for a happier example, all the birth announcements you send via e-mail). Word gives you a number of choices for the way in which you select your main document. You can do any of the following:

- Use the current document

- Start from a template

- Start from an existing document

Using the Current Document

If you decide to use the current document as the main document for your merge operation, you can simply type the text for the document as you want it to appear. You can omit the address information and the greeting at this point because Word provides the means to do that automatically when you add the merge fields to your document. Figure 26-3 shows an example of a form letter used in a merge print.

One consideration, however: If you're creating an e-mail message you want to broadcast in a merge operation, remember that many graphic images and special text formats can create larger files and possibly require more time for downloading. For the convenience of your readers, consider going light on the graphical enhancements if you're creating an e-mail message.

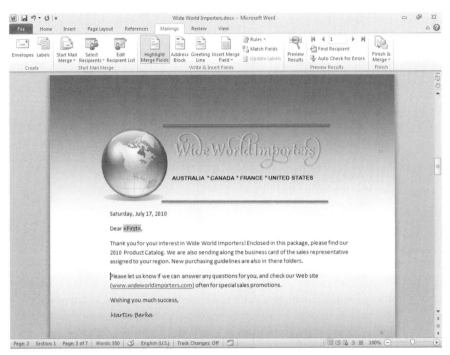

Figure 26-3   The main document stores the boilerplate text you'll use for the body of the message.

Starting from a Template

If you don't want to work with the current document, you can choose a template instead. Word gives you access to a number of mail merge templates you can start with and then modify to fit the document you want to send. To do this, perform the following steps:

1.   Click the File tab to display Backstage view.

2.   Click New. Click in the Search Office.com For Templates box, type merge, and then press Enter.

      Word searches Office.com for templates that include merge fields and displays the results in the Search Results area (see Figure 26-4). You'll find everything from post-cards and brochures, to labels and reports.

3.   Click a template you'd like to see; the item is displayed in the preview panel on the right side of the dialog box.

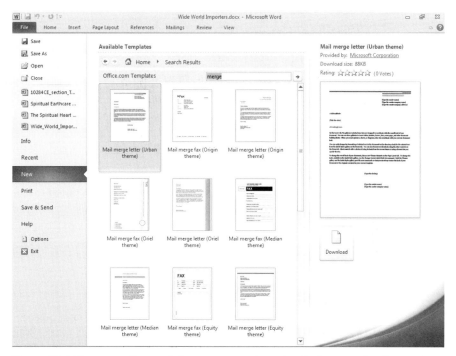

Figure 26-4 You can easily search for merge templates that fit the type of project you're creating.

4. When you find the template you want to use, select it then click Download.

The template opens in your document window.

5. Press Ctrl+S to display the Save As dialog box, enter a name for the document, and click Save.

Now you can begin filling in your own information and tailoring the document for your merge project.

Starting from an Existing Document

If you've used a letter in the past that was particularly effective, or if you want to save time by converting some of your marketing copy to content for a mailing, you can simply open that document and use it as the main document. A main document can include text, images, borders, colors, shades, tables, and more—anything a traditional Word document can contain.

> **Tip**
> If you used a form letter in a past mail merge operation, you can always use it again, even if it was created in an earlier version of Word. Simply open the existing document, and then on the File tab, click Convert. This converts the legacy file into Word 2010 format. Now you can add and modify information and fields as needed.

> **Tip**
> If you want to send a simple merge document but don't want to invest the time in creating a document from scratch, you can open an existing merge document and simply modify it with your own text.

Choosing Your Recipients

Who will you send your project to, and where do you store your contacts? These questions are part of the next step in the merge process. To choose the recipients of your merge document, use the Select Recipients command in the Start Mail Merge group (you might have seen the recipient list called the data source or source list in previous Word versions). Your choices are to use an existing list, choose Outlook Contacts, or type a new list (see Figure 26-5).

Figure 26-5 You select recipients by choosing the contact information of the people who will receive your mailing.

Creating a New List

If you have only a few recipients for the mailing you're preparing, you might want to use the Type A New List option to enter the names and addresses and save the information with the document. You might use this option, for example, when you are creating a merge template for the minutes of your monthly board meeting. You can enter the names, street addresses, and e-mail addresses for the board members once and then save and use the file for all the board meeting minutes throughout the year.

Here's how to create the new list.

1. On the Mailings tab, click Select Recipients in the Start Mail Merge group. Select Type New List from the options.

2. In the New Address List dialog box, type the information for the first recipient.

   You can press Tab to move the selection from field to field (see Figure 26-6).

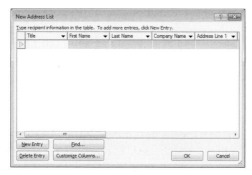

Figure 26-6 Type information for the recipient list in the New Address List dialog box.

3. To start a new recipient entry, click New Entry.

   The selection moves to the next row in the new address list.

4. Continue entering the information for each recipient, and then click OK when you're done.

After you click OK, the Save Address List dialog box appears, with My Data Sources selected as the current folder, as shown in Figure 26-7. Enter a name for the file then click Save.

Figure 26-7 Microsoft Office Address List files are stored by default in the My Data Sources folder, where they can be accessed by all Office applications.

Chapter 26

Customizing Address List Items

If you want to change the items listed in the New Address List dialog box, click Customize Columns. The Customize Address List dialog box appears. You can make the following changes to the Field Names list:

- To add a field name, click Add. The Add Field dialog box appears. Type the name for the field you want to create then click OK.

- To delete a field and all the field information, select the field, click Delete, and then click Yes in the confirmation message box.

- To rename a field, select it then click Rename. Enter a new name for the field then click OK.

- To move a field, select it, and then click either Move Up or Move Down to change its position in the list.

When you're finished making modifications to the field list, click OK to return to the New Address List dialog box. Add or edit your data as needed and then click Close to return to the document.

Using an Existing Recipient List

To select a list you've already created, click Use Existing List in the Select Recipients list. The Select Data Source dialog box appears, from which you can choose a data list you've already created. Navigate to the folder containing the file you want and then click Open. If the file includes more than one data table, the Select Table dialog box will appear; choose the data table you want (see Figure 26-8).

Figure 26-8 If more than one table is used in your data source, Word will prompt you to choose the table containing the data you want to use.

Choosing Outlook Contacts

The easiest way to add up-to-date contact information is to use your contact manager: Outlook. Because contacts in Outlook are updated as you work, your Outlook contact information might be more current and complete than static data lists. You can add e-mail addresses easily from messages you receive and send, which means you are gathering data continually while you go through your daily routine. Of course, the most complete data records—for example, client information that includes name, address, home and office phones, e-mail address, Web pages, and spouse names and birth dates—are available only because you add the information yourself. This means that the degree to which Outlook can actually help you will depend on how consistently and diligently you've entered contact information.

To select your Outlook Contacts list, simply click Select From Outlook Contacts in the Select Recipients list. The Select Contacts dialog box appears, as shown in Figure 26-9. Click the contacts list you want to use then click OK. The entries in your Contacts list appear in the Mail Merge Recipient dialog box.

Figure 26-9 You can easily import your Outlook Contacts for use in your Word mail merge operations.

Choosing and Sorting Recipient Information

Now that Word knows where to find the information you want to use in the merge operation, you can narrow things down further by clicking Edit Recipient List in the Start Mail Merge group on the Mailings tab. Use the Mail Merge Recipients dialog box to choose, sort, and edit the information in your data source file (see Figure 26-10). If you plan to make changes, such as updating the address of a particular client, changing a company name, or deleting customer information you no longer use, you can use the commands in this dialog box to carry out those tasks. Table 26-1 lists the various ways you can work with merge data.

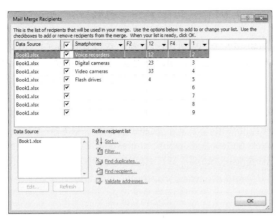

Figure 26-10 Use the Mail Merge Recipients dialog box to select the recipients for your mailing and to edit information as needed.

Table 26-1 **Working with Merge Data**

Action	Result
Clear the check mark in the selection column.	Removes a recipient from the merge operation.
Select the check box in the selection column.	Adds a recipient to the merge operation.
Click the arrow in the heading of the column by which you want to sort (for example, Last Name).	Reorders recipient records based on a particular field (if the listing was A to Z, clicking the heading will arrange the list Z to A).
Click a Data Source entry and click Edit. When the address list dialog box appears, click New Entry and enter the new recipient data. Click Close to close the dialog box.	Adds a new recipient to the list.
Click Sort.	Displays the Filter And Sort dialog box, which you can use to choose the field(s) by which you want to sort the information.
Click Filter.	Displays the Filter Records tab of the Filter And Sort dialog box which you can use to enter the fields and values by which you want to filter the data used.
Click Find Duplicates.	Locates and displays any duplicates in your data list and enables you to deselect them to leave them out of the merge operation.
Click Find Recipient.	Displays the Find Entry dialog box so that you can search for a specific word or phrase in your data list.
Click the Validate Addresses link.	Checks the data validity for your address data, if you have a validation program installed.

Filtering Your Recipient List

Most of the items in the Mail Merge Recipients list are straightforward, but one needs a bit more explanation. If you want to filter the information in your current recipient list, click the Filter link in the Mail Merge Recipients dialog box. When you click Filter, the Filter And Sort dialog box appears, as shown in Figure 26-11. To filter the records and create a specific subset (for example, all recipients who live in Denver, Colorado), click the Field arrow then choose the field you want to use as the first filter (in this example, State).

Figure 26-11 Use the Filter And Sort dialog box to create a subset of recipients you want to use in the merge.

Figure 26-12 shows the filtering criteria used to locate all recipients in the database who have purchased an HTC smartphone. In this example, click the Comparison arrow to display the list of choices to assist you in filtering the data. Choose from among the 10 different items (in this case, Equal To). Then, in the Compare To field, type the value you are looking for (which here is HTC).

Figure 26-12 Enter the filtering criteria in the Field, Comparison, and Compare To fields.

When you click OK, the recipient list in the Mail Merge Recipients dialog box changes to reflect only the subset of data returned as a result of the filtering. Click OK to return to the merge document.

Adding Merge Fields

So now you've selected the document you want to use and you've identified the people to whom you want to send it. The next group in the Mailings tab involves adding the place-holders in the document where the data will be inserted for the individual recipients. The Write & Insert Fields group includes the following merge fields that you can insert in your document.

- **Address Block** Displays the Insert Address Block dialog box, in which you can add the name, street address, city, state, and postal code at the insertion point.

- **Greeting Line** Displays the Greeting Line dialog box. Use this to select the saluta-tion you want to use as well as the format for the recipient name.

- **Insert Merge Field** Displays options listing the fields available in the recipient list you've selected for the document. Use this to add specific fields in your document as needed.

- **Rules** Offers a number of conditional controls with which you can add program-ming capability to your merge form. For example, if you want to prompt the user to enter information at a particular point on a form, you can use the Fill-In rule. When you click Rules and then click Fill-In, the dialog box shown in Figure 26-13 appears. You can enter the information you want to appear to prompt the user. You can also provide default fill-in text. Select the Ask Once check box if you want the user to be prompted only one time. Click OK when you're done.

Figure 26-13 The Insert Word Field: Fill-In dialog box enables you to provide both a prompt and default text.

- **Match Fields** Use this to match up the fields in your recipient list to the fields in your database. See the section titled "Matching Fields with Your Database," on page 778, for details.

- **Update Labels** Updates changes you've made in the recipient list and the labels you're creating. (This command is available only when you select Labels as the docu-ment type you're using for the merge process.)

Inserting an Address Block

The Address Block includes the collection of data you're likely to use most often. The block includes the recipient name, street address, city, state, and postal code. You can also include the company name and the country and region in the address if you choose. To add the Address Block to your main document, follow these steps:

1. Place the insertion point where you want to insert the Address Block.

2. Click the Insert Address Block command in the Write & Insert Fields group on the Mailings tab.

The Insert Address Block dialog box appears, as shown in Figure 26-14.

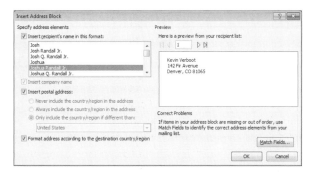

Figure 26-14 In the Insert Address Block dialog box, specify the address format you want to use.

3. Scroll through the Insert Recipient's Name In This Format list to choose the format you want to use for the recipient name, and then select the style you want to use.

4. If you want to omit the company name from the Address Block, clear the Insert Company Name check box. (Note, though, that this option is available only if your recipient list includes a Company field.)

5. To hide the postal information in the Address Block, clear the Insert Postal Address check box.

The Preview section shows your current selections. You can advance through the recipient data by clicking the Next button above the preview window.

6. If you don't see the fields you want to include, click the Match Fields button to match up the data names in your recipient list with the field names used in the merge operation. (For specifics, see the section titled "Matching Fields with Your Database," on page 778.)

7. Click OK to close the dialog box. Word inserts the following code at the insertion point.

```
<<AddressBlock>>
```

Chapter 26

> ## Tip
>
> How do they format postal codes in Denmark? On which line should you put the primary and secondary addresses? You can take some of the guesswork out of sending international mail and let Word take care of those and other details for you. To do so, when you use the Insert Address Block feature in the mail merge process, be sure to select the Format Address According To The Destination Country/Region check box.

Choosing a Greeting Line

The Greeting Line merge field is where you can say hello in the language and format you want. To add a greeting line, follow these steps:

1. Place the insertion point in the document where you want to add a greeting line.

2. Click the Greeting Line command in the Write & Insert Fields group.

   The Insert Greeting Line dialog box appears, as shown in Figure 26-15.

Figure 26-15 Use the Insert Greeting Line dialog box to choose the salutation and name format for your greeting.

   For those recipients that show an empty or invalid name entry, you have the option of adding a generic phrase. Choose either Dear Sir Or Madam, To Whom It May Concern, or type your own phrase in the text box.

3. Preview the greetings by using your recipient list data (similar to the Address Block entry). Then use Match Fields to correct any problems in the way information is being displayed.

4. Click OK to close the dialog box and insert the greeting line.

   Word inserts the following code at the insertion point.

   ```
   <<GreetingLine>>
   ```

Inserting Merge Fields

Word offers a number of preset merge fields that you can insert by pointing and clicking. You can further personalize your main document by adding address or database fields. To display the additional merge fields you can use in your document, click Insert Merge Field in the Write & Insert Fields group. The Insert Merge Field dialog box appears, as shown in Figure 26-16.

Figure 26-16 Use the Insert Merge Field dialog box to insert either Address Fields or Database Fields.

If you want to use fields available in your Address Book, click the Address Fields option. You'll see quite a list of offerings, from basic contact information, to a spouse's name, to a nickname. When you click the Database Fields option, you'll see traditional database fields, including Title, First Name, Last Name, Company Name, Address Line 1, Address Line 2, City, State, ZIP Code, Country, Home Phone, Work Phone, and E-Mail Address.

To insert one of the additional merge fields, follow these steps:

1. Place the insertion point where you want to add the field.

2. Display the Insert Merge Field dialog box by clicking the Insert Merge Field command in the Write & Insert Fields group.

3. Click Address Fields or Database Fields.

4. Click the field you want to add then click Insert.

5. When you're finished, click Close to return to your main document.

Figure 26-17 shows a form letter after two merge fields have been added. Note that Highlight Merge Fields was used so they would be easy to spot on the page.

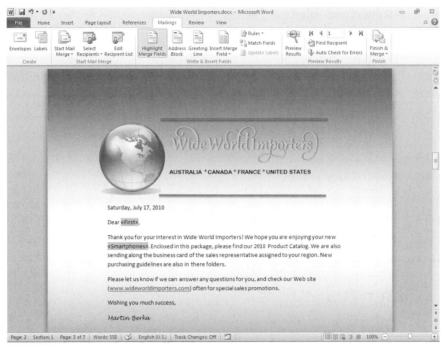

Figure 26-17 You can add database and address fields in the body of your document as needed.

TROUBLESHOOTING

I'm having trouble getting my merge fields to line up.

When you're adding merge fields to your document, hidden spaces can affect the field alignment. To fix the problem, turn on paragraph marks by going on the Home tab and clicking Show/Hide in the Paragraph group. Displaying paragraph marks shows all paragraph marks, spaces, and tab characters so that you can better control the placement of merge fields in your document.

Matching Fields with Your Database

With Word 2010, you can use data you've entered and organized in other programs—such as Access, Excel, other database programs, or compatible e-mail utilities—to serve as the source for your mail merge. If the fields you've created in your database don't match the fields in the address list, don't worry—you can use the Match Fields tool to equate the fields so data automatically flows into the appropriate places.

You can display the Match Fields dialog box in several ways.

- Click the Match Fields button in the Write & Insert Fields group on the Mailings tab.

- Click the Match Fields button in the Insert Address Block dialog box.

- Click the Match Fields button in the Greeting Line dialog box.

Designate how you want Word to match fields by clicking the arrow of the field you want to match. For example, in the example shown in Figure 26-18, the field name Word is looking for is Address 1, but in the database, the address is called Home Street. Click the Address 1 arrow and choose Home Street from the list.

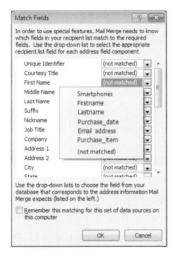

Figure 26-18 Use the Match Fields dialog box to direct Word how to import the data you've created in other programs.

Continue to match up other fields as needed. After you make your matches, click OK to close the dialog box and return to the document.

Mail Merge Quick Tips

Here are a few tips to help your merge projects go smoothly:

- Keep a listing of your data fields on hand so that you can draft your merge documents to use your available data most effectively.

- Save merge documents as templates that you can use regularly to cut down on the time spent on your merge operation.

- Perform a test print of envelopes, labels, and letters on inexpensive printer paper (as opposed to special stationery, labels, or company envelopes) to confirm that the placement of the fields is correct.

- When printing envelopes and labels, print an extra set if you regularly send mailings to the same group.

- If you update your data list, reattach the most current version of the data file to the document by choosing Use Existing List in the Start Mail Merge group, and then reselecting the name of the data file.

Adding Word Fields

Along with the merge fields presented in the Mail Merge Wizard, you have another set of fields at your disposal. You can use Word fields to personalize your document, message, or form even further. You might want to add a Word field, for example, that skips a record based on the data in a particular field.

To add a Word field to your main document, follow these steps:

1. Place the insertion point in your document where you want to add the field.

2. Click the Rules button in the Write & Insert Fields group on the Mailings tab.

   A menu appears, listing the Word field choices. Click your choice; Word prompts you to add additional information. Table 26-2 gives you an overview of the Word fields available in mail merge operations.

Table 26-2 **Word Fields for Mail Merge**

Field	Description	Options
Ask	Adds a customized dialog box that asks for more information during a merge	You can use a predefined bookmark or add a new one to mark the placement of the Ask field.
Fill-In	Prompts user for additional information	You can choose to have Word ask for information with each merged record or only once, at the beginning of the process.
If...Then...Else	Creates conditional text segments that insert one phrase in one situation and another phrase in another	You can control the fields you want to compare as well as the qualifier (Equal To, Not Equal To, Less Than, Greater Than, Less Than Or Equal, Greater Than Or Equal, Is Blank, Is Not Blank).
Merge Record #	Adds the number of the current record to the merged document	Place the insertion point where you want the number to appear; no dialog box is displayed.
Merge Sequence #	Inserts numbering for all documents in the merge	Place the insertion point where you want the number to appear; no dialog box is displayed.
Next Record	Includes data from the next record in the current record	You can include several records at once; however, to list many records, create a directory.
Next Record If	Includes data from the next record if a certain condition is met	You can include record data if a field contains a value you seek.
Set Bookmark	Adds a bookmark and attached text in every merged document	You can use existing bookmarks or add new ones to accommodate the merge.
Skip Record If	Omits records depending on a specific condition	You can choose the fields to compare and the qualifier (Equal To, Not Equal To, Less Than, Greater Than, Less Than Or Equal, Greater Than Or Equal, Is Blank, Is Not Blank).

Chapter 26

Previewing the Merge

The next step in the merge process involves reviewing the data merged into your document. The Preview Results group contains the commands you need to do this. Click Preview Results to start the process. The first document is displayed by default with the data of your first recipient displayed in the Word window (shown in Figure 26-19). You can page through the recipients by clicking the previous (<<) or next (>>) button in the wizard task pane.

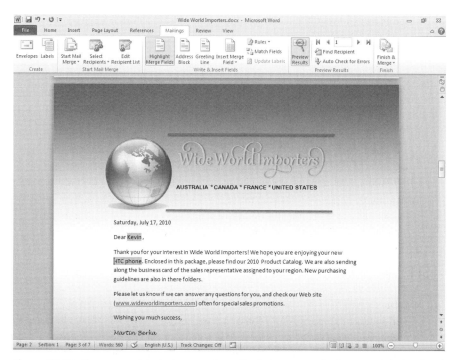

Figure 26-19 The merge data is shown automatically in your main document during Preview.

Finding a Specific Entry

If you want to locate a particular recipient in your list, click Find Recipient in the Preview Results group. The Find Entry dialog box appears, in which you can type the data you'd like to locate. Specify the field you want to search, if necessary, and then click Find Next. Word locates the text you indicated in the merge document.

Checking for Errors

If you're preparing a merge operation with hundreds or even thousands of records, it's an especially good idea to run a test before you perform the actual merge. Word gives you an easy way to run a quick check for errors by simply clicking the Auto Check For Errors button in the Preview Results group. The Checking And Reporting Errors dialog box appears (shown in Figure 26-20). You can test your merge in three different ways: You can simulate the merge and save the errors in a new document; you can go ahead and run the merge operation, but have Word stop and alert you when an error is found; or you can complete the merge without pausing for errors and have Word report the errors in a new document.

Figure 26-20 Select an error-checking method in the Checking And Reporting Errors dialog box.

The difference between these options is that one runs a "practice test" that reports on errors it finds but does not make changes in the document. The second option, the default, performs the merge but alerts you immediately whenever an error is found. If this is the first time you've used the mail merge utility in Word, it's a good idea to test it out using the simulation until you feel comfortable proceeding with the real thing. With the third option, you can go ahead and print, but Word collects any errors in a separate document that you can review after the merge is complete.

Merging the Documents

The final step in the mail merge process involves printing, sending, or saving your document with the data intact. The actual merge is a bit anticlimactic. To finalize the merge, you simply click Finish & Merge in the Finish group on the Mailings tab. Three choices appear: Edit Individual Documents, Print Documents, and Send E-Mail Messages. The first option saves the merge operation as individual files, the second sends the documents to the printer, and the third prepares and sends e-mail messages with your merge information included.

Merge to a New Document

When you click Edit Individual Documents in the Finish group, the Merge To New Document dialog box opens. Here, you can choose whether you want to merge all records, the current record only, or a range of records you specify. Make your choices, and then click OK to complete the merge.

Choosing Merge Print Options

To prepare your merge documents for printing, click Print Documents in the Finish group. The Merge To Printer dialog box appears, from which you can choose from the following options:

- **All** Prints all records in the current document.

- **Current Record** Prints only the displayed record.

- **From And To** Prints a range—from record 2 to 5, for example—so that you can select only those records you want to print.

Chapter 26

TROUBLESHOOTING

Instead of values, fields are printed in my mail merge document.

You went through all the steps in the merge process, checked the merge for errors, and selected the merge process you wanted. Everything looked fine. But when you printed the merged documents, you saw the merge field names instead of the values in the document. What's going on?

It might be that the Print Field Codes Instead Of Their Values check box has been selected in your Word options, which by default causes fields, rather than the values they store, to be displayed. To check this option and change it if necessary, on the File tab, click Options at the bottom. In the Word Options dialog box, click the Advanced category in the left panel. Scroll down to the Print options and clear the Print Field Codes Instead Of Their Values check box. Click OK to close the dialog box and return to the document.

Merge to E-Mail

If you choose Send E-Mail Messages in the Finish group on the Mailings tab, the Merge To E-Mail dialog box appears. Before you send the messages, you can specify whether you want to send the e-mail in HTML or text format, or send the message as an attachment. You can also choose the field you want to use in the To line (this is helpful if you have more than one e-mail address in a recipient list) and add a Subject line to describe the content to the recipient.

After you enter these choices, select which records you want to send in the Send Records area. Similar to the printing options, you can choose All, Current Record, or enter a range of records you want to use. Click OK when you're ready to send.

Creating a Directory

All the merge operations in this chapter thus far have involved taking multiple data items and pluging them into documents that you can replicate easily. There will be times, however, when you will want a complete listing of the records in your source file. You might, for example, want to keep a listing of all the people you sent a catalog mailing to last fall.

To create a directory of records from your data source, you can use the Directory document type. Here are the steps.

1. On the Mailings tab, in the Start Mail Merge group, click Start Mail Merge then click Directory.

2. Using the Select Recipients command in the Start Mail Merge group, choose whether you want to type a new list, use an existing list, or select Outlook Contacts.

3. If necessary, click Edit Recipient List and filter, sort, or edit the data to be used in the directory.

4. In the Write & Insert Fields group, click the fields you want to insert (most likely you'll want only Address Block).

   If you want to add additional fields, click the Insert Merge Field command then make your choices.

5. Click Preview Results to see how the directory entry will look.

   Don't worry that only one record is shown in the document window to preview; you'll see an entire list when the merge is completed.

6. Click Edit Individual Documents in the Finish & Merge command in the Finish group. Choose All to include all records in the merge, and then click OK.

   The merge is completed and the directory is displayed in your document window. You can now save the directory file and use it for future merge operations.

> **Tip**
> You can quickly add a two-column format to your directory by going on the Page Layout tab and clicking Columns in the Page Setup group. In the Columns list, choose the number of columns you want to use. The document is instantly reformatted to reflect your selection. Remember to save your changes by pressing Ctrl+S.

Printing Envelopes and Labels

In some cases, you might want to print only a single envelope or an individual sheet of labels. In such a situation, working with the data source and inserting fields in a document isn't necessary—no merge is needed. When you want to print a simple envelope, click Start Mail Merge on the Mailings tab and choose Envelopes. The Envelopes Options dialog box appears, as shown in Figure 26-21.

Figure 26-21 The Envelopes Options dialog box enables you to create and print individual envelopes.

> **Note**
>
> If you're working with an open document that has an Address Block inserted (or a default address you've entered yourself), the selected address is the one that will be used.

To print an envelope, simply follow these steps:

1. Select the recipient address and then display the Envelope Options dialog box.

2. Click the Envelope Size arrow then choose the size of the envelope you will be printing.

3. Click in the Delivery Address area then click Font to select the font you want to use.

   Use the From Left and From Top controls to set the amount of space between the printed address and the edge of the envelope.

4. Set the font and spacing settings for the return address as well.

   The Preview area shows you how your envelope will look when printed.

5. Click the Printing Options tab to determine how you should position the envelope in the printer.

6. Click OK. Word saves your information, and your envelope is displayed in the Word window as you specified.

Creating Labels

Instead of printing directly on envelopes, you might want to print mailing labels. Word makes it easy for you to print labels in a wide range of shapes and sizes. If you want to print single (or a few) labels and don't want to use mail merge to do it, you can use the Label Options dialog box to create them quickly. Here's how to do it:

1. Start by selecting the data you want to use to create the labels.

2. On the Mailings tab, choose Labels from the Start Mail Merge command list.

   The Label Options dialog box appears. Use the options here to enter the vendor of the labels you are using, then choose the way the labels are arranged on the page.

3. Click the Details button if you want to change the page size or enter a different dimension for the label.

4. Click OK to save your changes.

> **Tip**
>
> If you have a number of labels that you want to print quickly, it's best to use the Mail Merge Wizard to lead you through the steps for printing labels. To start the wizard, on the Mailings tab, click Start Mail Merge in the Start Mail Merge group. Choose Step by Step Mail Merge Wizard. Choose Labels in the Select Document Type area then follow the prompts on the screen.

TROUBLESHOOTING

> *I can't feed envelopes from a loaded tray.*
>
> If you've loaded envelopes in a paper tray and Word keeps prompting you to feed your envelopes to the printer manually, make sure that you've selected the correct paper feed choices. To check the settings, display the Label Options dialog box by clicking Start Mail Merge and choosing Labels. In the Tray field, choose the name of the tray in which you loaded the labels. Click OK to save your changes.

Chapter 26

What's Next?

This chapter took you through the process of creating a variety of mail merge projects with Word 2010 so that you can share your documents with donors, teammates, board members, and prospective customers all over the world. The next chapter moves into the customizable document realm by showing you how to add Word 2010 content controls to your Word documents.

CHAPTER 27

Customizing Documents with Content Controls

Understanding the Word 2010 Content Controls..... 789

Creating the Document........................... 790

Adding and Formatting Static Text 792

Adding Content Controls 794

Changing Content Control Properties 799

Using Content Controls........................... 805

Protecting Documents............................ 805

Adding Legacy Controls 808

Adding ActiveX Controls.......................... 808

What's Next? 810

O FTEN when we're planning documents, we typically think about what we want to include *today* on the page. We're trying to meet a specific goal—like inspire people to increase their donations this year, or enticing folks to come take a closer look at our product Web site. But the content you create can live beyond the purpose you've planned for today's documents. And in some cases, a document that meets today's goal would be made even better if you added room for variable information—or interactive elements—that engage your readers. Word 2010 content controls can help you build that kind of functionality into your pages, and although it takes a bit more planning, the whole process is nearly as simple as point-and-click.

If you previously read the chapter on mail merge (Chapter 26, Creating Mailings Large and Small), you remember that part of that process involves choosing the data items you want Word to insert in your document. Those items were actually content controls, the variable tools Word uses to gather and display the data that merges with—or changes—your pages. This chapter introduces you to content controls and shows you how to add them to your document.

Understanding the Word 2010 Content Controls

Previous versions of Word included a collection of form controls used to add form fields to documents. With form fields, you can, for example, create an invoice document, a travel expense report, or a registration form that a user could fill out electronically and submit. The data was saved with the document and could then be used in other data applications. Those form controls are still available in Word 2010—but now they are referred to as Legacy Form controls.

The content controls in Word 2010 give readers control over the type of content displayed in a document, populating specific selections based on the choices that they make. Someone reviewing your document can click a content control item at the top of your annual report, choose their name from the list, select the date, and leave a comment before they save and close the document. Content controls are XML-based, which means that the data and the presentation of the data can be stored separately.

When might you use content controls in your Word documents? Here are a few ideas:

- You are creating a training document with a short quiz at the end to evaluate if organization volunteers have learned key elements of your program.

- You want to add a routing system to standardized documents that automatically shows the user who to send their report to once it is finished.

- You want to create a boilerplate template for a document you plan to create often that includes all the styles and formats already applied.

- You need to standardize the documents used across your organization to streamline the way information is collected, shared, and used in your business processes.

Creating the Document

You can create the document that you want to use with content controls in one of three ways: you can start with a Word template (most templates include content controls of some kind), modify an existing document, or create a new document from scratch.

You can choose to add the content controls first and then drag them to any point in the document where you want them to appear, or you can create the body of the document—with its theme, styles, and illustrations, as appropriate—and then add the content controls last. Either way, the process is straightforward.

Displaying the Developer Tab

Your first step in creating a document that includes content controls involves displaying the Developer tab. The Developer tab is hidden by default because its function is specialized. To display the Developer tab, follow these steps:

1. On the File tab, click Options.

2. Click Customize Ribbon and, in the column on the right, select the Developer check box then click OK.

The Developer tab appears on the far right side of the Ribbon, as you see in Figure 27-1.

Figure 27-1 The Developer tab includes the tools to add content controls to your documents.

The Developer tab includes six different groups:

- **Code**   This group includes the tools you'll use to record macros, and write and edit Microsoft Visual Basic for Applications code.

- **Add-Ins**   With this group you can set up any add-ins you use with Word, using the Add-Ins or COM Add-Ins tools.

- **Controls**   The Controls group contains the Content Controls you add to the document. From within this group, you can add a number of different control types (including Legacy Controls and ActiveX controls), change to Design Mode, modify control properties, and group controls.

- **XML**   This group includes tools for displaying the XML structure of the current document, adding an XML schema, attaching transforms, and adding expansion packs.

- **Protect**   The Protect group offers only one tool—Protect Document—which displays the Restrict Formatting And Editing task pane so that you can control the permissions that others have to modify your document.

- **Templates**   The Templates group includes a single tool—Document Template—which you use to add templates, schemas, and other add-ins to the current document.

Word Content Controls vs. InfoPath Forms—Which Is for You?

You can add content controls on your Word documents to take care of all kinds of data collection needs. Whether you create an invoice, a data list, a travel log, or an expense listing, you can add the content controls to your Word document and update the document as needed.

Some Office 2010 suites include a program called Microsoft InfoPath 2010. This application is a sophisticated form-generation program with which users can create custom forms and share them in a variety of ways. InfoPath 2010 is intended for users and businesses that rely heavily on form technologies to carry out their day-to-day work. You can add an InfoPath form to an e-mail message you create in Outlook 2010, design one to send data to a SharePoint list, or convert one of your Word documents into an InfoPath form. InfoPath also offers centralized management of the forms you create, which is helpful if forms are a big part of your work. If you use content controls only occasionally, the content control features Word provides are probably enough for your needs. On the other hand, if your requirements call for more sophisticated form management, check out InfoPath 2010 by going to *http://office.microsoft.com/en-us/infopath/default.aspx*.

Adding and Formatting Static Text

The beauty of content controls is that they are so easy to use; the process feels just like creating an ordinary document. The content controls simply add to the functionality of the document and elevate it beyond a flat, read-it-once-and-put-it-away purpose. Now you can read the document, respond to questions or information items, or add to the information by selecting your choices within the body of the document. In this way, a simple document becomes "smart." Here are a few examples of ways you can transform a traditional document into a document that makes use of content controls:

- In a document that helps prepare your volunteers or staff members for travel, you might want to use the first page as an information-gathering section in which the user enters information items such as Name, Address, Phone, and more. Additionally, you'll record travel and passport information. On the next page, you might want to include a how-to guide to travel reporting, country-specific site-seeing tips, or information about customs in the area.

- In a document you're preparing that describes your plan for an upcoming project, you will include the purpose for the project, an overall description, as well as a list of team members and contact info, and areas on the form for the various tasks and stages in the project. The list of team members, their contact items, and their assigned tasks can all be placed in content controls, so the information for the team members is continually updated and in sync with your organization's data (see Figure 27-2).

- In the patient records in your small medical office, you have a number of items that would appear on a traditional form—such as name, birth date, address information, and social security number—but you also want to include your privacy policy and other information related to your practice in the file. In this way, the traditional form and document merge to become one: easy to update, track, and secure.

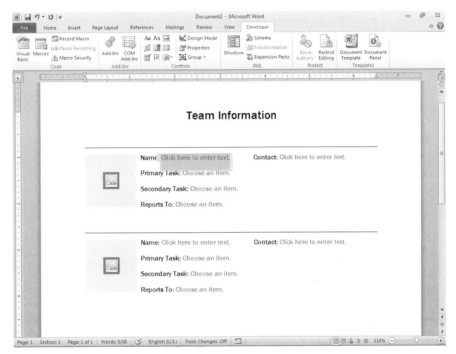

Figure 27-2 You can easily add a team contact form in your shared document using content controls.

You might want to simplify the form's formatting by choosing a theme and then assigning specific Quick Styles to the various elements. You can also add Quick Parts, objects, photos, and more to spruce up the form any way you'd like. If you have designed letterhead for your company and want the form to resemble your other business documents, you can use the letterhead as the basis for your form. Figure 27-3 shows several formatting enhancements that have been added to the team information form.

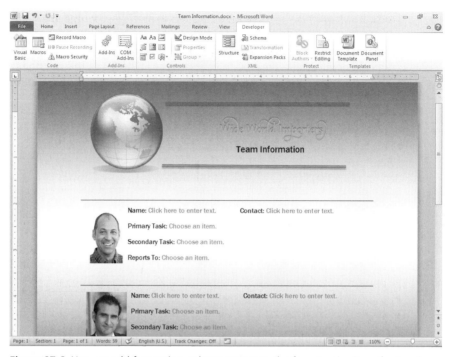

Figure 27-3 You can add formatting enhancements to the form to give it professional appeal.

Adding Content Controls

Content controls are so simple and flexible that you can add them at any point during the creation of your document. If you want to add them as you type, go ahead—you can just drag them to the point in the document you want them to be used. If you decide later that you want to move the control to a new spot, simply drag it there.

Here's a quick list of ways readers of your document can use the content controls you enter to provide information:

- Enter simple text in a comment box

- Choose from among a series of options in a list

- Select one of several pictures to cast votes for their favorite new logo design

- Add their own information in addition to the list items presented

- Select a date they choose from a visual calendar

- Format the text they enter on the form

You'll find everything you need to add those items to your form in the Controls group on the Developer tab. Table 27-1 gives you an introduction to the various commands, and the sections that follow provide more detail on each control type.

Table 27-1 Word 2010 Content Controls

	Name	Description
Aa	Rich Text	Users can enter text with most types of formatting, as well as tables and images
Aa	Plain Text	Accepts plain text or text with simple formatting only
	Picture	Use this control to add a picture to the form
	Combo Box	Creates a text list in which the user can edit list items unless you specify otherwise
	Drop-Down List	Lets you create a list in which the items are non-editable
	Date Picker	Adds a calendar object so users can select a date
	Check Box	Add a check box control to the page
	Legacy Tools	Displays a palette of tools that includes Legacy Forms (form controls available with previous versions of Word, such as text box, check box, or drop-form fields) and ActiveX controls
Design Mode	Design Mode	Displays the document in Design Mode so that you can arrange and edit content controls in the document
Properties	Properties	Opens a dialog box containing options you can change for the selected control
Group	Group	Groups the items within a selected region of a form

Chapter 27

> **Tip**
>
> It's helpful to have an idea of the types of content controls you want to add to your document before you add them. You might want to sketch out the document on a piece of paper or use an existing document as a guide.

Control Types in Word 2010

You can use the content controls in Word 2010 to gather and connect the information you need to make your business processes run smoothly. In addition, they offer people reading your document specific and easy-to-understand ways to interact with the items on your page. Word 2010 includes a number of different content controls, each of which collects a different type of information. The sections that follow provide a closer look at the different types of content controls.

Rich Text Control

With the Rich Text control, you can add an item to your document that the user can then format as real text. For example, suppose that you want users to have the ability to change the format of the text they enter in a control. When you add a Rich Text control to the form, the Mini Toolbar appears whenever the user enters text in the control and then selects it (see Figure 27-4).

Figure 27-4 A Rich Text control lets users format text after they enter it.

Rich Text controls also accept larger amounts of text (multiple paragraphs) and can include tables and graphics. When you need to provide the flexibility of gathering information in a variety of forms and formats, Rich Text controls will give you what you need.

Plain Text Control

The Plain Text control command inserts a simple Text control at the cursor position. When might you want to use a Text control? This control is useful for all kinds of things: you can record comments, names, addresses, volunteer projects, campaigns, staff member names, and more. Text controls can accept a minimal amount of formatting; basically, any text your users need to enter that doesn't require special formatting capabilities can be entered in a Text control. In Figure 27-5, the Contact field is a Text control.

Figure 27-5 With Text controls, users can enter plain text—no formatting required.

Picture Content Control

A Picture control comes in handy when you want to add special images in a document. For example, the team information document includes picture controls so each team member's photo can be added (see Figure 27-6).

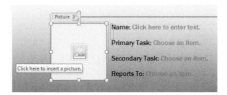

Figure 27-6 The Picture content control gives users the option of adding images directly into the document.

Combo Box Control

Use a Combo Box control when you want to give users a range of choices from which they can select, while also giving them the option of entering a new item not represented on the list. For example, in the control shown in Figure 27-7, the primary task list shows the various tasks you can assign to a team member. Or, if you don't see the task you want to select, you can click in the text box and type the task that you want to include.

Figure 27-7 Combo boxes provide users with a list from which they can choose, or they can also enter their own information.

Drop-Down List

Use a Drop-Down List control to create a list from which users can select an answer. Unlike the combo box, which gives you the option of allowing users to add their own entries, a drop-down list constrains users to only the answers you provide. The sample drop-down list in Figure 27-8 shows the managers available to the team. You can choose the manager you want to assign to each team member by clicking the appropriate name on the list.

Figure 27-8 A drop-down list provides users with a range of choices.

Date Picker

The Date Picker control makes it easy for you to select the date relevant to the information you are entering. You can type a date in the text box or click the arrow to display a calendar that shows the current month (see Figure 27-9). You can display different months by clicking the left or right arrows in the Date Picker title bar. To select a date, simply click the day you want (or click Today to enter the current date).

Figure 27-9 The Date Picker control displays a calendar you can use to insert a date in the document.

> **Tip**
>
> The Date Picker doesn't provide a way to show a range of dates, so if you want to include information about a span of time (to record the amount of time spent on a volunteer assignment, for example), create Start Date and End Date fields to record the beginning and the completion dates of the project.

Adding a Control

Now that you know what to expect from the various controls, you can begin adding them to your document. When you are ready to add a control, the process is simple, and no matter which type of control you are adding, the process is the same. Follow these steps:

1. Click at the point in the document where you want to add the Content Control.

2. On the Developer tab, click the control in the Controls group that you want to add to your form.

   For example, to add a Combo Box control to your form, click the Combo Box control.

3. Word adds a Combo Box control to your form and inserts the text, *Choose an item.*

When the user clicks the arrow to the right of the prompt text, a drop-down list appears, but only the prompt text appears in the list. You add the items for the list by working with the control's properties (which is the subject of the next section).

Changing Content Control Properties

After you've created a Content Control, you can tailor it to include the information you want users to enter. You will change control properties when you want to do one of the following:

- Add a title to the field

- Specify a tag so that you can locate the field easily

- Choose a formatting style to apply to the displayed text

- Control whether the field contents can be edited or not

- Choose the format of the content

- Select a locale and calendar type (Date Picker control only)

- Determine how to store the date if the control has an XML mapping (Date Picker control only)

- Indicate whether you want Word to allow multiple paragraphs (Text field only)

- Add and arrange items in a list (Combo Box and Drop-Down List only)

- Assign Document Building Block Properties, such as a gallery and category, to populate a list of choices (Building Block Gallery control only)

To display the properties for a control you've added to the document, click the control, and then click Properties in the Controls group (or, in some cases, right-click the control). The Content Control Properties dialog box appears, in which you can customize the settings for that particular control.

Each control type has its own set of options. For example, when you add a Combo Box content control and then choose Properties, you see the dialog box shown in Figure 27-10. When you display the properties for a Rich Text content control, the dialog box shown in Figure 27-11 is displayed.

Chapter 27

Figure 27-10 When you add a Combo Box content control, you add list items in the Properties dialog box.

Figure 27-11 The Content Control Properties dialog box for a Rich Text content control.

Adding Titles and Tags

Adding a title to a control on your form can help give users a little more information about the type of data you want them to enter. When you add a control title, the title appears on a tab above the control when the user clicks it.

To add a title to a control, select the control and click Properties in the Controls group. In the Content Control Properties dialog box, click in the Title text box and type the control title you want to use. Click OK to save the change.

You can also add tags in the Content Control Properties dialog box. When you add a tag, the control is enclosed in a set of tags that helps you locate, sort, and easily work with that data. Add a tag by clicking in the Tag box in the Content Control Properties dialog box.

Type the tag name then click OK. By default, the tag is not visible on the form. To see the tags, click Design Mode in the Controls group. Figure 27-12 shows both the control title and tags displayed in Design Mode.

Figure 27-12 You can display the tags used to mark each Content Control by clicking Design Mode in the Controls group.

> **Tip**
> When a Content Control is mapped to a data store, the tags will appear orange in Design Mode. Content Controls that are not mapped will have blue tags in Design Mode.

Styling Your Control

You can control the way the text in your control looks in Word 2010 by setting style options. You can use an existing style for the control items or create a new style for the look of the text. The great thing about this is that you can automate the formats you use regularly in forms text. You can create a style you like and then choose it each time you create a control so that all your controls have a similar look.

To choose an existing style for your content control, follow these steps:

1. Click the control you want to change.

2. Click Properties in the Controls group on the Developer tab.

3. Select the Use A Style To Format Contents check box. The Style selection becomes available.

4. Click the Style arrow to display the available styles (see Figure 27-13).

Figure 27-13 You can apply an existing style to document control text.

5. Click the style you want to use for the control text then click OK.

If you want to create your own style for the text users will see in the document, follow these steps:

1. Click the control you want to change and display the Content Control Properties dialog box by clicking Properties in the Controls group.

2. Select the Use A Style To Format Contents check box.

3. Click the New Style button.

    The Create New Style From Formatting dialog box appears.

4. Type a name for the style in the Name box, and then select a Style Type and Style Based On settings if necessary.

5. Click the Formatting arrow then choose the font you want from the displayed list.

6. Apply additional formatting settings, such as size, style, font color, or alignment, and more, using the controls in the Formatting area of the dialog box.

    The preview window shows you how the style will look in your document.

7. Click OK to save the new style. Click OK a second time to apply the settings to your control and return to the document.

For more information on styles, see Chapter 12, "Applying and Customizing Quick Styles."

Locking Controls

By default, no locking features are in effect for the content controls you create, meaning that for controls where editing is allowed (Rich Text controls and Combo Box controls), users can edit the control itself as well as the control's content. Word offers you two different kinds of locking capability for the controls on your document. You can opt to lock the content control so that it cannot be deleted, or you can lock the contents so that they cannot be edited. When would you use these different options?

- Select Content Control Cannot Be Deleted when you want to ensure that the user of your document will not be able to intentionally or unintentionally delete the document control.

- Click Content Cannot Be Edited when you want to limit users from modifying the content displayed in the Content Control. For example, you might want to lock a text control to prohibit users from changing content that has already been added to the control.

You can also use the Contents Cannot Be Edited option to force a particular selection on a document. For example, suppose that you ordinarily allow users to order one of three versions of your annual report—PDF, Web, or print. For now, however, you're out of your print reports, and you want to offer the PDF option only.

You can select the PDF option and then click the Contents Cannot Be Edited check box. This locks the selected item in place so that users cannot choose a different item in that particular control. When you print reports are back in stock, you can display the control's properties and clear the Contents Cannot Be Edited check box in the Content Control Properties dialog box so that users once again have a range of choices.

Adding Content to Lists

This last setting in the Content Control Properties dialog box might be one you'll want to use first. When you create a Combo Box control or a Drop-Down List control, the whole idea is to give document users a range of choices from which to choose. But when you initially create the control, only prompt text appears—which isn't going to serve your purpose very well. To add the items to the lists, follow these steps:

1. Select the Combo Box or Drop-Down List control to which you want to add list items.

2. Display the Content Control Properties dialog box by clicking Properties in the Controls group.

3. In the Drop-Down List Of Properties area, click Add.

   The Add Choice dialog box appears (see Figure 27-14).

Figure 27-14 The Add Choice dialog box is where you add both a Display Name and a Value for your list items.

4. Type the text you want to appear in the list then click OK. The item is added to the list. Repeat Step 3 and this step until you've entered all the items you want to appear in the list.

5. Arrange the items in the list the way you want them to appear in the control by using the Move Up and Move Down buttons in the Content Control Properties dialog box. Additionally, you can edit an item by selecting it in the list then clicking Modify. Or, you can delete an item by clicking it then choosing Remove.

6. Click OK to save your changes.

Try out the list by clicking the arrow to the right of the control on the document. The list should appear in the order you specified.

> **Note**
>
> The Combo Box control enables users to add their own items into the text list. If a user chooses to take advantage of this feature, the latest added item is automatically displayed at the top of the list if the control is mapped to a data store.

Mapping Controls to XML

When you click Design Mode on the Developer tab, the tags that are displayed indicate the start and end of content controls and help you see what's going on in your document, but they don't automatically provide XML functionality for the data you are displaying or capturing. To map the data to the XML data store, follow these steps:

1. Right-click the content control to display the Controls contextual menu.

2. Point to Apply XML Element. A list of XML tags available in the current document appears.

> **Note**
> You must have an XML schema attached to the document before these tags will appear. To attach a schema, click Add-Ins in the Add-Ins group, click the XML Schema tab, click the Add Schema button, choose the schema you want to use in the Add Schema dialog box, click Open, and then OK.

3. Click the XML element you want to apply to the content control.

Now the information displayed through or gathered by that content control is mapped directly to the XML data, and the latest information will be reflected by that control.

Using Content Controls

Designing a document with content controls is the first part of the story; using the controls is the second part. Working with a document that includes content controls is so simple it feels just like working with any traditional document (which is one of the main points of content controls). To use content controls in a document, follow these steps:

1. On the File tab, choose New.

2. Choose the document or template you want to use for the current document.

3. Create, modify, and format your document normally.

4. Each time you encounter a content control, click in the control and then type the requested information (or choose it from the displayed list).

5. Save your document as you normally would.

Protecting Documents

When you're working specifically with forms, the Protect Document tool is an important item on the Developer tab. You'll use this type of protection when you want to safeguard all information in the document, allowing users to enter data only as you've specified in the individual content controls.

Chapter 27

When you protect a form, you lock the controls in place so that no further changes can be made to formats or specifications. This also protects other items on the form—titles, help text, photos, and more. Of course, users will still to be able to use the lists as intended and enter text in text and legacy fields. To protect a document that includes content controls, follow these steps:

1. Click the Restrict Editing command in the Protect group.

2. Select the Allow Only This Type Of Editing In The Document check box.

3. Click the list arrow then choose Filling In Forms (see Figure 27-15).

Figure 27-15 You can protect the form but allow users to fill in form fields as needed.

4. Click the Yes, Start Enforcing Protection button to protect the form.

   The Start Enforcing Protection dialog box appears, offering you the chance to enter a password for the form. If you want to add a password, type it in both text boxes in the dialog box. If not, leave the text boxes blank.

5. Click OK to put the protection settings in effect.

TROUBLESHOOTING

My Building Block Gallery Content Controls are disabled, or I cannot paste in a content control.

If your document is protected for Filling In Forms you might find Building Block Content Controls are disabled and you cannot use Paste In A Rich Text control, Plain Text control, or a Combo Box control.

The following provides two workarounds for this issue:

- Use a selective protection method described in the following Inside Out tip.

- Use the No Changes (Read Only) protection option and mark each content control as an exception.

INSIDE OUT   Nested Content Controls and Selective Document Protection

If you find the Protect Document method of document protection is too restrictive, you can protect portions of your document using nested content controls. The general procedure is to place static text and content controls used for data entry in a Rich Text control. Then for the Rich Text control, enable both Locking options: Content Control Cannot Be Edited and Content Control Cannot Be Deleted. The result is only the nested content controls can be edited and the static text cannot be modified or deleted. Here are the specific steps:

1. For each content control you want to protect, display the Content Control Properties and verify the Locking option Content Control Cannot Be Deleted is selected.

2. Select the Content Controls and all static text that you want to protect.

3. On the Developer tab, click the Rich Text Content Control. A Rich Text control should be placed around the selected data.

4. Select the newly added Rich Text control and then click Properties.

5. Select both Locking options (Content Control Cannot Be Edited and Content Control Cannot Be Deleted) and then click OK.

If you need to edit the static text or content controls after you enable the Locking options for the Rich Text control, simply click the Design button and make your modifications.

Adding Legacy Controls

Legacy controls are available in Word 2010, but unless you have a specific reason for using them (for example, one of your remote offices is still using a previous version of Word), the new content controls in Word 2010 are a better choice. You can add the following legacy controls in Word:

- The Legacy Text control is a basic text input tool. When you add a Legacy Text control, Word 2010 inserts the {FORMTEXT} field at the current cursor position in the document.

> **Note**
> The field codes that Word inserts automatically can't be modified. To change the settings for the inserted field type, double-click the field.

- Use the Check Box control to create a list consisting of multiple check boxes. The {FORMCHECKBOX} field is inserted at the cursor position.

- Use the Drop-Down control to provide a list of choices for the user in a legacy document. {FORMDROPDOWN} is added at the cursor position.

> **Tip**
> If you want to see which code Word is inserting in your document when you add legacy controls, simply press Alt+F9. The display changes to show the field codes. When you're ready to return to the original display, press Alt+F9 again. Be sure to protect the form once again before you begin using it. Although this is not required for content controls, form fields will not work properly until the form is protected.

Adding ActiveX Controls

For special situations, you might want to use an ActiveX control to carry out actions when your user selects an item on your form. You might use an ActiveX control, for example, to run a macro that automates a task. ActiveX controls can add flexibility and power to your forms, but you need to be careful using them. Because of the type of objects they are, ActiveX controls can potentially access your local files and even be used to modify your registry. As such, you need to be careful to use ActiveX controls in a secure environment to ensure that hackers don't find a doorway into your network through an unsecured ActiveX control.

ActiveX Controls and the Trust Center

The Microsoft Trust Center, which was introduced in Microsoft Office 2007, is one line of defense against those who might want to tamper with ActiveX controls. The Trust Center automatically reviews any document when you open it, looking for macros from sources not on your Trusted Publishers list, as well as ActiveX controls. For more information on the Trust Center and the Trusted Publishers list, see Chapter 20, "Securing Your Word Documents." To review the ActiveX settings currently in effect on your system, follow these steps:

1. On the File tab, click Options.

2. Click Trust Center then click the Trust Center Settings button.

3. Choose ActiveX Settings.

    The range of settings for ActiveX controls is displayed in the Trust Center window.

4. Review the settings and click the one that works best for your application.

5. Click OK to save any changes.

> **Note**
> If you include ActiveX controls on your form and plan to deploy the form so that it can be used on other computers, be sure to include some explanatory text to inform readers how to change their ActiveX settings. This way you can ensure that the controls of your form will work properly on other systems.

Adding an ActiveX Control

To use ActiveX controls, you should be comfortable with Microsoft Visual Basic for Applications (VBA). To add an ActiveX control to your form, follow these steps:

1. Open the template to which you want to add the control.

2. Click the Restrict Editing tool then clear the check boxes in the Formatting And Editing options to unprotect the form.

3. Place the insertion point where you want to add the control.

4. Click the Legacy Tools command in the Controls group on the Developer tab.

5. Click the ActiveX control button on the Legacy Tools gallery that you want in the document. Word adds the control to your form and changes the display to Design Mode.

Changing Control Properties

You can change the way an ActiveX control appears by modifying the control's properties. To do so, display Design Mode, right-click the control to display the shortcut menu, and then choose Properties. The Properties dialog box appears, as shown in Figure 27-16.

Figure 27-16 Change the way a control looks by making changes in the Properties dialog box.

Click the Categorized tab to see the various properties organized by category. If you want to make a change—for example, you might change the font—double-click the setting in the right column. When you double-click the font selection, for example, the Font dialog box appears, in which you can make the necessary changes then click OK.

Programming a Control

Although an in-depth discussion of using VBA to program an ActiveX control is beyond the scope of this book, you can easily access the code window for programming your control. To access the code window, follow these steps:

1. Right-click the ActiveX control then click View Code.

   Word displays the Visual Basic Editor.

2. Enter the code for the control's event procedure.

3. Click File then Close And Return To Microsoft Word to exit the editor and return to your document. Alternatively, you can simply press Alt+Q.

What's Next?

This chapter introduced you to the content controls in Word 2010 and walked you through the simple process of adding content controls to your Word documents. The next chapter finishes up the book by taking a closer look at creating and working with macros.

Working with Macros in Word 2010

A Bit About VBA and Macros 812

Saving Macro-Enabled Documents and Templates. . . . 813

Recording a Macro 814

Running Macros 818

Editing Macros 826

Additional Macro Options. 830

Protecting Your Macros. 835

Digitally Signing Macros 835

What's Next? 839

M ENTION the word *macro* at a dinner party, and folks automatically assume you're a Word expert (well...OK, maybe at a dinner party where the guests spend *way* too much time on their computers). But in reality, a macro can be a very simple set of formatting choices (like "indent this and italicize it") or a complex operation that helps automate common procedures that you use often. Although the behind-the-scenes operation of a macro comes from instructions written in the Microsoft Visual Basic for Applications (VBA) programming language, you don't have to be a programmer to write a macro. You can simply turn on the macro recording tool and let Word keep track of your operations while you complete the steps you want to include in the macro. You can then play back the macro whenever you want to perform those steps, and Word takes care of the process for you. You might create a macro to perform the following chores:

- Speed up routine editing and formatting, such as using Find and Replace to clean up data copied from another source that contains manual line breaks and multiple paragraph marks.

- Automate a complex series of tasks—for example, inserting a table with a specific size, table style, and certain table options (such as including a total row and banded columns).

- Make an option in a dialog box more accessible, such as turning on and off the display of text boundaries.

- Work around various limitations in Word, such as inserting a static date (one that does not update to the current system date) with a single click or keyboard shortcut.

- Combine several repetitive tasks, such as switching to a specific document view, modifying the Zoom Level, and setting other view options.

If the idea of speeding up cumbersome tasks with a simple click of a button or keyboard shortcut is appealing, then read on. You do not need any previous programming knowledge to benefit from this chapter. However, you do need to be familiar with the content contained in this book, or at least be familiar with those areas in which you want to automate specific tasks.

This chapter covers the basic fundamentals of macros by showing you how to automate several of the tasks previously listed. We'll start by using the Macro Recorder to create a few macros, cover some simple editing tasks, and then take a look at sharing macros with others (either ones you create or those that you obtain from someone else).

> **Note**
> Full exploration of macros and VBA is beyond the scope of this chapter—entire books are dedicated to this subject. Those who want to learn more will find a list of recommendations in the section titled "What's Next," on page 839.

A Bit About VBA and Macros

When you start working with macros, understanding a few concepts and some terminology is helpful, even if you do not plan to go beyond recording macros and simple editing. For starters, Visual Basic for Applications, or VBA, is a subset of Microsoft Visual Basic. The primary distinction between the two is that VBA is dependent on a host application, such as Word. This means that if you share macros created in Word with other users, they must also have Word installed to use them.

A macro is actually a VBA procedure, and the terms are used interchangeably. A *procedure* is a series of statements, or actions, that are grouped together to form one specific set of instructions that is associated with a specific name, or what is referred to as a macro.

Macros can be saved in macro-enabled documents or templates. When a document or template contains macros, they are contained in a specific portion of the file called a *VBA Project* (also known as a project). A VBA Project stores objects, such as a *module*, and a module stores macros. If this seems confusing, consider how documents are stored: they are stored on a specific drive (VBA Project), they are placed in a folder (module), and they are assigned a name (macro).

When you create a template that contains macros, documents that are attached to the template are able to use macros stored in the template, and you can access the template's VBA Project through the document. This means you can modify and create new macros in the attached template without actually opening the template in Word. However, like most features, the default behavior can be changed, and you can disable the editing capability, which is discussed in the section titled "Protecting Your Macros," on page 835.

Saving Macro-Enabled Documents and Templates

A document containing macros must be saved using the Word Macro-Enabled Document file type (.docm). Templates containing macros must be saved using the Word Macro-Enabled Template file type (.dotm). If you save a document or template using the macro free file types, Word Documents (.docx) or Word Templates (.dotx), any macros contained in the files will be removed. If you inadvertently try to use a macro-free file type to save a document or template that contains macros, a message box appears, alerting you that your VBA project cannot be saved in a macro-free document.

> **CAUTION!**
>
> If you answer Yes to confirm that you want to save the file using a macro-free file type, the VBA Project will be discarded when you close the file. However, prior to closing, if you modify the VBA Project, such as editing an existing macros or recording a new one (which you will learn how to do in this chapter), you can recover the macros by using a macro-enabled file type to save the document or template.

To save a document or template containing macros, follow these steps:

1. On the File tab, click Save As.

2. In the Save As dialog box, display the Save As Type list and select either Word Macro-Enabled Document or Word Macro-Enabled Template.

3. Provide a File Name and Save In location then click Save.

New macros and changes to existing macros are automatically saved when the document or template is saved.

> **Note**
>
> If you are saving a file in an older file format, such as a Word 97-2003 Document (.doc) or Word 97-2003 Template (.dot), there is no distinction between macro-enabled and macro-free files; macros are saved directly in the file when using these file types.
>
> Additionally, when you save a macro-enabled file, the macros are not converted to XML, they are saved in a binary format. For those interested in knowing more about the document parts that comprise an Office Open XML file, macros are stored in a document part named vbaProject.bin.

Recording a Macro

As mentioned earlier, a macro can be as simple as recording steps, or actions, you already perform in Word—you don't even need to learn a programming language. You can also use the Macro Recorder to record the bulk of your macro and later edit it in the Visual Basic Editor. This section of the chapter eases you into the realm of macros, starting with how to plan a macro, considerations you should take into account, and using the Macro Recorder to record a macro.

Setup and Planning

Before you start working with macros, make sure the Developer tab is displayed on the Ribbon, shown in Figure 28-1. The Developer tab contains options in the Code group for recording and running macros.

Figure 28-1 The Developer tab contains access to advanced features, such as macros, but it is not displayed by default.

> **Tip**
> To display the Developer tab, on the File tab, click Options, and then click Customize Ribbon. In the list on the right, select the Developer check box then click OK.

You also need to check your Macro Security settings and ensure that you are able to allow your macros to run after they are created. To check Macro Security, follow these steps:

1. On the File tab, click Options, and then click Trust Center.

2. Click the Trust Center Settings button then click Macros Settings. Your macro security options will display as shown here:

3. Select the option Disable All Macros With Notification if necessary.

   You can use any option except Disable All Macros Without Notification, but Disable All Macros With Notification is the recommended setting.

4. Select the Message Bar section and verify the option is selected for Show The Message Bar In All Applications When Active Content, Such as ActiveX Controls and Macros, Has Been Blocked.

5. Click OK to close the Trust Center Settings and then click OK to accept your changes and close Word Options.

If you have not disabled the Message Bar and your Macro Security settings are set to Disable All Macros With Notification, when you open a document or template that contains macros (or open or create a document based on a template that contains macros), the macros are initially disabled. To enable them, click the Options button that appears in the Message Bar. In the Microsoft Office Security Options dialog box, select Enable This Content then click OK.

> **Note**
>
> If you want to disable macros, display the Microsoft Office Security Options dialog box and select Help Protect Me From Unknown Content (Recommended), as opposed to closing the Message Bar.
>
> Some macros have been known to cause the Message Bar to redisplay when opening or creating new documents, even if the document or template you are opening or creating does not actually contain macros.

For more information on Macro Security, see Chapter 20, "Securing Your Word Documents."

Prior to recording a macro, consider the following:

- First, practice the steps that you will record. The macro recorder is similar to a video recorder, and every action will be captured, including switching document views and moving your insertion point—even your mistakes are recorded. For macros that will involve several steps, consider jotting down a few notes to help you remember the correct sequence of steps.

- When you are recording, the mouse cannot be used to select text or move the cursor—you will need to use the keyboard instead. You can review navigation and text selection methods in Chapter 8, "Navigating Your Document."

- If you are creating a macro for a specific template, and the macro will navigate to specific locations in documents based on the template, then consider adding Bookmarks in the template. Then in your macro you can use Go To (F5) to navigate to the correct location. For more on using Bookmarks, see Chapter 8.

For our first simple macro example, we will insert the current system date as a static date in your document. If you've ever inserted a date by using the Date And Time dialog box, more than likely practice is not necessary. To use the Macro Recorder and record a new macro, follow these steps:

1. Create a new document and use the Word Macro-Enabled Document file type (as described in the preceding section) to save it in My Documents as MyFirstMacros.docm.

2. Navigate to the Developer tab and in the Code group, click Record Macro. This will display the Record Macro dialog box shown in Figure 28-2.

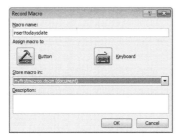

Figure 28-2 The Record Macro dialog box provides all of the options for creating a macro, including assigning the macro to a button or keyboard shortcut.

3. In the Macro Name text box, type a name for your macro, such as **inserttodaysdate**.

> **Note**
>
> Naming a macro is similar to naming a document, and you should use descriptive names. Macro names are limited to 80 characters when using the Record Macro dialog box; they must start with a letter; they can include letters and numbers; and they can't include most special characters or spaces (you can use the underscore character to represent a space).
>
> If you give your macro the same name as an existing macro, you will be prompted to replace the existing macro. You can click Yes to replace the macro, click No to return to the Record Macro dialog box and modify the name, or click Cancel to cancel the macro recording.
>
> Additionally, if your macro uses the same name as a built-in command, your macro will replace the built-in functionality. For more on viewing built-in Word commands or replacing them with your own macro, see the Inside Out tip titled "Viewing Word Commands," on page 834.

4. In the Store Macro In list, select MyFirstMacros.docm.

   If you save the macros in Normal.dotm, they will be available to all documents. However, it's recommended that you initially save your macros in a separate document during the learning stages.

5. Provide a description for your macro, if desired, and then click OK to begin recording.

   Your mouse pointer displays with a cassette tab, indicating that your actions are being recorded. The Record Macro button on the Developer tab will change to a Stop Recording button (you'll use this button when you are finished recording your macro).

   > **Tip**
   >
   > While you are recording a macro, you can click the Pause Recording button to perform any steps you do not want to record in your macro. When you are finished, click the Pause Recording button again to resume recording.

6. On the Insert tab, in the Text group, click Date & Time to display the Date & Time dialog box.

7. Select your preferred date format, clear the Update Automatically option if necessary, and then click OK.

   Do not add any additional steps unless you want your macro to contain other actions. For example, if you want to start a new paragraph after inserting the date, press Enter.

8. On the Developer tab, click Stop Recording in the Code group.

9. Test the macro.

   To test your macro, delete the previously inserted date, then on the Developer tab in the Code group, click Macros (or press Alt+F8) in the Macros dialog box, click Insert-TodaysDate, and then click Run. The current system date should be inserted in your document at your insertion point.

   > **Tip**
   >
   > For a one-click method to start and stop recording a macro, right-click the customizable status bar then click Macro Recording. Then, to access the Record Macro dialog box, click the Record Macro button on the status bar. Like the Record Macro button on the Developer tab, the Record Macro button will change to Stop Recording when you are recording a macro.

Chapter 28

You might be wondering how navigating to the Developer tab, clicking the Macros button, selecting the macro from the list, and clicking Run can save time. You are correct in thinking it's not necessarily any faster than inserting a date by using the Date & Time dialog box. For simple macros, the time-saving steps occur when you add the macro to your Quick Access Toolbar or assign it to a keyboard shortcut. Accomplishing both of these tasks is covered in the next section.

Running Macros

As you might have gathered in the previous section, using the Macros dialog box is not the most efficient way to run your macros. Ideally, running a macro should be as simple as clicking a button or pressing a keyboard shortcut. This section of the chapter covers how to add a macro to your Quick Access Toolbar, how to assign a keyboard shortcut to your macro, and how to use specifically named macros that will automatically run without being assigned to a button or keyboard shortcut.

Macros can also be added to the Ribbon. However, doing so requires some XML knowledge, and this capability isn't found within the Word application. For more information on customizing the Ribbon, see "How to: Customize the Ribbon" in MSDN's Developer center (*http://msdn.microsoft.com/en-us/library/aa942954(VS.80).aspx*).

Adding a Macro to the Quick Access Toolbar

As you might know from reading previous chapters, the Quick Access Toolbar can be easily customized with commands that are not on the Ribbon or with commands you prefer to have visible at all times. The Quick Access Toolbar can also be used as a one-click method for running macros. To add the previously created macro to your Quick Access Toolbar, follow these steps:

1. Open MyFirstMacros.docm, if it's not already open.

2. Click the More button at the end of the Quick Access Toolbar.

3. Click More Commands to open Word Options with the Customize section displayed.

4. In the Choose Commands From list, select Macros.

   The macro, inserttodaysdate, will appear as Project.NewMacros.inserttodaysdate in the list of commands, as shown in Figure 28-3.

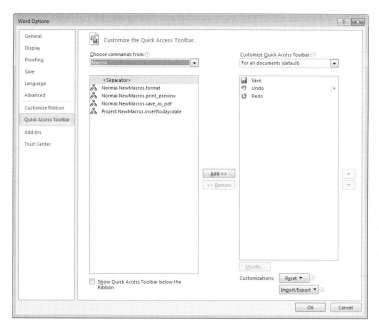

Figure 28-3 Click the macro you want to add to the Quick Access Toolbar, click Add, and and then click OK.

> **Note**
>
> The name of the macro, Project.NewMacros.inserttodaysdate, provides the loca-
> tion where the macro is stored, as previously discussed in the section titled "A Bit
> About VBA and Macros," on page 812. Project is the name of the VBA Project, New-
> Macros is the name of the module (which is automatically created when you use
> the Macro Recorder), and inserttodaysdate is the name of the macro.

5. In the Customize Quick Access Toolbar list, select For MyFirstMacros.docm.

You should store your Quick Access Toolbar customizations in the same location as
your macro. Use For All Documents (Default) if the macro is stored in your Normal
template.

> **Note**
> The list of current Quick Access Toolbar commands will disappear after you select For MyFirstMacros.docm from the Customize Quick Access Toolbar list. When you customize the Quick Access Toolbar for a specific document or template, the customizations will merge with the commands listed under For All Documents (Default) when the document, template, or a document attached to the template is opened.

6. Select the macro (if it isn't already selected) and then click Add to add it to your Quick Access Toolbar.

7. Click the Modify button to open the Modify Button dialog box, shown here.

8. Select a symbol, or icon, for your macro, such as the Appointment Book icon. Then to modify the ScreenTip, change the Display Name for your macro. For example, type **Insert the current date**.

9. Click OK to accept the changes in the Modify Button dialog box, and then click OK to accept the Quick Access Toolbar customizations.

Your custom macro button appears on your Quick Access Toolbar, as shown here.

When you close MyFirstMacros.docm, the custom macro button will be removed from the Quick Access Toolbar. You can also use the macros you created and stored in MyFirstMacros.docm with other documents by using the fileas a global template. For more on working with templates, see Chapter 4, "Templates and Themes for a Professional Look."

INSIDE OUT   When Is a Macro Actually Warranted?

In past versions of Word, macros were typically created for every repetitive task, such as inserting frequently used text, graphics, tables, and formatting text and paragraphs. Now, with all of the new features Word has to offer, alternate methods for reusing data are available. At the beginning of this chapter, the list of tasks for which you could create a macro included the example of inserting a table with a specific size, table style, and certain table options. Depending on your needs, a macro is not the only way to accomplish this task. If you need precisely formatted content, such as a graphic, table, or frequently used text, consider creating a building block instead. For example, a specifically formatted table can be turned into a building block and be placed in the Quick Tables gallery, as shown here:

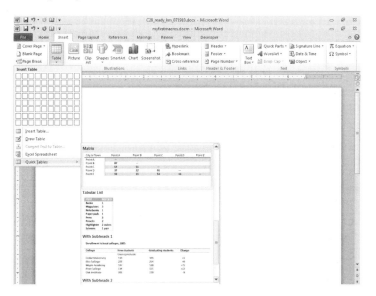

A building block provides more flexibility than a macro, especially when it comes to modifications. To modify a macro, you need to either record the macro again or manually edit the code. To modify a building block, you can insert the building block, make your modifications, and then redefine the building block with your modified content.

If you want to add a single building block to your Quick Access Toolbar, use a combination of building blocks and macros. For instance, create a building block in which the content is inserted in a document and record a macro for inserting the building block.

If you want to create a keyboard shortcut for a building block, a macro isn't necessary. Building blocks are available in the Customize Keyboard dialog box, which is described in the next section, under the AutoText category.

If the purpose of your macro is for text or paragraph formatting, consider using a style instead of a macro. As with building blocks, formatting can be easily redefined in the style without having to record the macro again or manually edit the code.

Keep in mind that the key to undertaking any task is to first determine the easiest route and then to use the most efficient tool for the job.

Assigning a Keyboard Shortcut to a Macro

In addition to adding your macros to your Quick Access Toolbar, you can assign keyboard shortcuts to your macros. The initial steps are similar to the steps used to add a macro to your Quick Access Toolbar. First, open MyFirstMacros.docm, display Word Options, and then click the Customize Ribbon tab. Then follow these steps:

1. Click the Customize button to display the Customize Keyboard dialog box, as shown in Figure 28-4.

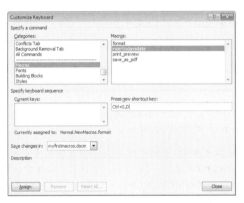

Figure 28-4 Use the Customize Keyboard dialog box to create keyboard shortcuts for your macros.

2. In the Categories section, scroll to the bottom of the list then select Macros.

3. Click the Save Changes In list and select MyFirstMacros.docm.

    InsertTodaysDate should now be visible in the Macros list, as shown in Figure 28-4.

4. Place your cursor in the Press New Shortcut Key text box, and then press your desired keyboard shortcut on the keyboard, such as Ctrl+Shift+D.

    Note that Ctrl+Shift+D is a built-in keyboard shortcut and is assigned to Double Underline. If you use this keyboard shortcut to add double underline, select an alternate keyboard shortcut for your new macro and press those keys on the keyboard instead.

CAUTION !

Depending on which combination you use, custom keyboard shortcuts may override built-in keyboard shortcuts, so be sure to check if the shortcut you want to use is available (or you don't mind overwriting the built-in shortcut). You can check to see if your intended keyboard shortcut is currently assigned by looking below the Current Keys list after the keys you want to use are pressed.

5. Click Assign then click OK to assign the keyboard shortcut. Close the Customize Keyboard dialog box then click OK to close Word Options.

Tip

After you are familiar with the steps for adding a macro to your Quick Access Toolbar, or assigning a keyboard shortcut to a macro, you can select one of these options when you start recording a new macro. In the Record Macro dialog box (shown in Figure 28-2), click the Button option to add the macro to your Quick Access Toolbar or click the Keyboard button to assign a keyboard shortcut.

TROUBLESHOOTING

My macro cannot be found or is disabled.

If you try to run a macro and encounter a message indicating that your macro cannot be found or has been disabled because of your Macro Security settings, the first thing to check is your Macro Security settings, which are described in the section titled "Setup and Planning," on page 814.

If you're still having trouble after you have verified that your Macro Security settings enable you to run macros, and if you are trying to run the macro from your Quick Access Toolbar or a keyboard shortcut, try running the macro by using the Macros dialog box, which is found on the Developer tab in the Code group (or press Alt+F8). If the macro does not appear in the list, your macro is missing. Either the document or template in which the macro is stored is not open, or the macro was inadvertently deleted. If you can successfully run the macro from the Macros dialog box, try recreating the keyboard shortcut or the button on your Quick Access Toolbar.

Running a Macro Automatically

Most macros require you to click a button or use a keyboard shortcut to run the macro. However, a few macros will run automatically when a specific event occurs, such as when Word starts; when you open, close, or create a document; and when you exit Word.

A macro must be stored in your Normal template in order for it to run automatically when a document is created, opened, or closed. It must also use a macro name listed in Table 28-1, which also describes the events associated with the macros.

Table 28-1 **List of Automatic Macros**

Auto Macro Name	Description
AutoExec	Runs when Word starts
AutoOpen	Runs each time a document is opened
AutoNew	Run each time a document is created
AutoClose	Runs each time a document is closed
AutoExit	Runs when Word exits

> **Note**
> You can use other events, called Document-Level Events, to cause a macro to run automatically. However, they are out of the scope of this chapter.

For our automatic macro example, we'll take a look at another task listed at the beginning of this chapter—combining several repetitive procedures, such as switching to a specific document view and modifying the Zoom Level.

Word users often need to open documents in a certain view and at a specified Zoom Level. In recent versions, if you create a new document based on the Normal template, Word uses the current view settings and Zoom Level, as opposed to older versions that use the settings stored in the Normal template. But you still can't open documents in certain views and at specified Zoom Levels when you're accessing previously created documents. However, a simple macro and the power of VBA gives you the tools to specify which view, Zoom Level, and any other viewing options will be applied. And these settings will be in effect for every document you open automatically using a macro named AutoOpen. To create the macro, use the following steps:

1. On the Developer tab, click Record Macro.

2. In the Macro Name text box, type **AutoOpen**. From the Store Macro In list, select All Documents (Normal.dotm)—if it isn't already selected—as shown here.

3. Click OK to start recording. In the View options (on your status bar), click your desired view.

   Even if it's the view you are currently using, the action will still be recorded.

4. Click Zoom Level to open the Zoom dialog box and select your desired Zoom settings. (Changes made using the Zoom Slider are not recorded.)

5. Make any other desired changes to your view then click Stop Recording.

6. Test your macro by opening a document.

To fully test your macro, create a new document, switch to another view, change your view settings, and make another editing change, such as typing a space in the empty document and then pressing Backspace to delete the space. Then, save the document, close it, and reopen it.

> **Note**
> Why type a space just to delete it? Because altering your view or zoom settings by itself does not qualify as a change to the document. An action must appear in your Undo list for Word to actually save changes to your view.

Alternatively, you can verify your recorded macro by viewing the recorded code in the Visual Basic Editor, which is covered in the next section.

Chapter 28

TROUBLESHOOTING

The Macro Recorder did not record all of my actions.

When you use the Macro Recorder, you might find that not all of your actions are recorded, such as when you use the Zoom Slider to alter your view or select various options in a dialog box (for example, Open, Print, or Save As).

In general, Word can record the result of your choices in a dialog box but not the steps used to obtain the result. And if the steps are not part of the end result, they will not be recorded. In some instances, unfortunately, there is no valid reason for you to be unable to record specific actions. Thankfully, each version of Word adds more capabilities to the Macro Recorder. For example, in Word 2010, when you use the Macro Recorder to record a change to an option in Word Options, only the option you changed is actually recorded—that alone is a significant and welcome change from previous versions. But some areas still need to be tweaked.

However, just because you are unable to record an action, doesn't mean it's impossible to accomplish your goal. For these situations, you might need to find an alternate method. In the example given here, it might mean using the Zoom dialog box instead of the Zoom Slider, or manually editing the macro and making the necessary additions. For the latter, VBA knowledge is required, but the more you learn about Word and VBA, the easier it will become.

Editing Macros

Depending on the macro you record, sometimes you might need to edit and refine the results of the recorded macro. The beauty of VBA is that the syntax is fairly easy to read and comprehend. If you are interested in learning more about macros, viewing recorded code is a good place to start. For our editing example, we'll take a look at another task discussed at the beginning of this chapter—making an option in a dialog box more accessible. This example will clear the Show Picture Placeholders option, which speeds scrolling through a document that contains a large number of inline images in Print Layout view, and we'll make a simple edit to the macro so that each time you run it, the option will toggle on or off depending on its current state. To get started, follow these steps:

1. Open MyFirstMacros.docm, navigate to the Developer tab, and click Record Macro.

2. In the Macro Name text box, type **TogglePicturePlaceholders**. From the Store Macro In list, select MyFirstMacros.docm, add a description if desired, and then click OK to start recording.

3. On the File tab, click Options then click Advanced.

4. Select the Show Picture Placeholders option, which is located under the Show Document Content heading.

5. Click OK to accept the change and close Word Options. (If the option is already selected, clear it; all we need is to have a change recorded.)

6. On the Developer tab, click Stop Recording then click Macros.

7. Select TogglePicturePlaceholders in the list of macros then click Edit.

   The Visual Basic Editor will open, and you will see both recorded macros, as shown in Figure 28-5.

Figure 28-5 The InsertTodaysDate and TogglePicturePlaceholders macros shown in the Visual Basic Editor.

Prior to editing, take a closer look at the macro you just recorded (you will take a closer look at the Visual Basic Editor in the next section) and note the following:

- Each macro, or *procedure*, begins with the statement Sub, which stands for subroutine, and ends with End Sub. The text in between these lines is the code that is executed when you run the macro.

> **Note**
>
> Another set of paired statements you'll see in recorded macros is *Function* and *End Function*. This structure groups related statements together, such as a group of options in a dialog box. And like *Sub* and *End Sub*, the group begins with the statement *With* and ends with the statement *End With*.

- The green text, preceded by an apostrophe, is called Comment Text. As the name implies, this text is used for purposes of notes and documentation, which you can use to identify the macro, describe what it does, or give instructions as to its use. Comment text is ignored when the macro runs. You can safely delete these lines if you want. You can add an apostrophe anywhere in the macro, but any text that follows it (until the end of the current line) will be treated as Comment Text.

- ShowPicturePlaceholders is set to a True/False (Boolean) value, as are all check boxes. `True` means the check box is selected, and `False` means the check box is cleared.

As mentioned earlier in this chapter, you do not need to know VBA to follow the syntax. Take the statement in the TogglePicturePlaceholders macro, for example. In the active window, the view option—Show Picture Placeholders—is selected, or turned on.

Because the Show Picture Placeholders option is a True/False (Boolean) value, to use the macro to toggle the view of Picture Placeholders, all we need to do is set Show Picture Placeholders to the reverse of its current value. To make the edit, follow these steps:

1. Locate the TogglePicturePlaceholders macro. It should appear similar to the code here.

   ```
   Sub TogglePicturePlaceholders()
   '
   ' TogglePicturePlaceholders Macro
   '
   '
       ActiveWindow.View.ShowPicturePlaceHolders = True
   End Sub
   ```

2. Select `ActiveWindow.View.ShowPicturePlaceHolders` and copy it.

3. Replace `True` at the end of the line with `Not` and then paste the previously copied statement. The revised statement is shown here.

   ```
   ActiveWindow.View.ShowPicturePlaceHolders = Not ActiveWindow.View.ShowPicturePlaceHolders = True
   ```

   > **Note**
   > When you reference only an option (in VBA this is called a Property), as opposed to changing the value of the option, the current value of the option is returned. The *Not* operator reverses the current value, and if the current value is *True*, the `Not` operator toggles the value to change to *False*, and vice-versa.

4. From the File menu, click Close And Return To Microsoft Word.

5. Assign the macro to your Quick Access Toolbar by using the steps provided in the section titled "Adding a Macro to the Quick Access Toolbar," on page 818.

6. Verify that you are using Print Layout view, insert an inline image (Text Wrapping is set to Inline With Text) in your document, and try out your new macro. The macro should toggle between viewing empty placeholders and viewing the image in the document.

The Visual Basic Editor

The Visual Basic Editor is a powerful automation tool. As mentioned earlier, covering all aspects of VBA and the Visual Basic Editor is beyond the scope of this chapter; entire books are dedicated to this subject alone. This section will discuss the elements of the Visual Basic Editor, many of which are used in this chapter. A diagram of the Visual Basic Editor is provided in Figure 28-6, and Table 28-2 describes each element in the diagram.

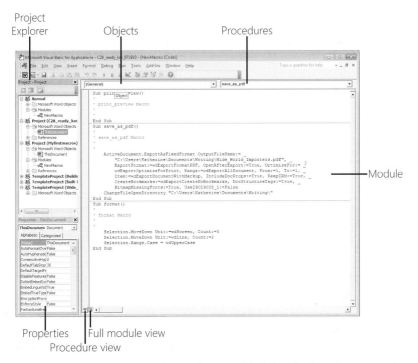

Figure 28-6 The Visual Basic Editor is the central hub for all of your macro needs; you can use it for creating, editing, and deleting macros.

Table 28-2 **The Visual Basic Editor**

Element or term	Description
Project Explorer	Provides access to all available VBA Projects including open documents, templates, Normal template, loaded global templates, and an attached document template. The name of the file that contains the project is enclosed in parentheses next to the name of the project. Double-click a VBA Project—or an object, such as a module—in the VBA Project to open it and view the contents. If the Project Explorer is closed, from the View menu, click Project Explorer or press Ctrl+R.
Properties Pane	Displays properties of the selected object in the Project Explorer. Can be used to change the name of a module or project. The Properties pane is primarily used for other types of objects available in VBA, such as a UserForm, which is also called a dialog box. If the Properties pane is closed, from the View menu, click Properties Window or press F4.
Module	Contains a collection of macros. Each macro in the module is visually separated by a horizontal line.
Procedure View	Displays only the active macro in the module.
Full Module View	Displays all macros in the module.
Procedure List	Provides quick navigation between macros in the module. To quickly jump to another macro, select the macro from the Procedure List. This option is useful if you have several lengthy macros, or if you are viewing the module in Procedure view.

Additional Macro Options

As you become more familiar with using macros, you might find that you have macros that could use a more descriptive name, macros you do not want (it's not unusual to have several failed macro recording attempts when you are in the learning stages), and macros that you want to use in other documents or templates. How to deal with each of these situations is covered in this section.

Renaming a Macro, Module, or Project

The easiest way to rename a macro, module, or project is to use the Visual Basic Editor. Note that the previously provided rules for naming macros still apply—names must start with a letter and they cannot contain spaces or special characters, except for the underscore character (which you can use in place of spaces). An exception to the rules previously provided is the character limit. You can use up to 255 characters in the macro name if you are naming or renaming it in the Visual Basic Editor; names for modules and VBA Projects are limited to 30 characters. Additionally, similar to documents, macros contained in the same module must have a unique name, and modules in the VBA Project must likewise be uniquely named.

To rename a macro, simply change the name of the macro after the line that begins with Sub.

To rename the module or VBA Project, select the module or VBA Project in the Project Explorer. In the Properties pane, change the name in the (Name) text box.

CAUTION

If your macro is assigned to a button on your Quick Access Toolbar or a keyboard shortcut, changing the name of the macro, module, or VBA Project will disable the button or keyboard shortcut. You need to remove the disabled button from your Quick Access Toolbar and create it again. For a keyboard shortcut, you will need to reassign the keyboard shortcut to the renamed macro.

TROUBLESHOOTING

I've encountered an "Ambiguous name detected" error.

If you try to run a macro and Word displays an error that states an Ambiguous Name is detected, you have two macros with the same name in your module.

To resolve the error, first note the name of the macro listed in the error message. If the Visual Basic Editor does not automatically open and locate the macro for you, then, on the Developer tab, click Macros to open the Macros dialog box, select the macro in the list, and click Edit. The Visual Basic Editor will open with the macro displayed.

If you cannot find another macro with the same name, click the Procedure list; you should see two macros with the same name. Click either macro in the list to navigate to the macro in the module. To correct the error, you need to rename one of the macros and provide a unique name. Or if it is a duplicate macro, delete one of the duplicates by using the steps provided in the next section.

Deleting and Exporting Macros and Modules

To delete a macro, you can use one of the following methods:

- Display the Macros dialog box, click Macros on the Developer tab or press Alt+F8, select the macro in the macros list then click Delete.

- In the Visual Basic Editor, select the entire macro—starting with the line that begins Sub, through End Sub—and press Delete on the keyboard.

Deleting a macro does not remove the macro from your Quick Access Toolbar (you need to manually remove the button). If you assigned a keyboard shortcut to the macro, no further action is required.

To delete a module, select the module in the Project Explorer. From the File menu, click Remove *ModuleName*. You will be prompted to export the module before removing it, as shown in Figure 28-7.

Figure 28-7 You are asked whether you want to export a macro before removing it.

If you click Yes, the Export File dialog box will display, in which you can provide a name and location for your exported module, as shown in Figure 28-8.

Figure 28-8 Use the Export File dialog box to export your module and save it prior to deleting and removing the module from your VBA Project.

You can use standard file naming rules for your exported module because it will be saved as an external file. Note that the file uses a .bas file extension. However, it is nothing more than a text file, and you can use Notepad to open it and view the contents.

> **Tip**
> If you want to delete an entire VBA Project, save the document or template in a macro-free file format, such as Word Document (.docx) or Word Template (.dotx). Doing so will remove the entire VBA Project from the document or template. If you want to preserve the macros, export the modules from the VBA Project prior to saving the file in the macro-free file format.

Importing Macros and Modules

There might be a time when you want to add your exported module back to the VBA Project, or import a module for use in another VBA Project. To import a previously exported module, in the Project Explorer, select the VBA Project to which you want to add the module. Then, from the File menu, click Import File. The Import File dialog box will display (it is similar to the Export File dialog box that is shown in Figure 28-8). To import the module, navigate to your saved module, select it, and then click Open. The module should now be added to your VBA Project.

If you want to use a single macro from the exported file, you can use Notepad to open the previously saved file, copy the macro, and paste it in any module. Alternatively, you can import the entire module and delete any macros you do not want to keep.

Another way to share macros between documents and templates is to open both files and then copy and paste the macros between the modules, just as you would copy and paste content between documents.

> **Note**
> You can also use the Organizer—available in the Macros dialog box on the Developer tab—to copy, rename, and delete modules. However, if you are comfortable using the Visual Basic Editor, you will find it is more flexible than the Organizer because the Organizer is limited to working only with modules and not individual macros. For more information on using the Organizer, see Chapter 4.

Chapter 28

INSIDE OUT   Viewing Word Commands

If you give a macro the same name as a built-in Word command, your macro will run instead of the built-in command. To access the list of built-in Word commands, on the Developer tab, click Macros. Then in the Macros In list, select Word Commands, as shown here:

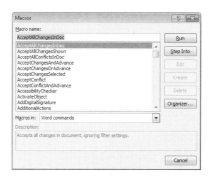

Many of the built-in Word commands are named according to how they are accessed in previous versions of Word. For example, if you are looking for Print Preview, use FilePrintPreview. (To quickly jump to a specific Word command, type the first few letters of the name in the Macro Name text box.)

If you find a Word command you wish to intercept with a macro, you can change the name of a previously recorded macro to match the name of the built-in Word command.

Alternatively, if you want to view the code used in the built-in Word command so that you can copy it and use it in another macro, learn more about VBA, or append additional code, select the command from the Macros list, click the Macros In list, select your document or template, and then click Create.

Keep in mind, if you add a macro with the same name as a built-in command and are not planning to replace the built-in command with your macro, you need to delete the macro or modify the macro name. Otherwise, Word will use the macro in place of the built-in command. For more information on deleting macros, see the section titled "Deleting and Exporting Macros and Modules," on page 832.

Protecting Your Macros

You can protect your macros from alteration by assigning a password to your VBA Project. To do so, follow these steps:

1. Display the Visual Basic Editor (click the Visual Basic button on the Developer tab or press Alt+F11).

2. From the Tools menu, click Project Properties.

3. Click the Protection tab, as shown in the following image, then select Lock Project For Viewing.

4. In the Password text box, type a password and then type it again in the Confirmation text box. (The Password and Confirmation are both required.)

Once your VBA Project is protected, you will be prompted to enter the password the first time you access it, such as when you double-click the VBA Project in the Project Explorer to open it, or use the Macros dialog box to edit or delete the macro after the file has been closed and reopened.

As with passwords in general, keep in mind that if you lose the password, you won't be able to access the VBA Project. Though some password cracking utilities are available, there are no guarantees they will work, and their success depends on the complexity (or more accurately, the simplicity) of the password you used to secure the VBA Project.

Digitally Signing Macros

Macros are digitally signed for a couple of reasons. The primary reason is to provide authentication for the macros when you share them with others. Another reason is so a user can disable all macros except for those that are digitally signed for security reasons. Even if you do not intend to digitally sign your macros, this section of the chapter will still

Chapter 28

be beneficial to you. You might come into contact with macros that have been digitally signed, and the more you know about digital signatures, the more you can make informed decisions when it comes to macro security.

In the tools that came with your version of Microsoft Office 2010, you'll find a program called SelfCert, a digital signature utility. This utility will help you digitally sign the macros and VBA projects you create, whether you are sharing your macros with others or they are for your own personal use in documents and templates.

Creating a Self-Signed Digital Signature

You can use SelfCert to create a digital signature yourself; it is intended to be used for macros that you use in your personal documents and templates. With a SelfCert digital signature, you can disable all macros except for those that are digitally signed. (For more on security settings, see Chapter 20.)

A digital signature created using SelfCert can be shared with others. However, it relies more on trust than true authentication. When SelfCert is used to create a digital signature, no authentication is required, and any name can be used for the digital signature. As you have likely surmised, anyone can easily create a digital signature using someone else's name or a corporation's name. It's for this reason that an authenticated digital signature can be provided only by a Certificate Authority.

Third-Party Digital Signature

If you are sharing your macro with others, you need to obtain a third-party digital signature for code signing to ensure that the macro is truly secure. A digital signature for code signing is issued by a third party which is called a certificate authority (CA). This third party validates the identity of the applicant for the digital signature before it is assigned and later keeps track of the digital signature to determine if it has expired or been revoked. Microsoft maintains a list of all third-party certification authorities, and you can view or download the list by visiting this Microsoft Office site at *http://support.microsoft.com/kb/931125*.

CAUTION

If the other user does not have your digital signature when you use SelfCert.exe to digitally sign a VBA Project and they later share your macros with others, they will be prevented from enabling the macros. For more information, see the Troubleshooting tip titled "I can't enable macros," on page 838.

To create a digital signature using SelfCert, follow these steps:

1. Click the Start button then click All Programs. Choose Microsoft Office and point to Microsoft Office 2010 Tools.

2. Click Digital Certificate for VBA Projects.

    The Create Digital Certificate dialog box appears, as shown in Figure 28-9.

Figure 28-9 The Create Digital Signature dialog box is where you create a digital signature for your personal use.

3. In the Your Certificate's Name text box, type a name for your digital certificate then click OK.

Your digital signature has been created, and you can now use it to sign your macros for personal use.

Digitally Signing a VBA Project

When you digitally sign your macros, you are actually providing a digital signature for the VBA Project, which as previously mentioned is the primary container for your macros. After you have obtained a digital signature or created one for your personal use, you can digitally sign your VBA Project as follows:

1. Open the document or template you want to sign.

2. On the Developer tab, click Visual Basic or press Alt+F11.

3. In Project Explorer, select your VBA Project.

Chapter 28

4. From the Tools menu, click Digital Signature to display the Digital Signature dialog box, shown here:

5. Click Choose, select your digital signature from the Select Certificate dialog box, and then click OK.

   The digital certificate name will display in the Digital Signature dialog box.

6. Click OK to digitally sign your VBA Project and close the Digital Signature dialog box.

> **Note**
> If you previously selected a digital signature, you do not need to click Choose and select the digital signature again. To use the current digital signature, click OK in the Digital Signature dialog box.

After your VBA Project has been digitally signed, depending on the type of digital signature you used, you might need to digitally sign the VBA Project again if you create new macros or modify previously created macros.

TROUBLESHOOTING

I can't enable macros.

If you open a document or template—or if you create a new document based on a template—and you find you cannot enable the macros, first check your Macro Security settings, as described in the section titled "Setup and Planning," on page 814.

If your macro security settings are correct, the likely cause of the problem is macros that were signed with a digital signature created using SelfCert. To resolve this issue, use one of the following methods:

- If the digital signature is one you previously created or a digital signature you trust, you can install the digital signature on your system. Click the Show Signature Details link, click View Certificate, click Install Certificate, and then follow the steps in the Certificate Import Wizard.

- If you do not want to install the digital signature, you can remove it to enable the macros. Allow the macros to be disabled, display the Visual Basic Editor (Alt+F11), click Digital Signature on the Tools menu, and then click Remove. Save the file, close it, and reopen it. You will then be allowed to enable the macros.

Of the two methods provided, the second is recommended if the digital signature is not one you created. Once you install a digital certificate on your system, it is considered a System Root Certificate, which doesn't display in the Trusted Publisher dialog box in the Trust Center, and it could potentially be exploited. Note that you can use Internet Explorer Options to remove a previously installed digital certificate by viewing Certificates on the Content tab.

What's Next?

Now that you know the information in this chapter, you might be amazed at how much you can do using the Macro Recorder and a little knowledge about the Visual Basic Editor.

If this chapter has whet your appetite for macro knowledge, several resources are available to help you learn more. Here are two recommendations:

- The Word MVP Site (*www.mvps.org/word*). This Web site contains answers to frequently asked Word questions and provides tutorials and articles for using VBA in Word.

- The Microsoft Developers Network (MSDN; *msdn.microsoft.com/en-us/office/aa905482.aspx*). This Web site isn't strictly for developers; it includes topics for beginners, too. It also contains a wealth of sample code that you can copy and paste in your VBA Projects. Some samples can be used as-is, whereas others might need to be tweaked to fit your needs.

As you continue to explore and expand your experience with Word 2010, I hope you'll enjoy the creative, collaborative, and flexible ways in which you can create projects large and small. Be sure to check Office.com from time to time for new articles, templates, and tools, and if you have questions or curiosities about Word features you rarely use, visit the Word Solution Center (*http://support.microsoft.com/ph/11377#tab0*) to get the latest fixes, product guides, and how-to advice.

Chapter 28

Index

A

accessibility 35, 50, 638
ActiveX content controls
  adding 809
  programming 810
  properties, changing 810
  Trust Center and 809
  when to use 808
ActiveX, security settings for 67, 635
add-ins
  Add-ins group on the Developer tab 791
  managing 63
  security settings 67, 634
address lists, customizing 770
advanced options, how to change 63
aligning text
  Alignment Tabs 166
  Drawing Grid, overriding 341
  first line and hanging indents 341
  headers and footers 166
  index alignment 725
  left and right indents, adjusting 340
  Paragraph Dialog box, using 341
  in table cells, changing 479
  tools and shortcuts for 338
  types of alignment 223
  using the ruler 339
  vertically, between margins 157
All Caps Font effect vs. uppercase 221
Annual Reports, designing 96
AppData folder, displaying 106
area charts 500
Arrange All documents command 29
arrows symbol set 564

art
  artistic borders 599
  artistic effects, applying 532
  art position, choosing 556
  Clip Art task pane 164
  distributing vs. aligning 555
  Drawing Grid, working with 530
  object layering, controlling 556
  objects, aligning 553
  objects, grouping and ungrouping 555
  Snap Objects To Grid feature 555
  text wrapping, controlling 557
  wrap points, adding and editing 558
authoring
  adding authors, and permissions 43
  improved features for 5, 7–10
AutoCorrect feature
  adding entries 309
  case sensitivity and 309
  controlling changes 308
  exceptions, entering 311
  function of 290, 307
  Math AutoCorrect 568
  replacing and deleting 311
  setting options for 307
  symbols 226
AutoFit, for tables 487
AutoFormat feature
  adding to the Ribbon 338
  as you type 335
  choices, adjusting 336
  managing 334
  options, changing 336
automatic update to date and time 229

AutoText
  AutoText Gallery, how to use 242
  printing entries 452
axes of charts, working with 513–515, 518

B

backgrounds
  adding and customizing 179
  colors and gradients 179
  custom, and fill effects 180
  matching colors 180
  patterns and pictures, using 182, 537
  removing from photos 538
  textures 182
backing up files, turning on automatic backup
      feature 53
Backstage view
  customizing 68
  fast commands 34
  Groups area 36
  Help tab 36, 61
  Info tab 35, 37, 38–51
  justification of text, tightening of 224
  new features in 5, 7
  New tab 35, 57, 70, 70–72, 109
  opening documents 76
  Options command 36, 52, 62
  Preview and Properties area 37
  Print tab 35, 36, 37, 57, 436
  purpose of 33
  Recent tab 35, 55, 75
  Save & Send tab 36, 58, 93
  Save & Share tab 642
  where to locate 34
balloons, track changes 677
  showing and hiding balloons 681
  size and location of, adjusting 682, 683
  text styles 681
bar charts 500
bibliographies
  building blocks for 230
  description of 314
  generating 319

saving to previous version of Word 51
  styles, use of 315
bidirectional text, working with 282
binding documents, margins and 147
Blogger, blogging services 755
blog posts
  blog accounts, configuring 755
  categories, adding 753
  Microsoft Office 2010 blogs 749
  new post document 70
  new, starting 750–752
  pictures, adding 755
  reusing content in 203
  saving to Windows Live SkyDrive 757
  text, entering 752
  web links, inserting 752
  what to blog about 754
  who's blogging 747
boilerplate text, templates for 111
boldface text 212, 215–216
Book Fold page settings 151
booklets, page setup features for 145
bookmarks, document navigation via 260
borders
  adding to pictures 542, 600, 604
  adding to sections and paragraphs 600
  adding to tables 605
  adjusting while previewing 441
  artistic, using Art Page Border feature 599
  blank lines, adding 601
  border spacing 601
  clearing, using No Border 588
  creating 597
  customizing 588–596
  first page, changing 599
  horizontal lines, inserting 603
  page or section 158
  partial borders, creating 596
  printing problems with 603
  reasons to add 587
  simple, adding 587
  to a single page 598
breaks, controlling page 156–159

Browse Objects feature 26
bubble charts 500
building blocks
  about 102, 208
  Building Blocks.dotx, troubleshooting 232
  Building Blocks Organizer 231, 232
  categories 236
  content controls and 234
  content, reusing 203
  cover pages, creating new 210
  Create New Building Block dialog box 235
  creating and using 230, 234–237
  customizing 237–238
  deleting 239
  descriptions for 236
  Document Building Blocks folder 237
  downloading from Microsoft Office Online
      239
  galleries 230, 232
  ideas for types of 240
  inserting existing building blocks 232
  vs. macros 821
  Modify Building Block dialog box 238
  naming 235
  paragraph formatting, including 235
  properties, modifying 238
  quick access to 242
  saving 51, 236
  themes, enabling 235
  Word Startup folder 237
Business Letterhead, designing 97
business plan documents, page setup features
      for 145

C

capitalization 220
  AutoCorrect feature
    case sensitivity and 309
    exceptions, entering 312
    options, setting 308
  Changing Case command 220
  small caps, how to apply 220
captions, adding to pictures 543

center alignment of text 224
Center tool, Mini Toolbar location of 212
certification authorities, working with 629
Change Case command 220
character formatting
  character styles 382
  keyboard shortcuts 257
  linked styles 382
  spacing, condensing 443
  Style Inspector 401
charts
  basic 501
  changing the type of chart 503
  chart templates 503
  chart tools, understanding 505
  data
    arrangement of, changing 508
    Chart Tools Design tab, working with 506
    data labels, working with 517
    datasheets, working with 507
    external, using 508
  defaults, setting 503
  editing and enhancing
    axes, working with 513–515, 518
    chart styles, applying 511
    Chart Styles gallery 511
    Chart Tools, using 509
    data labels, working with 517
    fonts, changing 512
    gridlines and trendlines, adding 515
    legends, displaying and positioning 516
    new layouts, choosing 510
    titles, adding 512
  formatting
    adding shadows and glows 521
    chart elements 519
    chart objects 518
    shapes 520
  ideas for using 499
  saving to previous versions of Word 51
  titles, adding 512
  types of 499
Check for Issues tool 50

citations
description of 314
editing 318
inserting 317
placeholders, adding and using 318
saving to previous versions of Word 51
Clear Formatting command 223
Clip Art task pane 164
Clipboards
Office Clipboard and system Clipboard 83
viewing the contents of 430
co-authoring
adding and modifying 42
collaborative features of Word 2010
blocking co-authors 700
contacting co-authors 700
using SharePoint Workspace or Windows
Live SkyDrive 697
simultaneous editing and saving 698
troubleshooting 701
comments, adding and managing
commas, inserting 675
deleting comments 688
description of 668
navigating comments 686
printing 684–686
responding to 687
reviewing 685–687
voice and handwritten comments 676
comparing and combining documents
combining revisions from multiple authors
696
compare (Legal Blackline) and combine
668
comparing two versions of same document
694–696
markup tools, description and table of
668–671
master documents and subdocuments 206
new features for 5, 7
revision process
comments and revisions, viewing 673
confidential revisions 696

organization of 667
reviewers, configuring colors for 672
sharing techniques 643
tags, creating together 39
tracking changes
accepting and rejecting changes 689–692
balloon and reviewing pane options
680–683
changed lines, customizing appearance of
680
description of 668
display options 677
printing tracked changes 684–686
reviewing tracked changes 685–687
while you edit 678
colors
backgrounds, applying colors and gradients
to 179
for borders, choosing 593
color palettes 89, 223
Custom Colors dialog box 548
highlighting tool 221
matching, using RGB or HSL values 180, 594
pictures, color adjustments 534
shadows, coloring 550
text, changing 222
themes and 89, 131, 135
underlining 215
columns
column breaks, inserting and removing 196
column charts 499
column layouts
flowing text into 194
new, beginning 195
Column Tool, using 189
default column widths 188
for directories 785
in indexes 726
lines between columns 190
multicolumn documents 188–190
for part of a document 191
planning 187
seeing columns, in Print Layout view 189

spacing between 194
specs, in the Columns Dialog box 190
unequal column widths, creating 192
when to use 187
widths, changing 193
Combo Box content controls 797, 803
commands, built-in, viewing 834
comments
managing
commas, inserting 675
deleting comments 688
description of 668
navigating comments 686
responding to 687
printing 684–686
reviewing 685–687
voice and handwritten comments 676
Community Server program 755
compatibility
Check for Issues tool
Check Accessibility 50
Check Compatibility 50
Inspect Document 50
Compatibility Checker 639
Compatibility Mode 46
document converter 46
Protected View
file validation, changing 617
what's displayed in 616
working with 615
tests for, from the Info tab 35
compressing pictures 534
concordance files, for indexes 728
confidential document revisions 696
content controls
ActiveX controls
adding 809
programming 810
properties, changing 810
Trust Center and 809
when to use 808
adding 798
building blocks and 234, 807

Content group on the Developer tab 791
vs. InfoPath forms 791
Legacy Form controls 789, 808
properties, changing
lists, adding content to 803
locking 803
mapping controls to XML 804
styling 801
titles and tags, adding 800
when to use 799
protecting documents 805, 807
saving to previous versions of Word 51
static text, adding and formatting 792
types of
adding 794, 798
combo box control 797
date picker 798
drop-down list 797
nested 807
picture content control 797
plain text control 796
rich text control 796
using 804
when to use 790, 792
content creation
borders, applying behind content 606
building blocks
creating new 234–237
custom galleries and the AutoText gallery
242
ideas for creating 241
inserting 208
for complex documents 174
goals for 175
handwriting with mouse or stylus 78
ideas for 3
importing documents 204
inking, for long-hand content 204
inserting content from another Word
document or text file 77
objects, placing 207
publishing options for 201
reusing 202

content creation, *continued*
  Snipping Tool, using 420
  speech recognition, using 77
  text, entering 203
content delivery, possibilities for 178
content formatting. *See also* text formatting
conversion, document
  Compatibility Mode 46
  free converter 46
cover pages
  adding 208
  building blocks for 230
  Cover Page Gallery 210
  creating your own 210
  galleries 233
crashes, system
  corrupt Normal template 108
  Document Recovery task pane 53
cropping pictures 535
cross references, document
  adding 326
  deleting 328
  error messages 328
  hyperlinks as, for web pages 327
  modifying, moving, and updating 327
  reference types 326
  relative 328
cross references, index 722
Customer Experience Improvement Program
  68
Customize Status Bar list 31
cutting, copying, and pasting
  how to, including keyboard shortcuts 80
  Paste with Live Preview 6
  table data 474

D

data
  chart data
    arrangement of, changing 508
    Chart Tools Design tab, working with 506
    data labels, working with 517
    datasheets, working with 507

    entering 506
    external, using 508
    hidden, removing from documents 625
    merge data, working with 772
    table data, sorting 486
database programs, as used in mail merge
  778
date and time elements
  Date Picker content control 798
  how to add 228
  in headers and footers 164
  recording a macro to insert 816–818
Decrease Indent tool, location of 212
defaults
  date and time 229
  Document Defaults 388, 407, 408
  document properties 44
  Font Color button 222
  new document 383
  Quick Access Toolbar 16
delivery delay, for e-mails 661
design
  assessing regularly 73
  characteristics of a well-designed document
    95
  features to help with, summary of 102
  importance of 101
  layout and design fundamentals 175–178
  redesign considerations 73, 113
Developer tab, displaying 790, 814
dialog boxes, access to launchers 17
dictionaries
  adding to 301
  custom
    accessing and modifying 301
    adding dictionaries 304
    adding terms to 304
    creating new 303
    default, choosing 305
    default location of 304
    disabling, removing, and deleting 306
    limitations of 303
    lists of terms, converting into custom

dictionary 305
digital signatures and stamps
  adding a stamp 631
  attaching to files 48, 630
  certificate authorities and security adminis-
    trators, working with 629
  digital IDs
    creating 629
    how to get 628
  macros
    reasons for signing 835
    self-signed signatures, creating 836
    third-party signatures 836
    VBA projects 837
  removing signatures 632
  signing 628
  viewing signatures 631
directory of records, from data sources 784
display options
  how to change 63
  mathematical equation display, controlling
    565
documents
  Arrange All command 29
  browsing, using the Navigation Pane 25
  comparing and combining 693–697
  complex documents
    factors to consider 173–175
    outlining, reasons for 415–417
  displaying only current document styles 398
  Document Defaults 388, 407–409
  Document Grid
    Drawing Grid, displaying 285
    language settings 149
    settings, specifying 284
    turning feature on 284
    working with 283
  Document Inspector 693
  Document Quick Styles, resetting 389
  Document Recovery task pane 53
  Documents Building Blocks folder 237
  expiration dates for documents, setting 637

inspection
  from the Info tab 35
  quality control tools 290
length and current page, as shown in Status
    Bar 30
mail merge documents, types of 764–768
multiple, working with 28
new, creating
  default Normal template 383, 389
  from the New tab in Backstage view 35, 57
orientation of, changing 147, 441
planning 142–144
properties
  customizing display 44
  printing 451
  setting, from the Info tab 35
  working with, from the Info tab 38
protection 47–49
readability level 306
recent documents
  locating, in Backstage view 34
  options for list 35, 55
section formatting, Reveal Formatting pane
    402
short documents, page setup features for
    143
Split command 29
style changes and 383
Trusted Documents, setting up 67
views, changing 21–24
View Side By Side command 29
double spacing, setting 345
double strikethrough of text 220
doughnut charts 500
Draft document view 24
draft versions of documents
  AutoRecover feature 52
  Background Saves feature 52
  editing and reviewing 175
  recovering and deleting
    from the Info tab 35
    Recover Unsaved Documents feature 54

drawings
  Drawing Canvas, working with 530
  Drawing Grid
    displaying 285
    overriding 341
    Snap Objects To Grid feature 555
    using 531
  freehand
    adding text to 552
    tables 468
drawing tablets 204
drop caps, creating 357
Drop-Down List content controls 797
duplicating documents, using the New
        Windows tool 29

E

Ecma Office Open XML format 103
editing tools
  AutoCorrect
    adding entries 309
    case sensitivity and 309
    changes, controlling 308
    exceptions, entering 311
    function of 311
    options, setting 307
    replacing and deleting entries 311
    symbols 311
  comparing and combining documents
        693–697
  copying, cutting, and pasting 80
  editing restrictions, applying 622–624
  editing time, total 38
  Edit Links To Files selection 44
  formatting inconsistencies, checking for 291
  grammar, checking
    activating the grammar checker 295
    as you type 296
    Do Not Check option 297
    grammar rules, setting 300–302
    hiding grammar errors, when to use 296
    options, configuring 298–300

macros, editing 826–830
overview 289
permissions and restricting 48, 125
preventing editing, Mark As Final 297
proofing your document
  complex documents 175
  flagged errors, fixing 292–294
  proofreaders, necessity of 297
  Spelling and Grammar dialog box 295
  suppressing proofing marks 296
quality control checks 290
saving documents 91–95
simultaneous editing
  co-authoring 698–700
  new features for 5, 7
spelling, checking
  as you type 296
  contextual 291
  Do Not Check option 297
  error notifications 291
  hide spelling errors, when to use 296
  importance of 290
  options, configuring 298
text selection and shortcuts for 79
undoing, redoing, and repeating 85
e-mail attachments
  sharing files
    delaying delivery 661
    flagging messages 660
    priority, setting 659
    receipts, requesting 660
    sending securely 658
    voting buttons 662
  options for 642
e-mail attachments, setting preferences for
        64
e-mail, merge to 784
embedding vs. linking objects 583
embossing text effect 220
encryption
  how to 620
  passwords 48, 620

removing protection 621
templates 125
energy saving features 435
engraving text effect 220
envelopes, printing 456–458
equations, mathematical
  building blocks for 230
  calling attention to 570
  creating from scratch 563
  equation display, controlling 565
  Equation gallery 562
  Math AutoCorrect, using 568
  options, setting 566
  saving
    to previous versions of Word 51, 562
    to the Gallery 567
  symbol sets and descriptions 564
errors, checking from the Status Bar 30
ESL (English as a second language)
  Microsoft Research ESL Assistant 285
Excel spreadsheets, inserting into a table 470

F

fast commands
  in Backstage view 34
  Recent Documents, changing number of 55
faxes, sending
  choosing a service 664
  creating and sending 663
  multiple faxes, using Mail Merge Wizard
    666
  troubleshooting 665
field codes, controlling 167
File Block settings 67, 635
file extensions
  of backup files 53
  displaying, how to set default 113
  for macro-enabled documents 813
  for macro-enabled templates 813
  macro-free 813
file formats
  available in Word 2010 60, 94
  converters for, how to locate 46, 94

for converted documents 47
for previous versions of Word 51
for templates 102
file sharing
  compatibility issues 50
  converters for additional file formats 94
  converting from earlier versions of Word 46
  via e-mail
    delaying delivery 661
    flagging messages 660
    priority, setting 659
    receipts, requesting 660
    sending securely 658
    voting buttons 662
  via fax
    choosing a service 664
    creating and sending 663
    multiple faxes, using Mail Merge Wizard
      666
    troubleshooting 665
  file validation, changing 617
  Mark As Final feature 618
  network locations
    accessing resources in 655
    creating 654
    FTP sites, linking to 654
    saving documents to 655
  new options for, in Word 2010 644
  protection, preparing 47–49
  Save & Send tab in Backstage view 58
  SharePoint Workspace 2010
    documents, checking in and out 649
    Groove workspaces 646, 648
    new documents, creating 650
    new workspaces, creating 646–648
  with Windows Live SkyDrive 59
  Windows Live SkyDrive
    co-authoring in 697–701
    saving to a shared space 653
    setting up and using 651
    sharing files 652
  with Microsoft SharePoint 59
  workgroup templates, using 656

file size of document, locating 38
fill effects
  Fill Effects dialog box 181
  gradients for backgrounds 180
Find and Replace
  Find and Replace dialog box 253
  floating objects vs. inline objects 257
  formatting settings 256
  search parameters 254
  special characters 257–259
  wildcards 255, 256
flagging e-mail messages 660
Flesch-Kincaid Grade Level scores 306
Flesch Reading Ease scores 306
folders
  creating new 94
  shared 647
fonts
  All Caps Font effect 221
  availability on your system 213
  changing, using the Mini Toolbar 512
  default settings 407
  Font Color tools
    Font Color button 222
    Mini Toolbar location of 212
  Font dialog box 220
  Font list
    how to use 213
    Theme Fonts section of 214
  font size
    Font Size list 214
    Font Size tool 212
    how to specify 214
    Keyboard shortcuts for 215
    table Styles, troubleshooting 483
  Font tool 212
  OpenType fonts 216, 217
  Reveal Formatting pane 402
  specifying 213
  themes and 89, 131, 136
  troubleshooting, printing 446
footnotes and endnotes
  adding 320

  customizing 321
  deleting 323
  description of 314
  Footnote and Endnote dialog box 321
  inserting 321
  margins and 325
  moving and copying 323
  separator lines, creating new 324
  visible in which views 322
  on web pages, as hyperlinks 323
  when to use 320
formatting text
  additional formats 220
  as you work 210–212
  clearing formatting 223
  comparing text formats 403
  for complex documents 174
  default settings 407
  effects, deleting 220
  finding instances of 256
  Format Painter tool, location of 212
  formatting lost, when saving to previous
      version of Word 51
  formatting marks, controlling the display of
      473
  inconsistencies, tracking 404
  in index entries 722
  quick, using the Mini Toolbar 20
  resricting and protecting 125
  styles, how to inspect 400
  text attributes, applying 215
  text effects, applying 219
  using the Font dialog box 220
form controls 789
FTP sites, linking to 654
Full Screen Reading document view 22, 64
functions in tables, working with 490
fundraising materials, ideas for 240

G

galleries
  building blocks 230, 232, 235, 237
  custom building blocks 241

custom galleries and the AutoText gallery 242

dialog box launchers, access to 18

Equations gallery 567

Header, Footer, and Page Number 163

previewing choices 20

Quick Parts 235

Styles 381

Table of Contents gallery 707

Text Box gallery 572

Theme Colors gallery 135

Theme Effects gallery 133

themes and 130

Themes gallery, how to find 87

working with, options for 19

geometry symbol set 564

glow styles for text, applying 219

Go To command 259

grade level scores, for document readability 306

gradients, for backgrounds 181

grammar check

activating the grammar checker 295

as you type 296

contextual spelling feature 9

Do Not Check option 297

grammar rules, setting 300–302

options, configuring 297–299

other languages 270

Status Bar, checking from 30

grant proposals, page setup features for 145

Greek letters symbol set 564

gridlines

adding, in charts 515

how to display and hide 26

Groove workspaces 646, 648

groups

in Backstage view 36

objects, grouping and ungrouping 555

types of, on the Ribbon 14

Grow Font tool

Mini Toolbar location of 212

for text size adjustment 214

H

gutter settings

for bound documents 147

customizing 145

handwritten content 78, 204

headers and footers

alignment tabs 158

building blocks 230

creating 158

deleting 158

editing 158

field codes 158

galleries 158

Go To 164

themes, changing to match fonts and colors 158

viewing 158

headings

browsing, in the Navigation Pane 25, 248

built-in styles for 706

in Outline View 418

styles, keyboard shortcuts to apply 409

and the table of contents 706

Help

finding Help, summary of 60

Help tab in Backstage view

information available 36

Word version and product ID 37

hidden data, removing from documents 625

hidden text, how to create 220

highlighting text

hide and show highlighting 222

how to 221

Home tab

Clipboard group 84

Font group

Clear Formatting command 223, 393

Font Color arrow 222

fonts and sizes, specifying 213

Font Size list 214

text effects, applying 218

Text Highlight Color command 221

Home tab, *continued*
  formatting commands 211
  Styles group
    formatting lists and text 380
    Styles gallery 381
    Styles Pane 390, 391
  text alignment commands 224
hyphenation
  automatic 355
  manual 356
  non-breaking
    formatting 356
    how to insert 227
  options for 354
  text in other languages 355

I

ID (product), how to locate 37
importing documents 204
Increase Indent tool, location of 212
indenting
  changing 372, 441
  first line and hanging indents 341
  Indents and Spacing tab 342
  left and right, adjusting 340
  types of 350
indexes
  cross-references, adding 722
  entries, AutoMarking with a concordance file
    728
  entries, formatting 722
  entries, marking 719
  formatting the index
    alignment 725
    columns 726
    indented or run in 725
    options, formatting 724
  generating the index 723
  good indexes, qualities of 717
  long entries, and bookmarks 721
  page ranges, specifying 722
  repeated entries, selecting 721

  reviewing your document 723
  subentries, creating 720
  troubleshooting, error messages 726
  updating or adding entries 727
InfoPath Forms vs. Word Content Controls
    791
Info tab in Backstage view
  co-authors, adding and contacting 42
  document compatibility
    checking and preparing for 50
    Compatibility Mode 46
  document properties 37, 44
  Help tab 61
  options 35
  Permissions, setting 48–50
  Recover Unsaved Documents feature 54
  Related Files area 44
  tags and comments, adding 39–42
ink
  adding content longhand 204
  expanded capabilities of 11
Insert tab
  building blocks 230
  Quick Tables 233
  Symbols group and list 224
  Text group
    Date and Time tool 228
    Quick Parts 231
    Text From File command 77
inspection, document
  for sensitive information, hidden comments,
    and XML data 50
  from the Info tab 35
international mail codes and formatting 776
italics
  Home tab command and keyboard shortcut
    216
  how to apply 215
  Italic tool, location of 212

J

justified alignment of text 224

K

keyboards
  adding, for other languages 271
  current configuration, checking 274
  setting up, using current language 269
  Windows Keyboard Layouts tool 271
  Word Options 271
keyboard shortcuts
  Apply Styles Pane 390
  assigning your own
    printing list of 452
    symbols 226
  Building Blocks, inserting existing 233
  built-in commands, viewing 834
  character formatting 257
  copying, cutting, and pasting 81
  macros 822
  navigation through documents 265–266
  Open dialog box 76
  overriding 823
  paragraph align and formatting tools 339
  Reveal Formatting pane 401
  styles
    applying styles 409
    creating your own shortcuts 410
    Style Inspector 401
    Styles Pane 390, 391
  symbols, inserting 225
  text alignment 224
  text attributes and effects 216
  text case, Change Case options 221
  text selection 80
  text sizing, incremental 215
  Undo 85
keywords, for indexing your document 717

L

labels, data 517
labels, printing 458
languages
  adding 269
  Asian 286
  automatic detection of 271
  bidirectional text, using 282
  changing
    as you type 273
    from the Status Bar 31
    from Word Options 63
  Document Grid, working with East Asian
      languages
    drawing grids, displaying 285
    locating 283
    settings, specifying 284
  keyboards, adding 271
  proofing language, setting 270
  translating
    custom translations 281
    definitions, real-time 276
    documents 278
    Microsoft Engkoo 286
    Microsoft Research ESL Assistant 285
    Mini Translator, using 274–276
    selected text 277
    tools, improvements in 274
    Translation Services, changing and adding
        279–282
    WordLingo service 278
  Windows Language Bar 273, 274
layering of objects, controlling 556
layout, displaying Layout Options 186
left alignment of text 224
Legacy Form controls 789
legends, displaying and positioning 516
letterhead, designing 97
letter-like symbols set 564
letters, page setup features for 143
ligatures
  definition 216
  using 217
line and page breaks, controlling 353
line charts 499
line numbers
  adding and controlling 170
  adjusting while previewing 441
lines, horizontal
  adding to documents 601, 603
  graphical lines, creating 604

line spacing, specifying 345
linked styles 382
linking vs. embedding objects 583
lists
  automatic, controlling 361
  bulleted lists
    bullet font, changing 365
    Bullet Library 364
    bullet symbols, changing 366
    converting to numbered list 371
    custom bullets 364
    new bullet, choosing 364
    picture bullets 367
    when to use 359
  content controls, adding to 803
  creating
    ending a list 363
    quick, from existing text 361
    space between items, adding 363
    while you type 362
  formatting problems 363, 373
  indents, changing 372
  list styles
    displaying 380, 392
    legal style numbering 377
    new, creating 375–378
    paragraph formatting in 383
    using for complex numbering 370
  multilevel 373–375
  numbered lists
    converting to bulleted list 371
    numbering, continuing 370
    numbering, restarting 371
    numbering schemes, choosing 368
    style, modifying 368
    when to use 360
  Reveal Formatting pane 402
Live Preview, setting preferences for 64
Locations, Trusted
  description of 634
  specifying 66
locking content controls 803
long documents
  building block ideas for 241

column layouts, switching between 195
complex documents, what to consider
    173–175
features of 732
master documents
  creating 740
  getting started with 738
  problems and workarounds 737
  subdocuments, creating 741
  tools for 739
  when to use 736
  working with 742–744
planning 143
table of authorities
  citations, adding manually 734
  generating 736
table of figures
  captions, adding 732
  figure numbering, controlling 733
  generating 734
tips for 207, 208
lowercase text, changing 220

M

Mac and PC compatibility 39
macros
  Code group on the Developer tab 791
  digitally signing
    reasons for 835
    self-signed signatures, creating 836
    third-party signatures 836
    VBA projects 837
  disabling 815
  editing
    examples 826–828
    Visual Basic Editor 829
  lost or disabled macros, troubleshooting
    823
  macro-enabled and macro-free documents,
    file extensions 47
  options, additional
    deleting and exporting 832
    importing 833

renaming macros, modules, or projects
830
password protecting 835
recording
examples 816–818, 824
naming 816, 834
one-click method 817
pause recording 817
setup and planning 814–816
storing 817
testing 817
troubleshooting 826
resources for further learning 839
running
"Ambiguous name detected" error 831
automatically 824–827
keyboard shortcuts, assigning 822
Macro Security settings, checking 814
Quick Access Toolbar, adding to 818
troubleshooting 823, 831
ways to use 818
saving macro-enabled documents and
templates 813
security settings for 67, 635
and VBA, explanation of 812
when to use 811, 821
mail merge
directories, creating 784
envelopes and labels, creating 785–787
Mail Merge Wizard 763
merge fields
address blocks, adding 775
greeting lines, choosing 776
inserting 777
matching with database 778
tips for 780
types of 774
word fields, adding 780
merging the documents
print options, choosing 783
to a new document 783
to e-mail 784
overview of 762

planning your project
document type, selecting 764
existing documents, using 767
main document, current document as 765
templates, using 766
types of projects 763
postal codes and formatting 776
previewing the merge
errors, checking for 782
Preview Results group, using 781
specific entries, finding 782
recipients
choosing and sorting information 771
creating a new list 768–770
existing lists, using 770
filtering lists 773
merge data, working with 772
New Address List dialog box 769
Outlook contacts, choosing 771
terms, understanding 763
Mail Merge Wizard 666
margins, document
adjusting
changing margin settings 145
on the Ruler 146
suppressing top and bottom margins 22,
145
while previewing 441
aligning content vertically between 145
binding documents, and 145
custom, creating 145
Margins gallery 145, 146
Margins tab 145
measurements units, changing the default
145
Mirror Margins 151
multiple pages, settings for 151
white space, showing 145
marketing materials, ideas for 240
markup features 670–672
master documents 206
creating 740
getting started with 738

master documents, *continued*
  problems and workarounds 737
  subdocuments
    collapsing 743
    converting 744
    creating 741
    expanding and displaying 743
    importing data for 741
    merging 744
    separating 744
  tools for 739
  when to use 736
  working with 742–744
merging table cells 477
Message Bar, settings for 67, 635
Microsoft Developers Network website 839
Microsoft Engkoo 286
Microsoft Exchange, co-authors online 43
Microsoft Genuine Advantage
  downloading templates 72
Microsoft InfoPath 2010 791
Microsoft Office Help 61
Microsoft Outlook 771
Microsoft Research ESL Assistant 285
Microsoft support, contacting 61
Microsoft Translation 279
Mini Toolbar
  enabling 212
  formatting choices, quick 20
  text selection and formatting 212
  turning off and on 21
Mini Translator tool
  setting preferences for 64
  using 274–277
modules
  deleting and exporting 832
  importing 833
  the Organizer 833
  renaming 830
Multilevel Lists
  applying 373
  creating a new list style 375–378
  list styles 383, 392

multiple documents, working with 28
multiple page settings 150

N

name and initials in files, setting preferences
      for 64
navigation, document
  bookmarks 260
  Browse Object tool 252
  Find and Replace dialog box
    floating objects vs. inline objects 257
    formatting settings 256
    Go To tab 259
    special characters 257
    text strings 253–256
  keyboard shortcuts and function keys
      264–266
  Navigation Pane
    browsing by headings 248
    browsing by page 249
    browsing by search results 251
    content, ways to find 246–251
    how to use 24
    search box 247
    vs. Outline View 433
    ways to use 6, 248
  overview of, in Word 2010 245
  windows, displaying and arranging
    commands, locating 262
    multiple windows, switching among 264
    splitting the document window 262
    viewing pages side by side 263
  Zoom tools 261
negated relations symbol sets 564
nested tables 471
network locations, and file sharing
  accessing resources 655
  creating a network location 654
  FTP sites, linking to 654
  saving documents to 655
Newsletters, designing 99
New tab in Backstage view
  new files, starting 57

options for 35
  templates, working with 70–72
New Windows tool 29
non-breaking hyphens
  formatting 356
  how to insert 227
non-breaking spaces, inserting 227
Normal Style, understanding and modifying
    408
numbers
  legal style 377
  number forms 217
  number spacing 217
  page number style and placement 230

O

objects
  aligning 553
  Browse Object feature 252
  distributing vs. aligning 555
  embedded
    linking vs. embedding 583
    saving to previous version of Word 51
  grouping and ungrouping 555
  inserting
    existing objects, adding 585
    new object, creating 584
    Object dialog box 584
    placing, procedures for 207
    positions, choosing 556
  layering, controlling 556
  OLE (Object Linking and Embedding)
      technology 583
  text wrapping, controlling 557
  wrap points, adding and editing 558
Office 2010 and themes 127
Office.com
  checking 839
  Templates area 71
  themes, downloading 130
Office Communicator, co-authors online 43
Office Online, additional templates 71
OneNote notebooks, reusing content in 203

Open Document format 206
opening files
  in Backstage view 34
  Open And Repair 77
  Open dialog box 76
  in Protected View 67
  related files, opening 44
OpenType fonts
  how to use 216
  saving to previous version of Word 51
operators symbol set 564
Organizer, the
  modules, working with 833
  templates, modifying 123
orientation of documents, changing 147, 441
orphan/widow control 353
outlines
  basics of good outlines 414
  changing
    cutting and pasting 430
    dragging to new location 430
    expanding and collapsing the outline 429
    moving topics up and down 429
  complex projects, reasons to make an
      outline 415–417
  exploring outlining tools 419
  headings
    adding 426
    outline levels, applying 426
    promoting and demoting 426
  how to 219, 220
  importing, from a text file 427
  new, creating 421–423
  Outline View
    customizing 422
    displaying, along with Print Layout View
        428
    displaying levels of text 423
    first line of text, showing 424
    formatting, removing and showing 425
    headings, alphabetizing 433
    restructuring your document 431
    snipping tool and 420

Outline view, *continued*
   symbols in 418
   troubleshooting 418, 422
   viewing 24, 417
   vs. the Navigation Pane 433
   printing 431
   types of 414
Outlook, Microsoft 771

P

page setup and pagination
   basic page setup, options for 139
   borders, page and section 158, 597–599
   browsing, with the Navigation Pane 25, 249
   custom settings
      backing up 169
      and the Normal template 169
      saving as template 155
   document types 143
   headers and footers
      alignment tabs 166
      creating 159
      deleting 167
      editing 163, 165
      field codes 167
      galleries 163
      themes, changing to match fonts and
         colors 163
      viewing 162
   headlines and 156
   line numbers
      adding and controlling 170
      deleting 171
      troubleshooting 171
   margins
      adjusting, on the ruler 146
      aligning content vertically between 157
      binding documents, and 147
      changing margin settings 145
      custom, creating 145
      Margins gallery 145, 146

   Margins tab 142
   measurement units, changing the default
      147
   multiple pages, settings for 151
   suppressing top and bottom 22
   white space, showing 156
multiple pages
   settings 150
   viewing 28
options for, in the Page Setup dialog box
   142
orientation of documents 147
page breaks, controlling 156, 157, 353, 438
Page Layout tab
   building blocks 230
   Themes group and gallery 87
page numbers
   adding 159
   style and placement 230
page ranges, specifying in indexes 722
Page Setup dialog box 140
paper size and source
   Document Grid 149
   paper size, choosing 148, 441
   paper source, selecting 149
planning your document 140, 142–144
sections, document
   borders, adding 600
   and columns 191
   creating 153–155
   headers and footers, removing and editing
      168
   section types 154
   when not to use 152
   when to use 151
setup defaults, saving to the current
   template 168
text wrapping breaks, inserting 155
paragraph formatting
   aligning and indenting text
      Drawing Grid, overriding 341

first line and hanging indents 341
left and right indents, adjusting 340
Paragraph Dialog box, using 341
tools and shortcuts for 338
using the ruler 339
AutoFormat feature
  adding to the Ribbon 338
  as you type 335
  choices, adjusting 336
  managing 334
  options, changing 336
borders, adding 600
building blocks 235
Document Defaults 407
drop caps, creating 357
formatting markers, viewing
  Reveal Formatting pane 402
  Show/Hide button 333
hyphenation
  automatic 355
  manually 356
  options for 354
  text in other languages 355
line and page breaks, controlling 353
linked styles 382
paragraph styles 382
parameters of 333
spacing issues
  addressing 343
  empty paragraph marks, cleaning up 344
  line spacing, specifying 345
  space above and below paragraphs, adjusting
    346, 442
Style Inspector 401
Styles and 334
tabs
  carrying from one paragraph to the next
    350
  default Normal template 348
  manual, clearing 352
  role of 347
  setting, using the Tabs Dialog box 351
  setting with the Ruler 349

shifting text, and 348
  tab and indent types 350
  understanding 332
parental controls, how to set up 68
passwords
  encryption 48
  file-sharing 125
  macros, protection for 835
pasting content
  Ignoring paste options 82
  paste options 81
  Paste With Live Preview 82, 83
patterns for backgrounds 182
PC and Mac compatibility 39
PDF files
  saving documents as 627
  and secure sharing 658
  understanding 626
permissions
  Add A Digital Signature 48
  for co-authors 43
  content controls, locking 803
  customizing 637
  Encrypt With Password 48
  Mark As Final 48
  Restrict Editing 48
  Restrict Permission By People 48
  setting 48–50, 636
  user permissions, setting from the Info tab
    35
  Windows rights management 125
personal information, removing from
    documents 625
photos
  for backgrounds 182
  editing and adjusting 534
  improvements and enhancements for 9
pictures
  arrangement on page
    aligning objects 553
    distributing vs. aligning 555
    grouping and ungrouping objects 555
    object layering, controlling 556

pictures, *continued*
  Position tool 556
  text wrapping, controlling 557
  wrap points, adding and editing 558
for bullets 367
Clip Art task pane 164
editing
  artistic effects, applying 532
  backgrounds, removing 539
  cropping 535
  image adjustment 534
  resizing 537
  rotating 538
enhancing
  captions, adding 543
  picture borders 542, 600
  picture effects 543
  pictures styles, applying 541
inserting
  borders 604
  screenshots and clippings 553
macro to toggle Show Picture Placeholders
    828
obtaining, using the Snipping Tool 420
as page backgrounds 537
Picture content controls 797
Picture dialog box, opening 164
Picture Effects, adding 542
shapes and lines
  shadows and 3-D effects 549
  shape fills, changing 546
  shape styles, applying 545
  shape text, adding and formatting 546
  transparency 548
  vs. pictures 544
watermarks as 185
pie charts 500
placeholders for citations and sources 318
Plain Text content controls 796
points (unit of measure) 214
postal codes, formatting 776
power outages, and recovering unsaved files
    54

printing
  cancelling a print job 446
  envelopes 785–787
  greener printing 435
  images, color or black and white 551
  labels 787
  merge documents 783, 785–787
  options, setting
    backgrounds, printing 179, 183
    copies, number of 447
    document elements 450
    document orientation, changing 441
    margins, adjusting 441
    odd and even pages 449
    page numbers, formatted vs. physical 449
    printing ranges 448
    printing several pages per sheet 452
    Print tab in Backstage view 35
    scaling printed documents 453
    semi-transparent option 186
  paper size, changing 441
  paper source, selecting 149
  previewing your document
    importance of 438
    making changes while previewing 441
    Print and Preview tools 57, 439
    zooming in on details 439
  Print Layout View
    changing to a different printer 437
    default view 22
    displaying, along with Outline View 428
  Print tab in Backstage view
    preview and page through documents 37,
      57
    productivity features 436
    setting options for 35
  .prn files 448
  specialized printing
    envelopes 456–458
    labels 458
    options available 454–456
  tables, printing without row and column
      lines 487

text
  "fitting" text 442
  hidden text 445
  selected text 444
Tracked Changes lists, printing 445
troubleshooting
  borders 603
  characters cut off 454
  extra blank pages 445
  fonts, wrong 446
  markup lists, non-functioning 452
  two-sided printing, and paper jams 450
priority for e-mail messages, setting 659
product ID, how to locate 37
proofing options
  complex documents 175
  display and exceptions, controlling 296–298
  flagged errors, fixing 292–294, 294–296
  how to change 63
  proofing notifications
    flagged errors, fixing 292
    jumping to the next 294
    types and descriptions of 292–294
  Proofing Status display 291
  proofreaders, necessity of 294, 297
  setting a language 270
  Spelling and Grammar dialog box 294
  spelling and grammar options, configuring
      298–301
  suppressing proofing marks 294, 296
Protected View 67
protection of documents
  digital signatures and stamps
    adding a stamp 631
    attaching to files 630
    certificate authorities and security adminis-
      trators, working with 629
    digital IDs, creating 629
    digital IDs, how to get 628
    removing signatures 632
    signing 628
    viewing signatures 631
  editing restrictions, applying 622–624

encryption
  how to 620
  passwords 620
  removing protection 621
features in Word 2010 614
forms, working with 805–807
hidden data, removing 625
macros
  Macro Security settings 814
  passwords, assigning 835
Mark As Final feature 618
PDF and XPS files, preparing 626
personal information, removing 625
preparing files for 47–49
privacy options 635
Protected View
  choosing what is displayed in 616
  file validation, changing 617
  working with 615, 635
Protect group on the Developer tab 791
security warnings, checking for red X 633
Windows rights management 125
Publishers, Trusted
  adding to list 634
  specifying 66

Q

Quick Access Toolbar
  Alignment Tabs, adding to toolbar 166
  custom galleries and AutoText galleries 242
  display
    location 17
    resetting default 16
  function and customization of 16, 63
  macros 818–820, 831
  Mini Translator, adding 277
  opening documents 76
  Open Recent File, adding 56
  Print Preview and Print, adding 439
  Quick Print, adding 443
  Redo button, adding 86
  Styles Combo Box, adding 391
  templates, access to 117

Quick Parts
  building blocks 230
  headers and footers 164
Quick Styles
  designs available 384
  Quick Style gallery
    Apply Styles Pane 390
    create new style 397
    Modify a style 397
    Select All # Instances of Style Name 394
    styles, applying and modifying 385–387
  QuickStyles folder, location of 389
  resetting 389
  SmartArt diagrams 498
  themes and 129
  understanding 102, 384
Quick Style Sets
  about 211
  custom, creating 387–389
  custom, deleting 389
  resetting 389
  switching and modifying 386
  themes and 387, 388
Quick Tables
  adding a table 465
  Quick Tables gallery 233, 466

R

radar charts 500
readability level of documents 306
read-only files
  permission 48
  templates, suggested for 125
receipt requests, for e-mails 660
Recent Documents
  Quick Access Toolbar, adding to 56
  Recent tab in Backstage view
    file status, changing 75
    locating 34, 75
    options for 35, 55, 76
    pinning a document to the list 75
recovery, document
  draft versions of 52–54

  unsaved files 54
Redo or Repeat, how to use 86
red X on documents, meaning of 633
references
  bibliographies
    description of 314
    generating 319
    style, choosing 315
  citations
    description of 314
    editing 318
    inserting 317
    placeholders, adding and using 318
    Track Changes, using 318
  cross-references
    adding 326
    deleting 328
    error messages 328
    as hyperlinks, for web pages 327
    modifying, moving, and updating 327
    relative 328
  footnotes and endnotes
    customizing 321
    deleting 323
    description of 314, 320
    inserting 321
    margins and 325
    moving and copying 323
    separator lines, creating new 324
    views, and visibility of 322
    on web pages 323
  Reference tab
    building blocks 230
    groups and types of references 313
  sources
    adding and managing 315
    description of 314
    editing 318
    other source lists, incorporating 317
    placeholders, adding and using 318
  types of 312
reflection options for text, applying 219
Related Files area of the Info tab 44

reports
  building block ideas for 241
  page setup features 143
resizing pictures 537
reusing content
  how to features 203
  ideas for 204
  understanding 202
Reveal Formatting Task Pane 401
Reverse Book Fold page settings 151
review process
  balloon and Review Pane options, configuring
    680–683
  comments and revisions, viewing 673
  confidential revisions 696
  organization of 667
  reviewer name, setting 671
  reviewers, configuring colors for 672
  versions of documents, how to view 697
Ribbon, the
  AutoFormat, adding 338
  custom galleries and 241
  customization of 5, 63, 64
  Developer tab, attaching templates 118
  dialog launchers, access to 17
  disappearance of 29
  display and minimization of 15
  features of 14
  galleries on 19
  macros, adding to 818
  new features in 5
  Outlining tools, viewing 419
  Page Layout tab 140
  purpose of 33
  Quick Access Toolbar and 17
  Quick Styles button 384
  resetting 65
Rich Text content controls 796
right alignment of text 224
rotating pictures 538
rulers and gridlines, displaying and hiding 26
Ruler, the
  aligning paragraphs 339
  setting tabs 349

S

Safe Mode, starting Word in 108
sales reports, ideas for 240
saving files
  AutoRecover 52
  Background Saves 52
  changing options for 63
  fast command for 34
  file types 94
  macro-enabled documents and templates
    813
  to network locations 655
  Save As Dialog Box 92
  Save & Send tab 36, 58–60, 93
  Save to Web 59
  to a server 11
  in SharePoint Workspaces 650
  to a SharePoint Site 94
  simple save 91
  to Windows Live SkyDrive 653
scaling printed documents 453
Scatter (XY) charts 500
screenshots
  adding 553
  Screenshot feature 10
ScreenTips
  displaying in a different language 268
  setting preferences for 64
scripts symbol set 564
scrolling, synchronous 30
search function
  based on tag and comment information 40
  Browse Objects feature 26
  Search Document box 25, 251
  text search using the Navigation Pane 26
security administrators, working with 629
sentence case, changing 220
shading
  behind content, applying 606
  behind table data 485
  considerations for using 608
  of color effects 181
  tables and paragraphs, applying 607

shadows
  adding and controlling 549
  coloring shadows 550
  position and appearance of, changing 550
  shadow settings for text 219, 220
shapes
  in charts, formatting 520
  Drawing Canvas option 530
  Drawing Grid, using 531
  shape fills, modifying 547
  shape text, adding and formatting 546
  styles, applying 545
  as text containers 572, 576
  transparency 548
SharePoint accounts
  co-authoring in
    contacting co-authors 700
    editing and saving simultaneously 698
    setting up and using 697
    troubleshooting 701
  explanation of 59
  reusing content 203
  saving to 60, 93, 94, 643
  SharePoint blog 755
  SharePoint Workspace 2010
    documents, checking in and out 649
    Groove workspaces 646, 648
    new documents, creating 650
    new workspaces, creating 646–648
sharing building blocks 237
single spacing, setting 345
size, document 38
small caps 220
SmartArt diagrams
  creating 494
  formatting, making changes to 497
  Quick Styles 498
  saving to previous version of Word 51
  text, adding and formatting 496
Snap Objects To Grid feature 555
Snipping Tool 420
social media sites, reusing content for 203
software updates 61

sources, referencing
  adding and managing 315
  description of 314
  editing 318
  other source lists, incorporating 317
  placeholders, adding and using 318
spacing issues
  addressing 343
  border spacing, adjusting 601
  empty paragraph marks, cleaning up 344
  line spacing, specifying 345
  space above and below paragraphs, adjusting
    346
  table cell spacing, changing 479
special characters
  inserting 224, 227
  locating, using the Find and Replace dialog
    box 257–259
speech recognition
  for content creation 77
  training Office 2010 to recognize your voice
    77
spelling
  AutoCorrect 293
  checking, as you type 296
  checking, from the Status Bar 30
  contextual spelling feature 9, 404
  Do Not Check option 297
  error notifications 291
  hide spelling errors, when to use 296
  options, configuring 298–300
  other languages 270
Split documents command 29
splitting table cells 478
splitting windows, using the splitter 262
startup options, how to change 63
Status Bar
  language and keyboard preferences 31
  options, adding or removing 31
  Page area 30
  spelling and grammar 30
  understanding and tailoring 30
  word count 30

stock charts 500
strikethrough of text
  double strikethrough 220
  Home tab command and keyboard shortcut
    216
styles
  aliases, assigning 394
  applying
    Apply Styles Pane 390, 394
    automatically 119
    chart styles 511
  clearing and deleting 393
  comparing formatting 403
  and content controls 800
  creating and modifying
    automatic updating, enabling 399
    based on existing styles 398
    based on existing text 395
    modifying existing styles 397
    styles for following paragraphs 399
    templates, adding a style to 400
  font formatting 223
  fundamentals of 381
  images, applying picture styles to 541
  line styles, for borders 592
  management tools
    Reveal Formatting pane 401
    Style Inspector 401
  Manage Styles dialog box
    Edit tab 405
    Recommend tab 406
    Restrict tab 406
    Set Defaults tab 407
    when to use 404
  printing document styles 452
  purpose of 379
  Reveal Formatting Task Pane 401–403
  selecting and changing all instances of 394
  shape styles, applying 545
  source of, how to locate 404
  Style area, how to display 380
  Style Inspector 401
  Styles Combo box 391, 394

Styles Pane
  Clear All option 393
  creating new from formatted text 395
  Disable Linked Styles 392
  display only current document styles 398
  Manage Styles 392, 404
  Modifying a style 397
  New Style 392
  Options 393
  recommended list of styles 406
  Show Preview 392
  Style Inspector 392
  Styles list 392
  working with 390–394
  table of contents (TOC) styles 707, 715
  table styles 480–483
  Text Effects gallery 219
  underlining 215
  watching as you work 380
subdocuments 206
subscript, text 216
superscript, text 216
surface charts 500
symbols
  adding 224
  automatic insertion 226
  Symbol dialog box 227
  types of, in Outline View 418

T

table of authorities
  citations, adding manually 734
  generating 736
table of contents, building blocks for 230
table of contents (TOC)
  creating
    customized 708–710
    manually adding entries 710
    TOC styles 707
  customizing
    defaults, resetting to 716
    entry styles, matching to TOC levels 715
    styles, changing 715

table of contents, *continued*
    Table of Contents Options dialog box
        708–710, 714
   formatting
     changing the format 712
     choosing a format 711
     editing and updating 712
   headings for, effective 706
   necessity of 705
   removing a TOC 713
   troubleshooting, missing headings 712
   for the Web 713
table of figures
   captions, adding 732
   figure numbering, controlling 733
   generating 734
tables
   cells
     deleting 477
     inserting 476
     merging 477
     selecting 474
     spacing and alignment, changing 479
     splitting 478
   columns and rows
     adjusting, after splits and merges 478
     deleting 477
     distributing data evenly 489
     inserting 476
     moving 477
     widths and heights, changing 489
   creating
     drawing a table 468
     Excel spreadsheets, inserting 470
     inserting, and AutoFit Options 467
     methods for 464
     Quick Tables 465
     Row and Column Grid, using 467
     size considerations 479
     text, converting to a table 469
   editing
     converting a table to text 470
     copying and pasting table data 474
     formatting marks, displaying 472

     options for 472
     selecting table cells 474
     selecting table segments 474
   formatting
     AutoFormat feature 480
     borders, custom 484
     borders, options for 605
     default, setting 483
     displaying formatting marks 472
     font size, troubleshooting 483
     Reveal Formatting pane 402
     shading behind data 485
     table styles 380, 383, 480
     table styles, custom 482–484
     Table Styles gallery 392
     Table Tools contextual tab 380
     themes and 482
   functions, working with 490
   nested tables 471
   planning 464
   positioning in documents
     flowing text around tables 485
     indenting the table 485
     options, how to 485
     table breaks, controlling 491
   printing without row and column lines 487
   resizing
     AutoFit, testing 488
     AutoFit, understanding 487
     column width and row height, changing
       489
     distributing data evenly 489
     entire tables 488
     options for 487
     preset and percent table sizes, setting 488
     text direction, changing 489
     view options 488
   tabbed vs. borderless 347
   table data, sorting 486
   and web page design 490
Tablet PCs and handwritten content 204
tabs
   carrying from one paragraph to the next
     350

contextual
  Chart Tool tabs 505
  purpose of 15
default Normal template 348
Developer tab 790
manual, clearing 352
Options command 36
on the Ribbon
  customizing 64
  types 14
role of 347
setting
  using the Tabs Dialog box 351
  with the Ruler 349
shifting text and 348
tab and indent types 350
tagging documents
  adding to content controls 800
  how to 40
  purpose of 39
  tips for 39
templates
  adding and removing 115
  attaching to documents 117–119
  boilerplate text for 111
  building blocks, built in 231
  building blocks, sharing 237
  chart templates 503
  custom
    backing up 107, 169
    based on existing document 112, 114, 155
    based on existing template 112, 114
    design considerations for 113
    elements of 114
    managing 63
    page setups, saving 168
    saving 115
    from scratch 112, 114
    single click access to 117
    testing 116
  Custom XML feature 104
  design, consistent 72
  existing
    changing the template file 122

changing while working in a document
  123
created in previous versions of Word 105
modifying 122
renaming, deleting, and copying styles
  123
global
  loading, automatically 120
  loading, manually 120
  Normal and Building Blocks templates as
    119
  troubleshooting 121
  unloading 121
  working with 119
how they work 105
how to find 70–72, 109–111
macros and 812
for mail merge 766
managing
  the Organizer 123
  protecting 125
  troubleshooting 124
My Templates folder 71, 74
Normal template
  adding styles to 400
  automatic macros and 824
  damaged, replacing 107
  default for new documents 383
  default settings, changing 169
  Quick Style Set as default 389
  renaming 107
  tab default 348
  troubleshooting 106, 108
  understanding and using 106–108
Office.com Templates 110
options, summary of 110
previewing 72
purpose and operation of 102–105, 105
Recent Templates 71, 72
Reset To Quick Styles From Template 389
reusing content 203
Sample Templates 71
saving favorites 74
saving keyboard shortcuts in 411

templates, *continued*
  storage location, changing 106
  storing online 111
  style change in documents 383
  styles, adding to templates 400
  Template group on the Developer tab 791
  Workgroup Templates 110, 656
  XML formatting of 103
text
  alignment 223
  attributes, applying 215
  bidirectional, working with 282
  clearing formatting 223
  color, changing 222
  columns, flowing text into 194
  converting to a table 469
  entering 203
  "fitting" or condensing, methods for 441
  formatting of
    as you go along 210–212
    comparing formats 403
    inconsistencies, tracking 404
    Style Inspector 401
    styles 380, 382
  hidden, printing 445
  highlighting tool 221
  new features for enhancement 10
  OpenType fonts, using 216
  Rich Text and Plain Text content controls
    796
  selecting text, and shortcuts for 79
  shape text, adding and formatting 546
  size, changing 28
  tables
    flowing text around 485
    text direction, changing 489
  Text From File command, to import
    documents 204
  Text Highlight tool 212
  text size
    Keyboard shortcuts for 215
    points as unit of measure 214

text watermarks 185
text wrapping breaks, inserting 155
text wrapping, controlling 557
  wrap points, adding and editing 558
text boxes
  adding 572
  building blocks for 230
  drawing canvases, creating 580
  formatting 574–576
  inserting text into 574
  linking, to flow text 578–582
  saving to previous versions of Word 51
  text wrapping 576
  when to use 570
text effects
  additional formats 220
  applying 218
  deleting 220
  saving to previous versions of Word 51
  Text Effects gallery 219
  Text Effects tool 218
textures
  custom 182
  for page backgrounds 182
themes
  changing
    applying a new theme 130
    colors 131
    font selection 131
    what to be aware of 127
  charts and 504
  colors and 89
  custom
    color schemes 135
    font sets 136
    saving 137
  default 129
  downloading 130
  effects and 90, 133
  experimenting with 87
  font colors and 223
  fonts and 89

formatting changes and 211
galleries and 130
overriding theme settings 132
purpose of 126
Quick Styles and 129, 384
Quick Style Sets and 387
settings 134
table styles and 482
Theme Fonts 213
what they include 102, 128
thesaurus, function of 290
3-D effects, applying and customizing 551
time and date elements 228
titles
adding to content controls 800
chart titles, adding 512
displayed on the Info tab 39
Title Case, applying 220
toggle commands
text attributes and effects 216
toggle case, applying 220
Track Changes edits
accepting and rejecting changes 689–692
balloon and reviewing pane options
    680–683
changed lines, customizing appearance of
    680
citations 318
comparing and combining documents
    693–697
description of 668
display options 677
printing lists of 445, 451, 684–686
reviewing tracked changes 685–687
saving to previous version of Word 51
viewing, in the Navigation Pane 250
while you edit 678
translating content
custom translations 274
definitions, real-time 274
documents 274
Microsoft Engkoo 274
Microsoft Research ESL Assistant 274

Mini Translator, using 274–276
overview 268
ScreenTips in a different language 268
selected text 274
translation services
adding new 281
changing and adding 274–277, 280
custom 281
Microsoft Translation 279
WordLingo service 274, 278
translation tools 8, 274, 285
transparency
of color effects 181
shapes 548
trendlines, in charts 515
Trust Center
accessing 63, 633
ActiveX Settings 67
Add-Ins, third party 67
categories in 634
File Block 67
Macro Settings 67
Message Bar 67
parental controls 68
permission levels
    applying permissions to documents 638
    customizing 637
    setting 636
Protected View option 67
setting privacy and protection levels 63,
    66–68
setting up 66
Trusted Documents 67
Trusted Locations 66
Trusted Publishers 66
viewing and removing trusted sources 635
typography, OpenType fonts 216

U

underlining
Home tab command and keyboard shortcut
    216
how to apply 215

underlining, *continued*
  removing 216
  Underline button 215
  Underline tool, location of 212
Undoing, Redoing, and Repeating, using 85
units of measure
  changing, on the Ruler 340
  changing the defaults 147
  conversion to points 346
unsaved files, recovering 54
updates, software 61
Uppercase text
  changing, using the Change Case command
    220
  vs. All Caps Font effect 221
user account options, changing 63

V

VBA (Visual Basic for Applications)
  Editor
    Comment Text 828
    elements of 829
    modules and views 830
    Procedure List 830
    Project Explorer 830
    Properties Pane 830
    structure of statements 827
  and macro creation 812
  projects 812
  syntax of 826
versions of Word
  Compatibility Checker 50
  Compatibility Mode 46
  free document converter 46
  macro-enabled and macro-free files, saving
    813
  tips for tags 39
views, document
  changing, how to 21
  draft view 24
  full screen reading view 22
  number of pages, locating 38
  outline view 24
  print layout view 22

View Ruler button 26
View Side By Side documents command 29
View tab
  document views, changing 21
  Navigation Pane, accessing 24
  rulers and gridlines, displaying and hiding
    26
  size and number of pages, changing 28
  web layout view 23
viruses, protection from 108
voting buttons 662

W

watermarking
  adding, to printed documents 183
  building block styles 230
  custom 184
  editing 184
  picture watermark 185
  text watermark 185
  troubleshooting 186
  Watermark gallery 183
web pages
  cross-references as hyperlinks 327
  design, using tables 490
  TOCs, preparing for the Web 714
  Web Layout document view 23
  Word Web App, features of 11
widow/orphan control 353
wildcards, using 255, 256
windows
  displaying and arranging 262
  document, splitting 262
  multiple, switching among 264
  New Windows tool 29
  side by side viewing 263
  Switch Windows tool 29
Windows Live accounts
  reusing content 203
  signing into or signing up for 59
  Windows Live Spaces 755
Windows Live SkyDrive 59, 93
  co-authoring in 697–701
  saving to a shared space 653

setting up and using 651
sharing files 652
and the Word Web App 757
Windows rights management 125
Windows Snipping Tool 420
Windows Vista and Windows 7 106
Word 2010 new features
  authoring features, improved 7–11
  color scheme, setting 64
  dialog launchers, using 17
  document views, changing 21–24
  energy saving features 435
  galleries, working with 19
  Mini Toolbar 20
  multiple documents, working with 28
  Navigation Pane 24–26
  pages, viewing more than one at a time 28
  Protected View 67
  Quick Access Toolbar 16
  the Ribbon, exploring 14
  rulers and gridlines, displaying 26
  Status Bar, understanding and tailoring 30
  user experience, enhancing 5–7
  user interface 13
  using Word anywhere 11
Word commands, built-in, viewing 834
word count statistics
  shown in the Info tab 38
  shown in the Status Bar 30
  for text box content 581
Word Mobile 2010, flexibility of 12
Word MVP Site 839
Word Options
  automatic backup feature, enabling 53
  Background Saves, enabling 52
  Editing Options 404
  General Program preferences, changing 64
  how to change
    from Backstage view, tabs column 62
    Options link on the Help tab 61
  Paste commands, setting default for 83
  Recent Documents, how to change number
    of 76

for text selection 79
Word Solution Center 839
Word Startup folder 121, 237
Word Web App
  and blogging 757
  how to use 757–760
  opening documents in 757
  using anywhere 757
  working with 758
Word Web App, features of 11
workgroup templates, using 656
WorldLingo translation tool 278, 279

X

XML-based formats
  Ecma Office Open XML format 103
  and macro-enabled files 813
  Open Document format 206
  reusing content 203
XML data, mapping controls to 804
XML group on the Developer tab 791
XPS files
  saving documents as 627
  for secure sharing 658
  understanding 626
XY (Scatter) charts 500

Z

Zoom dialog box
  document display options 28
  document navigation in 261
  options in 441
Zoom tools
  in Draft and Outline views 440
  modifying Zoom levels, creating a macro for
    824
  on Print Preview tab or View tab 439
  Zoom slider, and document display 21

About the Author

Katherine Murray wrote her first book about Microsoft Word back in the dark ages when it was only available in a DOS version (remember that?). Over the years, Word has been her favorite program, and she's seen it grow from a mind-blowing word processing program (*that actually shows line breaks on the screen!*) to a full-featured, complex (and overweight, some might say) program that does everything you could ever want a word processor to do, including sewing a button on your shirt. Finally she's seen Word mature into an elegant, smart, efficient program that provides the flexibility to produce content for a variety of platforms, graphic design tools to help even art-challenged writers look good, and enough high-end features that proficient users can streamline their tasks and produce smart content that hits the mark but doesn't gobble up their creative time.

Katherine writes about all sorts of Microsoft Office technologies, and, true to what she writes about, she outputs the content she writes through multiple channels: As books, e-books, presentations, video demonstrations, articles (for CNET's TechRepublic and Microsoft.com), and online learning courses with Microsoft Learning. She also blogs regularly (her Office blog is called, appropriately, BlogOffice) and loves gardening, cooking, and doing just about anything under the sun with her kids, grandkids, and animals.

What do you think of this book?

We want to hear from you!

To participate in a brief online survey, please visit:

microsoft.com/learning/booksurvey

Tell us how well this book meets your needs—what works effectively, and what we can do better. Your feedback will help us continually improve our books and learning resources for you.

Thank you in advance for your input!

Stay in touch!

To subscribe to the *Microsoft Press® Book Connection Newsletter*—for news on upcoming books, events, and special offers—please visit:

microsoft.com/learning/books/newsletter